Knowledge Innovation on Design and Culture

Knowledge Innovation on Design and Culture

Proceedings of the 3rd IEEE International Conference on Knowledge Innovation and Invention 2020 (IEEE ICKII 2020)

Kaohsiung, Taiwan 21 – 23 August 2020

Editors

Teen-Hang Meen
National Formosa University, Taiwan

Chun-Yen Chang
National Taiwan Normal University, Taiwan

Cheng-Fu Yang
National University of Kaohsiung, Taiwan

World Scientific

NEW JERSEY • LONDON • SINGAPORE • BEIJING • SHANGHAI • HONG KONG • TAIPEI • CHENNAI • TOKYO

Published by

World Scientific Publishing Co. Pte. Ltd.
5 Toh Tuck Link, Singapore 596224
USA office: 27 Warren Street, Suite 401-402, Hackensack, NJ 07601
UK office: 57 Shelton Street, Covent Garden, London WC2H 9HE

British Library Cataloguing-in-Publication Data
A catalogue record for this book is available from the British Library.

KNOWLEDGE INNOVATION ON DESIGN AND CULTURE
Proceedings of the 3rd IEEE International Conference on Knowledge Innovation and Invention 2020 (IEEE ICKII 2020)

ISBN 978-981-123-871-0 (hardcover)
ISBN 978-981-123-872-7 (ebook for institutions)
ISBN 978-981-123-873-4 (ebook for individuals)

For any available supplementary material, please visit
https://www.worldscientific.com/worldscibooks/10.1142/12327#t=suppl

https://doi.org/10.1142/9789811238727_fmatter

Preface

The 3rd IEEE International Conference on Knowledge Innovation and Invention 2020 (IEEE ICKII 2020) was held in Kaohsiung, Taiwan on August 21–23, 2020, which was organized by the IEEE Tainan Section Sensors Council (IEEE TSSC), the International Institute of Knowledge Innovation and Invention (IIKII), and the National University of Kaohsiung, Taiwan. This conference provided a communication platform for researchers on the topic of knowledge innovation and invention. It aimed to enable interdisciplinary collaboration and international networking between researchers, technologists, educators, and experts from various areas in the academic and industrial fields. The papers related to the IEEE field have been published on IEEE Xplore® (https://ieeexplore.ieee.org/xpl/conhome/9318770/proceeding) and indexed by EI (Engineering Index). This volume *Knowledge Innovation on Design and Culture* includes 95 excellent papers on the following topics:

- Knowledge Innovation
- Design with Intelligence
- Design Education
- Design Ethics
- Design Thinking
- Design and Management
- Heritage and Design
- Design Psychology
- Design and Marketing
- Design Culture
- Design History
- Life-Style Design
- Fashion Design
- Industrial Design
- Smart Healthcare System Design
- Cultural and Creative Research

The proceedings reveals how social scientists and engineers collaborate interdisciplinarily and network internationally. The IEEE ICKII keeps providing the platform for establishing an international network to integrate social sciences and engineering technologies in the academic and industrial fields.

Distinguished Professor Dr. Teen-Hang Meen
Department of Electronic Engineering, National Formosa University, Yunlin, Taiwan
Chair of IEEE Tainan Section Sensors Council (IEEE TSSC)

https://doi.org/10.1142/9789811238727_fmatter

Contents

https://doi.org/10.1142/9789811238727_0001

A Brief Analysis of the Functions and Principles of Chinese Contemporary Art Criticism

Zhang Xiaoyan

School of Art and Design, Wuhan University of Technology, Wuhan, Hubei Province, China
School of Design, Fujian University of Technology, Fuzhou, Fujian Province, China
Design Innovation Research Center of Humanities and Social Sciences Research Base of Colleges and Universities in Fujian Province
Email: 610491762@qq.com Tel: 19906932766

Abstract

This paper expounds the functions and principles of Chinese contemporary art criticism. By analyzing the definition, significance and principles of art criticism, the paper concludes that art criticism should play a leading role in culture and expound the value and significance of contemporary art.

Keywords: contemporary China, art criticism, principle, significance

Introduction

In today's society, traditional and modern art forms coexist, and art has entered a diversified era. Different artistic concepts intersect and various forms of expression and artistic styles emerge in an endless stream. This complex and diversified situation leads to vague criteria for judging artistic works, nature of artworks and artists. Therefore there is a need to actively participate in the practice of artistic creation and theoretical thinking on contemporary art issues, to correct the wrongs and guide viewers to appreciate and correctly understand art works.

Definition

Wolff, an American art critic, defines art criticism as "an evaluation of the quality and meaning of art works." According to Wolff, art criticism is more concerned with assessing value and significance. This evaluation is usually based on accepted critical criteria and explains how to arrive at evaluation results. Through Wolff's explanation, we can better understand the meaning of art criticism.

So it seems, art criticism includes art theory research, comments, appreciation, the comparison of art works, and other fields. It requires knowledge of history, theory, artists and art judgment, explanation, and evaluation system research. One of the main functions of art criticism is to confirm that new art can be understood and evaluated fairly, no matter how bizarre, unartistic or even against the trend.

Significance of art criticism

The main function of art criticism is to judge and evaluate. In contemporary times, the development of art has changed. The change of artistic concept and the update of formal language make it more difficult to judge artworks and non-artworks. In the development of western modern art, there have been several times when art theorists have thought deeply and explored the concept of art and artist. For example, in the 1960s, American philosophers Arthur Danto and George Dickey put forward the views of "art world" and "conventionalism" on the measurement standard of artworks and non-artworks, and called for the end of art. In fact, Danto and Dickey's theoretical discussion on the definition of art is a response to the issues of art and non-art and the identity of artists at that time. Today, when art is gradually aestheticized in daily life, the boundary between art and non-art and the nature of artists has become blurred, which have troubled art theorists. Hence, it is more necessary for making contemporary art criticisms. Art criticism is the bridge and guide between art works and viewers. Through the understanding and elaboration of artistic works, art criticism tells viewers the value and significance of artistic works.

In the development of contemporary art, art criticism has become the growing point of artistic theory innovation. Art criticism directly faces the status quo of art development and creative practice. It takes art works as the main research object, analyzes and evaluates them. At the same time, it also includes the investigation and study of various artistic phenomena. And there is no denying that art criticism is a practice supported by theory. It is an activity of judging and evaluating works of art guided by theories and using the research results of art history and new research methods. Therefore, art criticism constitutes the main content of art theory.

Art criticism has always been a major innovation of art theory. Research shows that art criticism always focuses on new artistic phenomena, works of art and schools. In order to enrich and develop the research achievements of art theory and history, we should constantly find and solve new problems and summarize new experiences in the development and practice of artistic creation, so as to make art theory and history obtain new materials from actual practice. The solution of new artistic problems requires not only new methods in line with the requirements, but also new ideas. It is the new research methods and concepts for the new problems that constitute the new artistic theoretical factors. Throughout the development the Western history, it is not difficult to find that art criticism constitutes a theoretical achievement. From the original art ontology generated by many original theories to the development of epistemology generated by many art compositions and the law of artistic creation; from realism, positivism and naturalism since the 19th century to formalism, existentialism, Anglo-American new criticism, structuralism and new historicism after the 20th century, they all start from the status quo of art and realistic problems faced by art and are carried out with art criticism. It is an inevitable fact that art criticism has become the major innovation of art theory since the 19th century. In today's art pluralism, both social progress and artistic development need art criticism more than ever. Art criticism should be an objective and honest expression of evaluation, which can make many people's fuzzy problems clear and even guide people to think in the right direction.

Principles of art criticism

The history of product design criticism determines that there should be different critical views in different periods. For example, Chinese technology and design adhere to the value standard of applicable, economic, beautiful. It is in line with ancient Chinese concept of creation, which stresses adapting to the right place at the right time, the right people, the right materials and the right circumstances. In the post-industrial society, product criticism and culture have become very important evaluation elements. However, no matter which period, design criticism has some common characteristics, which are reflected in the following aspects:

A. Practical and Theoretical Characteristics

Design criticism is the criticism of the object or process and events. It is the criticism of the design fact and object, which has obvious practical purpose and value. It is also a theoretical form of criticism, which is from the design practice and can guide or act on it. Its principles, norms, standards, values and other aspects have theoretical significance, which can form the design philosophy and therefore also has the function of education and guidance.

B. Ideal and Future Characteristics

The standards of design criticism are often excellent standards that can only be achieved through efforts, which are often higher than the general requirements and have the characteristics of idealism. Ideality must have characteristics of the future, which is the expression of people's hope for the future.

C. Periodic and Historical Features

The standards and norms of design criticism are not universal and may not be practical for graphic design or interior design if they are applicable to product design. What is practical for one stage is not necessarily practical for another historical stage. The standards of modern design are not practical for postmodern design.

D. Diversity and Multiplicity

Design critics, designers and governments formulate certain standards for design practice, which may adjust, modify and improve the norms. Design practice and criticism flow and integrate in both directions. The design criticism and the appraisal itself also contains the history, the present situation and the future.

E. Classical and Authoritative

Standards and norms have a certain classical significance, as a model. Sometimes it has a kind of authority. Only standards that conform to classic characteristics can be convincing. The five characteristics of design criticism provide useful references for us to construct today's critical standards.

Conclusion

In a complex art situation, art criticism should take the lead. Art criticism should actively participate in the practice of contemporary art creation, and judge and lead artistic creation and appreciation with its own unique vision, and reveal the law of artistic creation. It should explain the value and significance of contemporary art. In particular, art criticism should play the role of cultural guidance in the thinking and evaluation of contemporary art. With a unique identity, art criticism should improve contemporary society's level of art appreciation and judgment, and play a positive role in social development and cultural prosperity.

Funding

1. The 2017 Science and Technology Research Project in Hubei Provincial Department of Education, Project Number: B2017388
2. Fujian University of Technology Research Foundation Project in 2018, Project Number: GY-S18016

References

[1] Victor Margolin, Design, *The Future and the Human Spirit* [J]. Design Issues, 2007.

[2] Von Hippel, Eric. *The Sources of Innovation* [M]. Oxford and New York: Oxford University Press, 1988.

[3] Fang Ning, *The Unavoidable Problem* [J]. Review of Contemporary Writers, 2011.

[4] Christopher Alexander, *The Timeless Way of Building* [M]. New York: Oxford University press, 1999.

https://doi.org/10.1142/9789811238727_0002

Case Study of Indigenous Restaurant Culture on the Creation and Protection of Traditional Wisdom of Taiwan Indigenous Peoples

Tengfei Ma[1,2], Changwei Chai[1*], and Jifang Shang[2]

[1]Chinese Culture University
[2]Northwest Normal University
*Corresponding Author Email: changwei.chai@gmail.com

Abstract

This research discusses the creation and protection of the traditional wisdom of indigenous peoples. By taking the food culture of indigenous peoples as a case study, the spiritual connotation and value of the food culture of indigenous peoples are summed up and proposed to pass on as a way of educating others about indigenous peoples' food culture. In this study from February 12, 2020 to April 21, 2020, a total of 400 questionnaires were sent out and 392 were returned. The recovery rate was 98%. Questionnaires were filled out by 165 men and 227 women. Through a preliminary understanding of people's general feelings about indigenous restaurants, the phenomenon of the traditional food culture of indigenous peoples was discovered. The research results showed that most consumers recommend indigenous restaurants to people around them, which fully reflects that the popularity of indigenous restaurants is still high and meets the needs of the public. The charm and cultural atmosphere of other restaurants are different, and the general public does have a sense of freshness about the indigenous food culture.

Keywords: Taiwan indigenous, restaurant culture, traditional wisdom

Introduction

Taiwan has pleasant scenery and is located near the Tropic of Cancer. Its unique geographical location has enabled Taiwan to nurture fresh fruits and vegetables between the tropical monsoon climate and the subtropical climate. The surrounding seas bring abundant precipitation and provide a variety of seafood. Taiwan's special historical background has given opportunities for a variety of cultural integration. A large number of immigrants has allowed Taiwan's indigenous people's culture to spread to the world and made Taiwan's indigenous people's food culture more diverse.

Indigenous peoples have a long and ancient history on the land of Taiwan and have brought culture to Taiwan in continuous historical changes. At the same time, traditional and ethnic culture is disappearing from mainstream culture. Moreover, Taiwan's indigenous rarely have their own words. The inheritance of all cultures is carried on by word of mouth and examples. Although it continues a certain history, it is difficult for following generations to study and the social environment is changing. It is difficult to ensure the stable inheritance of culture.

In the 1960s, Taiwan's socio-economic production model slowly shifted to labor-intensive industries, which resulted in a large number of people concentrated in urban industrial areas. The shrinking of the traditional agricultural area along with the deepening of the currency economy market, the increase in employment opportunities on the flat land, the gradual loss of reserved lands by the indigenous peoples, the increase in the population of the tribe, intermarriage, the pursuit of a new life and state, and other subjective and objective factors, have made residents of many flat or mountainous plains move to live and work in cities and towns. For example, mountain-less natives who have mountain reservations and tax reductions worsened economic conditions. The ethnic population continues to increase, and traditional agricultural land production cannot be loaded. Thus, they migrate and settle in non-indigenous towns, which brings out a high proportion of ethnic groups in urban areas. [1]

Since then, the term "urban indigenous" has been widely used, which is a product of the background of the collision of tradition and modernity. Nowadays, indigenous ethnic groups are under various cultural impacts of globalization, which gradually drains the traditional culture of the indigenous and allows the urban indigenous to constantly wander between mainstream and traditional culture. With the efforts in recent years, indigenous culture has shown signs of importance and began to flourish. However, this seemingly thriving indigenous culture, on the other hand, are at a constant loss. Deliberately held indigenous festivals or food events become commercialized and consumerized products of tourism, and food is globalized. The current situation that causes everyone to eat out blindly develops economically and loses precious culture. Thacker Afu pointed out that the capitalist market economy has had an impact on indigenous food culture. Under the cover of cultural tourism market, indigenous food has been reduced to a "flavored meal" that only satisfies the appetite. Eating is extremely common, but it is also extremely important. It is related to everyone's daily life. An anthropologist said: "The tongue is the most direct way to understand a culture." [2]

The definition of indigenous people was drafted by the Taiwan Provincial Documentation Association based on history, culture, language, and customs, and reported to the Taiwan Provincial Government and the Ministry of the Interior. The Ministry of the Interior of Taiwan approved the name of the indigenous people as nine ethnic groups on March 14, 1954, including the Atayal, Saixia, Bunun, Tsou, Rukai, Paiwan, Puyuma, Amis, and Dawu. The Executive Yuan officially approved the Thao as the tenth indigenous ethnic group on

August 8, 2001. Later, the Taroko, Sakilaya, Saidiq, Kavalan (actually Pingpu), Laalwa, and Kanakanafu tribes were added. There are currently 14 ethnic groups in their language and culture with a total number of 575,067 people, which accounts for 2.44% of the total population of Taiwan (as of August 2020).

Research Methods

This questionnaire survey was started from February 12, 2020 to April 21, 2020 for 69 days. 400 questionnaires were sent out and 392 were returned with a 98% recovery rate. 165 men and 227 women filled out the questionnaire. The questions were gender, age, whether you are an indigenous person, occupation, education level, marital status, monthly income, whether you have been to an indigenous restaurant, the number of meals in an indigenous restaurant in the past year, the name of the indigenous restaurant you have visited, and meals information sources, dining companions, dining motivation, willingness to repurchase, whether to recommend indigenous restaurants, places that indigenous restaurants attract, the dining environment of the indigenous restaurants where you go, the theme style, and suggestions for the protection of indigenous food culture. 10 multiple-choice questions, 3 multiple-choice questions, and 6 fill-in-the-blank questions, a total of 19 questions. Through a preliminary understanding of the general public's general feelings about indigenous restaurants, we can discover the problems associated with preservation of indigenous culture.

Results

A. Gender

The respondents to the questionnaire included 165 men (42.09%), and 227 women (57.91%). They included 27 indigenous males (52.49%) and 24 indigenous females (47.06%).

TABLE 1
Gender of respondents

Gender	Male (Number of People)	Female (Number of People)
Total	165	227
Indigenous Peoples	27	24

B. Whether Participant is an Indigenous Person

The respondents to the questionnaire included 51 indigenous people (13.01%) and 341 non-indigenous people (86.99%). All respondents lived in Taipei or New Taipei City.

TABLE 2.
Ethnic group of the respondents.

Whether You Are An Indigenous Person	No	Yes
(Number of People)	341	51

C. Profession

The respondents to the questionnaire included 16 occupations, 6 directors, 11 catering, 9 publishing houses, 22 services, 2 self-employed, 5 studio managers, 53 teachers, 4 laborers, 15 businessmen, 136 students, 2 marketing planners, 7 employees, 19 freelancers, 13 unemployed people, 49 retired people (22 retired teachers, retired service industry 18 people, 9 people retired from other occupations). The occupational status of the indigenous people in the questionnaire were: 1 director, 2 catering, 1 publishing house, 3 service industry, 1 self-employed, 1 studio manager, 10 housekeepers, 3 teachers, 1 laborer, 1 businessman, 11 students, 0 marketing planner, 1 employee, 5 freelancers, 2 unemployed, 8 retired (4 retired teachers, 3 retired service industry, 1 retired from other occupations).

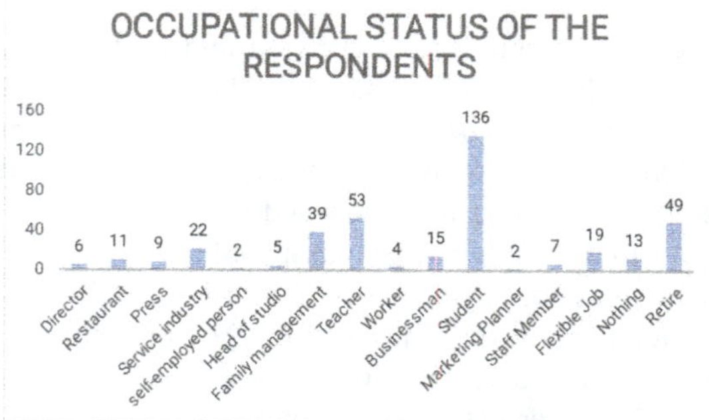

Fig. 1 Occupational status of the respondents.

Fig. 2 Occupational status of the respondents who were indigenous.

D. Age

The respondents comprised 109 people of under the age of 20, 64 of 20 to 30, 101 of 30 to 40, and 40 over 40. 76 people were 50 years old and 42 people were over 50 years old.

The status of the indigenous people in the questionnaires returned: 8 under 20 years old, 5 between 20 and 30 years old, 8 between 30 and 40 years old, and 9 over 50 years old.

TABLE 3
Data of age of the respondents

Age	Under 20	20-30	30-40	40-50	Over 50 years old
Total	109	64	101	76	42
Indigenous Peoples	8	5	21	8	9

E. Education Level

The respondents included 20 people with the education level of elementary school and below, 20 with junior high school, 50 with senior high school, and 181 with junior college/university. There were a total of 121 people from research institutes with the largest respondents from associates/universities. There were 6 indigenous people with education level of elementary school and below, 5 of middle school, 14 of high school, 19 of college/university, and 7 of graduate school or above.

TABLE 4
Data of education level of the indigenous people

Education Level	Under Elementary School	Junior High	Senior High	College/ University	Graduate School or Above
Total	20	20	50	181	121
Indigenous	6	5	14	19	7

F. Monthly Income

The respondents included 162 people with a monthly income of less than NTD 20,000 and 108 people with a monthly income of NTD 20,001–40,000. There were 68 people with a monthly income of NTD 40,000–60,000, 29 with NTD 60,000–80,000, and 25 with NTD 80,001. There were 20 indigenous people with monthly income below 20,000 NTD, 20 with between 20,000 and 40,000 NTD, 7 with monthly income between 40,000 and 60,000 NTD, 3 people with income between 60,001 and 80,000 NTD, and one person had a monthly income of more than 80,000 NTD.

TABLE 5
Monthly income of indigenous peoples surveyed

Monthly Income	Under 20,000	20,001-40,000	40,001-60,000	60,001-80,000	Above 80,000
Total	162	108	68	29	25
Indigenous Peoples	20	20	7	3	1

G. Whether the Respondent has been to an Indigenous Restaurant

Among the respondents, the number of people who had been to an indigenous restaurant was 311 and the number of people who had never been to an indigenous restaurant was 81. The number of indigenous people who have been to an indigenous restaurant was 47, and the number of people who have never been to an indigenous restaurant was 4.

TABLE 6
Whether the respondent has been to an indigenous restaurant

Whether the Respondent has been to an Indigenous Restaurant	yes	no
Total	311	81
Indigenous Peoples	47	4

H. Number of Meals at Indigenous Restaurants in Past Year

81 people ate 0 times in indigenous restaurants in the past year, 107 did 1 or 2 times, 82 did 4 times, 30 did 5-8 times, and 92 did 8 times.

4 indigenous people ate 0 times in the indigenous restaurant, 11 did 1 time, 4 did 2 times, 18 did 4 times, 8 did 5 times, and 16 did 8 times.

TABLE 7
Number of visits to indigenous restaurants in the past year

Number of Visits to Indigenous Restaurants in the Past Year	0	1	2-4	5-8	8 or more
Total	81	107	82	30	92
Indigenous Peoples	4	11	18	2	16

I. Dining Information Sources (Multiple Choice Questions)

The number of respondents who selected TV reports as information source was 30 people, and 10 people selected broadcast introduction as the information source. 20 people were introduced by newspapers, 40 by magazines, 50 by a website, and 190 by relatives and friends. Restaurants were selected through flyers (50 respondents), through recommendation (40 respondents), through government page (20 respondents). The highest number of people selected the restaurants by relatives and friends' recommendation.

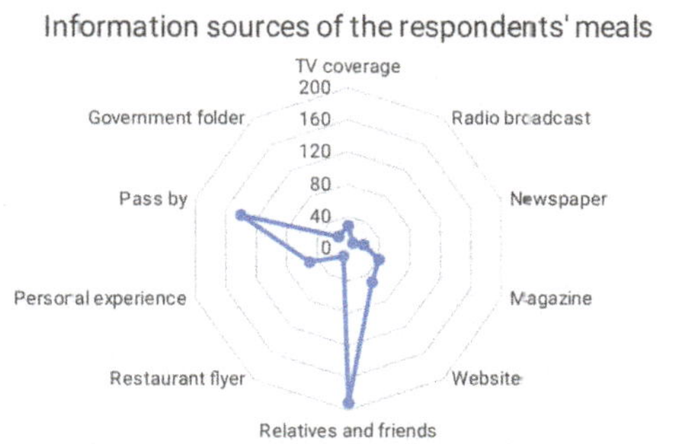

Fig. 3 Information sources of the respondents' meals

TABLE 8
Information sources of the respondents' meals

Dining Information Sources	TV	Broadcast	Newspaper	Magazine	Website
	30	10	20	40	50
	Relatives and friends	Restaurant flyer	Personal experience	Passing by	Government folding introduction
	190	10	50	140	20

J. Dining Companion (Multiple Choice Questions)

80 respondents chose their family members as dining companions, 197 chose friends, 203 chose classmates, 21 chose colleagues, and 45 chose a couple.

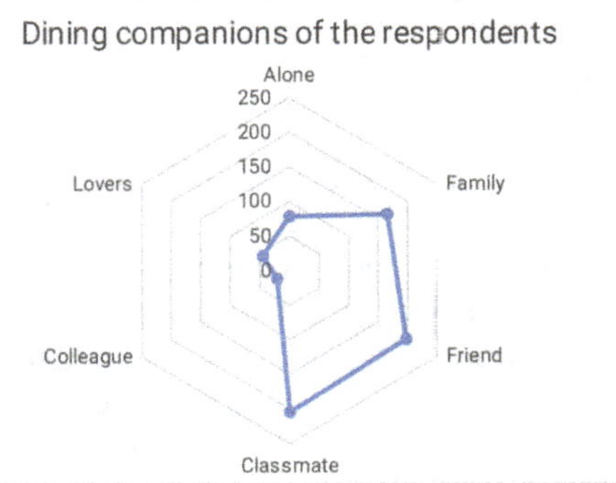

Fig. 4 Dining companion of the respondents

TABLE 9.
Dining companion of the respondents

Dining Companion	Alone	Family	Friends
	80	166	197
	Classmate	Colleague	Couple
	203	21	45

K. Dining Motivation (Multiple Choice Questions)

44 respondents chose curiosity as the motive for dining, 27 chose appointment, 170 chose family and friends gathering, 179 chose the experience of indigenous food culture, and 148 chose coincidence.

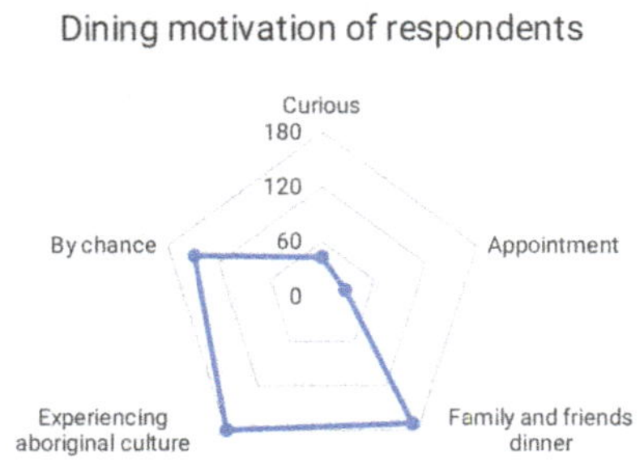

Fig. 5 Dining motivation of the respondents

TABLE 10
Dining motivation of the respondents

Dining Motivation	Curious	Appointment	Family and Friends' Dinner
	44	27	170
	Experience Indigenous Culture	Passing By	
	179	148	

L. Repurchase Intention

343 respondents had revisit intention (87.50%), while 49 did not (12.50%). 49 indigenous respondents expressed their willingness to revisit (96.08%), and 2 did not (3.92%).

TABLE 11
Repurchase intention of the respondents

Repurchase Intention	Yes	No
Total	343	49
Indigenous Peoples	49	2

M. Whether Participants would Recommend Indigenous Restaurants

49 respondents highly recommended indigenous restaurants, 222 people recommended, 105 not necessarily recommended, 10 did not recommend, and 6 never recommended. 16 indigenous respondents strongly recommended, 30 recommend, 4 people did not recommend, and 1 never recommend.

Fig. 6 Do respondents recommend indigenous restaurants

Fig. 7 Do indigenous people recommend restaurants

TABLE 12.
Cronbach reliability analysis

Name	Number of Items	Sample Size	Cronbach αcoefficient
Dining Companion	6	392	0.968
Dining Motivation	5	392	0.968
Information Source	10	392	0.989

Questionnaire Data Analysis

A. Questionnaire Reliability

The reliability coefficient of dining companions and dining motivation was 0.968, and the information source reliability coefficient was 0.989, both of which were greater than 0.9. This indicates that the reliability of the research data is good and used for further analysis.

B. Questionnaire Validity

The KMO and Bartlett test was used to verify the validity. The KMO values are 0.916, 0.888, and 0.936 respectively, and all are greater than 0.8. The research data has a good level of validity.

TABLE 13
Validity analysis

Name	Test Result		
Dining Companion	KMO value		0.916
	Bartlett Sphericity Test	Approximate chi-square	3363.678
		df	15
		p value	0.000
	KMO Value		0.888

Name	Test Result		
Dining Motivation	Bartlett Sphericity Test	Approximate chi-square	2732.228
		df	10
		p value	0.000
Information Source	KMO Value		0.936
	Bartlett Sphericity Test	Approximate chi-square	9819.638
		df	45
		p value	0.000

TABLE 14
Linear regression analysis results

	Regression Coefficients	95% CI	VIF
Constant	2.628 (17.704**)	2.337 ~ 2.919	-
Monthly Income	-0.081 (-1.341)	-0.198 ~ 0.037	1.000
Sample Size	392		
R^2	0.005		
Adjustment R^2	0.002		
F Value	F (1,390)=1.797,p=0.181		
Dependent Variable: Number of Meals			
D-W Value：1.084			
* p<0.05 ** p<0.01 t value in brackets			

C. Linear Regression

a. Monthly income does not affect the number of meals

The model *R* square value is 0.005, which means that monthly income explains the 0.5% change in the number of meals. The *F* test of the model found that the model did not pass the *F* test (F=1.797, p=0.181>0.05), which means that the monthly income does not affect the number of meals.

b. Ethnicity does not affect whether to eat in indigenous restaurants

The model *R*-square value is 0.001, which means that the family explains the 0.1% change of the meal. When the *F* test was performed on the model, it was found that the model did not pass the *F* test (F=0.386, p=0.535>0.05), which means that the family does not affect the meal.

TABLE 15
Linear regression analysis results

	Regression Coefficients	95% CI	VIF
Constant	1.417 (10.507**)	1.152 ~ 1.681	-
Clan	-0.044 (-0.621)	-0.183 ~ 0.095	1.000
Sample Size	392		
R^2	0.001		
Adjustment R^2	-0.002		
F Value	F (1,390)=0.386,p=0.535		
Dependent Variable: Meal			
D-W Value: 0.471			
* p<0.05 ** p<0.01 t value in brackets			

TABLE 16
Linear regression analysis results

	Regression Coefficients	95% CI	VIF
Constant	2.087 (10.471**)	1.696 ~ 2.477	-
Profession	0.037 (1.974*)	0.000 ~ 0.074	1.000
Sample Size	392		
R^2	0.010		
Adjustment R^2	0.007		
F Value	F (1,390)=3.898, p=0.049		
Dependent Variable: Number of Meals			
D-W Value：1.081			
* p<0.05 ** p<0.01 t value in brackets			

c. Occupation has a significant positive impact on the number of meals

The model *R*-square value is 0.010, which means that occupation explains the 1.0% change in the number of meals. When the *F* test was performed on the model, it was found that the model passed the *F* test (F=3.898, p=0.049<0.05), which means that occupation significantly affected the number of meals. (The formula of the model is: number of meals = 2.087 + 0.037 * occupation)

d. Age has a significant negative impact on the number of meals

The model *R*-square value is 0.041, which means that age explains the 4.1% change in the number of meals. When the *F* test was performed on the model, it was found that the model passed the *F* test (F=16.510, p=0.000<0.05), which means that age significantly affects the number of meals. (The number of meals=3.032-0.203*age)

TABLE 17
Linear regression analysis results

	Regression Coefficients	95% CI	VIF
Constant	3.032 (19.108**)	2.721 ~ 3.343	-
Age	-0.203 (-4.063**)	-0.300 ~ -0.105	1.000
Sample Size	392		
R^2	0.041		
Adjustment R^2	0.038		
F Value	F (1,390)=16.510,p=0.000		
Dependent Variable: Number of Meals			
D-W Value：1.201			
* p<0.05 ** p<0.01 t value in brackets			

Discussion

A. Indigenous Restaurant Business Philosophy

The business philosophy is the direct presentation of the restaurant to customers, which determines the characteristics and development of the restaurant. At the same time, it attracts consumers and obtains economic benefits. The questionnaire survey result showed that respondents were attracted by the indigenous restaurant. Most of them were attracted by "indigenous cultures". The answers to the restaurant cultures of different ethnic groups were similar without direct ethnic-cultural characteristics. The differences between ethnic groups are ambiguous. It is only reflected in the name, but not a deeper understanding of culture. There is a situation of blindly following the trend. In the restaurant design, the decoration features are prominent, and there is no related experience area or activity for consumers to experience the national culture. At present, there are three types of indigenous restaurant business concepts that are ubiquitous in the market: sharing indigenous cuisine, enhancing cultural exchanges between groups, and providing indigenous employment space.

B. Indigenous Restaurant Design

Most indigenous restaurants' capital is mainly raised by their funds. In addition to the flow of people, they consider rental costs, location, the acquisition of ingredients to ensure the authenticity of indigenous cuisine and convenience. The respondents generally liked the decoration. To show the characteristics of indigenous culture, the decoration should attract consumers' attention with display except for traditional indigenous cultural relics, Totems, handicrafts (weaving, woodcarving, bamboo), and so on. The characteristics need to be diversified, not limited to monotonous cultural relics. The respondents suggested that hands-on projects be added to allow interested consumers to have a cultural experience in restaurant workshops, and the food culture can also be shown to consumers through various methods such as films, restaurant music, and commentary.

C. Respondent Questionnaire Data Feedback

a. Some people have never been to an indigenous restaurant or do not know. Among 392 respondents, 33% have never visited indigenous restaurants, nor have 37% of the indigenous people. The indigenous restaurant has failed to obtain a wider range of customers but has a certain degree of understanding. More than half of the respondents, including indigenous people, have visited indigenous restaurants.

b. Among the respondents, most dining consumers visit for the first time. In the past year, the respondents have visited indigenous restaurants 1–4 times, of which only 1 time visitors account for 27.29%. 30 respondents have visited 5–8 times (7.65 %). Customers who were familiar with or prefer indigenous restaurants visited indigenous restaurants frequently and the number was relatively high (23.46%). Most of the respondents visited the restaurants for the first time.

c. Indigenous restaurants have a higher return rate. 392 respondents expressed their willingness to return (96.08%), while 2 did not have the willingness (3.92%). Only a small number of respondents were not willing to patronize again, and a majority of people patronized indigenous restaurants again, so indigenous restaurants have certain development potential.

d. Sixty-one percent of respondents would recommend indigenous restaurants. Most respondents recommended indigenous restaurants to people around them, which reflected that the popularity of indigenous restaurants was high, in line with the needs of the public and experiential cultural services, with its unique cultural charm, the differences from the cultural atmosphere of other restaurants, and the freshness of their national culture for ordinary people. Another factor is the result of changes in the market.

Conclusions

The development potential of the indigenous restaurant lies in the lack of publicity, while the advantage in an interpersonal promotion. The analysis of the questionnaires showed that 190 respondents obtained the information from relatives and friends, 140 from public advertisement, and the rest from the main consumer's dining information. Indigenous restaurants adapting to the needs of the people is a necessary condition for the development of indigenous restaurants. 166 respondents chose their family members as their dining companions as, 197 chose friends, and 203 chose classmates. 31.51% of the respondents chose the motivation to experience the indigenous culture, 87.50% expressed their willingness to revisit, and 69.13% strongly recommended or would recommend. Thus, indigenous restaurants need to focus on experiential restaurants. Although the experience of cultural experience mode varies from person to person, participating in cultural experience activities or workshops greatly expand the cultural living space of indigenous restaurants.

For the age and number of visits, the model R-square value was 0.041. This means that the age of the respondents affected the number of visits. Gathering and entertainment are an extended function of indigenous restaurants in addition to experiencing the main functions of indigenous culture. To expand the cultural influence and survival of indigenous restaurants, space has a certain positive meaning.

Although the monthly incomes of the respondents were different, it was an important independent variable. The model R square value was 0.005, indicating that monthly income did not affect the number of visits. Similarly, the indigenous restaurant is not a "single-use restaurant" for the indigenous people. With the family as the independent variable and the number of visits as the dependent variable, the model R square value is 0.001, which means that the family did not affect the number significantly. The model did not pass the F-test (F=0.386, p=0.535>0.05), which means that being an indigenous retaurants did not affect the number.

After considering all aspects of the dietary culture of indigenous peoples, the characteristics of visiting indigenous restaurants were identified, which helps the restaurants. The result leads to the future development of the culture of indigenous people and contributes to its preservation. The result allows improving relevant measures. The indigenous people's food culture needs the protection of food and retention of national memory in order for people to realize the unique charm of the food culture of Taiwan's indigenous people.

References

[1] Cao Ruitai. Research on the Legal System Planning of Taiwan's Indigenous Rights and the Development of Autonomous Regions [J]. Unity Forum, 2017(06):57-60.

[2] Xu Xun. Research on the Expansion of Taiwan's In-Depth Tourism Market in Zhejiang - Based on the Perspective of Food Culture [J]. Journal of Jilin Radio and Television University, 2014(10):44-45.

[3] Chen Jianyue. "Ethnic Tourism" or "Foreign Tourism": A Comparison of Related Studies on Both Sides of the Strait [J]. Journal of the Central University for Nationalities (Philosophy and Social Sciences Edition), 2017, 44(01):17-25.

[4] Luo Xiaonan. Seeking all the wild from ritual failure - the wisdom inheritance of Taiwan indigenous culture and Chinese traditional culture [J]. Journal of the Yunnan Institute of Socialism, 2017(01):112-114.

[5] Dong Jianhui, Huang Mingsong. The Tradition and Future Prospects of Taiwan Indigenous Studies at Xiamen University [J]. Journal of Hubei University for Nationalities (Philosophy and Social Sciences Edition), 2017, 35(01):5-11.

[6] Ren Na. The norms and practices of the protection of the rights of indigenous peoples in Taiwan in my country [D]. South-Central University for Nationalities, 2018.

[7] Ma Juli. A summary of the "Seminar on the Development and Cultural Inheritance of Mainland Minorities and Taiwan Indigenous Peoples" [J]. Southwest Frontier Ethnic Studies, 2016(02):252+250.

[8] Zheng Siyang. A review of changes in Taiwanese food culture since the 20th century [D]. Zhejiang Gongshang University, 2015.

[9] Liu Yingdou. Random Talk about the Food of the Gaoshan People (2)—Ami and Atayal [J]. Chinese Food, 1992(11): 38-39.

[10] Zhu Lin. A study on betel nut bags of the Ami and Puyuma in Taiwan. Fujian Normal University, 2016.

[11] Zeng Yaling, Li Lao. From "Sedek Bale" to see the culture of the aborigines of Taiwanese Saidiq., "Film Literature", (2014(01): 47- 48 pages).

[12] Wang Meng. A Summary of Taiwan Kavalan Studies. Journal of Guangxi University for Nationalities (Philosophy and Social Sciences Edition), (2006(S1): 23-26).

[13] Zhu Zhilin. Survival in the Cracks: An Ethnological Investigation of the "Rectification" of Southern Tsou People. "Xiamen University", (2017).

[14] Yang Mingduo, Sun Wenying. Research on the status and path of the protection and inheritance of China's food and beverage intangible cultural heritage. Journal of Sichuan Institute of Tourism, (2020(02): 6-9 pages).

[15] Li Weiying. Changes in the traditional food culture of the Ami in Taiwan. National History Research, 2017(00): 368-378.

[16] Shen Songmao. Taiwan's Food Culture and Future Direction "Business Economy and Management", 1995(03): 56-57.

[17] Ye Yupei. Discussion on the relationship between livelihood and ecology: Taking the Bunun tribe in Tannan Village, Xinyi Township, Nantou, Taiwan as an example.

[18] Mao Daizong. Thao Customs. "Art Garden", 2019(01): 1310.

[19] Mount Modai. The industrialization of ethnic culture and the protection of characteristic ethnic villages under the background of tourism: A case study of the "Kele Tribe" of the Taroko nationality in Taiwan.

[20] Zheng Weibin, Wang Hongtao. Fracture and continuity: The ethnic maintenance and cultural reconstruction of the Sakilaya after the name rectification.

[21] Bush Bunanan. The culturally rich Paiwan ethnic group. Taiwan Sound, 2016(01):102-107.

[22] The SPSSAU project (2020). SPSSAU. (Version 20.0) [Online Application Software]. Retrieved from https://www.spssau.com.

[23] Eisinga R, Te Grotenhuis M, Pelzer B. The reliability of a two-item scale: Pearson, Cronbach, or Spearman-Brown [J]. International Journal of Public Health, 2013, 58(4):637-642.

[24] Emanuel, D. (1974). Psychographics And From Where It Comes. Lifestyle and Psychographics, Chicago: AMA, 22.

[25] Engel, J. F., Blackwell, R. D. & Miniard, P. W. (1978). Consumer Behavior, Hinsdale: Drydoll Press.

[26] Hansen, R. A. & T. Deutsher (1978). An Empirical Investigation of Attribute Importance in Retail Store Seletion. Journal of Retailing, 53(4).

[27] Jaime, C. D. & F. K. Mahajan. (1998). Know your Place. Marketing. , Apr.

[28] Jones, N. (1983). The Restaurant, A Place for Quality Control and Product Maintenance. International Journal of Hospitality Management, 2(2), 93-100.

[29] Khan, M. A. (1991). Concepts of foodservice operations and management, New York: Van Nostrand Reinhold.

[30] Kotler, p. (1994). Management Analysis, Planning, Implementation and Control (7th ed.)., New Jersey: Prentice Hall, Inc., pp.164-170.

[31] Lundberg, D. E. (1984). The Hotel and Restaurant Business. New York: Van Nostrand Reinhold, pp.264-266.

https://doi.org/10.1142/9789811238727_0003

A Comparative Study on the Parental Music Literacy of Preschool Children-Taking Taiwan and Southern India as Examples

Hsiao-Fang Lin*, Liza Lee, Vasistha Bhargavi

Chaoyang University of Technology
168, Jifeng E. Rd., Wufeng District, Taichung, 413310 Taiwan
*Corresponding Author Email: snoopystock100@cyut.edu.tw

Abstract

The purpose of this research is to compare the music literacy of parents in Taiwan and South India, and the use of 3C products in music activities with preschool children. The subjects of this study were parents of children aged 3–6 years old in Taiwan and Southern India. There were 84 valid samples by using the online sampling method, including 55 cases in Taiwan and 29 in Southern India. The research tool was the "Music Literacy Questionnaire of Preschool Parents" edited by the researchers using descriptive statistical analysis, Mann-Whitney U test, and χ^2 test of nonparametric statistics for data analysis. The results of the study found that there were significant differences in parenting encouraging exposure to music and in e-music literacy between Taiwanese and South Indian parents. The main difference came from mothers, while there were no significant differences in fathers. Secondly, in parent-child music activities, the use of 3C products was particularly different. Fathers preferred to use the Internet, while mothers preferred music CDs. Mothers played CDs to children, while fathers listened to CDs and watched TV with children. This research was a transnational preliminary survey, and initial results found that there were cultural differences in family music activities and the use of technological products between Taiwan and South India.

Keywords: parental music literacy, preschool children, transnational comparative study, e-music literacy, 3C products in music activities

Introduction

In a child's developmental stages, preschool age is considered the most important stage for the family. This is the place where children grow up, the family environment is important to shape children's habits, and the parents are the initial mentors in the child's life and the relationship with children. Human languages and symbols originate from music and performance. For most people, learning music means learning musical instruments and having a skill, or cultivating temperament through music, or opening up a different life for the future. In any case, music exists in our lives, but there are questions: can people have the ability to accept, understand or enjoy it? Does the musical literacy of a parent or caregiver affect the musical environment of a child's childhood, will it contribute to the development of musical potential, or music preferences? The parental music literacy defined in this study consists of two parts: the parent's ability to accept, understand, perceive and appreciate music as well as e-music literacy that refers to the experience of using technology to interact with children in music.

Hansen *et al.* thought that music literacy relates to reading and writing traditional music notation. However, the notion has expanded exponentially since the development of technologies and other forms of notation such as graphic scores and those used in other cultural contexts (Martin, 2018; Barton, 2019). In the Ecological Systems Theory (Bronfenbrenner, 1979, 1986), the family is the micro-system in the lives of children and the most frequent and direct environment that children come into contact with. Family activities are also one of the standards for testing family lifestyle and quality of life, as well as an important dimension to measure the level of children's activity participation and cognitive development (Jin and Hao, 2018). In a quantitative study, we sought to determine the connection between music literacy and music-related background variables of parents. This study defined three aspects of parental music literacy: 1. Parents' music educational attitude, 2. Parenting encourages exposure to music, 3. Parent-child attachment.

Methodology

A. Participant and Setting

The subjects of this study were parents of 3–6 years old children in Taiwan and Southern India. By using online sampling methods, a total of 84 effective samples were obtained: 55 in Taiwan, 29 in southern India; and 26 were fathers and 58 were mothers. It is inferred that most of the caregivers of preschool children are mothers, so the number of mothers who filled out the questionnaire was higher than that of fathers. About 70% of the parents have taken music lessons at school, and more than 80% of the parents have a college degree or above. The descriptive statistical analysis of participants' music background information is presented in Table 1.

TABLE 1

Descriptive statistical analysis of participant's background information

Varable	Item	Taiwan	Southern India	Total
Parents	1.Father	12 (21.8%)	14 (48.3%)	26
	2.Mother	43 (78.2%)	15 (51.7%)	58
Parent's music experience	1. Graduated from the Department of Music	4 (7.3%)	1 (3.4%)	5
	2. Non-music graduate, but currently working in the music field	3 (5.5%)	1 (3.4%)	4
	3. Participate in school music courses during school, learn instruments after school time	39 (70.9%)	18 (62.1%)	57
	4. No contact with music at all	9 (16.4%)	7 (24.1%)	16
	5.Other	0 (0.0%)	2 (6.9%)	2
Parent's education level	1. Senior high school, Higher vocational school	4 (7.3%)	0 (0.0%)	4
	2. Five-year or two-year technical school	5 (9.1%)	1 (3.4%)	6
	3. four-year technical school, colleges, university	30 (54.5%)	16 (55.2%)	46
	4. Master	15 (27.3%)	9 (31.0%)	24
	5. Ph. D	1 (1.8%)	3 (10.3%)	4
Total		**55**	**29**	**84**

B. Research Framework

There is one independent variable in this study: participants' background information. The dependent variables are parent-child e-music activities and parental e-music literacy. This research intends to explore the parent-child music interaction of different genders and countries and parents' e-music literacy. The family music interaction refers to parents using 3C products for parent-child music activities. The research structure is shown in Figure 1.

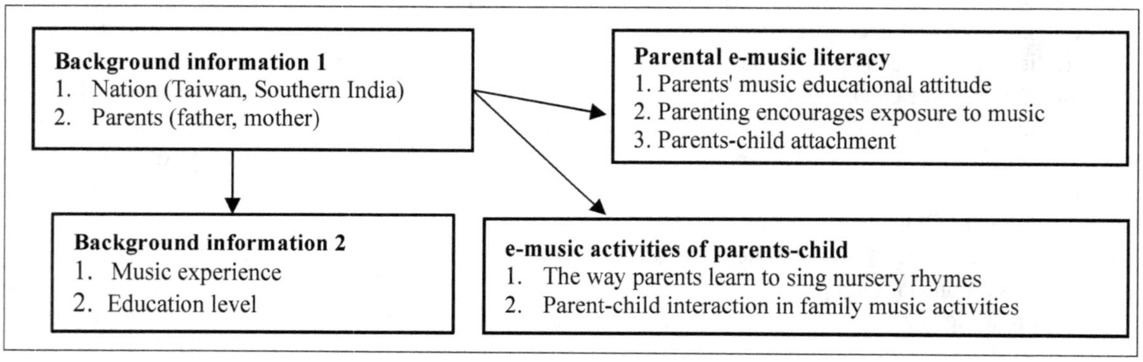

Fig. 1 Research structure

C. Research Tool

The research tool was the "Preschool Parents' Music Literacy Questionnaire" edited for this research. The questionnaire contains three parts: the background information of parents (3 items: child's father/mother, educational level, music experience), the music interaction experience between parents and children (1 item: how did you learn to sing songs for your baby?), and parental music literacy (1 item: the most common music-related activities or the way of listening to music at home). The questionnaire contained 18 items in the Likert 5-points scale. The standard Cronbach's α was 0.990 and the construct validity was 0.860.

D. Statistics Analysis Methods

Due to the small number of samples in this survey, to avoid errors in statistical analysis, the Mann-Whitney U test and χ^2-test of nonparametric statistical methods were used for data analysis.

Results

In this study, a researcher's self-compiled questionnaire was used to conduct a cross-cultural survey of Taiwan and South India, and the results were initially presented from the following three aspects.

A. Compare the Parental Music Literacy of Fathers and Mothers in Taiwan and South India

The parents' attitudes toward music education has three aspects: parents' attitudes towards children's exposure to music, encouraging children to learn music, and playing music games or activities with children (parent-child attachment). The results of this study found a significant difference among these aspects (Mann-Whitney U=579.50, p=.014). The mother's parenting encourages exposure to music (Mann-Whitney U=212.00, p=.048) and all parenting encourages exposure to music (Mann-Whitney U=544.50, p=.017) showed significant difference. The differences in the other two aspects and between the two national's fathers were not significant. The results are shown in Table 2.

TABLE 2
Mann-Whitney U-test results of father and mother's e-music literacy of in Taiwan and South India

		Parents' music educational attitude	Parenting encourages exposure to music	Parent-child attachment	Total
Mother	Rank Mean	Taiwan=31.19; India=24.67	Taiwan=32.07; India=22.13	Taiwan=31.10; India=24.90	Taiwan=31.91; India=22.60
	Mann-Whitney U	250.00	**212.00***	253.50	219.00
	p	.193	**.048**	.215	.065
Father	Rank Mean	Taiwan=15.29; India=11.96	Taiwan=16.25; India=11.14	Taiwan=15.25; India=12.00	Taiwan=15.75; India=11.57
	Mann-Whitney U	62.50	51.00	63.00	57.00
	p	.264	.087	.273	.164
Total	Rank Mean	Taiwan=45.57; India=36.67	Taiwan=47.10; India=33.78	Taiwan=45.14; India=37.50	Taiwan=46.46; India=24.98
	Mann-Whitney U	628.50	**544.50***	652.50	**579.50***
	p	.108	**.017**	.168	**.040**

*$p<0.05$

B. The Way Parents Learn to Sing Nursery Rhymes

There are different development and progress of 3C products. Therefore, it is necessary to understand how fathers and mothers in different cultures learn nursery rhymes and sing to their children. The item in the questionnaire was "How did you learn to sing songs for your baby". Table 3 showed that the way fathers and mothers in Taiwan and South India learn nursery rhymes, childhood memories and the Internet are common. The χ^2 test results showed that the fathers of different nationalities had significant differences in "From internet (e.g., YouTube)" (χ^2=6.003, p =.014), while the mothers in "Music CDs or music textbook" (χ^2=5.613, p =.018). In terms of overall comparison, the fathers and mothers also had significant differences in "Music CDs or music textbook" (χ^2=7.849, p=.005).

C. Parent-Child Interaction in Family Music Activities

The music activities of parents and children at home were investigated through the use of 3C products. The fathers had significant differences between Taiwan and Sothern India in three items: "Play music CDs and listen with children" (χ^2=4.338, p=.037); "Play DVD or TV program for children to watch (χ^2=8.211, p=.004)", "Use the computer or mobile phone to play music or videos to watch with children (χ^2=5.539, p=.019)". For mothers, there is a significant difference in the performance of Taiwan and Southern India in "Play music CDs for children (χ^2=4.432, p=.035)". The results are shown in Table 4. The Taiwanese fathers and South Indian fathers showed the difference in accompanying their children in musical activities, while mothers had no difference.

TABLE 3
χ^2-test of "How did you learn to sing songs for your baby"

	Taiwan (N=55, Nm=43, Nf=12)		Southern India (N=29, Nm=15, Nf=14)		χ^2		p		Total (N_{Taiwan}=57, N_{India}=30)	
	Mother	Father	Mother	Father	Mother	Father	Mother	Father	χ^2	p
Learn during school	13	1	4	2	.068	.224	.794	.636	.231	.631
Childhood memory	31	7	7	7	3.182	.181	0.074	.671	2.833	.092
From internet (e.g., YouTube)	26	10	8	5	.233	**6.003***	.629	**.014**	3.140	.076
Music CD or music textbook	17	3	1	2	**5.613***	.478	**.018**	.490	**7.849****	**.005**
From mother or elders in the family or relatives	7	2	5	5	1.971	1.192	.160	.275	4.839	.028
Self-edited	3	0	3	1	2.034	.891	.154	.345	0.939	.333

Note: N_m means sample size of the mother, N_f means sample size of the father

TABLE 4

χ^2-test of "The most common way of music activities for parents and children at home."

	Taiwan (N=55, Nm=43, Nf=12)		southern India (N=29, Nm=15, Nf=14)		χ^2		p		Total (N_{Taiwan}=57, N_{India}=30)	
	Mother	Father	Mother	Father	Mother	Father	Mother	Father	χ^2	p
Play music CD for child	15	3	1	1	**4.432***	1.583	**.035**	.208	**7.633****	**.006**
Play music CD and listen with child	14	5	2	1	2.058	**4.338***	.151	**.037**	**6.361***	**.012**
Play DVD or TV program for child to watch	5	0	1	7	.295	**8.211***	.587	**.004**	**6.560***	**.010**
Play DVD or TV program to watch with child	5	1	2	4	.030	1.704	.861	.192	2.537	.111
Use computer or mobile phone to play music or video for child	10	3	7	4	2.942	.042	.086	.838	1.890	.169
Use the computer or mobile phone to play music or videos to watch with child	8	7	0	2	3.237	**5.539***	.072	**.019**	**4.827***	**.028**

Note: N_m means sample size of the mother, N_f means sample size of the father

Conclusions and Suggestions

With the rapid development of 3C products and changes in parents' lifestyles, the music interaction between parents and children has also changed greatly. In the past, most mothers raised their children at home, but mothers need to go out to work now. Thus. there is little time to spend with their children. In the busy modern life, music activities between parents and children begin to rely on the Internet and 3C products. The results of this research found cultural differences in parent-child music interaction patterns between Taiwan and Southern India and between the fathers and mothers in the musical activities of young children.

This research is a transnational preliminary survey. In South India, the sample size was small in the questionnaire survey. It was limited in terms of understanding the interaction of family music in depth. However, cultural differences were found. Parents need to spend more time communicating with their children in music. Even if the parents have no experience in musical instrument learning or are not good at singing, with the aid of 3C products, these are no longer the key points. e-music literacy and attitude guide and encourage children to come into contact with music to cultivate their mind.

References

[1] Barton, G. (2019). *Developing Literacy and the Arts in Schools.* Routledge.

[2] Bronfenbrenner, U. (1979). *The ecology of human development.* Cambridge, MA: Harvard University Press.

[3] Bronfenbrenner, U. (1986). Ecology of the family as a context for human development: Research perspectives. *Developmental Psychology, 22*(6), 723-742.

[4] Hansen, D. Bernstorf, E.& Stuber, G. M. (2014). *The music and literacy connection.* New York, NY: Rowman & Littlefield.

[5] Jin, F., & Hao, S. (2018). The Relationship between Children's Participation in Family Activities and Parental Company. *Journal of Shaanxi Xueqian Normal University, 34*(7), 9-13.

https://doi.org/10.1142/9789811238727_0004

A Preliminary Study on the Obstacles of Dementia Examination for Retired Elderly Based on Service Experience Survey - Mainly on MMSE

Sei-Wo Tseng*, Chia-Chen Wu, Wei-Cheng Huang

National Yunlin University of Science and Technology, Douliou, Yunlin, Taiwan
*Corresponding Author Email: tsengws@gemail.yuntech.edu.tw

Abstract

An aging society leads to the growth of the mentally retarded population. According to the statistics of the Taiwan Association of Dementia in 2019, nearly half (34) of the 74 mentally retarded people were not diagnosed with dementia when they suffered financial losses. More than 90% (65) were not declared to be assisted or supervised. As most of the family members of patients do not understand the symptoms of dementia, and the patients themselves are unwilling to admit and refuse to be tested for dementia. In this study, a tool for examining the medication payment for dementia in Taiwan was used to test the mini-mental state examination (MMSE) for retired elderly people. The potential design requirements are proposed by contextual observation: (1) changing the type of dementia test, such as taking board games, and integrating MMSE questions into the game can reduce the subjects' vigilance, (2) changing the presentation and interaction mode of topics, using the agricultural products (space), festivals (time), and celebration activities (space) in Taiwan to test the topics of space, time, memory, calculation and drawing, and interacting and testing them in a non-verbal way to increase understanding and interest, (3) using nostalgic elements to connect the elderly with memory, and (4) examining the living environment at home and promoting family interaction.

Keywords: Product design, Table games, Contextual inquiry, Dementia, MMSE

Introduction

In 2017, the world's population of dementia reached 50 million [1]. According to Taiwan's demographic data at the end of December 2018, 626,026 out of 3,433,517 people over the age of 65 were diagnosed with mild cognitive impairment (MCI). 269,725 people were diagnosed with dementia and 109,706 with extremely mild dementia [2]. Dementia is a disease of acquired memory and other brain dysfunction [3]. Usually, in mild cognitive impairment, the patients consciously degrade their memory, which causes occasional getting lost, putting things in the wrong place, losing the sense of time, or changing personality, emotional ups and downs, delusion, suspicion, and unclear logic of language expression [4].

However, when the elderly have mild cognitive impairment, family members may not necessarily associate it with dementia.

Moreover, due to the self-esteem of patients with suspected dementia, they are not willing to admit that they have dementia and refuse to be tested for dementia. When financial losses occurred in September 2019 [5], nearly half (34) out of 74 dementia patients were not diagnosed with dementia. More than 90% (65) did not have the declaration of assistance or guardianship with no legal recourse. Most of the family members of the patients do not understand the early symptoms of dementia, and easily misunderstand some of the symptoms. Patients themselves do not feel that they are already dementia patients and are unwilling to admit, so the disease worsens and the opportunity to see a doctor earlier is delayed. The disorder behavior in the early stage of dementia has a great impact on society and family. For various problems and threats of early disorder behavior of dementia, many experts believe that home-based dementia detection is necessary [6]. The dementia assessment tool helps the family members of the elders to understand the degree of the disease in their families and seek medical treatment and control as soon as possible.

At present, the commonly used dementia tests in Taiwan include Mini-Mental State Examination (MMSE), Clinical Dementia Rating (CDR), Informant Questionnaire on Cognitive Decline in the Elderly (IQCODE), Ascertain Dementia 8 (ad-8), and Cognitive Abilities Screening Instrument (CASI). MMSE is currently the most widely used tool in clinical and research. Though it takes a longer time it is more efficient [7]. It is an important basis for Taiwan to review the drug payment for dementia [8], which is detected by nurses or family members. To find out the obstacles and potential opportunities during the evaluation of dementia in the retired elderly, the method of context observation and the analysis of five behavioral models were conducted.

Method

The design of the research process in this study is divided into the exploration and definition of demand [9]. Through the observation of the elderly in Douliu elderly care center and Keelung rehabilitation center, we aimed to find out potential and unmet needs and integrate the design policy and framework of the prototype product.

A. Demand Exploration Stage

In the demand exploration stage, ten participants (half male, over 60 years old, unlimited educational background and personality), were recruited in an elderly care center of Douliu City, Yunlin County and a Keelung rehabilitation center. They were interviewed in a semi-structured way for about 30 minutes to define the personality and the target group of the experiment.

After that, 30 participants were recruited and tested with MMSE. In the process of testing, the experimenters observed the context of participation and found out the interactive behavior problems, obstacle points, and emotions of retired elders by using MMSE in five dimensions of activities, environment, interaction, objects, and user. Finally, according to the behavioral information of dementia detection collected in the context insight stage, five working models including interaction, sequence, utensil, culture, and physical environment model [10] were analyzed for obtaining the model behavior.

B. Demand Definition Stage

In this stage, the affinity graph method [11] was used to summarize the potential needs of the participants. The interdisciplinary experts including nurses, designers, mechanical and electrical engineers, and dementia specialists were recruited to form a focus group. By using the behavior information collected by the context insight method, the service requirements and opportunities are summarized and the subsequent design specifications are defined as shown in Fig. 1.

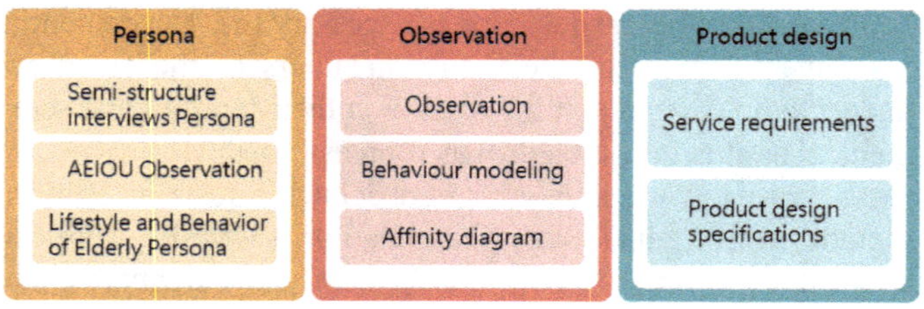

Fig. 1 Experimental planning steps.

Results

A. Demand Exploration Stage

Through observation and interview with 10 recruited participants, the group characteristics were summarized as follows: (1) free use of the upper limb, (2) the retired elderly, and (3) the age of over 60 years old.

B. Contextual Observation and Analysis

Based on the result of the demand exploration, we recruited 30 participants who had the group characteristics and performed MMSE tests and interviews. Then, the five dimensions of Activity, Environment, Interactive, Object, and User were analyzed.

C. Working Models

Based on the behavioral information of dementia detection collected in the context insight stage, five working models such as interaction, sequence, utensil, culture, and physical environment model [10] were used to analyze model behaviors.

(1) Interactive model: The interaction model is to observe the interaction and post-interview process among the participants during the MMSE test. Then, the interaction model was used to analyze the interaction process in three aspects of people, things, and objects (Fig. 2). The following are the obstacles for the MMSE test in the interaction model.

a. Participants were afraid of writing and refused the experiment.
b. Participants were influenced by self-esteem and refused the experiment.
c. Participants often needed repeated explanations of the experimental questions.
d. Participants often can't answer smoothly due to presbyopia's vision problems.
e. Some participants had poor reading comprehension.
f. Some participants had problems with writing or drawing.

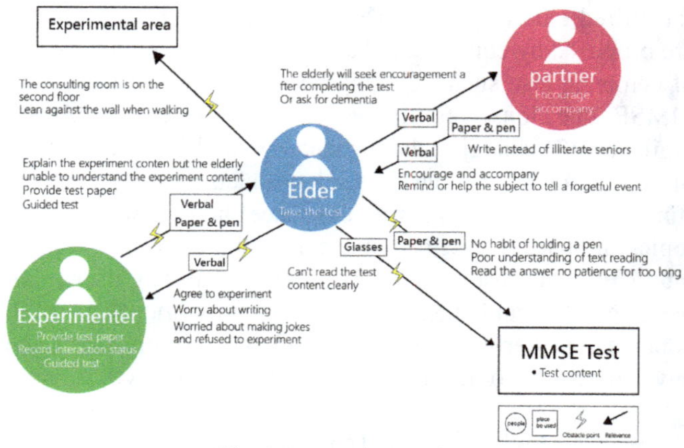

Fig. 2 Interactive model

(2) Sequence model: The obstacles of the sequence model observation were as follows (Fig. 3).

a. Some participants thought that they did not need the dementia test.
b. Family members also felt uneasy and unfamiliar when explaining the topic to participants.
c. Some participants did not want to answer the questions when they had no confidence.
d. Some participants used their fingers for calculation.
e. After completing the test, some participants sought the support of the experimenter or companion.

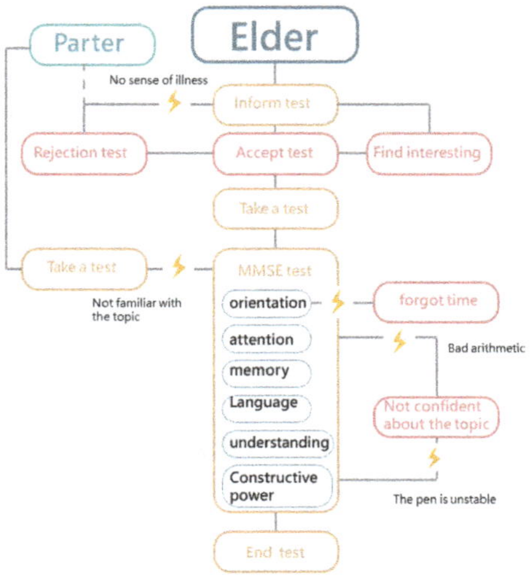

Fig. 3 Sequence model.

(3) Tool model: All the objects were recorded by participants during the test (Fig. 4). The interaction between participants and objects was described as follows.

a. Some participants had difficulty in reading the words of MMSE due to their lower educational background.
b. Some participants used fingers for calculation.
c. Some participants had difficulty when drawing.
d. Some participants needed to wear presbyopia glasses.

Fig. 4 Tool model.

(4) Cultural model: The cultural model explored the participants' attitudes towards the MMSE dementia test under the influence of cultural background and recorded the lack of behavior and barriers. For example, when a participant does not want to be diagnosed with dementia, self-esteem affects the willingness to be tested as shown in Fig. 5.

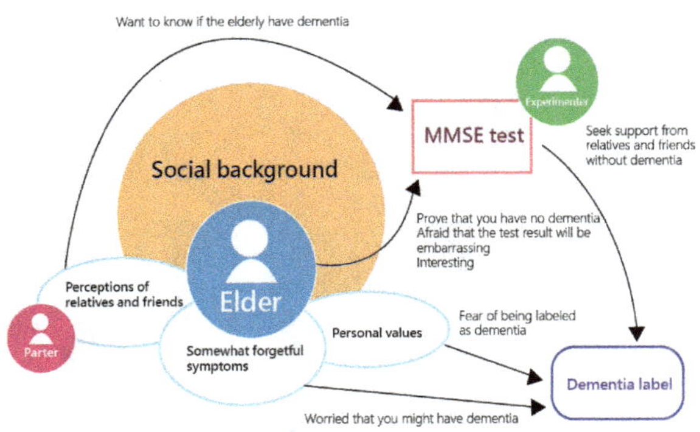

Fig. 5 Cultural model.

(5) Environment model: The physical environment model presents the plan of the test site as shown in Fig. 6. The following is a description of the test environment. The test area was on the second floor. The participants walked without obstacles by using handrails. During the test, the surrounding objects should be clear to avoid participants' distraction.

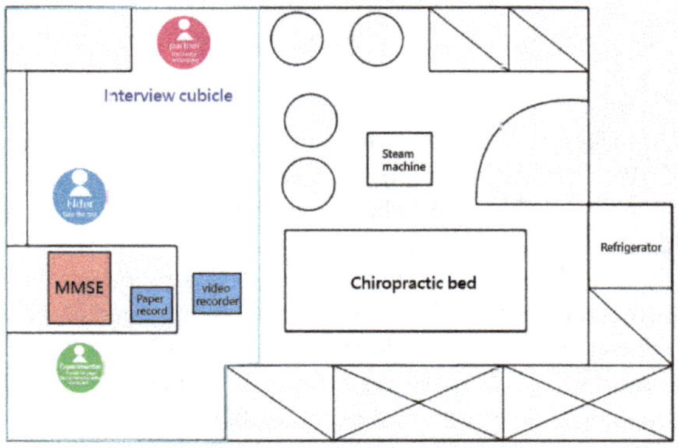

Fig. 6 Environment model.

D. Demand Definition

In this study, five behavioral models were used to analyze the content of context observation, and the obstacle points were sorted in the affinity graph method. The problems were grouped and summarized from complexity to simplicity. The potential needs of retired elderly and their families were identified as design points. The following are five common problems in this study.

a. Lack of information on the early symptoms and behaviors of dementia.
b. Self-awareness and self-esteem affect the willingness to test for dementia.
c. The difficulty in reading and understanding for some of the retired elderly was found in the test.
d. The form of dementia test results in the psychological exclusion of some retired elderly.
e. The related objects and environment affect the willingness and result of the test.

Conclusions

In this study, we analyzed and summarized the data from five behavior models such as activity, environment, interactive, object, and user observation points. The affinity graph method was used to summarize and analyze all the key points. The potential design requirements are summarized as follows.

(1) Changing the type of dementia detection, such as taking board games, and integrating MMSE questions into the game can reduce the participants' vigilance.
(2) By changing the presentation and interaction mode of topics, the special products (space), festivals (time), and celebration activities (space) in Taiwan can be used to test the topics of space, time, memory, calculation, and drawing for interacting and testing them in a non-verbal way to increase understanding and interest.

(3) Using nostalgic elements to make the cognitive connection between elderly subjects and memory is necessary.
(4) The overall presentation mode examines the living environment at home and promotes family interaction.

References

[1] International., A.s.D., World Alzheimer Report 2019: Attitudes to dementia. . 2019, : Alzheimer's Disease International: London.
[2] Association, T.A.s.D., How many people are mentally retarded. 2019a, Taiwan Alzheimer's Disease Association: Taipei.
[3] Guo, H., Delusional behavior in dementia. . Counseling and counseling, 2009(287): p. 20-23.
[4] Qiu, M., Code of practice for diagnosis and treatment of dementia. Journal of women's Association of endometriosis of the Republic of China, 2008. 15(3): p. 10-12.
[5] Association, T.A.s.D., It is everyone's responsibility to protect the financial security of dementia. 2019b, Taiwan Alzheimer's Disease Association: Taipei.
[6] Wang, C., Introduction and application of ad-8. Prevention and treatment of vascular medicine quarterly, 2013(16): p. 10-12.
[7] You, Z., A quasi experimental study on the effects of horticultural programs on the well-being of the mentally retarded elderly. , in Institute of education for the elderly, Department of adult and continuing education, . 2012, Chung Cheng University. p. 132.
[8] Qiu, M. and L. Tang, Guide to the care of dementia. 2009, Taipei: Raw water culture publishing.
[9] Tseng, S.-W., et al., An Indoor Gardening Planting Table Game Design to Improve the Cognitive Performance of the Elderly with Mild and Moderate Dementia, International Journal of Environmental Research and Public Health, 2020. 17(5): p. 1483.
[10] Beyer, H. and K. Holtzblatt, Contextual design: defining customer-centered systems. Vol. 1. 1998: Morgan kaufmann.
[11] Kawakita, J., The Original KJ Method. 1982, Tokyo, Japan: Kawakita Research Institute.

https://doi.org/10.1142/9789811238727_0005

A Public Problem-Based Case Study on the Practical Methodology of Social Design

Han-Xing Chen[1,2*], Wen-Huei Chou[2]

[1]Nanjing Normal University, Nanjing, Jiangsu, China
[2]Graduate School of Design, National Yunlin University of Science and Technology, Yunlin, Taiwan
*Corresponding Author Email: 523116181@qq.com

Abstract

The problems faced by social design are different from those of conventional designs that show more macroscopic, comprehensive, systematic, trans-disciplinary, and complicated features, which challenges the agility and capacity of existing design methodology. This study aims to analyze the challenges encountered by design methods in dealing with public issues and to provide references for improving social design methodology. Therefore, the Design Council's Framework for Innovation model and the tools commonly used in the conventional design was applied to a case of public interest. By reflecting and investigating this process and results, this study suggests the implementation of current practical design methods to accommodate coherently the many volatile aspects of social design.

Keywords: Social design, design thinking, public issues, double-diamond model, design methodology

Introduction

At present, people are generally optimistic to believe that design has been equipped with the methods and abilities to deal with social problems [1-3], which results in another policy-making method besides administration and management means [4]. However, the abilities advocated by design to pay more attention to experiences and to reveal values regarding economy and legislation face challenges in many policy-making procedures of governments and public sectors [3]. Social innovation led by governments and the public sectors focuses on issues such as the reform of polity [5], which is not consistent with the design's intent of transforming people's life and work style through emotions and experiences. Previous studies show whether the design methods, models, and tools derived from traditional design are suitable for social design and need to be examined through further research.

In 2019, a traditional market building in Taiwan was going to be demolished. The urban renewal caused conflicts between different stakeholders and formed a complex social public issue. The university as the research team participated in the research on the East Market dispute as a third party. Under the framework of social design, this study introduced an existing model of design thinking into the design practice of real-world public problems. The purpose of this study is to investigate and analyze the challenges encountered by design methods in dealing with social problems and to provide a reference for improving social design methodology.

Literature Review

A. Whose Needs Should Be Satisfied – The Complexity of Public Problems

The essence of the East Market dispute is a social public problem caused by urban regeneration. The sustainable development of cities and communities has been listed by the United Nations as one of the 17 sustainable development goals [6], of which economy, society, and environment are the three main dimensions of sustainable development [7]. However, social sustainability in urban regeneration is often neglected, but economic interests are mainly considered [8]. Consistent with the findings by Fu [9] and Ingram [10], the plan of using demolition or renovation of old buildings and relocation of the population as the main means damaged the interests of some stakeholders, especially the vulnerable groups [8,11], and could easily evolve into a unilateral act of the government [12]. Besides, the large-scale demolition of the traditional market resulted in the disappearance of regional culture, the rupture of emotional ties, and the loss of urban memory and local identity [11,13]. This shows that the complexity of social problems caused by urban regeneration lies in their need for comprehensive and systematic consideration.

B. Concept and Characteristics of Social Design

At present, there is no agreement on the definition of social design in the academic community of design. Faud-Luke [14] defined that social design increases the happiness and quality of society. Yamazaki [15] believed that the purpose of social design is to solve systemic problems in society. Manzini [16] emphasized that social design is different from traditional design and usually non-commercial. They indicate in common that the purpose and service objects of social design are different from those of traditional design.

The *Socio-ecological System Model* (SESM) is often used to discuss systems of social problems. According to Dalton and Wandersman [17], socio-ecological systems can be divided into five levels of categories from small to large scale: Individuals, microsystems, organizations, regions, and macrosystems. Levels 4 and 5 indicate that social problems may involve larger categories, such as communities, cities, public policies, laws, and cultures. Irwin [4] believed that usually, social problems cannot exist only at a single ecosystem level.

The characteristics of social design can be summarized as follows: (a) Social design involves systematic problems [18,19], (b) Stakeholders are more complex [1], (c) The scale of social design is larger [19], (d) Social design is a dynamic process, and (e) Social design requires interdisciplinary and cross-disciplinary collaboration.

C. Social Design Methods in Practice

The design methodology is a study on design processes, practices, and principles [20,21]. Its research scope includes design thinking, models, and tools that are widely discussed by contemporary design research. In the recent practices of social innovation design, Yang and Sung [22] and Lee [23] supported that traditional design models and tools can still play a positive role in some social design practices. Anand and Haag [24] transformed Double Diamond Model (DDM) into a more complex framework and believed that more rounds of divergence and convergence would help to ensure the consistency between the final results and the needs of stakeholders. Thus, the phenomenon of adjusting and reforming methods is very common. According to Martins [25], the research on design methodology has long neglected the problems arising from the actual implementation of design models and methods. Therefore, reflecting and improving traditional design models and tools in social design practices should become the focus of methodology research.

Methods and Process

A. Research Planning

The research team consisted of 9 researchers and a professor. This study adopted multiple methods from research methods and design thinking methods, models, and tools. The completeness of DDM [26] was chosen as the research framework in this study after being compared to other design thinking models. First of all, the challenges faced by the East Market were imported into DDM. Subsequently, the design process and results were reflected and discussed to explore the advantages and problems encountered by traditional design models and tools. Finally, this study attempted to suggest an improved methodology of social design.

B. Process of Social Design Project

Researchers referred to the '4D framework' of DDM, namely Discovery, Definition, Development, and Delivery [26].

a. Discover

The researchers drew Stakeholder Map to find key elements related to design research [27]. Firstly, it can be seen on the map that the East Market dispute involved a large number of stakeholders, and their interest relationships were complicated. Secondly, the systems and modes of operation among all levels of governments and their agencies had been formed. It was difficult for non-governmental organizations, vendors, local colleges, and universities to have a substantial impact on them. Therefore, we planned to interview the participants across different groups. As a result, this study collected a total of about 6 hours and 55 minutes of recorded interviews which had full-text scripts of 41,376 Chinese characters.

b. Define

Based on the interview data, the researchers understood and analyzed the stakeholders through the Empathy Map from the aspects of pain points, needs, views, thoughts, and so forth. Through conceptualizing and categorizing the expressions and opinions on the empathy maps of all stakeholders, the researchers found that they all paid attention to 'transformative development' and 'co-participation'. For these two common values, the research team defined the How Might We (HMW) problem through repeated iterations: How to integrate social resources, empower vulnerable stakeholders, and enable them to adapt to the changing world?

c. Develop

The User Journey Map revealed some hidden dangers like bad hygiene habits, poor management, and resistance to changes which had always existed before and after the East Market dispute and become the causes for the displaced vendors and their damaged businesses. From this, the researchers got the opportunities to design: (a) innovation of vendors' means to autonomy, (b) transformation of business concepts, (c) application of modern Internet technology, (d) strengthening communication with customers, and (e) development of innovative thinking (Fig. 5). Thus, this research proposed three steps to achieve the purpose of improving the adaptability of vendors in the Service Blueprint: (1) Introduction of modern market, (2) learning of new management concepts, and (3) market transformation practice.

d. Deliver

The 'Deliver' phase is the production and release of design outcomes. As different from the Prototyping in traditional design, a curriculum plan is developed based on the Service Blueprint by aiming to improve the adaptability of vendors. This plan is divided into four modules each of which contains two to three specific courses. The contents of these courses as well as the fore/back-stage operations correspond to the needs and values of the vendors and other stakeholders. Although this study has not yet made a comprehensive evaluation of the plan, the lecture on the East Market issue held by community universities provides significant references. The pre- and post-test results of the questionnaire before and after the lecture showed that the public's understanding of the history and local culture of the East Market improved through the teaching activities, thus enhanced the power and ability to plan the future development of the East Market.

Findings

The research results showed that innovative solutions were obtained for the East Market dispute through the use of DDM and eight tools commonly used in traditional design. The plan included almost all stakeholders and allowed them to create their value. However, the case study also revealed some imperfections in these tools and models.

A. Ways to Cope with the Complexity of the Real World

Social problems in the real world are complex and changeable, and there are events or accidents beyond the control of researchers. By being faced with these situations, the researchers could only passively return to the field to collect data under the changing situations and make repeated adjustments and iterations to the design process and results. According to design thinking, the methods and tools provided by design methodology include mainly interviews and observation. As social issues are becoming more complex, social design urgently needs the development of tools to cope with the variability of the real world.

B. Strategies for Dealing with the Attributes of Stakeholders

The characteristics of social design include the complexity of stakeholders. Although the existing methodology has already responded to this, the wicked problems faced by social design usually inevitably involve government agencies as well as marginal or vulnerable groups whose distinctive attributes often make it difficult to communicate and collect data. The diversity of stakeholders and the complexity of their social relationships are common in real-world research. The resulted incompleteness of data is likely to affect the quality of design practices and research. Therefore, social design methodology needs to develop specific strategies to deal with the attributes of stakeholders.

C. Skills of Deploying Researchers with Different Attributes

The attributes of researchers include dimensions like professional fields, skills, identities, and backgrounds. The observation revealed that the interviews by the researchers were rejected due to their identity as students. Some opinions that had the prospect of developing into larger-scale social innovation achievements were forced to be adjusted. These phenomena reflect the limitations in the attributes of researchers for social design research and the necessity of strengthening the cross-field cooperation. The methodology research of social design needs paying attention to how to coordinate the attributes of researchers of different types, fields, and backgrounds in the design team and use these attributes in their respective advantages.

D. The Pursuit of Certainty in the '4D' Framework

This study holds the logic that defines the correct problems of the pursuit of idealized 'certainty' in design methodology. The following phenomena require attention: a) It is presupposed that there were no differences in the situation and needs within each group of stakeholders. However, the actual situation was that there were various visions and values among them; b) to reduce the complexity of dealing with social issues, the researchers assumed the result of 'the demolition of the East Market', thus greatly limiting the variables faced by the solution; c) the interview scripts with over 40,000 characters were reduced to a few words in the empathy map, and converged to the 'correct' problem, which reduced variables and the loss of details. Under the framework of DDM, research problems and results related to certainty are achieved by reducing variables, presetting conditions, and limiting the scope of the problem.

How to Introduce Social Design Methods into Public Problems More Successfully

A. Introducing Relevant Theories in Social Science to Strengthen the Methodology of Social Design

This study suggests adopting strategies in anthropology and ethnography to enhance the ability of the existing methods to deal with the complexity of stakeholders. Also, the Actor Network Theory (ANT) provides enlightening guidance for diversified actors to realize the co-creation of values through common actions. This suggests that the theories and methodologies of other related disciplines be used to enhance and enrich the methodology of social design.

B. Guiding Broader Design Actors to Participate in Cross-domain Collaboration

Stakeholders involved in social problems should not be considered in passive roles. The social design should expand the influence of Participatory Design and Co-design, bring some qualified stakeholders into the research team as actors, and even train them into designers. Their participation makes it easier for the research team to have empathy for all types of stakeholders. Besides, they have the opportunity to bring novel insights into the collected data.

C. Adopting New Technologies to Improve Methods for Exploring Social Problems

Designing for real social problems means that research cannot always be carried out under the most ideal conditions. Traditional tools such as observation, interviews are thus challenged. With the development of the Internet and digital technology, more people leave traces of activities on websites or social media. Therefore, this study holds the view that the development of data collection tools and technologies based on forums or social media will help social designers to understand the thinking and behavior patterns of various stakeholders through big data, such as reviews and status sharing. Also, this will help deal with the problem of insufficient data brought about by the complexity of social problems and stakeholders.

D. Developing Constructive Frameworks for Social Design

The existing frameworks for design thinking generally pursue certain research issues and result through presetting, simplification, and restriction, thus limiting the value of social design. Therefore, social design methodology must reverse the thinking mode of seeking certainty. This study recommends adopting a constructive design thinking framework. That means researchers' understanding of social issues determines the scope and scale of research issues and their change with the increase of understanding. Therefore, this study changed the structure of DDM to illustrate the influence of the ever-changing understanding of the world over time on research issues and design results (Fig. 1). This suggests that designers should understand social design as a dynamic construction process and be open to the design process and results.

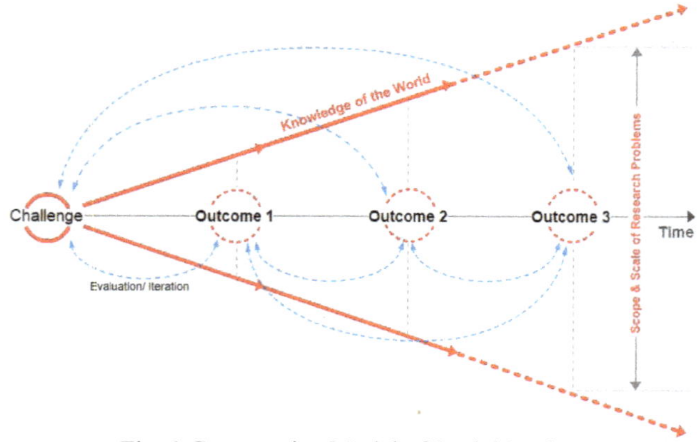

Fig. 1 Constructive Model of Social Design

Conclusion

Through the case study, we found that the design models represented by DDM and the traditional design tools responded to issues that are commonly seen in public problems relatively well. These problems include power inequality, exclusion of vulnerable groups, and unsustainable development of society and culture. In this process, the research results of social science like the social ecosystem theory played a positive role in expanding researchers' vision by promoting systematic thinking and enhancing the ability of design tools to deal with social problems.

However, this study also revealed that the methodology of social design is imperfect in research methods, means, and techniques when studying societal issues that hold great richness, variety of people and things in the real world. Therefore, this study suggested replacing the old way of thinking with the framework of constructivism and being open to the process and results of social design. The implication is that researchers should approach the essence of social problems continuously in the dialogue with the real world to gain insight into real problems.

The novel framework built in this study pointed out that the social design methodology focuses on the real world as well as its variability and richness, discovers real research problems, and makes real designs based on expanding the understanding of the real world.

References

[1] Jones, P. "Systemic design principles for complex social systems." *Social Systems and Design,* Gary M. Eds., Tokoyo, Japan: Springer, 2014, pp. 91-128.

[2] Buchanan, R. "Design research and the new learning." *Design Issues*, 17(4), 2001, pp. 3-23.

[3] Bason, C. "Design-led Innovation in Government." *Stanford Social Innovation Review*, 11(2), 2013, pp. 15-17.

[4] Irwin, T. "Transition deign: A proposal for a new area of design practice, study, and research." *Design and Culture*, 7(2), 2015, pp. 229-246.

[5] Sorensen, E. "Political innovations: innovations in political institutions, processes and outputs." *Public Management Review*, 19(1), 2017, pp. 1-19.

[6] United Nations (UN). "*Transforming our world: the 2030 Agenda for Sustainable Development* (A/70/L.1)." 2015, Retrieved November 26, 2019, from https://www.unfpa.org/sites/default/files/resource-pdf/Resolution_A_RES_70_1_EN.pdf

[7] United Nations (UN). "*Agenda 21.*" 1992, Retrieved November 26, 2019, from https://sustainabledevelopment.un.org/content/documents/Agenda21.pdf

[8] Darchen. S. and E. Ladouceur. "Social sustainability in urban regeneration practice: a case study of the Fortitude Valley Renewal Plan in Brisbane." *Australian Planner,* 50(4), 2013, pp. 340-350.

[9] Fu, Y. R. "The Value of Humanistic Emotional Factors in the Small-scale Renewal of Historic Buildings." *Housing & Real Estate*, 2018(9), 2018, pp. 80.

[10] Ingram, C. "Building between past and future: Nostalgia, historical materialism and the architecture of memory in Baltimore's Inner Harbor." *Philosophy and Social Criticism*, 41(3), 2015, pp. 317-333.

[11] Gonzalez, S. and P. Waley. "Traditional Retail Markets: The New Gentrification Frontier?" *Antipode,* 45(4), 2013, pp. 965-983.

[12] Lopez-Morales, E. "Gentrification in Santiago, Chile: a property-led process of dispossession and exclusion." *Urban Geography*, 37(8), 2016, pp. 1109-1131.

[13] Mi, M. N. and H. J. Yu. "Design Research on Optimization of Farmers Market under the Background of Urban Renewal." *Sichuan Drama,* 1, 2018, pp. 173-176.

[14] Faud-Luke, A. *Design activism: beautiful strangeness for a sustainable world.* London, UK: Routledge, 2013.

[15] Yamazaki, R. *Community Design*. Chuang, Y. -H Trans. Taipei City, Taiwan: Faces Publishing, 2015.

[16] Manzini, E. *Design, When Everybody Designs: An Introdection to Design for Social Innovation*. Cambridge, MA: MIT Press Ltd., 2015.

[17] Dalton, E. and A. Wandersman. *Community Psychology: linking individuals and communities*. Belmont, CA: Wadsworth/Thomason Learning., 2007.

[18] Wolf, G. and N. Mahaffey. "Designing Difference: Co-production of spaces of potentiality." *Urban Planning,* 1(1). 2016, pp. 59-67.

[19] Smith, R. and O. Iversen. "Participatory design for sustainable social change." *Design Studies,* 59, 2018, pp. 9-36.

[20] Cross, N. *Developments in Design Methodology*. Chichester, UK: Wiley., 1984.

[21] Löwgren, J., and E. Stolterman. "Methods & tools: design methodology and design practice." *Interactions*, 6(1), 1999, pp. 13-20.

[22] Yang, C.-F, and T. –J. Sung. "Service Design for Social Innovation through Participatory Action Research." *International Journal of Design*, 10(1), 2016, pp. 21-36.

[23] Lee, H.-K. "Revitalising Traditional Street Markets in Rural Korea: Design Thinking and Sense-Making Methodology." *International Journal of Art and Design Education*, 38(1), 2019, pp. 256-269.

[24] Anand, K., and J. Haag. "A framework for teaching Design for Social Impact." Paper presented at the Designing Design Education for India Conference, Pune, India, 2013, March, retrieved on Nov. 30, 2019, from http://cadi.lecoledesign.com/en/2014/01/english-a-framework-for-teaching-design-for-social-impact/

[25] Martins, R. "Analysis of Available Design Implementation Methods. A Study About Scarcity of Implementation Methods." *Design Journal*, 20, 2017, pp. S4730-S4733.

[26] Tschimmel, K. "Design Thinking as an effective Toolkit for Innovation." *Proceedings of ISPIM Conferences*, 23, 2012, pp. 1-20.

[27] Hanington, B. and B. Martin. *Universal Methods of Design: 100 Ways to Research Complex Problems, Develop Innovative Ideas, and Design Effective Solutions*. Beverly, MA: Rockport Publishers, 2012.

https://doi.org/10.1142/9789811238727_0006

A Study of Applying Bauhaus Design Idea into the "Body Workshop of Bauhaus"

Yi-Wen Ting*, Po-Shien Lin, Rung-Tai Lin

Graduate School of Creative Industry Design, National Taiwan University of Arts, New Taipei City, Taiwan
*Corresponding Author Email: ading1113@gmail.com

Abstract

Bauhaus, the most important art and architecture school in art history, was founded in Weimar, Germany in 1919 by artist Walter Gropius, and closed in 1933 under the Nazi regime. In less than 15 years, it had a profound impact on modern art, architecture, design, and other fields. Today's Bauhaus is not just the name of an architectural school, but also a style. The "Bauhaus Body Workshop" is based on the concept of Triadic Ballet. It enables students to re-examine the relationship between themselves and space and to experience the physical practice of the human body and space in the Bauhaus Theater 100 years ago.

Keyword: Bauhaus, Triadic Ballet

Introduction

In the Bauhaus School, the Bauhaus Theater Course hosted by the painter Oscar Schlemmer aims to enable students to understand the relationship between the human body and space and to stimulate students through experiments and creative displays of performing arts. The "Bauhaus Theater" in the Bauhaus series published in 1925 deconstructed the traditional concept of theater from two aspects: theater space and human body space. The four laws of human space proposed by Oscar Schlemmer break the traditional dance narrative form by making dance art creation no longer serve the role. However, it returns to the artistic creation itself, and through bold forward-looking experiments, reflects the modernism purity and abstraction of art.

At present, Bauhaus's research is mainly in the field of design and architecture. The Bauhaus Theater has relatively little research. The Bauhaus Theater extends the concept of shape, space, and color to the dance experiments of the human body and space, which also indirectly affects the entire field of post-modern dance. This research analyzes the core concept of its artistic coding from the most famous representative work of Oscar Schlemmer's work "Triadic Ballet". The core concepts are the triad of space, shape, and color bring the three concepts into the design of the curriculum and allow the crafts design students to understand the relationship between body and space through the way of workshops.

Literature Review

A. The Triadic Ballet of Bauhaus

The Bauhaus Theater Course was established at the beginning of the school's establishment in 1920. Later, when the school moved to Dessau in 1926, an exclusive theater was established, which was hosted by the painter Oscar Schlemmer (1888~1943)[1]. Its purpose was to enable students to understand the relationship between the human body and space through theater courses, and to create creative thinking for students through the creative display of performing arts. The American Bauhaus Dance Association (bauhausdance.org) pointed out: "Oscar Schlemmer, the theater concept has influenced the performance theories of modern and postmodern dancers such as Merce Cunningham, Ivan Nicholas, and Robert Wilson. [2]"

The research of Bauhaus is currently mainly in the field of design and architecture, while the research of Bauhaus Theater is relatively few. The book *Die Bühne im Bauhaus* of the Bauhaus series published in 1925 was translated into English and published as *The Theater of the Bauhaus* in 1961, which included Walter Gropius' introduction and four short essays: Oscar Schlemmer's "People and Art Modeling", "Theatre", "Theater, Circus and Variety Show" and "U-shaped Theater"[3]. The shock caused by the book *Bauhaus Theater* deconstructed the traditional concept of theater from two aspects of theater space and human body space. The theater space talks about the building of the theater itself and discusses the great possibility that the theater itself can produce performances, while the human body space talks about the maximization of performing arts as proposed by Oscar Schlemmer. "The four laws of human body space" broke the narrative form of traditional dance so that dance art creation no longer serves the role but returns to the artistic creation itself. Through bold experiments, it reflects the purity of art in modernism.

The "Triadic Ballet" has been tried by dancers in workshops as early as 1912 [3]. A part of the content was released in 1915. It premiered in Stuttgart in 1922 and was performed at the Weimar State Theater in 1923. In a ten-year experiment, Oscar Schlemmer used the metaphor of dance and machine to develop and explore the potential of theater. The ballet, which is least like ballet, has become an important text for understanding modern art changes and Bauhaus' stage thoughts[4] (Liu Chun, 2018). "Triadic Ballet" has different translation methods, all based on three acts and three dancers. German dance critic Ilona Landgrave explained that the "three" (triadic) in "Triadic Ballet" was derived from the Greek language and consisted of three acts and three dancers[4].

The performance is composed of solo, duet, and trio. The dance consists of three forms. The 12 dance segments include circles, triangles, and squares. The 18 sets of costumes are divided into three series. The whole play consists of three series in yellow, rose, and black. Two male and one female dancers change 18 sets of costumes and complete 12 dances, as shown in Figure 1 in Oscar Schlemmer's manuscript.

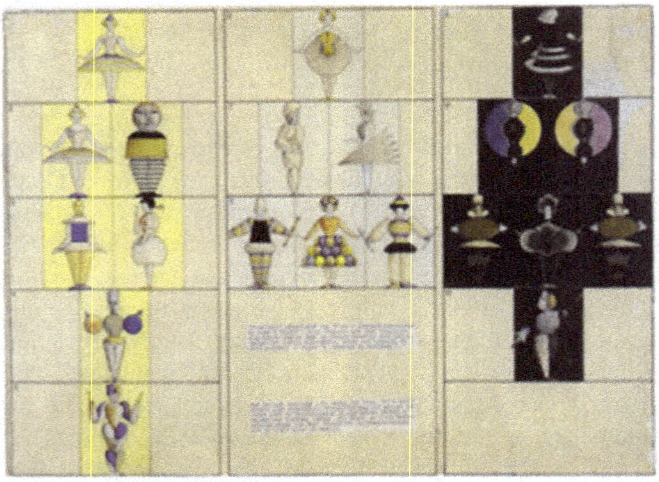

Fig. 1 Design diagram of Triadic Ballet [3]

Oscar Schlemmer said in The Theater of the Bauhaus: "Human organisms stand in the cubic and abstract space of the stage. People and space have different laws, Who will become dominant? One situation is that the abstract space faces the difference of natural persons and transforms itself in order to adapt to the latter. The other situation is that natural persons reshape their image to adapt to the abstract space" [3]. "These laws are involved in 'as a dance'., 'The person of the person', he follows the laws of the flesh and the laws of space, whether in abstract movements, in symbolic dance dramas, or an empty stage. This person as a dancer will be excessive. The medium of the great world of theater."

B. Space theory of body The Triadic Ballt.

German modern dance began to develop gradually under the influence of expressionist with western thinking. It is especially known as the founder of German modern dance: Rudolf von Laban (1879-1958) and his students. The exploration of the human body and space has established a good research foundation. Rudolph Laban is regarded as the father of dance theory. He made an in-depth analysis of human movements in terms of content and form and put forward the theory of "Effort", which consisted of four basic principles of element composition: gravity, time, space, and fluency [5] (Rodolf von Laban, 1947). Space refers to the relationship between the human body's movement and the external world. In the form of movement, Laban performs various elements of the human body's movement in space. After analyzing and proposing the famous concept of "sphere space", he regarded the space of human movement as a cube space of three dimensions. The human body has two attitudes towards space: hug and repulsion which bring about the movement by centripetal or centrifugal force.

Laban pointed out that the human body moves on two "three planes": high, middle, and low planes, and door, table, and wheel planes (Figure 2). If the human body is regarded as a central point, the six orientation points of up, down, left, right, front, and back can be obtained [6] (Liu Qingyi p.42).

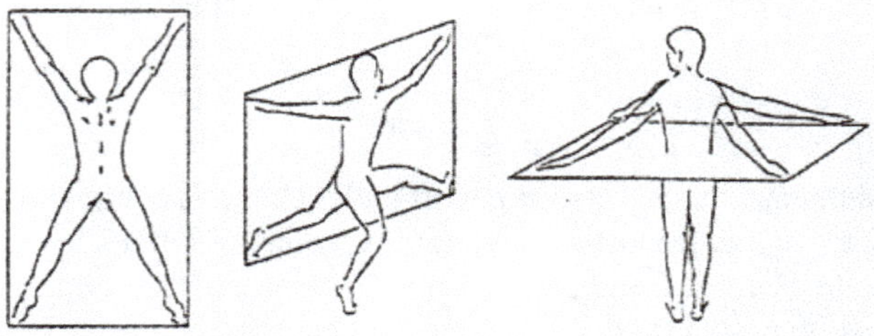

Fig. 2 Three planes of the human body [5]

Mary Wigman (1886-1973) had a deep understanding of the various basic elements of dance, especially the understanding of space. She wrote a thesis on 《Space Theory》. She proposed that as long as the dancer is in the space middle, the body is the center, high and low, front and back, parallel right and left, front and back, and radiates into the space from the center of the body. Mary Wigman insisted that the dancer be the soul of space, the receiver of space vibrations. These space vibrations gather into the inner initiative that is released in the swing of the body to accept and give. This is a kind of eternal communication. The space for composition, creation, and dance comes from nothingness. In this space, the concealed and searched form circulate and coil around each other, waiting for the time to come, to give them color and outline, and add brilliance to the image [6]. Mary Wigman's thoughts on dance space deeply influenced her student Kurt Jose whose 1932 award-winning work "Green Table" is considered to be the foundation of German dance theater.

Oscar Schlemmer believes that the law of the organic human body lies in its inherent invisible functions: heartbeat, fluid circulation, breathing, brain, and nervous system activities. The decisive factor is that human beings create an imaginary space under motion and radiation (Figure 6). The three-dimensional abstract space is only the horizontal frame and the vertical frame of the flow of generation. As invisible, the "person as a dancer" obeys the laws of the flesh and the laws of space. He follows his feelings about himself. His feeling of immersing in space created almost endless ways of expression, whether in free abstract movement or a dance drama full of symbolic meaning, whether in an empty stage or an environment full of scenery [3]

Method

A. Research structure

This research is based on the most famous work "Triadic Ballet" of Oscar Schlemmer, the most important artist of the Bauhaus Theater. The core concepts of the Triadic Ballet are the triad of space, shape, and color. In the triad, "space" includes height, depth, and breadth, "shape" includes circles, triangles, and squares. "color" includes red, yellow, and blue. Therefore, the entire form of the Triadic Ballet is formed around the core concepts of three large triads and three small triads, present these concepts and triads in Figure 3.

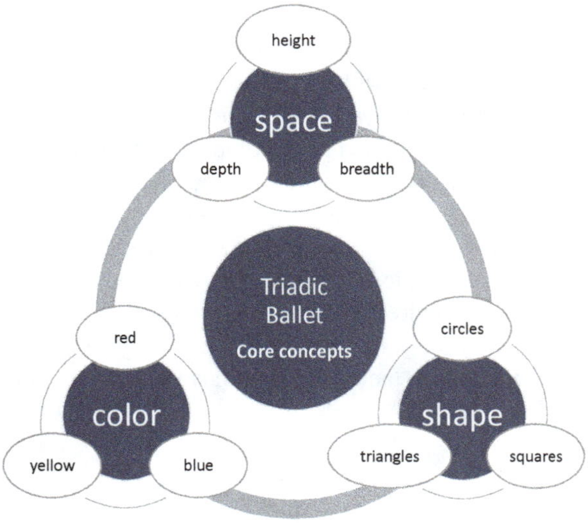

Fig. 3 Core Concepts of the Triadic Ballet

The research process is shown in Figure 4.

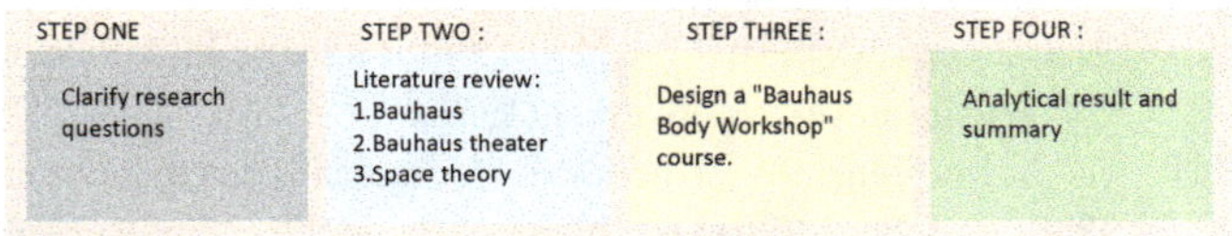

Fig. 4 Research process

Result and discussion

According to the core concept of "Triadic Ballet" design themes of the workshop, the course is divided into three parts: warm-up activities, main activities, and discussion. The lesson plans in the workshop are shown in Table 1.

The number of participants was a total of 13 graduate students from the Department of crafts design, including 1 male (7%) and 12 females (93%). The self-assessed knowledge of Bauhaus scored 3.7 points while the knowledge of Bauhaus Theater scored 2.8 points (on a 5 point scale).

Participants' feedback on the course is as follows: 1. Today's activity content can experience how the body is shaped: the average score is 4.7 points, 2. Today's activity content helps to understand the relationship between body and space: average score 4.9 points, 3. Today's activity content helps to think about the appearance of shapes in three-dimensional space: the average score is 4.8 points, 4. Overall, today's activity participation feeling: the average score is 5 points, and the feedbacks of students shows in Table 2.

TABLE 1
The workshop plan.

Body Workshop of the Bauhaus			
Date	2020.12.28 09:30-11:00	**Place**	Dance Studio
Teacher	Ting, Yiwen	**Student**	Graduate students from the Department of Crafts Design

Workshop goal

A. From the workshop process, experience how the body is shaped.

B. Experience the relationship between body and space.

C. Try to transform from two-dimensional plane modeling to three-dimensional space.

Workshop content

A. Warm up

a. Extend the body to a large extent, and get used to stretching.

b. Use music and walking to gradually enter the state of the course. When adding tambourine beats, point (body parts) line (to bring flowing lines with body parts) to three of the surfaces (to touch classroom objects such as floor walls and other surfaces with body parts)

B. Main activities

a. As a group of three people, discuss how to use the points, lines, surfaces of the body and partners to create circles, triangles, and squares.

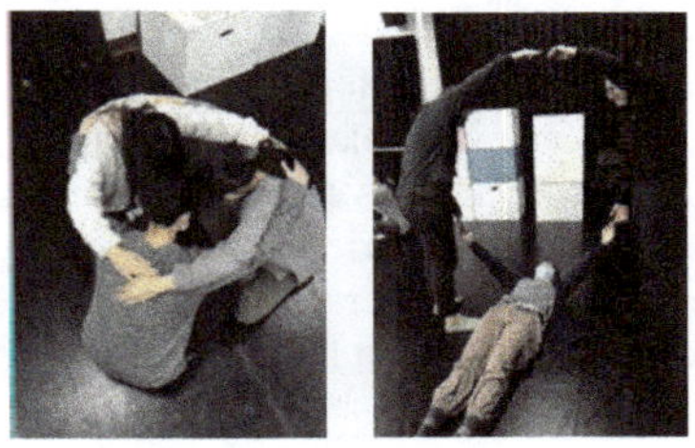

b. Personally think and express how to create a shape with a moving track.

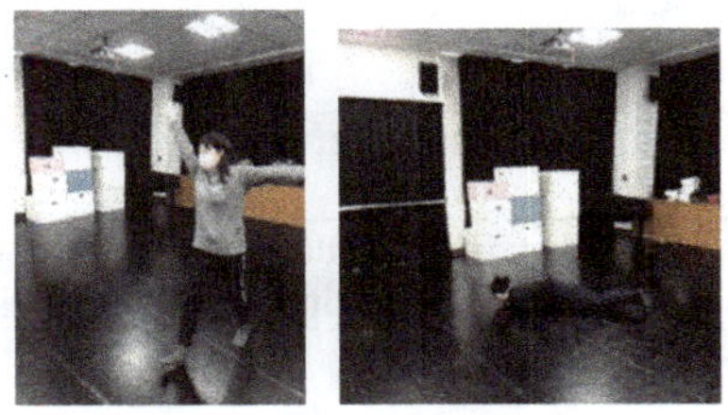

c. In groups of two, create shapes and trajectories that move in space.

C. DISCUSS

TABLE 2
Student experience

NO.	Student's Feedback
1	Great!
2	Wonderful
3	When there are more than two people, the interaction of the shape is very fun
4	The process transition from flat to three-dimensional (or even to four-dimensional space) is very interesting.
5	The concept of triadic ballet gives the shape more imagination, like it!
6	Use the points, lines, and surfaces of the body to deliberately form a three-dimensional shape. On the contrary, it is found that all body actions usually have shapes.
7	It's very interesting. I usually focus on handwork. I have never thought of using my body to think, coupled with the relationship between cooperation and space, so that my creation is not just from my heart.
8	Thank you teacher today for giving us the opportunity to get in touch with the rhythms of the body and space that we don't usually touch, and we also intuitively associate it with the time trajectory! It's very interesting~ In addition to the original idea, there will be unexpected effects when performing actions. The use of body shape and space is relatively diverse, and there is a lot of room for development.
9	Dance is somewhat related to time, space, rhythm and craftsmanship. It turns out that the human body can present many geometric figures similar to the points, lines and surfaces of craftwork creations. After dancing, the body also feels comfortable and it feels great experience!
10	We cannot see myself shape but seeing other students reflection can tell what is our shape, so this class needs me and others. This is the most interesting thing.
11	Interesting!
12	The points, lines, and planes of the human body are interesting!
13	It's very interesting. I usually focus on handwork. I have never thought of using my body to think.

Conclusion

Students' feedback suggested their familiarity with the principles of form. They were good at applying design elements of point, line, and plane in their creations. However, the core concept of Triadic Ballet inspired students to explore the relationship between the human body and outer space. Timely guides and repeated practices were helpful for students to get rid of conventional two-dimensional thinking and to achieve the goal of cross-domain learning about the rhythm of body, space, and time. This research is conceived based on Oscar Schlemmer's most famous "Triadic Ballet". The core concept of shapes, spaces, and colors are extracted to develop the course of the workshop, through which the students experience Bauhaus's idea of course that was created a hundred years ago. Students' final evaluation demonstrated their high satisfaction with the course of the workshop. The students of art and design major were prepared for applying their professional knowledge to complete three-dimensional dances to express various themes of body, space, shape, and color. They stated that the body workshop was helpful to increase creative thinking in future design creation. The idea of Schlemmer's Triadic Ballet, which advantaged the Bauhaus students one hundred years ago, is still admired by contemporary young students. All the changes of culture, government, region, and language have not been able to obscure his glory.

References

[1] Smock, W.: The Bauhaus ideal then and now: An illustrated guide to modernist design. Chicago IL: Academy Chicago Publishers (2004).

[2] Bauhaus dance, http://bauhausdances.org/2019/1125

[3] Schlemmer, O.: Man and art figure. In W. Gropius & Ar. S. Wensinger (Eds). The Theater of the Bauhaus. Middletown, CT: Wesleyan University Press (1961).

[4] Chun, L.: Humanity Dance and Mechanical Principles-From Tridic Ballet (2018). https:// kknews.cc/zhtw/culture/pgkz88j.html. Accessed 10 Dec 2019

[5] Rudolf Laban: The language of movement. Plays, Inc.(1974).

[6] Liu, Q.: Outline of History of Modern Western Dance. Shanghai Music, Shanghai (2014).

https://doi.org/10.1142/9789811238727_0007

A Study of the Development of Animal Conservation Multimedia Aids in an Industry-University Cooperative Course

Yu-Horng Chen

Department of Learning and Materials Design, University of Taipei, Taipei, Taiwan
Email: horng@utaipei.edu.tw

Abstract

The impact of natural environment degradation and the loss of species has simplified the biodiversity on Earth. Thus, modern zoos (in this study we particularly work with Taipei Zoo) have become one of the most important shelters for some natural species. Furthermore, zoos are important environmental education areas for cultivating modern citizens with environmental literacy and having enough knowledge and behavior related to environmental issues. Therefore, together with Taipei Zoo, this research proposes a cooperative course and multimedia aids for environmental education (in particular in the field of animal conservation). The course and multimedia aids are useful to educate the university students about environmental issues by applying their knowledge and skills to design these aids and help zoo visitors (learners) to learn conservation messaging by navigating through these aids in the zoo (on-site). The multimedia aids are designed for zoo visitors (learners) of all ages to foster an appreciation for wildlife in an attractive, amusing, and easy-to-understand way. It is expected that the aids deliver wildlife conservation and environmental messaging to the visitors (learners) and help them perceive a better experience while walking around the zoo.

Keywords: zoo, conservation education, environmental literacy

Background

The extinction and decline of wildlife species are lessons for people to learn, and it is a warning alarm for a worsening environment. The rich ecosystem generated from the biological diversity of nature is the foundation of the sustainable development of the Earth. However, with the destruction of nature and the endangerment of species, natural environment protection and animal conservation have become important current issues [1]. Modern zoos use their wildlife management, medical care, conservation, and scientific research to continue to promote cross-border conservation programs to support the survival of endangered animals. Zoos have the opportunity and responsibility to lead visitors (learners) to understand the threats and challenges faced by species through education, learn the importance of biodiversity conservation, and improve people's environmental education and conservation literacy. The unique resources and the immersive environment of the zoos allow visitors (learners) a great place to observe the wild species and generate a connection between emotion and life experience [2].

Since its foundation over a hundred years ago, Taipei Zoo has been designed as a place to enjoy nature, a teaching museum to display the lives of species, a research base of wild animals, and a stronghold for wildlife conservation [3]. Taipei Zoo has proposed the principle of 'learning from life' in 2014 and has been recognized in the field of environment and education by providing diversified environmental education courses and activities. It is expected that the wide range of educational courses and activities developed by the zoo allows visitors (learners) to learn about animal conservation. It is hoped that people learn to care about animals and preserve their habitats. In the course cooperation between the zoo and universities, the development process of animal conservation learning materials offers the chance to observe the feelings and gains of the learners in the process of operating and applying the learning content.

Literature Review

With the importance of biological diversity and environmental conservation, zoos have become the nature conservation institution of the world. Moreover, zoos have the responsibility to perform four major roles [4]:

1. conservation – to actively participate in conservation work inside and outside the territory to strengthen the welfare of wildlife;
2. tourism – to provide visitors with the experience activities of nature and education;
3. research – to constantly improve professional development through nature conservation and the study of social science;
4. education – to take education as an important conservation work and influence people's awareness and behaviors toward natural resources and conservation education and to encourage visitors to cultivate their sense of responsibility and participate in the work of conservation.

The purpose of conservation and environmental education is to enhance people's environmental literacy and enable them to conduct themselves in ways that are friendly to the environment, including cultivating awareness, knowledge, skills, and action, and creating a society that coexists in harmony with nature [5]. A zoo is equipped with a unique environmental field and learning resources to provide an informal environmental learning center for conservation and environmental education. Furthermore, a zoo is committed to providing visitors with a close-to-nature experience, promoting meaningful learning, and promoting a platform for conservation-related social interaction.

Zoos provide a wealth of knowledge on nature, ecology, conservation issues, and strategies. This particular environment also enables visitors (learners) to appreciate the beauty of animals, establish connections with wild animals, and develop environmental ethics for caring for animals and environmental friendliness. The environmental education activities in zoos promote social interaction and expand social horizons through interactive communication between learners and zoo caretakers and teamwork among learners. The experience and activities in zoos are learner-oriented and free-choice learning which enhances learning motivation and gives opportunities for self-exploration and self-confidence training. Zoos are the places that provide learners with opportunities to build a bridge to science, environmental education, and conservation activities.

The Curriculum Guidelines of 12-Year Basic Education also expects to cultivate students in core literacy areas such as autonomous action, interaction, communication, and social participation and to enable students to become lifelong learners in life situations with social adaptability and resilience [6]. It is expected that educators pay attention to the development of students' cognition, emotion, and skills related to the environment. The emphasis should be put on the social interaction between people and the internal self-growth of individuals to cultivate the ability of self-learning and independent thinking. It is also important to cultivate students to understand how to interact with others and the environment and cooperate with others to build a mutual good society and environment.

Structure of Design

The purpose of this research is to understand the current development of conservation education of the cooperation between Taipei Zoo and the students from the Department of Learning and Materials Design, University of Taipei. The subjects, content, and learning objectives of the educational activities planned by the Taipei Zoo caretakers are used with the assistance of digital learning content designed in line with educational activities and an app interface suitable for learners to click and read anytime and anyplace developed by the university students. The design of apps uses Smart App development software to generate the teaching app for animal conservation educational activities and integrates the concept of knowledge testing for the learning content. Experts are invited in different stages to review and provide suggestions for revisions during the process of development. Then, college students bring the app to elementary schools and pre-test Grade 5 class of students (22 participants) who provide feedback suggestions after experiencing the app operation. Based on the feedback from the students, the app is amended again and then visitors (30 participants) use the app to learn more about animal welfare and environmental conservation. Visitors are interviewed and asked to fill in a questionnaire after using the app. Finally, the opinions and suggestions on the app from the visitors are collected and analyzed.

Taking one group of apps, for example, the content of the app 'capybaras go to school' include the following three key design aspects:

(1) Introducing the physiological structure and living habits of capybara through picture books and stories.
(2) Arousing the learning interest and motivation of learners, and deepening their learning impression through cartoons, pictures, audio media, and so on.
(3) The designing of interactive games utilizes the asking of questions at knowledge points as checkpoints in the learning process to understand the learning situation of learners on animal conservation knowledge.

Discussions

Taipei Zoo's educational displays and the conservation education plans to guide visitors (learners) to observe the rich and diverse environment of the animal displays (for instance, animal behavior and imitating the wild habitat). With the assistance of a digital learning app, visitors (learners) become observers who build connections between the observed environment and animals with the content of information descriptions and learn relevant knowledge at the same time. While observing, they enjoy the beauty of nature and wildlife. The awareness and sensitivity of beauty improve the development of attitudes and values toward the environment.

Taipei Zoo has positioned itself as an animal teaching museum that showcases and learns from life. The Zoo is full of knowledge. Thus, the development of apps helps people understand how the species interact with the environment and its habitat in the ecosystem by learning content and observing the shape and behavior of animals on-site. It is a perfect place for learning the concepts of biological diversity. However, the complex system knowledge and open learning environment require the assistance of instructors and learning content to connect the background knowledge with learners. Therefore, the apps designed in this study have received overwhelmingly positive feedback as the apps are helpful to the learners in establishing connections with wildlife and conservation through true stories and emotional and vivid descriptions. Only when learners take the initiative to connect knowledge to life, meaningful learning is developed.

Conclusions

The ultimate goal of conservation education is to cultivate citizens to aware of conservation and support conservation with their actions to create real change in conservation and allow society to coexist with nature. Conservation education is a student-centered education for 12-Year Basic Education. It triggers learning motivation and interest as well as to create interaction between the environment and people in real-life. The development of digital learning materials about animal conservation and environmental education aims to provide an interactive environment for university students to learn from the real-world and cultivate their attitude, knowledge, skills to face real-world problems. Also, the ability of coexistence should be demonstrated by building one's sense of self-worth. For example, critical thinking and teamwork cultivated in the course of exploring conservation issues are the qualities required for self-learning and social participation.

References

[1] WWF (2018). *Living Planet Report - 2018: Aiming Higher*. Grooten, M. and Almond, R. E. A. (Eds). WWF, Gland, Switzerland. [online] Available at: https://livereport.protectedplanet.net/pdf/Protected_Planet_Report_2018.pdf

[2] Pearson, E. L., Dorrian, J., & Litchfield, C. A. (2013). Measuring zoo visitor learning and understanding about orangutans: Evaluation to enhance learning outcomes and to foster conservation action. *Environmental Education Research, 19*(6), 823-843.

[3] Taipei Zoo (2014). *White Paper on the Policy of the Taipei Zoo 2015~2024*. Retrieved from https://www.zoo.gov.taipei/News_Content.aspx?n=1A7199F880AAB2CB&s=6586F9308833C7EA

[4] Patrick, P. G., Matthews, C. E., Ayers, D. F., & Tunnicliffe, S. D. (2007). Conservation and education: Prominent themes in zoo mission statements. *The Journal of Environmental Education, 38*(3), 53-60.

[5] Trombulak, S. C., Omland, K. S., Robinson, J. A., Lusk, J. J., Fleischner, T. L., Brown, G., & Domroese, M. (2004). Principles of conservation biology: Recommended guidelines for conservation literacy from the education committee of the society for conservation biology. *Conservation biology, 18*(5), 1180-1190.

[6] The Ministry of Education (2014). *Curriculum Guidelines of 12- Year Basic Education: General Guidelines*. Retrieved from http://12basic.edu.tw/12 about-3-1.php

https://doi.org/10.1142/9789811238727_0008

A Study on Belief of Dragon-Eye Water and Temple Design in Biyun Temple in Liuqiu Township, Pingtung

Shu-Heng Liu[1*], Chen-Fu Wang[2]

[1]Doctoral Program Student of Graduate School of Design,
National Yunlin University of Science and Technology, Yunlin, Taiwan
[2]Professor of Graduate School of design, Graduate School of Design,
National Yunlin University of Science and Technology, Yunlin, Taiwan
[*]Corresponding Author Email: z6210770126@gmail.com

Abstract

Liuqiu Township in Pingtung is a small island full of religious beliefs. Folk beliefs provide spiritual support for the whole island. The most prosperous temple is the Biyun Temple. The Guanyin Buddha is a god in whom the whole island believes in and the faith center of the whole island. Both spirituality and divine power have important status. Biyun Temple's unique Feng shui "Crab Den" is even more indispensable. This research aims to understand the importance of Biyun Temple's unique Feng Shui through literature review, interview, and discussion. As the island resembles a crab, there is a unique Dragon-Eye water which plays a major role in the inheritance of religious ceremonies and customs. Biyun Temple also changed the way of sacrifice, color matching, and regulations of the temple. The development of Biyun Temple has expanded to other places via the blessings of natural terrain and the efficaciousness of the temple.

Keywords: Biyun Temple, Crab Den, Dragon-Eye Water, Religious belief

Introduction

Biyun Temple, a center of faith for the entire island, is the largest temple in Liuqiu Township. The deity enshrined in Biyun Temple is Guanyin Buddha. Biyun Temple has a very long history in Liuqiu Township. In the hundreds of years of history, Guanyin Buddha has blessed every islander, and the people's devotion to the gods also made Biyun Temple become popular. Islanders are used to calling her "Guanyin Ma" as everyone comes to Biyun Temple to ask for her permission about everything from weddings to funerals. Without the permission or guidance of Guanyin Buddha, people do not take any risk. Therefore, in the folk beliefs of Liuqiu Township, the Guanyin Buddha is not only the belief of the entire Liuqiu Township, but also the patron saint of everyone. Just like a mother, she looks after everyone. Therefore, the Guanyin Buddha is also known as the mother Guanyin. Biyun Temple is also known as "Guanyin Ma Temple" (Fig. 1).

In history, the entire human life is related to culture [1]. The power of beliefs is indispensable in Taiwanese society. Folk beliefs are a consolation to everyone. There are different kinds of temples in Liuqiu Township, which is proof of the belief and piety of the local people. In the development and spread of religion, temples have a lot to do as a medium of communication. Therefore, the function of the temple itself is to connect religious beliefs with religious cultures and communities as a new composite culture [2].

Fig. 1 Biyun Temple.

A. Motivation

In the history of temples, each of them has its stories and development characteristics, which come along with many experiences in nature, coincidences, and harmony. These beneficial conditions have greatly contributed to the prosperity of a temple, spreading its reputation, and traditional folk beliefs to future generations. In addition to the meticulous care and blessing of Guanyin Buddha, the support and enthusiasm of the believers also conduce to the development of Biyun Temple in Liuqiu Township. The place where Biyun Temple is located has a very special Feng Shui. In folk beliefs, the location, like the construction of buildings, plays an important part in Feng Shui, and it affects people's success. Feng Shui has been developed as a means of self-improvement to unify their own harmony and changes with the nature. Its main purpose is to improve people's living quality and living environments [3].

Biyun Temple has had a special Feng Shui called "Crab Den" which is important in the natural Feng Shui of the temple. For Biyun Temple, the crab cave is an important Feng Shui owing to its geographical environment and religion. The geographical Feng Shui accompanies the whole building. Thus, it is not only the geographical environment but also religious influence. The development and promotion of the temple transformation have become smoother. The history of the temple complements its geographical environment. "Dragon-Eye Water" is an important natural landscape among crabs. It is spring water that gushes out naturally. Lombok Water arranges water for the entire Liuqiu Township folk belief ceremony. To cooperate with the Feng Shui of the crab cave, Biyun Temple has made different changes in the temple's expansion, color design, and folk beliefs. In addition to the permanent benefits of Feng Shui, the temple has many different customs and beliefs (Figs. 2 and 3).

Fig. 2 Dragon-Eye Water-1.

Fig. 3 Dragon-Eye Water-2.

B. Purpose

The layout of geomancy, which is believed to affect people's health, living qualities and financial conditions, is crucial to the design of a place. Therefore, an assessment is indispensable to the layout of geomancy. By maintaining and protecting the Feng Shui of the Crab Den and Dragon-Eye Water, Biyun Temple shows the importance of Feng Shui to Liuqiu Township and explains how they develop their popularities and status quo.

This study, through interviews and literature review, discusses the influence Crab Den has on Biyun Temple, the importance of Dragon-Eye Water to the religious ceremonies in Liuqiu Township, and the changes and construction that Feng Shui brought to the temple. With these changes, the profits can be maximized. Besides, changing the way we worship our ancestors can be compatible with the belief of crab dens. Moreover, Dragon-Eye Water can be developed as a publicity stunt to maintain the long-term operation of the temple.

Literary Review

Religious beliefs have several vital functions in human society such as survival, integration, and cognition. They provide the courage that human society needs to face challenges as well as consolation through folk beliefs. In this way, people can overcome challenges through meeting their psychological needs. Furthermore, beliefs unite people and make a better society [5]. Beliefs also reinforce the cohesive force of a harmonious society.

In addition to the psychological advantage given by religion, there is also unique knowledge in the Feng Shui of Biyun Temple. Feng Shui is related to personnel as well as to houses, cemeteries, and temples. As for the geographical environment, it is often mentioned in the local records. [6]

Based on the universal concept and theory that man is integrated into nature, Feng Shui is a form of environmental aesthetics studied in ancient China for towns and affects interior design [7]. In Chinese culture, five elements are generated and controlled by each other. The reconciliation of yin and yang and the natural cycle affects the magnetic field and Feng Shui. Feng Shui was also the environmental science of ancient China. Feng Shui provides a theoretical basis for future construction and layout of the location and natural environment [8]. Therefore, Feng Shui is a belief that includes the auspiciousness of the environment and helps people with strategies, career, local development, and so on [9]. Consequently, Biyun Temple, together with Feng Shui of Crab Den and the special environment of Dragon-Eye Water, has gradually developed with the help of Feng Shui and become the largest center of faith in Liuqiu Township.

Method

Biyun Temple in Liuqiu Township has cooperated with many religious ceremonies.

A. Crab Den

It is named "Crab Den" as the terrain is like a big crab, and the big claws of the crab are faced with the two mountains which surround Biyun Temple. The crab cave is a "living cave" as its mouth spits to maintain its life. In geomancy, dragon-eye water is equal to the crab's mouth. Moreover, the dragon-eye, a larger spring in Liuqiu Township, has never dried up, so the local people are dependent on it. It is a lifeblood of the whole crab in folk beliefs, so Dragon-Eye Water has become a special Feng Shui landscape that concerns the entire Biyun Temple and the Crab Den.

B. Dragon-Eye Water

Dragon-Eye Water, a natural and clean spring, is widely used in folk religion. In the dragon eye pool, there are many aquatic living things such as shrimps, crabs, and fish that appear at night (Fig. 4).

Fig. 4 Dragon-Eye Water Pool

Dragon-Eye Water is widely used for diseases. A few people use it as a medical collocation. When dispensing medicine in the temple, it is recommended to use Dragon-Eye Water. In the belief of Liuqiu Township, as long as people add a single drop of it, their illness is healed at once. The ingredients in the medicine swabs include shrimps and other creatures. After consulting Guanyin Buddha, more people want the shrimp as ingredient. Moreover, there are also many miracles. In large religious ceremonies of Liuqiu Township, such as the gods of Welcome Royal Lord Festival, and the preparation rituals, Dragon-Eye Water is used. There are also many examples of the use of Dragon-Eye Water by followers from other places to worship.

Another half-moon-shaped pool is built next to Dragon-Eye Water. In geographic Feng shui, it is supposed to have a side towards people, and vice versa. This is the concept of geographic Feng Shui. As the water pressure leaves the heat in a hexagram, the semicircle pool is believed to eliminate heat and prevent fire [10]. Its main function is to prevent Liuqiu Township from a flood, too. The bottom of it is connected to a dredging water pipe to maintain its water volume (Fig. 5).

Fig. 5 Half-moon-shaped pool

Additionally, another mesocosm is built to make Dragon-Eye Water a new tourist attraction. When people are taking a walk by it, they hear the messages of the temple's history by the docents of the temple (Figs. 6 and 7).

Fig. 6 Mesocosm-1

Fig. 7 Mesocosm-2

C. The Changes in the Belief and Feng Shui

Regarding the changes in rituals, "temple" as the name of Buddhist temples is used, especially for Buddhist sacrifice ceremonies. The naming of palaces and temples depends on gods. For example, the common temples use the names of gods for palaces, halls, shrines, altars, and so on. [11]. "Temple" serves vegetarian food in Buddhism, but Biyun Temple isn't. They use meat as sacrifices as they feed the crabs in Crab Den.

As for the design of the temple, the color red must be avoided as it represents death for crustaceans. Therefore, yellow is used instead as it is the color for crabs. Yellow is believed to make the crab hole nutritious and strong, which has a lot to do with this geographical geomantic image (Fig. 8) [12].

Fig. 8 Roof

Conclusion

Liuqiu Township is a coral reef island surrounded by the sea. As the soil on the island is suitable for farming, the main way for residents to make a living is fishery. When the business is not going well or the weather changes, the only consolation for frustrated fishermen is folk beliefs. Biyun Temple is a spiritual haven for believers, and also the place where the native consciousness gathers. Through the believers' devotion to gods, Biyun Temple has also become a place where everyone feels connected. By uniting people, the entire village can be connected with the Taiwanese native consciousness of the entire island. A better cohesive force makes the social model of the residents of Liuqiu Township more harmonious.

The establishment of a temple not only reflects the needs of followers but also presents cohesion among the residents [13]. Liuqiu Township residents' faith and their devotion to the Guanyin Buddha is not only reflected in the prosperous incense but also the temple authority's attitude. The authority of the temple is prudent, and believes in "Man prays, Gods hears." The entire temple and people are highly dependent on the Feng Shui of Crab Den. The functions of Dragon-Eye Water affect Liuqiu Township significantly.

Furthermore, Biyun Temple has been making much progress as a tourist attraction for Dragon-Eye Water's distinctiveness and universality. Therefore, everyone who is going to begin construction is supposed to obtain permission from gods to avoid changing the whole Feng Shui. This emphasizes that Guanyin Buddha takes care of the entire Liuqiu Township, and the residents also believe in gods. This has been passed down through the years as a precious culture, so its promotion is important for people to understand the Feng Shui better.

Feng Shui and Biyun Temple complement each other, so much publicity is observed by changing the old customs under special circumstances. These are also the temple's innovations. With publicity, the power of gods and the effect of geographical Feng shui makes Biyun Temple well known.

References

[1] Hofstede, G.,(2001), *Culture's Consequences: Comparing Values, Behaviors, And Organizations Across Nations Sage Publications,* Thousand Oaks Institution.

[2] Duan,Yu-Ming, *Chinese Temple Culture*. Shanghai: People's Publishing House, p.29.

[3] Guo,Yun-Xia (2007), *Application of Feng Shui in Residential Buildings*, Architecture Forum, Iss.139

[4] Chang, Ping-Teng & Lee, Jung-Hua & Hung, Kuo-Chen & Tsai, Jen-Teng & Chyung Perng (2009), Applying fuzzy weighted average approach to evaluate office layouts with Feng-Shui consideration, *Mathematical and Computer Modeling*, Vol. 50, 1514-1537.

[5] Li, Yi-Yuan (1985), *Belief and Culture*, Taipei: Chuliu Publisher, p.33.

[6] Tang, Hui-Yun (2003) , *China Feng Shui Studies*, Chinese Culture University, Graduate School of Chinese Literature, Paper, p.24.

[7] Mak, Michael Y. & Ng, S. Thomas (2005), The art and science of Feng Shui - a study on architect's perception, *Building and Environment*, Vol. 40, 427-430.

[8] Lee, S.H. (1986), *Feng Shui: Its Context and Meaning*, Ph.D. Dissertation, Cornell University.

[9] Qiu, Bi-Lian (2015), *A Discussion on the Evaluation Criteria of Space Design and Planning from the Perspective of Feng Shui Theory*. National Yunlin University of Science and Technology. Graduate School of Design, Master Program Paper, p.3.

[10] Li, Qian-Lang (2003), *Taiwan Ancient Architecture Illustrated Collection*, Taipei: Yuan-Liou Publishing Co., Ltd.

[11] Wu,Ying-Tao (1998), *Taiwanese Folklore*. Taipei: Jonwen Publisher, p.42.

https://doi.org/10.1142/9789811238727_0009

A Study on the Activities and Strategies of Citizen Participation during the Creation Process of the Hua-Zhai Cultural Cluster in Wangan Township

Shu-Yan Wang*, Shyh-Huei Hwang**

Graduate School of Design, National Yunlin University of Science and Technology
No.123, Sec. 3, University Road, Douliu City, Yunlin County 640, Taiwan
*Corresponding Author. Email: *susanwsy@gmail.com, **hwangsh@gemail.yuntech.edu.tw

Abstract

Hua-Zhai Village is a clustered settlement located in Wang-An Township, Penghu County, Taiwan. Hua-Zhai Village is believed to have existed as a settlement since the Han Chinese from Mainland China began settling there three centuries ago and is the first registered important historical settlement by the Taiwanese government. Hua-Zhai Village went through a period of exodus during the 1950s with people looking for work in more populated areas, and buildings became dilapidated afterwards. Now the village intends to restore their community and buildings, and an executive team formed by the Ocean Cultural Creative group from Graduate School of Design, National Yunlin University of Science and Technology (NYUST) has been commissioned to conduct village revitalization. With the challenges of outlying archipelago geographic disadvantages and little population, Hua-Zhai Village is stuck in a difficult situation of being a "super marginal village." In order to facilitate the community living functions and revitalize neighborhood social network, the NYUST executive team pursued the perspective of regional revitalization. Through the discovery of social issues that Hua-Zhai village encountered, the NYUST executive team investigated and developed an integrated problem-solving strategy based on regional context, viewing the cultural settlement from different perspectives to further preserve, transform and regenerate, aiming to support settlement revitalization of Hua-Zhai Village.

The purpose of this research are to analyze the issues, strategies and specific actions of Hua-Zhai Village revitalization, and to explore the core values of village revitalization through the process. Participant observation was applied to collect and analyze data, in-depth interviews and interactive discussions were applied to deepen the study and generate benefits. The research developed four problem-solving strategies, eleven concrete action plans and three implementations. Based on the process of Hua-Zhai Village revitalization, this research has three conclusions: 1) collaboration and exploration with residents, taking revitalization as re-innovation by working with them to explore new possibilities; 2) active participation from residents by inviting them to be hands on; 3) cooperation with government resources, from dependence to collaboration.

Keywords: important village settlement Wang-An Hua-Zhai Village, cultural reconstruction, citizen participation

Research Background and Motivation

Hua-Zhai is the old name of Zhongshe Village and is one of the four villages located in Wang-An Township, which is the largest archipelago among the south sea hydrographic system in Penghu, Taiwan. It has about 300 years of history, and is among the first registered important historical buildings by the government. There are around 150 households, and most of them live in traditional residential architectures, the four-fold compound. Often the building materials were obtained locally, and most of them are coral stones. Residents started moving to Taiwan for offshore fisheries or other related work owing to economic and education needs in the 1950s. This resulted in the out-migration and disintegration of buildings in Hua-Zhai Village.

The major two challenges of Hua-Zhai Village revitalization are offshore geographical disadvantages and severe population loss. It is difficult to maintain the community living functions with few and aging population. Hua-Zhai Village is stuck in a difficult situation of being a "super marginal village." Now the village intends to restore their community and buildings, and commissioned an NYUST executive team to participate in the revitalization. This is the first time NYUST executive team tried to facilitate community living functions and restore neighborhood social network through the perspective of regional revitalization. NYUST aimed to explore the social issues that Hua-Zhai Village encountered and find a solution based on the principle of assisting the village, aiming to support settlement revitalization of Hua-Zhai Village.

Research Purpose

This research is to explore the issue of revitalization of clustered village. Two purposes of this research are as follows.

1. Analysis of the topics, strategies and actions of Hua-Zhai Village revitalization.
2. Analyse the core values of Hua-Zhai Village revitalization and rejuvenation through the regional revitalization process.

Methodology

Participant observation was applied in this study. Researchers fully engaged in the promotion of strategic activities conducted by the executive team. Research data were collected during the participation. This research also interviewed stakeholders and held discussion to activate the promotion and generate benefits.

Literature Review

Clustered settlement refers to the environment that people live in, and is often thought as naturally formed. However, Hiroshi Hara suggested that clustered settlement is not formed naturally but carefully planned. According to Implementation Rules for Cultural Heritage Preservation, settlement is defined as buildings and area of accessory buildings with historical or regional characteristics, including aboriginal tribes, Dutch Formosa period neighborhoods, Han Chinese streets, foreign settlements during Qing dynasty, immigrant villages during Japanese government, modern dormitories, and military kindred villages, etc. Though formation of settlement varies with historical context including background and needs, there are four common elements of formation: people, organization and activity, buildings and area, and communication. A lack of any of the four elements will hurt the settlement and its culture. Settlement preservation has to look after both physical and invisible cultural heritage.

A. Cultural Reconstruction

The Comprehensive Community Development Program inaugurated in 1994 by the Council for Cultural Affairs (upgraded as Ministry of Culture of the Republic of China) aims at establishing community culture, developing community consensus, and building up community life experiences. This program tried to rebuild culture through interactions between people-to-people, to environment, and to community, and further facilitate the development of community. The community of life is built up through the development of consensus, the emotional memory attached to community life, and the collective historical memory. An essential of community development is community residents.

B. Regional Revitalization

The purpose of regional revitalization policy, proposed by Japanese Prime Minister Shinzo Abe, is to solve problems such as labor force decline, overpopulated city, and the industrial economic problems that regions encounter. National Development Council conducted the "Flipped Design, Regional Revitalization" pilot project in 2016. This project aimed at integrating geographical, industrial and human resources of a region and took creation, innovation, entrepreneurship, and revitalization as strategies to promote regional characteristics and industrial resources. This pilot project tried to let residents have a chance to shape new life experience that is different from their collective memory in the past through innovative intervention into community, settlement and remote areas. In his book, *Regional Revitalization*, Kinoshita Hitoshi shared the firsthand experience of regional revitalization, and deliberated on how to encourage people to discuss about value of region, and then turn the value into profit. Region is often connected to the impression of an aged society in a small and remote district. The cooperation between executive team and private sector should have a whole layout about responsibilities and concrete work division. The revision or enactment of new policy or system, should be predominated by the residents or the participants, instead of central or local government.

Introduction of Hua-Zhai Village and process of regeneration

A. Introduction of Hua-Zhai Village

There are four sectors of Hua-Zhai: Dingliao, Xialiao, Weiliao and Shan-zi-hou. Most of residents are seafarers and fishermen with some of them making their living from the mountains. Hua-Zhai had a good community function in early the early days. When cultural heritage researchers investigated traditional settlements in the 1980s, Zhongshe Village, where Hua-Zhai is located, in Wang-An Township and Erkan Village in Shiyeu Township were selected as important areas for developing cultural heritage tours of traditional settlements. However, the location of Erkan Village was superior to Hua-Zhai, and therefore the preservation project of Hua-Zhai was postponed.

Preservationists sent an application to the World Monument Fund (WMF), a private nonprofit organization dedicated to saving the world's most treasured places, in 2003 to put Hua-Zhai as an important settlement. They succeeded in having the settlement put on the 2004 World Monuments Watch List of the 100 most-endangered sites. The reason Hua-Zhai was selected is that it is considered as the most well preserved early Han Chinese settlement in Taiwan. Being listed by the WMF in 2004, Hua-Zhai was later announced to be the first national "important settlement" in 2010 by the Taiwanese government.

B. Settlement Revitalization and Strategic Action

Prior to being registered as an important settlement, Professor Lin Huei-cheng had started investigation of settlement space since the late 1970s. Lin had conducted several projects such as "Preliminary investigation of Hua-Zhai settlement preservation and early plan for community development" and "Pilot project of settlement preservation and building restoration of Hua-Zhai Village in Wang-An Township." In 2015, NYUST started the project of repurposing and management of unused space of Hua-Zhai Village. The executive team mainly assists in the preservation of traditional living wisdom and settlement revitalization. For the hardware, the authority administration needs to invest in buildings and physical outcomes. However, human resource, instead of concrete buildings, was the key factor of revitalization. Therefore, the executive team took intervention strategy to facilitate collaboration among residents. Based on the foundation of traditional culture, the executive team carried out the construction of new culture through concrete ways to trigger residents' identity.

The process led by the executive team was as follows:

- Step 1. Obtaining firsthand information through field research, and then conducting internal information integrating and analyzing.
- Step 2. Developing project items for practice.
- Step 3. Second round of field research, learning local living skills, exploring the wisdom, and further analyzing the core problem.
- Step 4. Revising operational strategies, reorganizing before action.

During the process of continued interaction and reflection, the executive team concluded the core problems that settlement encountered.

1. Residents were perplexed by the wrong guidance information provided by the tour agency.
2. The process of preparedness went slowly, causing uncertainty and ambiguity.
3. Aged residents and low population.
4. Weak community organization mobility.
5. Community industry chain fading.

Corresponding to the results of field research, the executive team took four strategies to solve problems, including network building, local empowerment, information dissemination, and description of industrial profile. The strategies are illustrated as follows:

1. Building network
    a. Set up Hua-Zhai settlement service center: serving as communication center for residents and tourist information center for visitors.
    b. Open up Facebook fan page: managing "Hua-Zhai settlement service center" Facebook fan page, and interact with netizens under the name of Wang-An. The page is mainly for sharing the activities and news of Hua-Zhai.
    c. Providing community service: attracting external resources to provide community services. For example, inviting residents to participate in re-grow after fallow, and the arrangement of settlement.
2. Local empowerment
    a. Training of volunteer guide: inviting residents to participate in the volunteer guide training course, and preparing teaching materials for training guide.
    b. Volunteering service: inviting residents to participate in volunteer services including environmental maintenance and repairing.
    c. Grounding program in education: compile documentary of oral history collected by residents or expatriated residents, and later inviting primary school students to transform into picture book and publish.
3. Information dissemination
    a. Special exhibition of Hua-Zhai No.111 restoration documentation: as the first finished restored settlement architectures, the No.111 restoration construction plays the role of cultural guide, assisting residents, expatriated villagers, and visitors to learn about the construction of traditional architecture and the formation of settlement. The documentation is published as an e-book online for reading.
    b. Making use of digital guide media such as QR code and iBeacon: inviting residents who are familiar with Hua-Zhai cultural history to film 12 guide videos and 17 audio guides, providing active and passive guide with the support of modern technology.
    c. Guide map: develop tourist map with local artists, and collect information including history background, guide of 17 designed sites, traffic information, local food information, etc.
    d. Photography exhibition of Hua-Zhai: take photographs as media to inspire residents viewing their ordinary living environment with new aspects and discovery.
4. Describing industrial profile
    The development of cultural creative product, Wang-An Hua-Zhai cookies, is meant to combine multi functions including local landscape, QR code for tour guide, the tour experience, and promotion of cultural and tourist resources. In addition, it is also a combination of land resources for experimental energy use research and development trying to describe industrial profile.

Hua-Zhai settlement service center	Exhibition of Hua-Zhai No.111 restoration documentation

Hua-Zhai settlement service center Facebook fan page	Guide map

Volunteering service	Photography exhibition of Hua-Zhai

C. Overall Characteristic of Strategies

Taking various perspectives toward settlement revitalization.

1. Residents' participation is the center of the project. With the support from NYUST's multi-field design profession, the executive team explored the life wisdom from field research, and transformed the resources obtained locally with modern technology.
2. Making use of both virtual and physical internet: villagers moving out for work is a lifestyle phenomenon of outlying archipelagos. Population is the first problem of revitalization. The NYUST took both virtual and physical gateways to promote community development with the hope to attracting expatriated villagers to come back and on the other hand, building resident's identity for mobilization.
3. Turning disadvantages into opportunity: disadvantage could turn out to be an opportunity. Transforming

ordinary life or disadvantages into the energy of future industry, describing community industrial profiles. For example, there are Leucaena leucocephala that would harm the landscape of village and also destroy the construction of historical buildings. It would take a lot of effort and budget to eradicate all L. leucocephala. However, if the residents could turn the resource into sustainable energy, it will construct community industrial profiles, and turn the disadvantages into opportunity.

Conclusion

This research focused on settlement revitalization, and aimed at repurposing of unused space of case study. Through the investigation of characteristics and problems of Hua-Zhai village, NYUST executive team concluded with four problem-solving strategies and 11 concrete actions that were relevant to settlement sustainability. The value of sustainability is another issue that will be discussed and developed by residents in the near future. Target at recruiting youth returning back home, NYUST suggested four strategies, including building network, local empowerment, information dissemination and description of industrial profile. It is expected through the implementation of these four strategies, the exodus youth can learn their identity and culture from a different perspective, facilitating the living function and further revitalizing the economy, which is the core value of settlement revitalization at this stage. The current stage of Hua-Zhai village revitalization can be viewed as a process of being scattered to assembled, and from assembled to united. For NYUST executive team, this is an implementation of societal innovation design. The research has three conclusions from the process.

1. **Collaboration and exploration: the village revitalization could be viewed as a process of re-innovation with the collaboration of university students and local residents.**
   The field research was conducted by NYUST team, but local residents were the main actors. The role and attitude of NYUST team affected the level of participation and motivation of residents. NYUST went out to invite residents in person to join a project to help elder residents get rid of exotic trees. Through collaboration residents found the beauty of ordinary life.
2. **Practical and visible action. During the process of revitalization, NYUST invited residents to actively participate in the project in person.**
   The NYUST team brought up 4 problem-solving strategies and 11 concrete action plans. The NYUST invited residents to participate hands on. It is expected that through the action, residents would start to take care of their community and participate in the development. The feedback from residents are as follows. "*My house is cleaned up. My house is No. 114. See, it is tidy and pretty, isn't? It is great to tidy up my own house.*" "*This time our entire family member worked together. They came back and we work to fulfill our bounden duty. After that we had chit chat over our childhood memory and the fun story with elders. Though it was tiring, I feel satisfaction and a sense of achievement inside*"
3. **Collaboration with government resource: Support from government is an important force for village revitalization, but the allocation of resources is even more important.**
   Hua-Zhai is registered as an important settlement by government, and its authority administration is Bureau of Cultural Heritage, whose mission is to preserve, restore, and provide administrative resources. The collaboration among NYUST team, residents and government, providing sufficient resources and communication, is crucial. Settlement is where people live, therefore, exploring the authenticity and uniqueness is the foundation of participating in revitalization, especially for human resource. Good communication and attitude toward the project is the best start up for collaboration.

References

[1] Jungshe Village, https://www.wmf.org/project/jungshe-village#.T8uHAic-nIc.facebook, 2017/8/27Access.

[2] Kinoshita Hitoshi, Zhang P. Y. (trans.), (2017), *Regional Revitalization*, New Taipei city: First Press.

[3] Lin Xin Hua (2009), Policy of Culture, New Taipei city: Yang-Chih Publishing.

[4] marginal village, https://ja.wikipedia.org/wiki/%E9%99%90%E7%95%8C%E9%9B%86%E8%90%BD, 2017/8/27 Access.

[5] Hara Hiroshi, Huang M. P., Lin Y. T. (trans.) (2011), *Settlement of 100 revelations,* New Taipei city: Common Master Press: A division of Book Republic Publishing.

[6] Chen Q. A. (1995), comprehensive community development and Cultural and Creative Industries, 《Culture Industry Seminar & Community Overall Creation of Sino-Japanese Communication Proceedings》, Taipei, P.5.

[7] Rong F, J., I have a dream: Lutheran Church as a modern heritage policy imagination, https://heritagenote.wordpress.com/2015/07/10/modernarch1/, 2017/8/27Access.

[8] Lin C. Y., 2006, *Delimitation of the Spatial Territory for Traditional Chinese Settlements in Quemoy: A Study of Ngó-iân Religion*, Shu-Te University(Taipei, Taiwan)

https://doi.org/10.1142/9789811238727_0010

A Study on the Adaptability of Art Majors in Guangdong Undergraduate Colleges under the Background of the Planning and Development of the Guangdong-Hong Kong-Macao Greater Bay Area

Wu Jun

Beijing Institute Of Technology, Zhuhai, China
Bangkok Thonburi University, Bangkok, Thailand
Email: 59249551@qq.com

Abstract

From the perspective of the planning and development of Guangdong-Hong Kong-Macao Greater Bay Area, we aim to establish art majors in schools, colleges, graduate schools, and companies. Five indicators are obtained through systematic analysis and research on the curriculum of art of colleges in Guangdong Province. Methods such as literature review and comparative analysis are adopted. The result shows that the opening rate of art majors in Guangdong undergraduate colleges is high, but the majors are not diverse. As the number of students between majors varies greatly, some majors are not chosen. The employment of graduates is concentrated in Guangdong Province. The degree of professional relevance is higher than that of the national average, and there is strong demand in the job market. For the mission of inheriting and promoting the culture and art, the goals of culture and leisure, and the development needs of the Greater Bay Area, the art majors should be freely offered and coordinated as follows: (1) the number of enrollment for art majors should be changed from “market concentration” to “planned decentralization”, (2) the training of professionals should change from “minority” to “popularization”, and (3) the setting of art majors should be changed from “discipline” and “In the planned catalog” to “future development and internationalization”.

Keywords: The Guangdong-Hong Kong-Macao Greater Bay Area, Undergraduate College of Guangdong Province, Art, Professional Settings, Adaptive

Introduction

In 2019, the Central Committee of the Communist Party of China and the State Council issued the "Guangdong-Hong Kong-Macao Greater Bay Area Development Plan Outline". The outline pointed out that it is necessary to strengthen cultural self-confidence, build a humanistic bay area, promote and support the inheritance and development of excellent Chinese traditional culture, especially the promotion of Lingnan culture. It also emphasized to improve the public cultural service system and cultural and creative industry system in the Greater Bay Area and promote the industry of publishing, multimedia, and music. Exchanges between art academies, performing art schools, and cultural and cultural institutions need to be increased in the Greater Bay Area by supporting cooperation in curating exhibitions and facilitating cross-border performances. Shenzhen was designated to have the world's high-end creative design resources and vigorously develop the fashion and cultural industry. The area needs to build a diversified tourism product system such as cultural history, leisure and vacation, health care, cruises, and yachts and accelerate the three-dimensional development of "ocean-island-coast' tourism by building characteristic towns in coastal areas [1].

The "Guangdong-Hong Kong-Macao Greater Bay Area Development Plan Outline" outlines the future development direction, ideas, and goals of the Greater Bay Area. The goals of the planning outline are inseparable from the joint efforts of various levels of government, enterprises, institutions, scientific research institutes, and other organizations and individuals. However, talents are the key to realize the above development plan. The Greater Bay Area plan proposes to create a highland for education and talent. For this reason, cultural and artistic professionals are particularly important in the Bay Area. The universities in Guangdong Province, as the core of the Greater Bay Area, not only have inherent geographical advantages but also undertake the mission of cultivating and developing talents.

Individuals or systems adapt to changes by improving genetic or behavioral characteristics and retain the corresponding adaptive characteristics through genetics [2]. From the background of "Guangdong-Hong Kong-Macao Greater Bay Area Development Planning Outline", we analyze and judge whether the setting and current situation of art majors in ordinary undergraduate colleges in Guangdong Province can adapt to this historical mission. The healthy development of art majors in universities and the realization of the goals in the planning outline are of great significance.

Research method

With the help of human capital theory, this research adopts a literature review, a comparative analysis method, an induction method, and other research methods. Through combing the art majors currently opened in all ordinary undergraduate colleges and universities in Guangdong Province and conducting a systematic comparative analysis, it is concluded that the art majors in provincial ordinary undergraduate colleges meet the development goals in the "Guangdong-Hong Kong-Macao Greater Bay Area Development Plan Outline" and attract the attention of relevant art education managers in Guangdong Province.

This study took 67 ordinary undergraduate colleges and universities in Guangdong Province as the research object. The data in the research are from the information disclosed by the Ministry of Education of China, the Guangdong Provincial Department of Education, the Guangdong Employment Guidance Center, and the official websites of various universities. Owing to the relative stability of university majors and enrollment, this study collected more than 70 employment reports of the colleges for 2018 graduates. The study used basic statistical analysis and extracted core elements such as "opening art majors majors", "the number of colleges and universities", "the number of majors opening art majors", "the number of graduates", "employment in Guangdong Province", and "employment professional relevance". The elements were analyzed and compared, then.

Status Quo of Art majors in General Undergraduate Universities in Guangdong Province

A. Number of colleges and universities offering art majors

Of the 67 undergraduate colleges and universities in Guangdong Province, 50 (74.63%) offer art majors. Among them, 27 (71.05%) of 38 public and 23 (92%) of 25 private universities offer the majors.

B. Number of colleges opened by major

According to the "Ordinary Colleges and Universities Undergraduate Specialty Catalog and Specialty Introduction" (2012 edition) by the Higher Education Department of the Ministry of Education of the People's Republic of China, there were 29 art majors. Among 50 colleges and universities, the major of visual communication design is offered, environmental design majors by 35, product design majors by 29, and music science majors by 22. No college offers sculpture, recording art, opera, film, television literature, and art history. Only one institution offers photography, theater film, television art design, theater film, television director, film studies, drama studies, composition and composition technology theory.

C. Number of 2018 graduates of art majors

In 2018, there were a total of 15,952 graduates with art majors. The top four were environmental design, music, visual communication design, and product design. The number of graduates exceeded 50% of the total number of graduates. There were eight majors in public art, performance, drama, film studies, the art design of drama, film and television, composition and technology, drama, film and television director, and photography which had less than 100 graduates. Among them, there were only 15 graduates of theater and film director and 17 photographers.

D. Proportion of 2018 graduates employed in Guangdong Province

In 2018, 91.97% of the graduates of the majors were employed in Guangdong Province. The employment rate of public and private colleges were 90.61 and 93.32%, respectively.

E. Employment professional relevance

In 2018, the employment rate with professional relevance of the graduates was 76.43%. The rate of public and private colleges were 80.60 and 70.78%, respectively.

Conclusion

Based on the above situation, the opening rate of the majors in Guangdong colleges and universities seems high, but the number of students between majors varies greatly. Several majors have a majority of the students. The employment of graduates is concentrated in Guangdong Province, and the degree of professional relevance is higher than the national level. The demand for the employment market for art majors in Guangdong Province is high.

Education investment should be based on market supply and demand [3]. In the long-term practice of professional setting, there are two influencing factors of setting a major: social demand and the level of education. These two factors have a long-term effect on professional standards. The influence of social demand is gradually weakening, while that of the education level is increasing [4]. Nowadays, the rapid development of China's economy changes society's demand for all professions, which demands colleges and universities to meet the demand in time. Nowadays, the major setting of colleges and universities should be based on the main principle of "focusing on disciplines and taking into account market needs".

The idea of the "Outline Development Plan for the Guangdong-Hong Kong-Macao Greater Bay Area" is the country's requirements and vision for the development direction, ideas, and goals in the next few decades. Colleges and universities in Guangdong Province have unique advantages to provoke the mission of building and developing the Greater Bay Area. Through the analysis of the setting of art majors, a development plan of education in art majors is provided for the prosperity and development of culture and arts. A scientific approach should be taken in terms of the professional placement of art majors.

A. Discipline of art majors: transition from "free setting" to "overall planning and linkage"

The art majors are offered by many undergraduate colleges in Guangdong Province. The number of art majors in schools has reached 74.63%, of which private schools have reached 92%. There are four leading majors in terms of student enrollment: visual communication design, environmental design, product design, and musicology. One of the main reasons for the concentration in several majors is that the admissions are decided by universities according to popularity. Thus, the education authority needs to plan for diversifying the majors, which strengthens the coordination and control for unpopular with appropriate investment and inheritance. The government also needs to encourage colleges to develop and offer various art majors.

B. The number of students enrolled in art majors: should shift from "market concentration" to "planned decentralization"

The number of students in each of the art majors varies greatly, and that in some majors is relatively small. Majors with a larger number of enrollments are allowed to have talent training, employment competitiveness, and education of quality. Majors with a small number of people lack talented students, which affects the construction and development of the industry.

For this reason, the number of enrolling students in art majors should be diversified to meet social demand. At the same time, supporting the majors of fewer enrollments needs to increase to cultivate professionals, improve students' learning and employment satisfaction, and increase the talent pool for the development of the Greater Bay Area.

C. *Cultivation of professional talents in art majors: the transition from "niche" to "popularization"*

To fulfill the requirements of the development of cultural and artistic heritage in the Greater Bay Area, not only a large number of professionals and students are needed, but also the residents need to understand the essence of art, accept its cultural and artistic forms, and consciously maintain them. The environment for the inheritance and development of culture and arts requires universities to provide superior resources to popularize the arts for society and improve the level of accomplishment. It can be carried out through the following. (1) opening the campus and providing art classrooms to attract non-professionals, (2) creating a strong artistic atmosphere from campuses to communities, (3) serving the communities with resources and accelerating the integration, development, and innovation with regional culture and customs, and (4) collaborations of colleges and universities with the for local folk culture and art. When the inheritance and development of the local government and the community are fully integrated, the local people learn, promote, and jointly maintain the development, inheritance, and innovation of local folk culture and art.

D. *Professional setting of art majors: should shift from "in the catalog of discipline planning" to "future development and internationalization"*

Guangdong Province is a relatively international province and China's window to the global society. The advancement of the Greater Bay Area planning enables new ideas to emerge such as artificial intelligence, 5G, big data, and so on. Along with the diversification of China's economic development, the barriers between academic disciplines are becoming low. The majors in the national professional planning do not fully contain the professional content, and the defined professions cannot satisfy people's future demands, which requires the innovative development of new professions and their directions. For this reason, universities in Guangdong province should diversify the majors for global integration and offer the majors that are in line with future development and international standards innovatively.

The planning and implementation of the development of the Guangdong-Hong Kong-Macao Greater Bay Area at the national level will surely turn the area into a vibrant world-class city cluster. It will also enhance the international competitiveness of the area that participates in international cooperation and competition at a higher level. The expansion is also a major measure to further promote the construction of the "Belt and Road". Universities in Guangdong Province need to bear the important responsibility of technical support and personnel training in this task. By facing a new era, tasks, demands, and challenges, it is necessary for the universities in Guangdong Province to further optimize and adjust the art majors for the better ground of art training, which helps to realize the development mission of the Greater Bay Area.

References

[1] The CPC Central Committee and the State Council issued the Outline of The Development Plan for The Guangdong-Hong Kong-Macao Greater Bay Area in February 2019

[2] Kitano H. Systems biology: A brief overview. Science, 2002, 295(5550): 1662-1664

[3] [US] Gary Becker, Human Capital, Translated by Chen Gengxuan, Machinery Industry Press, 2016.3

[4] Ji Baocheng, Research on Subject Setting in Chinese Universities [M], Renmin University of China Press, 2006:38

https://doi.org/10.1142/9789811238727_0011

A Study on the Analysis Method of Graphics

Zhong Yu*, Wang Yanfei**

School of Art and Design, Shanghai University of Engineering Science
Tongji University Shanghai Institute of Design and Innovation, Shanghai 201620, China
*Corresponding Author. Email: *ppdexyj@163.com, **895492168@qq.com

Abstract

This article analyses graphics from three aspects including historical background, contents and functions. It proposes three kinds of analysis methods: art analysis + historical situation, design thinking + imaginative thinking, design science + graphics capabilities. It offers analysis method support for curriculum design, disciplinary construction and design practices.

Keywords: graphic analysis, analysis method, design science

Design Science is a relatively new and emerging discipline in recent years. According to 2011 structural adjustment of the undergraduate majors of ordinary institutions of higher education in China, Design Science belongs to the category of Art, as one of the five first-level disciplines. With the development of Design Science in China, the major has been established, the contents have been growing, and the disciplinary task has turned from "Establishing Design Science" to "Constructing Design Science with local characteristics". Graphics is China's unique artistic and cultural resource. It is important to appreciate, analyze, re-design and re-use local graphics under the perspective of Design Science, which is also of great significance for "Constructing Design Science with local characteristics".

Graphics usually have a long history, excellent contents, wide-ranging functions and different forms of carriers. "These graphics possess the unique characteristics not only in China and also in the cultural history of the world, and have their own systems naturally."[1] Appreciating these Graphics requires the analysis of the historical background, contents, and functions.

This article is divided into four parts. The first three parts analyze graphics from the perspectives of historical background, contents and functions. The story of many graphics in history provides the theoretical and reference basis for the analysis methods. In the last part, under the perspective of Design Science, three methods of contemporary analysis are proposed.

Analysis of graphics from the perspective of historical background

China has a long history. It has been about 5,000 years since the Yellow Emperor, about 4,000 years since the Xia Dynasty and about 3,600 years since the Shang Dynasty. In the past thousands of years, the local culture has never been cut off. It has been a multi-ethnic fusion culture with the Han people as its main body. With the development of the times, the regional scope of being labelled as "China" has also been under constant changes. The civilization of the Pre-Qin period is based in the Yellow River basin, and the states of Chu, Yue and Wu during the Eastern Zhou period (770-221 BC) has developed the South. Then, Qin Dynasty established China's first large unified country, and determined the main body of China as the Yellow River basin and the Yangtze River basin. Later, China has gone through a number of dynasties including Western and Eastern Han, the Three Kingdoms, Western and Eastern Jin, Northern and Southern Dynasties, Sui, Tang, the Five Dynasties and Ten Kingdoms, Northern and Southern Song, Yuan, Ming, Qing, the Republic of China, until the People's Republic of China.

The so-called China sometimes expands, sometimes shrinks, is sometimes unified, sometimes split. The span of thousands of years and the spatial changes of millions of square kilometres, tells us that arts and culture has been deeply influenced by the political pattern, national folklore and philosophical thoughts of the region. Therefore, unlike many other countries in the world, the analysis of graphics must be based on the diversity of China, as one must take different era and the territories into concern.

The political pattern lays the tone of the graphics, ethnicity and folk custom determines the characteristics of the graphics, and philosophical thoughts give meaning to the graphics. In addition, in all ages of history, the level of productivity also has an impact on the carrier, contents and creative methods of the graphics. Overall, graphics are the creation of art, the record of history, and the symbol of culture. (TABLE I) [2] [3]

It can be seen that the artistic style of graphics is closely related to the background of the times.

TABLE I
GRAPHIC ANALYSIS OF DIFFERENT ERAS

Era	Political Pattern	Ethnicity and Folk Custom	Philosophical Thoughts	Main Carriers	Artistic Style
Primitive Times	Clan Commune in Yellow River and Yangtze River Basin	Primitive Society	Patrilineality and Matriarchy	Cave Painting, Porcelain, etc.	Primitive, for Decoration, Records and Communication
Pre-Qin Period	Territories Granted to the Nobles	Sinocentrism, First Wave of Ethnic Amalgamation	Philosophical Thoughts Thrived	Bronze Ware, etc.	Dignified and Majestic with Geometric Shapes

Qin and Han Dynasties (221 BC-220AD)	Period of the Great Feudal Unity	The Han Ethnicity Formed	Confucianism Became the Mainstream	Brick and Stone Relievo, Eaves-tile, etc.	Symmetrical with Abstract Shapes
Wei, Jin and the Southern and Northern Dynasties (220 - 589 AD)	Split v/ith Wars	South-bound Migration of the Han Ethnicity, Second Wave of Ethnic Amalgamation	Buddhism Prevailed, Mutual Influences Between Han and Other Ethnicities	Grottoes, Sculptures and Mural Paintings, etc.	Buddhist Culture Combined
Sui & Tang Dynasties (581- 907 AD)	Feudal Unity with Opening Politics	Fusion of Cultures with Strong International Communications	A Mix of Confucianism, Taoism and Buddhism	Grottoes, Porcelain, Architecture, etc.	Splendid and Elegant
Song & Yuan Dynasties (960-1368 AD)	A Fusion of Ethnic Regimes	Third Wave of Ethnic Amalgamation	Rapid Development in Technology	Porcelain, etc.	Delicate for Song Dynasty and Rough for Yuan Dynasty, Classic Patterns of Flowers and Plants Emerged
Ming & Qing Dynasties (1368-1912 AD)	Feudal State Declined and the Multi-exhnic Status Consolidated	Fourth Wave of Ethnic Amalgamation Enriches Folk Culture	Early Capitalist Emerged in Ming Dynasty and Seclusion in Qing Dynasty	Hand-crafts	Abundant Visual Language

Analysis of graphics from the perspective of content

"Xing Xiang", or form and image, is a commonly-used vocabulary for people that has different meanings in many contexts. There is an ancient saying that goes "Xiang, or images that carry meanings, lie in the sky yet Xing, or actual forms, lie on the ground." [4] which is often quoted by scholars in the fields of philosophy, social science, and art. The original intention is that when something severe is about to happen, there will be a sign sent off from the sky. In the field of art, people generally separate "Xing" from "Xiang" before combining them for further analysis. "Xing" refers to the shape of things that can be seen, and "Xiang" refers to the meaning of the forms. The thinking about "Xing Xiang" has greatly influenced the contents of graphics, as one "Xing" might refers to multiple "Xiang" and one "Xiang" might be reflected in multiple "Xing".

Taking "Eight Immortals" as an example, it is the collective name of the eight gods in local folklore, which generally refers to Tieguai Li, Han Zhongli, Zhang Guolao, Lu Dongbin, He Xiangu, Lan Caihe, Han Xiangzi and Cao Guojiu. The "Eight Immortals" graphic is a typical traditional figure, divided into "The Clear Eight Immortals" and "The Vague Eight Immortals". "The Clear Eight Immortals" is the image of these eight gods, and "The Vague Eight Immortals" is the image of the instrumental figures held by these eight gods above. The two forms of "The Clear Eight Immortals" and "The Vague Eight Immortals" actually express the same "image". [5]

It can be seen that the analysis of graphics contents need to be carried out in the mindset of "Xing Xiang".

Analysis of graphics from the perspective of function

Graphic design pays attention to the "function" of the images. A large part of the graphics' functions are to pray for "good luck". These graphics are called auspicious patterns.

The auspicious expression of the graphics has been around for a long time. "He Tu Luo Shu" is one of the earliest figures in China. Its appearance is considered an auspicious sign. In *Sui Chao Zi*, it says that when the emperor Ji comes to prosperity, the He Tu will come out of the Yellow River. [6] In *Zhou Yi Kou Yi*, an interpretation of Yi Ching written by scholar Hu Yuan, says He Tu is an auspicious sign from the sky. [7] These statements link the graphic to the destiny of the country.

In daily life, graphics are influenced by the willingness to yearn for a better life, which even reach the level that "graphics must have meanings, and the meanings must be auspicious". "Shou" is the first of the "five blessings" pursued in traditional culture. People are eager for longevity and happiness, so they have made the character of "Shou" an art pattern and an auspicious graphic. More than 300 kinds of Shou graphics have been handed down. [8]

Overall, graphics are functionally oriented and practical.

Contemporary analysis method of graphics from the perspective of Design Science

The discipline of Design Science emphasizes on the intersection of "art", "design" and "science", which forms a unique perspective of Design Science. Through the analysis of graphics from the perspectives of historical background, contents and functions, this article summarizes three kinds of analysis methods for experts in the field of design.

The first type: "art analysis + historical situation".

The teaching method of art analysis is currently widely used in traditional graphic teaching in design-related majors. The main way is for students to achieve emotional resonance through the experience of visual analysis under the guidance of teachers. However, the main problem is that through visual experience alone, the audience are not able to gain a sense of synonym, as they might lack of sufficient interest and are not able to form an understanding that is deep enough. Therefore, it is crucial to learn the historical situations of the graphic, including political pattern, national folklore, philosophical thoughts, main carriers, to form a kind of associative memory and an understanding that is deeper and broader.

The second type: "design thinking + imaginative thinking".

Design is generally divided into two aspects: planning and creation. This way of division in fact corresponds to the integration of the both "Xing" and "Xiang" of traditional graphic contents. Therefore, combined with design thinking and imaginative thinking, we can better understand the connection between the creative ideas of traditional graphics and contents expression.

The third type: "design science + graphics capabilities".

The scientific nature of design is reflected in the analysis of design ideas, the evaluation of design solutions, and the implementation of design projects. From the perspective of design science, we can analyze the creativity, performance, and use related environment and effects of traditional graphics to deepen the understanding of traditional graphics' functions.

Analysis of graphics in the perspective of Design Science should achieve three levels of purposes. The first level, to understand our own original art culture, to be the contemporary inheritor of traditional art culture; the second level, to understand the traditional graphic design thinking, to inspire contemporary design; the third level, to summarise the graphic analysis methods of Design Science, to construct design contents of local characteristics, build up the design context, and promote the development of Design Science.

References

[1] M. Xia, *The Application of Chinese Graphics in the Modern Logos,* Annals of Oncology Official Journal of the European Society for Medical Oncology, December 2012, Suppl 2(12):S47-S50.

[2] Mei Shu Da Guan Editorial Departmen, *The Chinese fine arts education academic symposium the art and design theory volume,* Shenyang: Liaoning Fine Arts Press, October 2016, pp.163-164.

[3] J. Liu, et al., *Development and Research of Traditional Crafts in Modern Lighting Design,* Changchun: Jilin University Press, July 2016, pp.109-111.

[4] J. Qi, *Zhou Yi Zheng Jiang*. Beijing: Xian Zhuang Shu Ju, September 2013. p.4.

[5] Z. D. Li, *China's Traditional Auspicious Graphics,* Shanghai: Shanghai Press of Science Promotion, 1989, pp.69-75.

[6] Q. Chen, et al., *Zhu Zi Ji Cheng•Volume 4,* Beijing: Tuanjie Press, 1996, p.69.

[7] Z. Liu, *Chinese I-Ching Studies,* Beijing: Central Compilation & Translation Press, May 2015, p.304.

[8] K. Ji, et al., *Journey of Folk Art,* Beijing China Textile Press, September 2015, pp.295-297.

https://doi.org/10.1142/9789811238727_0012

A Study on the Application of Computer-Aided Design for Space Lighting

Ching-Hua Chiu[1*], Chun-Wang Lee[2]

[1]Ph.D. Candidate, Graduate School of Technological & Vocational Education,
National Yunlin University of Technology and Science, Taiwan
[2]Ph.D., Graduate School of Technological & Vocational Education,
National Yunlin University of Technology and Science, Taiwan
*Corresponding Author Email: am8586ma@gmail.com

Abstract

We applied software to simulate the interior lighting layout and compile the lighting data to design an expert system. Users in a simulating interior lighting design quickly learn the reference values of the data and understand whether the lighting distribution follows the standard by simply inputting relevant parameters step-by-step.

Keywords: programming design, expert system (ES), lighting design, room index, illuminance values

Introduction

To adapt to the classroom environment, the eye muscles are overstretched, and long-term learning in a poorly lit condition causes visual diseases. The school classroom lighting is divided into psychological and physiological aspects for review and analysis [1]. In the psychological aspects, (1) a good lighting environment prevents fatigue, and (2) a well-lit environment stimulates students' motivation to learn. In physiological aspects, (1) a good lighting environment prevents problems of the visual organs, and (2) good lighting maintains the physical health of students and teachers.

The quality of classroom lighting has a great impact on students' eyesight. High lighting quality protects students' eyesight and improves their learning efficiency [2]. This study, by considering energy conservation and a comfortable lighting environment, aims to collect and review relevant literature on classroom lighting design and evaluate the design's performance and effectiveness in applications through a computer-aided software simulation. The objectives of this study are as follows:

(1) Aiming to improve the quality of existing classroom lighting which lacks an overall design and evaluation
(2) Conventional space lighting designing without lengthy calculation steps and queries and programming a set of lighting design interface to provide interior designers with a rapid design system.
(3) Assessing the feasibility of the design by computer simulation software.
(4) Providing with the lighting design instruction and helping to achieve accurate design for interior designers when designing the lighting system.

Research Design

We collected and compiled the related literature, norms, and theoretical foundations to propose a systematic simulation of the indoor lighting layout and construct a classroom experiment space for simulation [3,4,5,6]. The methods are as follows:

A. Literature Collection:

We collected classroom lighting-related norms and the relevant theoretical data as the basis of this study [7,8].

B. Establishment of Theories

The relevant theories, literature, and research papers were collected to analyze and compare the ideal lighting methods for the guidelines of perfect design [9,10].

C. Execution of the Lighting Calculations

The lighting equation was used to preliminarily calculate the number of lamps, average illuminance, power consumption (KWh), electricity bills, and lighting-related data.

D. Simulation Analysis and Programming

(1) DIALux 4.11: To simulate each indicator's efficiency when a light fixture is placed in the indoor space to ensure the designed light fixture achieves a required lighting quality in the classroom space.
(2) Visual Basic: To write a program, and enter the parameters to calculate the required data by executing the program.

Spatial Arrangement

A. Arrangement of Classroom Space Lighting

A small classroom was selected for a lighting layout simulation analysis. It had the dimension of 10, 8, and 3.6m in length, width, and height, respectively. The light source used a cool color temperature (4500K ~ 6500K). The content of the classroom lighting design simulation is sown in Table 1.

TABLE 1
Contents of the classroom lighting design

Parameter Project	Parameter Value	Remark
Work surface illuminance	500 Lux	CNS classroom lighting illuminance benchmark
CU	0.52	
M	0.8	
Ceiling reflection coefficient [%]	70	
Flooring [%]	20	
Expected Results		
Work surface average illuminance [Lux]	500	
Work surface light distribution uniformity	≥0.5	

B. Selection of Energy-Saving Lamps

The luminaires used in this study were PHILIPS TBS463 SQR 4xTL5-13WHFP AC-MLO [11-12]. The details are as shown in Table 2.

TABLE 2
Specification of the light fixtures (luminaires)

Light fixture Brand 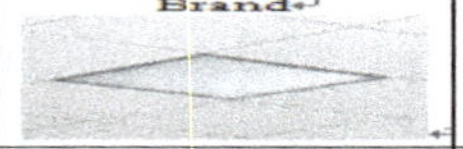	PHILIPS TBS463 SQR 4xTL5-13W HFP AC-MLO Dimensions: 0.622(M)x0.622(M)x0.105(M)	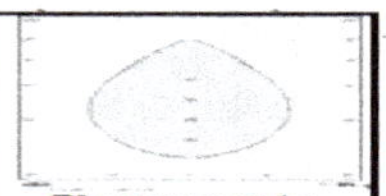 Photometric (Polar Coordinate)
Luminous flux (light fixture)	2668 lm	
Luminous flux (lamp):	4600 lm	
Light fixture power	59.0 W	
Light fixture classification standard of (CIE)	100	

C. Required Number of Light Fixtures

Based on Eq. (1), the number of classroom light fixtures required was calculated. The number of fixtures affects the aesthetics and lighting characteristics of the layout. To facilitate the arrangement and combination of luminaires, a total number of 25 light fixtures were arranged in 5 rows and columns.

$$N = \frac{E \times A}{M \times CU \times F} = \frac{500 \times 80}{0.8 \times 0.52 \times 4600} \cong 20.9 \quad (1)$$

D. Construction of Classroom Space Lighting

At this stage, DIALux software was used to draw the classroom space and construct relevant equipment. The parameter items were set as shown in Table 1. It shows the construction overview of the classroom lighting space. Figure 1 shows the editing parameters. Figs. 2 and 3 show the floor plan of the classroom space and the front view of the classroom space.

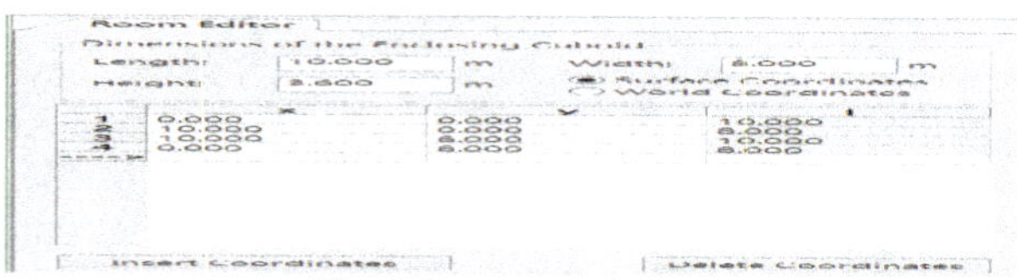

Fig. 1 Parameters items.

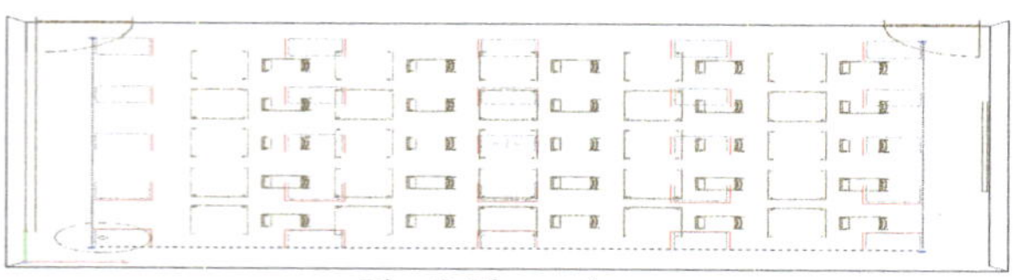

Fig. 2 Floor plan.

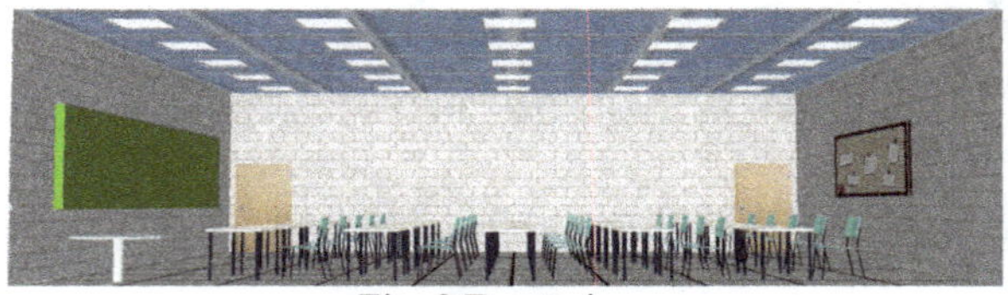

Fig. 3 Front view.

E. Analysis of Classroom Lighting

The classroom had a total number of 25 light fixtures. Each fixture had a luminous flux of 4600 Lm, and a power of 59 W. The desktop was set at a height of 85cm. The space height was 360cm, and The fixture installation height was 369.5cm. The maintenance coefficient (M) was 0.80. The simulation results were shown in Table 3 and Figs. 4 and 5. The working surface's average illuminance was about 593 Lux, and the illuminance uniformity was 0.503. The floor's average illuminance was 373 Lux, and the illuminance uniformity was 0.4. The ceiling's average illuminance was 149 Lux, and the illuminance uniformity was 0.43. The color temperature was divided into 2500 K and 6500K, and the visual effects were as shown in Figs. 6 and 7.

TABLE 3
Analytical projects of lighting.

	Name	F light fixture (Lm)	F Lamp (Lm)	P (W)
Light fixture	PHILIPS TBS463 SQR 4xTL5-13	2668	4600	59
Total		66700	115000	1475
Surface	r [%]	Average illuminance Lux	Illuminance uniformity	
Work surface		593	0.503	
Floor	20	373	0.4	
Ceiling	70	149	0.43	
Black board wall (5)	50	236	/	

Remarks: Space height: 3.6 M; installation height: 3.695 M; maintenance coefficient: 0.80

Fig. 4 Performance chart.

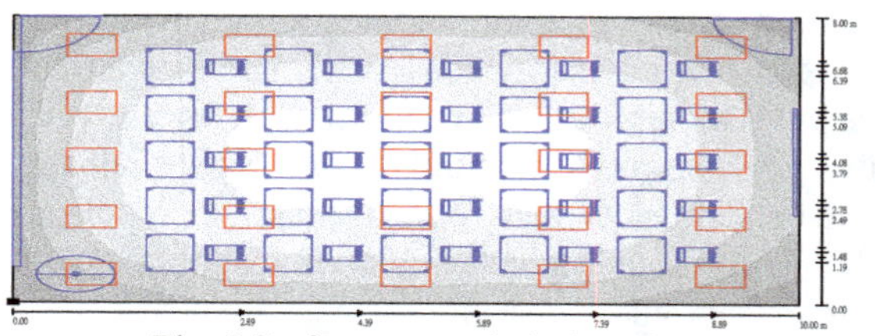

Fig. 5 Surface grayscale isolux diagram.

Fig. 6 Color temperature 2500 K

Fig. 7 Color temperature 6500 K

F. Electricity Charge Calculation

According to the analytical projects of classroom lighting (Table 3), a total of 25 light fixtures were used in the classroom. Each fixture had a luminous flux of 4600 Lm, and a power of 59 W by assuming the lighting of 8 hours a day and 22 working days a month. The electricity charge required for lighting the classroom this month was calculated with the details of the equations as follows:

Power (KWh) = (Total degrees in fixtures x Days of use x Daily lighting hours) / 1000
= (59x25x22x8) / 1000
= 259.6 KWh

From the non-business time pricing table, electricity below 120 degrees costs NT$ 2.1 per kilowatt. As the consumed electricity is 259.6 degrees, the pricing for over 120 degrees is NT$ 3.02 per kilowatt. For the classrooms to achieve an average illuminance of 593 Lux and an illuminance uniformity degree of 0.503, the monthly lighting electricity cost is NT$ 673.59.

Computer-aided Design

The above classroom lighting layout needs a lot of time to query the relevant data and manual calculations when calculating the number of luminaires and electricity consumption. This study developed a simple programming design to shorten the time spent on querying and calculating electricity consumption (Fig. 8).

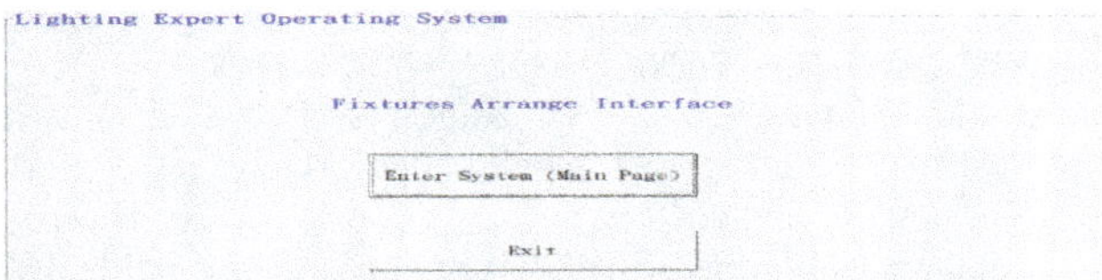

Fig. 8 Lighting expert operation system.

A. Room Index Conversion Program Design

When converting the number of light fixtures, in pre-operation, several parameters are needed, including the room index (RI), coefficient of utilization (CU), maintenance coefficient (M), and other parameters of the light fixtures (see Fig 9). The RI value can be obtained by entering the dimensions of the interior space into the table in the user interface of the room index conversion program. The room index is mainly used to determine the type of luminaire (e.g., wide illumination or narrow illumination luminaire) and the coefficient of utilization (CU) value to query.

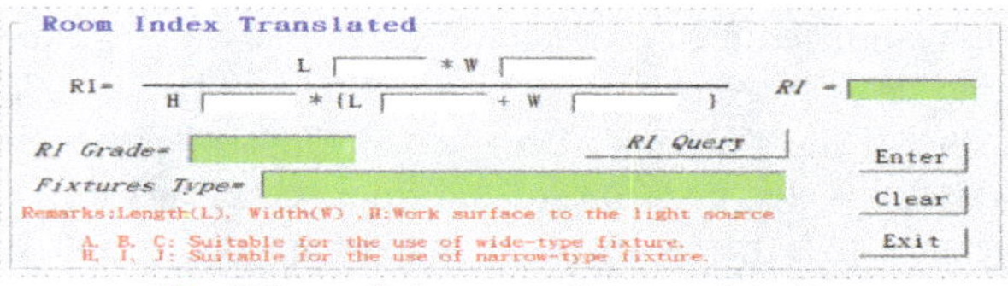

Fig. 9 Room Index operating user interface

B. Lighting Utilization Rate Programming

The lighting utilization rate is based on the room index data and set with space material reflectance with classroom lighting design content (Table 6). The reflectance of the ceiling, walls, and floors were 70, 50, and 20%, respectively. The light fixtures of PHILIPS TBS463 SQR 4xTL5-13W HFP AC-MLO showed the lighting utilization rates in the operation user interface (Fig. 10), which was provided for the following operational use.

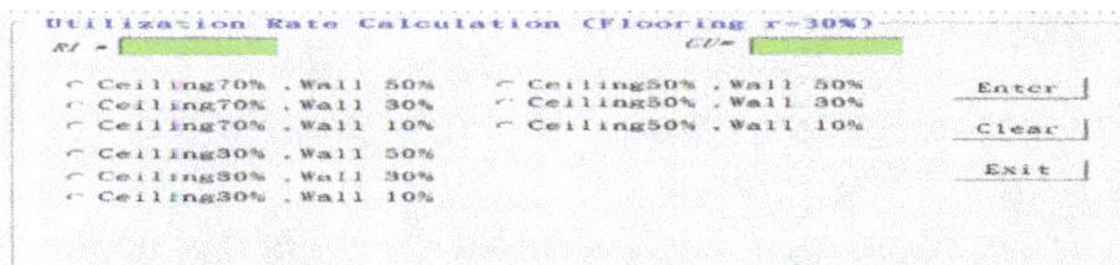

Fig. 10 Utilization rate in operation interface

C. Required Fixtures in Conversion Programming

To convert the number of light fixtures required, the maintenance coefficient requires a determinant. The program based on DIALux software numerical values has three options: (1) very clean with a low annual utilization rate of 0.8, (2) clean space and a three-year maintenance cycle of 0.7, and (3) indoor or outdoor installation, high pollution 0.5, and other options (Fig. 11).

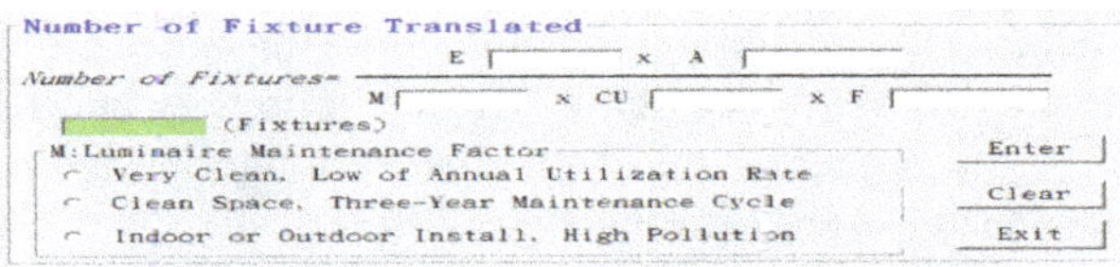

Fig. 11 Fixtures in the operation user interface

D. Consumption and Electricity Charge Programming

The design of the power factor and electricity tariff calculation is based on the current policy changes, so the power factor and electricity tariff operation interface is adopted. The tariff is divided into summer and non-summer season, and further divided into non-business and business purpose (Fig. 12).

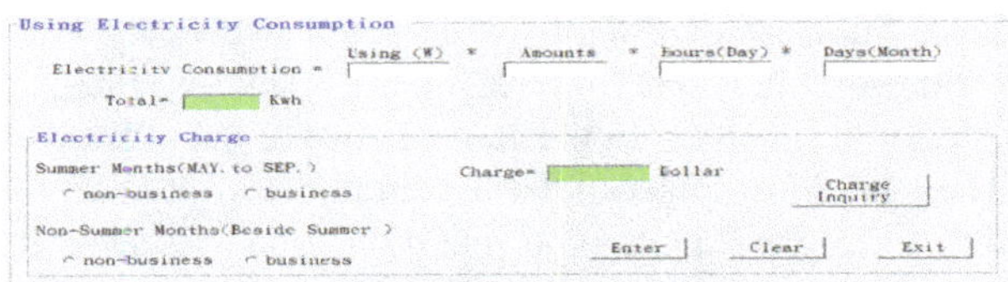

Fig. 12 Consumption user interface.

Results

A. Interior Lighting Design Simulation to Help Learn the Reference Value of the Data

To complete the programming, we used classroom lighting design contents as input parameters (Table 1). The RI value of the classroom was 1.6161. 70% of the ceiling, 50% of the walls, and 20% of the floor were chosen as the reflectance to achieve an average illumination of 500 Lux with 25 lamps for classroom lighting design and 5x5 arrangement. The average illumination of the classroom was 598 Lux (Fig. 13), and the lighting utilization rate was 0.52, which was the highest in the world.

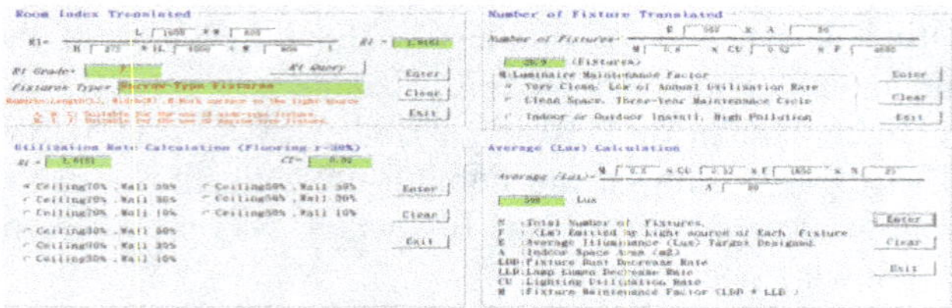

Fig. 13 Fixtures in conversion program execution.

B. Programming Execution To Help Implement Further Complicated Computation

The classroom needed a total of 25 light fixtures. This study further converted KWh consumption in classrooms into electrical charge through the computation. All the complicated steps of checking the meter table and calculating in the traditional lighting design were eliminated for time efficiency.

Conclusions

A computer-aided design software assists interior space lighting designing, improves designers' abilities to complete a lighting fixtures layout design based on their experience, and reduce the probability of human error in judgment and calculation. Besides, this study designed a friendly interface to meet the requirements of end-users or interior lighting designers and solved the problem of insufficient illumination to provide the convenience of calculating the electricity consumption in the interior lighting design. The following were the result of this study.

(1) By the staged color performance diagram on the lighting simulation, the working surface Isolux diagram, and the grayscale Isolux diagram, it was easy to identify the position of the fixture's illuminance distribution.
(2) From the grayscale Isolux diagram, the maximum value of the general interior space illuminance was in the center of the space.
(3) From the classroom light fixture simulation analysis, the location of the light fixtures in the space provided the interior designers with the convenience of installation.
(4) The use of computer-aided design and layout shortened the time for labor configuration and reduced the probability of human miscalculations.
(5) With the compiling of the parameters into the software programs, the room index (RI), the query of hat type of light fixture, and the CU values to use in a short period.
(6) The data of the room index was used to calculate the lighting utilization rate (CU), the maintenance coefficient (M), other parameters of the luminaires, and the number of luminaires, which reduced the traditional experiential conversion of lighting fixtures.
(7) To calculate power consumption and electricity bills, users simply entered the relevant parameters.

The lighting environment emphasizes sufficient, balanced, and stable illumination as well as low-glare visual surroundings. In conventional interior design, most of the relevant data are converted from experiential values, which are not systematic and easily lead to errors. This study represented the results of a program approach for the calculation of the relevant parameters, which saves time and reduces errors in manual calculation.

References

[1] D. C. Chou, *Construction Equipment*, Taipei: Maorong Books Ltd., 1998.8.

[2] Taipei City Government Department of Education, *Taipei Education Statistics*, Taipei: Taipei City Government, 1996.

[3] D. C. Chou, *School Classroom Lighting Promotion Manual*, Taipei: Architecture and Building Research Institute, Ministry of the Interior, 1998.6.

[4] Ministry of Education, *School Classroom Lighting and Energy-saving Reference Manual*, Taipei: Ministry of Education, 2004.5.

[5] D.C. Chou, *School Classroom Lighting Design Technology Handbook*, Taipei: Architecture and Building Research Institute, Ministry of the Interior, 1996.6.

[6] J. E. Kaufman, *IES Lighting Handbook : 1981 reference volume*, NY: Illuminating Engineering Society of North America, 1981.

[7] S.M. Berman, Energy Efficiency Consequences of Scotopic Sensitivity, *Journal of the Illuminating Engineering Society*. Vol.21, No.1, 1992, pp. 3-14.

[8] M. Navvab, Visual Acuity Depends on the Color Temperature of the Surround Lighting, *Journal of the Illuminating Engineering Society*. Vol.31, No.1, 2002, pp. 70-84.

[9] IES. *Guide for Educational Facilities Lighting (ANSI/IES RP3-1988)*, NY: IESNA, 1988.

[10] J. E. Flynn & A. W. Segil, Architectural Interior Systems: Lighting, Air conditioning, Acoustics, U.S:Van Nostrand Reinhold, 1992.

[11] Southern California School, Classroom Lighting Guide, U.S: Southern California Edison, 2004.9.

[12] J. B. de Boer & D. Fischer, *Interior Lighting*, Netherlands: Springer, 1981.11.

https://doi.org/10.1142/9789811238727_0013

A Study on the Detection of Semantic Discontinuity between Product Expression and Consumer Perception of Apparel Products

Kuo-Kuang Fan[1], Yi-Ting Chang[1*], Xiao-Yu Huang[2]

[1]Graduate School of Design, National Yunlin University of Science and Technology, Yunlin, Taiwan
[2]Xiamen Academy of Arts and Design, Fuzhou University, Xiamen, China
[*]Corresponding Author Email: twoeting@hotmail.com

Abstract

Under the impact of the COVID-19 pandemic, which has severely devastated the fashion industry, semantic discontinuity detection between product expression and consumer perception has become even more important than before. Many studies have investigated the semantic difference between designers and consumers in the last decade, but there are few studies on the key vector for semantic discontinuity detection of the product. We interviewed three apparel designers and developed a questionnaire with six different elements. The questionnaire was randomly distributed to 30 consumers to ask about two apparel products and their photographs. The results of the study indicate that consumers are more likely to perceive semantic continuity with a designer's physical product than photography and there is a significant difference between the expression of apparel products and consumer perception. The results provide a way of effective communication with consumers for designers and allow setting the goals for the intended semantic expression in design, decision-making, and establishing the basis for good communication between designers and consumers in the fashion industry.

Keywords: Clothing code, semantic discontinuity detection, research methods, communication

Introduction

As COVID-19 has spread around the world, especially in Europe and the United States, the "Big Four" fashion weeks (Milan, London, Paris, and New York) were impacted in 2020. According to NSS Magazine, fashion houses lost between €3 billion and €40 billion in sales with decreasing stock price losses. "I think the epidemic has brought the fashion industry to a standstill," Wintour, editor-in-chief of Vogue US, said on CNBC's Closing Bell show on 21 March, "and everybody is rethinking what the fashion industry stands for, what it means and what it should be." According to a report by the CNA, Inditex Group, the parent company of fast-fashion leader ZARA, expects to have a revenue of €3.3 million in 2020 which is decreased by 44% from that in 2019. A loss of €409 million in the first quarter of 2020 was reported, and Inditex would close 1,200 stores. However, during the same period, online sales grew by 50%. The data showed that off-line stores in the fashion industry are experiencing a severe impact, and the detection of the semantic discontinuity between product expression and consumer perception became more important than ever. The main motivation of this study is to develop a well-established semantic detection tool during this recession in the fashion industry. The purpose of this study is to detect and analyze the semantic discontinuity between apparel products and consumers to establish better communication between designers and consumers.

A two-stage questionnaire was completed to address the potential semantic issues between consumers and designers. In the first stage, the questionnaire identifies whether products or product photos help consumers understand the intended semantic expression of the designer. In the second stage, we explored the semantic gap between consumers and designers and tried to identify and analyze the issues.

Literature Review

Semantics is used in linguistics, logic, cognitive science, psychology, and many other fields. Lai [7] mentioned that psychologists, philosophers, and linguists paid special attention to semantics. The understanding and interpreting mechanisms involved in this study focus on the philosophical concerns about how people perceive various facts and how they relate to each other. We attempt to understand how semantics works and how it becomes an effective bridge between designers and consumers. Although there are some commonalities in semantics research across research fields, specific research methods and contents differ greatly. In this study, we searched for published semantics-related research in the past decade and compared semantic intentions and realization in product design. The examples of semantic studies in the last decade include the following: (1) the study of high-end furniture impressions uses product photos as the main objects [1], (2) conveying specific information, (3) exploring designers' capability of embodying design concepts by the product forms and whether there is a semantic gap in the transmission of information by using photos of various types of electronic products as the main objects [2], (4) exploring the semantic differences between designers and consumers of automobiles by using photographs of automobiles as the primary objects [3], and (5) designers of semantic discontinuity detection, using physical chairs as the primary objects [4]. In semantic research, we found that product photos were preferred by researchers. However, it is still unknown if photography can be a tool for semantic detection in the apparel industry. To reduce the semantic distance between apparel designers and consumers, the detection tool is designed for reducing semantic discontinuity.

Barthes [6], a French literary critic on semiotics, argued in The Fashion System that fashion is not only an instrumental value used to cover up and keep out the cold but also an image-clothing. By extension, fashion is one of the signs of people's identity. Every garment, fabric, and silhouette has symbolic meaning conveyed by the designer, which in this study is called "clothing codes". Clothing codes play an important role in communication between the designer and the consumer, when the consumer's interpretation of the clothing code does not meet the designer's intentions, that is, the semantic discontinuity. The semantic discontinuity is critical to designers. Responding to the semantic discontinuity requires a well-developed two-way detection tool for detecting semantic meanings understood by designers and consumers. This study uses two-way questionnaires and interviews to examine the differences.

Research Methods

This study assumes that an appropriate research vector reduces the semantic discontinuity between designers and consumers and that consumers' preference of the vector is conducive to the detection of the semantic discontinuity between product expression and consumer perception. Interviews were conducted with three fashion designers, and the questionnaires were designed based on the "clothing codes" mentioned by Roland Barthes in his book "*The Fashion System*", which were sizes, styles, visual imagery, lines, tactile impression, and fabrics.

A two-stage detection tool was designed for semantic discontinuity.

Stage 1: Data collection and interviews with designers

An interview was conducted with a designer who provided products and product photographs of two research objects (Figs. 1 and 2). The designer's answers to the questionnaire were collected and analyzed.

Stage 2: Evaluation and expression of participants' product perception

With the two objects as apparel products, 30 participants (customers) were selected at random as the subjects.

The explanation of questionnaire A: According to a subject's choice, the subject was provided either a real product or a photograph and filled the questionnaire A.

The explanation of questionnaire B: A questionnaire survey with 6 elements was conducted on garments in Figs. 1 and 2. The data and evaluation were collected and analyzed (Table 1).

Fig. 1 Design A

Fig. 2 Design B

Results and Analysis

22 of 30 subjects chose the physical product as the research vector for the evaluation and product expression. More participants believed that the physical product was better than the photograph to understand the product semantics that the designer tried to convey.

For the questionnaire A, there was no significant difference by gender between selecting the photograph and the physical product. The age of the participants showed a significant difference. Nine of 23 subjects whose age was 21–30 years old chose the photograph, while all of seven participants at the age of 51-60 years old preferred the physical product to perceive the semantics. According to the analysis of the interviews, this generation barely shopped online and their consumption behaviors were still based on visiting off-line stores.

For the questionnaire B, the average score of 22 subjects who chose the physical product as the research vector was calculated to figure out the conformity of product semantics with consumer perception. The result indicated that nearly half of the subjects understood the designers' semantic intentions on styles, tactile impressions, and fabrics but not on lines that had a significant semantic difference between designers and consumers. The results of the study are shown in Table 1.

Some of the subjects did not understand the meanings of the terminologies used in the questionnaires, such as fabrics, fabric composition, and specific terms for describing lines in garments, which caused semantic gaps with the designers. 10 of the 22 subjects understood the semantic intentions of the designers. The result proposes a reference for designers to design their apparel products in the future.

TABLE 1
Semantics discontinuity detection (unit: average number of participants)

Design / Question	Question 1	Question 2	Question 3	Question 4	Question 5	Question 6
Design A	12	8	10	4	10	11
Design B	7	14	6	7	13	15
Average.	9.5	11	8	5.5	11.5	13

Discussion

The number of people who chose the physical product as the research vector was 22 and the number of product photographs was 7. The difference in the number of people was caused by the limitation of this study. Therefore, it was not possible to explore which of the two factors was closer to the designers' semantics. Therefore, we compared the data of semantic meanings of 22 subjects who chose the physical product as the research vector with the semantic intentions of the designers. The following comments were made in the questionnaire B.

(1) They cannot know the size of a garment just by looking at the photo, so it is good to communicate if you provide the photographs with a proper proportional scale.

(2) They think that Design A is both fashionable and individualistic, and Design B is both casual and urban-stylish. The style of apparel is ambiguous to make a proper decision.

(3) For Question 4, it is easy to understand the designer's question by only using adjective phrases. It is very possible to misunderstand the meaning of the question by using more technical terms such as Y-shaped lines and A-shaped lines.

(4) The participants who choose the product photographs as the research vector determine the fabric and its tactile quality by referring to the details of the design. For example, the zipper in Design A makes it look stiffer, while the collar in Design B makes it look softer.

(5) The participants said they did not know what cellulose acetate was, so they could not know what it smelled like. When you buy a garment, you do not pay much attention to the ingredient labels. People mostly use their hands to determine the quality of the fabric.

The above is the feedback given to the designers by the participants during the interviews.

22 of 30 participants believed that the physical product conveyed the semantic intentions of the designer better than the photograph. The result represented that the epidemic did not change the decision. However, the fashion industry has been devastated by COVID-19 pandemic. It is not only making challenges for designers responding to the situation but also provides a new prospect for physical stores. It turns out that consumers think that the physical product is the best vector to understand the product semantics by the designer. Two-way communication between designers and consumers helps designers understand consumer perspective on products through research and consumers understand product semantics through semantic detection.

Conclusions and Recommendations

22 out of 30 participants thought that the physical product as the research vector was better to understand the designer's product semantics than the photograph. The results indicate that nearly half of the participants understood the designers' semantic intentions on styles, tactile impressions, and fabrics but not on lines. The subjects believed that they could know more details of the size, material, and tactile quality of the garment through the physical product, which could not be given from the product photos. They even thought that there was a huge gap between the photographs and the product. These semantic discontinuities affect brand perception, so designers must take into account the comments made by the subjects. The results of this study provide designers a pertinent recommendation that the semantic detection settings of products, whether using physical products or photographs, must take into account the background of consumers or add some description on the terminologies in the questionnaire to reduce the semantic discontinuity generated by the participants' different backgrounds [5]. For future research on detecting semantic discontinuity, researchers need to overcome the limitations of this study and further explore whether the research vector is a physical product or a photograph. Better communication between designers and consumers is achieved and established with the basis between designers and consumers in the fashion industry.

References

[1] Hu, T., Zhao, J., and Zhao, D., A study on the semantic gap between designer and user in automobile design, *the IASDR 5th international congress of international association of societies of design research,* Tokyo, Japan, 2013.

[2] Khalaj, J. and Pedgley, O., *International Journal of Design,* 8(3), pp. 79-96, 2014.

[3] Shigemoto, Y., and Moultrie, J, Delivering messages: exploring the ability of designers to embody concepts in product form, *the 10th spring conference of the Japan society of Kansei engineering,* Kyoto, Japan, 2015.

[4] Khalaj, J. and Pedgley, O., *International Journal of Design,* pp. 36-39, 2019.

[5] Chang, Yi-Ting, Delivering messages: exploring the ability of designers to embody concepts in product form, *the 7th IDSFC 2020,* Yunlin, Taiwan, 2020.

[6] Roland Barthes, *The Fashion System,* New Taipei City: Laureate Books, 1998, pp. 275-279.

[7] Lai, Hui-ling, *Semantic,* Taipei: Wunan Press, 2017, pp. 10-30.

Appendix

The questions in Questionnaire A are shown as follows:
This questionnaire is designed to help designers and consumers detect product semantics. In your opinion, which of the following options can help you better understand the

semantics of the product that the designer is trying to convey?
1.Product photographs
2.Physical products

About the six elements of product semantics of apparel, the questions in Questionnaire B are shown as follows:

Question 1:
What size do you think this design is?
1.S Size 2.M Size 3.L Size 4.XL Size

Question 2:
What do you think the designer wants to convey?
1.Fashionable 2.Individualistic 3.Casual 4.Urban-stylish

Question 3:
Which imagery of four seasons do you think the designer is trying to express?
1.The warmth of spring. 2.The keeping out the cold and the heavy look of winter. 3.The loneliness and desolation of autumn. 4.The freshness and breathable feeling of summer.

Question 4:
Which of the following options do you think the designer would like to express in the form of clothing codes?
1.Y-shaped: gentle and graceful. 2.H-shaped: tough and strong. 3.A-shaped: dignified and elegant. 4.S-shaped: a sexy female.

Question 5:
How do you feel about the tactile properties of this fabric?
1.Smooth 2.Tough 3. Fluffy 4.Stiff

Question 6:
What do you think the fabric smells like? 1.Cotton 2.Plastic 3.Cellulose Acetate 4.No smell

https://doi.org/10.1142/9789811238727_0014

Action Research on Teaching of Design Appreciation of Postmodern—A Case Study of the Post-Pop Design Appreciation Activity of Elementary Students in Taiwan

Li-Chun Huang[1*], Ming-Chuan Ho[2], Yung-Chia Chiu[3]

[1]Graduate School of Design, National Yunlin University of Science and Technology, Taichung 40041, Taiwan
[2]Department of Industrial Design, National Yunlin University of Science and Technology, Taiwan
[3]Department of MICE Marketing & Event Management, Shu-Te University, Taiwan
*Corresponding Author Email: lichun666888@yahoo.com.tw

Abstract

The pop design movement is derived from pure art. Pop art emerged in the UK in the 1950s, prevailed in the US and the UK in the 1960s, and influenced design activities. It became weaker in the 1970s. After the death of Andy Warhol in 1989, pop culture has risen again, and critics call it "Post Pop". Today, in the design of space, visual communication, fashion, advertising, digital media, film, traces of post-pop art can be seen. With the changing trend in art education, the curriculum of design education in Taiwan adopts an educational view that emphasizes creation and appreciation. With a class of art and design education in an elementary school, the action research method is adopted in this study to understand the trend of post-postmodern design. In addition to conducting a teaching activity of design appreciation for senior students of the elementary school, the first writer uses the samples revised by an expert questionnaire and tests the students for the identification ability of T-shirts with Post Pop design. The results of the questionnaire survey were analyzed with SPSS 18.0. Besides testing the teaching effectiveness of the appreciation activity, the teacher establishes a teaching model for design appreciation to enrich the design education of current elementary schools in Taiwan and enhance students' resilience ability of new art in the 21st century.

Keywords: post-pop design, design appreciation, elementary school design education

Introduction

Pop design was derived from pure art. Scholars thought pop design was an art activity of modernism with the creative skill and technique of duplication, attention to teenagers' secondary culture, and the taste of common people. Pop design belongs to postmodernism. Pop artists or designers often make use of other people's works by amplifying, narrowing, dismantling, collaging, and making a part of personal creations. These techniques of deformation, displacement, fragmentation in non-tradition ways led to the controversy about "Who is the author" or "creative arts". In the digital and post-modern times, the creative approaches of copying, appropriating, and re-building are found everywhere with mechanical reproduction.

T-shirts are clothes that people often wear. Children are familiar with T-shirts. The students at the sixth grade of Li-Ming elementary school wear class uniforms (T-shirts) in routine school activities. This study carried out the creative teaching of a T-shirt design for senior elementary school students. When designing a T-shirt, sample designs were selected by experts to test students' ability to distinguish the design style of Post Pop. The result of the questionnaire survey was analyzed with SPSS. The research on the design appreciation activity provides a method for the current elementary school art teaching in Taiwan and enhances the students' ability to adapt to post-modern art.

Literature Review

A. Glossary clarification

a. Action Research

Action Research emerged from Kurt Lewin's work in social psychology in the 1940s [1]. Action research suffered a decline in favor during the 1960s due to its association with radical political activism [2]. Subsequently, action research gained a significant foothold both within the realm of community and participatory action research as a form of practice oriented to the improvement of educative encounters [3].

b. Modern Art and Post-Modern Art

The MOMA Museum's website says that artists broke the tradition in the 19th century to create modern art. The birth of modern art can be traced back to the Industrial Revolution and lasted through the 19th century. Modern art included artistic work produced during the period from the 1860s to the 1970s and denoted the styles and philosophies of the art produced during that era [4]. The art after the 1960s is so different from previous modern art and is referred to as post-modern art [5]. Then, as soon as Duchamp openly displayed ready-made objects as artworks, postmodern concepts disappeared. Later in the 1960s and 1970s, pop artists intentionally turned to popular vulgar culture in contradiction with the rules of modernism. Conspicuous changes could be seen in many artworks during the period and postmodern thinking started to flourish [6]. Back then, the "post" in "postmodern art" no longer purported an extension from modern art. It was a reactionary movement against modern art.

B. Pop Design Movement

Fashion, commercial products, and advertising design are equally important ideas in pop art [7]. Applying pop art ideas into furniture and decoration was mostly favored at the time. The term "design" became an approach and was improved into the pop design movement [8].

a. Pop Design Movement in the UK and the US (1950-1970)

Dominion of art from the "Industrial Art movement" in the 19th century of the UK was crashed in the 1950s. False policies of culture encouraged the artists to leap out of the weak market by pop ideas in the 1960s. Pop ideas especially caught people's eyes in fashionable dress, furniture, and interior design. They broke traditional British style, even Modernism and Internationalism conventions. Sharp shape, vivid color, particular mode, playing characters, and cynical attitudes towards life were new approaches in pop design. Pop perspectives became popular in Britain and Europe in the 1960s. American pop artists, such as Jasper Johns and Andy Warhol, were famous for their works such as the American Flags series (1954), Marilyn Monroe (1962), and Green Coca-Cola Bottles (1962). They enlightened designers on pop ideas with collages, flowers, whirlpools, and circles, and so forth. Yvs Saint Laurent (1936-1998), a fashion designer, pushed pop spirits onto fashion dresses, which advanced commercial culture mixed with fine arts.

b. Post Pop Design Movement (1980-2000)

Post Pop was revealing again when Andy Warhol died in 1989. Post Pop was widespread in the world. By paying more attention to the concepts of time, medium, and reproducibility, it became an international cultural movement.

c. Pop in the 21st Century (2001-)

Pop design remains popular in the 21st century. Both imagination and creative ideas provide rest to the soul. Pop design started to cooperate with neo-Dada, street art, graffiti art, radical art, minimal style, and luxurious style. Pop design is seen everywhere nowadays: plastic lamps in orange, colorful desks in simple shapes, T-shirts or blankets with cartoon characters, the cover of the CD, the posters of the rock-en-roll bank, and so on. New-age consumers such as teenagers and young working women are apt to anti-tradition and personal style.

Study Method

A. Study Objectives

This study has two purposes. The first one is to find out whether T-shirt samples in the styles and aesthetic qualities of Post Pop design help achieve the goal of verifying students' art appreciation performance. The second one is to understand students' ability in identifying the styles of Post Pop design and the results of the identification.

B. Methods

a. The content analysis method: literature related to the Pop and Post Pop design, styles, and aesthetic qualities were summarized and presented.

b. The questionnaire survey method: 12 specialists and scholars (Table 1) were invited to divide 30 T-shirts into two groups, one with Post Pop styles and aesthetic qualities and the other with non-Post Pop styles and aesthetic qualities. Afterward, we used the selected samples to perform a specifically designed test to verify the students' appreciation ability to identify Post Pop design styles.

c. The action research method: The students were given lessons on design appreciation and responded to a questionnaire. The students' learning result was analyzed by using SPSS.

TABLE 1
The academic background and teaching experience of the specialists and scholars

No.	Name	Teaching Experience (years)	Highest Educational Qualification
1	Li O Jie (M)	27	PhD in science of design
2	Lin O Sen (M)	26	MA in art
3	He O Zhou (M))	27	MA in art
4	Li O Ying (F)	10	PhD in science of design
5	Huang O O (F)	28	MA in art
6	Zhu O Hua (F)	13	MA in art
7	Chen O Di (F)	26	BA in art education
8	Huang O Ru (F)	26	BA in art education
9	Wu O Xin (M)	23	BA in art education
10	Wu O Ren (M)	24	BA in art education
11	Chen O Xing (F)	25	MA in art
12	Chen O Fang (F)	23	BA in art education

The study procedure is shown in Table 2.

TABLE 2
The study procedure

*Confirmation of study contents, methods and steps *Confirmation of teaching procedures and teaching material contents	→	*Collection and arrangement of related literature and data →
*Preparation of teaching materials *Selection of identification samples by specialists and scholars and modification	→	*Completion of the questionnaire survey on students(Dec. 2009) →
*Quantification and analysis of questionnaire data * Documentation and presentation of study results (Oct. 2020)		

C. Questions

a. What are the standards (styles and aesthetic qualities of Post Pop design) adopted by the specialists and scholars in the selection of identification samples?

b. What did the identification samples selected by the specialists and scholars include?

c. How was the performance of students in identifying the Post Pop design styles of the T-shirts and the results?

d. Could the identification samples selected by the specialists and scholars help achieve the goal of verifying the appreciation ability of students?

E. Study Targets

The questionnaire survey was performed for specialists and scholars between June and August in 2010. The teaching and the questionnaire survey on students were carried out in November 2010. 57 students participated from an elementary school in Taichung City.

Study Results and Finding

A. Postmodern Aesthetics in Pop Design

According to the contents of postmodernism, Hassan argued that the elements of postmodernism included indeterminacy, fragmentation, decanonization, self-lessness, depth-lessness, irony, hybridization, carnivalization, performance, participation, and immanence [9]. This study adopted Hassan's opinions for the aesthetic characteristics of the pop design.

B. Identification Samples Selected by Specialists and Scholars

The experts participating in the questionnaire survey included elementary school art teachers with over ten years of teaching experience and professors from departments of art and design. They selected T-shirts with Post Pop and non-Post Pop design styles. Among 30 T-shirts, 3 T-shirts were selected by 67% of the participants, 3 by 75%, 6 by 83%, 7 by 92%, and 2 by 100% (Table 3). The T-shirts selected by the experts were divided into 10 sample groups which were labeled with Post Pop style and non- Post Pop style to test the students. Among the ten sample groups, Group 3 showed the worst test result with the correct answer rate of 31.6% (Fig. 1). 92% of the experts thought the T-shirt on the left in Fig. 1 displayed a strong Post Pop style with a creative Pop technique. The T-shirt on the right also showed postmodern art qualities such as decanonization, fun, and playability. The animal patterns in the animation design on the T-shirt were not only closer to the daily life of children but also had emotional resonance with children. Therefore, Group 3 could not be used in the official test.

TABLE 3
The Probability of T-shirt being selected

No.	POP	No	Probability of being selected	No.	POP	No	Probability of being selected
1	1	11	92%	14	11	1	92%
2	3	9	75%	16	2	10	83%
3	10	2	83%	18	2	10	83%
4	11	1	92%	19	11	1	92%
5	11	1	92%	20	1	11	92%
6	3	9	75%	22	0	12	100%
7	2	10	83%	23	10	2	83%
8	8	4	67%	24	11	1	92%
9	8	4	67%	25	0	11	100%
10	8	4	67%	27	2	10	83%

Fig. 1 Group 3 of the ten sample groups

C. Performance of students in identifying Pop design styles

The results of the test for the students showed the correct identification of Post Pop design styles as 87.7% (Fig. 2). This indicated that prior teaching activities improved the students' learning performance. At the same time, the survey also proved the samples selected by the experts could effectively measure the ability of the students to identify Post Pop design styles.

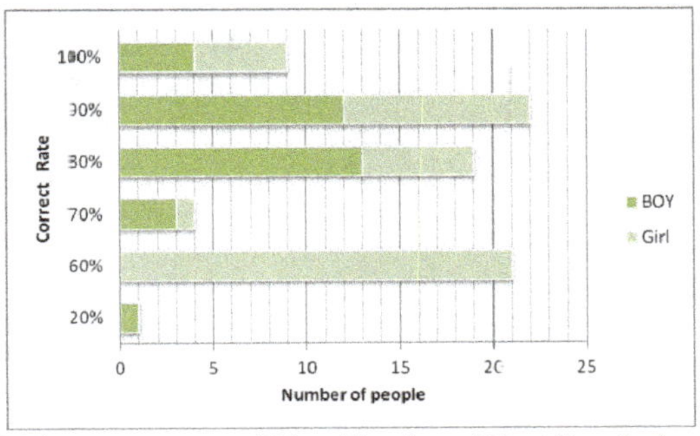

Fig. 2 The correct rate of identification of Post Pop design style

Conclusions

As a consequence of the changes in art education around the world, art education has not only continued to focus on guidance through creative teaching but also increased the contents and ratio of art appreciation teaching. This has been a common tendency in Taiwan and other countries. Creativity and appreciation are emphasized in the design and planning of art education courses. The creative art techniques and expressiveness of 11- to 12-year-old children have reached the pseudo-realistic stage. By guiding the children through appropriately designed appreciation activities, their aesthetic experience is enriched and design ability and expressiveness during the adolescence period develop. The study result reveals that action research has established an effective teaching method of design appreciation as well as a research model. The result also shows that teaching appreciation of Post Pop upgrades students' design appreciation ability. This study helps to enhance the contents of current art education at the elementary school level in Taiwan as well as improve children's capability to adapt to the developments of postmodern art.

References

[1] Kemmis, S. & McTaggart, R., The Action Research Planner. Geelong, Victoria: Deakin University Press, 1998.

[2] Stringer, E. T., *Action Research:A handbook for practitioners 3e*, Newbury Park, ca.: Sage. p.304, 2007.
[3] Carr, W. and Kemmis, S., Becoming Critical. Education, knowledge and action research, 1986.
[4] Atkins, Robert, Artspeak: A Guide to Contemporary Ideas, Movements, and Buzzwords. New York: Abbeville Press., p.102, 1990.
[5] Liu Fengrong, An Enlightenment from Postmodernism for Contemporary Art Criticism Education, A Collection of Papers from the InSEA (International Society for Education through Art) Asia Regional Congress, Department of Fine Arts, National Changhua University of Education, pp.177-185, 2001.
[6] Lu Rongzhi, Postmodern Art Phenomena, Artist Publishing, Taipei, 1990.
[7] Zhao gui-ying, Culture as a Painting-Pop Art's Popular and Postmodern Culture, Master Thesis, Department of Sociology at Tunghai University, 1992.
[8] Wang shou-zi, Modern Design 1864-1996, Taipei: Artists Press, 1997.
[9] Ihab Hassan, The Postmodern Turn: Essays in Postmodern Theory and Culture, Ohio: Ohio State University, p.20, 1987.

https://doi.org/10.1142/9789811238727_0015

An Empirical Study on Activating Small-scale Multifunctional Community Care Facility Space Based on Service Design

Wan-Li Wei*, Li-Ya Lin

Department of Product Design, Ming Chuan University, Taoyuan 333, Taiwan
*Corresponding Author Email: wanliwei@mail.mcu.edu.tw, Tel: +886 3 350-7001

Abstract

This study explored older adults' preferences and needs for small-scale multifunction care centers through a questionnaire survey. Before then, the customer needs and the relevant construction features were investigated using the quality function deployment. A spatial plan for small-scale multifunction care centers was then proposed on the basis of the research results, with the assistance of service design tools. A 100-ping (a Taiwanese unit of area equivalent to 3.3 m^2) small-scale multifunction care center was planned to verify the case. The center was designed with six major spaces, namely a health examination and exercise area, reading area, recreation area, dining service area, and teaching area, the use of which would enable the center to meet the diverse needs of older adults. Finally, design evaluation and verification were conducted through a questionnaire survey. The results demonstrated that the spatial planning for small-scale multifunction care centers should consider factors such as safety, situations involving the use of assistive devices, and the old's psychological aspects to create a truly diverse and friendly environment for aging in place.

Keywords: aging in place, service design, community care, quality function deployment (QFD), small-scale multifunction

Introduction

A. Research background and motive

Aging in place is a concept originating from northern Europe in the 1960s that maintains that the aging process should occur in a familiar living environment. According to a survey of older adults lived in Taiwan conducted by the Department of Statistics of the Ministry of Health and Welfare in 2011, aging in place can overcome the shortage in the labor force and be the preferred aging model for older adults. Japan has developed small-scale multifunction care centers, and Taiwan also has approved a 10-year long-term care project in 2007 to promote a home-based and community service–based care model [1]. In recent years, service design has been valued and widely applied in numerous fields. The tools of service design are employed to identify the optimal solution using multiple reflections from the users' perspective. Results can be used to improve existing services or create new ones, thereby enabling the provision of more comprehensive services. In response to changing demographics and a need to create a society friendly to older adults, the advantages of service design can be usefully applied to design spaces that can meet the needs of an aging population.

B. Research objectives

Aging in place is a response to the urgent need to accommodate an aging society. In this study, space design plans and design specifications were proposed for small-scale multifunction care centers in communities to serve as a reference for future designs. Accordingly, the purposes of this study are as follows: (1) to explore the trend of aging in place and the needs of small-scale multifunction care centers in communities through a literature review and analysis. (2) to understand older adults' expectations and needs for small-scale multifunction care centers through a questionnaire survey, outline design goals, and formulate design specifications for said centers. (3) to propose a spatial-planning program based on the design objectives and verify the feasibility of implementing the small-scale multifunction spatial planning program in communities to enable older adults to benefit from more friendly service spaces and resources.

Literature Review

A. Research framework

Despite offering professional care to older adults, institutional care has caused older adults to lose their freedom [2]. Therefore, countries view aging in place as the ultimate goal of enabling older adults to age in places they have lived for a long time and maintain their customary lifestyle [3].

B. Theories and application of service design

Service design entails thinking that begins from the customers' perspective and seeking to understand their feelings and needs, with the goal of providing a more complete service experience. It consists of four major stages (inquiry, design, implementation, and evaluation) and five essential milestones (service gap, concept co-creation, visualization, reflection, and review). Appropriate service design tools must be employed at each stage of service design to help improve the service processes and the end results. Fig. 1 depicts the diverse classes of service tools-their flexible application is extremely crucial in service design.

Older adults' needs can be understood and included as the primary consideration through the user-centered characteristics of service design. Additionally, co-creation in service design considers all stakeholders and allows them to participate in design. This reveals problems from different perspectives, and new solutions can be created through the collaboration of talents from different fields. Design that takes users into account not only meets the needs of older adults, but also considers those of the stakeholders, thus achieving the most complete design plan.

Service design tools are as follows. (1) A stakeholder map, which can be plotted through interviews and questionnaire surveys to understand the interactions among stakeholders and the importance of each role in the service. Moreover, it may also be used to discover unappreciated roles that are actually critical. This tool can be used to adjust work content to produce a smoother service process [4]. (2) A customer journey map, which is plotted according to the process of customers receiving services and characterized by the inclusion of customers' emotions when they are in contact with the provided services. It identifies the possible touchpoints using sweet spots and pain points to identify subsequent service improvement areas and visualize the application process, which facilitates re-examination of the service process and enables the stakeholders to rapidly and clearly understand the content. Therefore, the customer journey map is used to understand customers' needs and pain points, after which relevant improvements can be made [5]. (3) The service blueprint is a visualization of the service process that is often used in the design field as a tool for service innovation. Based on customers' perspectives, service processes are drawn stepwise into flowchart and used to evaluate and analyze the service "error points" and improve the imperfect service process, thereby establishing a standard operating procedure for service personnel to implement [6].

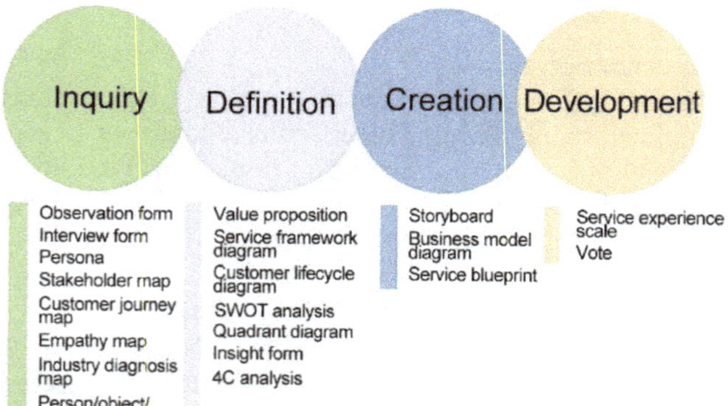

Fig. 1 Service design processes and tools [4].

Research Method and Procedures

A. Research method

Questionnaire survey: We conducted two questionnaire surveys in this study. The first survey was conducted with participants aged 55 years and older using online questionnaires, inquiring into design assessment and verification. Older adults' needs and preferences for space use were explored through a semi-structured questionnaire in which a seven-point Likert scale was used. For the design assessment and verification questionnaire in the second survey, design field personnel and space users (caregivers and older adults aged 55 years and older) were recruited as participants. The questionnaire was semi-structured, and a seven-point Likert scale was employed. The test results were then integrated into the space design specifications and formed the basis of conclusions and suggestions.

The expert questionnaire survey involved five participants (three care service experts and two design field scholars) and was conducted anonymously through offline and online questionnaires. The aim of the questionnaire was to explore the importance of customers' needs for the space of small-scale multifunction care centers. The survey results were then used to produce a house of quality (HoQ), which revealed customer needs and the importance of each of them, by using the quality function deployment (QFD).

QFD: Through QFD, customer needs can be ranked according to their importance, and construction characteristics can also be considered, both of which enable the realization of design. Additionally, applying an HOQ can reduce the time required for design and improve product development efficiency as well as ensure the design results meet customers' needs and expectations.

Service design tools: Service design tools such as the stakeholder map and customer journey map were used to assist the design process. Service users, service providers, and potential stakeholders were identified through stakeholder maps and selected for use as the references for subsequent design and research. According to the design results, the authors proposed how the design program enhanced older adults' aging in place and explained the expected resources that older adults can receive.

B. Research procedure

The research procedure in this study was divided into three stages. In the first stage, older adults' physical conditions and the current situation of the care institutions were ascertained through literature review and the first questionnaire survey to identify the spaces requiring improvement to serve as references for subsequent designs. The questionnaire survey was administered to older adults aged 55 years and older to determine older adults' preferred services provided by care centers. In the second stage, the QFD was employed to construct a HoQ for small-scale multifunction space planning as well as to establish customer needs, construction characteristics, a relationship matrix, and a technical correlation matrix. In the third stage, the constructed HoQ was used in determining the design specifications. After performing a simulation using 3D computer modeling software, the second questionnaire survey was then conducted for design evaluation and verification.

Results

A. Service provision

According to the questionnaire survey results, the spatial planning in this study was expected to include spaces such as a sports activities area, dining service area, and recreation area.

With respect to the preferred venues provided by the small-scale multifunction care centers, statistical results in Table I indicated that the multifunction activity room had the highest score, followed by the pantry, recreation area, and dining space.

TABLE I
TEST RESULTS FOR FACILITY PROVISION

No.	Items	Total score	Ranking
1	Multifunction activity room	90	1
2	Pantry	89	2
3	Recreation area	87	3
4	Dining space	86	4
5	Health examination site	86	4
6	Reading area	85	5

Test results for spatial planning in Table II revealed that safety was the top priority, followed by favorable ventilation and smoothness of spatial circulation. Moreover, in addition to lighting and choice of material that were also emphasized by the participants, situations involving older adults' use of assistive devices such as canes, walkers, and wheelchairs should also be considered.

TABLE II
TEST RESULTS FOR SPATIAL PLANNING

No.	Items	Total score	Ranking
1	Safety	100	1
2	Smooth spatial circulation	98	2
3	Favorable ventilation	98	2
4	Favorable lighting	95	3
5	Choice of materials	95	3
6	Green plants	94	4
7	Versatile use	91	5

B. Quality function development (QDF)

Customer needs were realized through their conversion into construction project items using QDF, which identified the items that are prioritized in customer needs as well as approaches to satisfying customer needs with consideration of engineering construction and features. HoQ was divided into the following three categories. (1) Customer needs: the expert questionnaire was rated on a seven-point Likert scale and was administered to a total of five participants (three care service experts and two service field scholars). The final results were divided into five major categories and 22 items. (2) Construction features: The possible construction features corresponding to customer needs were identified through a literature review, after which the KJ method was used for streamlining and classification and dividing construction features into five main categories. (3) Relationship matrix and technical correlation matrix: the relationship matrix between customer needs and construction features was established through expert experience, and the technical correlation matrix was determined according to the correlation between measures. HoQ was constructed using QFD and thus served as the design reference for the spatial planning of small-scale multifunction care centers as illustrated in Fig. 2.

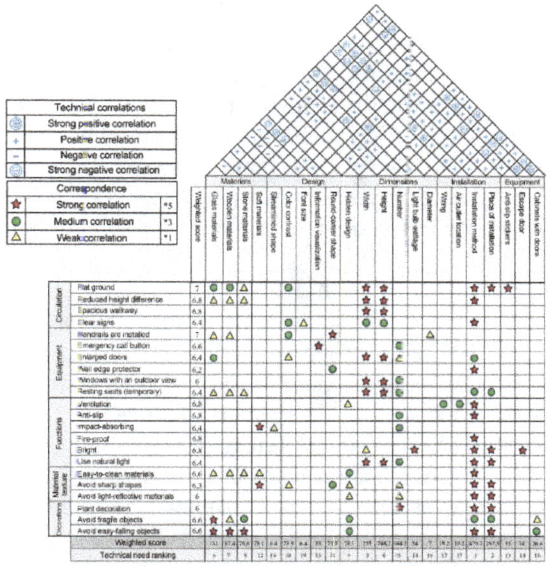

Fig. 2 HoQ for the spatial planning of small-scale multifunction care centers.

C. Design proposal and description

To practice the ideal of aging in place, namely older adults visiting small-scale activity centers during the day and returning home at night, this study focused on small-scale multifunction care centers and proposed the following design in Table III.

TABLE III
DESIGN SPECIFICATIONS FOR SPATIAL PLANNING

Total space (ping; a Taiwanese unit of area equivalent to 3.3 m3)	100-ping (six main spaces, 11-ping each)
Maximum capacity	37–40 people
Space setting location	Idle space in communities, public space in buildings
Target users	Healthy older adults (60–80 years old)
Multifunction space mode	Four field modes (small classroom, large speech space, dining space, large activity space)
Spatial functions	Reading, health examination, exercise, teaching, socializing, discussion, games, dining, consultation, toilet, exhibition, chess
Design features	• Open space for the convenience of older adults' activities • Multifunctional tables and chairs • Green plants provide extra vitality to the space • A warm color can add a sense of warmth to the space • Provision of all four field modes through spatial rearrangement • Decoration by creating an artwork display area of paintings by older adults

The spatial design specifications for small-scale multifunction care centers were determined on the basis of the research findings in this study, and a design plan is proposed in Fig. 3. The space in the proposed plan mainly consists of one mode from which three additional spatial modes are derived through changing the spatial arrangement and structure. Each mode possesses its own spatial features and can be adjusted by users according to the activity content, enabling the space to meet diverse needs.

With respect to location functions, a round table can be installed to facilitate users' communication and interaction. To accommodate a large group of participants for speeches or classes, several spaces can be converted into a single large space for such purposes. The spaces for reading and health examination and exercise are retained in all four main space modes to enable older adults who do not participate in the main activities to nevertheless visit the small-scale multifunction care centers for daily routine health examination and exercise.

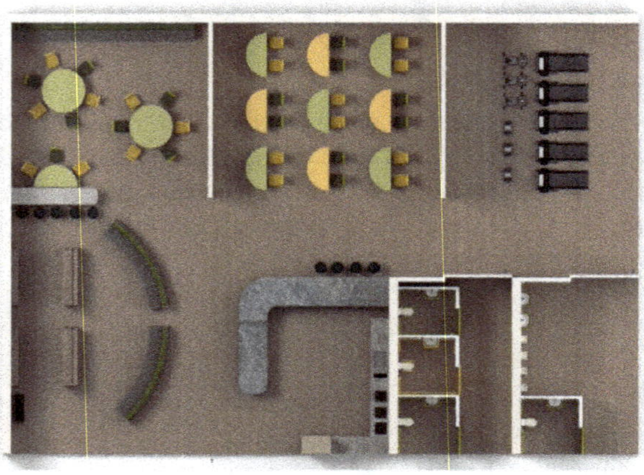

Fig. 3 Proposed design for small-scale multifunction care centers.

D. Expected service experience in the proposed small-scale multifunction care center

A customer journey map as shown in Fig. 4 was produced according to the results of the multifunction spatial planning. The research objective is to create a space that facilitates an ideal daily life mode for older adults, which involves visiting small-scale multifunction care centers during the day and returning home at night.

In this study, older adults' activities were arranged in various time slots, and a mood curve and schematic of the space used by older adults were drawn. Care centers can provide favorable resources and care for older adults as well as satisfy their needs for learning and making friends, thereby creating a friendly environment for older adults and achieving the ideal of aging in place.

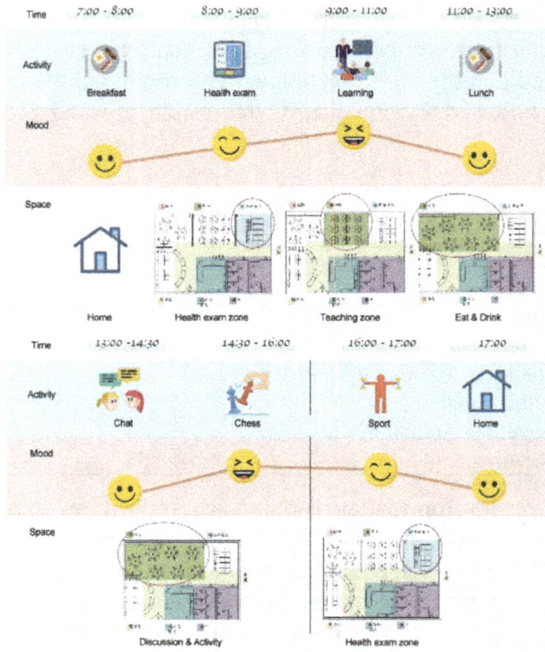

Fig. 4 Customer journey map.

Acknowledgements

The authors gratefully acknowledge the financial support provided by the Ministry of Science and Technology, R.O.C., under Research Project MOST106-2410-H-130-041-MY2.

References

[1] H. J. Chien, "Comprehensive Community Care: Small-Scale and Multifunctional Service", *Journal of Chang Gung University of Science and Technology*, 23, 2015, pp.15-22. [in Chinese, semantic translation]

[2] Ecusbook, "Is It Undesirable to Live in Nursing Homes? These Two Words Are the Key!", *Business Today*, August 12, 2018. Retrieved from https://www.businesstoday.com.tw [in Chinese, semantic translation]

[3] iLong-Term Care, What is "Aging in Place?" Necessity of Community Environment and Home Space - *Senior life*, August 12, 2018. Retrieved from https://www.ilong-termcare.com/Article/Detail/2400 [in Chinese, semantic translation]

[4] Ian Jang, "Supporting Innovation with Tools and Methods". April 13, 2017. Retrieved from https://www.slideshare.net/uxstudio/f-70005190 [in Chinese, semantic translation]

[5] Kate Kaplan, "When and How to Create Customer Journey Maps. "April 8, 2017. Retrieved from https://www.nngroup.com/articles/customer-journey-mapping/

[6] C.Y., Ting, "The Research of College Textbooks Publishing Plan and Market from Service Blueprint.", (Unpublished master's thesis). Minghsin University of Science & Technology, Hsinchu, Taiwan. [in Chinese, semantic translation]

https://doi.org/10.1142/9789811238727_0016

Application of Actor–Network Theory to Explore the Transmission and Innovation of Local Cultural Industry of Rush-Weaving Craftsmanship in Yuanli

Fang-Ching Liu*, Shyh-Huei Hwang**

National Yunlin University of Science & Technology, Yunlin, Taiwan
*Corresponding Author Email: *D10930007@gemail.yuntech.edu.tw, **hwangsh@gemail.youtech.edu.tw

Abstract

Local craftsmanship revitalizes the local economy and passes down cultural memory in Taiwan's community-based craft industry. Through the actor-network theory, this study explored how the Taiwan Yuan-Li Handiwork Association and Yuan-Li Town Triangle Rush Exhibition Hall were related to the development of rush-weaving craftsmanship in Yuanli. The feasibility of rush-weaving craftsmanship transmission and cultural industry innovation was investigated, too. The objectives of this study are to (1) explore and analyze the roles and social functions of the Taiwan Yuan-Li Handiwork Association and Yuan-Li Town Triangle Rush Exhibition Hall in the local cultural industry and (2) identify how the two organizations revitalize local rush-weaving craftsmanship differently through their heritage education for transmission, production development, and sales activities. In compliance with the obligatory passage point for the revitalizing of transmission and innovation in the rush-weaving craft industry, the two organizations have distinct attributes, orientations, and business models which were identified through case studies and interviews. The Taiwan Yuan-Li Handiwork Association has gradually transformed to pioneer rush-weaving craftsmanship revitalization to various R&D organization that promotes heritage education and product innovation. Yuan-Li Town Triangle Rush Exhibition Hall, a quasi non-governmental organization, positions itself as a local cultural museum that enhances the transmission of Yuanli's unique rush-weaving culture through mass tourism. The two organizations exhibit ostensibly different platforms and development patterns, but their interwoven relationship represents heterogeneous and diverse ways of transmitting and innovating rush-weaving craftsmanship and offeres possibilities and prospects for the industry.

Keywords: Yuanli, Rush-Weaving Craftsmanship, Actor-Network Theory, Local Cultural Industry

Introduction

The implementation of the Comprehensive Community Development Policy by the Taiwanese government in 1994 has progressively established connections between the community, culture, and craftsmanship by driving the craft industry development under the Comprehensive Community Development Policy. The promulgation of the Policy for Cultural and Creative Industries in 2002 has further promoted the gradual transformation of community craft activities. Many traditional handicrafts have begun to incorporate modern designs and developed a business model on the basis of fine crafts. Through tourism and marketing, local residents have fostered the cultural and creative industry within their community. The support of the Comprehensive Community Development Policy and the Policy for Cultural and Creative Industries and the inclusion of the design and design education fields facilitate the revitalization of the local economy and the transmission of cultural memory with Taiwan's local craft industry [1]. Rush-weaving craftsmanship has 300 years of history. The development of Taiwan's local rush-weaving craftsmanship, culture, and economy in Tongxiao, Yuanli, and Dajia constitutes a significant part of Taiwan's history. On the basis of the actor–network theory (ANT), this study explored the roles of the two nongovernmental organizations (i.e., the Taiwan Yuan-Li Handiwork Association and Yuan-Li Town Triangle Rush Exhibition Hall) in local rush-weaving craftsmanship development and possibilities for transmission and innovation in the rush-weaving cultural industry. The research objectives include exploring and analyzing the role and social function of the Taiwan Yuan-Li Handiwork Association and Yuan-Li Town Triangle Rush Exhibition Hall in the local cultural industry and identifying how the two organizations revitalize local rush-weaving craftsmanship differently through heritage education, production development, and sales activities.

Developmental of Rush-weaving Craftsmanship in Yuanli and ANT-based Innovative Thinking

A. Development of Taiwan's craft industry in community

The development of Taiwan's craft and cultural industry during the postwar period from 1940 to 2004 demonstrates the evolution of Taiwan's culture, politics, society, and economy. The development of Taiwan's craft industry in the community is achieved in four stages: (1) the 1940s–1970s: local craftsmanship continued to be categorized as a traditional handicraft industry. The Executive Yuan listed "community development" as one of the seven major social welfare items in 1965, and the Ministry of Interior promulgated the Regulations on Community Development Work in 1968, both of which signified the gradual development of community awareness. After the 1970s, the innovative mass production technique posed great challenges to traditional handicrafts, craftsmen, and factories. (2) the 1980s: the establishment of the first Cultural Heritage Preservation Act and then the Council for

Cultural Affairs and Taiwan's democratization since the lifting of martial law in 1987 both promoted the enhancement and development of comprehensive community development. In the 1980s, the Council for Cultural Affairs began to implement the 12 Major Cultural Construction Projects and formulate goals to industrialize of local culture. (3) the 1990s: implementation of the Comprehensive Community Development Policy and the "Culture and Industry Seminar" jointly organized by the Council for Cultural Affairs and the National Taiwan Craft Research and Development Institute encompassed research and proposal of ideas to foster local industries, communities, and cultural development. The objective was to provide local employment and achieve self-sustainable development. (4) After 2000: the formulation of the Policy for Cultural and Creative Industries prompted the development of models fostering cultural and creative industry within the community. The combination of local industries with creative designs gradually guided developments in the creation and sale of high-end fine cultural artifacts. In 2004, the National Taiwan Craft Research and Development Institute launched the "Incubation Project to Support Community Crafts with Local Characteristics" to assist with the sustainable development of the craft and cultural industry in local communities [1,2].

B. Evolution and development of rush-weaving craftsmanship

Rush-weaving craftsmanship can be traced back to as early as 1727 when Taokas women discovered wild triangle rushes in the lower reaches of Da'an River and weaved them into practical products such as rush mats and halters. Rush-weaving craftsmanship developed rapidly among coastal tribes. In 1756, Han people began learning the weaving technique from indigenous women. The rush mat weaving technique was thus introduced by the indigenous people of the Shuang-liao Tribe to Han villages such as Dajia Street and Yuanli Zhuang [3,4]. Table 1 shows the developmental history of rush-weaving craftsmanship from the Japanese colonial period to the formation of the Republic of China.

TABLE 1
The development history of the rush-weaving craftsmanship

Year	Event
1901	Dajia Hoko Bureau Director CHU Li formed a joint venture with the local gentry including TU Ching, LI Cheng, and LI Tsung-ho to establish Yuan Tai Co., the first rush straw hat shop in Dajia. LI Tsung-ho sold two thousand hat bodies to Osaka, Japan, and set the record for the earliest export of Taiwanese rush straw hats.
1903	Dajia Straw Hat Limited Partnership Corporation was established; Dajia straw hats were promoted at the fifth National Industrial Exposition in Osaka, Japan; the export of Dajia straw hats to Europe and the United States began in this year.
1911	Yuan Tai Co. established a branch in Kobe, Japan, which was a major step toward the development of the industry's export sales.
1933	Export sales ceased due to an economic downturn in the United States.
1945	After the retrocession of Taiwan, rush straw hats and mats were shipped to and sold in China, opening up another major market for the straw hat and mat industry.
1949	The end of the Chinese Civil War ceased the cross-strait trade. Subject to changes in the international trading system, the export sales of the rush straw hats and mats stagnated, causing the industry to suffer a severe blow.
1955	Through the promotion effort of Madame Chiang, the director of the Miaoli County branch of National Women's League of the R.O.C., TSOU Ching, increased the sales of rush straw hats and mats by advocating the use of straw hats as Scouts' hats across the province.
1971	The Miaoli County Straw Hat and Mat Marketing Cooperative was terminated following tax evasion lawsuits, which caused relevant companies to shut down. Moreover, social changes and the advancement of the industrial and commercial industry enabled women to enter factories and earn higher wages. The hat and straw industry thus weakened.
1981–1991	Due to the relocation of industries in Taiwan, predatory dumping of cheap straw hats from Southeast Asia, China, and South Korea to Taiwan rendered the survival of the local straw hat and mat industry even more difficult.

Data sources: [3] and [4]/compiled by this study

C. ANT summary

The ANT asserts that the world is composed of nonhuman actors (e.g., architecture, technology, tools, or microorganisms) in addition to human actors. These human and nonhuman actors are placed in the same network constructing and shaping one another. Results of the flow relationship are derived from the development and evolution of the relationships between interacting and linked actors. According to the ANT, the construction of knowledge and technology is not determined by humans but, rather, is entirely dependent on the connections and interactions between human and nonhuman actors. In the ANT, the nature and form of actors are presumed to be changeable, and society as a whole contains multiple connections resulting from the interactions between human and nonhuman actors [5].

Research Methods and Steps

Through case studies, we compiled field notes with relevant literature and analyzed them based on interview records. The action context of rush-weaving craftsmanship organizations, such as the Taiwan Yuan-Li Handiwork Association and Yuan-Li Town Triangle Rush Exhibition Hall, was organized and analyzed. Specifically, the roles and social functions of the two organizations in the local cultural industry were explored, and the differences in their use of heritage education, production development, and sales to revitalize local rush-weaving craftsmanship were addressed. The steps for the execution refer to the literature review on Taiwan's community-based craft and cultural industries, the development history of rush-weaving craftsmanship, and the

ANT. Subsequently, a preliminary field investigation of individual cases was conducted to clarify the context and the status of the rush-weaving industry in Yuanli. Textual data were organized and interview records were analyzed according to the ANT.

Use of ANT for Analysis of Transmission and Innovation in Yuanli's Rush-weaving Craft and Cultural Industry

A. Distinction between Yuanli's two actors in the local rush-weaving craft and cultural industry

According to ANT, all actors of a network undergo translation to be able to connect and negotiate, thereby form an action model that is mutually acceptable. The four phases of the translation process are (1) problematization, (2) interessement, (3) enrolment, and (4) mobilization.

This four-phase circular process enables actors to obtain relevant resources and mutual support by accelerating the formation of actor-networks [6]. Through ANT translation analysis, the Taiwan Yuan-Li Handiwork Association and Yuan-Li Town Triangle Rush Exhibition Hall were defined as actors, and the revitalization of the local craft and cultural industry (i.e., rush-weaving craftsmanship in Yuanli) was an obligatory passage point (OPP) which motivated the two actors to engage in a network mechanism. The objectives were to analyze the roles and social functions of said two organizations and identify how they revitalize local rush-weaving craftsmanship differently through heritage education, production development, and sales activities (Tables 2 and 3).

TABLE 2
Roles and social functions of the Taiwan Yuan-Li Handiwork Association and Yuan-Li Town Triangle Rush Exhibition Hall

Actor	Profile, role, and social function
Taiwan Yuan-Li Handiwork Association	1. In 2003, Shanjiao Community commenced revitalization of local industry to implement comprehensive community development action. Because rush-weaving craftsmanship is a professional field that requires a craftsperson-in-residence, the Taiwan Yuan-Li Handiwork Association was established in 2009. The association aims to promote the innovative design and transmission of rush-weaving craftsmanship. 2. The connection between the association and Yuanli is such that the association serves as the educator responsible for knowledge delivery to the local community (i.e., Yuanli). Through cooperation with local kindergartens and elementary schools to establish a local cultural curriculum, the association implements education in rush planting and weaving craftsmanship among young children in Yuanli. 3. In addition to a focus on the transmission of local rush-weaving knowledge, activities such as certification examination for rush-weaving craftspeople, curriculum offering rush-weaving experiences, and local trips are used to promote the development of rush-weaving culture in Yuanli. 4. Features of rush-woven products: Professional managers are responsible for product research, development, and sales. In terms of product characteristics, innovative designs have been incorporated into traditional rush-woven products.
Yuan-Li Town Triangle Rush Exhibition Hall	1. This exhibition hall is managed by a quasinongovernmental organization founded in 2004 by the Yuanli Farmers' Association. 2. This exhibition hall, focusing on the ecology and weaving technique of rush, serves as a local cultural museum. In indoor and outdoor areas, this exhibition hall offers a rush experience section, rush hat and mat cultural section, rural grain display section, and DIY classroom. 3. Its primary role as a local museum enables local residents and external visitors to learn more about the history and value of rush-weaving craftsmanship. 4. Features of rush-woven products: The product design style remains traditional, and no professional product designers are involved.

Data sources: Compiled from interview records

TABLE 3
Distinctions between the Taiwan Yuan-Li Handiwork Association and Yuan-Li Town Triangle Rush Exhibition Hall regarding the rush-weaving craft and cultural industry in Yuanli

Actors	Taiwan Yuan-Li Handiwork Association	Yuan-Li Town Triangle Rush Exhibition Hall
Problematization: defining organizational orientation and identifying countermeasures to transmission of rush-weaving craftsmanship	1. Established a rush workshop and hired professional craftspersons to restore the traditional work pattern of rush-weaving. 2. Focus on the development of rush-weaving craftsmanship in Yuanli. 3. The Love Rush Craft Awards were established to recognize the creative capacity of craftspeople. 4. Heritage education for transmission of rush-weaving craftsmanship by craftspeople is implemented with the objective of revitalizing and restoring the rush-weaving industry.	1. The exhibition hall offers sightseeing and recreation activities as well as selling rush-woven products. 2. Train local older adults who excel at rush-weaving to become instructors and pass on rush-weaving craftsmanship. 3. The beauty of the local rush-weaving culture and craftsmanship is promoted through tours provided by exhibition hall staff to sightseeing groups.
Interessement: organizational management and sales channels	1. Rush-woven products are sold at the Village Life Shop of the association, department stores, consignment stores, and the Pinkoi online shop. 2. Promote beginner-, elementary-, intermediate-, and advanced-level courses for	1. Sightseeing groups and external visitors are the target audience of the exhibition hall. 2. Products are sold at the exhibition hall's own shop as well as at other farmers' associations. 3. A rush-weaving curriculum

	rush-weaving experiences. By planning local trips, the association stimulates peoples' interest in rush-weaving craftsmanship.	implemented at the exhibition hall focuses on providing mass experience.
Enrolment: Alliances formed between actors in the network	No official alliance had been established between the two organizations, but we discovered, through visits and field surveys, that both organizations promote each other to visitors. In addition, the Taiwan Yuan-Li Handiwork Association invites members of the Yuan-Li Town Triangle Rush Exhibition Hall to serve as judges for the Love Rush Craft Awards. Last, both organizations cooperate with nearby communities to promote rush-weaving craftsmanship, forming an additional network for revitalizing the community-based cultural industry.	
Mobilization: role and task for each actor	The focus of the Taiwan Yuan-Li Handiwork Association is on education for the transmission of rush-weaving craftsmanship, rather than profiting from products sales or experience courses offered to the public. Moreover, the Taiwan Yuan-Li Handiwork Association gradually transformed from an actor, pioneering rush-weaving craftsmanship revitalization, to a diversified R&D organization that promotes heritage education and product innovation in rush-weaving craftsmanship. The Taiwan Yuan-Li Handiwork Association aims to provide a platform for the cultural industry of Taiwanese rush-weaving craftsmanship to attract people to join the industry.	The Yuan-Li Town Triangle Rush Exhibition Hall is primarily responsible for introducing Yuanli's rush-weaving culture through tourism and mass experience provision. In addition, the exhibition hall has been invited to participate in the New Taipei City Archaeology Festival held by the Shihsanhang Museum of Archaeology multiple times to collaborate on the promotion of rush-weaving craftsmanship. By collaborating with other museums to organize relevant events, Yuan-Li Town Triangle Rush Exhibition Hall enhances the exposure of Yuanli's rush-weaving culture and industry.

Data sources: Compiled from interview records

B. Transmission of and prospects for rush-weaving craftsmanship in Yuanli

Through the translation analysis of the ANT, this study used the revitalization of rush-weaving craftsmanship in Yuanli as the OPP to explore how the Taiwan Yuan-Li Handiwork Association and Yuan-Li Town Triangle Rush Exhibition Hall differ in their orientations, roles, social functions, and business and sales models. The Taiwan Yuan-Li Handiwork Association has gradually transformed from an actor that pioneered rush-weaving craftsmanship revitalization to a diversified R&D organization for promoting heritage education and product innovation in rush-weaving craftsmanship. The association has even set the goal of providing a platform for the rush-weaving cultural industry for Taiwan to attract aspirant individuals to join the industry. Yuan-Li Town Triangle Rush Exhibition Hall, a quasi non-governmental organization, defines itself as a local cultural museum that passes on knowledge regarding and appreciation for the rush-weaving culture in Yuanli through mass tourism. Through exchanges and interactions with other museums, rush-weaving craftsmanship can be more widely promoted and prevalent. Despite differences in the platforms and development, the two organizations have collaborated to offer heterogeneous and diverse approaches to the transmission of and innovations in rush-weaving craftsmanship in Yuanli. The revival of the local cultural industry promotes local culture as well as creating more possibilities for community redevelopment and revitalization.

Discussions

The ANT was applied to explore two actors (i.e., the Taiwan Yuan-Li Handiwork Association and Yuan-Li Town Triangle Rush Exhibition Hall in Yuanli) and their development within the networks they have formed. Despite the lack of official alliance between the two actors, positive interaction was observed. With the same OPP of revitalization, transmission, and innovation in Yuanli's rush-weaving industry, both organizations expanded their respective action networks through participation in the Love Rush Craft Awards and community-initiated events by enhancing their capacity to revitalize the rush-weaving cultural industry in Yuanli. Operationally, both organizations have financial and capital constraints, which pose several challenges. The Taiwan Yuan-Li Handiwork Association does not have its premises, whereas the Yuan-Li Town Triangle Rush Exhibition Hall in Yuanli lacks museum professionals responsible for comprehensive and strategic planning to upgrade its collections. An official alliance between the two organizations fosters rush-weaving craftsmanship talent and the industrial establishment of rush-weaving craftsmanship in Dajia, Taichung, and constitutes various methods of revitalizing the cultural industry. The Art Weaving Festival organized by the Miaoli County Government in 2019, the Yuanli Rush Culture Festival organized jointly by the Yuanli Township Office and Chung Chou University of Science and Technology in December of 2019, and the Yuanli Township Office's proposals for the regional revitalization of the rush-weaving cultural industry in Yuanli in 2020 all signify further possibilities and prospects for the cultural industry resulting from the participation of diverse actors.

References

[1] Zhuge Zheng, *The process and significance of the communityization of the craft industry. Community craftsmanship*, Taiwan craft, Vol. 49, pp. 12-17.

[2] Cultural Environment Foundation, *The track of overall community construction in Taiwan*, Cultural Construction Committee Press, 1999, pp. 23-43.

[3] Shyh-Huei Hwang, *Taichung City Registered Traditional Craft-Rush Weaving Preservation, Maintenance and Investigation Plan*, 2020, unpublished, pp. 6-11.

[4] Official website of the Taiwan Yuan-Li Handiwork Association, quote from: https://reurl.cc/MvxdVv (Search date:6,19,2020)

[5] Hong Rongzhi, *The entrepreneuring process of cultural and creative industry clusters activate depleted communities: From the Perspective of Actor-Network Theory*, PhD thesis, 2016, unpublished, p.13, pp.45-46.

[6] Zhuang Kaiyong, *Analyzing the Service Innovation Processes and Outcomes of BigHillNorthMoon Based on the Actor Network Theory*, Thesis, 2015, unpublished, pp.9-12.

https://doi.org/10.1142/9789811238727_0017

Application of Configuration Design with Model of Design-Creating-Thinking on Cultural and Creative Product Design

Being-Cheng Chen

Department of Fashion Design, Tainan University of Technology, Tainan City 71002, Taiwan
Email: tp0013@mail.tut.edu.tw

Abstract

This research intends to use cultural and creative design techniques and introduce the Model of Design-Creating-Thinking, and integrate the research process into a set of easy-to-understand cultural and creative design patterns to be applied to product design. First, through the literature review of cultural and creative design data, the compilation of design elements, and the establishment of research methods, this research introduces cultural symbol decoding, coding tables, and form design to create the element evolution design of Model of Design-Creating-Thinking. Finally, through the creation and analysis of practical works, the design mode of cultural and creative products is constructed to achieve the research purpose. The research results are as follows: (1) A design model of cultural and creative products is constructed as a design approach so that the design process can be organized and procedural and exemplify contextual basis for designers' reference; (2) Model of Design-Creating-Thinking is imported to promote designers to create more new forms of product shaping, which is an innovative design thinking method; (3) In addition to reflecting the characteristics of cultural and creative design and the transformation of elements, the works show the effect of alternation and fusion of tradition and modernity. It also conveys the innovative vocabulary of the evolution of shapes.

Keywords: cultural and creative industry, cultural and creative product design, configuration, model of design-creating-thinking

Introduction

In 2002, the Taiwan government began to implement the cultural and creative industry policy, which prompted many traditional industries to face transformation. With understanding the "full" use of cultural creativity and taking "creativity" as the core concept of every project, Cultural and Creative Product Design has become the goal of Taiwan's efforts to expand internationally in recent years.

Cultural diffusion of globalization not only induces people to reflect on and recognize their respective cultures but also facilitates designers to develop identifiable product design with distinguishable cultural characteristics on the basis of cultural differences. That is, the focus on local cultural design and applications to develop products with unique identification and differentiation enables consumers to have fabulous and sentimental cultural experiences [1,2,3].

According to the background and motivation of the previous research, the primary objectives are divided as follows: (1) to primarily analyze the cultural connotation of Kinmen Jinshui Elementary School's building(s) based on literature review, (2) to induce design factors based on the decoding and encoding of cultural symbols for the evolution design of design-creating-thinking model elements, (3) to apply the characteristics thereof and transformed elements in product design, (4) to build a cultural and creative product design model to facilitate product design, and (5) to make the design process organized, procedural and contextual as a reference.

Literature Review

A. Cultural and Creative Product Design

a. Definition and design connotation of culture and cultural and creative products

The term "cultural and creative products" implies products derived from cultural traits and primarily existed in forms of economic benefits. From the aspect of literal meaning, "culture" is the core spirit of creative products and the main factor that forms cultural and creative products. Human lives are mostly influenced by culture [4] which is an anthropological term by referring to the basic values, faith, code of conduct, and other social constituents of culture. This study, therefore, defines culture as "various explicit and implicit behavior patterns learned or inherited with the use of symbols and a sharable human symbol system used to guide individual behaviors and achieve group recognition". For designers, product design refers to the process that transforms inner-thinking into specific results, and their mission is to translate different product functions into symbols. However, the symbol system thereby must also be constructed based on the common social culture to be meaningful.

b. Problems of cultural and creative product design

According to the literature review, image authorization is commonly adopted in Taiwan as the primary design method for cultural and creative products. Although woodcut effect produced reprints and duplications, morphological imitations or even emblazonry reproduction can be directly associated with culture, and designs created using these techniques not only lack creative presentations and fun elements, but also limited designers' creativity in product shape design [5,6,7]. This is the reason that, with foresight, Mitchell [8] thought that disputes over the theory of cultural entities in the past shall be abandoned, and it is necessary to focus on how the evolution and development of various cultural concepts to make culture a tool that dominates people for power and interests. The focal point of his argument lies in the study of the "design process and methods" of cultural products. Therefore, from the above-mentioned problems currently encountered in the design and development of cultural and creative products in Taiwan, it is known that the only opportunity to create high quality cultural and creative products provides a good environment. Besides, the core value of the cultural and creative industry is to attract consumers with a design that tells stories, adds cultural value, and features original content. This is also the biggest strength of Taiwan.

c. Cultural and creative product design methods

Concerning the design methods for cultural and creative products, the design concept of this study is based on the three levels of the spatial perspective of culture proposed by many scholars including Leong [9]. It is also divided into three layers according to the connotation of cultural and creative products, including the outer (up) layer (tangible and material), middle layer (use behavior, ritual, and custom related), and inner (down) layer (identity and intangible). Each layer of the cultural space represents different levels of cultural product design. Thereafter, in "Cultural Creativity · Added Design Value", Lin [10] further divided Leong's "three cultural space levels" into a three-identity-level framework based on factors that must be considered when designing a cultural and creative product.

B. Design-Creating-Thinking Model

In "A Study on the Relation of Interaction between the Model of Design-Creating-Thinking and Variations", the authors mentioned that the so-call creating mode is a circular operation of import, process, output, and feedback [11]. The creating-thinking model generally operates in three stages, including the conceptualization, concretization, and practice stages [12,13] plus several involved steps therein: planning, analysis, evaluation, decision-making, control, and so on [14]. Besides, the design is also considered as a product of information. There are many information and restraints that must be integrated and handled throughout the entire design process. Therefore, some scholars established, for example, a "model of the design creation process" [13] and a "General procedural model of the design process" [12] by utilizing the control and information communication theory. Based on them, the authors thus proposed their ideas towards the "design-creating-thinking model" (Fig. 1) at the end of this article.

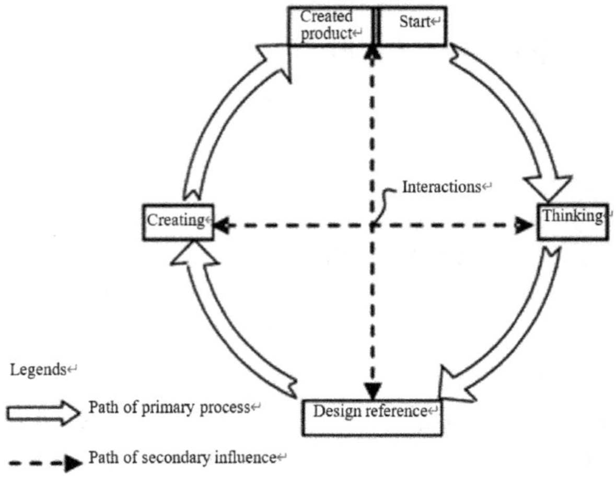

Fig. 1 The design-creating-thinking model [11]

The design method described in "A Study on the Conceptual Discourse and Practical Design of the Design-Creating-Thinking Model" emphasized the design factors of natural organisms (plants and animals) such as action or morphology to capture symbols or images therefrom. The source data are then analyzed, processed, and verified with bionic design elements to create the entity's evolution process based on the shape. This innovative design concept is used in this study for the analysis of morphological design applications.

Research Methods

A. Study Procedure and Method

For the study objectives, the study process was generally divided into three stages. In the first stage, we summarized and classified the application forms of cultural and creative product design through the literature review of qualitative research, and discussed fundamental theories. In the second stage, case studies in cultural and creative product designs were carried out. Apart from collecting a wide range of design cases to study the design and constituents of cultural and creative products, the decoding and encoding of the cultural symbol table and the element transformation design table were adopted to the thinking of cultural and creative product design in product creation. In the third stage, practice in creations using practical design methods was carried out. The final product was then evaluated and examined by experts to build a design model for cultural and creative products. This helped designers or professionals understand the design context and constituents in design.

B. Study Target

This study confirmed the cultural and creative product design target primarily based on the study motivation and objective characteristics. In this study, the historical buildings of Kinmen County's Jinshui Elementary School were selected as the study target owing to its representation of local culture. The old building's unique style and morphology were transformed into design elements. Through the applications of the design-creating-thinking model, cultural and creative products break through the original frame and create new products for the contemporary society and the new design brings out the cultural characteristics and spirit of Kinmen's historical sites.

C. Study Process

The above-mentioned study process, tools, and methods are summarized in Fig. 2.

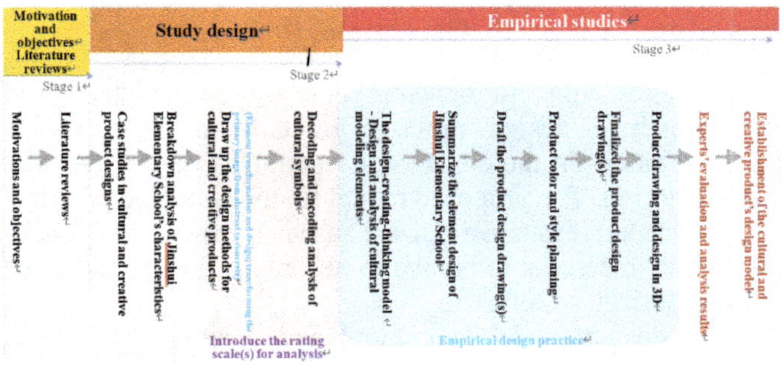

Fig. 2 Study process

Results and Discussion

A. Introduction to Jinshui Elementary School

The "Kinmen Battlefield Culture" is one of the renowned world heritage sites and currently in the "peaceful coexistence" stage. As a perfectly preserved and demonstrating site, Kinmen has plentiful historical buildings, traditional settlements, battlefield culture, and natural resources. After battlefield administration affairs were lifted from the region in 1992, Kinmen National Park was officially launched on October 18, 1995, to promote the region's tourism industry. Jinshui Elementary School in Shuitou Village of the southwestern part of Kinmen Nain Island, on the other hand, was completed in 1932. This representative architecture was founded by overseas Chinese and Kinmen's first western Baroque architecture (Fig. 3). Jinshui Elementary School is the only school in a hollow square in Kinmen County. The square-shaped buildings contain the classrooms, administration office, teachers' boarding house, and circular space, the assembly hall. The entire architecture was designed in a south-eastern style (Fig. 3). The architectural feature of Jinshui Elementary School contains the western gable in the front, columns, a five-foot way arcade, and classroom tables and chairs. We considered the schools' western gable, columns, and bottle-shaped railing objects as the elements of morphological design. Upon transformation through designing, these elements were used to create new morphological products, styles, and terms.

Fig. 3 The school gate gable side and building layout to assume ring shape [15]

B. Establishment and Evaluation of the Cultural and Creative Product Design Model

a. Analysis of Jinshui Elementary School's historical and cultural symbols

When designing a creative and cultural product, the first thing is to know about objects, including local culture and knowledge, ancestors' history, and accumulated cultural experiences. All of these not only create external physical intuition and inner psychological emotions but also generate a sense of identity from the historical, storytelling, representative, and symbolic features of local culture. Being familiar with the connotation of cultural characteristics and language symbol of the product is important as it facilitates the "transformation of design thinking" during the design process. These cultural characteristics introduce the design and development of cultural and creative products. In this study, the cultural symbol analysis of Jinshui Elementary School is primarily based on the three levels of the spatial perspective of culture proposed by Leong [9], followed by the use of cultural symbol decoding and encoding table. This table deconstructs and reconstructs the elements of the objects for analysis and application. Finally, the design elements are captured to carry out a practical design and finalize the product creation.

b. Encoding and encoding analysis of cultural symbols

Deconstruction (encoding) does not refer to the disassembling or breaking of an object. It refers to the act of releasing "combination rules" that do not comply with the social reality through the custom (cultural) system and then generating principles and knowledge from current social conditions to actively use them again. This study targeted Jinshui Elementary School to carry out an element deconstruction analysis mainly for the application of cultural symbol decoding and encoding table. This table was designed with the two major functions of "studying the design" and "resolving image symbol or product" and verified with empirical analysis. The function of "resolving image symbol or product" enables decoding and encoding analysis with an entity's image symbol or product and understanding the designer's design concepts. The function of "studying the design", on the other hand, captures and uses the design elements through the decoding and/or encoding of an abstract or concrete symbol for product design. Therefore, these two functions help understand the designer's design concepts while capturing design elements to study the design [16].

c. Element evolution design of design-creating-thinking model

With cultural and creative product's shape and design thinking, this study emphasizes the discussion of object elements. The adopted methods, on the other hand, are based on the design methods proposed by Chen [17]. The symbols and images of the target object are captured from the natural biological system or phenomenon. By pulling, squeezing, and rotating the elements, the simplified symbols are recreated through the transformation design process. As the innovative modeling design concept is applied for the product morphological design, this study summarized relevant literature review and combined various design methods to create the modeling element rating scale and apply it to design targets. The design elements are summarized as follows. Figure 4 is the modeling element design process of Jinshui Elementary School. Figure 5 is the final products, the Jinpingmei watch, and earphones. Figure 6 is the artwork exhibition board design.

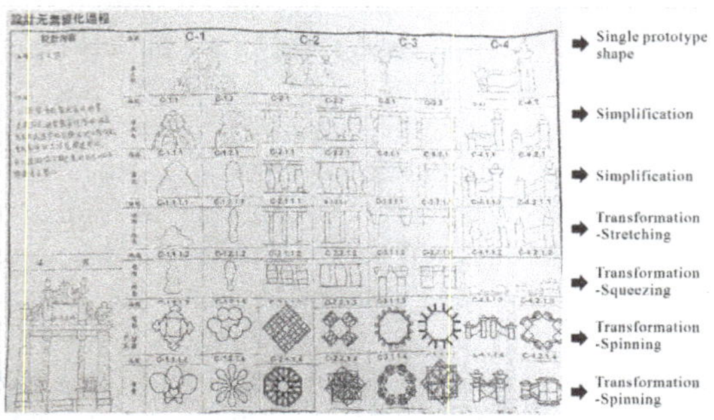

Fig. 4 The modeling element design process of Jinshui Elementary School. Designer: Li,You-Syuan

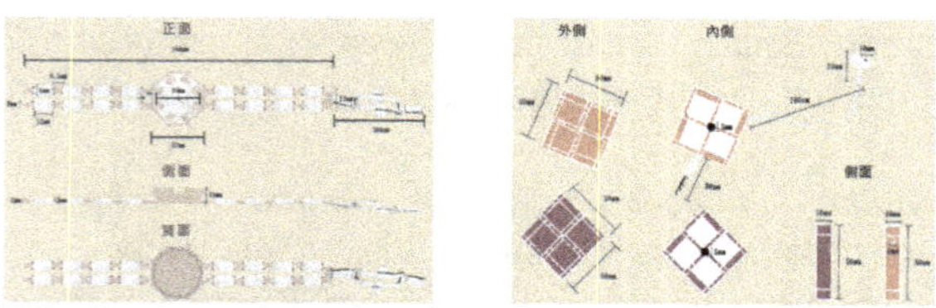

Fig. 5 The Jinpingmei watch and earphones. Designer: Li,You-Syuan

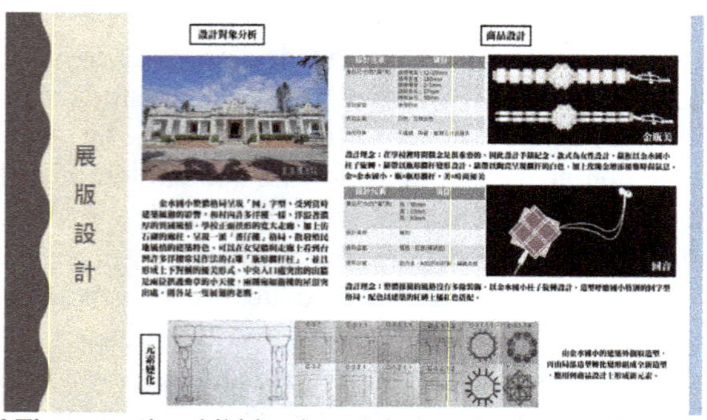

Fig. 6 The artwork exhibition board design. Designer: Li, You-Syuan

d. Establishment of the cultural and creative product design model

With the use of cultural symbol decoding and encoding analysis table and element evolution design rating scale of the design-creating-thinking model, this study divided Jinshui Elementary School's product design model into 3 stages and 10 steps as illustrated in Fig. 7.

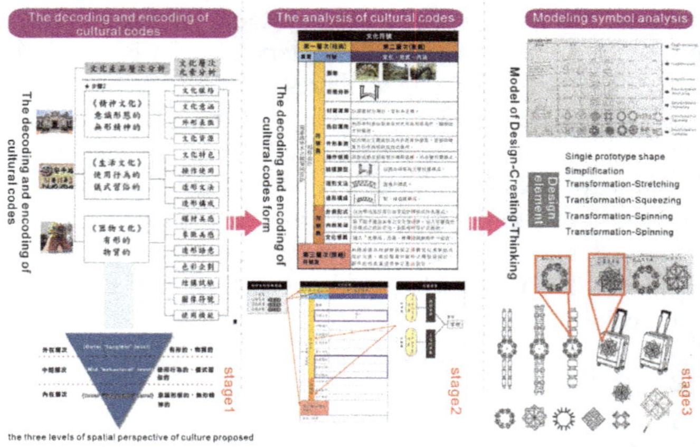

Fig. 7 Cultural and creative product design model

Conclusion

This study aims to develop an easy-to-understand and easy-to-operate design process for cultural and creative products based on the design concepts and to apply them in product design. The proposed model firstly evaluated practical designs and surveys and modified based on experts' feedbacks. The results offered a reference to designers. The conclusions are summarized as follows:

(1) A design model of cultural and creative products is constructed as a design approach so that the design process is organized and exemplified procedural and contextual basis for designers' reference.

(2) Model of Design-Creating-Thinking is imported to promote designers to create more new forms of product shaping, which is an innovative design thinking method.

(3) In addition to reflecting the characteristics of cultural and creative design and the transformation of elements, the works show the effect of alternation and fusion of tradition and modernity. It also conveys the innovative vocabulary of the evolution of shapes.

References

[1] V Raaij, F. W, *Applied consumer behavior*. London: Longman, 2005.

[2] L. Rung-Tai and L. Po-Hsien, A Study of Integrating Culture and Aesthetics to Promote Cultural and Creative Industries, *Journal of National Taiwan College of Arts*, 2009, 5(2), 81-106.

[3] C. Chi-Hsiung and C. Being-Chenem, The Industrialization Model Study of Cultural Creative Product Design and Development, *Journal of Science and Technology*, 2014, 23(1), 11-24.

[4] G. Hofstede, *Culture's consequences: comparing values*, behaviors, institutions, and organizations across nations Sage Publications. Thousand Oaks Press, 2001.

[5] L. Rung-Tai, Cultural creativity added design value. *Art Appreciation*, 2005, 1(7), 26-32.

[6] L. Ju-Ching and H. Ming-Chyuan, Rethinking about the Cultural Products of a Museum: Perspectives Across Disciplines, *Journal of Design*, 2007, 14(4), 69-84.

[7] T.Y. Chang and Y.J. Chuang, Innovation Rooted in Culture: A Preliminary Investigation of the Design Model of Cultural Products, *Journal of Cultural and Creative Industries Research*, 2011, 1(3), 151-164.

[8] D. Mitchell, There's No Such Thing as Culture: Towards Reconceptualization of the Idea of Culture in Geography. *Transactions of the Institute of British Geographers*, 1995, 20, 102-116.

[9] B. D., Leong, & H. Clark, Culture-based knowledge towards new design thinking and practice - A dialogue. *Design Issues*, 2003, 19(3), 48-58.

[10] L. Rung-Tai, Creative learning for designing cultural products. *Art Appreciation*, 2005, 1(11), 52-59.

[11] C. Chi-Hsiung and C.Ying-Ping, A Study on the Relation of Interaction between the Model of Design-Creating-Thinking and Variations, *Journal of Design*, 2004, 9(2), 71-86.

[12] S., Joseph, "Design systems and paradigms", *Design Studies*, 1996, Vol. 17, 227-239.

[13] V. V., Kryssanov, H., Tamaki, & S., Kitamura, "Understanding design fundamentals: how synthesis and analysis drive creativity, resulting in emergence", *Artificial Intelligence in Engineering*, 2001, Vol.15, 329-342.

[14] J., Stempfle, & P., Badke-Schaub, "Thinking in design teams: an analysis of team communication", *Design Studies*, 2002, Vol. 23, 473-496.

[15] C. Chao-Hui, *The Research of Using Virtual Reality for Historic Site: Take Kinmen Ancient Building of Jinshuei Primary School as an Example*, 2019, Department of Arts and Design, dissertation, 8-15.

[16] C. Chi-Hsiung and C. Being-Chenem. A Study on the Decoding and Encoding Design Methods of the Cultural Codes Framework Applications, *International Journal of Tourism Leisure Cultural Creative Fashion Design*, 2016, 1(2), 11-20.

[17] C. Chi-Hsiung Design with Model of Design-Creating-Thinking on Ideas discuss and practical design research, SongHe Press, 2004.

https://doi.org/10.1142/9789811238727_0018

Application of Service-Dominant Logic and Value Co-Creation into Flower Store Service to Produce Positive Interactive and Esthetic Experiences

Hsiu-Tan Chu[1], Li-Shiue Gau[2*], Chieh-Ju Wu[3], Jong-Chae Kim[4]

[1]Doctoral student, Department of Business Administration, Asia University, Taichung, 41354, Taiwan
[2]Asia University, Taichung, Taiwan, Taichung, 41354, Taiwan
[3]Doctoral Candidate, Department of History, SUNY Binghamton, U.S.A.
[4]Associate Professor, Fairleigh Dickinson University, U.S.A.
[*]Corresponding Author Email: lsgau@asia.edu.tw, Phone: 886-4-23323456

Abstract

This study is to examine the correlation between customers' interactive experience with flower stores and their purchase intentions through the aesthetic experience along with the examination of customers' brainwaves. Among a total of 56 effective questionnaires, 10 random participants are chosen to give electroencephalogram (EEG) examinations and interviews. Regression analyses showed the explained variance 57.9% and the regression coefficients 0.415 (interactive experience) and 0.422 (esthetic experience). The EEG in interactive experiences varied case by case, but delta tended to increase in aesthetic experiences.

Keywords: service dominant logic, experience, purchase intention, EEG

Introduction

This study attempts to apply concepts of service-dominant logic, value co-creation, and experiential marketing into a flower shop's customer service management. The theory of service-dominant logic and co-creation of value can emphasize the importance of interaction and service, which leads to esthetic experiences for the customer when receiving the flowers. Both self-reported questionnaires and physiological signals from electroencephalograph readings were adopted to examine interaction and esthetic experiences in the purchase process of flower shop consumption.

By means of experiential marketing, customer experience has been designed in this research with three dimensions including the interactive experience, aesthetic experience, and purchase intentions. This study simultaneously explores interactive and aesthetic experiences and their influence on consumer behavior to increase customers' purchase intentions. The research adopts questionnaire surveys, interviews, and a portable noninvasive electroencephalogram (EEG) device as tools to test on customers of a flower store, A Dan's Flower Shop, in Huatan Township, Changhua County, Taiwan.

We apply service-dominant logic [1] beyond customer-oriented marketing philosophy along with value co-creation to come out with the idea of interactive experiences when visiting a flower shop and buying flower. Service-dominant logic provides a framework for explaining value co-creation between service users and service providers. Moving away from static transactions, service-dominant view emphasizes exchange processes and relationships and moves toward dynamic exchange relationships in which value is co-created with customers [1].

Because a service-centered view is dynamic and participatory [1], service provision or service users' values developed by the users' interactive learning process and experiences with service providers can be certainly maximized as the flower shop engages in an exchange and interactive relationship with customers. In the interactive experiences, we used the experiential marketing's five aspects [2] to create five dimensions of interactive experiences: sense, act, think, feel, and relate. Through an interactive and iterative learning process, the value of flowers can be co-created to meet higher-order needs such as enjoyment of the beauty with an esthetic experience.

Experiential marketing is a key that creates customer engagement via service and product experiences. Engagement experiences will eventually help customers build their trust on the product. Marketers need to pay more attention on customer experiences about the service and products they received through exchange behaviors. Customers' experience-based relationships with their chosen service and product will have a positive influence on helping customers more immersed in the beauty of the flower.

That is, following the interactive experience in the process of shop owner's introduction for the customer, esthetic experiences are expected to occur when customers receive the final product of the flowers. Here, the esthetic experience used one E (esthetic) of experience economy's 4E model [3] to scale. Both the interactive experience and esthetic experience were also measured by EEG signals in addition to a questionnaire. For the dependent variable, purchase intention, its data is only collected by questionnaires.

Research Method

A. Research Design

Based on the theory of service-dominant logic, value co-creation, experiential marketing, and the 4Es model of experience economy, this study hypothesized positive correlations among the three following variables: Interactive experience, aesthetic experience, and purchase intention. The first hypothesis (H1) is: The influence on emotional relaxation and delight of customers' aesthetic experience by interactive experience is positive. The second hypothesis (H2) is: The influence on purchase intentions by customers' interactive experience with a flower store is positive. The third hypothesis (H3) is: The influence on purchase intentions by customers' aesthetic experience is positive. The fourth hypothesis (H4) is that EEGs will be induced by interactive and aesthetic experiences (Fig. 1).

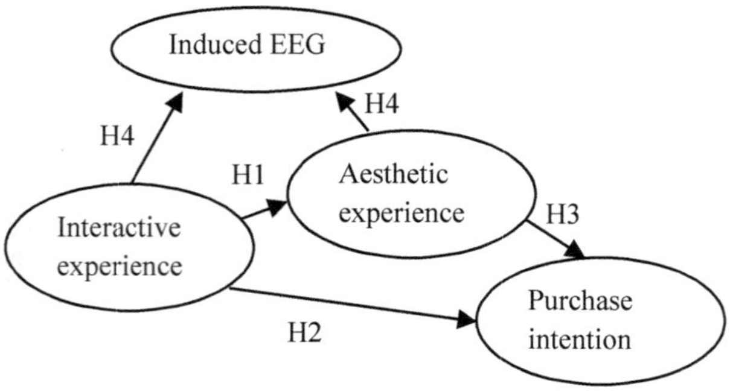

Fig. 1 Research framework

To test these hypotheses, our researchers have collected 56 valid questionnaires filled out by some random customers of a certain flower store, A Dan's Flower Shop, in Huatan Township, Changhua County, Taiwan. Among all effective questionnaires, 10 random participants were selected to conduct EEG examinations and interviews. BioGraph Infiniti version 6.1 equipment made by Thought Technology Ltd. was used to collect the data by the EEG channel.

The EEG examinations included a pretest, a subsequent test, and a posttest. The pretest collected brainwave signals for one and half minutes when the participants opened and closed eyes respectively. While the EEGs were collected, a Youtube screen (audio only) with a static photo of Hsun Chiang, a Taiwanese author and art historian, talking about beauty was shown [4]. This tried to lead all participants' minds in the same direction as a baseline for comparison analyses.

The subsequent test collected the participants' EEGs after they interacted with the manager of the flower store about the introduction of flower names, meanings, ways of flower preservation, and how to take care of flower. The participants had 25–30 minutes to choose flowers and interacted with the manager during the period. While EEGs were collected, participants sitting in front of all flower materials were instructed to recall the engaging process of the consumption. The EEG collection lasted one and half minutes.

The posttest collected the same participants' EEGs after the flower store completed the final product using various types of flowers chosen by the participants. The flower store spent approximately 10–20 minutes arranging flowers for the participants. While appreciating the flower product, participants were measured with their EEGs for 1.5 minutes. In order to understand the participants' experience in undergoing the three parts of the EEG collection, a brief interview was conducted after the EEG examinations. Then, the participants responded to the questionnaire.

B. Instruments

The interview primarily asked participants about whether they felt uncomfortable during the process of the EEG collection, how they felt in general, and what they thought during the process. The questionnaire had two parts: Personal information and research variables. The former included gender, age, education, marital status, religion, income, frequency of flower store visits, purchase purpose, and preferred flower style. The latter consisted of three sections for the three scales measuring the variables.

The first section focused on customers' interactive experience with the flower store. The survey questions of this section have been designed with the five aspects of the experiential marketing, such as feel, think, sense, act, and relate. In terms of feeling and sensual aspects, an example of a statement was: The cozy environment of the flower store makes me feel joyful and relaxed. For think, an example of a statement was: The introduction by the flower store helps me realize what kind of flowers I would like to purchase.

For the aspect of acting, an example of a statement was: The introduction by the flower shop makes me want to join more experiential DIY (do it yourself) activities related to flowers. For the aspect of relating, we had a statement such as "the information offered by the flower store helps me understand the different meanings of flowers in various social occasions." A total of 13 items were used to measure the variable of interactive experience. The scale of interaction experience was created based on the theory of experiential marketing and relevant Chinese literature review along with field experiences.

The second section investigated customers' aesthetic experience. Examples of items were: The flowers I purchase makes me appreciate the beauty, be immersed in the beauty, and keep me in a good mood. There were three items used to measure the variable of the aesthetic experience. The scale of the aesthetic experience was created based on a previous study [5].

The last section examined customers' purchase intentions. Two examples of statements were: I will share my purchase experience in the flower store with others; I recommend the flower store to others. Three items were used to measure purchase intentions. A five-point Likert scale was used for all items of these three variables: 1 = strongly disagree, 2 = disagree, 3 = neutral, 4 = agree, 5 = strongly agree.

Results and Discussion

A. Pilot Study

A pilot study was conducted beforehand by 32 participants from college students and 50 participants from researchers' friends, who answered the survey based on their previous flower purchase experiences. The results helped to revise the questionnaire. For example, the wording of two items for measuring interaction experience was revised to make them more straightforward and easier to understand.

B. Questionnaire

The profile of the sample consisted of 35 females and 21

males. 16 participants were older than 60 years old and 25 were between 41 and 60 years old. 37 respondents had educational level of college or higher. 34 participants were married. Most participants had religious belief in Buddhism (n = 11), I-Kuan Tao (n = 10), and Taoism (n = 9). The family income per month in Taiwan dollars was higher than 100,000 for 13 people and between 30,000 and 99,999 for 28 people. For frequency of flower store visits, 20 respondents answered at least once a season or more. The major purposes of purchasing flower were regular decoration (n = 10) and for congratulations (n = 8). The preferred flower style was elegant and artistic (n = 31). The most popular types of flower were orchid, lily, and rose.

The means of the 13 items for the interactive experience were between 3.79 and 4.38; for the esthetic experience, the means of the 3 items were between 4.20 and 4.34; as for the 3 items for the purchase intention, the means were between 3.95 and 4.11. Reliabilities of the three variables as measured by Cronbach's alphas were between 0.88 and 0.92. The correlation coefficients among these three variables were between 0.70 and 0.71.

Using the interactive and esthetic experience as two independent variables and the purchase intention as the dependent variable, a regression analysis showed that the regression model was significant; the explained variance was 57.9% in terms of adjusted R square; the standardized regression coefficients were 0.415 for the interactive experience and 0.422 for the esthetic experience. These results indicated that H1, H2 and H3 were supported. The variable of the esthetic experience played a mediating role.

C. EEG

For the ten participants in collecting EEG signals, 8 were females and 2 were males. 6 were between 41 and 50 years old; 3 were between 51 and 60 years old. 5 had a junior college or a college degree; one had a senior high school degree; one was a middle school student and one had a middle school degree; two were blue collar workers.

All participants' theta and alpha waves of EEG in the state of closed eyes were higher than those in the state of opened eyes during the pretest. The paired-samples t test showed that the comparisons were significant ($p < .001$). This met nomological validity, indicating that the equipment for recording EEG signals was valid.

The ratio of the EEG signals in interactive experiences compared to those in the open-eyes resting condition did not show consistent results among the ten participants. The respondents 7 and 10 seemed to be the most aroused participants while the respondent 3 might be relaxed without working on too much mental activity. Table 1 shows the ratios, which were calculated by the following equation: (EEG signals in interactive experiences − EEG signals in the open-eyes resting condition) / the open-eyes resting condition.

TABLE 1

Ratios of the EEG signals in interactive experiences compared to those in the open-eyes resting condition

	theta_ratio	alpha_ratio	SMR_ratio	beta_ratio	delta_ratio
case 1	-0.034	-0.073	-0.135	-0.193	0.094
case 2	-0.032	-0.056	-0.049	0.032	-0.063
case 3	0.000	0.143	-0.101	-0.087	0.035
case 4	-0.057	-0.050	-0.162	-0.140	0.063
case 5	-0.011	-0.024	-0.100	-0.110	0.031
case 6	-0.010	-0.060	0.000	0.009	0.152
case 7	0.004	0.364	0.414	0.462	-0.028
case 8	-0.210	-0.202	-0.007	0.005	-0.224
case 9	0.073	-0.063	0.014	-0.002	0.129
case 10	0.174	0.849	0.238	0.106	0.374

The ratio of the EEG signals in esthetic experiences compared to those in the open-eyes resting condition showed a consistent tendency in a delta increase except for respondent 7. At the current stage of this study, it was difficult to explain the reason of the delta increase. Whether delta waves were induced due to deep relaxation or because of more body movement when appreciating the flower product was unclear. Additionally, respondent 5 seemed to be the most aroused participant in the esthetic experience. She had a very strong preference to the color of purple. Table 2 shows the ratios, which were calculated by the following equation: (EEG signals in aesthetic experiences − EEG signals in the open-eyes resting condition) / the open-eyes resting condition.

TABLE 2

Ratios of the EEG signals in aesthetic experiences compared to those in the open-eyes resting condition

	theta_ratio	alpha_ratio	SMR_ratio	beta_ratio	delta_ratio
case 1	0.105	0.073	0.068	-0.084	0.354
case 2	0.126	0.132	0.100	0.217	0.223
case 3	0.142	0.056	-0.060	-0.043	0.226
case 4	-0.148	-0.116	-0.022	-0.061	0.324
case 5	0.566	0.239	0.254	0.315	0.662
case 6	0.182	0.057	0.093	0.029	0.444
case 7	-0.043	0.108	-0.003	0.033	-0.028
case 8	-0.029	-0.085	-0.012	-0.008	0.018
case 9	0.033	0.000	0.167	0.121	0.099
case 10	-0.033	-0.088	-0.150	-0.111	0.201

D. Interview

Most of the interviewees mentioned that at the beginning they might feel a little bit nervous or uncomfortable due to the first try for measuring EEG. Nevertheless, most participants felt informative and enjoyed the florist's enthusiasm in the interactive experience; as for the esthetic experience when receiving the final flower product, most participants felt delighted, happy, excited, and relaxed. During the process, a few participants might recall some memories or enjoy spacing out. This might be related to personality.

E. Cross Analysis

The cross analysis was conducted using different sources of data such as subjective questionnaire responses and objective EEG signals. The correlation between the means of interactive experiences and the ratios of theta/alpha was significant, positive, and high (0.67, p = 0.035) (Fig. 2). This might indicate that basically the higher participants' perceived interaction experiences, the higher ratio of theta/alpha in terms of decrease in alpha. That is, higher interaction experiences might not mean relaxation.

Another cross analysis between the means of esthetic experiences and delta waves showed that the coefficient was significant, positive, and high (0.65, p = 0.043) (Fig. 3). However, Fig. 3 seemed to indicate that when participants' perceived aesthetic experiences were low, the delta mean cannot be high. The relationship seemed to be asymmetrical.

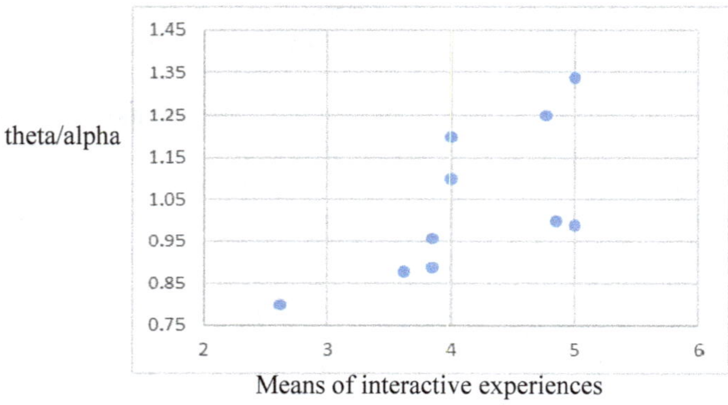

Fig. 2 Scatterplot between means of interactive experiences and the ratios of theta/alpha

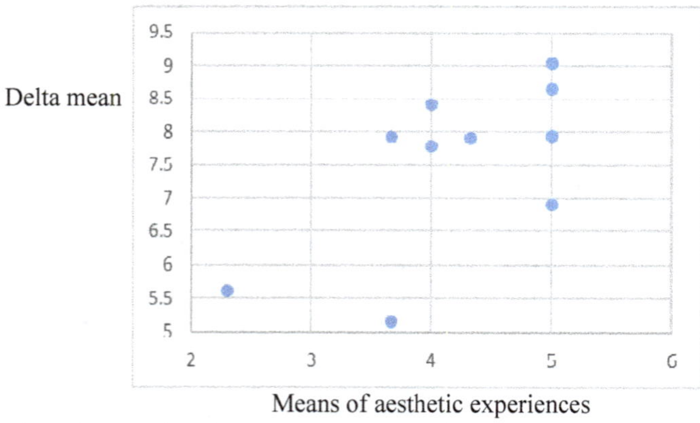

Fig. 3 Scatterplot between means of aesthetic experiences and delta mean

F. Conclusion

The analysis of the questionnaire and EEG data shows statistical significance and strong positive correlations in terms of the following assumptions: The positive influences on customers' aesthetic experience and their purchase intentions by customers' interactive experience with the flower store; the positive influence on purchase intentions through customers' aesthetic experience. The results help flower stores understand customers' purposes, preferences, needs, experiences and purchase intentions. Through the questionnaire data, flower stores realize the types of service and assistance that customers expect. The interview data also give flower stores an insight into customer requirements. This study concludes flower stores can successfully apply service-dominant logic and value co-creation to produce positive interactive and esthetic experiences for customers.

Acknowledgments

This research project appreciates some financial support from Ministry of Science and Technology (MOST 106-2410-H-468-020) and Asia University (106-asia-17). Our gratitude also goes to anonymous reviewers and Michael Burton, Asia University for the English editing.

References

[1] S. L. Vargo and R. F. Lusch, Evolving to a new dominant logic for marketing, *Journal of Marketing, 68*(1), 1-17, 2004.

[2] B. H. Schmitt, *Experiential Marketing*, New York: The Free Press, 1999.

[3] B. J. Pine II and J. H. Gilmore, *The Experience Economy*, Boston, MA: Harvard Business School Press, 2011.

[4] H. Chiang, *Talking about Beauty*, from https://youtu.be/KFReCP3kXPs, 2017.

[5] L. S. Gau, M. I Chen, W. C. Lu, H. F. Lin, Cross-validation of physiological and psychological signals at induced educational and esthetic experiences. *Proceedings of the 2017 IEEE International Conference on Information, Communication and Engineering: Information and Innovation for Modern Technology, ICICE 2017* (pp. 101-104), DOI: 10.1109/ICICE.2017.8479258, 2018.

https://doi.org/10.1142/9789811238727_0019

Applying Board Games on Curriculum Design for Elementary School — A Case of Integrative Activities Curriculum

I-Chun Hung*, Chun-Chih Chen, Tung-Long Lin

National Kaohsiung Normal University, Kaohsiung 807, Taiwan
*Corresponding Author Email: ginger97117@gmail.com, Phone: +886-963167515

Abstract

Board games are games that can be played on a desk or other flat surfaces. It is an emerging educational technology. Because of education reform, learning is no longer limited to school. In terms of the learning process, the best way to learn and retain knowledge is to combine learning content with life experience. Therefore, ways to learn are no longer limited to textbooks. The purpose of board games in learning is to integrate the flow experience and digital learning through experiencing the game, so as to enhance learners' motivation and interests in learning and encourage learners to participate in learning. Students can not only learn through the whole process of the game, but also produce a flow in that situation. In addition, they can learn new knowledge and skills naturally.

In recent years, board games are more and more popular in the educationese. Through board games, learners can cultivate their mind, enhance learner's motivation and interests, and promote enduring learning. Besides, board games with digital technology can increase the games' variability and enjoyment. In recent times, teachers have started introducing board games as a teaching method that is interactive and informative. Learners can learn to think and to adapt in various subjects, such as mathematics, language, history and science. In addition to intellectual disciplines, board games also provide opportunities for students to be collaborative, explorative and think critically. Besides, through the games, students can be trained to resolve conflicts and to apply strategies to learn. This study is based on the Evaluation Grid Method and questionnaires to research students' willingness in learning, in-depth interviews to evaluate students'satisfaction surveys by promoting the students' cognition, affection, behavior. The purpose of this study is to understand students' acceptance of board games in integrative activities and to discuss the relationship among environmental factors, curriculum factors and students' using behaviors on board games. Therefore, the results of the follow-up verification study can be used as a reference to board games in teaching design in the future.

Keyword: Board Game, Experience, Evaluation Grid Method, Bloom's Educational Objectives

Research Background and Motivation

In today's societal makeup, due to the increase in new immigrants and underprivileged households, 1/3 of elementary students suffer some form of difficulty in learning, many to the point of learning disability; no student starts education on an equal foot. The application of board games is to motivate learning; student's response can identify their level of engagement, enthusiasm, and passion; those that do not respond well or show a lack of participation, other methods can be subsequently arranged to customize and aid their education.

Board games naturally promote positive competition, exercise in learning, training and teamwork that are vital lessons in education. It is highly interactive with games designed to match curriculum, decisions open for discussion and without informational biases, which are all aspects that are essential for learning. This study investigates whether the integration of board games can elevate elementary students' willingness to learn, their acceptance of the games and the resulting increase in learning ability.

Research Question

Board games can invoke a meaningful experience that promotes willingness to engage from the students, which prompt the students to actively construct their sense of concept and find the purpose to explore. Furthermore, it can motivate their learning and accumulation of knowledge. Enumerated below are the research questions:

1. Can the integration of board games within the curricular effectively increase in student's perception of concept?

2. Can the integration of board games within the curricular bring positive learning motivation for the students?

3. Can the integration of board games within the curricular clear up the concepts that students normally find confusing?

4. Can the integration of board games within the curricular aid in student's logical thinking and reaction capability?

The research is based on the concept of "Evaluation Grid Method" (EGM), in combination with a derivative of the "Technology Acceptance Model" (TAM) and the aid of Likert Scale to evaluate the student's willingness to learn with the integration of board games within the curricular, how their sense of conceptualization are improved and further discussion into the factors that affect acceptance. The purpose is to understand the relationship between curriculum, board games, how the circumstance in which board game is applied and the student's behavior in use.

Literature Review

"Evaluation Grid Method" is a research method whereby highly engaged targeted audience are being interviewed, concrete behavioral cases and features are compared and studied to summarize into dependable evaluation and opinion. What may have been hard to map out previously in the relationships between the abstract such as feelings in comparison to something concrete, organization using this method is reliable. The research applies the Evaluation Grid Method (EGM) from Miryoku Engineering with the perspectives from Kano two-dimensional quality model to identify the educational designs behind different boardgames with respect to the experience satisfaction levels relevant to learning effectiveness. This can determine the game's characteristic of design and quality classification to induce games that are beneficial to attract and promote learning into elementary curriculum.

Research Samples and Measure

The samples are selected according to locally sourced board games that are readily available for purchase. Board games include 2Plus Formosa, Flashlights & Fireflies and Bzz Out, the details are shown below:

1. Flashlights & Fireflies – An interactive boardgame with stereographical cards. The game emphasizes learning about insects and various knowledge within the field. *Purpose:* students learn about knowledge of insects and also the importance of safety in regard to returning home, it promotes interaction with peers, motivates learning and interpersonal relationships.

2. Bzz Out – An interactive teamwork based boardgame that teaches the ecology of the honey bee.

Fig. 1 Bzz Out game cover.

Purpose: Contrary to common board games where players are squared up against one another, this boardgame requires teamwork. The success of others is vital for the success of oneself. It is in essence a revision on the negative impact of pure competition and converting that into a teamwork game with a common goal.

3. Plus Formosa – Utilizing cards to mimic as camera lens of different depth of field to capture wildlife and protected species in turn learning about the general knowledge of the said animals. Through the interactive gameplay with peers, the concept of wildlife preservation is smartly ingrained.

Fig. 2 2Plus Formosa game cover

Fig. 3 2Plus Formosa card flash card types

Experiment

The interview conducted by the EGM will be categorized under three parts, "Original Reason", "Specific Matters" and "Abstract Reason". Understanding their original reason will be followed by their abstract feelings then asking for more precise specific matter.

The original reason is categorized into five parts according to elementary student's attraction to the board games which includes: art, stylistics, interaction, story and force; specific matter is categorized under: color composition, equipment styles, friendship systems, story continuity and the mechanism of force action/defend systems. These five specific matter will then be stretched in the EGM interviews to extract abstract attraction factors such as: fun factor, fantasy, uniqueness, special factor, interactive level, excitement level, starting difficulty, interpersonal relationships, relaxing factor, challenge factor and sense of achievement.

Research Results

Through the interviews, the grid will be layered out according to the boardgames' Evaluation Grid as follows:

TABLE 1
EGM Interview content description sample table

Original Reason	Specific Matter	Abstract Reason
Art	1. Colorful 2. Vivid Characters 3. Distinctive Features 4. Fancy Color Scheme 5. Flash Card Design 6. Clear Roles	1. Fantasy 2. Handsome 3. Unique 4. Attitude 5. Dazzling 6. Exciteful
Stylistic	1. Enticing Equipment 2. Gorgeous Outfit 3. Attractive Body Image 4. Exquisite Art 5. Identifiable Equipment Roles 6. Distinctive Themes	1. Elegant 2. Noble 3. Romantic 4. Cute 5. Playful 6. Unique
Interaction	1. Equipment Systems 2. Teamwork 3. Good Equipment Meta 4. Realistic Setting 5. Friendship Systems	1. Interactive 2. Excitement 3. Interesting 4. Interpersonal Relationship 5. Starting Difficulty
Story	1. Story Continuity 2. Character Back Stories 3. Gradual Difficulty Increase 4. Believable Fantasy 5. Character Arc Simulation	1. Vividness 2. Relaxation 3. Uplifting 4. Challenging 5. Acceptance 6. Achievement
Force	1. Weapon Choice 2. Attacking Methods 3. Equipment Arrangements 4. Defensive Mechanism 5. Illogical Transformation	1. Fresh 2. Funny 3. Happy 4. Difficulty Levels 5. Realistic 6. Protection

The research has shown that there are five major attracting categories in determining the feasibility of the application of boardgames to the curriculum; they are: Art, Stylistic, Interaction, Story and Force.

Through the samples we have gathered and the scores accumulated according to the evaluation table we have observed that the middle intermediate grade students have a difference in preference compared to the higher grade students; middle grade students prefer flash card type boardgames whereas the higher grade students prefer a design that is more three-dimensional.

Conclusion, Discussion and Limitations

The research has shown that through the application of methods of teaching and careful design of classroom events an environment that provokes students' willingness to learn can be induced. The environment will gradually consolidate and mature into personal interest and behavior. In other words, interest in learning can be nurtured.

According to the researchresults, the clear-cut attractive factor for any selection of boardgames by our specific target audience (elementary students) is the Stylistic appeal followed by other factors such as Art, Interaction, Story and Force.

References

[1] Greenburg, P. (1989). Ideas that work with young children. Learning self-esteem and self-discipline through play. Young Children, 44(2), 28-31.

[2] Swacha, J., Skrzyszewski, A., & Syslo, W. A. (2010). Computer game design class: The students' and professionals" perspectives. Informatics in Education, 9(2), pp. 249-260.

[3] Thomas, W. J. (2000). A review of research on project-based learning. Retrieved December 24, 2010, from The Autodesk Foundation: http://www.bie.org/files/researchreviewPBL_1.pdf

[4] Virvou, M., Katsionis, G., & Manos, K. (2005). Combining software games with education: Evaluation of its educational effectiveness. Educational Technology & Society, 8(2), pp. 54-65.

[5] Vries, d. A., & Roodenrijs, E. (2010). Playtesting: part of game design and development. Testing Experience, (10), pp.60-62.

[6] Wikipedia contributors. (2010, December). Board Game Retrieved December 11, 2010, from Wikipedia, The Free Encyclopedia: http://zh.wikipedia.org/zh-tw/%E6%A1%8C%E4%B8%8A%E9%81%3A%E6%88%B2

[7] Winn, B., & Heeter, C. (2007). Resolving conflicts in educational game design through playtesting. Innovate Journal of Online Education, 3(2).

[8] Zimmerman, E. (2003). Play as research. In L. Brenda (Ed.), Design Research. Cambridge, MA: The MIT Press.

[9] Zimmerman, E. (2009). Gaming literacy: Game design as a model for literacy in the 21st century. In B.Perron & M. J.

[10] P. Wolf (Eds), The video game theory reader, 23-32. New York: Routledge.

[11] Siraj, S. (2005). Project-based learning (PrBL): for CurriculumEnrichment: Malaysia experiences. Paper presented at Project-based Learning Conference. Taiwan.

https://doi.org/10.1142/9789811238727_0020

Augmented Reality to Enhance Interactive Graphic Card Design and Students' Learning Perspective

Mei-Chun Chang

Department of Digital Media Design, Tungnan University, New Taipei City, Taiwan
Email: sprinachang@gmail.com

Abstract

The purpose of this study is to investigate the impact of augmented reality (AR) on design learning for college students of design departments by introducing augmented reality (AR) technology application into an interactive design course and discussing students' problems in AR learning and creation. 45 senior students in a digital media design department of a university of science and technology were invited as the research objects to collect the data through observation, questionnaire, and retrospective interview. It was found that students benefit from the application of AR for their learning attitude and aesthetic experience in interactive design, and students with low academic achievement prefer AR learning more than those with high academic achievement. Students generally accepted AR software for interactive design. They were also satisfied with the learning and design results. In terms of learning motivation, when compared to traditional teaching, AR also helps students improve their learning efficiency, increase their creative motivation, and concentrate on the class.

Keywords: Augmented reality (AR), Augmented Reality Learning Experiences (ARLEs), Cognitive theory of multimedia learning (CTML), Visual design

Introduction

Augmented reality (AR) technology has become more popular in the application of information technology into teaching. AR assisted learning also increases research diversity and feasibility [1]. The use of digital media integrated into traditional teaching methods has become the mainstream of learning design at present [2]. AR has become an emerging technology with great potential in education [3]. In particular, AR is becoming increasingly popular in education, as it provides an interactive learning experience. Teachers are committed to digitizing learning content and designing learning situations in a digital environment so that students have a rich learning experience via mobile devices.

According to the research, AR technology is currently used in learning fields such as architecture, interior, product, game, interaction, engineering, and textbook design to provide a multi-level visual dynamic information experience. For the application of AR to design courses, most students have the motivation to learn and improve their learning results. Through AR teaching, students have a sense of surprise and maintain their concentration [4]. An AR teaching module is used as auxiliary teaching material by saving teachers' time to supplement content and students' time to copy notes. AR technology is applied in product design courses to solve structural defects [5]. One can use the spatial identification method of 3D furniture AR to assist the learning of plane configuration planning [6]. According to the literature, AR provides new learning opportunities but also brings new challenges and tests in people's learning technologies. The courses of a digital media design department cover various technologies from the graphic, web, video, and animation to digital content design. However, the link between digital technology and artistic design is ignored, and the promotion of a course covering a teaching scene faces potential challenges. Therefore, in current practical teaching, students are guided and stimulated to use appropriate methods and textbooks, and innovative teaching approaches are employed with novel media materials.

Based on the above, the purpose of this study is to explore the following: (1) understanding the impact of AR interactive graphic cards on the learning attitude of college students in a visual design department, (2) discussing how students design and make AR interactive graphic cards, and (3) presenting the impact of AR interactive graphic cards on students.

Literature Review

A. Application of AR in Design Teaching Practice

The principle of AR technology is to capture a real image through a mobile phone in combination with identification and positioning technology so that the real scene on the screen augments the virtual object generated by the computer. Thus, users have the visual experience of the coexistence of the real and virtual world simultaneously. Previous studies were used to explore the learning orientation of AR design. For example, Büttner *et al.* proposed an augmented and virtual visual method to evaluate space [7] by supplementing all the insufficient information in real activities to experience the immersive context, reduce complexity, and provide visual effects to complete tasks such as assisting disabled or unskilled personnel to complete relevant space design work.

In "Augmented Visual Design: Designing Ever-changing Classrooms", Sinfield and Cochrane allowed students to create things by using virtual and AR technologies [8]. By combining visual songs and dynamic images in their portfolios, Sinfield used AR technology to generate different visual experiences and redesigned the course content to enhance the educational experience of college students. AR utilized the spatial identification method of 3D furniture AR to assist the learning of plane configuration planning [9].

B. Discussion on Cognitive Theory of Multimedia Learning

Mayer proposed the cognitive theory of multimedia learning based on Miller's research on information processing ability [10] as shown in Fig. 1. Multimedia teaching materials (Mayer, 2001) are presented in the form of texts [11], pictures, and various types of learning activities, including the following three cognitive processes: selection, organization, and integration. The cognitive processes that learners experience include: perceptual memory, working memory to long-term memory, selecting text and picture information through multimedia, organizing them into image context mode, and integrating with the relevant prior knowledge of learners to produce meaningful knowledge understanding.

Among them, the key to learning success is the link between language and visual models as well as the quality of integration. According to the multimedia design principle proposed by Mayer (2003) [12], complete learning material information is an effective way to assist learners to acquire knowledge, which includes an appropriate learning reference template, focused and coherent teaching materials, and simplified operation instruction steps. If a work can be completed in a short time, then its effective learning can help students.

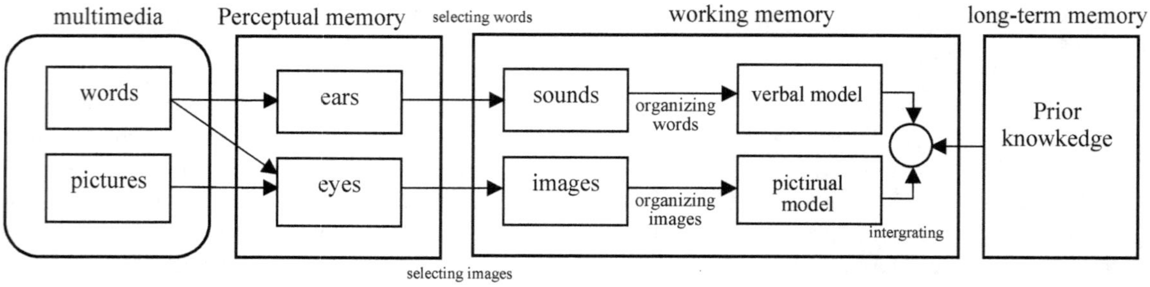

Fig. 1 Cognitive Theory of Multimedia Learning (Mayer, 2001)

C. AR Graphic Card Content Design

AR editing platform is free to create AR and virtual reality. The techniques of AR identification include marker-based AR, marker-less based AR, and location-based AR. Marker-based AR is also known as image recognition-based AR. An AR editing platform includes image identification and spatial identification. Currently, AR is produced by computer editing software and mobile applications, which offer the most convenient and easiest way for AR image identification with graphic cards as the medium. Identifying images is usually produced by shooting, scanning, computer graphics, or image processing.

The particularity of AR application in design lies in the "combination of virtuality and reality" of real-time, three-dimensional, dynamic, and creating other features. The link between "shooting script" and "art design" is important. The style, dynamics, and vision of art design affect the picture presented by AR. Therefore, the priority of the AR effect is the visual experience of interaction and context. In design, users must be immersed and sympathetic. In AR production, one must pay attention to the following design elements: seamless transition, integration of context, and multi-sensory interaction [13].

To make AR have the effect of creating a surprise, a graphic card is a most commonly used medium. Graphic card recognition is applied to cards, posters, paper, flyers, book covers, billboards, clothes, and so on. The technique of seamless transition is to make the first frame of an AR material film in the AR trigger medium. Triggered AR transits between virtuality and reality just like the visual effect of Harry Potter's moving newspaper.

Research Method

Based on the convenience sample, this study selected 45 senior students in a university of science and technology in New Taipei City as the research objects to collect qualitative and quantitative research data through observation records, questionnaires, and retrospective interviews. The overall research process and approach were divided into the following three stages.

(1) Stage 1 - AR course teaching and learning: The AR editor (Makar) was imported into the design course, and the design consisted of three units: (1) image recognition basics, (2) birthday cards, and (3) language learning cards. The observation method and retrospective interview were used to collect students' situations in AR art design from these three units.

(2) Stage 2 - Questionnaire survey on students' experience: After students finished making AR interactive graphic cards, they filled the questionnaire immediately. The content of the questionnaire was divided into three levels for data collection, and the topics or problems corresponding to each level were discussed.

(3) Stage 3 - Retrospective interview for students with high and low achievements: After the preliminary analysis of observation records and questionnaire data, the design teacher of this class selected 5 students with high academic achievement and low academic achievement, respectively, and conducted the interviews on this total of 10 students to obtain in-depth descriptions of their experience in learning and creation.

Fig. 2 Course unit and student work

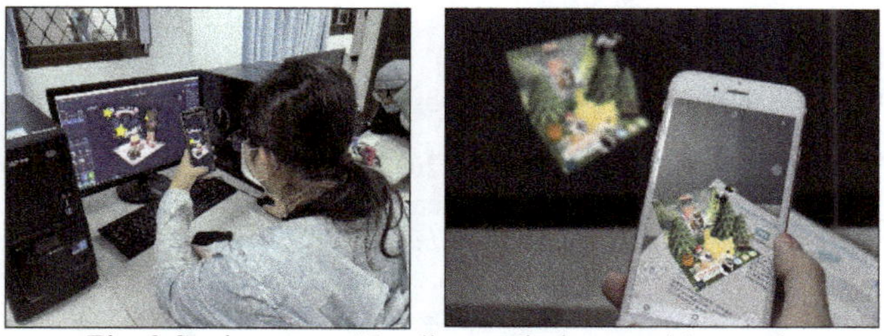

Fig. 3 Students use AR editor to design graphics cards

Research Findings and Discussion

A. Students' Learning Attitude towards AR Graphic Card Design

As shown in Table 1, as for "students' views on the effect and impact of AR technology on learning AR" in terms of motivation, most students agreed that the interactive design of the AR editor in this study enhanced their interest in learning. Among them, students with low academic achievement had lower learning satisfaction with the AR editor than students with high academic achievement. All (N=45) students agreed that AR technology stimulated their interest in learning, and learning with the AR editor was very attractive (question 1.1); 82% (n=38) of students agreed that they concentrated when learning AR with the AR editor (question 1.2); nearly 11% (n=5) of students agreed that it was boring to learn AR with the AR editor (question 1.3). According to the interview data, the high-achieving students (n=5) indicated that they could complete the graphic card design without reading the teaching videos back and forth, while the low-achieving students (n = 5) indicated that they could only complete all the graphic card design with the assistance of others, as hoping to complete the assignment with more convenient operations.

TABLE 1
Students' Learning Attitude on the AR Editor and Interactive Design (N=45)

	Question	Agree (Person-time)	Disagree (Person-time)	Percentage of Agreement (%)
1.1	It is very attractive to learn about interactive design with "AR".	45	0(0%)	100.0
1.2	When learning "AR" with the AR editor, I can concentrate.	38	7	82.4
1.3	I find it boring to learn "AR" with the AR editor.	5	40	11.1

Source: Compiled by this study.

This study finds that most students held a positive attitude towards learning AR interactive design, though several low-achieving students felt confused about instruction in teaching videos and the lack of design integrity and believed that identification interaction was enough. One reason could be that the design of the AR interactive graphic card developed in this study in terms of the difficulty of the interactive design and the content of the teaching materials could not fully conform to the cognitive development level of each student. This result was pointed out by Mayer and Moreno as they found that the gap in cognitive development levels between learners led to individuals' learning process with high-level knowledge by using multimedia teaching materials with considerable obstacles [14].

B. Students' Learning Effect on AR Graphic Card Design

As shown in Table 2, most students agreed that the AR interactive design in this study improved the design application as for "students' learning on the augmented effect of AR editor" in terms of personal relationship. Students with low academic achievement had lower learning satisfaction with AR software than those with high academic achievement. All (N=45) students agreed that learning the "AR" technology of the AR editor was helpful to the application of project production (question 2.1). 71% (n=32) of students agreed that they could learn the effect of AR with the AR editor (question 2.2). Nearly 84% (n=38) of students agreed that unexpected augmented interactive effects could be learned from the AR editor (question 2.3). According to the observation data, more than 70% of the students thought that learning from the AR editor increased the learning effect of interactive design.

According to the interview data, three students indicated that the AR editor covered a large number of materials, which could effectively and conveniently complete the content of the screen. Low-achieving students (n = 5) were all interested in augmenting the interactive effect through mobile phones. The findings of this study echo relevant research results before. The application of AR technology in multimedia design reflects that AR technology plays a more significant role in learning effectiveness and attractiveness for students with low academic achievement compared to students with high academic achievement [14].

TABLE 2
Technical Effects of Students on the Interactive Design of the AR Editor (N=45)

	Question	Agree (Person-time)	Disagree (Person-time)	Percentage of Agreement (%)
2.1	Learning the "AR" technology of AR editor is helpful to the application of project production.	45	0	100.0
2.2	I know how to learn the effect of "AR" with the AR editor.	32	13	71.0
2.3	Some unexpected augmented interactive effects can be learned from the AR editor.	38	7	84.3

Source: Compiled by this study.

Conclusion and Suggestions

The results of this study show that AR interactive graphic cards have positive effects on most students' learning attitude and creative process in design, and students have high acceptance of the learning application of AR combined with interactive technology in project production.

(1) In the study of "students' views on the effect and impact of AR technology on learning AR", the results show that students generally believe that AR interactive graphic cards make them more willing to participate in the study of design than without it. AR technology enhances their interest in using interactive graphic cards. The free editing of an augmented interactive graphic card without the need of programming ability, intuitive simple operation, and a large number of materials drive students to continue to create and further explore other application technologies within the editor and the augmented interactive effect in the graphic card increases the enjoyment of students' learning experience.

(2) In the study of "students' views on the cognitive impact on the augmented effect of the AR editor in learning", the findings note that most students agree that AR technology is conducive to the interactive effect presentation of works. AR can be used in the design of peripheral products for thematic production, such as picture books, souvenirs, posters, various cards (postcards and business cards), and so forth. By using the integration technology of virtuality and reality of AR, students can focus on observing the modeling, color, dynamic effect, and layout of three-dimensional space, and the production of the interactive function of the AR editor enables students to learn more augmented interactive effects.

In addition to the above positive responses, the following findings in this study are worthy of attention and discussion and can be applied in an AR interactive design course. Although Mayer and Moreno [15] proposed that the differences in the level of individual cognitive development may result in the obstacle of cognitive understanding in the independent use of multimedia teaching materials by learners, students have exhibited different cognitive situations for aesthetic expression and the creation of design courses. Students with high learning achievement made extensive use of and patiently search for 3D online materials, and the designed products were more complete and beautiful than before using AR.

Students with low learning achievement downloaded several materials and completed the setting as soon as possible for the augmented effect test, but the designed products were simple and incomplete. The teaching of the course revealed that students presented different levels of performance in the spatial arrangement. It is suggested that supporting mechanisms and measures be taken to assist students with low learning achievement in their study process, or that some learning scaffolding be developed. This helps students have teaching plan references to follow and assists students in their aesthetic design performance ability.

References

[1] Ibáñez, M. B., & Delgado-Kloos, C. (2018). Augmented reality for STEM learning: A systematic review. *Computers & Education*, 123, 109-123.

[2] Catrambone, R., & Seay, A. F. (2002). Using animation to help students learn computer algorithms. *Human Factors*, *44*(3), 495-511.

[3] Akçayır, M., & Akçayır, G. (2017). Advantages and challenges associated with augmented reality for education: A systematic review of the literature. *Educational Research Review*, *20*, 1-11.

[4] Chun-Di Chen & Chih-Tang Lee. (2013). The Practices and Vision of Digital Technology for Design Practical-Learning. *Elementary Education*, *53*(6), 53-61.

[5] Lai, Y. C. (2017). IS AUGMENTED REALITY A NEW PARADIGM IN DESIGN EDUCATION WHEN EDUCATIONAL SUBSIDY DECREASES?. In *DS 88: Proceedings of the 19th International Conference on Engineering and Product Design Education (E&PDE17), Building Community: Design Education for a Sustainable Future, Oslo, Norway, 7 & 8 September 2017* (pp. 549-554).

[6] Chang, Y. S., Hu, K. J., Chiang, C. W., & Lugmayr, A. (2020). Applying Mobile Augmented Reality (AR) to Teach Interior Design Students in Layout Plans: Evaluation of Learning Effectiveness Based on the ARCS Model of Learning Motivation Theory. *Sensors*, *20*(1), 105.

[7] Büttner, S., Mucha, H., Funk, M., Kosch, T., Aehnelt, M., Robert, S., & Röcker, C. (2017, June). The design space of augmented and virtual reality applications for assistive environments in manufacturing: a visual approach. *In Proceedings of the 10th International Conference on Pervasive Technologies Related to Assistive Environments* (pp. 433-440).

[8] Sinfield, D., & Cochrane, T. (2020). Augmenting visual design: Designing the changing classroom. *E-Learning and Digital Media*, *17*(5), 365-387.

[9] Chang, Y. S., Hu, K. J., Chiang, C. W., & Lugmayr, A. (2020). Applying Mobile Augmented Reality (AR) to Teach Interior Design Students in Layout Plans: Evaluation of Learning Effectiveness Based on the ARCS Model of Learning Motivation Theory. *Sensors*, *20*(1), 105.

[10] Miller, G. A. (1956). The Magical Number Seven, Plus or Minus Two Some Limits on Our Capacity for Processing Information. *Psychological Review*. *101*(2), 343-352.

[11] Mayer, R. E. (2001). *Multimedia Learning*. New York, NY: Cambridge University Press.

[12] Mayer, R. E., & Moreno, R. (2003). Nine ways to reduce cognitive load in multimedia learning. *Educational Psychologist*, *38* (1), 43-52.

[13] Bai, Bi-Zhen , 2020. *Are you AR today? AR augmented reality innovative thinking*. Sbooker Publications.Wei, X., Weng, D., Liu, Y., & Wang, Y. (2015). Teaching based on augmented reality for a technical creative design course. *Computers & Education*, *81*, 221-234.

[14] Mayer, R. E., & Moreno, R. (1998). A cognitive theory of multimedia learning: Implications for design principles. *Journal of Educational Psychology*, *91*(2), 358-368.

https://doi.org/10.1142/9789811238727_0021

Background and Prospect of the Application of Artificial Intelligence in Design

Xiaojie Zhu

[1]Shandong University of Art and Design, Jinan 250300, Shandong, China
Email: zhuxiaojie@sdada.edu.cn

Abstract

Current research on design science has gone through several stages from desire to doubt, through practical research, and finally into the research of design process, design method, and design pattern. The results of these studies, such as pattern language, and axiomatic design, provide an important methodological basis for automated design and the application of artificial intelligence in design. At present, the successful application of artificial intelligence in design mostly focuses on design assistant tools, while the design of intelligent system is facing the challenge of "wicked problems". This paper attempts to sort out the process of scientific design research from the perspective of design science, to summarize the achievements of scientific research and the current status of the application of artificial intelligence in design, and lastly, to discuss future directions of application of artificial intelligence in design.

Keywords: design, research through design, scientific design, artificial intelligence

Introduction

The design of reality systems, such as architectural design, industrial design, interaction design, and service design requires systematic and complex procedures. After analyzing the design problems, experienced designers can propose the most appropriate solutions through design cases and experience hubs. However, it often takes many years of study and practice to become a qualified designer, and diverse design projects are often accompanied by new difficulties and challenges. Therefore, design has always been considered as a highly skilled task that only human beings can complete. However, in recent years, due to the development of high-performance GPUs and the surge of machine learning, artificial intelligence (AI) has developed rapidly and has been successfully applied in many fields. So how about the application and prospect of AI in the field of design?

The objective of AI is to solve problems with higher efficiency and better results. AI users need to accurately identify problems, abstract them, and input them into AI programs. The complexity of design is because there are too many complex problems in design requirements and design process [1]. To apply AI, we must first have a more objective and systematic analysis of the design activity itself. Based on this, we can sort the development process and application status of AI in design, then explore the future directions.

Design Science

The research on design science can be traced back to the modernism design movement in 1920s. At the beginning of the 20th century, the development of industrial technology in Europe and America stimulated the demand for more predictable and cooperative design methods [2]. Peter Berens said that art should not be regarded as a personal affair, or as an individual artist's self-delusion or fantasy. The representative of De Stijl, Theo van Doesburg, proposed that: "The new spirit, which already governs almost all modern life, is opposed to animal spontaneity, to nature's domination, to artistic flummery." It needed objective methods and systems to design and create[3]. Bauhaus school concentrated on these thoughts and explorations, gradually formed a rational and rigorous teaching system and design style, pushed the modern design movement to a new height, and became a pioneer of modern design education.

After the Second World War, the migration of Bauhaus faculties transmitted these ideas to the United States. Le Corbusier, described his house as a "living machine" and envisaged an objective and rational way of design. Buckminster Fuller advocated the establishment of design science, which can minimize the use of energy and materials by making the most of human advantages. In the 1960s, the pursuit of design science was concentrated in the research of design process and design method based on science, technology, and rationality. The Conference on Design Methods, held in London in September 1962, is regarded as the beginning of design methods as an independent research area. In 1965, Sidney Gregory first defined design science in his paper, "Design science is concerned with the study, investigation, and accumulation of knowledge about the design process and its constituent operations. It aims to collect, organize, and improve those aspects of thought and information which are available concerning design and to specify and carry out research in those areas of design which are likely to be of value to practical designers and design organizations[4]." Herbert Simon, the Nobel laureate, also put forward specific demands for "design science", expecting to develop an intellectual, analytical, and teachable theoretical system about the design process [5].

In the 1980s and 1990s, a large number of journals on design methods emerged in the United States and Europe. In the process of research, people gradually discovered that there was still a big gap between science and design. In the process of design thinking research, Schön and Cross, etc., believed in the ability of designers that the cluttered and troublesome problems in design also brought innovation and uniqueness to the solution [6]. Dixon argued that cognitive research involves too many uncertain variables. It was too early to form a fixed theoretical model. However, he also believed that computer-based research, if properly used to discover and interpret the knowledge and strategies needed for design, may form an ideal theoretical basis [7].

Nevertheless, during that period, the American government and public showed great enthusiasm for design research, and a large number of design research institutions emerged. Many universities around the world also started to offer doctoral education in design, and the relationship between design theory and practice has become an important research topic. These researches on design process, design method, cognitive psychology, and behavior of designers help us to understand designers and their design process. A large number of models and methodologies formed by research have gradually played a more important role in design practice and design teaching, which also lays a foundation for the connection between information technology and designers, and provides theoretical support for the application of AI in design.

Theory, Model, and Method

In 1965, L. Bruce Archer, head of the Design Research Unit of Royal College of Art, published the book *systematic methods for designers* [8], and proposed a design method based on critical path analysis. He believed that design was a goal oriented problem-solving program and a planning process, focusing on goal setting, problem division, and process methodology, and the design method must be systematic. He divided the design process into three stages: analysis, creation and realization. He is regarded as the pioneer of design method and scientific design method.

In 1977, Christopher Alexander published *A Pattern Language: Towns, Buildings, Construction.* He discussed how urban planning and architectural patterns support human activities and interactions. The book introduced 253 architectural design patterns, "each pattern describes a problem which occurs over and over again in our environment, and then describes the core of the solution to that problem" [9]. This book was not only widely valued by the construction industry, but also gave an important method to solve complex problems and summarize design experience.

Many researchers have studied design patterns. Ullman et al. summed up a task/epsilon accumulation model (TEA model) through the design empirical research of a group of mechanical designers, in order to explain how the design was unfolded, hoping this model can predict the success or failure of the design under specific resources [10]. The authors also believed that the development of design model was helpful to the development of design aid tools, the improvement of design education, and the complete automation of some design tasks, so as to ultimately improve the efficiency and quality of design. Perlman et al. believed that design could be studied from the perspective of behavioral science, "there are many well-known guidelines and methodologies to study human behavior, and design patterns can be summarized and verified through multiple experiments" [11]. Hoover et al. in *Models and Abstractions in Design* proposed that the most useful abstract concept was to help designers understand and predict the relationship between the required behavior and the physical properties of design objects [12]. Designers could use theories from different perspectives to create models to predict the behavior of design objects and help improve design.

Around 1963, Horst Willhelm Jakob Rittel, Christopher Alexander, and others launched the Design Method Movement. They advocated a systematic view of design projects and proposed a series of design methods which emphasizes on rationality or science (such as definition, prototype, evaluation, etc.). In 1973, Rittel proposed the concept of "wicked problem"[13], which considered that most design problems, that were wicked problems, were incomplete, contradictory, difficult to identify and define, and often could not be solved by standard or known methods. He also proposed the Issue Based Information Systems (IBIS), which can objectively record the principles and context behind group decision-making. Rittel's research became the basis for design rationale research in computer science [14].

Nam P Suh proposed Axiomatic design in *The Principle of Design* in 1990. The author believed that the so-called design was actually a mapping between "what we want to achieve" and "how we want to achieve it". The author also proposed that a good design should be able to independently and simply meet various functional requirements. The core of the idea was multi-domain mapping, that was, design activities were divided into user domain, functional domain, physical domain, and process domain [15]. This system has become a design model for many researchers. Finger et al. focused the design model on parametric design, configuration design, and conceptual design. They systematically sorted out related research content and made a basic theory for the establishment of parametric design models [16].

Current Status of Ai in Design

From the perspective of function and role in the design process, the application of AI can be roughly divided into two categories. One is design assistant, which can support the designer's design expression; the other is design system, which can complete the whole design task independently or relatively independently.

A. Design Assistant Tools

Since the 1970s, computer scientists have been interested in system design methods and design science. They tried to prove scientific design decisions by programming and evaluating building performance, during which CAD has made great progress. In recent years, with the development of deep learning, some AI design assistant applications have emerged in some small functional areas. Limpaecher et al. collected user's hand-painted sketches through the "DrawAFriend" game to let AI learn user's painting style. Through deep learning, the algorithm can modify the user's handwriting in real time to achieve the ideal painting effect [17]. The drawing assistant can extract bones and structural lines from the target image, and then use polygons to simulate the target shape, so as to help users draw [18]. "Portraitsketch" can automatically adjust the parameters of strokes, improve the aesthetic quality of sketches, and help users create recognizable portrait sketches[19].

Researchers from the University of California, Berkeley and Carnegie Mellon University designed and developed the SILK (Sketch Interfaces Like Krazy) system. It can recognize the user's interface sketch drawn through the Handwriting Tablet and convert it into a prototype. The use of SILK can help designers ensure the rapidity and creativity of hand drawing, while saving the time of prototype design [21]. Coincidentally, Airbnb has also developed an artificial intelligence tool, which can identify user's hand drawn interface sketch through camera, and transform it into High-fidelity prototype by using deep learning [22]. In addition, there are some tools for user testing using AI in the market. For example, VisualEyes can automatically generate the product's attention heat map, reducing the time of artificial eye movement test. It is said that the accuracy rate has reached 84% of the real person test.

B. Intelligent Design System

The Department of Artificial Intelligence at the University of Edinburgh has been conducting theoretical and applied research on AI since 1984. They designed the Edinburgh Design System (EDS)[23], which can generate, record, and organize various types of design knowledge to assist the designer to deal with the poorly structured problem and make the appropriate design decision.

Kumara et al. tried to create an artificial neural network, trained two-layer perceptron through algorithm, and searched the matching design solution [24]. Kim et al. created "virtual design assistant" with deep learning tools, and tried to use the "hybrid intelligence" combined by artificial intelligence and designers to assist the early analysis and creative process in design. The main functions of virtual design assistant are as follows: 1. understand user requirements and extract functional requirements; 2. provide design decision suggestions based on "axiomatic design"[15]; 3. accumulate design data. The first function is verified by experiments. By using word clustering, the design requirements of user's natural language are extracted into vectorized design requirements [25].

In 2017, Alibaba's artificial intelligence "Luban" system designed 400 million posters, and the visual and commercial effects of the posters have "reached the level of middle and senior human designers", making it possible for "thousands of people and thousands of faces" of advertising resources in the Singles Day promotion [26]. The system consists of four parts: design framework, element center, actor, and evaluation network.

C. Research Framework of AI Application in Interaction Design

Unlike other design categories, interaction design was born to solve the design problem of human-computer interaction interface. The code used for interaction can even reach 50% of the total code. This makes interaction design combine with AI naturally. In order to summarize artificial intelligence based interaction design, first, it is necessary to analyze and sort out the application cases of artificial intelligence in design, especially in the design of digital products, to understand the current application ways and methods of artificial intelligence in the design, to understand the development path of artificial intelligence, and to have a basic understanding of the technical and application conditions of artificial intelligence; second, it is necessary to study human-computer interaction, the development and evolution of the interface, the trend of technology development and application in the industry; third, to restudy the current interaction design methods , to grasp the specific practice in the industry, and to comprehend the opinions of the practitioners; fourth, to study and summarize the application of artificial intelligence to improve the efficiency and quality of interaction design, finally, to carry out the user research and effectiveness test of this method.

The research should focus on four aspects: (1) The construction of a design model to systematically review the research results of the application of artificial intelligence in design, focusing on the theoretical and modeling research process of design methods. (2) The characteristics of human-computer interaction in the era of artificial intelligence. Only when we understand the media characteristics and development trend of human-computer interaction can we have a specific framework for human-computer interaction in the era of artificial intelligence. (3) AI assisted user research. User research is an important part of interactive design. How to improve the efficiency and quality of user research by using artificial intelligence is an important factor to promote the development of interactive design. (4) Interactive design method driven by artificial intelligence. In the era of artificial intelligence, whether the interaction design methods follow the existing logic and paradigm or explore new ideas and methods is still worthy of in-depth discussion and further investigation.

Based on the above research path, the following two research objectives can be achieved. First, the application path and technical basis of artificial intelligence in interactive design are systematically investigated and analyzed at the current level. Second, the improvement of interactive design method driven by artificial intelligence is planned and predicted at the development level. The innovation of new technology to the interface and the improvement of intelligence can greatly improve the user experience. Big data, machine learning, emotional computing and other technologies can improve the efficiency and quality of interactive design. Therefore, theoretical and prospective research should be done for the application of artificial intelligence in interactive design as early as possible.

Conclusion

Since the beginning of the 20th century, the research of scientific design has accumulated numerous achievements in the design process, design method, and designer cognition and behavior. Although there is still a great controversy in the academic circles about whether design is a science, these research results have laid a theoretical foundation for parametric design, automatic design, and even the application of AI in design. Therefore, in order to carry out research on the application of AI in design, it is necessary to exploit research on scientific design. At present, most of the application of AI in design focuses on design aids, which help designers to complete links in the design process more efficiently. For example, relying on the image generation of machine learning can quickly generate high-quality design drawings through sketches. We believe that in the near future, such tools will make a very significant impact on product design, architectural design, interaction design, visual communication design, and other fields. From the perspective of design system, choosing appropriate design model and parameterizing design requirements and design elements are the key elements, which depend on the collaboration and progress of design science and AI. On the one hand, the application of AI in design can greatly improve the productivity of design but, on the other hand, it also has an impact on the design industry. Understanding the feasibility and development directions of AI application in design can help the design industry to adjust its business models, as well as to help the design training programs, and to cultivate professional talents for intelligent design.

Acknowledgments

Authors gratefully acknowledge the grant from Philosophy and Social Science Foundation of China (#19BG113). We also thank professor Victoria Chi of North Carolina State University for her help in proofreading English translation.

References

[1] D. H. Jonassen, "Toward a design theory of problem solving," *ETR&D*, vol. 48, no. 4, pp. 63–85, Dec. 2000, doi: 10.1007/BF02300500.

[2] J. Zimmerman, J. Forlizzi, and S. Evenson, "Research through design as a method for interaction design research in HCI," in *Proceedings of the SIGCHI Conference on Human Factors in Computing Systems - CHI '07*, San Jose, California, USA, 2007, pp. 493–502, doi: 10.1145/1240624.1240704.

[3] N. Cross, "Designerly Ways of Knowing: Design Discipline Versus Design Science," *Design Issues*, vol. 17, no. 3, pp. 49–55, Jul. 2001, doi: 10.1162/074793601750357196.

[4] S. A. Gregory, "Design Science," in *The Design Method*, S. A. Gregory, Ed. Boston, MA: Springer US, 1966, pp. 323–330.

[5] H. A. Simon, *The Sciences of the Artificial*. MIT Press, 2019.

[6] D. A. Schön, "The reflective practitioner," *New York*, vol. 1083, 1938.

[7] J. R. Dixon, "On research methodology towards a scientific theory of engineering design," *AI EDAM*, vol. 1, no. 3, pp. 145–157, Aug. 1987, doi: 10.1017/S0890060400000251.

[8] L. B. Archer, *Systematic Method for Designers*. Council of Industrial Design, 1965.

[9] C. Alexander, *A Pattern Language: Towns, Buildings, Construction*. Oxford University Press, 1977.

[10] D. G. Ullman, T. G. Dietterich, and L. A. Stauffer, "A model of the mechanical design process based on empirical data," *AI EDAM*, vol. 2, no. 1, pp. 33–52, Feb. 1988, doi: 10.1017/S0890060400000536.

[11] P. Y. Papalambros, "The design laboratory: Interdisciplinary research and education," in *Proceedings of the 1988 NSF Grantee Workshop on Design Theory and Methodology*, 1988.

[12] S. P. Hoover, J. R. Rinderle, and S. Finger, "Models and abstractions in design," *Design Studies*, vol. 12, no. 4, pp. 237–245, Oct. 1991, doi: 10.1016/0142-694X(91)90039-Y.

[13] H. W. Rittel and M. M. Webber, "Wicked problems," *Man-made Futures*, vol. 26, no. 1, pp. 272–280, 1974.

[14] C. Rith and H. Dubberly, "Why Horst W. J. Rittel Matters," *Design Issues*, vol. 23, no. 1, pp. 72–91, Jan. 2007, doi: 10.1162/desi.2007.23.1.72.

[15] N. P. Suh, *The principles of design*. New York: Oxford University Press, 1990, 1990.

[16] N. Bayazit, "Investigating Design: A Review of Forty Years of Design Research," *Design Issues*, vol. 20, no. 1, pp. 16–29, Jan. 2004, doi: 10.1162/074793604772933739.

[17] A. Limpaecher, N. Feltman, A. Treuille, and M. Cohen, "Real-time drawing assistance through crowdsourcing," *ACM Transactions on Graphics (TOG)*, vol. 32, no. 4, p. 54, 2013.

[18] E. Iarussi, A. Bousseau, and T. Tsandilas, "The drawing assistant: Automated drawing guidance and feedback from photographs," 2013.

[19] J. Xie, A. Hertzmann, W. Li, and H. Winnemöller, "PortraitSketch: face sketching assistance for novices," in *Proceedings of the 27th annual ACM symposium on User interface software and technology*, 2014, pp. 407–417.

[20] J. Choi, H. Cho, J. Song, and S. M. Yoon, "SketchHelper: Real-Time Stroke Guidance for Freehand Sketch Retrieval," *IEEE Transactions on Multimedia*, vol. 21, no. 8, pp. 2083–2092, Aug. 2019, doi: 10.1109/TMM.2019.2892301.

[21] J. A. Landay and B. A. Myers, "Sketching interfaces: toward more human interface design," *Computer*, vol. 34, no. 3, pp. 56–64, Mar. 2001, doi: 10.1109/2.910894. [22] B. Wilkins, "Sketching Interfaces," *Airbnb.Design*. https://airbnb.design/sketching-interfaces/ (accessed Jan. 17, 2020).

[22] K. Millington, "The Edinburgh Designer System," in *IEE Colloquium on Alvey "Design to Product" Demonstrator Project*, Mar. 1990, pp. 4/1-4/3.

[23] S. Kumara and I. Ham, "Use of Associative Memory and Self-Organization in Conceptual Design," *CIRP Annals*, vol. 39, no. 1, pp. 117–120, Jan. 1990, doi: 10.1016/S0007-8506(07)61015-4.

[24] S.-G. Kim, S. M. Yoon, M. Yang, J. Choi, H. Akay, and E. Burnell, "AI for design: Virtual design assistant," *CIRP Annals*, vol. 68, no. 1, pp. 141–144, Jan. 2019, doi: 10.1016/j.cirp.2019.03.024.

[25] Celia Chen and Sarah Dai, "Alibaba lets AI, robots and drones do heavy lifting on Singles' Day," *South China Morning Post*, Nov. 11, 2017. https://www.scmp.com/tech/innovation/article/2119359/alibaba-lets-ai-robots-and-drones-do-heavy-lifting-sing les-day (accessed Oct. 15, 2019).

https://doi.org/10.1142/9789811238727_0022

Characteristics of Taiwanese Food Banks and Their Potential to Reduce Food Waste and Achieve Sustainability Goals

Chuan-Ching Hwang

Department of Social Work, Chaoyang University of Technology, Taichung, Taiwan
Email: chuanching.hwang@gmail.com

Abstract

Food banks collect the surplus food and then distribute it to the poor. They aim to reduce food waste and feed the needy. The main purpose of this paper is to analyze the potential and capability of Taiwanese food banks to reduce food waste and improve sustainability. Though food banks have been established in most parts of the country, the potential of Taiwanese food banks for reducing food waste has been limited due to their dry food orientation. However, the Taiwanese food bank has shown a greater possibility to solve the problem of food waste in recent years. Even in developed countries, food banks' ability to solve the problem is still extremely limited. Without the goal of helping people, food banks have difficulties in obtaining broad social support. This prevents them from legalizing their operation and therefore, achieving their goal of sustainability.

Keywords: Taiwanese food banks, food waste, sustainability, community refrigerators

Introduction

Due to the limitations of global resources, it is important to reduce food waste to achieve sustainability on planet Earth. According to a 2011 report by the Food and Agriculture Organization, about one-third of the world's annual food production was wasted. If the wasted food was properly consumed, it would be enough to feed about one billion people, many of whom suffered from absolute poverty [1]. According to a report in the Taiwanese magazine "Common Wealth" in 2013, the total amount of food wasted in a single day in Taiwan could be piled up to a height almost 70 times taller than Taipei 101, the tallest building in the country [2]. In other words, the food shortage of the world does not come from insufficiency, but from inconsistency of distribution.

There are many strategies to tackle food waste. Ideally, it would be more efficient and reasonable to distribute, manage, and allow consumers to reduce the waste in production and sales processes. However, it is impossible to completely reduce food waste at every stage. Food waste is caused by overproduction, packaging errors, aesthetic problems, excessive overbuying, and so on. Most of the surplus or wasted food can be consumed before being disposed of in garbage bins. The food banks collect the surplus food and distribute it to the poor, aiming to reduce food waste and feed the needy. If food banks operate to their fullest potential, we might be able to save the earth's resources significantly and improve sustainability.

The main purpose of this paper is to analyze the potential and capacity of the Taiwanese food bank to reduce food waste. For these purposes, we introduced the development and the current size of today's Taiwanese food bank and analyzed their major operational characteristics. This study is based on qualitative observations, interviews with food banks' staff and literature reviews.

Development and Size of Food Banks in Taiwan

Since the establishment of the first non-profit organization named "Food Bank" in the United States in 1967, food banks have been established all over the world for more than half a century. The USA has the longest-running and largest food banks in the world. For example, there are around 3.7 million people (12% of the total population) who have benefitted from food aid supplied by food banks. In France, Italy, Poland, and other European countries, it is estimated that more than 3 million people use food banks [3]. Today, the United States Food Bank Federation "Feeding America" is one of the top three non-profit organizations (NPOs) in the United States. The German food bank "Die Tafeln" has flourished since its inception in 1993 and is considered one of the most influential social movements since the 1990s.

In Taiwan, the first food bank was established in the early 2000s. In the beginning, it mainly collected surplus bread and distributed it to disadvantaged people. However, the operation was limited to small communities in terms of the recipients and the scale of services. Since 2008, several local governments have started to create food banks as a food aid program, mostly for people who were not eligible for public assistance. After 2010, food banks have mushroomed all over Taiwan by local governments and non-governmental organizations. In 2010, the Taichung Red Cross took the lead in setting up a physical "supermarket-style" food bank that allowed recipients to choose the food or materials from the shelves as if they were shopping in supermarkets. This practice has affected many food banks established later in Taiwan.

In 2016, the "Alliance of Taiwan FoodBanks" (ATF) was established with the aims of policy-making, concept advocacy, and resource links. The ATF has played an important role in the expansion of further food banks across the country. The key figures encouraged many NPOs to establish food banks or community refrigerators and provided instructions. Through the organization, the ministry of agriculture established a country-wide organization to utilize surplus products such as fruit and fish. The ATF is active in coordinating their member food banks to collect surplus food from super- and hypermarkets. Currently, the alliance has more than 60 food bank members that are located in most parts of the country.

How do the food banks work?

There are many types of food banks by service in three major categories [4]. The first category is called "business to business" (B2B), also known as the "logistical model". The model is for distributing the collected food to social welfare organizations or food banks. There is a big difference in the size of the organizations. In general, most "Food Banks" in the United States adopt the B2B model, and the size is large. However, in Asia, the size is relatively small. Only a few institutions, such as the "People Food Bank" located in Taichung, tend to operate in a sizable way. The second category is called "business to customers" (B2C), also known as the "Front-line model" in which the collected food is delivered directly to clients at a fixed time. This type is called "Food Pantry" in the United States and "die Tafeln" in Germany. Most of the Taiwanese food banks or "community refrigerators" belong to this category. The third category is a hybrid model in which the collected foods are provided either to the client or other social welfare organizations.

Characteristics of Food Banks in Taiwan

In comparison to food banks in other Asian countries, Taiwanese Food Banking has the following characteristics [5].

(1) Diversity: Taiwan's food banks are diverse. At present, around half of the cities and counties have either actively created their food banks or cooperated with local food banks. Purchased or donated foods are distributed once a month by community organizations. The other half of the local governments have small storerooms to provide the needy with "consolation" services when they are not eligible for public monetary assistance. Most of the government-run food banks are set up in the Social Assistance Section of the Social Affairs Bureau for social assistance. The majority provide dry or processed food such as cans, noodles and rice. Eligibility is determined by tests. The duration is limited normally to 3-6 months with an extension of the service decided under further examination.

Private Food Banks have been established all over the country. There are around 100 B2C private local food banks. Most of them do not have large warehouses. Furthermore, several soup kitchens provide free meals for the needy, especially for homeless people. As most of the foods are collected from the market or donated by the people, their operation is similar to food banks. Soup kitchens can therefore be classified as food banks. Some agencies also collect excess supplies, such as clothes, toys, and so on, and operate in a similar way to food banks in terms of providing surplus materials to the underprivileged.

(2) Strong community-based: Most food banks provide services within one city, township, or district. Some run for an entire city, such as the Kaohsiung Charity Federation. The People Food Bank, the 1919 Food Bank, and the Andrew Charity Organization serve the needy across the whole country. The People Food Bank runs mainly a B2B model. The 1919 Food Bank sends food parcels to the needy families, while the Andrew Charity Organization sends food packages to children aged under 15 with the cooperation of schools, churches, and NPOs.

(3) Dry-food oriented: Most of the Taiwanese food banks provide dry or processed food, such as cans, noodles, rice, milk powder, and so forth. Most of the food banks do not have enough volunteers to collect surplus food and deliver it every day. Therefore, they prefer non-perishable foods as they can be preserved for longer and distributed at any given time when volunteers are available.

(4) Community refrigerators: Several social welfare institutions, churches, and community centers have refrigerators. These are among the few food banks that provide perishable food mainly to the needy living in the same community. Most of these community refrigerators have been established over the past four years, and as of December 2020, there are approximately 200 refrigerators in the country [6].

Eligibility

Food banks created and promoted by the local governments of counties and municipalities solve issues caused by the lack of flexibility in the social assistance system in Taiwan. Many of the poor may not be eligible for the subsidies of low-income families due to strict criteria such as real property, an income of a household, savings, and so on. Even if the government's welfare is obtained, around 80% of the needy families can only receive an allowance for their children. This subsidy is usually not sufficient to meet the demand. Therefore, many local governments use the food bank to make up for the lack of governmental assistance. Most food banks in Europe and the United States do not strictly limit the period for the needy to receive food aid. However, not only the government but also private food banks in Taiwan usually grant food aid to their clients for a limited period. When granted for the first time, clients are usually eligible for food assistance for three to six months, which can be extended for another term if necessary. This indicates that food banks in Taiwan tend to define their aid as assistance for urgent needs.

Potential of Reducing Food Waste

In terms of food sources, some local governments adopt budgets to purchase food for distribution. The potential of governmental food banks for reducing food waste falls short of the demand. Many private food banks raise funds by donations to purchase food or ask companies to donate non-perishable foods that are valid for more than six months. The non-governmental food banks lack manpower, space, and finance. They have been providing dry or processed foods for more than a decade, so their potential to solve food waste problems cannot be overestimated.

In recent years, however, Taiwanese Food Banks have shown a greater interest in solving the problem of food waste. Some hypermarkets and supermarkets including PX Mart and Carrefour, have begun to donate surplus food to the food banks. The Alliance of Taiwan FoodBanks (ATF), established in 2016, actively promotes the idea of reducing food waste and links different food resources to organizations. The ATF has been helping its members gather surplus food and establish so-called "community refrigerators". According to the ATF, 50 community refrigerators have been set up in 2020 alone [6]. Though the amount of surplus food that a single community may save is limited, this shows good potential to solve the problem of food waste.

Conclusion

The food banks' capability to solve the problem of food waste is still limited. According to Grahm [7], even in the USA, the largest food banking country in the world, only 3% of food waste can be saved. Therefore, food banks must place more emphasis on helping the needy while providing surplus food. When ignoring the goal of helping people, food banks have difficulty in obtaining broad social support. To legalize their operation and therefore achieve the goal of sustainability, food banks must carry out the functions of environmental protection and helping people.

References

[1] Food and Agriculture Organization, Food wastage footprint. Impacts on natural resources. Summary report. Rome: FAO, 2013.

[2] F.J. Hsia, New good food movement, Common Wealth 219, April 2013, Retrieved Dec 2, 2020, from https://www.cw.com.tw/article/5048262,

[3] U. Gentilini, Banking on food: the state of food banks in high-income countries, IDS Working paper, 2013:415.

[4] S. Baglioni, B. De Pieri, and T. Tallarico, Surplus food recovery and food aid: The pivotal role of non-profit Organizations. Insights from Italy and Germany. VOLUNTAS: International Journal of Voluntary and Nonprofit Organizations, 28(5), 2013, pp.2032–2052.

[5] C.C. Hwang, Toward multidimensional and destimatization of food banks. Community Development, 150, Oct. 2015, pp. 260-270 (in Chinese).

[6] E. Lin, Alliance of Taiwan FoodBanks, working paper presented at the annual symposium of the Asian Food Banks on Nov. 30 2020, unpublished.

[7] R. Grahm, Food Banks Nations: Poverty, Corporate Charity and the Right to Food. Oxon: Routledge, 2018.

https://doi.org/10.1142/9789811238727_0023

Condensation and Dissipation on the Visual Processing of Fear Elements in Animation

Miaolian Chen, Lingxuan Wang* and Qiaoliang Li

Xiamen Academy of Arts & Design Fu Zhou University Xiamen, China
No.852, Ligong Road, Jimei District, Xiamen, Fujian
Xiamen, Fujian Province, China
*Corresponding Author Email: zellwlx@sina.com

Abstract

In animated works, visual elements with terrifying functions are used widely. These terrifying elements not only serve the theme of terror, but are also used to convey non-terrified emotions and other themes. For example, *The Skeleton Dance, Coco* and *Tim Burton's Corpse Bride*. The same symbol of terror, if handled in different ways, can give the audience different feelings. Taking the image of skeleton as an example, this paper discusses how this terrifying factor brings viewers different visual perceptions when dealt with differently. As for the visual perceptions generated by terrifying elements in animations, we intend to discuss how images of terror are treated in a non-terror oriented way.

Keywords: Animation, Fear elements, Visual processing

Introduction

Nowadays, images of terror are frequently used in animations and films with non-terror themes. When expressing non-terror themes, traditional symbols of terror usually undergo a process of artistic embellishment in order to reduce the feelings of terror they might generate in the viewers. However, how effective can this artistic treatment be in soothing the viewers? There is no way we can find it out. By using the same research methods used to evaluate the scale of semantic difference, this paper attempts to find out how the audience's visual perception is influenced if the terrifying elements in the "skeleton image" are weakened.

Fear Shapes in Animation

Terrifying elements are ubiquitous in animations just as the feeling of terror is born with every human being. For example, the earliest animation film about skeletons was the 1979 film The Wall released by Disney. By inserting 5 animation clips into the traditional film as a way of expression, the maker of this movie gave a post-modernistic touch to it. Each of the five animated segments used dim colors to convey a sense of depression and terror. 7 is an animated comedy put on screen in 2001. Terrifying elements are ubiquitous in the movie. The look of the characters alone can give the viewers a sense of terror. For example, the president of the monster company has the eyes of a spider and 8 legs which are a feature of a crab. His dark and withered skin even adds to his creepiness.

The emotion of terror also develops as human society proceeds. Before the industrial age, the ancient people, who hadn't yet developed a clear sense of identity, tended to feel terrified of the almighty nature. The film *The Croods* was a reflection of that age. The Croods family dwell in caves. Timid and cautious, they rely on their father to survive in the primitive society. The family live in a cave most of the time, and they only come out when they have to search for food. For the Croods, everything beyond the cave seems to be filled with terror. When the industrial age arrived, the relationship between human beings and machines became the focus of social discussion. The Japanese cartoon master Katsuhiro Otomo expressed his reflection on modernism and his worries in the form of animation. In Work termination order, only a bunch of robots are left to construct the building mechanically. All they know is to 'continue the construction'. The order will never change for any robot. When human beings use man-made machines to satisfy their insatiable desire, their humanity is lost, and their use of machines only bring them negative effects. In Akira, Katsuhiro Otomo underlined the undesirable consequence caused by Akira, a concrete epitome of technology.

Reasons for Choosing the Skeleton Model

It is hard to identify characters with terrifying elements in animated work due to their marginality or criticality. When it comes to the classification of terrifying roles and characters, ghosts and demons in the eastern culture, werewolves, spirits, vampires, zombies and half-human monsters in the western culture, even including kids and dolls are all typical examples of terrifying images that are capable of generating feelings of terror in the viewers. However, they are simply an external representation of human beings' terror. Instead, "skeletons" are the most real objective existence under the terror of death.

The skeleton is one of the most terrifying and most primitive symbols of death. skeleton dance or Dance of the Dead is a much-favored theme in Middle Ages literature and art. In the 1540s, the plague broke out in Europe, killing almost one third of the people in Europe; in 1337, the hundred-year-war between England and France brought another huge blow to the two countries. Fear of death became a major source of terror haunting the Europeans around the 16th century. On one hand, people were scared of death; on the other hand, they longed for eternal peace after their death, and the skeleton dance was a reflection of such a mentality. After the beginning of the Renaissance, the skeleton dance gradually faded out of people's sight. It was not until the rising of romanticism in the 1830s that the image of skeleton was used again by the artists to convey their brand-new artistic theories and philosophical thoughts.

Many animation masters have chosen skeletons as a material for their creation, and some even made jokes about this deadly image that were supposed to convey terror. Movies featuring skeletons as the major character can date back to the magical short film produced by Disney in 1929 -*The Skeleton Dance*. The movie had black and white hand-drawn Figures matched with music adapted from Saint -Saen's Dance of skeleton. As the night falls, the cold wind is howling. In a cemetery outside the town, four skeletons are dancing merrily. Set in Mexico during the day of the dead, animation *Coco* tells the story of the hero's accidental intrusion into the world of the dead and getting enlightenment on the love of family and the pursuit of dreams. The animation master Tim Burton shows a preference over terrifying elements. Animations *The Nightmare Before Christmas, Tim Burton's Corpse Bride, Frankenweenie* all employ the terrifying symbol of skeleton. The need for survival is the most fundamental need of human beings. Our fear of death is born with us. Therefore, I treat skeleton, the most primitive symbol of terror, as the object of this research.

Design and Implementation of Semantic Difference Scale

I did a preliminary research by making interviews and laid a foundation for the experiment. Then I selected skeleton images from animation or films, based on which I designed a scale of semantic difference. The next step was to do the test and data analysis.

Fig. 1 From *Tim Burton's Corpse Bride* skeleton girl.

A. The Selection and Design of Figures

Prior to the research, I analyzed the most commonly seen animation styles in the market. Based on the needs of the experiment, I finally decided to choose images of skeletons from stop-motion animations, 3-dimension animations and 2-dimension animations. In terms of Figures, I preferred characters whose shape and look would not remind people of terror. Besides, unpopular films or non-major characters in popular films were perfect choices for me so that people would not form any stereotype on these characters. Finally, I chose panoramic view and processed all images with Photo-Shop to give them a unified background.

Fig. 2 From *Coco* Aunt of Miguel Rivera.

Fig. 3 From *Holiday Party*.

Figure 1 shows the image of the child skeleton in the animation *Tim Burton's Corpse Bride*. The character of the stop-motion animation was re-created with real materials. Her orange hair, purple dress, one of her hands carrying a flower basket and the other scattering the pedals indicate that she was a flower girl. Figure 2 features the aunt of the protagonist in animation *Coco*. The skeleton went through 3-dimensional processing. Her head appeared fuller. Wearing a pink dress, blue and brown accessories, and a flower on her head, she beamed with smile. Figure 3 chose a skeleton image from *Holiday Party*. It was a 2-dimensional animation co-produced by Disney and Giant Ant.

B. Design of Semantic Difference Scale Form

In the preliminary research, interviews were mainly done on Wechat in the form of word-to-word communication. The interviewees were asked to describe how they feel over the visual image of skeleton with an adjective and give a word opposite to that adjective. I summarized the words mentioned by the interviewees into the following: Devilish, dead, Gypsum,head,Gothic,creepy,vicious,bleak,scrawny,undone,to rturous,bloodcurdling,fearful,tenebrous,quirky,heretical,ice-c old,alone,terrible,sick,fragile,weak,shadowy,gruesome,ugly,d ry,eccentric,piquant,extraordinary.The antonym issummed up

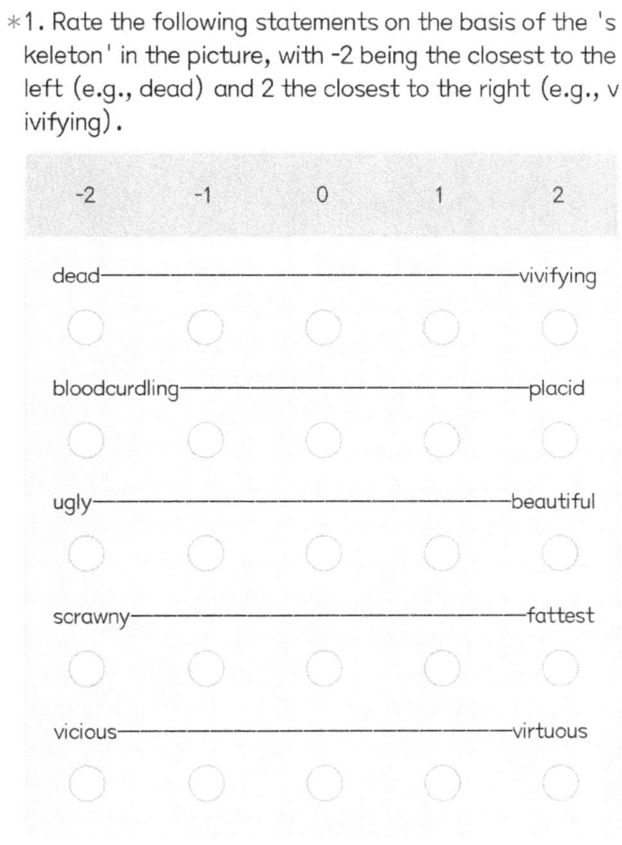
*1. Rate the following statements on the basis of the 's keleton' in the picture, with -2 being the closest to the left (e.g., dead) and 2 the closest to the right (e.g., v ivifying).

-2	-1	0	1	2

dead———vivifying

bloodcurdling———placid

ugly———beautiful

scrawny———fattest

vicious———virtuous

Fig. 4 Questionnaire on perceptual words and semantic differences of "skeleton".

as seraphic, material, saintly, bright, vivifying, prosperous, hopeful,beatific,busy,warm,cute/relaxed,comfortable,stiff,fat, beautiful,placid,firm,serene,funny,virtuous,cozy,fearless,humi d,nononsense.

The following five words were used frequently by the interviewees to describe their feelings over "skeleton": bloodcurdling, dead, scrawny, vicious, ugly. I chose antonyms for each of the five words and placed them on the other end of the scale. The opposites of the five words are: placid, vivifying, fattest, virtuous, beautiful. Together with the five adjectives, they made up five word pairs. The preset values are: -2 represents 1 point, -1 represents 2 points, 0 represents 3 points, 1 represents 4 points and 2 represents 5 points. The design of the scale form is indicated in Figure 4.

C. Selection of the Research Object

As the research involves a great many concepts related to animation, I chose 48 students of digital media in the College of Crafts and Arts of Fuzhou University and social figures aged between 20 and 35 years old as the subject of my test. The participants were divided into professional and amateur groups. They were required to fill in the form within three minutes. In order to eliminate the effect that the participants' overthinking might have on the test result, the participants were kept from one another and thus free of the influence of one another.

The test subjects, who were grouped according to whether they were professionals in art or design or not, were required to grade the five word pairs. Altogether 48 forms were collected. Among the 43 valid forms collected, 22 were from design professionals and the other 21 were from non-art professionals.

Data Analysis

The results of semantic difference are represented with mean

TABLE I
DIFFERENT "SKELETON" SHAPE OF THE 5 MATERIAL TO THE SCORE COMPARISON

Paired Elemental Words	Art and design		
	Fig1	Fig2	Fig3
dead-vivifying	2.05±1.28	3.50±1.37	3.05±1.35
bloodcurding-placid	2.41±1.07	3.32±1.55	3.45±1.33
ugly-beautiful	2.14±0.90	3.01±1.44	2.82±1.10
scrawny-fattest	2.55±1.12	3.77±1.30	2.00±0.92
vicious-virtuous	2.77±1.09	3.10±1.50	3.14±1.09
Paired Elemental Words	Nonartistic design		
dead-vivifying	2.63±1.31	3.58±1.27	3.74±0.96
bloodcurding-placid	2.53±1.23	3.42±1.43	3.58±1.04
ugly-beautiful	2.32±1.22	3.21±1.40	3.47±1.14
scrawny-fattest	2.26±1.07	4.05±0.76	2.32±1.03
vicious-virtuous	2.68±1.34	3.16±1.60	3.53±0.94

value±standard variation. As Table I indicates, there exists a huge difference in the mean values of the five word pairs. If compared vertically, the two groups of test subjects tended to give negative comments on Figure 1, while their comments on Figure 2 and 3 were more positive. No distinct orientation was shown in any of the three kinds of figures. But comparatively, Figure 2 was more apt to arouse positive feelings. Therefore, having the image of skeletons going through visual processing can reduce the extent of terror it might bring to the audience. However, it still fails to completely eliminate the feeling of terror the audience might develop at the sight of a skeleton image. Horizontally, both groups held similar opinions on the word pair of "fat and thin", and the dispersion degree remained tiny. Among all bodily features of Figure 2, "fat" has the highest score. Compared with the statistics related to the other two Figures, statistics of Figure 2 tilt towards the positive area. So we believe that the visual perception of "fat" has a positive correlation with the other factors.

Conclusion

With regard to a visually processed skeleton image, people with art background do not differ much from people with no artistic background in their opinion towards the image. Therefore, we believe that a visualized processing of the skeleton image meets with the visual and psychological needs of most people.

Among all the visually processed "skeleton" images, the scores of Figure 1, a stop-motion cartoon image, differ greatly from those of Figure 2 and 3 due to the differences in their shape, materials and color. There are several reasons accounting for this: firstly: terrifying images of children and dolls are usually associated with fear; secondly, made with realistic materials, the girl skeleton in Corpse Bride was almost identical to a real figure, which added to its terror; thirdly, grades also diverged due to the differences in color and light. Compared to Figures 2 and 3, Figure 1 is not as bright and its color saturation is lower, therefore, it enhances the feeling of depression and creepiness that the audience may feel. In this research, as the characters varied, there may be some errors in the figures or statistics collected. In the next experiment, I will try to unify the three types of characters and eliminate possible errors brought by different characters.

We believe that movement is an effective way to reduce the feelings of terror. In the next research, I will conduct a quantitative research combining the carnival theory put forward by the famous Soviet Union literalist and psychologist Mikhail Bakhtin and the approach to evaluating semantic difference. I will explore the differences in the movement of "skeletons" in my next experiment.

References

[1] B.Zhou. Fear and literary expression.
[2] J.Wu, L.L.Li. Influence of model differences on audience brand impression in male formal dress print ads. 2009.
[3] C.G.Jung. *Psychology and Literature*. Trans.Chua Feng, Ke Su. Jiangsu: Yilin press. 2011.
[4] Z.G.Yi. *The Anthropology of Art*. Shanghai: Shanghai Art Publishing House. 2001.
[5] L.Svendsen. *The Philosophy of Fear.* Tran.sJ.J.Fan..Beijing: Peking University Press. 2009.
[6] M.M.Baxtnh.Volume 6 of the complete works of Baxtnh. Trans. Z.L.Li, Z.X.xia et al. Shijiazhuang: Hebei Education Press. 1998.

https://doi.org/10.1142/9789811238727_0024

Creative Thinking to Resist the Challenges of Pandemic — Research on Colorant as Example

Meiho Chen

Department of Communication Arts, Chaoyang University of Technology, 168, Jifeng E. Rd., Wufeng District, Taichung, 413310 Taiwan
Email: meiho@cyut.edu.tw

Abstract

After the Industrial Revolution, in the 21st century, mankind is facing the harsh test of economic growth and environmental protection. Colorant research contains cross-field creative thinking that has been added to develop our Cultural Creative Industry to reduce the pollution by artificial dyes. The extensive usage of biomaterials is not only for natural dyeing but also for the development of biotechnology and pharmaceutical products to fight viruses.

Keywords: Colorant, Cultural Creative Industry, Intangible Cultural Heritage, Biomaterials

Introduction

Creative thinking comes from different fields, such as Sir William Henry Perkin (1838–1907), who synthesized quinine to suppress the virus, and unexpectedly, discovered the first aniline dye which is an important invention for artificial colorant in the age of mass production of the Industrial Revolution. He successfully changed the history of the fashion and textile industry in the 19th and 20th centuries. Industrialized mass production creates capitalism and causes inequality. After 165 years, chemical dyes are polluting rivers and oceans. UNESCO has called on all countries for Sustainable Development Goals (SDGs) to make improvements for economic growth and social progress with environmental protection. We expect that the cultural and creative industries protect cultural heritage from frequent loss, as they cannot compete with industrialized products. The extensive use of biomaterials resolves this situation.

World History of Infectious Diseases

The worst disease pandemic in history claimed hundreds of millions of lives happened in 541. After that, an infectious disease, the black death prevailed between 1346−1353. Fortunately, this epidemic disease was eliminated by the British Medical Scientist Edward Jenner. The cholera virus survives through contaminated food and water and is still common in low-income countries with poor sanitation since 1817. During the First World War, Spanish flu by H1N1 quarantine measures slowed the spread of the virus and turned it into a mild seasonal flu from 1918−1920. The Ebola virus first appeared in Africa in 1976. Since 1981, HIV and AIDS which attack the human immune system have not been cured until now. Their high mortality is due to the symptoms that take a long time to appear. However, the SARS and MERS have infected people from 2002−2012 which have been easily subdued. Unfortunately, they have influenced the beginning of the COVID-19 virus pandemic. [1]

Infectious diseases have existed since ancient times. The important thing is how we learn lessons and develop advanced technology to stop these diseases. We need to divert the attention and continue to work professionally. Sir William Henry Perkin (1838−1907) (Fig.1) discovered the first aniline dye and founded a science-based industry. Perkin successfully changed the history of the fashion and textile industry in the 19th and 20th centuries. These are examples of how to fight the virus. [2]

Fourth Industrial Revolution

Since the steam engine invention in 1776, fundamental changes were brought by the Industrial Revolution, which is often referred to as The Age of Machines. Steam engines were used in the age of the first industrial revolution. When Perkin found aniline dye as an artificial colorant in 1856, the second industrial revolution added mass production with the electronic machine. Gradually, this artificial dye replaced natural ones such as magnolia and madder. After 165 years, rivers and oceans are polluted by chemical dyes. Computers and automated production caused the third industrial revolution in 1969. Industry 4.0 has made one smart factory since 2013. Through the Internet world, robots serve humans in the application of the Internet of Things, Big Data, Advanced Analysis Control Systems, and Autonomous Robots. [3] These bring a better life from now on than before.

Sustainable Development Goals (SDGs)

In the present world, people move around so much and suffer from COVID-19. [4] Since the Industrial Revolution in the 19th century, capitalism has been formed in many countries, and gaining wealth is the goal of the public. However, people tend to be unscrupulous to obtain wealth and damage the natural environment. Recently, people began to realize the importance of protecting the environment. The research on natural colorants is also a way to promote well-being under the International Symposium and Exhibition on Natural Dyes (ISEND) and the World Eco-Fiber and Textile Forum (WEFT) initiated by UNESCO. The first ISEND-WEFT was held in Hyderabad, India in 2006, and was organized by UNESCO and the Crafts Council of India. Since then, five more events have been held in Korea (2009, organized by Kim [5], Cardon and Sayette [6], and Ong [7], National Taiwan Craft Research and Development Institute), and the Symposium/Festival on natural colorants "Plants, Ecology and Colors" held in Antananarivo, Madagascar (2017).

After more than 10 years of practical research on natural colorants, the key issues in the 17 SDGs [8] advocated by the United Nations include the following: local care (to promote local natural plant dyeing), sustainable environment (natural vegetation dyeing replaces chemical dyeing to avoid water pollution), industry linkage and economic sustainability (creating natural dyeing industry management), health promotion and food safety (natural organic plants should be used for food dyeing), hair dyes instead of PPD (p-phenylenediamine may cause cancer), cultural sustainability (inheriting ancient natural plant dyeing technology), and social practice (women set up dyeing workshops with the independent economic ability to achieve gender equality). Colorants research is a comprehensive science that needs interdisciplinary cooperation. Such as physical research emphasizes to study the role of light, the wavelength of the color light, and the mixing of shades. Chemical research is about the source of the colorant. In ancient times, colorants were mostly made from animals, plants, and minerals. Chemically synthesized colorants have replaced the color materials of animals and plants since the 19th century.

Physiologists study how light and color produce functions and effects on human visual organs and research on color vision adaptation. They believe that the reaction of human sense perception to color is greatly related to the living environment and personality growth. Important questions are as follows: How does the color's light affect people's minds and spirit and how does the color's light affect humans? Aestheticians research the appearance of colors and their inner feelings. The artist's attention to the perspective of color is based on aesthetics, color beauty, contrast, blending, and color matching. In summary, three basic procedures for understanding colors are as follows: to explore colors with a scientific spirit of seeking the truth and to use actual experience to understand the colors. The third step is to enter the world of applied color.

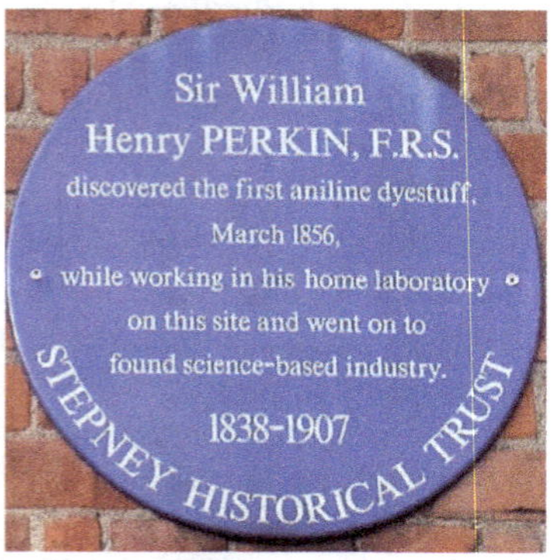

Fig. 1 William Perkin Blue plaque in Cable Street, London, England.

Cultural and Creative Industries

After the Industrial Revolution, a society of capitalist thought was formed. Capitalist society creates inequality between the rich and poor. A big consortium does not resist the challenges of pandemics that last too long. Cultural and creative industries make up for these deficiencies, as they encourage the establishment of small studios. The study of colorant serves as a model for examining this concept of research. Industrial foundry experience in Taiwan society in the 1970s.

This is an important reason for Taiwan's economic takeoff to which dyeing and weaving work made a major contribution. Taiwan's economic failure in 1990 was mainly due to China's policies that attracted Taiwanese businessmen to set up factories. The processing industry started from imitation. After learning the skills, a brand is created so that the foundry maintains its business. Japan and Germany are successful in brand creations. Since the discovery of synthetic fibers and colorants at the beginning of the 19th century, natural dyes and handmade products were in less demand. This change became a serious setback for Taiwan's society and the economy as manual labor could not compete with mass production. Silk tapestry [9] has played an important role in the preservation of Chinese painting and calligraphy and has continued since the Song Dynasty (960–1279). Unfortunately, due to the complexities of techniques, craftspeople eventually stop using them. If this is not preserved, it will ultimately disappear. The declaration of the United Nations Educational, Scientific and Cultural Organization (UNESCO) on the importance of the intangible cultural heritage protection concerned with ancient knowledge and traditional craftsmanship on nature dyeing. Joint education, the seventeenth session of UNESCO General Assembly, held in 1972 stated that through the World Cultural and Natural Heritage Protection Convention [10], inherent interdependence between cultural and natural heritage must be preserved. The thirty-second session in 2003 decided the intangible cultural heritage protection and stated that intangible cultural heritage is a living heritage of skills, technology, and knowledge. Traditional crafts masters in China have since then been protected. Since 2003, UNESCO has considered the deep-seated interdependence between intangible cultural heritage and tangible cultural and natural heritage.

Cross-field Integration

Interdisciplinary integration is the current direction of education by removing the barriers of knowledge to stimulate creative thinking. Knowledge and wisdom are obtained from the Internet but need a correct teaching and guidance process. When people and ideas in the network system are naturally connected in the creative network world, the changes in the thinking/training model of the teachers and students are possible. For example, thinking Hats, Mind Mapping, and The World Café lead us to contemplate the innovations in education. De Bono [11] developed the six thinking hats methods that are thinking methods that combine group discussion with individual thinking. In 2007, Tony and Bazun [12] published the "Mind Map Bible" as an image learning method that is more impressive than text. By drawing images, knowledge, concepts, or ideas are expressed visually. In a brainstorming method, it is easy to make irrelevant things through the way of making stories and deepen the memory of the brain to improve the students' learning effectiveness. The initiators of creative thinking in the World Café are Brown and Isaacs [13], as they advocated using dialogue to find answers. Their seven principles are setting the scene, creating a pleasant and hospitable environment, sharing the results of collective exploration, exploring the really important questions, listening to the insights, encouraging active contributions, and connecting different perspectives. According to the aforementioned, the teaching and learning activities are replaced by distance teaching as a teaching aid. Although, in this digital age, the teachers' original task of transferring prodigious knowledge is challenged. A college education is cultivating the students' rational knowledge in logic, ethics, willpower, and the aesthetic cultivation of perceptual knowledge, which leads to professional skills. The conditions for success include curiosity, intuition, and practicality.

Combination of Humanities and Technology

During the industrial revolution of the 19th century, people invented steam engines and cameras, but artists did not invent anything. However, those machines are aged and replaced by electrical and digital ones, while the paintings are not. Paintings in different periods reflect the ideas of people in different periods, their feelings of light and air, and in the long run, retain the dreams of mankind. These do change with the development of social sciences. If the most fundamental and simplest curiosity is retained, the advantage of the artist's "function" is placed in the relatively long development of mankind. Every year, more than one million well-known museum visitors help the country's economic growth. Invention comes from creative thinking and imagination that do not exist in humanity and art [14].

Extensive Use of Biomaterials [15]

Since the industrial revolution, the shortage of energy and the environmental pollution caused by traditional fossil fuel energy such as coal, oil, and natural gas brings a crisis to the sustainable survival of mankind. In the 21st century, mankind faces the dual pressure of economic growth and environmental protection. The development of environment-friendly materials makes the 21st century an era of biotechnology. We look forward to the development of biotechnology [16] and pharmaceutical products to fight viruses and the extensive usage of biomaterials. We have a philosophic Chinese interpretation of immortality that consists of the continuous transmission of virtue as a protection against destruction. This continuity is not assured by the immortality of inanimate objects, but by successive generations. The attitude of the Chinese is faced towards the past. Thus, the Chinese choose to neutralize their attitude to give an impact of time. They transferred the problem. The eternity does not have to live in the architecture, she has to live in the architect. The passing nature of the monument is as an offering made for the "greediness of time", and it is at the prize of this sacrifice that the manufacturer ensures the continuity of his spiritual intention [17].

References

[1] William Hardy McNeill, *Plagues and Peoples*, Garden City, New York: Anchor Press/Doubleday, 1976, Yang Yuling Translation, Commonwealth Publishing Co., Ltd., Taipei, 2016, pp.252–350.

[2] Gavin Weightman, *The Industry Revolutionaries, the creation of the Modern World 1776-1914*, United Kingdom, Atlantic Books Ltd., 2007, Jia Shiheng Translation, Goodness Publishing House, 2010, pp.339–357.

[3] Klaus Schwab, *The fourth Industrial Revolution*, World Economic forum, 2016, Commonwealth Publishing Co., Ltd., Taipei, 2016, pp.20–30.

[4] Hiroyuki Ishi, *World history of infectious diseases*, Tokyo: Kadokawa corporation, 2014, Li Hanting Translation, Amann Co., Ltd.,Taipei, 2018, pp.77–92.

[5] Kim, Ji-Hee, *Natural Dyeing, tradition and Innovation*, Int. Symp. & Exhibition on Natural Dyes, Taegu, Korea, 22–27 September, 2008.

[6] Dominique Cardon, Anne de la Sayette, *Colors for a greener world*, Int. Symp. & Exhibition on Natural Dyes, La Rochelle, France, 25–30 April 2011.

[7] Edric Ong, *Waste to Wealth*, Int. Symp. Exhibition on Natural Dyes & World Eco-Fiber and Textile forum, Kuching, Sarawak, Malaysia, 27 September– 1 October 2012.

[8] UNESCO, Sustainable Development Goals (SDGs), retrieved from : https://en.wikipedia.org/wiki/Sustainable_Development Goals

[9] Meiho Chen, *Natural Dye in the Application of Silk Tapestry in view of the preservation of its intangible cultural heritage*, International Journal of Liberal Arts and Social Science, Vol. 2 No. 8 October, 2014, ISSN: 2307-924X, pp. 67–68.

[10] UNESCO, the World Cultural and Natural Heritage Protection Convention, retrieved from : http://www.unesco.org/culture/ich/index.php?lg=en&pg=00005

[11] Edward De Bono, *Six Hat Thinking*,retrieved from : https://fr.wikipedia.org/wiki/Méthode_des_six_chapeaux

[12] Tony Bazun and Barry Bazun, *Mind Map Bible*, retrieved from : https://en.wikipedia.org/wiki/Tony_Buzan, and https://en.wikipedia.org/wiki/Barry_Buzan

[13] Juanita Brown and David Isaacs, *the World Café*, retrieved from : http://www.theworldcafe.com/about-us/history/

[14] The Best Artificial Intelligent Movie- list of artificial intelligence films, retrieved from: https://en.wikipedia.org/wiki/List_of_artificial_intelligence_films

[15] Yao Xiangjun, Tian Yishui , *Biomass Energy: Developing Green Gold*, 21 Century Sustainable Energy Series, New Wun Ching Developmental Publishing Co., Ltd., 2008, pp.38–43.

[16] Sharon Walker, *Biotechnology Demystified, a self-teaching guide*, McGraw-Hill Companies, Inc., 2007, Zhang Linglan Translation, Chang-Shang Publishing. Ltd., 2008, pp.199–227.

[17] Victor Segalen, retrieved from : https://fr.wikipedia.org/wiki/Victor_ Segalen

https://doi.org/10.1142/9789811238727_0025

Design and Development of Augmented Reality Technology Applied to Teaching Tool in Campus Environmental Education for Primary School Students

Chu Yu Cheng, Yan Wang*, Wen Zhe Yu

South Taiwan University of Science and Technology, Tainan, Taiwan
*Corresponding Author Email: ma81c401@stust.edu.tw

Abstract

This research applied augmented reality (AR) technology to the curriculum of elementary students. The interactive teaching was designed for understanding dengue fever mosquitoes ecologically. Students could learn by using mobile devices. It provided virtual characters to guide students to explore biological knowledge. The learning was no longer limited to a classroom with computers, and turned out to be creative and ubiquitous. The research solved the problems of inconsistency and weakness of environmental education. With this learning method, the ability of learning, observation, and interactive experiences were obtained.

Keywords: environmental education, biological science, interactive teaching tool, augmented reality

Introduction

Flipped learning emphasizes student-centered learning. Flipped learning contains two aspects: "Individuals use computer-related vehicles for learning outside the classroom" and "Group study by individuals in the classroom" [1]. It turns passive learning into active learning. It improves learning skills in issues finding, problem analysis, problem-solving, and individual creativity. Flipped learning starts from pre-class preparation and pre-subject study in advance. It attempts to have students away from the original classroom learning. Natural science related contents are appropriate for flipped learning.

This study demonstrates a new learning aid for mosquito prevention and biology learning for primary school students. Dengue fever has been increasing in recent years all over the world and attracted attention in Taiwan as it is becoming one of Taiwan's significant public health issues. Dengue fever is infected by *Aedes aegypti* and *Aedes albopictus*. The local outbreak consumes a lot of resources and threatens human health. Therefore, effective epidemic prevention and understanding the habits and characteristics of the mosquitoes are the main issues, too. In elementary schools, the lessons on dengue fever are insufficient. Students need to understand the disease and the biological behavior of the mosquitos which cannot be observed. Therefore, the goal of this research is to build interactive, immersive, and imaginative interactive teaching tool that integrate AR technology the learning.

Augmented Reality

Augmented reality (AR) is an interactive technology that supports or makes up a visual deficiency for physical environments. The virtual layer is positioned between the physical environment and the user. Texts, images, videos, or other virtual items can be added on smartphones, tablets, wearable devices (such as headsets), and projectors [2]. Extensive research of AR technology has been conducted in the fields of computer technology and human-computer interaction, and also developed in various fields such as medicine, industry, games, military, art, education, tourism, and construction. AR was initially proposed to be on the "reality-virtuality continuum". It uses real and virtual environments at both ends of the "real-virtual continuity" and is positioned as "mixed reality" in the middle of AR and augmented virtuality (AV) [3]. Azuma proposed that AR is a visualization technology that contains three characteristics: (1) physical and virtual objects, (2) real-time interaction, and (3) precise 3D technology to locate virtual and physical objects. In short, AR is the integration of virtual objects into real reality through instruments, which enriches scenes of reality, promotes real-time interaction, and allows users to obtain immediate feedback [4].

In education, AR has gained the attention of many researchers in teaching applications. In particular, the New Media Alliance of America, which released the "2017 Horizon Report" pointed out that maker space, analytical technology, artificial intelligence, robotics, and virtual realization affect the development of basic education in the next five years. Many studies have been carried out on the potential and trend of AR in teaching. AR as a computer-aided tool has a considerable and comprehensive impact on learning [5]. Abdüsselam pointed out that AR technology realizes the visualization of the magnetic field and helps concretize the object for teaching demonstration in physics courses [6]. Students learn through the 3D perspective in AR to strengthen cognitive content and enhance procedural operations. Furthermore, AR technology in interactive learning education enhances participation and motivation by making a vivid and interesting integration of text, sound, pictures, web pages with subject knowledge [7]. AR technology reduces the drawbacks of education. In other words, it helps solve the problems of non-interactive traditional learning, lack of sense, interactivity of participation, and involvement in the design of teaching materials.

Related Works

There are various teaching tools with AR in the market, such as NEOBEAR Pocket Zoo 3D animals AR stereo cards. It shows the different relationships between animals in the zoo and the ecological environment by integrating AR into cards. The research results showed that it provided students with an understanding of three-dimensional images of animals and increased their enthusiasm and ability to learn and explore. However, it cannot attract senior students to repeatedly use and keep using for a long time. AR can be used with books to transform the original text into an animated form. It offers a personal firsthand experience and attention. The currently published book on AR is "Augmented Reality flipping applied to science education applied to high school textbooks" by Professor Qiu Meihong of National Taiwan Normal University. It includes topics such as basic biology, elective biology, basic chemistry, elective chemistry, basic physics, and geography which aim to prove students' understanding of the subjects and interests in science learning. AR technology has been applied in a real-time translation APP. For example, the mobile game Pokémon GO by Niantic has a large number of players and shows the charm of AR. The Pokémon GO requires users to walk outdoors to obtain rewards. The research result of this study shows that teaching tool with AR have a significant improvement in the learning motivation and effectiveness of students with autism [8].

Design Method

There is not much research and development of AR technology for educational content for elementary school learning. In the "Outline of the Twelve-Year National Basic Education Course" in Taiwan (2018), the scientific learning methods in natural sciences should start from stimulating students' curiosity and willingness to learn and guide them to conduct active exploration, experimental operations, and diverse learning based on their experience. Students become to have core knowledge, inquiry practice skills, scientific argumentation, and communication skills. However, most students only learn in the classroom using passive tools and are unable to approach the natural environment through self-exploration. To meet the needs of learning and practical design theories, this research adopted a design method to develop teaching tool. The design process was divided into five stages: emphasize, define, idealize, prototype-make, and test. (Fig. 1) Therefore, the process started from background research, investigation to user understanding for confirming the design requirements and summarizing ideas, then drawing the ideas to implement.

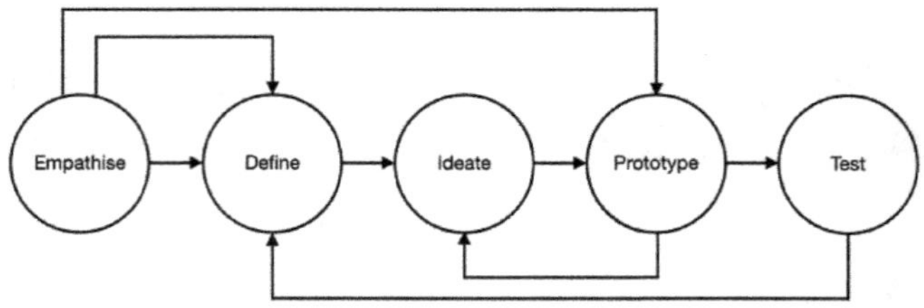

Fig. 1 Design process.

Design and Development

This study applied AR to the subject learning of "Environmental Biological Exploration System" with mobile devices. The main learning tasks for basic biological sciences include "environmental exploration", "biosignature", "biologic behavior", "disease prevention", and "implementation of environmental sanitation". These are from representative research and development results of the new era molding project designed by flipped learning materials of biological science in elementary schools. Through 3D modeling and AR technology, the teaching tool solve the problems of the insufficiency of accurately biological features and re-strengthen the geographical clues of the biological environment. They combine flipped learning to anchor point teaching, exploratory learning, game learning, practical operation, and online sharing. All are breakthroughs from the traditional one-way teaching. They also combine the concepts and technologies to an exploratory teaching plan, help students complete the learning by combining practical actions such as cleaning up the environment physically.

The biological science aid demonstrated the breeding process of the mosquitoes in 3D animation. Three stages of eggs, larvae, and pupae were designed in the interactive tool. For example, the "egg" could be learned by the following: (1) "color touch label" on the top was used to scan and bring out teaching plans and 3D animation contents, (2) the main double-layer construction of teaching kit box allows students to activate the sensor for showing how the water rising reveals the mosquito eggs on the shore and they are soaked for incubation, and (3) when the activation sensor is operated, the signal is transmitted to the database, then the information is delivered by the digital carrier. At the same time, the teaching plan with animation film fragments, text, and special images of the "eggs" on the screen. Teachers could place the tool next to the gutter or standing water on the campus. The content of larvae and pupae were included in the same design.

The tool with the existing AR teaching tool on the market provides diversity of science education teaching materials. The survey of previous research related to AR and education showed all teaching tools were mainly given to students at grade K7 and above. There is little research on AR textbooks for elementary school students. Especially for teaching tools on dengue fever, there are no similar teaching materials.

Thus, this tool provides a new way of teaching about dengue mosquitoes [9]. The teaching process is offered by teachers on their campus. Students must use an APP to do online learning tasks and specific clues or missions. They explore and learn biological sciences through a game-like interaction for practical action and learning effectiveness (Fig.2).

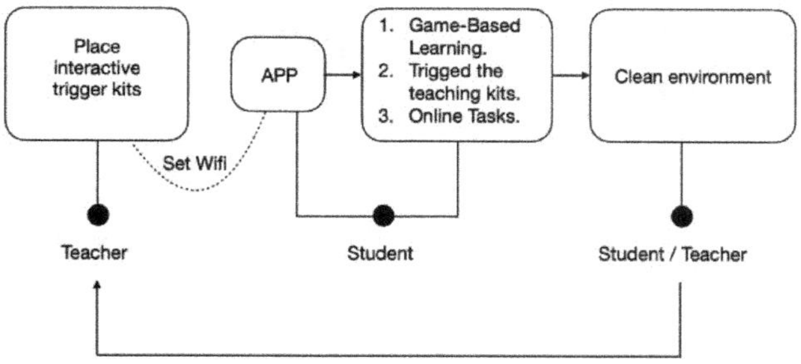

Fig. 2 Teaching Process.

This design enhances students' observation ability and increases their interest in learning in biology education.

Conclusion

The new tool enhances the learning ability of students such as observation on campus and increases their interest in biology education. The purpose of improving the teaching efficiency of biological sciences in elementary schools can be fulfilled. Through AR technology, students transform passive learning into active learning. The ultimate goal is to improve the ability of flexible learning which corresponds to the campus environment. The new tool provides teachers with a high degree of autonomy in biology education and diversified and digitized materials. It also enhances environmental awareness and makes learning interest and confidence.

Acknowledgements

The study is part of an ongoing research project (MOST 108-2511-H-218 -005 -MY2) funded by Ministry of Science and Technology, Taiwan.

References

[1] J.L. Bishop & V. Matthew, The Flipped Classroom: A Survey of the Research, American Society for Engineering Education, 2013.

[2] J. Carmigniani, B. Furht, M. Anisetti, P. Ceravolo,E. Damiani, M. Ivkovic, Augmented Reality Technologies, Systems and Applications. Multimed Tools Appl. 51, 2011, pp. 341–377.

[3] U. Akira, M. Paul, T. Haruo & K. Fumio, Investigation of Errors in Perception of Stereoscopically Presented Virtual Object Locations in Real Display Space,October 1, 1994,38 issue: 4. pp. 250-254.

[4] R.Azuma, A Survey of Augmented Reality, In Presence: Teleoperators and Virtual Environments-6, August, 1997,pp. 355-385.

[5] J.Delello, Insights from Pre-service teachers Using Science-based Augmented Reality, Computers in Education Journal, 2014, pp.1,295-311

[6] S. Mustafa & K. Hasan, The Effect of Using Augmented Reality and Sensing Technology to Teach Magnetism in High School Physics Technology, Pedagogy and Education, 2020, 29:4, pp. 407-424.

[7] Di Serio, Á., Ibáñez, M.B. & Kloos, C.D. ,Impact of an Augmented Reality System on Students' Motivation for a Visual Art Course, Computers & Education, Elsevier Ltd, November 10, 2013, 68, pp. 586-596.

[8] C. Pin-Fang, The Study of the Effect of Applied Augmented Reality Teaching Materials on Autistic Students, 2017.

[9] M. kcayir,G. kcayir., H.M.Pektas, & M A.Ocak, Augmented Reality in Science Laboratories: The Effects of Augmented Reality on University Students' Laboratory Skills and Attitudes Toward Science Laboratories, Computers in Human Behavior,2016, 57, pp. 334-342.

https://doi.org/10.1142/9789811238727_0026

Design and Research of Interactive Storytelling in Children's Digital Picture Books

Nan Zhang, Jun He*, Jing Lin

Xiamen Academy of Arts & Design Fuzhou University, Xiamen, China
*Corresponding Author Email: dr.hejun@qq.com

Abstract

With popularization of mobile intelligent terminal equipment, there has been a new method of digital reading provided for children that adopts Multimedia and Human Computer Interaction technology. This paper studied the interactive storytelling in children's digital picture books. Through analyzing the modularization and improving discussion about the feasibility of altering the linear narrative mode, it aimed to enrich the reading mode and increase the usage in children's digital picture books to improve the digital reading experience and emotional communication for children.

Keywords: children's digital picture books, interactive storytelling, reading experience

Introduction

With the rapid development of digital media technology, the types of information have become diversified.Paper books are no longer the main role of the media. The way children obtain information has also changed dramatically. Interesting stories are an indispensable role in children's picture books. Multimedia technology and interactive technology make stories presents in picture books in a new way – interactive storytelling. By means of characteristics of intelligent terminal devices and interactive means, interactive storytelling decompose the stories into modules in the creation. So, children can choose the stories independently while reading, and promote the story development. interactive storytelling which based on digital technology not only enriches the reading and interaction methods of digital picture books, enhances the interest of reading digital picture books, but also helps children to improve their creativity and thinking ability.This paper will explore the feasibility of interactive storytelling in children digital picture book.

Features of Children's Digital Picture Book

A. Current situation of children digital picture book

Children's picture books convey information mainly dominated by pictures and supplemented by texts. The vivid and interesting stories that are composed of pictures and texts create a relaxed and pleasant reading for children, foster their interest in learning and provide conditions for children to read, think and imagine. With some limitations, early children's picture books use paper as the medium and have simple stories, which causes a decrease in interest and low interaction after = reading.

With development and popularization of mobile intelligent terminal equipment, digital products have been popularized among people of all ages, thus children's digital picture books have evolved. Based on the fact that all over the world importance is attached to children's digital literacy education and the application of digital interactive learning, children's digital picture books gradually become a new way to read picture books. At the same time, in order to meet the needs of the times and the market, mobile intelligent terminal devices are used as medium to produce digital drawing books for children endlessly. But there are many similarities and differences in the design of content and interaction modes, such as clicking, stroking and other interactive modes, which would be a lack of differences to stimulate children's vision, hearing and touch. To satisfy the expectations and needs of children and parents for children's digital picture books, children's digital picture books need to be diversified in order to have a huge potential.

B. Features of children's digital picture books

The medium of the books has changed from traditional paper media to mobile intelligent terminal devices. On the basis of traditional reading forms, books have become an interactive media by using multimedia elements such as sounds, animation, special effects and so on. Based on the features of the carrier, the books have the following features.

(i) Diversity of choices: Under the background of new media, the reading of children's picture books is no longer restricted by traditional ones. Children can freely choose picture books from various digital platforms and would not miss their favorite ones due to limitation of resources, time or space.

v(ii) Interaction: The most obvious feature of children's digital picture books is interaction. Unlike electronic picture books, digital picture books are not storage boxes of traditional children's picture books. The books are also different from the way that children's picture books play presentations automatically on TV. It can produce interactive behaviors when children are reading by multimedia technology and interactive technology. For example, clicking the small games related to the stories in the picture books, children can experience immersive reading, which is good to better understand the content of picture books for children.

(iii) Interesting: Compared with children's picture books in other mediums, children's digital picture books greatly enrich the form of story expression, enhance interactive experience, and bring better reading experience and emotional communication for children.

Concept of Interactive Storytelling

A. Features of interactive storytelling

With rapid development of science and technology, traditional literature, animation and films and television works are constantly seeking breakthroughs in content and presentation form. Users are increasingly pursuing the senses of substitution and immersion experience when they are reading and watching movies. Interactive storytelling emerges as the times require.

Interactive experience is the core of interactive digital products. In the narrative settings of traditional literature, animation, film and television works, users can only passively accept the fixed plots and experience a single linear reading mode. Interactive storytelling works bring users a new way of reading. By reorganizing the plot modules, users can freely choose the stories and influence the outcome. (Fig. 1) This interactive mode allows users to change from spectators to story participants and promoters, to participate in the construction of follow-up development, and to have more dominance rights and free space.

Another feature of interactive storytelling is immersion. Traditional narrative works often require users to integrate themselves into the stories through imagination, so as to stimulate emotions and achieve resonance effect. Interactive storytelling works to create a visual, audible and interactive virtual world for readers or viewers. Users choose their own directions in the stories, dominate the plots, have emotional communication and immersive experience from their hearts and get the feeling of "being in the situation".

From the above points of view, interactive storytelling allows users to participate and influence the development of stories by interacting with the plot and bringing users an immersive experience like being in the situation. It has a great potential to apply to children's digital picture books.

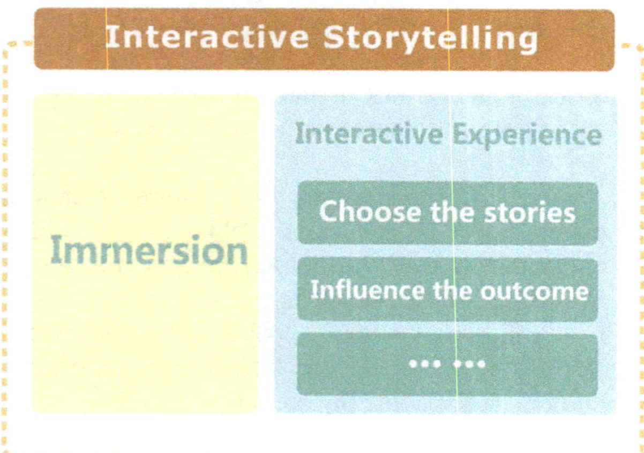

Fig. 1 Features of interactive storytelling

B. Application of interactive storytelling

Interactive storytelling is widely used in games and interactive movies. At the end of last year, the British drama *Black Mirror* launched the Christmas story *Black Mirror: Bandersnatch*. The application of interactive storytelling in film and television has led to hot discussion, which became a hot topic. The replaying rate of the Chinese interactive drama *The Origin of Buddha Head in the Bureau of Antiquities* exceeded 25% in five days, which showed the audience's strong interest in interactive storytelling. In interactive scenario games that are dominated by stories, designers write modular texts and animation films. When a particular scenario is going on, players can make their own choices to promote the scenarios. Different choices will lead to different scenario trends and different endings. For example, in the interactive movie game *Detroit: Changed Person*, there are three characters for players to choose. The three different storylines lead to different endings. There are also a lot of scenario options in the game, in which players need to make choices constantly and explore different worlds by selecting different routes. The selected interactive storytelling avoids the discomfort caused by the designer's original mode of thinking, improves the sense of substitution and immersion, and gives players more freedom to play.

Design Methods of Interactive Storytelling in Children's Digital Picture Book

A. User demand

The readers of children's digital picture books are preschool children. This group has its own features and particularities. Preschool age is an important period for development of children's thinking, when children's basic abilities, intelligence and emotional quotient are formed at this stage. Preschool children know the world through hands. Reading books is like playing with toys for them, and their creative thinking is active and psychological plasticity is great. They are curious about new things, eager to explore, willing to imagine and keen on raising questions, thinking and studying. Therefore, there is a great development space for preschool children's thinking. Their thinking is concrete. The combined audio-visual reading form makes reading simple, easy to accept and understand. Interactive storytelling can meet children's sensory needs of realizing the world by touch, arouse their interest in reading and help preschool children develop creative thinking.

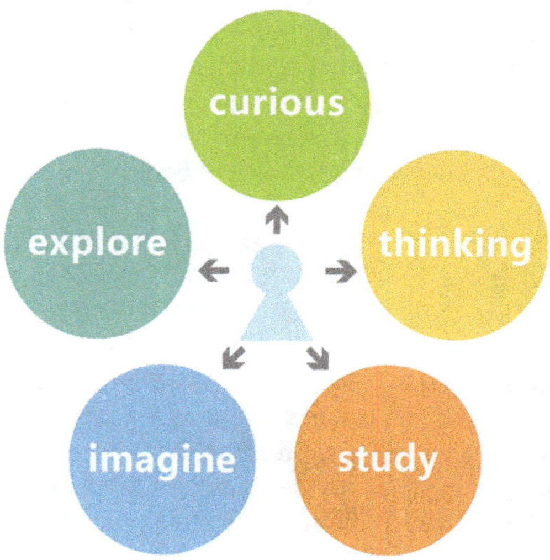

Fig. 2 User demand

B. Design of story modularization

Interactive storytelling works adopt the non-linear narrative mode. Unlike the linear mode, interactive storytelling works have multiple story development modes, and can lead to the same ending or different endings. In the interactive storytelling design of children's digital picture books, the stories of picture books are decomposed into various event modules or individual story module. The modules are recombined according to the stories, themes and elements of the picture books, which can be selected as the relevant points, turning points or the resulting endings to promote the stories. In reading picture books, whether it is the roles of the picture books, story development or ending is a story module. It provides children with interactive choices in the process of reading. There will be two or more story module choices, which can form different non-linear narrative structures. There are three typical non-linear narrative structures.

a. Tree-shaped structure

In the tree-shaped structure non-linear narrative mode, stories can be extended infinitely with the possibility of story development, and the story module is chosen according to children's interest in the development of the story, so as to promote the development of story. The story development of the tree narrative structure is straightforward, and there will be no cross-repetition. This structure enables children to read repeatedly, discover every different ending and improve children's interest in reading and encourages repeated reading of the children's digital picture books. (Fig. 3)

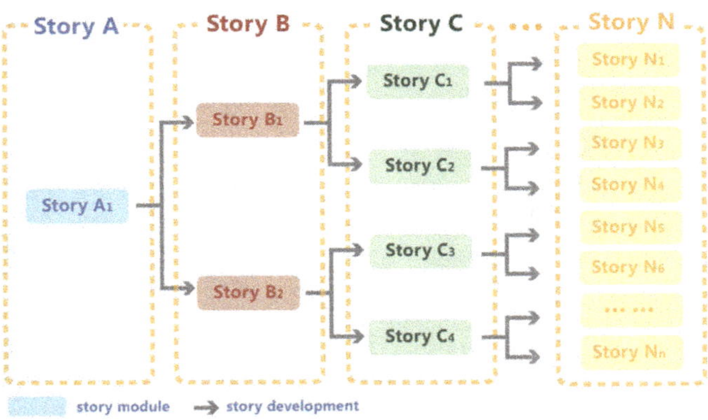

Fig. 3 Tree-shaped structure

b. Parallel structure

Similar to the linear narrative mode, the parallel narrative structure chooses different role modules. After experiencing different stories, it ultimately leads to the same ending. Such a narrative structure ensures the narrative integrity of the picture book stories, retains the interaction in interactive storytelling and gives children the right to choose. At the same time, it controls the direction and the end of stories, which is suitable for the children's digital picture books with clear educational significance. (Fig. 4)

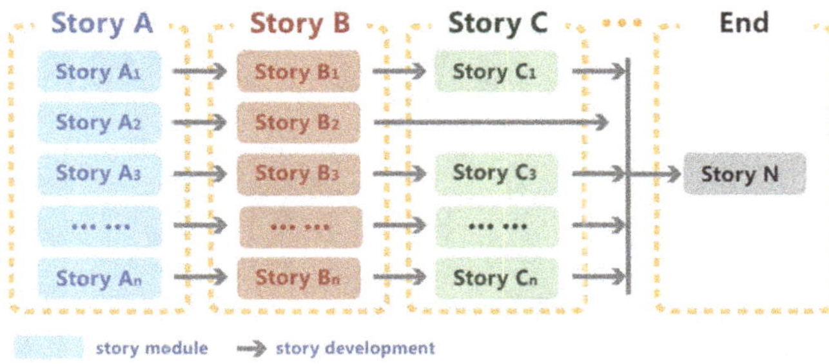

Fig. 4 Parallel structure

c. Fragmentary structure

Fragmentary structure has no fixed sequence of time and space. Children can combine story modules on their own and form different stories. The books with such a structure have no exact requirements for story development and the final expression themes. The books bring more interesting reading experience to children, which is conducive to develop their divergent thinking and imagination. (Fig. 5)

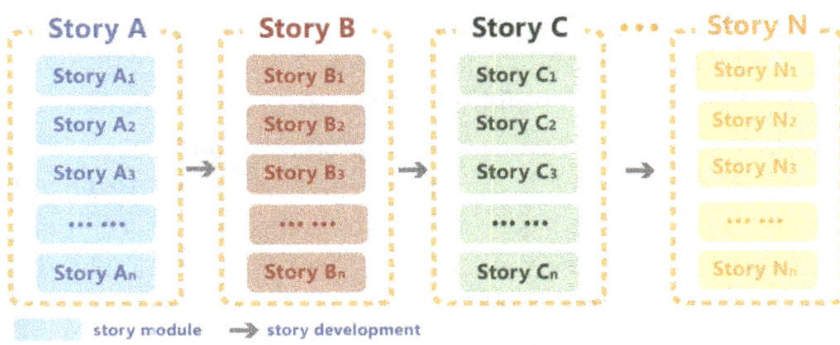

Fig. 5 Fragmentary structure

C. Analysis of reading experiences

Children's digital picture books pay more attention to children's behavioral and psychological needs, improving the interaction of picture books through interactive storytelling, optimizing and upgrading the reading experience of picture books. After interactive storytelling are integrated into children's digital picture books, it realizes more forms of interaction. Each reading choice brings a different reading experience, which makes story form of picture books dull and singular no longer. The non-linear narrative structure makes the contents of picture books colorful and more exciting. New contents will be produced after children make different choices. Each reading can experience a different story, which prolongs the timeliness of reading picture books and improves the repeated reading of the books. On the premise of guaranteeing the integrity of picture books' stories, it makes children's digital picture books more interesting, stimulates children's strong interest in reading /learning and satisfies children's participation and enthusiasm to a certain extent.

Interactive storytelling gives children the optional combination and play-based interactive mode. It brings children immersive experience and emotional experience when they are reading picture books and improves children's concentration, which is good to develop children's creative thinking and divergent thinking and improve their abilities to read, think and imagine (Fig. 6).

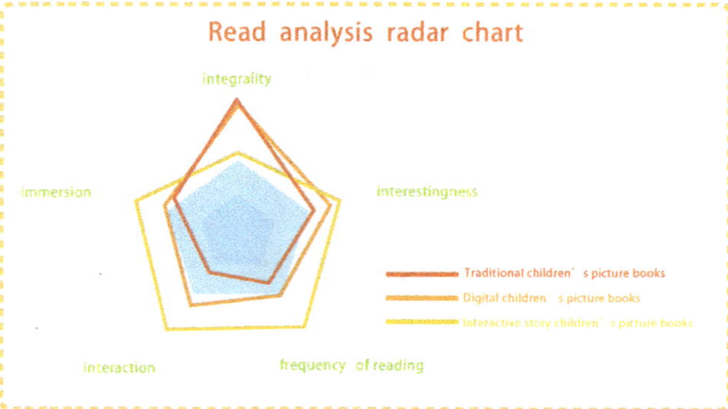

Fig. 6 Read analysis radar chart

Conclusion

By studying the interactive storytelling design process of children's digital picture books and analyzing the design methods of interactive storytelling, this paper hopes to improve the interestingness and interaction of children's digital picture books and develop a diversified narrative mode to meet children's reading needs. With the popularization of mobile intelligent terminal devices and the rapid development of the digital era, children's digital picture books are fast-emerging. Children's digital picture books have very broad prospects for development and great potential for development. On the basis of children's digital picture books, this paper analyses the modularization of the stories, changes to the original linear narrative modes, and forms a picture book narrative mode under free choice so that children can actively participate in the development of the stories and promote the development of stories. Meanwhile, ending of stories is uncertain and mysterious. It can stimulate children's curiosity and provide them with more open, freer, more interactive way of reading picture books. Children can get an emotional experience and sense of achievement in the process of participating in the development of stories. Each reading provides children with a different experience, develops their perceptual thinking and logical thinking, so that children can feel the joy of reading in different scenarios. Repeated reading of the children's digital picture books is increased and the life cycle of the books is prolonged.

References

[1] Luo Haotian, Research on Interactive Design of Children's Digital Picture Book. Jiangnan University, 2014

[2] Yan Junhu, Study on the Narrative Model of Video Game. Chongqing University, 2014

[3] J.Huang Lin, Xu Xingbiao, N*omadic Narration from Multi-choice Perspective: Narrative Model and Characteristics of Interactive Films in the Digital Media Age*. National Art Research, 2013.

[4] Jia Yunpeng, Xiao Mengxue, *Interaction and Interaction Interface of Films.* Research Topic on Future Image Technology and Impact Creation", 2016

[5] Sheng Yinyi, Hu Xinyi, *Research on Design Characteristics of Children's Interactive Picture Book in Digital Age.* Decoration, 2016

[6] Guo Shuxian, Analysis on Advantages and disadvantages of paper and Integration Development on Electronic Books in the Context of New Media. China National Expo, 2018

[7] Zhao Shuang, *Orff's Music Teaching Method for the Development of Preschool Children's Thinking.*. Shandong University, 2014

[8] Betty Sargeant, What is an ebook? What is a Book App? And Why Should We Care? An Analysis of Contemporary Digi*tal Picture Books,* Children's Literature in Education, 2015

[9] Fred Charles, *From computer games to interactive stories: interactive storytelling,* The Electronic Library, 2013

[10] C. Stapleton, C. Hughes, *Interactive imagination: Tapping the emotions through interactive story for compelling simulations,* IEEE Computer Graphics and Applications, 2003

https://doi.org/10.1142/9789811238727_0027

Design Method of the Form of Fantasy Game Characters

Kai Gao, Shuai Zheng*, Dong Lyeor Lee, Dong Yeop Lee, Hai Biao Huang

Kongju National University, South Korea
*Corresponding Author Email: zhengshuai93@naver.com

Abstract

The term "fantasy" in games may refer to a set of virtual magic worlds created by a designer or his or her team, and game characters generally are abnormal figures with human characteristics. These enable players to experience the joys that real life cannot offer for they incorporate fantastical connotations and surreal elements. In recent years, fantasy games thrive rapidly, as a large number of classic online games, including *World of Warcraft*, *League of Legends* and Aion Online, gaining popularity among numerous players with its great imaginary world. For a game, characters are the soul of the whole game and the visual focus of the players, and they can even directly influence game experience. Hence, the design of characters is a top priority in game design, but there are a lot of types of characters of fantasy games. All characters need to be designed by creators on their own. By analyzing a multitude of cases, the author tries to review from imagination-directed design thinking of creators, and constructs a design flow and method for the form of fantasy game characters.

Keywords: fantasy games, game character design, element synthesis

Introduction

Fantasy games are digital games with a fictional magic world of spiritual things with nonscientific interpretations as the arena and non-real images with humanity as objects, and fictional plots as the content. With rapid growth of digital entertainment technology in recent years, a character in a game is the form of existence of a player in a virtual world. They exist in entire developing process of the game, promoting the plot developments and subjective consciousness of players as an indispensable element of game progression developments [1].

Characteristics of Characters in Fantasy Games

Characters in fantasy games own supernatural power. Here supernatural power means all magic powers existing in legends and myths that science cannot explain or extraordinary talents. It includes witchcraft, magic arts, sorcery, summoning, invisibility, healing, and so forth.

Fantasy game characters are different from reality and exaggerated. Another feature of the magic game styling is "from reality, different from reality." In the design process, some materials are referenced from the reality and historical documents and are added as design elements in the character styling for exaggeration. For example, the character's body features, costume props, and other styles are exaggerated. Exaggeration processing can also play a role in strengthening the original intention of the design [2].

Design Flow of Fantasy Game Characters

Fantasy games are video games with a fictional magic world of supernatural things with nonscientific interpretations as the arena and non-real images with humanity as objects, and fictional plots as the content. With the rapid growth of digital entertainment technology in recent years, many video games on PC-based and household console have attracted countless game enthusiasts with their bold imagination, winding plots and gorgeous visual effect, allowing the video game industry to become a new rising force that thrives. In this febrile game development industry, fantasy themes such as fantasy and mythology become the first choices for game developers owing to their absolute advantages in geographical condition and fantasy games represented by occidental mythology. Oriental Xianxia have dominated the domestic game market and have become the most vital type of game in the game industry.

Generally, in mainstream European and American realistic and fantastical games, men are tall and strong musclemen, heroes are strong and robust, while women are normally plump and beautiful. Psychologically, such routine design can satisfy people's wish to realize their dreams in the virtual world. In fantasy games, except normal and healthy characters, there are lots of abnormal human and monsters, to give players different game experience. In fantasy games, there are many characters with multiple attributes as well as human, animals, and plants in reality. For instance, MOBA online game the *League of Legends*, which was developed by American company Riot Games and operated by mainland Chinese company Tencent Games, there are over a hundred distinctive heroes, such as human, beast and alien. Various kinds of heroes present us with a whole new magic world. For another example, the *World of Warcraft* produced by famous game company Blizzard Entertainment has designed 13 races including night elf, human, orc, undead, troll, tauren, and pandaren since it was released, whose appearance and style are different. However, it is characters non-existing in the real world that add more magic color to the games [3].

But the design of these characters is the greatest challenge for the imagination of designers. In human thinking, left brain tends to reason, such as logic, language, and analysis, while the right brain tends to sensibilities, such as painting, creativity, and emotion. Generally, the thinking process of a character design is going on both left brain and right brain simultaneously to get an image. As for how to design a fantasy character that does not exist in reality and make those who see it experience expected sensory stimuli, the author believes that we may symbolize the objects in real life and design more fantasy game characters by shaping and combining forms, costumes, and personality (see Fig. 1).

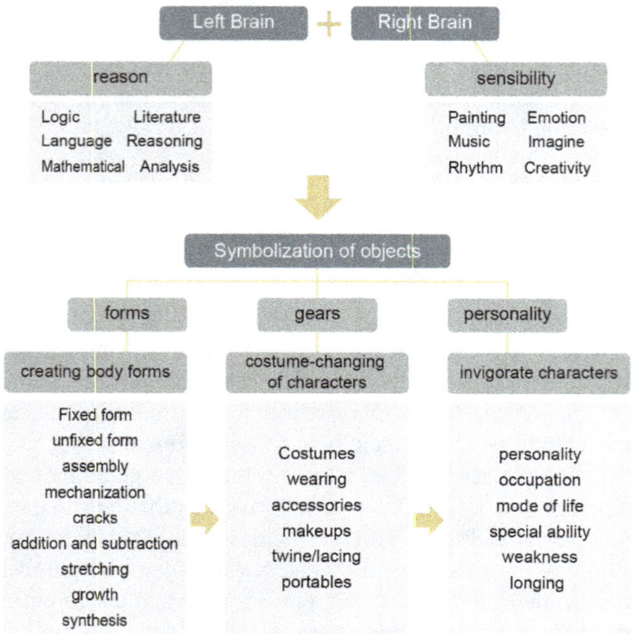

Fig. 1 Design flowchart.

Design Method for Fantasy Game Characters

Game character designers can refer to the setting of historical background for characters in the process of designing. For example, some mythical creatures in myths, but fantasy games have an extremely wide range of characters, which more require the independent design of designers. But design with imagination alone is a tough thing, no matter how outstanding a designer is [4].

In fact, we can symbolize all articles when designing game characters. We divide playthings of the articles into two types-living creature and the lifeless. Living creatures include human, mammals, birds, reptiles, amphibians, fishes, insects, plants and so on while the lifeless include machines, architectures, props, puppets, elements, etc. We name them A, B, C, D, E...as basic types of body. Then, we divided different types of body into components. For example, human can be broken down into head, neck, trunk, arms, legs and so forth, while birds are broken down into wings, tails, feathers and so on. They are marked as A_1, A_2, A_3, A_4...or more detailed marks. In this way we can assemble these basic types of body or components, for example, a combination of human and bird is A+C, or a combination of human and mammal with a bird's wings, which is A+B+C_3, and so forth. In this way, we can form an infinite number of combinations and create interesting figures beyond imagination (shown in Table I).

TABLE I
CATEGORY TABLE FOR OBJECTS

	Used as a base body type	Components that are grouped together on the body
Living beings	A.Human	A_1Head, A_2Neck, A_3Torso, A_4Arm, A_5Leg, A_6Feet...
	B.Mammals	B_1Horn, B_2Ears, B_3Eyes, B_4Teeth, B_5Tail, B_6Skin...
	C.Birds	C_1Eyes, C_2Mouth, C_3Wings, C_4Tail, C_5Feathers...
	D.Crawling Class	D_1Horn, D_2Teeth, D_3Tail, D_4Claws, D_5Leather, D_6Pliers...
	E.Amphibian	E_1Eyes, E_2Tongue, E_3Claws, E_4Tail, E_5Skin...
	F.Fish	F_1Eyes, F_2Tail, F_3Leather, F_4Teeth...
	G.Insect	G_1Tentacles, G_2Eyes, G_3Teeth, G_4Tongue, G_5Wings
	H.Plants	H_1Root, H_2Neck, H_3Leaves, H_4veins, H_5Flowered...
Inanimate body	I.mechanical	I_1Screws, I_2Battery, I_3Wire, I_4Gear...
	J.Building	J_1Structure, J_2Texture...
	K.Dummy	K_1Nose, K_2Cape, K_3Ear, K_4Eyes, K_5Body...
	L.Elements	L_1Fire, L_2Electricity, L_3Water...
	M.Props	...
	...	...

A. Forms of characters

The so-called form is body form or structure of a character. We can take any bodies and divide them into parts, creating new living creatures through synthesis. For instance, a flyable castle or stone that can talk, personating, or animalizing these lifeless articles to create images.

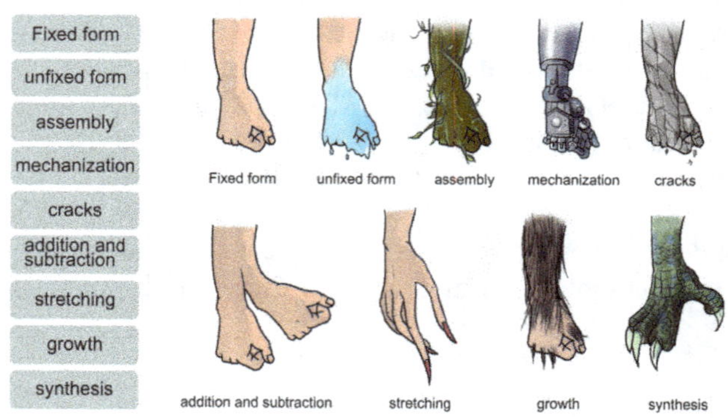

Fig. 2 Changes in nine forms.

First of all, there are various supernatural phenomena with existing physical law in a fantasy. Fantasy game characters require breakthroughs more, even if we have learned the physical form and structure of all kinds of creatures. However, characters are not changeless in fantasy games. So more importantly we need to break fixed ideas to change body structure. When the character is human, we will break the human down into the upper part of the body and the lower part, more specifically, head, neck, trunk, arms, waist, legs, and so on. Then we change decomposed parts morphologically. For instance, a fixed form, namely standard, like biological bodies in the real world are changed to un fixed form, which is made up of matters such as water or silt. Assembling, generating a form by assembling heterogeneous materials like batten and cirrus. Then we mechanize the physical form and add some cracks to the basic form. Then we add or subtract body parts. Some body parts are stretched for growth and growing other matters on the body. Then we synthesize with a part of another biological body (as shown in Fig. 2).

TABLE II
CLASSIFICATION TABLE

A. Human	Male/female (infant, toddler, child, teen, teen, middle-aged, old)
B. Mammals	Dogs, rabbits, monkeys,foxes, bears, pandas, pigs, elephants, giraffes, horses, sheep, leopards, lions, bats, kangaroos, seals, whales...
C. Birds	Eagles, swans, pigeons, swallows, crows, owls, chickens, seagulls, penguins, cranes, ducks, peacocks...
D. Crawling Class	Snakes, lizard, Gecko, Chameleon, turtle, crocodile...
E. Amphibian	Frog, Newt
F. Fish life in water	Shark, puffer fish, goldfish, tropical fish, octopus, squid, crabs, crayfish, shellfish, jellyfish, coral...
G. Insect Invertebrates	Butterflies, bees, dragonflies, flies, spiders, lizards, Mantis, beetle, snails, earthworms...
H. Plants Fruit/Vegetable	Tulip, Rose, mushroom, cactus, cherry tree, fir, apple, pumpkin...
I. mechanical	gears, light bulbs, clocks, telephones, computers, trams, cars, bicycles, airplanes, rockets, spacecraft...
J. Building	Castles, towers, apartments, dwellings, spiral stairs, factories...
K. Dummy	Clown, Tumbler, puppet, Straw Doll, Scarecrow, rag doll
L. Elements	Moon, stars, earth, clouds, rain, fire, water, ice, snow, rock, smoke, electricity, gold, copper, iron...
M. Props	Weapons, musical instruments, medical appliances, makeup props, magic props, cooking utensils...
...	...

This table is a list of objects in the universe that are roughly sorted into categories, which are listed as things that are often used in character design, and of course, items also can use that are not listed in the table.

The design of fantasy game character mostly uses synthesis, as synthesizing human and animal, human and plant, and so on to create the images of new beasts and sub-humans. There are two kinds of synthesis. One is the synthesis of different species, while the other is the synthesis of species and components.

We categorized all objects in the universe and listed them in a table. On this basis, we can synthesize different species to create the body of characters. New fantasy characters are generated through combinations. Moreover, the process of choosing types can be more concrete. For instance, from human beings, we can choose man, woman, kid or old person, while from mammalians we can choose cat, dog, or monkey as the physical basis. Such further detailed symbols make the process of designing characters more orderly (shown in Table II).

For instance, Zyra, the Rise of the Thorns in the *League of Legends*, is a synthesis of human and plant, namely A+H mentioned in the above table, while werewolf in the *World of Warcraft* is a synthesis of mammal and human, namely A+B (see Fig. 3).

Fig. 3 Zyra (*League of Legends*), werewolf (*World of Warcraft*), Draenei (*World of Warcraft*).

The synthesis of species and components is decomposing the basic types of the body into components and then combining them on the body. For instance, human grows the animal's tail, namely $A+B_5$, a fish grows on human feet, namely $F+A_6$, while stone has eyes, namely $L+B_3$. Draenei in the game *World of Warcraft* is designed by adding animal's horns, elf's ears, and so on (see Fig. 3). Taking human and components as an example, we can take humans as the basic form and then make a single or multiple combination of human and cases like ox's horn, cat's eyes, pig's nose, elephant's ears, and rabbit's mouth, to form a whole new fantasy character (as shown in Fig. 4).

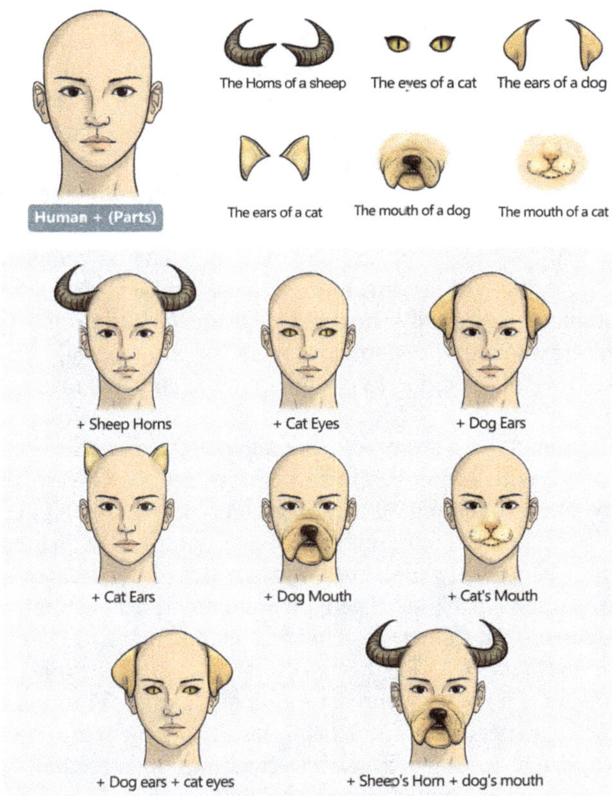

Fig. 4 Human+ (Parts).

B. Gears of characters

We get a naked form like a newborn baby from the above creation of physical form. On this basis, we can put any costumes and props in character. Costumes and props of game characters are an important part in a game, for players may acquire a feeling of freshness and a sense of joy from game experience by changing costumes and props. We can design for a character in depth from head to foot by designing costumes, wearing/covering, ornament, makeup, twine/lacing, and the way of carrying. A character may wear a swimwear, formal dress or uniform; or wear a hat, glasses, gloves and more; or wear necklace, bracelets, earrings and other accessories; or wear eye shadow, nail polish, tattoo and other makeups; or tie to bandages, ropes, iron chain and so on; or carry weapon, musical instrument, magic items and the like (as shown in Fig. 5).

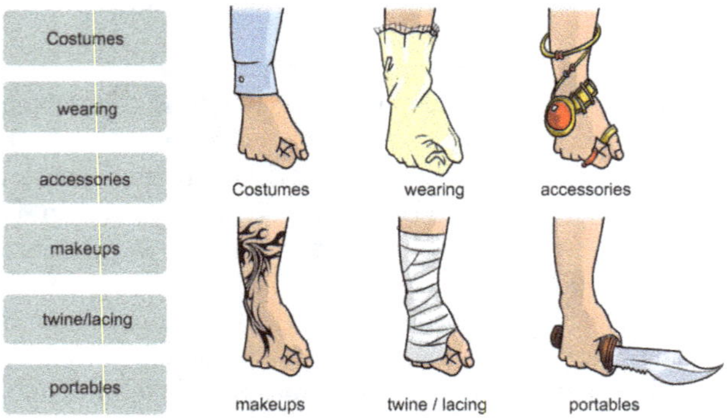

Fig. 5 Six ways of equipment.

C. Personality of characters

Among fantasy game characters, every character has a different personality. They may be an adorable and clever Lolita, or a righteous and brave archer, or a vicious and atrocious monster. Different character designs and settings make the whole character more ethereal. So-called personality is inherent characteristics of a character. Broadly speaking, form, or garment design is also included in the category of personality. This is because one may speculate on personality or occupation of a person even from physical features or costumes. Here, we summarized characterization into six items- personality, occupation, mode of life, special ability, weakness, and longing to invigorate the characters (as shown in Fig. 6).

Personality represents the characteristics of a character in emotion, will, action, and other aspects. He may be irritable, fiery and full of cunning tricks, or lachrymose, mild and cute. While occupation represents the social status of the character, he may be a king, general or a wizard, archer, and hunter, or a master and disciple. Then, we summarized habitats of characters, time slots of activities, eating habits, and other surroundings to define his mode of life, for example, this character is a nocturnal predator living in a cave. Most fantasy game characters have special abilities that living beings do not have, such as transfiguration, cloaking, resurrection, and synthesis. If a character does not have any weakness, this character will be boring, and game players will not experience a sense of superiority derived from the victory in the game. Moreover, characters also need longings. Conflicts come with longings. One may long for money or food, and so on [5].

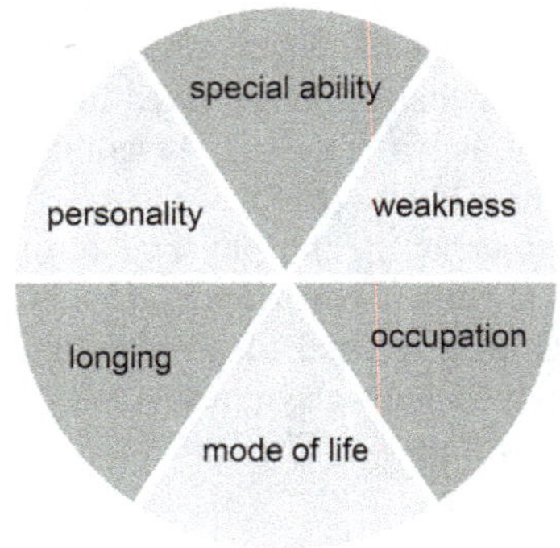

Fig. 6 The hexagonal table of individual character.

Conclusions

In the era of mobile internet, numerous game products emerge constantly and are replaced and updated at a much-too-fast speed. As operating cycle and operating time of fantasy games continuously decrease, fantasy games constantly add and update new characters, skins, and more to help prolong the life of the game to increase the stickiness of players. Although the design of fantasy game characters gives game designers great room for creation, yet aspirations are more likely to dry up in a completely free designing process. Therefore, this study aims to put forward a specific design approach and flow, improving forms, customs, and personality with extraction through symbolization, to guide character designers for sustainable design of fantasy characters. Of course, when designing fantasy game characters, designers should also choose corresponding creative elements according to specific background of the game and by the overall style of this game, thus reaching the goal of sustainable design.

References

[1] Peach Pit, Principles of Game Design, Pearson Education, 2013, pp. 100.

[2] Khaterine Isbinter, Phd, Better Game Character by Design (Pshycological Approach), Morgan Kauffman Publisher, 2006, pp. XVIII.

[3] Wong N., Tang A., Livingston I., Gutwin C., Mandryk R. (2009) Character Sharing in World of Warcraft. In: Wagner I., Tellio 刿 lu H., Balka E., Simone C., Ciolfi L. (eds) ECSCW 2009. Springer, London.

[4] Ernest Adams, Fundamental of Game Design, Third Edition Pearson Education, Inc, 2014, pp. 84.

[5] You, F.: The Creation of Characters that Have or Convey Emotion and Personalities with the Context of a Computer Game. OMSc. Dissertation, University of Bradford, UK (2005).

https://doi.org/10.1142/9789811238727_0028

Discourse Research on the Spread of Animation on We-Media

Ling-Xuan Wang

Xiamen Academy of Arts and Design, Fuzhou University, Xiamen, Fujian, China
Email: zellwlx@sina.com, Tel: +86 15996233625

Abstract

With the development of policies and markets, Chinese animation has transferred from a single film and television market to an interactive space in new media. This is a space containing multiple entities, such as artists, investors, governments, and subcultures, that is, what Bourdieu called "field". Context reflects the rules of the field in discourse activities. So we adopted discourse analysis as a method to investigate animation and related fields, focusing on discourse activities. We collected discourse data by verbal questionnaires and in-depth interviews, searching established topics, evaluation methods, terminology and diversified interests in the context of discourse about animation. The goal is to set up common and stable discourse model and efficient interaction mechanism among subjects in the field. The conclusion benefits commercialization and diversify creation of animated products.

Keywords: animation, discourse, field theory, context

Introduction

As a typical example of digital visual art, animation products are active in public communication and consumption, driven by commercial interests. About animated videos, creation, dissemination, purchasing, watching and comment constitute a social activity space, which include artists, investors, governments and subcultural groups, just as what Bourdieu called "field", and mostly operates in discourse activities, such as propaganda and commentary. In China, comments from individuals or small groups in the field of we-media have become a very important form of discourse. By selecting specific topic and communication techniques, tweets perform universal influence and consumption guidance ability. This is noticed and utilized by business and the administration, by packing their intention as spontaneous commentary behavior from individual media users. Although this refers the balance of discourse ability between subjects in spite of different economic resources, power and status, bad tendency still appears that spontaneous commentary discourse is abused to fool or deceive public, viciously attack rivals.

In the social research based on field theory, it is a typical tendency to make the minority groups with less discourse power speak directly through interviews. In the discourse research on animation, how context influences normalization and understanding of animated videos. We tried to use a unified discourse model to communicate the preliminary design of animation and the evaluation of investors and consumers. In the discourse analysis of animation, in addition to the traditional language analysis and elaboration paradigm, we also learned from protocol analysis to transform recommendation task into design thinking methods.

Methods

A. Design of research

Discourse data of we media was obtained through interviews of animation consumers. In order to collect material in natural ways, we tried to make the respondents' verbal behavior follow the normal way as they did everyday via mobile devices. At the same time, we tried to unify the form and scale of material with the least restricts, to make sure feasibility and the comparability of discourse analysis.

During initial tests, we decided to use voice short message of WeChat instead of selfie video to reduce stress. But still some respondents' recommendation was too short without further interaction.

Finally, the interview is carried out as follows, a task description was provided with a little non-mandatory constraints and guidance. Respondents will receive the following messages:

"*Recommend a movie or television cartoon to friends that have not watched it. send a voice message to make introduction, take your own step and talk freely, only limit length no more than two minutes.*"

First of all, voice message is a common form of daily communication on WeChat platform, so it relieved the pressure of being recorded for interviewees. And also, the voice message can be easily converted into text records in Wechat. Via voice message, interviewees would not expect to get feedback during sending message. The two minutes limit, which seems as max length, in fact guided respondents to control their messages to an appropriate period. Since the maximum of each voicemail message is one minute, most records lasted between 1 to 2 minutes.

B. Process

As the method of discourse data collection is still in experiment, we chose 16 interviewees between 20 and 30 years old, 8 males and 8 females. All interviewees were experienced in watching and consuming animation and related products. In order to distinguish whether the animation education background affect tendency of preference and

TABLE I
ANALYSIS OF MS. XU'S DISCOURSE

Timing	Recorded voices	Keywords	Notes
3s	*In recent years, Chinese animation is also well developed.*	Chinese （Classification, Country of origin）	
12s	*I want to "Amway" you "The King's Avatar", adapted from phenomenal online novel of the same title, by Hudielan in 2017.*	"Amway" (Attitude, Recommendation) Adapted (Serial, Original works)	"Amway" means recommend on Chinese Internet
14s	*"The King's Avatar" is now out of season, then the second season and its OVA version will be online in July this year.*	Out of season, The second season, OVA (Serial, Episode)	
Interval Between Messages			
21s	*Compared with the second season, I personally prefer the style of character painting in the first, for the recognition will be a little higher. In the second season, characters' faces is mostly in "bun style", possibly the reason I don't like.*	Character painting, Bun Style (Picture, Painting style) Prefer (Comparison, Self) Don't like (Attitude, Like (-))	
14s	*Then as adapted from online game novel, its fight is a important part. Then, so I personally think that the fight, and then the fluency of the shots, are not bad.*	Adapted (Serial, Original works) (2nd) Fight (Picture, Motion) (twice) Fluency of the shots (Picture, Shot design) Not bad (Attitude, Praise)	Focusing on quality rather than style

evaluation during discourse behavior, interviewees were divided into two groups (with or without relevant background).

As interviewees' discourse behaviors were conducted in the form of recommendation tasks, we referred to the method of protocol analysis to deal with the collected oral data. Typical protocol analysis aims to the process of accomplishing design tasks and verbal behavior related. We adopted the structure of protocol analysis in order to transform the oral activity of "recommending excellent films" into the thinking of Animation early stage. We focused on highly-frequent words and connections between paragraphs, in order to explain more deeply after structuring the discourse data.

A typical example of interviewee with animation educational background: Ms. Xu, 24 years old, master of digital media arts. Her discourse data recorded and analysis process is as follows:

Timing	Recorded voices	Keywords	Notes
10s	*Then it should have used 2D render. Now, 2D render is common in animation.*	2D render (Quality, Techniques) (twice) Common (Objective)	
10s	*Then I think the best part about "The King's Avatar" is "seiyuu", the seiyuu is very sensational, and very close to the role.*	Best part (Attitude, Outstanding) Seiyuu (Sound, Voice)(twice) Sensational, Close to the role (Perceptual impression, Sense)	Seiyuu is Japanese way of calling voice actor.
Interval Between Messages			
22s	*Now, big novel "IP" adapted as comics or games is a popular trend. As adaptation, according to the original works, restoration is a very important aspect for animated films. I feel that "The King's Avatar" did not bad in promoting "reduction degree".*	IP, Adapted （Serial, Original works) (3rd） Restoration (Perceptual impression, Emotion) (twice) Not bad (Attitude, Praise)	"Reduction degree" is adopted as evaluation
End of interview			

Ms. Xu chose a Chinese animation to recommend, however, she used much descriptions and vocabulary of evaluation from Japan, which are common among animation fans. Due to the educational background of animation, her discourse focused more on quality and technique during recommendation. She gave a special evaluation standard called "degree of restoration" to describe the consistency between adapted animation and original works.

Similar structuring and analysis were carried out for each interviewee's voice recorded. We only did structural coding on the general discourse strategies and organization, ignoring specific cartoon they recommended, to facilitate the unified analysis and evaluation.

ABLE II
MODEL OF DISCOURSE ABOUT ANIMATION

Introduction								
Classification	Story	Character	World view	Picture	Theme	Quality	Serial	Sound
Country of origin Topic Production Age orient	Narration Conflict Touching episode Classic plot Suspense	Gender Age Characteristic Behavior	Rule History	Painting style Shot design Motion	Doctrine Meaning Principle Education Inspiration	Techniques Skill	Original Works Episodes Prequel and sequel Frequency of update Derivative works	Voice Song Music

Evaluation					Comparison
Subjective				Objective	
Preferences	Personal experiences	Perceptual impression	Attitude	Popularity Award Favorable comment Profit, market feedback	Self Similar Contrast
(Same as "Introduction")	Life experiences Filming experiences	Sense Emotion	Like Praise Recommend		

Results

A. Model of discourse

According to the collected discourse materials of recommending cartoons, we classified all relevant information involved, and get the following table.

B. Differences related with animation educational background

Interviewees without animation background are more inclined to recommend cartoons by retelling the story content. Those with animation background prefer to offer recommendation with techniques, quality and emotional impressions.

Interviewees with animation background tend to avoid Japanese TV animation works, which are mostly recommended by the other group.

Interviewees without animation background would use more subjective preferences and personal experience to explain the reasons for recommendation, but the same strategy is less common among those with animation background.

Conclusion and Discussion

(1) The behavior and strategy obtained in this research basically cover the discourse patterns of young animation fans' recommendation of their favorite cartoons. The discourse model is close to the promotion process of animation products in the we-media environment. It also reflects people's thinking process and expectations for excellent animation works.

(2) Interviewees with animation educational background appeared to have potential consideration of "professionalism" about their discourse. It is reflected in the tendency to avoid typical commercial works, especially Japanese TV animations. They also tend to emphasize objective evaluation such as techniques instead of subjective impression. This implies the general value orientation and the discourse power structure in Chinese animation education, which differs animation fans as so called "professional" or "non-professional".

The discourse mode of animation needs to be further improved in larger scale interviews. It also should be tested in relevant contexts such as investment evaluation, political propaganda and art appreciation, so as to form a common discourse model that fits the context of the whole animation field.

References

[1] P. Sarkar, A. Chakrabarti, "A Support for Protocol Analysis for Design Research", *Design Issues*, 2013, 29(4), pp. 70-81.

[2] S. Atoof, "Context from a social semiotic perspective: a discourse analytical study of the children TV show, Bubble Guppies", *Social Semiotics*, 2015, 25(5), pp. 558-577.

[3] A. Pulos, "Confronting Heteronormativity in Online Games: A Critical Discourse Analysis of LGBTQ Sexuality in World of Warcraft", *Game and Culture*, 8(2), pp.77-97.

[4] J. P. Gee, B. Z. Yang translation, *An Introduction to Discourse Analysis: Theory and Method*, Chongqing, China, Chongqing University Press, 2011.

[5] G. Wang, "Dimension. And Film: Media culture field and strategic industry landscape", *Contemporary Cinema*, 2016, 8 pp.140-142.

https://doi.org/10.1142/9789811238727_0029

Establishing a Tea Industry Brand from the *Camellia Formosensis* of Kaohsiung

Chia-Mei Liang

Future College, National Yunlin University of Science and Technology, Yunlin, Taiwan
Email: liangchiamei@gmail.com

Abstract

Since the Japanese colonial period, there have been tracts of mountainous forests that have bred *Camellia formosensis* trees in the Liugui District of Kaohsiung City. These camellia trees are large-scale tree tea trees at mid-elevation levels. The picking completely requires manual climbing of tree trunks or using ladders. At present, most of the land where the camellia trees grow in southern Taiwan is mostly forest owned by the state or reserved by aboriginal people. In the district, most of the tea merchants and pickers maintain the basic raw material supply by renting the hillside land legally from the government. A small number of them are landowners with aboriginal status. After picking, the green tea is sold to tea merchants. At present, Taiwan's *Camellia formosensis* in Liugui District, by the efforts of tea merchants, each has its brand, marketing channels, and commodity markets. However, raw tea is not entirely from the same place of origin. Once the market demand is large, a very small number of tea merchants often mix with low-altitude teas, or other countries' teas, which results in the brand and goodwill of camellia tea fall. This article discusses the process of establishing a tea brand, the production of the story, the packaging of the image, and the design. The natural environment and geographical conditions of production are all important influencing factors. The output is usually inversely proportional to the price. This is a very natural phenomenon. However, once the brand strictly controls the manufacturer's technology and manufacturing procedures through production history, various quality inspections of the origin, the identification and charter system of the government promote. In future, the regional economic activity of the production area and environment of tea farmers are guaranteed to a certain degree, and the development of foreign markets and the establishment of consumer confidence will be more helpful than now.

Keyword: Camellia formosensis, digitize, brand establishment, production history, Taiwanese wild tea

Introduction

In the tea industry, the production process, the skills of tea, tea seats, "Gongfu" tea(A), and tea art are important. This forms the complete tea culture. Taiwan currently does not have an evaluation system and license assessment with cup testers and tea testers who are specialized in the tea. The identification mainly involves the part of the game tea. Among the current domestic teas, such appraisers are recommended by the tea industry improvement field, and there is no special assessment and charter system as a basis. Therefore, this article discusses the current situation and needs of Taiwan's *Camellia formosensis* in three parts, and look forward to the institutionalized and systematic establishment of a unique brand of rural camellia in Taiwan. Establishment of an examination system and professional evaluation certificates such as a digital production system and identification for *Camellia formosensis* are proposed.

Main producing areas of Taiwan *Camellia formosensis*

Camellia grows naturally in the south of the Central Mountain Range, as well as the Sun Moon Lake in the middle. These tea trees belong to the arbor type. Most of the growing environment is between 500-800 meters above sea level. The native tea trees in the mountainous areas of Pingtung even grow at 800-1200 meters above sea level. The tea has a faint fragrance after brewing, and the aroma stays in the mouth for a long time. This is the same as the quality of green tea picked from low-altitude tea gardens planted on flat or hilly land. Very different from fragrance. In 1771, it was recorded in ancient documents that some people in Sun Moon Lake once drank this camellia tea. The taste was special and the color was like pine. It relieves heat, dryness, and headache. It was also published in the newspapers of Kaohsiung in the Japanese era. People in the mountainous area once sold camellia, and most of the tea produced at that time was Assam black tea from Chadingshan. The bitterness of camellia is very high. Bitterness comes from normal internal raw material. The appearance of *Camellia formosensis* has a special feature when compared to other tea species. The leaf surface of *Camellia formosensis* has no fluff, and the two sides of the leaves are convex, with an oval heel leaf shape. Needle-shaped camellia has many buds of the same shape in each position and different tastes.

A. Overview of Taiwan tea species and Camellia formosensis species

There are a total of 14 tea districts in Taiwan from south to north. The southernmost is Port Tea and the northernmost is Beigan Tea from Matsu. Each tea district has its representative tea species, such as Taitung's Red Oolong and black teas of Sun Moon Lake in Nantou. All teas are associated with tea-producing areas. Therefore, Liugui is currently promoting *Camellia formosensis*. Tea leaves are grouped by the production season. The quality of camellia tea in spring is the best. The price of spring tea even reaches 300 to 400 yuan per catty. The price is low in summer.

"Wuyi" was a popular tea tree cultivated by the folk from 1970 to 1980. It is suitable for making fire-prepared tea and roasted heavily. In the past, Tieguanyin also produced Wuyi. Now, Tieguanyin has its independent method to ferment Wuyi. Light roasting is for raw tea, while heavy roasting for ripe tea to make black tea of unique fragrance.

The native tea tree is a large-leaf species. Under the condition of unmanned pruning and natural growth, the average height of trees is 3 to 10 m, and the length of mature leaves reach 10cm. Tannins of large-leaf species are higher, and the small green leafhoppers attract fewer pests. Therefore, the native tea tree has good resistance to diseases and insect pests, good adaptability, and easier to take care of. It is a native tea tree that fits Taiwan's climate and suitable agriculture.

B. Tea picking and tea making

Tea pickers go up the mountain before the sun is irradiated and the leaves are still moist. Before going there, they observe whether there is dew on the leaves. The part of tea picking varies according to the type of tea. Young leaves are usually picked. April to June are busy harvesting months for tea farmers. When the rain falls, the tea trees and the tea buds grow fast. If it is too late to pick, it grows into mature leaves that have more photosynthesis. If too many are picked, it affects the growth of tea trees. Therefore, 80% of young leaves are picked and 20% are for growing. When the number of tea leaves is too small, tea farmers do not pick for allowing tea plants to grow and sprout to increase the amount of tea. Generally, the production of *Camellia formosensis* in Taiwan is limited by the natural environment, the type of hillside, and the altitude. The harvested output of camellia planted by tea farmers, in terms of raw tea, is usually 100 jin which is about 25 jin of dried tea (products of tea leaves).

C. Overview of tea planting agricultural methods

The management methods of Taiwan's tea gardens are divided into four categories. Liugui's camellia mainly adopts wild methods without pesticides or fertilization. The camellia is an arbor-type tea tree species, which is originally adapted to Taiwan's climate and environment. The other two of the four categories are organic farming and customary farming. The customary farming is the terraced field method, which is convenient for picking and pulling tea. The customary method is to care for and manage the tea. For organic tea, organic fertilizers are used. For food safety, they cannot be harvested after a fixed time.

D. Overview of the ingredients and tea making process of Camellia formosensis

Camellia is rich in polyphenols and catechins, which are higher than other teas. Studies have shown that the catechins of camellia are 1.3 times higher than other teas. The tea-making process starts with the picking of the greens, and after the picking, it begins with indoor withering (Fig.1 and Fig.2), tossing (disruption, Fig.1), fermentation, panning (pan-firing), rolling (Fig.3), mass breaking (unravel, Fig.4), drying, package in stages, and making finished products. Camellia is mainly hand-picked by hand, and machine-picked is a common method of conventional farming. A temperature of 250 to 300°C is required to bake the green teas. As the stems are not dried, they need the second baking. For heavier tea flavor, baking three times is necessary. Fully fermented tea, such as black tea, needs a longer baking time.

The meaning of tea art and tea table representative

The meaning of tea art and feasts includes two levels: one is tea making and the other is tea tasting. The former emphasizes how to make a good pot of tea, and the latter focuses on how to enjoy a good pot of tea. In the process of making good tea, the most important part is how to choose tea. Taiwan's tea industry is prosperous. Whether it is non-fermented, semi-fermented or fully-fermented tea, it can be found everywhere. There are many types of tea to choose. Tea-drinking culture is diverse, and different utensils are used for different teas according to whether it is brewing or daily preservation. The way of brewing tea is what most people care about, and it is also the most fascinating place in the development of tea culture for so long.

In the history of traditional Chinese tea culture, tea was for eating not drinking. Tea was added to the dish as a part of the Chinese soup and boiled in porridge. Later, it gradually developed into a form of Leicha. In the Song Dynasty, drinking tea was developed as a tea culture and became a familiar way. Tea making appeared only after the emergence of Ming's pot making method. The good tea should be tasted carefully in an elegant environment. In the Song Dynasty, tea shops appeared, and drinking tea in the Ming Dynasty became diverse, richer, and interesting with artistic forms were added. The tea-making techniques and tea-drinking concepts were developed through the ages and became the tea art and tea feasts in Taiwan today. With the contemporary aesthetics of life, a contemporary Taiwanese tea drinking method that emphasizes beauty and practicality was developed.

Fig. 1 Adjust the thickness of the tea leaves on the bamboo mesh screen according to the weather.

Fig. 2 Observe the dehydration of tea.

Fig. 3 Knead, twist and loosen the tea leaves.

Fig. 4 The last turning and loosening of the tea pile.

Dilemma for tea farmers in southern Taiwan

A. Technical holdings

Raw tea leaves from Camellia trees are at the bottom of the tea industry with the lowest economic value and profit. Usually, the age of tea farmers who have land ownership and traditionally harvest camellia is relatively high, generally in the middle-aged and elderly between the ages of 50–75. Therefore, due to their age, tea farmers are less likely to learn and invest in the production chain of the tea industry. They cannot have all the technologies of a complete production chain. As a result, these tea farmers always stay at the bottom of the production chain.

B. Problem of output and acquisition

Since the output of tea farmers is directly proportional to the land area they own. The larger the land area, the more tea output harvested. However, as the process of tea production is complicated and requires a large space with modern machinery and equipment, it demands a lot of investment.

C. Problem of rapid labor shrinkage

In recent years, Taiwan's birth rate has dropped rapidly, and the original population is aging. A population who relied on camellia tea for their livelihoods is not a small minority. However, the age of tea harvesters continues to increase, and young people do not want high labor works. As a result, the production area of Taiwan's tea is not increasing but declining.

D. Problem of tea blending after tea merchants purchase

Tea farmers cannot create profit from every step of the production process such as packaging and marketing. As the entire tea-making process belongs to a production system, the farmers can trade teas only. Most factories mix the high-altitude Taiwan camellia teas with other teas and sell them under the brand of *Camellia formosensis.*

Discussion and conclusion

Through the respective needs of the production, manufacturing, and sales of native camellia, the establishment of the brand, the enhancement of the digitization of the production history, and the completeness of various certification systems, you can see the correlation between each other through Figure 5.

Establishing brands in the tea industry in Taiwan is usually based on place names and brand stories. As a brand name, a place name has its social responsibilities and risks. The digitization of the production history and the establishment of the system record the growth environment of the tea, all the processes of harvesting and manufacturing, and even the packaging and storage of the products. The information is transparent owing to the establishment of the digital system. The certification system is divided into two parts: the professional certification system and the chartering system of tea quality and origin. Both need to rely on the government's intervention and authorization to handle such a certification system to help private enterprises and regional agricultural development obtain guarantees.

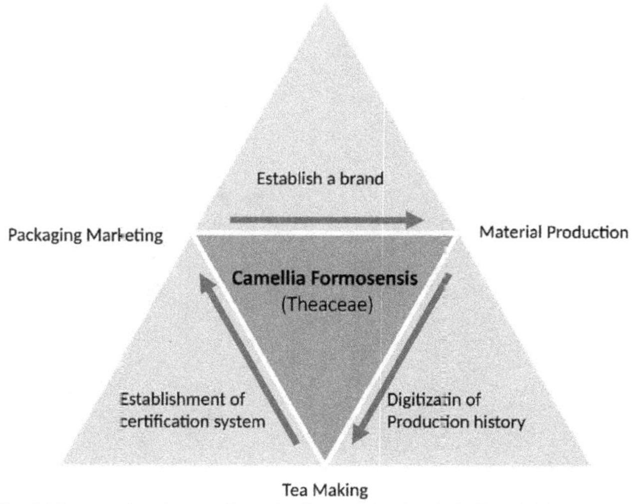

Fig. 5 The production and marketing ecological chain of this research.

References

[1] Mong-Huai Su, Chang-Fu Hsieh, Chih-Hua Tsou. 2009. The Confirmation of Camellia formosensis (Theaceae) as an Independent Species Based on DNA Sequence Analyses. Botanical Studies, 50(4), pp. 477–485.

[2] Hsieh, C. F., L. K. Ling, and K. C. Yang. 1996. Camellia, Theaceae. In D. E. Boufford, C. F. Hsieh, T. C. Huang, H. Ohashi and Y. P. Yang (eds.), Flora of Taiwan, second edition, Vol. 2. Editorial Committee of Flora of Taiwan, Taipei, pp. 662–693.

https://doi.org/10.1142/9789811238727_0030

Discussion on Conversion of Voice into Taste

Tzu-Heng Liu*, and Tsun-Hung Tsai**

Shih Chien University, Taipei City, Taiwan
*Corresponding Author Email: *h3621000@gmail.com, **otaru@g2.usc.edu.tw

Abstract

This study discusses the conversion between the sense of hearing and taste, in order to create an interactive installation based on it. There are many types of research and works about sound and vision. This study attempts to use voice and flavor as an interactive element, to make an installation that can convert voice into different tastes. First, we use a voice analysis tool that can recognize different emotions from voice feature recognition. After participants input their voices, we recognize their emotions. These correspond to different proportions of flavor, including sour, sweet, bitter, spicy, salty. Finally, different kinds of drinks are mixed based on the proportion, to achieve the effect of converting voice into flavor. Participants can experience their voices coming back into their mouth in another way during the interaction. This study then proposes some suggestions about conversion and exhibition, to provide a better experience.

Keywords: Voice, hearing, taste, interactive installation

Introduction

Conversion of different senses is often taken as a topic of many artworks. Wassily Kandinsky, one of the pioneers of abstract art, had tried to express music with visual graphics. Also, his book *Concerning the Spiritual in Art* mentions the association between the color red and the sound of a trumpet [1].

According to the development of technology, sound, smelling, and other kinds of senses also become elements of artworks, like sculptures with mapping, space with sound and image, or interactive installations where audiences can participate in the works. Conversion and association of different senses can be expressed in more and more ways because of this development.

There have been many designs and artworks about food and taste, but less interactive installations show this concept. Unlike vision or hearing that can be felt directly in most environments, to have a sense of taste, audiences should put something into their mouse on their initiative, in other words, to "taste" something themselves. We tried to use another element: voice. Voice comes out from one's mouth then back to their mouth in other forms. To let participants have an experiment like this, our purposes include:

1. Discuss the association and conversion of voice and taste.
2. Create an interactive installation that can convert voice into a sense of taste
3. In this creation, we use different kinds of drinks to represent a sense of taste.

Literature review

A. Interaction

The connection of participants and creation is built on the conversation through the interactive structure of the works, by moving their body or control it with their body, or contribute their body, action, and experience. Integrate themselves into the frame of the work according to the creator's intention. Trigger the creation's feedback and interaction after they deliver their information [2]. In this work, we hope to produce interaction by letting participant import their voice into the installation, and the installation will give gustatory information.

B. Previous works

Here we list some interactive art installations with sound. Reaction Wall (Fig. 1) is an artwork by artists Mojoko and Shang. When audiences yell or whistle, a lot of images of fashion culture spurt and spread on the wall. It shows the overflow of fashion culture today.

Pulsate (Fig. 1) is made by Japanese artists Sachiko Kodama and Minako Takeno. They fill a dinner plate with a liquid magnet. When audiences close to it and make some noise, the liquid magnet changes its shape according to the sound and back to initial form when there is no sound. It symbolizes the action and conversation of human.

Both these two creations are about importing a sound message to installations and get visual effects, no matter in image or object. Different from making visual effects, we hope to give audiences gustatory information.

Pianococktail (Fig. 2) is a concept created by Boris Vian, a musician and a writer from French. In his book" Froth on the Daydream "indicated a piano that can make a cocktail [3]. Géraldine Schenkel made a prototype according to the book in 2005. You can control the placement of the glass and open bottles of drinks by piano keys. After playing a song, you can get a glass of cocktail. In this work, the sound isn't regarded as a message given to the installation, but as an addition when the drink is produced. We refer to this installation to design the way to make different kinds of drinks. Instead of playing a musical instrument, participants only need to import sound information to get taste information.

Fig. 1 Reaction Wall (left) and Pulsate (right)

Fig. 2 Pianococktail by Géraldine Schenkel

Method

A. Sound, emotion and gustation

In 2010, Charles Spence and Alberto Gallace's research indicated an association between the sense of taste and sound. In their experiment, they let participants taste different commercially-available food and drink items, like water, juice, chocolate, etc. Then prepare paper-based line scales, anchored at either end with a nonsense word, like "maluma" and "takete". Fig.3 shows examples of line scales. Participants can mark on the line to show their perception near to which side. Results show that there are some associations between food's flavor, texture, and audio frequency of these nonsense words. For example, water, Brie cheese, and chocolate with caramel have a stronger correlation with the words "bouba" and "maluma" [4]. However, when audiences interact with the installation, they may not always speak some nonsense words with different audio frequencies. As a result, we need a tool that can analyze more features of one's voice.

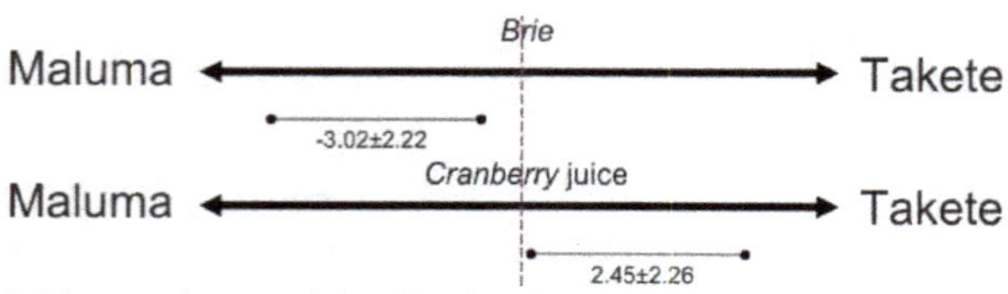

Fig. 3 Line scales used in Charles Spence and Alberto Gallace's research

Emotional speech recognition systems are tools for optimizing the Human-computer interface. They can analyze the different features of a human's voice and calculate which emotion it may express.

Fig. 4 illustrates a two-dimensional picture based on Thayer's emotion theory [5]. It is separated into four classes by the vertical axis showing the extent of energy/arousal and the horizontal axis showing the extent of tension/valence. In this picture, the class of "positive, high arousal" represents happy, exciting emotions. The class of "negative, high arousal" represents anxious, angry emotions. The class of "positive, low arousal" represents relaxed or calm emotions. The class of "negative, low arousal" represents sad or depressed emotions. Then we connect different classes with different flavors. After analyzing the emotions of one's voice, we place on two-dimensional picture to decide the percentages of different flavors. For example, the class of "positive, high arousal" corresponds to sweetness. The portion of sweetness according to how emotion data closes to this class. We convert voice into a sense of taste with this process.

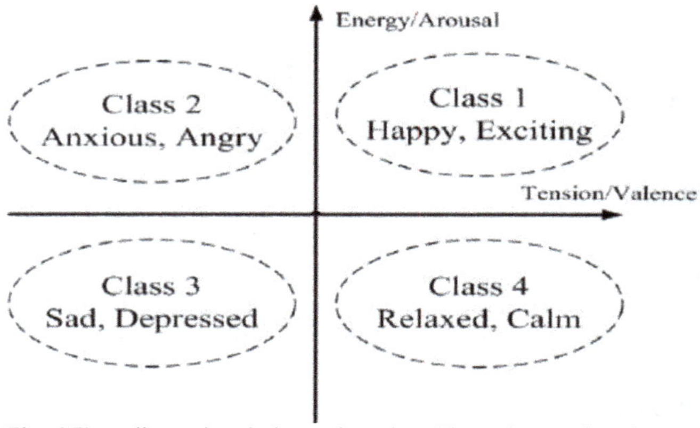

Fig. 4 Two-dimensional picture based on Thayer's emotion theory

B. Analysis of voice

We use Vokaturi as an emotional speech recognition tool. It can analyze at short notice and isn't limited by language. OpenVokaturi is an open-source software Vokaturi provides. OpenVokaturi can analyze nine features of voice, including average pitch, Pitch dynamics, intensity dynamics, etc. Then, data is analyzed with the Neural network. After that, we can get percentages of five emotions of a given voice: happiness, anger, sadness, fear, and no emotion.

C. Deciding on flavors

After getting the proportion of emotions, according to the two-dimensional picture we mentioned before, we use different percentages of sourness, sweetness, bitterness, spiciness, saltiness, and water to make different flavors.

Research by Qian Wang et al. in 2015 indicated that bitterness has negative and low- arousal, and sweetness has characteristics of negative and high-arousal. However, there is no obvious bias in sourness and saltiness [6]. Research by O. Robin et al. also showed that sourness and saltiness have more complex emotional characteristics [7]. Therefore, based on analysis by OpenVokaturi, we use sweetness to represent happiness and bitterness for sadness. Sourness and saltiness are taken as additions in some situations.

Narrowly, since there are no taste buds of spiciness on the human tongue, spiciness isn't classified into gustation. It is a combination of senses of pain and heat. This just corresponds to some physiological responses like rising of body temperature and heart rate, so we use spiciness to represent anger.

We add some sourness when high percentages of happiness, anger, or sadness. Except for gustation, sourness can cause a little irritation to the oral mucosa. This can correspond to strong and intense emotions. Besides, we also add some saltiness for sadness to represent some choked, hoarse features of voice. On the two-dimensional picture of emotion, fear and anxiety are placed between anger and sadness. To represent these emotions, we combine bitterness, sourness, and saltiness. We also add some spiciness when the percentage of fear is high enough. Complete details are showed in Table 1.

In this installation, we use lemon acid, sugar, bitter melon, chili, and salt to represent sourness, sweetness, bitterness, spiciness, and saltiness.

TABLE I
EMOTIONS CORRESPOND TO FLAVORS

	Base	Addition
Happiness	Sweetness	Sourness
Anger	Spiciness	Sourness
Sadness	bitterness	Sourness and saltiness
Fear	Sourness, bitterness and saltiness	spiciness
No emotion	water	-

D. Development tools

Python is a widely-used programming language. One of the Packages, Pyaudio, can be used to record and play sound. This installation uses this package to record a participant's voice, and then use OpenVokaturi we mention before to analyze percentages of five emotions. Different proportions of flavors are calculated based on these data.

Arduino is an open-source software and hardware company. They design and produce single-board microcontrollers and microcontroller kits for building digital devices. This installation uses Arduino Uno to control relays to turn on and off solenoid valves. Solenoid valves are installed below six tanks respectively. Each tank contains one of sour, sweet, bitter, spicy, salty, and water liquid. Different flavors of drinks are created by turning on or off solenoid valves. Fig. 5 shows the whole conversion process.

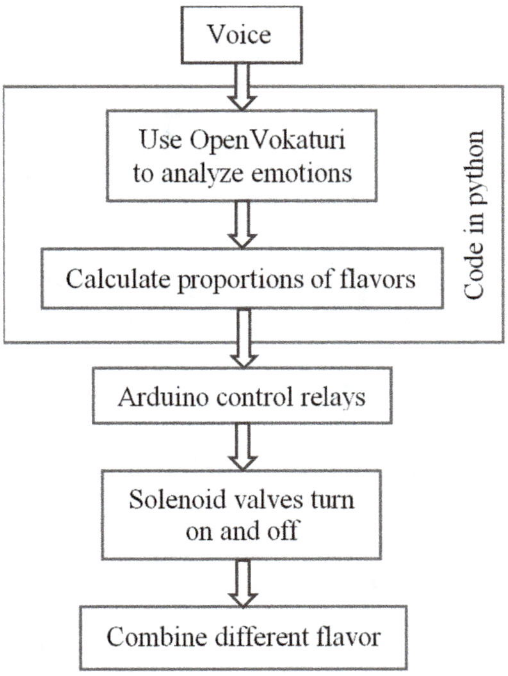

Fig. 5 Conversion process

E. Structure and operating procedure

To avoid the different amounts of drink retained in pipes, we arrange tanks in a circle, and pipes go to the center. Fig. 6 shows the structure of the installation. Board, relays, and power are placed below the installation to keep the cylindrical appearance. The microphone and button are placed on the other smaller cylinder as a console.

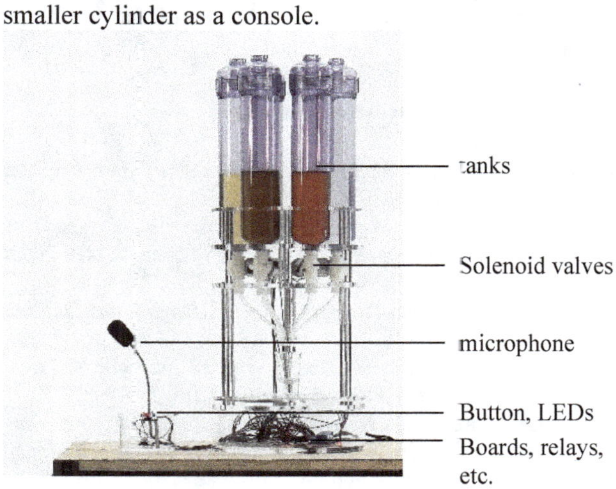

Fig. 6 Structure of the installation

Valves, wires, pipes, and other components are exposed, boards are also placed in a transparent shell. A transparent product can break the mystique of a device's inside, let people know it's structure and give it a kind of freshness and interest [8]. Besides, through the transparent shell, audiences can see LEDs on the board and relays blinking. With sounds of relays and valves and flowing of the drink through transparent pipes, audiences can feel the conversion process.

There are two LEDs on the smaller cylinder with a button. When pressing the button, the red LED turns on and starts recording. As long as the audience releases the button, it stops recording and starts to make the drink with the blue LED turning on.

Discussion

This study introduces some interaction artworks associating with sound and discusses the association between sound and gustation. We recognize features of voice base on emotion. To analysis the emotion of voice, this study uses an emotional speech recognition system and then matches emotion data to different flavors. The drink is used to represent different flavors. After some tests, audiences' feedback shows that the conversions are approximately similar to their intuition, but it still needs more statistics to verify.

After exhibited it for few times, we got some feedback. The installation should be placed in a quiet environment, or the microphone may get some noise and cause deviation. Besides, the operating procedure or the guide may be done better since some audiences can't understand the procedure immediately, even if there is a staff.

Also, cleaning of the installation is vital because drink should meet the standard of food safety. In the future, we may need better designs for convenient cleaning instead of removing each part to wash.

Here we list some possibilities

1. Change drink in the tanks according to requirement.
2. Get more feedback or questionnaire for better conversion.
3. Add more flavor or texture like umami, sense of chewing, creaminess, sparkle, and so on.
4. Organize associations between features of sound and flavors, to create an attractive audio effect for food advertisements.

References

[1] Kandinsky, W. *Concerning the spiritual in art.* Courier Corporation Press, 2012

[2] Tseng, Yu-Chuan, Lai, Wen-Shu, & Chuang, Ming-Chuen. *The Characteristics of Contemporary Digital Interactive Art*, 2009 (Doctoral dissertation).

[3] Vian, B., & Chapman, S. *Froth on the Daydream.* Quartet Books Press, 1988

[4] Spence, C., & Gallace, A. *Tasting shapes and words.* Food Quality and Preference Press, 22(3), 2011, pp. 290-295.

[5] Yeh, C. H., Lin, H. H., & Chang, H. T. *An efficient emotion detection scheme for popular music.* IEEE International Symposium on Circuits and Systems Press. pp. 1799-1802. May 2009

[6] Wang, Q. J., Wang, S., & Spence, C. *"Turn up the taste": assessing the role of taste intensity and emotion in mediating cross modal correspondences between basic tastes and pitch.* Chemical Senses Press, 41(4), 2016, pp.345-356.

[7] Robin, O., Rousmans, S., Dittmar, A., & Vernet-Maury, E. *Gender influence on emotional responses to primary tastes.* Physiology & behavior Press, 78(3), 2003, pp. 385-393.

[8] Fang, Yi wen. *The application of transparent plastic in product design - A case study on i-mac computer design.* 2003 (Master's thesis).

https://doi.org/10.1142/9789811238727_0031

Discussion on Promoting the Sustainable Development of Human Dignity among School Children through Design Education

Kuo-Kuang Fan, Chia-Lin Chang*

Graduate School of Design, National Yunlin University of Science and Technology
*Corresponding Author Email: pipi12345677@gmail.com

Abstract

Human-centered design provides practice and application in various fields. Among them, how to promote the sustainable development of human and social medicine, care for the needs of the disadvantaged and different classes, and make human dignity aware have gradually become the main research focus. With the rapid development of the economic networks today, human-oriented moral essences are gradually being ignored and violated. It is necessary and urgent to promote the sustainable development of human dignity through design education. In the research process, five visual cultural images of contemporary issues on human development guide students to express their views and ideas. Secondly, students discuss the human dignity issues behind these images and finally propose a design-thinking method. Through the study, students become caring for others and developing a way to realize the morality and value of human dignity.

Keywords: design education, human-centered design, human dignity, sustainable development

Introduction

In recent years, the research perspective of social design has been constantly mentioned, emphasizing the core spirit of "human-centered" in which opinions and thoughts of the people are valued. In communities, the voices of social networks need to be respected as well. The social design brings new possibilities to civic consciousness, human dignity, and human rights development. The value and importance of "people" themselves have become an essential and inseparable part of design education in the future. Secondly, the United Nations has proposed many goals related to human dignity in their Sustainable Development Goals (SDGs), such as staying away from poverty, avoiding starvation, right to education, gender equality, health, well-being, and so on. To realize these goals based on sustainable development, it is important to guide students to take these fundamental rights of human dignity into account through education. Therefore, using education with personal experiences to cultivate students' ethical values of human dignity to instill the notion of human dignity development protection is a direction that we can strive towards.

According to the trends, the direction of design practices and design education slowly moves towards caring for people and human dignity. The aim of caring has transitioned from "material" into "people" in design education, and further extended to the level of education itself. Students explore the numerous issues of human dignity in the learning process of design education, thereby proposing meaningful solutions with critical thinking to realize the sustainable development of human dignity. After then, the following is discussed between students: (1) How the "human-centered" design education is put into practice are discussed by the students, (2) performance that students have in the process, and (3) the changes and differences in regards of protecting human dignity after the course of design education. In summary, the purpose of the study is as follows.

A. Discussing what the important teaching perspectives and procedure are in the "human-centered" design education.
B. Discussing what the learning performances are in the learning process of "human-centered" design education.
C. Proposing what changes students have towards values and ethical perspectives of human dignity are after the "human-centered" design education.

Development and Current Condition of Study on Human Dignity and Design Education

Nowadays, many studies on human dignity have been proposed. Caring for the sustainable development of human dignity has become an obvious trend. How we can protect such development as well as face other issues extended from it are the focuses of this study. Allan Borowski believes that dignity is the foundation of human rights and we must strengthen social workers' understanding of dignity and raise their awareness and morality of dignity at work [1]. Roger Brownsword explores the relationship, state responsibilities, and human dignity among migrants [2]. Vasil Gluchman explores the nature of dignity and reflects on the reason why human beings are the highest form of life and we have the highest level of dignity [3].

The studies on human-centered social design emphasize the connection and respect between people as well. Through relevant exploration of social design, many studies are centered on promoting and advocating human dignity or ethical values that are co-created by communities. Richard Buchanan believes that design is not only based on human dignity and human rights but also an important means for everyone, especially women and children to implement and embody the principles of the Constitution in their daily lives. He also thinks that design provides a way to think about the world to solve many contemporary cultural problems faced by mankind [4]. Rebecca Walton proposes that we need to regard human dignity and human rights as the first principles and foundational values in the practice of technical and professional communication (TPC) [5].

We have to introspect whether changes are made for students' attention to human dignity in the learning process of design education. The introspection includes the following questions: (1) what are the factors affecting them, (2) why are learning of design education and their caring consciousness upon human dignity connected, and (3) which part should we enhance to improve students' sharpness and awareness of protection towards human dignity in the process of design education,? Respect for an individual should not vary by gender, class, and culture. That's the fundamental human rights, as well as an essential part of human dignity. Under such a world trend, scholars have begun to explore the relationship and connection between justice, human dignity, and human rights [6,7]. We pay attention to respecting individuals at different levels in this general environment. Through discussion of relevant studies, many focuses are found in terms of issues of protecting human dignity. This is important when we layout courses of human-centered design education.

Human-centered design education curriculum implementation approach

The subjects involved in this research are 22 senior students in an elementary school in central Taiwan, with an equal ratio of male and female. The students generally clearly express their ideas and concepts. We guide these students to approach human dignity issues in international human development through a "human-centered" design education curriculum. The issues include mainstream and common issues, as well as minority and less cared. Teachers show visual cultural images in the classroom and guide students to discuss continuously and discover the problems. Then, they guide students to think critically about the issues and explore the reasons behind the problems, and ask students to present their opinions and comments. When students have a certain level of understanding and remarks, we guide students to discuss how to maintain and improve human dignity. Finally, through design thinking, we invite students to propose plans or drafts for solving these human dignity problems with design strategies and techniques and evaluate the effectiveness and potential amendments of the content of the design via peer feedback. The main teaching steps are divided into the following six parts.

A. Identify human dignity issues:

Students explore issues related to human dignity through visual images of culture and discuss with students how they discover the issues.

B. Explore the causes of dignity issues:

Through group discussions, students discover the reasons for these human dignity issues.

C. Present critical thoughts:

Students express their thoughts, feelings, and comments on the causes of these human dignity issues.

D. Propose solutions to maintain human dignity:

Students come up with methods or strategies to maintain human dignity and discuss with students how to put it into practice in design.

E. Solve problems with designed strategies:

Design thinking or creation is presented in the process and results of solving the problem of human dignity and ask students to express their design concepts.

F. Evaluate the effectiveness of the design plan implementation:

Students discuss the advantages and disadvantages of implementing design plans of different groups and the possible results. After that, each group of students revises the design plan to reach more conducive to human dignity development. This is repeated until the students agree that the best design solution has appeared. The procedure of teaching is as shown in the flow chart below (Fig.1).

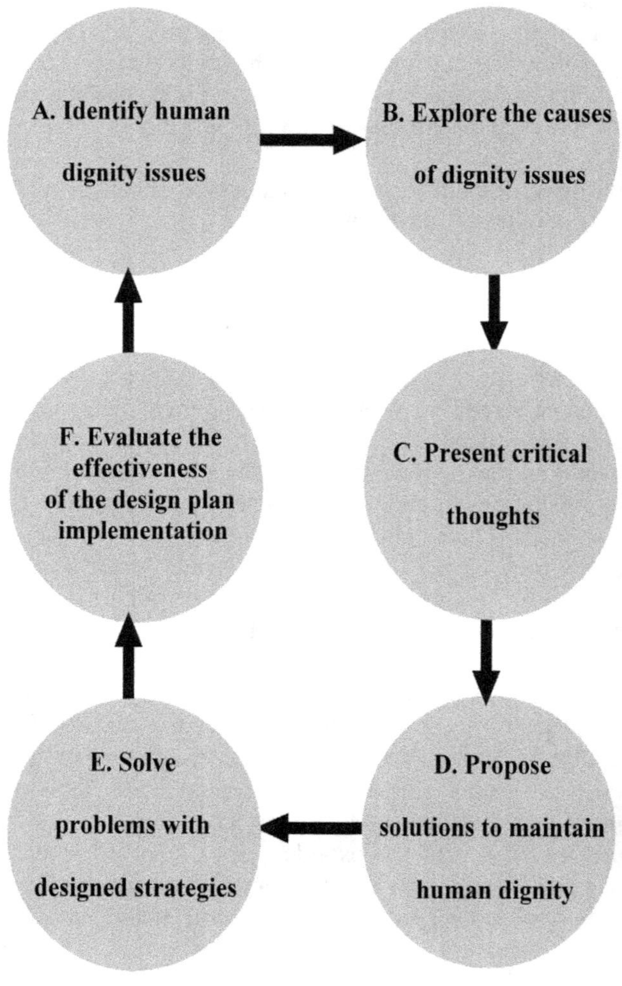

Fig. 1 The teaching procedures of human-centered design education.

Moreover, every step of the teaching is interlinked with each other. Through the design education courses, students start from the discovery of human dignity issues, and finally propose and evaluate solutions and strategies to solve the problems. During this process, students propose design strategies for maintaining human dignity and accumulate knowledge, empathy, and skills. The purpose is not just to cultivate the students to be designers, but also to be human dignity supporters.

Students' performance and feedback on the protection of human dignity

This research aims to enhance elementary school students' awareness of the importance of sustainable human dignity development through design education. During the research, we use five visual cultural images of contemporary human development issues to guide students to express their views and opinions. Afterward, we further discuss with students the human dignity issues behind these images and finally guide them to propose feasible solutions to these issues with a design-thinking approach. Such a course design enhances students' care for others and cultivates their morals and values for human dignity.

A. Providing ideas via critical thinking on the issues of human sustainable development:

Concerning the issues of human sustainable development, students use their critical thinking and put forward many ideas through the gaze, analysis, and discussion of visual cultural images, combined with their cultural values. Throughout the implementation of design education, from the shallow identification in the beginning and gradually to the cores of the problems, students continuously collect and clarify the information related to the sustainable development issues, so that they become to comprehensively understand the core of the problem.

B. Regarding human needs, shifting from a more convenient life to a more meaningful life with emotional connections:

The students' thinking about human needs turns deep and focused from being superficial and simple. In the beginning, most students believe that the most important human need should be a convenient life. In the second half of the design education curriculum, however, students begin to change their minds and think that emotional connection is more important for human sustainable development than a convenient life. Many students realize that emotional estrangement creates conflicts and contradictions between people and countries. That is why human sustainable development should focus on emotions. Students also discover that excessively pursuing a convenient life makes the scramble for resources more aggressive, which will be detrimental to human development and connection.

C. Students finding creative solutions through design thinking to the problems of human sustainable development:

Through the Human-centered spirit of design thinking, almost all of students' final design concepts and works include creative ways to solve the problems of human sustainable development. In the draft stage of thinking, everyone is still inclined to designing functional products. Nevertheless, after a series of critical thinking and brainstorming, students' considerations of humanism become more condensed than before, and the display of creativity begins to combine with more elements of care and empathy. Students gradually get rid of single functionality in their designs, and in turn, add more human experience and feelings into their design creativity for human sustainable development.

D. Altruistic beliefs, attitudes, and values becoming more obvious:

In the human-centered design education curriculum, students talk a lot about the concept of altruism. Altruistic beliefs, attitudes, and values continuously emerge in the discussion of human development issues, the choice of solutions, and the adjustment during the design implementation process. In the design process, students are interviewed on some of their selected subjects, such as the elderly, new residents, the disabled, and the poor. Through this learning process, students begin to think about how to help these people, change their lives, and help them connect with people and have intimate interactions in life. At this point, students' ideas of human dignity include obvious altruistic values.

E. The moral concept of human dignity being integrated into students' lives and becoming a core of design thinking and implementation

Through the above-mentioned learning and experiences, students attach much importance to human dignity. Through care, acceptance, empathy, and contribution, they become to understand the difficulties encountered and help needed in the lives of people of different genders, cultures, and classes. Through design thinking and implementation, human rights issues, human development dilemmas, and the possibilities of sustainable development worthy of attention are observed, and the light of human dignity can be manifested. This is a precious lesson for both students and teachers.

Discussion

During the process of "human-centered" design education, students' competence shifts from the implementation of functional design works to the connection with human emotions. They learn to understand the core of human development with critical thinking and realize the people-oriented spirit with design thinking. In that way, their altruistic beliefs, attitudes, and values become pronounced, and the moral concept of human dignity becomes deeply rooted in their mind. Via design education, students explore and discuss issues regarding human sustainable development and then understand, interpret, and identify the causes and relations of the issues with their critical thinking. Finally, in the implementation of design and creation, they look for possibilities and strategies to protect human dignity. Various learning approaches connect them deeply with the sustainable development of human dignity. The function of design education here is more than just teaching students to value and practice human dignity. What is more important than the teaching is to make them students, thinkers, advocates, and designers who value human dignity. In this "human-centered" design education learning process, students accumulate their competence in terms of cognition, empathy and skills for improving human dignity and opening doors for the sustainable development of human dignity.

Design education needs to guide students to discover dignity issues in human development and transform these issues into extended topics or platforms by allowing students to explore and internalize the knowledge. Only by deepening students' awareness of the topic, they have the opportunities to have more in-depth thinking and practice on the development of human dignity. Otherwise, the results of the teaching remain only in superficial cognition and criticism. Moreover, the human dignity of different genders, cultures, and classes and help and support for development are what students easily overlook during the overall design education. Teachers and researchers need to help students get in touch with both mainstream and minority issues of human dignity so that they integrate more comprehensive concepts and enhance their sensitivity to human dignity.

Conclusion and Suggestion

A. "Human-centered" design education can help students implement the development of human dignity:

After the implementation of "human-centered" design education, students have made significant progress and improvement in their thinking, critique, creation, and practice of human dignity. This process helps students contribute to the development of human dignity through design. The process of design education is not about guiding students to make beautiful or interesting design works, but to immerse them into the experience of design learning and cultivating them into practitioners of exploration, communication, identification, selection, and creation. Then, they make correct and valuable design practices for the development of meaningful human dignity. As students manifest the value of human dignity through design learning from an early age, they support and advocate for human dignity when they grow up. Such education complements their growth, which is very important and cannot be ignored.

B. Cultivating students to become advocates and designers for human dignity:

The design education process not only sparks students' sensitivity and creativity to human dignity issues but influences their mentality and makes them become advocates for human dignity. In other words, what we wish to cultivate through design education is a designer and a supporter of human dignity. A lot of design education at the elementary school level simply guides students to make aesthetically beautiful (and maybe some functional) design works but rarely any in-depth discussions or extensions of social issues. Such a situation equips students with good design skills, but they are inadequate in the expression of perception, emotions, and values, not to mention for them to advocate human dignity through design. It is important to return to a "people-centered" mindset. What is cultivated is not designers who know how to design, but ones who are willing to connect with people, contribute to society, and realize human dignity sustainability.

C. To cultivate a more comprehensive view of human dignity and morality in students, teachers should also pay attention to human rights issues that have been less cared for:

Nowadays, since the "people-centered" points of view have received increased attention, the importance of human dignity is constantly demanded. Such a phenomenon is not just in the field of design education, but also in other disciplines and subjects. With such a trend, poverty, starvation, education, and other issues that the mainstream society is concerned about are easily seen and advocated. On the other hand, human dignity or human rights issues of the minority such as education rights and the right to work of new residents are easily overlooked. Only through continuous discussion and clarification, students pay attention to and think about the human rights issues through critical and design thinking in the educational process. Designers and planners who learn through the process propose solutions for such issues and fulfil the sustainable development of human dignity.

References

[1] Borowski, Allan. "On Human Dignity and Social Work." The British Journal of Social Work, 2021, pp. 1–15.

[2] Brownsword, Roger. "Migrants, State Responsibilities, and Human Dignity." Ratio Juris, 2021, pp. 1–23.

[3] Gluchman, Vasil. "Nature of Dignity and Human Dignity." Human Affairs, vol. 27, no. 2, 2017, pp. 131–144.

[4] Buchanan, Richard. "Human Dignity and Human Rights: Thoughts on the Principles of Human-Centered Design." Design Issues, vol. 17, no. 3, 2001, pp. 35–39.

[5] Walton, Rebecca. "Supporting Human Dignity and Human Rights." Journal of Technical Writing and Communication, vol. 46, no. 4, 2016, pp. 402–426.

[6] Sołtan, K. Edward. "Justice, Human Dignity and Human Rights." The Good Society, vol. 26, no. 2-3, 2018, pp. 354–369.

[7] Kleinig, John, and Nicholas G. Evans. "Human Flourishing, Human Dignity, and Human Rights." Law and Philosophy, vol. 32, no. 5, 2013, pp. 539–564.

https://doi.org/10.1142/9789811238727_0032

Discussion on the Teaching Mode of Cooperative Learning from the Perspective of Design Department Students

Jui-Che Tu, Ku-Hsi Chu*

Graduate School of Design, National Yunlin University of Science & Technology, Yunlin, Taiwan
*Corresponding Author Email: eason79@gmail.com

Abstract

Cooperative learning is a common teaching application in curriculum planning and learning in many departments in recent years. With students from different backgrounds at the department of design and questionnaire surveys, three dimensions of "Learning Motivation and Attitude", "Cooperative Skills and Peer Interaction" and "Teacher-Student Relationship" were investigated. The results of the t-test showed that genders affected significantly the teacher-student relationship. In an educational system, there were significant differences in the three dimensions between the students in full-time and the night school. Grade analysis and verification results from ANOVA showed the full-time juniors had the most active participation in the cooperative learning model, followed by the full-time seniors and night school seniors. The research results also revealed that the students at lower grades had low participation in cooperative learning. The results provide a reference for academic research in design education and teaching models.

Keywords: cooperative learning, design learning, teaching mode, design department, students

Introduction

Teachers use a variety of different teaching strategies and models in classroom teaching and try to make students more efficient in the process of learning classroom information and knowledge. Especially in recent years, there has been a gradual increase in the research on the teaching strategy and model innovation of higher education. In the teaching mode, cooperative learning is often used. It is desirable that the course contributes to competition and growth of students with the cooperative learning model and narrows the gaps in cooperative learning. Moreover, university education has always advocated freedom to learn, and students are responsible for their learning effectiveness. Thus, whether students can truly absorb knowledge and theories in a class is not considered seriously. This research chose and discussed the cooperative learning teaching model from the perspective of design education. The practical design course aims to train independent designers. Therefore, even though other design courses often see the leading-in cooperative learning teaching moded, the final design work is personal. It still takes time and investment to complete the works. However, through cooperative learning, the practical design ability of personal design works cannot be trained, and the learning effect is reduced. For design department students, there may be different attitudes toward cooperative learning.

Therefore, the main purpose of this research is to explore the teaching model of cooperative learning, analyze the teaching model and acceptance of cooperative learning of design department students, and then summarize the differences in gender and grade for the educational system of the design department. In addition to helping teachers apply cooperative learning strategies, the teachers also can adjust their suitable teaching models for students with different ability. Therefore, the objectives of this research are (1) discussing the influence of students' acceptance of the cooperative learning teaching model, (2) understanding the impact of students from different backgrounds in cooperative learning, and (3) analyzing the appropriate cooperative learning model for students.

Literature Review

A. Cooperative Learning:

The cooperative learning method has been developed in the past decades, and many different methods have been implemented in the United States, Canada, Israel, and other European regions [1]. These teaching models include five types: cooperative learning, student team achievement, team game, jigsaw puzzle, and group investigation. Its main application and selection are based on the type of course and the status of the class students with consideration and evaluation planning. The cooperative learning developed by Ref. [2] is a common teaching model. Many scholars such as Ref. [3] pointed out that the use of cooperative learning makes group members have positive dependence with the effectiveness of reflection and achievement. Ref. [4] mentioned that cooperative learning becomes more important for group or peer activities in a limited course time. Reference [5] showed that cooperative learning is appropriate for 2 to 6 students. In an actual course, it is adjusted flexibly according to the size of the class, the state of the course, and the teaching goals. To make cooperative learning go smoothly, two elements are usually required: face-to-face interaction and group processing. This allows students to have more interaction opportunities in the process of group cooperation and promote learning and growth [6,7].

B. Cooperative Learning Strategy:

The theory of cooperative learning teaching strategies includes four main types as "Social Learning Theory",

"Cognitive Theory", "Motivation Theory" and "Behavior Learning Theory". In the cognitive theory, Ref. [8] believed that the construction of cooperative learning theory needs cognitive development, cognitive refinement, and motivation theory. Cognitive development theory assumes that when students interact with each other in the execution of coursework, they gradually become more familiar with important learning concepts. Reference [8] pointed out that students and groups need to promote learning motivation in cognitive development theory and the learning motivation of individuals and groups can be promoted for individual and team achievement through the design of the reward structure. These allow students' learning performance to grow.

References [9] and [10] mentioned the key role of social learning theory in the cooperative learning process. Through the interdependent cooperation process generated by the team members, the common goals of the team can be actively achieved. Many studies indicated that interpersonal relationships and the skills of group members are important factors in social and cooperative learning. Interactive modes such as empathy, caring, respect, support, encouragement, or teamwork promote positive social relationships among the group members. They are basic values in cooperative learning teaching models [11-18]. Reference [9] believed that behavioral learning theory is an important factor for the success of cooperative learning. From the educational point of view, it is accompanied by the stimulus-response connection and enhancement, weakening, and other behaviors in the transmission of information which focuses on the influence of positive interaction between groups on learning.

C. Learning Engagement:

Reference [19] pointed out that learning engagement includes affective and behavioral engagement. Behavioral engagement refers to the basic learning behaviors of students, such as going to school and maintaining class progress and requirements. Emotional engagement mainly explores students' inner sense of identity with the school, trust, and preference between teachers and classmates. Learning engagement depends on the student's dedication in various dimensions such as coursework, school activities, and interpersonal interaction [20,21]. From the research progress of learning engagement theory, Astin proposed the theory of student involvement to discuss student involvement and self-development. However, Ref. [22] suggested that there is a difference between involvement and engagement. Engagement in particular emphasizes the relevance of school activities and students' successful experience and focuses on the discussion of students' behavior for a good educational environment. More students' engagement in learning increases the degree of self-esteem and confidence in themselves [20,21].

Reference [23] explained learning engagement in which students' academic and non-academic activities should be included. Learning engagement enables students to actively learn and engage values. In recent years, studies related to learning engagement have gradually focused on the internal concepts of students, which refers to the involvement of cognitive learning theory. Therefore, Ref. [24] summarized learning engagement in a more meaningful way into three elements: behavioral, emotional, and cognitive engagement.

Research Method

A. Research Steps,Objects, and Tools:

This research is mainly conducted through questionnaire surveys on the attitudes of students participating in the design of courses with cooperative learning. The cooperative learning questionnaire was compiled by the cooperative learning workshop of the Ministry of Education of the Republic of China. It had three dimensions: "Learning Motivation and Attitude", "Cooperative Skills and Peer Interaction", and "Teacher-Student Relationship". The questionnaire explained 62.97% of the total variation of the data of 5302 parameters in factor analysis. The internal reliability coefficient reached 0.91 in the "Learning Motivation and Attitude", and 0.89 in the "Cooperative Skills and Peer Interaction", which indicated that the reliability of the questionnaire selected was significant [25]. The research steps were carried out in four stages: (1) the literature review, the analysis of the research topic, and defining the research purpose and the object, (2) the questionnaire survey of cooperative learning, (3) processing the data and verification, and (4) analysis and discussion of the results.

The subjects in this study were students in full-time and night school from the design department of the university in the middle of Taiwan. The number of students was 252 including 8 sophomores, 83 juniors, and 91 seniors.

B. Information Analysis:

The questionnaires for this study were distributed in paper from October to November 2020. 235 questionnaires were received including 227 valid and 8 invalid ones. The effective recovery rate was 90%. The proportions of male and female students were 57.7% and 42.3%. The proportions of seniors, juniors, and sophomores were 37.4%, 33.9%, and 28.6%, respectively. Full-time students composed 59.9% of the total number of subjects, while students of night school were 40.1%. We used SPSS statistical software for statistical analysis. Independent sample T-test and ANOVA were used to detect the significance of the difference.

Results and Analysis

A. Reliability and t-test Analysis:

Cronbach's α values of each dimension for internal consistency reliability were between 0.856 and 0.899, which indicated that the research tool had good reliability. There was a significant difference between male and female students for "Teacher-Student Relationship" and "I often feel the teacher care about me". (Male- N=131, M=3.11, SD=0.675; Female- N=96, M=2.88, SD=0.684; p=.009). However, for "Learning Motivation and Attitude", "Cooperative Skills and Peer Interaction", there was no significant gender difference.

There were significant difference between the students in full-time and night school for "Learning Motivation and Attitude" and "I can focus on learning in class" (full-time student- M=3.11, SD=0.580; night school students- M=2.84, SD=0.703; p=.002), "I think my academic performance has improved" (full-time student- M=3.21, SD=0.585; night school students- M=2.95, SD= 0.603; p=.001) and "I think the overall academic performance of the class has improved" (full-time student- M=3.07, SD=0.658; night school students- M=2.84, SD=0.734; p=.014), "Cooperative Skills and Peer Interaction", "When I encounter difficulties in my own learning, I will take the initiative to ask for help" (full-time student- M=3.20, SD=0.569; night school students-M=3.03, SD=0.605; p=.037) and "I often feel the support or encouragement from my classmates" (full-time student- M=3.15, SD=0.665; night school students-M=2.95, SD=0.7080; p=.031), which is significant difference. In the "Teacher-Student Relationship", "I am close to my classmates" (full-time student- M=3.21, SD=0.614; night school students- M=3.01, SD=0.782; p=.030), "I interact closely with the teacher" (full-time student- M=3.16, SD=0.574; night school students- M=2.76, SD=0.735; p=.000) and "I often feel the teacher care about me" (full-time student- M=3.14, SD=0.669; night school students- M=2.82, SD=0.676; p=.001).

B. ANOVA in Grades:

For "Learning Motivation and Attitude" and "I am willing to participate in the activities the teacher wants us to carry out", the full-time juniors had a higher score than other grade students (with full-time seniors MD=.596, p =.001; with night school seniors MD=.525, p=.044). For "I have confidence in my ability to learn in this course", full-time juniors had higher scores than full-time seniors (MD=.488, p=.035). For "I often thinking in the class", the full-time juniors had higher scores than other groups (with night school sophomores MD=.590, p=.032; with full-time seniors MD=.527, p=.008).

For "Cooperative Skills and Peer Interaction", full-time juniors had higher scores than other groups (with full-time seniors MD=.522, p=.005; with night school seniors MD=.522, p=.005). For "I can accept the different opinions of classmates", the full-time juniors had higher scores than other groups (with full-time seniors MD=.611, p=.000; with night school seniors MD=.492, p= .006). For "I am willing to cooperate with others to help each other", full-time juniors had higher scores than full-time seniors (MD=.684, p=.000). For "I am happy to share my thoughts or collected information", full-time juniors had higher scores than other groups (with full-time seniors MD=.706, p=.000; with night school seniors MD=.515, p=.004). For "When I encounter difficulties in my studies, I will take the initiative to ask for help", full-time juniors had higher scores than night school seniors (MD=.434, p=.034). For "When the group has different opinions, I can discuss with my classmates, understand each other, and obtain common opinions", full-time juniors had higher scores than full-time seniors (MD=.592, p=.002). For "Teacher-Student Relationship", compared with "I interact closely with the teacher", full-time juniors had higher scores than night school seniors (MD=.535, p=.014). For "I often feel the teacher care about me", full-time juniors had higher scores than night school seniors (MD=.517, p=.047).

Conclusion and Suggestion

With different background variables, this research discussed the acceptance and views of design department students on the cooperative learning model. The results showed that design department students had significant differences in the three dimensions of "Learning Motivation and Attitude", "Cooperation Skills and Peer interaction", and "Teacher-Student Relationship". In "I often feel the teacher care about me" of the "Teacher-Student Relationship" dimension, male students had a higher score than female students. There were no significant differences in "Learning Motivation and Attitude", "Cooperative Skills and Peer Interaction" by gender. There were significant differences in the three dimensions of "Learning Motivation and Attitude", "Cooperative Skills and Peer Interaction" between full-time students (higher score) than night school students. There was no obvious difference between male and female students in cooperative learning. However, in the educational system, full-time students were more engaged in cooperative learning than night school students.

In the dimensions of "Learning Motivation and Attitude", the participation of full-time juniors was higher than the full-time seniors and night school seniors. For confidence in learning, full-time juniors had a higher score than full-time seniors. In the regular thinking of the courses, full-time juniors had a higher score than the night school sophomores and full-time seniors. In the dimension of "Cooperation Skills and Peer Interaction", full-time juniors had a higher score than full-time seniors and night school seniors in listening to others' speeches, accepting opinions, and sharing ideas. In the willingness to cooperate, proactive help, and understanding and approving opinions, full-time juniors had a higher score than full-time seniors. In the "Teacher-Student Relationship" dimension, full-time juniors had a higher score than the night school seniors in interaction and caring teacher. The participation and investment in cooperative learning by full-time juniors were higher. In the three dimensions, full-time juniors had higher scores than the seniors in full-time course and night school. The results showed that lower grade students in full-time course and night school had lower participation in cooperative learning, while full-time juniors were most active.

References

[1] Veenman, S., Benthum, N. V., Bootsma, D., Dieren, J. V., & Kemp, N. V. D. (2002). Cooperative learning and teacher education. *Teaching and Teacher Education*, 18, 87-103.

[2] Johnson, D. W., & Johnson, R. T. (1991). *Learning together and alone*. Boston: Allyn and Bacon.

[3] Putnam, J. W. (1997). *Cooperative learning in diverse classrooms*. Upper Sadddle River, N. J.: Merrill.

[4] Lundberg, C. A. (2003). Nontraditional College students and role of collaborative learning as a tool for science mastery. *School Science and Mathematics*, 103(1), 8-17.

[5] Davidson, N. (1994). Cooperative and collaborative learning. In J. S, Thousand, R. A. Villa, & A. I. Nevin. (Eds), *Creativity*

and collaborative learning (pp. 13-30). Baltimore: Paul H. Brooks Publishing Company.

[6] Darnis, F., and L. Lafont. (2013). Cooperative Learning and Dyadic Interactions: Two Modes of Knowledge Construction in Socio-constructivist Settings for Team-Sport Teaching. *Physical Education and Sport Pedagogy.*

[7] Smith, A., and M. Parr. (2007). "Young People's Views on the Nature and Purposes of Physical Education: A Sociological Analysis." Sport, *Education and Society*, 12 (1): 37–58.

[8] Slavin, R. E. (1995). *Cooperative learning: theory, research, and practice*. Boston: Allyn and Bacon.

[9] Johnson, D. W., & Johnson, R. T. (1994). *Learning together and alone: cooperative, competitive, and individualistic learning* (4th ed.). Boston: Allyn and Bacon.

[10] Huang, Z. J., and Lin, P. X. (1996) *Cooperative learning.* Taipei: Wunan Books.

[11] Bayraktar, G. (2011). "The Effect of Cooperative Learning on Students' Approach to General Gymnastics Course and Academic Achievements." *Educational Research and Reviews,* 6 (1): 62–71.

[12] Casey, A., B. Dyson, and A. Campbell. (2009). Action Research in Physical Education: Focusing Beyond Myself through Cooperative Learning. *Educational Action Research,* 17 (3): 407–423.

[13] Dyson, B. (2001). Cooperative Learning in an Elementary Physical Education Program. *Journal of Teaching in Physical Education,* 20: 264–281.

[14] Dyson, B. (2002). The Implementation of Cooperative Learning in an Elementary Physical Education Program. *Journal of Teaching in Physical Education,* 22 (1): 69–85.

[15] Dyson, B., and K. Strachan. (2000). Cooperative Learning in a High School Physical Education Program. *Waikato Journal of Education,* 6: 19–37.

[16] Goudas, M., and E. Magotsiou. (2009). The Effects of a Cooperative Physical Education Program on Students' Social Skills. *Journal of Applied Sport Psychology,* 21 (3): 356–364.

[17] Johnson, R. T., R. Bjorkland, and M. L. Krotee. (1984). The Effects of Cooperative, Competitive and Individualistic Student Interaction Patterns on the Achievement and Attitudes of Students Learning the Golf Skill of Putting. *Research Quarterly for Exercise and Sport,* 55(2): 129–134.

[18] Yoder, L. J. (1993). "Cooperative Learning and Dance Education." Journal of Physical Education, *Recreation and Dance.* 64 (5): 47–56.

[19] Marks, H. M (2000). Student Engagement in Instructional Activity: Patterns in the Elementary, Middle, and High School Years. *American Educational Research Journal*, 32 (1), 153-184.

[20] Astin, A. W. (1984). Student involvement: A development theory for higher education. *Journal of College Student Development*, 40 (5), 518-529.

[21] Newmann, F. M., Wehlage, G. G., & Lamborn, S. D. (1992). *The significant and sources of student engagement. In F. M. Newmann(Ed.), Student engagement and achievement in American secondary school*(pp. 11-39). New York: Teachers College Press.

[22] Roberts, J., & McNeese, M. N. (2010). Student involvement/engagement in higher education based on student origin. *Research in Higher Education Journal*, 7.

[23] Audas, R., & Willms, J. D. (2001). *Engagement and dropping out of school: A life-course perspective.* Hull, Quebec: Applied Research Branch, Strategic Policy, Human Resources Development Canada. Retrieved November, 04, 2020 from https://eweb.uqac.ca/bibliotheque/archives/15292281.pdf

[24] Fredricks, J. A., Blumenfeld, P. C, & Paris, A. H. (2004). School engagement: otential of the concept, state of the evidence. *Review of Educational Research*, 74, 59-109.

[25] National and Preschool Education Department of the Ministry of Education (2013). Teaching manual for group cooperative learning. Taipei: National and Preschool Education Department, Ministry of Education.

https://doi.org/10.1142/9789811238727_0033

Empirical Study of the Bridal Hair Style Design Factors Assessment Model

Shu-Ping Chiu[1], Ya-Chun Wang[2], Wei-Cheng Chu[2], Li-Wen Chuang[1*]

[1]School of Fine Arts & Design, Lingnan Normal University, Zhanjiang, China
[2]Graduate School of Applied Design, Shu-Te University, Kaohsiung, Taiwan
[*]Corresponding Author Email: sphill200406@163.com

Abstract

In current times of open and transparent information, wedding preparations follow ancient etiquette but the bride's hair style has jumped out of conventional framework. In this era of seeking novelty and variation, creativity and customization are more suitable for the demands of consumers. Taiwan is marching toward economic development of value-increment creativity and technology. In Taiwan, popular aesthetics has become a cornerstone of fine service. Cosmetology and the hairdressing industry present a prosperous trend. This study is aimed to enhance advantages of bridal secretary in workplace to construct the bridal hairstyling factor assessment model that is to serve as a reference for customers and an approach for bride secretaries to apply in hairstyling. The first phase of this study: using the KJ Method as an inductive approach to establish a bridal hairstyle assessment plan; second phase: adopting the Modified Delphi Method to establish a bridal hairstyling factor assessment framework and standard based on common decision-making of experts; third phase: employing the AHP method to construct the bridal hairstyling factor assessment model, where hairstyling options are ranked; fourth phase: using a decision-making and evaluation plan to elect the best feasible bridal hair styles.

Keywords: cosmetology, bridal hairstyling, bridal secretary

Introduction

The creative fashion industry changes with time. Due to the development of modern science, technology and networks, as well as the popularity of Korean and Japanese styles, traditional weddings cannot satisfy modern people's needs. Theme-based and overseas-holiday-type weddings allow new couples to generate distinctive creativity. Consumers have higher demands on aesthetics. Wedding dress companies, wedding staff and even bride secretaries try their best to meet consumers' requirements, to help new couples have the nicest memory in life. In preparation for wedding, new couples always play the role of asking questions. From match-making and engagement to marriage, the marriage market covers an extremely wide scope including wedding cake, wedding banquet, wedding invitation, wedding dress photography, jewelry, dowry, house repair, furniture, honeymoon, cosmetics, marriage loan, etc. Bridal styling is also one of the factors especially valued by new couples. Bridal wedding gown is the focus that attracts people's attention. Moreover, bridal hair style is utilized to achieve perfection and optimization of bridal overall style. Nowadays, new couples' wedding dress photos are presented in almost all of the wedding ceremonies in Taiwan, just like how a wedding cake is indispensable in wedding ceremonies of Europe and America. [1,2]. Most Taiwanese are accustomed to taking "beautiful" wedding photos. Taking wedding photos in advance is a unique "Made-In-Taiwan" phenomenon. Wedding dress photography is a very big industry in Taiwan, which drives other peripheral industries. This study aims to establish a mode of evaluation for bridal hair style design factors, and provide a set of objective, effective methods for a bridal secretary to choose the most suitable bridal hair style in order to reinforce the competitive advantages of a bridal secretary.

Literature Review

Along with the change in overall social economic structures and popularity of education in Taiwan, the wedding ceremony changes from previous simplicity into current complexity. Under influences of electronic communication media and internationalization, nubile young men and women show changes in independence consciousness and selection of marriage ceremony, wedding customs now emphasize delicate customization. Patterns of ceremony include traditional wedding, religious or church wedding, civil marriage, group wedding, Chinese-style simplified wedding, self-designed trendy wedding and other special wedding ceremonies [3]. Brides dress up to present a beautiful appearance and deportment as well as keep a nice memory in life. Bridal secretary is a common proper noun in Taiwan, and an emerging industry extended from stylist of wedding dress company. The bridal secretary is a personal secretary who exclusively serves the bride and is in charge of bridal styling and change of bridal apparel on the wedding day. Bridal secretary plays the role of planning and managing all of the dressing affairs by the bride's side. Bridal secretary is mainly responsible for hair style maintenance, dressing, facial makeup, bridal deportment and etc., and can even stabilize bride's mental status [4]. Bridal secretary is an industry appearing along with enhancement of market consumption ability and life quality. When consumption ability of the society gradually increasing, brides are willing to pay more to show different kinds of styles on their wedding day [5]. The wedding service industry of Taiwan not only dresses up Taiwanese brides but also determines the form and the connotation of contemporary Taiwanese wedding dress photography. It plays a key role. Compared with conventional photo studio, current wedding dress shop is most special in that it not only takes photos but also provides almost all of the wedding related services and integrates wedding dress, makeup, hair styling, shaping design and photography. In addition, wedding dress industry is special in that it contains production and sales and influences consumption patterns. The wedding industry includes a very extensive range. It mainly refers to a set of various industries which provide serial products and services to people who get married. It covers a range from pre-wedding to post-wedding.

The industry chain is shown in Table 1.

TABLE 1
WEDDING INDUSTRY CHAIN

Stage	Demand item	Contents and activities	Industry type/commercial form
Pre-wedding preparations	Singles matching	Sodality	Dating agency, marriage service corporation
	Loans for wedding	Wedding cost preparation	Banking, financing industry
	Wedding invitation	Content design and printing	Printing industry, advertisement design
	Wedding cakes and candies	Customization of wedding cakes and candies	Food retails, cake and pastry industry
	Wedding information	Electronic invitation and photo album, wedding ceremony planning	Information industry, wedding consultant, magazine industry
	Articles for marriage etiquette	Apparel and accessories (Western style clothes, business suit, wallet/leather bag, belt, watch, tie, socks, etc.)	Costume industry, timepiece industry, general merchandise industry
	Wedding ring and jewelry	Wedding ring, accessories (necklace, bracelet, etc.)	Jewelry industry
	Wedding photography	Wedding dress style, wedding photography, photo album production	Wedding photography, wedding consultant
	Cosmetology and hairdressing	Cosmetology, body shaping, hair cutting/hair care/perm	Beauty industry, hairdressing industry
	Health examination	Premarital examination	Health examination center, hospital
Holding a wedding	Style design	Personal styling/make-up	Beauty industry, hairdressing industry, wedding photography
	Leasing of wedding party place	Customization of church and banquet place	Hospitality industry, tourism
	Wedding decoration	Customization of balloons and flowers	General merchandise for wedding, flower shop, wedding consultant
	Limousine arrangement and shuttle transfer	Limousine rental, shuttle transfer for relatives and friends	Automobile rental industry (rental of car, tourist coach)
	Arrangement of wedding process	Wedding host	Wedding consultant industry
		Bride secretary	Wedding consultant industry
		Wedding recording/photography	Wedding consultant industry, wedding photography industry
		MV producing and playing	Photography industry
	Wedding banquet	Catering, banquet	Hospitality industry, catering industry
	Gift for wedding ceremony	Small gifts for guests	Wedding consultant industry, wedding merchandise industry
	Accommodation arrangement	Relatives and friends' accommodation	Lodging industry
Post-wedding life	Honeymoon trip	Domestic and foreign tour, accommodation and shuttle arrangement	Tourism
	Household appliances	Household appliances (purchasing TV, refrigerator, etc)	Household appliances retail industry
	New house purchasing and decoration	House purchasing and decoration	Real estate agency, interior design industry
	Furniture and bedding	New house furniture (bed, cabinet, etc) and bedding (bed sheet, quilt, etc)	Furniture, bedding, house ornament industry
	Insurances	Various types of insurances	Insurance industry
	One month after newborn birth	Feast and gift for one-month-old newborn	Food retail industry, cake and pastry industry
	Anniversary	Anniversary, special photos, party and tour for golden or silver wedding	Wedding photography industry, hospitality industry, tourism, lodging industry

Research Methodology

This study summarizes related literature and uses the Jiro Kawakita (KJ) method and modified Delphi method of qualitative research to establish bridal hair style evaluation scheme and bridal hair design factor evaluation framework. Then, it utilizes AHP of quantitative research to establish bridal hair style design factor evaluation mode, determine criterion weighting, and decide substitute scheme, to provide Taiwanese bridal secretaries or consumers with a set of objective, effective methods to choose the most suitable bridal hair style in the process of practical design.

Conclusion

This study uses KJ method to obtain seven schemes of bridal hair style design evaluation: romantic style, personalized style, classical style, fashionable style, magnificent style, sweet style and elegant style. At the second phase, this study uses modified Delphi method to establish a bridal hair style design evaluation framework. Through two rounds of expert questionnaire, 16 experts reach an agreement on the evaluation framework, and establish bridal hair style design evaluation criteria and key factors. Principal criteria of evaluation include personal background, external conditions, clothes and accessories and use timing and venue (Table 2). Six sub-criteria of the perspective "personal background" are as follows in order of importance: personal preference, personality, consumption ability, educational background, occupation and age (Table 3).

TABLE 2
THE WEIGHT VALUE OF MAIN CRITERIA FOR THE OPTIMAL BRIDAL HAIRSTYLE DESIGN SCHEME

Design scheme	Weight value	Order number
Personal background	0.321	1
External conditions	0.286	2
Use time and venue	0.249	3
Clothes and accessories	0.144	4
C.I.	0.00316	
C.R.	0.0035	C.I./R.I.
λmax	4.0009	m+(C.I.×(m-1))

TABLE 3
THE WEIGHT VALUE OF EACH DIMENSION INDEX UNDER THE PERSPECTIVE OF PERSONAL BACKGROUND

Design scheme	Weight value	Order number
Occupation	0.062	5
Age	0.060	6
Personality	0.280	2
Personal preference	0.378	1
Educational	0.077	4
Consumption ability	0.143	3
C.I.	0.00405	
C.R.	0.00326	C.I./R.I.
λmax	6.020	m+(C.I.×(m-1))

Six sub-criteria of the perspective "external conditions" are as follows in order of importance: facial form and forehead height, hair color, hair quality and amount, hair length, head form, body height and weight (Table 4). Four sub-criteria of the perspective "use timing and site" are as follows in order of importance: taking photos, engagement, getting married, visit the parental home, wedding party, approaching, toast, seeing off guests, outdoors or indoors, luncheon or dinner party (Table 5). Four sub-criteria of the perspective "clothes and accessories" are as follows in order of importance: dress style, dress pattern, accessory pattern and accessory style (Table 6). Practical verification of optimal decision making scheme of bridal hair style.

TABLE 4
THE WEIGHT VALUE OF EACH DIMENSION INDEX UNDER THE PERSPECTIVE OF EXTERNAL CONDITIONS

Dimension	Weight value	Order number
Height and weight	0.058	6
Head form	0.121	5
Facial form and forehead height	0.317	1
Hair length	0.134	4
Hair quality and amount	0.150	3
Hair color	0.220	2
C.I.	0.00405	
C.R.	0.00326	C.I./R.I.
λmax	6.020	m+(C.I.×(m-1))

TABLE 5
THE WEIGHT VALUE OF EACH DIMENSION INDEX UNDER THE PERSPECTIVE OF USE TIMING AND VENUE

Dimension	Weight value	Order number
Taking photos, engagement, getting married vi sit the parental home	0.375	1
Wedding party, approaching, toast, seeing off guests	0.330	2
Outdoors or indoors	0.155	3
Luncheon or dinner party	0.140	4
C.I.	0.007	
C.R.	0.0077	C.I./R.I.
λmax	4.021	m+(C.I.×(m-1))

TABLE 6
THE WEIGHT VALUE OF EACH DIMENSION INDEX UNDER THE PERSPECTIVE OF CLOTHES AND ACCESSORIES

Dimension	Weight value	Order number
Dress style	0.295	2
Dress pattern	0.440	1
Accessory pattern	0.145	3
Accessory style	0.120	4
C.I.	0.00572	
C.R.	0.00143	C.I./R.I.
λmax	4.017	m+(C.I.×(m-1))

Miss Qian will get married in October of this year and wants to receive services of pilot makeup and hair styling in terms of wedding dress photography, engagement styling and wedding styling. Three evaluation scales are used respectively, with the scores 1 to 9 representing extreme dissatisfaction to extreme satisfaction. Regarding the seven substitute schemes of this study, 20 evaluation criteria are given proper scores as original scores. Then, overall weighting is calculated to obtain a composite score. The style of bridal wedding dress photography is romantic; the style of the bride in engagement ceremony is classical; the bridal style in wedding ceremony is Magnificent (Figs. 1–3).

Fig. 1 The most suitable bridal hair style of Miss Qian in the process of practical design "Romantic style" (Wedding photo modeling).

Fig. 2 The most suitable bridal hair style of Miss Qian in the process of practical design "Classical style" (Bridal engagement).

Fig. 3 The most suitable bridal hair style of Miss Qian in the process of practical design "Magnificent style" (Modelling of marriage).

Acknowledgment

The work was supported by the Special Taiwan Talent Fund of Lingnan Normal University (ZW2008 and ZW2009).

References

[1] Charsley, Simon R., Wedding Cakes and Cultural History, London: Routledge, 1992.

[2] Lewis, Charles, Hegemony in the ideal: wedding photography, consumerism, and patriarchy, Women's Studies in Communication, Vol. 20, No. 2, Fall 1997, 167-187.

[3] Li Yu-Ying, The Bride Maker: The Formation and Development of the Bridal Industry in Taiwan, Feng Chia Journal of Humanities and Social Sciences, 2004, No. 8, P183-217.

[4] Wu Pei-Zhen, Investigation into Role and Market Demand of Bridal Secretary, National Chung Cheng University, Senior Executive Management Institute, master thesis, 2014.

[5] Lin Lu, Teach Lin Lu's guide for bridal secretary beginners; Taipei city, China Times Publishing Company, initial version, 2005.

https://doi.org/10.1142/9789811238727_0034

Establish Artistic Anatomy Knowledge in Digital Sculpture Courses

Hung Sun[1*], Chìn-Chun Chen[2]

China University of Technology, No. 56, Sec. 3, Xinglong Rd., Wunshan District, Taipei City 116, Taiwan
*Corresponding Author Email: arion3d@gm.cute.edu.tw

Abstract

Artistic anatomy involves the study of 3D forms which is related to the human body itself and its constitutive structures as the basis for 3D modeling of topographic line structures. Understanding artistic anatomy relies on visual and 3D spatial concepts and is the foundation of students' education in developing games and making animations. By combining graphical data of anatomical structures with the production of digital sculptures, students were provided a new way to interact with anatomical structures. Six human sculpture sessions were planned for the course and tested both before and after the sessions. The results showed that the digital sculpture course resulted in a consistent improvement in students' understanding and concepts of artistic anatomy and an understanding of the relationship between the line structure of the 3D model and the texture of the human body.

Keywords: artistic anatomy, digital sculpture, 3D modeling, topology

Introduction

Since the Renaissance, artists like Leonardo da Vinci shared their knowledge through their works, and the close relationship between anatomy and painting continues until today [1]. With the rapid development of 3D games and animation real-time algorithms, producing high-quality art is a basic requirement for 3D artists. In addition to basic 3D animation software, digital sculpture software for sculpting precise model details is a must-have skill for 3D learners. Anatomy is the basis of surgical and public health teaching and is taught through a combination of three main approaches: graphic-based learning, physical model learning, and learning through virtual models [2]. Digital media students have different needs than medical students in terms of understanding skeletal relationships and major muscle composition, which are applied in the creation of digital character models, where the 3D line structure of the model can conform to the human body's musculature. Previous studies on 3D visualization in anatomy teaching have pointed out that 3D physical modeling is an effective method to establish spatial relationships in anatomy teaching [3]. Therefore, this study brings the knowledge of artistic anatomy into the digital sculpture curriculum, combining digital clay and character creation processes. By combining the graphic data of anatomical structures with digital sculpture production, it can provide students with new ways to interact with anatomical structures and establish the basic concepts of 3D modeling framework.

When using digital sculpture, students are required to follow artistic anatomy in sculpting human models and derive the results into self-created characters. The course also incorporates 3D printing of students' works to enhance students' motivation and learning outcomes.

Literature Review

A. Artistic Anatomy

The foundation of the medical curriculum consists of anatomy, and therefore is essential for medical students to have a basic understanding of the structures and their interrelationships as part of their undergraduate training. Anatomy involves the study of three-dimensional entities related to the human body itself and its constituent structures. For medical students, it is important to understand two-dimensional medical imaging data and to reconstruct three-dimensional models in the mind [4]. Human anatomy is the science of the shape and structure of the human body, but most anatomy education is still based on book-based formats [5]. Therefore, appropriate resources such as modern digital meta-3D models should be used to enhance spatial ability and anatomical understanding through the interactivity of visual learning to promote the learning ability to understand anatomy [6].

In recent years, it has become common to use digital 3D models for lectures and teaching of anatomy. In addition to online 3D models, virtual reality is also used for teaching anatomy [7]. Even the social media Facebook is used to create human anatomy education pages [8], which effectively demonstrate multiple perspectives of anatomy by encouraging collaboration and providing learner participation and motivation. Artistic anatomy focuses on understanding the relationship between external muscle form and motor structure. In a previous study, a modeling approach similar to the discipline of artistic anatomy was used to develop an anatomy-based muscle model. That study pointed out that applying knowledge of human anatomy to the development of human models is necessary if a high degree of realism is to be achieved [9].

B. Digital Sculpt

The focus of the Digital Media Department is on 3D animation or games. Learning 3D modeling is the beginning of all 3D software. Unlike the point, line, and surface editing modeling method of general 3D software, digital sculpture is a form of digital clay sculpture with a high degree of freedom, which is especially suitable for character creation. The human body itself and its structure involves the study of artistic anatomy, which is the basis of 3D character modeling. Understanding of artistic anatomy is a fundamental education for digital media students to develop games and animation characters.

After forming the human body shape using digital sculpting, the structure is further simplified according to the knowledge of the structural components of artistic anatomy, which still follows the concept of artistic anatomy. The 3D scanned real human body can also be used as the basis for constructing a low-polygon geometric model of the human body that follows the main features of anatomy, considering the rules of traditional polygon modeling [10].

C. Curriculum Design

The curriculum is designed with reference to the "ORDER" process, an "Observe-Reflect-Draw-Edit-Repeat" circle process based on cognitivist and constructivist learning theories and the process of critical observation, reflection, and drawing in anatomical learning [11]. Replacing the "drawing" step with "doing" can facilitate the incorporation of alternative artistic techniques. In the course on human muscle sculpture, the above learning approach is integrated and students are asked to use digital sculpture to produce human structures containing details by observing pictorial data and thinking about steps and layers. Blended learning is used as the most basic teaching aid.

Research Methodology

A. Digital Sculpture and Artistic Anatomy

In this study, the steps of ORDER [11] were modified to observation-analysis-sculpting-modification-repeat. First, we collected human anatomy pictures using online resources such as "Pinterest" and integrated them into a reference picture for students as a basic reference, the relevant detailed pictures were then viewed at any time using "Pure Ref" software, and the surface was presented as Figure 1.

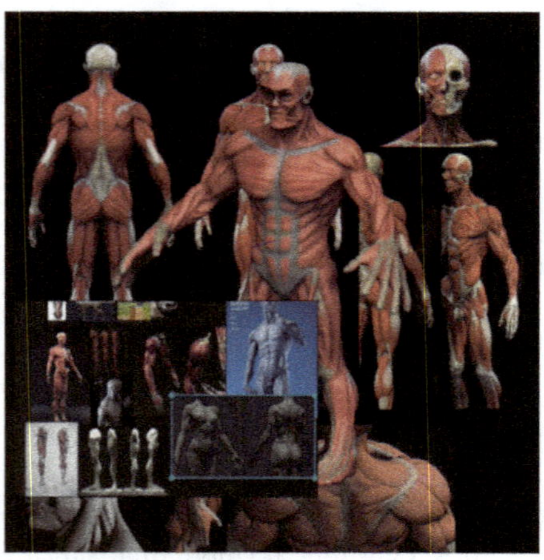

Fig. 1 Screen shot of an anatomical human sculpture in operation demonstration.

With the availability of various digital human generators or 3D scanned human model libraries, there is no need to build a basic human model from scratch. This study uses "Make Human ", an open source free software, as a starting point for generating a basic human body and understanding human body composition, which converts race, age, sex, and body shape, including detailed muscle size, into parameters for control. The basic physical appearance of Caucasians, Africans, and Asians can be explained together during setup. By adjusting the parameters, the students can understand the changes in body shape in terms of muscle mass and fat ratio. Students will be asked to develop their own human model materials to be used.

The muscle structure of each part is verbally explained during the demonstration of the sculpting method, and memorization is not deliberately required. Through the progression of each lesson, students are reminded repeatedly to sculpt themselves according to the reference pictures during the exercises. Blended learning offers additional learning possibilities, with classroom video recordings of all lectures and additional independent teaching modules as appropriate.

B. One-Group Pretest-Posttest Design

Since digital sculpture and 3D animation are professional courses in schools, it is not appropriate to implement a typical experimental design, i.e., randomly assigning to experimental group and control group, to avoid unfair effects on students' teaching. The basic design framework of this study is a one-group pretest-posttest design based on the researcher's previous teaching experience, in which the students were pretested before the experimental treatment and post-tested after the experimental treatment. The research structure is shown in Figure 2.

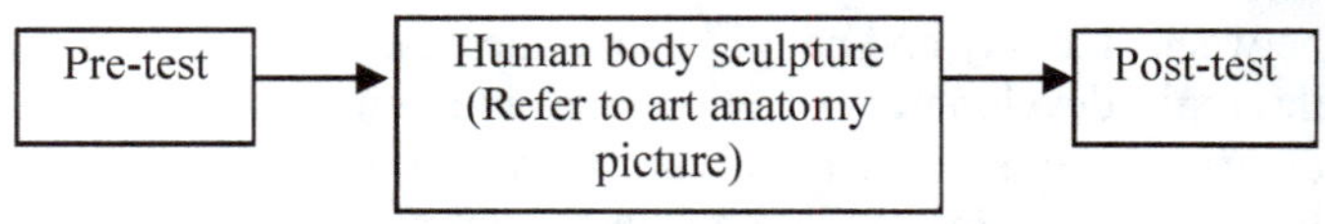

Fig. 2 Schematic diagram of the study design.

In its most common form, the One-Group Pretest-Posttest is a pre- and post-experimental variable test that measures changes in knowledge, attitudes, satisfaction, or skills of a single group of subjects [12]. The main weakness of this design is the lack of control groups for comparative comparisons, the limited control of validity, and the inability to determine the direct effect of experimental variables on the results [13, 14]. The responses to some of the threats of the One-Group Pretest-Posttest in this study are described in Table 1. The pre-posttest was administered with different levels of difficulty to reduce the effect of luck or statistical regression.

TABLE 1
Countermeasures For The Validity Of Single-Group Prediction-Post-test Designs.

Threats	Correspondence
History	Encouraging students to learn independently through other means may have some impact.
Maturation	The interval between pre and post-tests is short.
Testing	The difficulty level of the pre and post-test is different.
Instrumentation	Online exams are used instead of scale questionnaires.
Statistical Regression	The test subjects were anonymous and voluntary.

C. Test Design

The Artistic Anatomy Knowledge Test is divided into two stages: pre-test and post-test. The pre-test consists of 13 questions, which measure students' basic understanding of human muscles, the association of 3D models, and the names of muscles in various parts of the body. The post-test retains some of the questions with a higher error rate in the pre-test, and adds questions on muscle function and function, combined with 3D modeling, and more detailed muscle names, for a total of 16 questions.

Both the pre-test and post-test were reviewed by two industry experts and two university professors for difficulty and interpretation of the questions, and comments were given as shown in Table 2. The two industry experts were digital sculpture prototype designers and professional 3D designers, while one university professor taught clay sculpture and 3D game art, and the other taught 3D animation and game art.

It is expected that after 6 sessions of artistic anatomical sculpture practice, the post-test results will be improved.

TABLE 2
Expert Review Of Pre And Post Test Questions

	Pre-test	Post-test
Industry Expert A	This is very OK, it is basic common sense. In addition to muscle names may not remember.	I know the parts, but I don't remember the names on purpose. It should be difficult for students.
Industry Expert B	No problem, all should know.	You need to have studied the relevant knowledge to answer.
University Teacher A	The range is the basic knowledge of learning 3D modelling. Muscle names may be a challenge.	The subject matter is quite difficult and should not be taught without special instruction in artistic anatomy.
University Teacher B	All are the basic concepts of 3D character modelling.	The questions are distinguishable, and certain muscle names need to be memorized with special attention.

D. Data Collection

Before starting the human structure sculpture course, two classes of students were given a pre-test, which was filled in anonymously and freely, and the test was created by Google Forms. After six sessions, a post-test was conducted and the results of the sculpture assignments were collected and examined. Figure 3 shows the students' sculpture results following the anatomy of art.

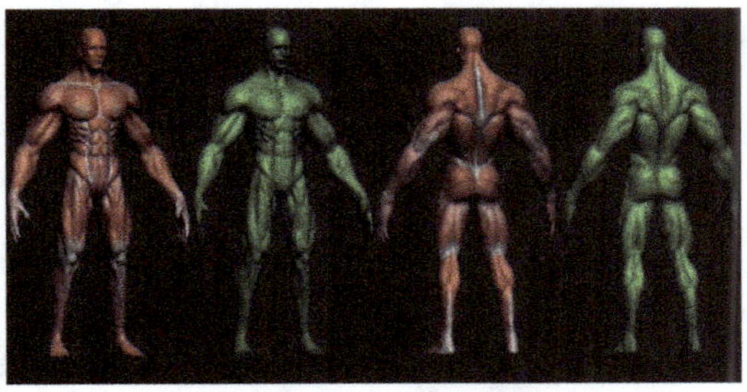

Fig. 3 Student's anatomy Sculpt homework.

TABLE 3
Group Statistics (Pre-Test)

	Category	N	Mean	Std. Deviation	Std. Error Mean
Score	Male	27	55.9259	12.66104	2.43662
	Female	65	45.1231	13.34109	1.65476
	Class A	51	45.7255	13.48047	1.88764
	Class B	41	51.4878	14.09277	2.20092
	Know	26	50.9615	15.64476	3.06819
	Unknow	66	47.2424	13.24800	1.63072

TABLE 4
Independent Sample T Test (Pre-Test)

		Levene's Test for Equality of Variances		t-test for Equality of Means	
		F	Sig.	t	Sig. (2-tailed)
Score	Gender	.001	.974	3.589	.001**
	Class	.005	.946	-1.997	.049**
	Know	1.101	.297	1.151	.253

**P<0.05

Result & Discussion

A. Pre-test analysis

A total of 99 student results were collected in the previous test, including 27 males and 65 females. Perform independent sample T tests on gender, class, and whether there is prior knowledge based on scores, as shown in Table 3 and Table 4.

The results of the F-test were all equal variances assumed. The two-tailed significance p-value for gender = $0.001<0.05$ and the two-tailed significance p-value for class = $0.049<0.05$, indicating that there was a significant difference between the pretest scores of gender and class, and that males were higher than females and class A was higher than class B. The knowledge of art anatomy was not significant, indicating that there was no difference.

B. Post-test analysis

After six sessions of human sculpting, the test was repeated by changing the questions. The mean and median scores of the pre and post-tests are shown in Table 5, which shows that the scores have improved.

TABLE 5

Comparison Of Mean And Median Of Pre And Post Test

Test	Mean	N	Std. Deviation	Median
Pre-test	48.2935	92	13.980	48.00
Post-test	57.58	67	18.986	58.00

The post-test was not only modified to increase the difficulty of the questions, but also added other questions. There are 68 students participating in the post-test, including 22 males and 45 females. The independent sample T test was performed on gender and class again with scores. The two-tailed significance p-value of gender=0.086>0.05, and the two-tailed significance p-value of class level=0.784>0.05, which is the rejection hypothesis, which means that after the course, there was no significant difference in post-test scores between gender and class.

Table 6 & 7 presents the two-tailed significance p-value of learning initiative=0.000<0.05, indicating that students who were active learners showed significant differences from passive learners in the post-test, with higher scores for students who actively sought information.

TABLE 6

Group Statistics (POST-TEST)

	Active Reserch	N	Mean	Std. Deviation	Std. Error Mean
Score	Y	37	64.70	17.133	2.817
	N	30	48.80	17.649	3.222

TABLE 7

Independent sample T test (Post-test)

		Levene's Test for Equality of Variances		t-test for Equality of Means	
		F	Sig.	t	Sig. (2-tailed)
Score	Active	.007	.932	3.728	.000**

Conclusion

The digital sculpture software presents the development trend of 3D digital technology, which can constitute the development of students' perception, imagination, and shaping power in modeling creation [15]. The students' final character creation results are presented in Figure 4 after learning to follow the concept of artistic anatomy through digital sculpture.

After six sessions of sculpting the human body, the gender and class no longer differed in the post-test, and the mean and median scores increased, indicating that the use of digital sculpture to sculpt the human body muscles can indeed improve students' knowledge of artistic anatomy on average. In addition, the results of the post-test, which included a question on self-initiated learning, showed a significant difference in scores between students who actively collected data and those who passively did so. It can be said that the course did have a good impact and motivated some students to learn, leading to more effective teaching.

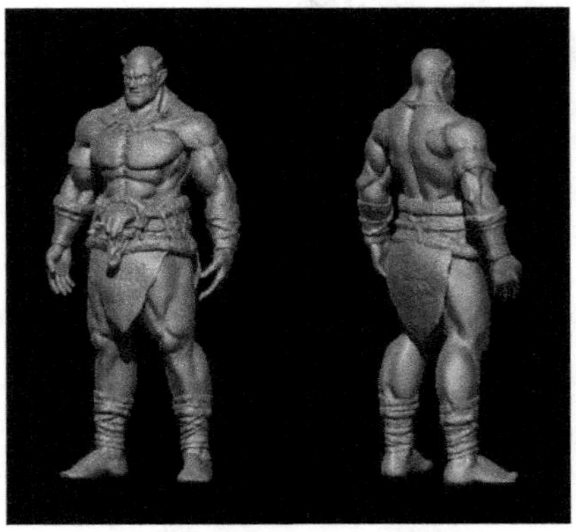

Fig. 4 Students' digital sculpture character creation.

Research limitations

Due to the One-Group Pretest-Posttest Design and anonymous free participation, it cannot be ruled out that students with poor learning tend not to participate in the post-test, resulting in a lower sample size and a skewed distribution of the sample in the higher score groups. In the future, a more rigorous experimental design is needed.

References

[1] Finn G M 2019 Painting, Pirouettes and Proving: A Tool-kit of Methods for Engagement in Anatomy. *The FASEB Journal*, ***33***(S1), 21-3.

[2] Avila F J 2016 Diseño de material didáctico para la enseñanza de anatomía. *Systems & design: beyond processes and thinking*, 1015-30.

[3] Estevez M E, Lindgren K A and Bergethon P R 2010 A novel three-dimensional tool for teaching human neuroanatomy. *Anatomical sciences education*, *3*(6), 309-317.

[4] Smit N, Hofstede C W, Kraima A, Jansma D, deRuiter M, Eisemann E and Vilanova A 2016 The online anatomical human: Web-based anatomy education. *Proc. Eurogr. Educ. Pap*, *2016*, 37-40.

[5] Nunn J F 2002 *Ancient egyptian medicine*. University of Oklahoma Press.

[6] Keenan I D and ben Awadh A 2019 Integrating 3D visualisation technologies in undergraduate anatomy education. *Biomedical Visualisation*, 39-53.

[7] Erolin C, Reid L and McDougall S 2019 Using virtual reality to complement and enhance anatomy education. *Journal of visual communication in medicine*, ***42***(3), 93-101.

[8] Jaffar A A 2014 Exploring the use of a Facebook page in anatomy education. *Anatomical sciences education*, *7*(3), 199-208.

[9] Scheepers F, Parent R E, Carlson W E and May S F 1997 Anatomy-based modeling of the human musculature. In *Proceedings of the 24th annual conference on Computer graphics and interactive techniques*, 163-172

[10] Azevedo H D and Araújo A 2020 Towards a canon for digital human anatomy 3D modeling. In *ARTeFACTo2020. International Conference on Digital Creation in Arts and Communication* 121-126. Edições Centro de Investigação em Artes e Comunicação.

[11] Backhouse M, Fitzpatrick M, Hutchinson J, Thandi C S and Keenan I D 2017 Improvements in anatomy knowledge when utilizing a novel cyclical "observe-reflect-draw-edit-repeat" learning process. *Anatomical sciences education*, ***10***(1), 7-22.

[12] Spurlock D R 2018 The single-group, pre-and posttest design in nursing education research: It's time to move on. *Journal of Nursing Education*, ***57***(2), 69-71.

[13] Campbell D T and Stanley J C 2015 *Experimental and quasi-experimental designs for research.* Ravenio Books.

[14] Knapp T R 2016 Why is the one-group pretest–posttest design still used?.

[15] Yuan Y 2018 Research on the Application of Digital Engraving Software in the Teaching of Digital Media Art Design Course. In *2018 13th International Conference on Computer Science & Education (ICCSE)* (pp. 1-5). IEEE.

https://doi.org/10.1142/9789811238727_0035

Exploration of Novice Designers' Modes of Thinking from the Perspective of Graphic Simplification

Hui-Ping Lu[1*], Hsin-Hung Lin[2]

[1]Department of Visual Communication Design, Asia University, Taichung 41354, Taiwan
[2]Department of Creative Product Design, Asia University, Taichung 41354, Taiwan
[*]Corresponding Author Email: jasmine@asia.edu.tw, Tel: 886-4-2332-3456 ext.6407

Abstract

This study reviewed a design case to explore novice designers' modes of thinking. The design case involved a graphic simplification process from the representation to the abstraction stages. The presentation of the resulting design work was analyzed to compile modes of thinking commonly used by novice designers. The study results revealed that novice designers demonstrated varying modes of thinking in different design stages. From the representation stage to the semi-representation stage, designers preferred preserving the composition of the original object, but the graphic and color of the object were simplified. From the semi-representation stage to the abstraction stage, various presentation approaches were adopted. One of the approaches involved changing the original composition, shuffling and rearranging design elements, and then forming a new composition. Another approach involved preserving the original composition, partially enlarging element features or changing the original viewpoint, and presenting the design from multiple perspectives. Gaining a further understanding on the common modes of thinking adopted by novice designers and providing adequate guidance during design processes can substantially facilitate the development of professional design ability.

Keywords: graphic simplification, modes of thinking

Introduction

Signs such as texts and images -as sources of inspiration- are crucial for stimulating design thinking and imagination (Cheng, 2010). The most effective forms of inspiration for designers are visual materials, specifically graphics and images (Menezes & Lawson, 2006). Studies have indicated that designers tend to search through a large quantity of visual materials and integrate them through mental imagery to develop design concepts (Schön & Wigins, 1992; Goldschmidt, 1994; McGown, Green, & Rodgers, 1998; Verstijnem, Hennessey, Leeuwen, Hamel, & Goldschmidt, 1998; Suwa, Gero, & Purcell, 2000; Dorst & Cross, 2001). At the beginning of a conceptual phase, referring to relevant materials benefits the design process (Herbert, 1993; McGown, Green, & Rodgers, 1998). The process of converting images to design concepts occurs in designers' brains and involves their personal intuition, experience, and preferences. Veteran designers have accumulated experience over time and can easily grasp the elements within images for inspiration, whereas novice designers typically find rapidly and smoothly creating concepts difficult without effective methodical aids. In the present study, designer tasks were given to novice designers to generate artistic works for observing such designers' processes of converting concrete images into abstract ideas. The methods these designers adopted were compiled for future comparison with those of veteran designers, providing a reference for training novice designers in simplifying graphics and conceptualizing design styles.

Literature

Two definitions of abstract exist as (1) imaginative images converted from concrete images, and (2) purely intuitive and imaginative illustrations with no concepts drawn from concrete objects. Abstract illustrations can be expressed in two forms. One involves simplifying concrete images of natural phenomena or extracting their expressive elements to form a simple abstract image, whereas the other incorporates purely abstract conceptualization without the basis of natural objects. In the present study, the first form was adopted. In the remainder of this section, methods of graphic simplification are described according to various fields.

A. Graphic Simplification in Arts

Pablo Picasso created 'Bull' around the Christmas of 1945. 'Bull' is a suite of eleven lithographs that have become a masterclass in how to develop an artwork from the academic to the abstract. In this series of images, all pulled from a single stone, Picasso visually dissects the image of a bull to discover its essential presence through a progressive analysis of its form. Each plate is a successive stage in an investigation to find the absolute spirit of the beast (Artyfactory, 2019). Picasso extracted critical information from a realistic image and simplified it into a near-abstract image (Fig. 1). Tree, a famous series of artworks by Piet Mondrian, was formed through the abstraction of concrete images using simplified lines and colors. The Red Tree (Fig. 2), inspired by the art style of Van Gogh, exhibits the clear outline of a tree but also features rough lines and contrasting colors. Mondrian replaced his previously realistic illustration style with the 2D image of a tree using line expression. The Gray Tree (Fig. 3), inspired by cubism, emphasizes compositional balance; numerous tiny branches are replaced with curves in the process of simplification. Based on the shape of a real tree, The

Flowering Apple Tree (Fig. 4) features further simplified line expressions; instead of a clear natural entity, an abstract expression consisting of basic geometric lines is displayed with novel compositional unity and balance.

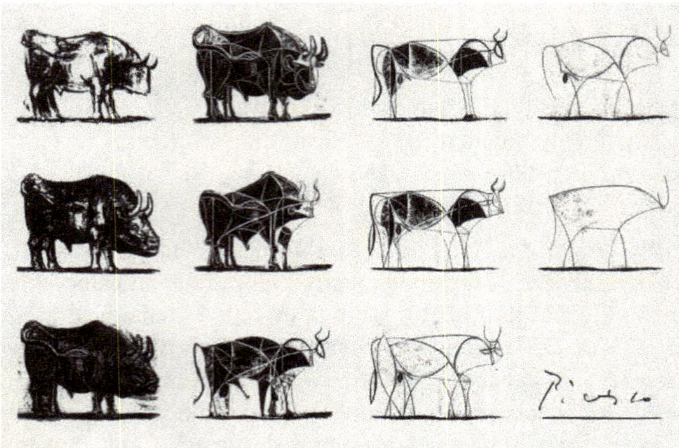

Fig. 1 Pablo Picasso (1881-1973) 'Bull', 1945.

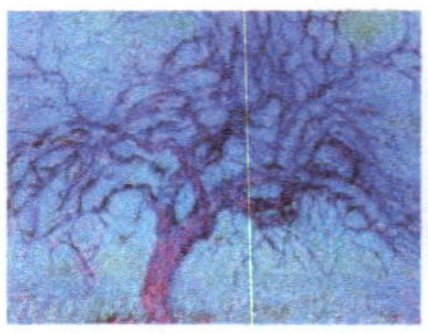
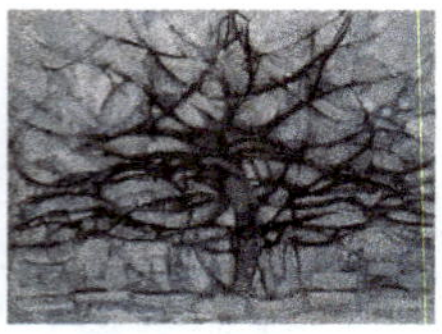
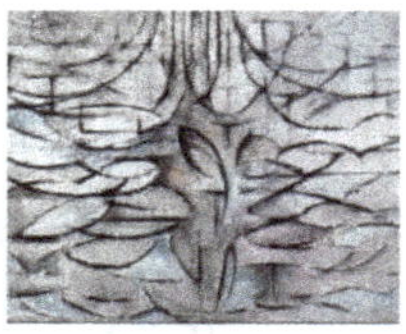

Fig. 2(left) Piet Mondrian (1908) 'The red tree'
Fig. 3(middle) Piet Mondrian (1912) 'Gray tree'
Fig. 4(right) Piet Mondrian (1912) 'The flowering apple tree'

B. Graphic Simplification in Comics

McCloud (1993) devised five steps of graphic simplification. Fig. 5 illustrates the transition of an image from realistic to iconic from left to right, revealing two representative directions. The image on the far left is most realistic, detailed, and identifiable, whereas that on the right is the most abstract, requires the highest level of perception, and provides the broadest room for interpretation. Different forms of expression enable readers to participate in the world of a comic and obtain enjoyable reading experience, which can be further enhanced by graphic simplification.

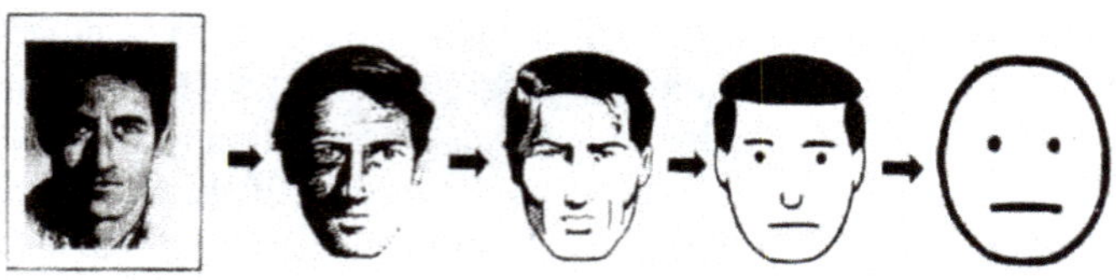

Fig. 5 Five processes of graphic simplification (from McCloud, 1993)

C. Graphic Simplification in Design

Simplification is a process of organizing a complex visual message into a simple one. In addition to removing small details, simplification involves adjusting an image's representation. Simplified graphics can be applied in various fields, such as logos, comics, illustrations, posters, and graphic designs. Studies have reported that simplified graphic designs attract greater viewer attention and are more identifiable than realistic graphic designs (Hsu, 2007). Because designers tend to process images emotionally and intuitively, in the research article

"Cognitive study on the design operation of graphic simplification," Hsu (2007) discusses methods for determining the identifiability of an image and facilitating favorable graphic designs. Rules and numerical values involved in the procedures are clarified to supplement designers' intuition and provide novices with guidance. Moreover, the same research classifies the approaches to graphic simplification into the abstract simplification of external visual stimulation and abstract formation of internal mental mechanisms, with the former emphasizing the abstraction of external objects and the latter focusing on the concretization of the internal part (Hsu and Wang, 2005). Figs. 6 and 7 illustrate the two most commonly adopted graphic simplification approaches, namely the extraction of complete form and extraction of partial features, which are typically jointly applied in design (Wang & Hsu, 2007).

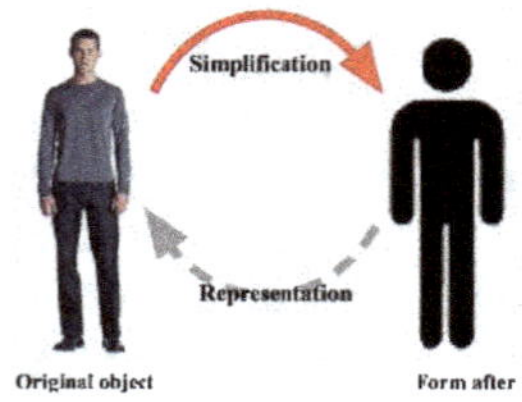

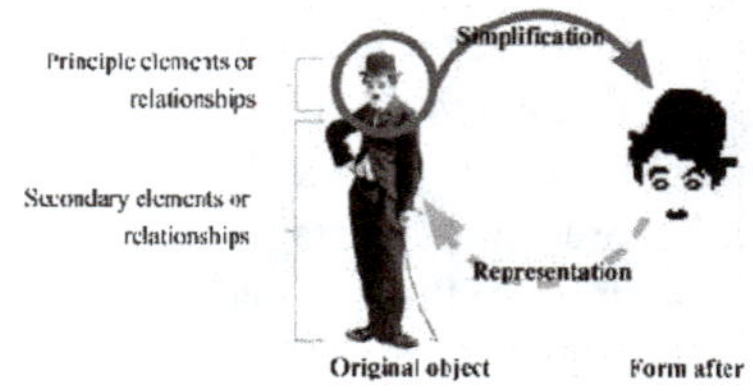

Fig. 6 (left) Extraction of complete form (from Hsu & Wang, 2010)
Fig. 7 (right) Extraction of partial features (from Hsu & Wang, 2010)

Method

This study employed a design task to investigate the transitional thought process of 60 novice designers. They were divided into 10 six-person groups, and each group was assigned with one of the following school attractions: (1) Art work, (2) Management building, (3) Information building, (4) Station, (5) Gymnasium, (6) Museum, (7) Rose garden, (8) Lotus pond, (9) Health building, (10) Administration building.

The three steps involved in the task, namely representation, semi-representation, and abstraction (Fig. 8), are described as follows:

1. Representation: participants cast lots to determine the site from top ten campus sites they will work in. Data were collected in the form of photographs, which could be taken repetitively and cropped according to their compositional needs.
2. Semi-representation: The photographs of the attractions were simplified into semi-representational images by removing lines of excessive details while retaining the attractions' shapes and colors.
3. Abstraction: The semi-representational images were converted into abstract images.

Most of the novice designers were inexperienced in design. Therefore, before the task started, the aforementioned art works Bull by Picasso and Tree by Mondrian were provided as examples for the participants to reference. After the task was accomplished, the design works with the same themes were compared for analysis.

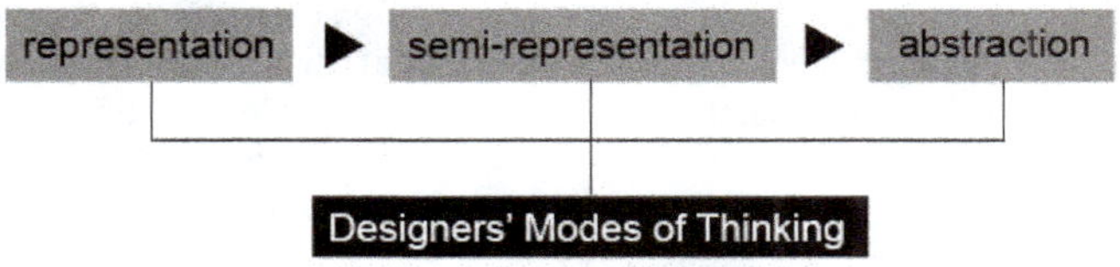

Fig. 8 Conceptual framework

Discussion

This study collected six works around the theme of lotus pond (Table 1). The following discusses these works from the perspective of three simplification processes:

1. Representation: The original photographs taken for the six cases displayed three modes of framing: close-ups (cases 1 & 2), medium shots (cases 3 & 4), and long shots (cases 5 & 6). In the close-ups, because the main objects filled the majority of the frame, details in the flowers and leaves were included for additional graphic variability. In the other four cases, because the main objects filled a relatively smaller portion of the frame, internal details were omitted in favor of simplification of the appearance; however, most of the cases retained the color schemes of the original photographs.
2. Semi-representation: In cases 1, 3, 4, and 6, the original photograph compositions were retained but the shapes and colors were simplified. In cases 2 and 5, the original compositions were altered for graphic reconstruction. In case 2, extensive lines were applied to segment the image to form blocks. Cases 2, 3, and 4 adopted points of view different from the original one taken by the camera, and the most characteristic parts of the objects were reassembled. For example, although the point of view of the lotus flowers was retained, that of the leaves was changed, forming a juxtaposition of different spaces. In case 5, the point of view was completely altered, creating an interesting contrast effect.
3. Abstraction: In cases 1 and 2, the works created in the semi-representation step were disassembled to create new images. In cases 3 and 4, the composition of these works was retained for further simplification. In cases 5 and 6, the composition was rearranged to create 2D graphic effects, forming graphics with notable color blocks. In particularly, in case 6, a grid was formed with graphic components within, creating a special decorative style.

Conclusion

The thinking patterns of the novice designers and phases of their graphic transition process were revealed through analyzing the aforementioned six cases.

1. The composition of an original photograph, particularly the proportion of the frame filled by the main object, affects the design concept and expression form of its abstract representation. When this proportion is relatively large, various textural details can be added for enhanced graphic variety. Otherwise, said details may be omitted in favor of graphic simplification of the appearance.
2. The semi-representation and abstraction phases primarily involved reducing the use of lines and colors. Occasionally, the camera's point of view of the original photograph can be partially altered for view-angle juxtaposition. Extensive lines can also be employed to segment the graphics or establish grids, and the main object can be re-placed in the grid.
3. The abstraction phase is primarily characterized by graphic recomposition, in which 3D spatial distribution is converted to 2D distribution. Components can be disassembled for rearranging. Examples are converting the original forms of the lotus flowers and leaves into simple blocks. Alternatively, the original composition can be retained for further simplification.

Design has widely been regarded as a secretive process, which is revealed only after the approaches employed are uncovered. In the present study, the transition process of the novice designers' thinking was examined. Future studies will compare this process with that of veteran designers to uncover the differences between them, providing a reference for training novice designers in graphic simplification.

TABLE 1
6 GRAPHIC SIMPLIFICATION CASES

	representation	semi-representation	abstraction
Case 1			
Case 2			
Case 3			
Case 4			

Case 5			
Case 6			

References

[1] Animals in art-Pablo Picasso (http://www.artyfactory.com/art_appreciation/animals_in_art/p ablo_picasso.htm)

[2] P. J. Cheng, *A study on designers' searching-retrieving behavior in the ideation process*. Unpublished doctoral dissertation, National Yunlin University of Science & Technology, Yunlin. 2010.

[3] K. Dorst and N. Cross, Creativity in the design process co-evolution of problem-solution. *Design Studies, 22*(5), 425-437, 2001.

[4] D. M. Herbert, *Architectural study drawings*. New York: Nostrand Reinhold. 1993.

[5] C. C. Hsu and W. Y. Redefining, Abstraction in Visual Art and Design. *Journal of Design, 10*(3), 81-100, 2007.

[6] C. C. Hsu, *Cognitive study on the Design Operation of Graphic Simplification.* Unpublished doctoral dissertation, National Taiwan University of Science and Technology, Taipei City, 2007.

[7] S. McCloud, *Understanding comics: The invisible art.* New York: HarperCollins, 1993.

[8] A. McGown, G. Green and P. Rodgers, Visible ideas: Information patterns of conceptual sketch activity. *Design Studies, 19*(4), 431-453, 1998.

[9] A. Menezes and B. Lawson, How designers perceive sketches. *Design Studies, 27*(5), 571-585, 2006.

[10] G. Goldschmidt, On visual design thinking: The vis kids of architecture. *Design Studies, 15*(2), 159-174, 1994.

[11] D. A. Schön and G. Wiggins, Kinds of seeing and their function in designing. *Design Studies, 13*(2), 135-156, 1992.

[12] M. Suwa and J. Gero, Unexpected discoveries and S-invention of design requirement: important vehicle for a design process. *Design Studies*, 21(6), 539-567, 2000.

[13] I. M. Verstijnem, J. Hennessey, C. Leeuwen, C. Hamel and G. Goldschmidt, Sketching and creative discovery. Design Studies, 19(4), 519-546, 1998.

https://doi.org/10.1142/9789811238727_0036

Exploratory Visual Field to Support Agent Analysis

Shaofu Li

Department of Architecture and Urban Planning, Chung Hua University, Hsinchu 30012, Taiwan
Email: shaofu@g.chu.edu.tw, Phone: +886-3-5186029

Abstract

While exploring new spatial environments, many configurations and functional properties of buildings are related with visibility between and across spaces. Efficient way finding is a clear and main focus on the design of space. In this paper, we present an agent analysis model that considers the effect of visual field that has led to complaints. To enable this analysis, a visibility and walkthrough simulation for predicting pedestrian movement pattern is conducted for the Museum of 21st Century, Kanazawa, Japan. This study attempts to make a comparative study of two unrelated analyses in visibility and physical (day lighting) environment.

Keywords: DepthmapX, Exploration, Wayfinding

Introduction

Observation analysis with simulation is widely used to analyze the movement patterns and visibility of public spaces. This method allows researchers to get reasonable results, but it mainly depends on the researcher's point of view. Since the architectural space cannot be seen all at once by its occupants, the space can be understood through a series of views obtained by moving (Peponis and Bellal, 2010). People tend to remember ntegrated spaces more frequently and include them in the cognitive map, if they are familiar with the environment. If people simply move randomly from a specified starting point, this familiar statistical pattern of integration space does not appear (Al-Sayed *et al.* 2014).

Most of the current visual analysis is limited to two dimensions and has not considered the changes of various physical environments. This experiment takes the analysis of natural light environment as an example to compare the visual differences.

A. Analysis Techniques of Connectivity

Radiance and DepthmapX software analyses are used to analyze visual connectivity inside a buidling environment with daylight. DepthmapX's spatial grammar technology is a graph-based auxiliary method, not a graph-based spatial description theory, which does not involve topology in the strict sense of word mathematics. Thus, radiance controlled by Ecotect Analysis is used to assist with the Agent Analysis. Radiance is a lighting simulation program based on light energy transfer that uses the backward ray tracing process to simulate. It allows specifying custom grid points for calculating the illuminance level in a room, and is not restricted by any geometric restrictions. This paper explores different types of analytical techniques for the connectivity within the built environment. The main purpose is reviewing each technology separately, the advantages and limitations of the connectivity within the building blocks. To understand the effect of changing spatial characteristics on the results of each method, the analysis was applied to three different locations in the same building and compared the results of the two techniques for further research.

B. Relationship between Exploration and Wayfinding

The 21st Century Museum was chosen because of its open layout, an intricate view of street corners restricted by roads. This paper deals with the intelligibility of spatial structure on the scale of urban spatial relations. Fig. 1 shows a circular pavilion-like structure with a diameter of 112.5m in four directions. The space requires relatively large movement to perceive the relationship within a relatively constant spatial reference range. All exhibition galleries are located in the center, surrounded by circle areas and intertwined with four courtyards of different sizes. It attempts to integrate the cognitive methods of the daylight environment through those courtyards into the modeling of wayfinding behavior. The main goal is creating a reasonable model for exploration tasks in indoor environments. Visitors roam freely in the maze, which is like a miniature city.

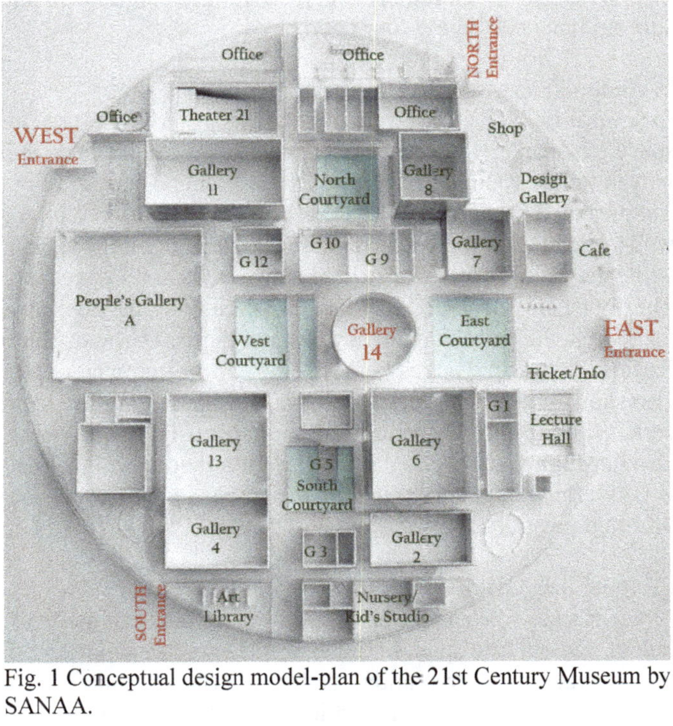

Fig. 1 Conceptual design model-plan of the 21st Century Museum by SANAA.

Space Syntax and Natural Movement

Space design is a decision-making process that forms the connection between people and place. Therefore, the methodology of designing space are required to establish a connection between the spatial dimensions of society and the social attributes of physical environments (Al-Sayed *et al.* 2014). This basic connection is the basis of the spatial grammar method, which proves the tangible analysis and interpretation of the complex social and spatial forms of human life. Space Syntax is a way to read and understand the city or architecture as a whole. DepthmapX's connectivity measures the number of direct connections in a space (Lee and Lee 2014). Physical or visual types of connectivity can enhance the way that visitors use the building. The conceptual models can be extended to practical applications in the social science, design and planning.

The analysis was performed with Space Syntax's DepthmapX software that analyzes the visual and physical connections inside the space through a variety of analysis methods. Being compared with visual analysis, ray traced analysis produces realistic visual effects to make up for the lack of two-dimensionality.

A. Visibility Graph Analysis (VGA)

Visibility graph analysis uses color codes to analyze visual connectivity. Fig. 2 shows VGA applied on the entrance level plan of the 21st Century Museum. The dark red area is the highly visible area, generally called the hotspot. The visibility area of the next level is shown in orange, and then yellow. Gradually from green to blue or dark blue, it represents areas that are less likely to be noticed. Therefore, general enclosed spaces, such as various exhibition halls, are mainly blue. And the pure white space represents any equipment space, which is stopped by tourists. It is clearly seen from this color codes that the areas with extremely high visibility surround the surrounding areas of the four courtyards.

B. Analysis of Isovist Area

Several field of view layers obtained from various points in space, and covered to represent a constant velocity line: the Isovist fields. The images taken from different positions in Fig. 3 show that the central part between obstacles (such as columns, walls, and blocks) represented in red and orange is most visible, while the visibility of the area behind these obstacles is weaker. The four courtyards and entrance area are obvious from any location in the building, but they obscure the area behind them. Part of the rounded edges (at both sides of the entrance areas) also show that there is very strong visual connectivity between certain points in the corridors. Simultaneously, the corridor also has high visibility to the circular glazed edge wall, which is very effective in enhancing the visual connectivity between different locations.

C. Agent Analysis in DepthmapX

Agent analysis is based on the analysis of the main body of indoor and outdoor spaces. The analysis also uses color codes to analyze the circulation patterns between spaces to distinguish areas with high and low spatial connectivity. The result shows the traces from red to blue.

Fig. 4 shows the possible route taken by 40 tourists (about a tourist coach) circulating from the ticket information counter (East Entrance Area) in the first 15 minutes. A large red area is found between the internal space of the east courtyard and the entrance area. The blue area also extends to the wide southwest side and connects to the same red area on the other side, behind Gallery 14. These are accessible areas with the strongest physical connectivity, and most of visitors move within these areas. The accessibility of other areas is significantly lower.

During a 15-minute period, this study found that most of agents only pass by, rarely entering and wandering even if they pass through the entrance of any exhibition hall. This is based on the results of the previous visibility analysis.

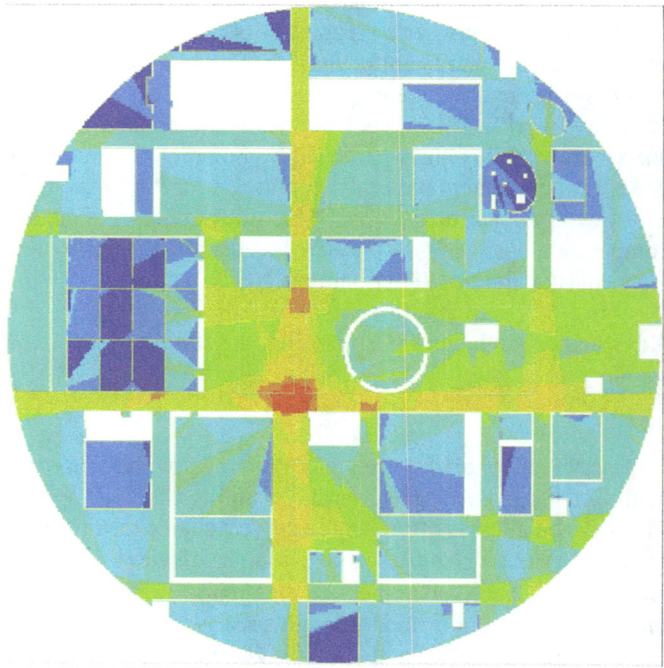

Fig. 2 Visibility Graph Analysis of the 21st Century Museum.

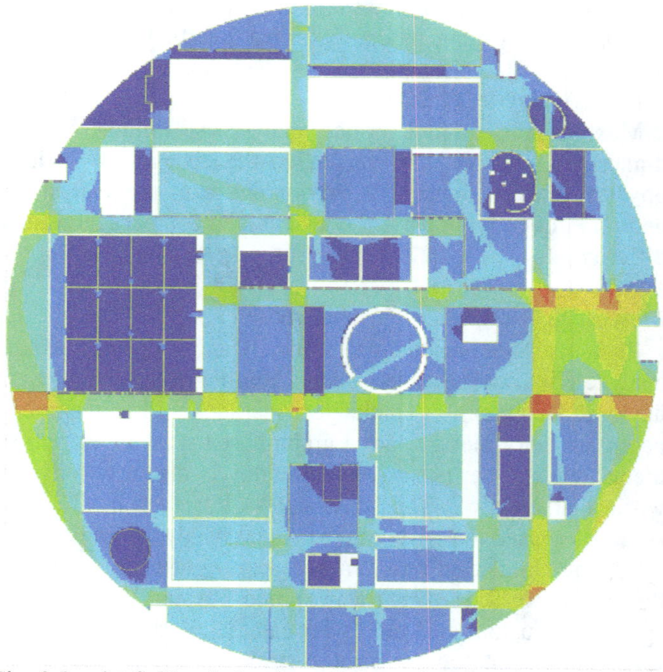

Fig. 3 Isovist fields of plan from different locations inside the 21st Century Museum.

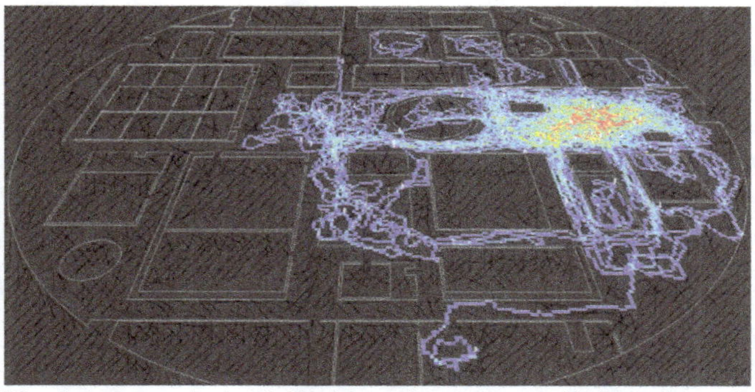

Fig. 4 Agent analysis of 40 visitors (a tourist coach) from the main entrance (east end) in the first 15 minutes.

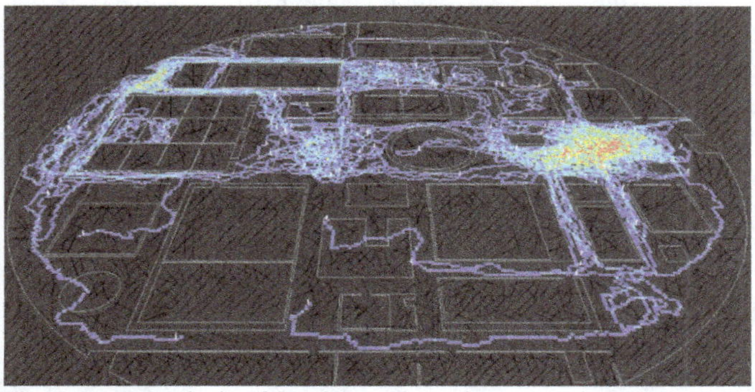

Fig. 5 Agent analysis of 80 visitors from the east and west entrances in the first 15 minutes.

The same experiment (Fig. 5) was applied to the two main entrances again with doubled number of agents. In the east entrance part, the analysis result was similar. Since the design of the museum is based on the entrance to the east, it is relatively time-consuming for tourists from the west to visit. Tourists spend a lot of time staying on the edge of the circular glazed walls. A very small number of tourists follow the various corridors, quickly away from the starting point. Most visitors move to the central area and wander in the courtyards of the northwestern districts. Interestingly, visitors to the west must pass through a long corridor to reach the wide courtyards. The circular outer ring boundary seems to guide the agents to move to the central.

D. Meanings of DepthmapX Analysis

Based on the spatial ontology, the VGA quickly predicts the trend of crowd movement. The formation of hotspots is an advantage of DepthmapX. The Isovist fields applied in the plan shows the overall visual connectivity of the area. Although the hotspots analyzed by the two overlap partially, they show different levels of high and low when compared with each other. The difference in this level is the strength of visual connectivity.

The calculation of the Agent Analysis combines the above analysis results in addition to superimposing and expanding the scope of application. Taking the experiment in Fig. 5 as an example, this research executed a dozen times to obtain the similar results of the calculations.

In general, the West Courtyard and the East Entrance Hall near the central area have the best visibility and accessibility, followed by the North and South Courtyards. It is difficult to explore the whole building, because a series of agents does not fill into the entire space with many gallery halls at the same time.

The best visibility of the ring-shaped edge glazed walls area is still from the East entrance. The West entrance has also better visibility. Owing to the openness, the courtyard area has stronger visual connectivity than the circular edge of the glass curtain walls. More areas with very strong visual connectivity are found in the East Courtyard. In addition, the visual connectivity of the South Courtyard that is larger than the other three courtyards is greatly affected as the area of this courtyard is smaller even though all four areas have similar obstacles.

Through comparative agent analysis, the traces of the west area cover more floor plans on the corridor, while the east area remains near the east courtyard. This shows that the main entrance zone is easier to navigate than the west zone, which means it has less circulation time.

Path of Exploration and Form of Observation

This study summarizes two points, among which the space syntax method has been used to re-examine the clarity and liveliness of the 21st Century Museum circulation system. The first method is to diagnose the nature of certain wayfinding problems encountered in the new space environment. The second is evaluating and exploring different galleries within a large exhibition zone.

For gaining a deeper insight in space syntax analysis, visual animation with daylight analysis tools is introduced to assist or support the results of agent analysis. As VGA is just a pure flat color codes, it only provides overall or rough evaluation like satellite images. Another agent analysis (Fig. 6) shows traces of the route that only 3 visitors take in the museum. It takes almost 8 minutes from the ticket counter. The result is shown as a blue trace. As shown in the plan, a large number of hotspots (footprints) are also found in the space between the entrance hall and the east courtyard.

According to the exploratory paths of these 3 agents with Radiance Analysis, we created a series of fixed-point views and finally animated the views. The reason for using fisheye lens (Figs. 7, 8(a), 8(b), and 8(c)) is to record the correct daylight and shadow changes precisely. The daylight environment is set at the Spring Equinox, Summer Solstice, Autumnal Equinox, and Winter Solstice in the four seasons, and at 09:30 in the morning when the museum opens.

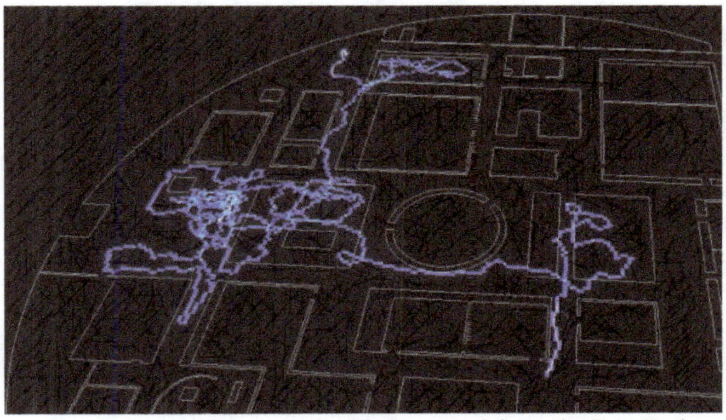

Fig. 6 Agent Analysis of 3 visitors started from the East End.

Fig. 7 Sample picture frame at eye level analyzed by Radiance.

(a) Agent-1 walking from ticket counter

(b) Agent-2 walking through the round glazed walls

(c) Agent-3 at museum shops

Fig. 8 Some samples needed to create movie-like visual motion

Conclusions: Configuration vs. Aesthetics

This research proposes to combine daylight analysis tools and execution measures with the space syntax analysis of a pavilion building and to assist the overall spatial cognition research based on a reasonable perspective. We discussed how to understand architectural and/or spatial configuration as an aesthetic way to solve the application of the theories.

Comparison of the results of each technology reveals that the Radiance technology is more accurate in larger-scale spaces and in determining the factors of connectivity, which may not be able to be identified using DepthmapX. Space Syntax Analysis is more accurate than observation in calculating visual and physical connections. In other words, even if DepthmapX analysis is accurate, it is more suitable for smaller scale spaces than for larger ones. Instead, it is necessary to observe the ray traces to verify the results (Fathy Alagamy *et al.* 2019). Both of the technologies seem to be dependent on each other and are not suitable for separate applications. The data retrieved from the Radiance analysis is sometimes more accurate than DepthmapX. However, due to differences in spatial configuration, the changes in visibility and accessibility can only be accurately identified through DepthmapX. This is different from Radiance, which is not easily recognized by the observers. Through Radiance, areas with high and low connectivity can be identified, but specific points cannot be accurately identified.

The reliability of the analysis results requires several considerations during the analysis. DepthmapX is a professional multi-layer analysis technique and a time-saving method. Space syntax can solve aesthetic problems. It shows how a method for architectural configuration allows a series of critical discussions from an aesthetic point of view. Space Syntax analysis contributes to understand architectural aesthetics and to configure efficiently with two technical systems. Then, time-saving and accurate graphics and reliable data are obtained with more reliable analysis results (Peponis *et al.* 1996).

The proposed method can promote students' interest, too. In addition to the training of analysis tools, it also allows students to quickly find problems and correct them without the guidance of instructors. With the help of tools, the application of physical built environment and spatial design can be both.

References

[1] Al-Sayed, K. et al., Space Syntax Methodology, 2014.

[2] Fathy Alagamy, S. et al., An Integrated Approach for Analyzing Connectivity in Atria. Alexandria Engineering Journal 58(1), pp. 315–324. doi: 10.1016/j.aej.2018.12.005., 2019.

[3] Lee, S.-J. and Lee, K.-H., Suggestion for a Visual Dynamics Analysis Model Using a Natural Movement Model. Journal of Asian Architecture and Building Engineering 13(2), pp. 381–388. doi: 10.3130/jaabe.13.381., 2014.

[4] Peponis, J. et al., New design technologies: using computer technology to improve design quality. Journal of Healthcare Design: Proceedings from the ... Symposium on Healthcare Design. Symposium on Healthcare Design 8, pp. 109–119, 1996.

[5] Peponis, J. and Bellal, T., Fallingwater: The Interplay between Space and Shape. Environment and Planning B: Planning and Design 37(6), pp. 982–1001. doi: 10.1068/b36052. 2010.

https://doi.org/10.1142/9789811238727_0037

Exploring and Studying the Attractive Experience Attributes of Cultural Tourism Project – Beijing South Luogu Lane as Example

Ying Liu[1] Chun-Chin Chen[2*] and Shu-Ming Wu[1]

[1]Dalian Art College, Tung Fang Design of University Institute of Cultural and Creative Design
[2]Kaohsiung Normal University, Dept. of Industrial Design
*Corresponding Author Email: ccchen@nknu.edu.tw

Abstract

Cultural tourism projects are strategic options for urban tourism seeking to improve and develop. They are based on the integration of culture and tourism, adding to creative experience services in order to satisfy the increasing needs of tourists for leisure and entertainment, and create a unique experience. This study is aimed at exploring the attractive experience attributes of cultural tourism project by using the example of Beijing South Luogu Lane, which provide the viewpoint of unique experience, and apply the evaluation structure method of Miryoku engineering to discuss characterisics of cultural tourism project by in-depth interviews with sampled tourists. The characteristics include seven attractive attributes, such as popularity, concern, uniqueness, entertainment, participation, culture, and self-realization. Among them, entertainment, uniqueness, and cultural performances are more obvious properties than others which can provide reference for future design of cultural tourism experience.

Keywords: Cultural tourism, South Luogu Lane, Experience, Evaluation Grid Method

Introduction

A. Research Background

Cultural tourism projects through the integration of culture tourism, leisure and entertainment experience aim to provide three-dimensional services for people's needs, and create a unique travel experience. Nowadays, many cities are striving to build cultural tourism projects to increase the charm of cities, and satisfy the intellectual and cultural needs of people (Zhou Mo, 2020). However, while cultural tourism has attracted much attention and rapid growth, problems such as serious product homogeneity, single industrial chain, and weak cultural awareness have appeared, which have plagued the development of the cultural tourism industry.

B. Research Purpose

Due to various problems, cultural tourism projects can no longer meet people's growing cultural tourism demands. The purpose of this research is to take the experience of tourists in Beijing South Luogu Lane cultural district as an example, which summarize the factors of urban cultural charm experience to provide references for future urban managers and related designers for urban cultural positioning and planning and design.

Literature Discussion

A. South Luogu Lane

South Luogu Lane is one of the oldest blocks in Beijing. Now it has become a famous urban cultural block in Beijing. It is a representative cultural tourism project full of old Beijing style and modern urban cultural characteristics.

South Luogu Lane not only retains the complete Yuan Dynasty Hutong courtyard and courtyard architecture, but also many popular food, specialty shops, and characteristic experience projects. It not merely allows tourists to experience the profound Beijing Hutong culture, but provides food, entertainment, shopping, travel services, and amazing experience of urban mass culture, as shown in Figure 1.

Fig. 1 Beijing South Luogu

B. Cultural Tourism and Experience Design

Personalization, experience and cultural connotation are the core of cultural tourism. Cultural tourism projects are much beloved because they can meet the higher level of tourist demand for tourism and leisure. Maslow's hierarchy of needs theory states that human needs rise in stages, from the basic needs of survival, safety, food and clothing, and sexual intercourse, to the gradually expanding demand for material enjoyment, and even higher-level personality development and self-realization needs, and experience is the level of self-realization needs, starting from life forms and situations, shaping sensory experience and thinking identity, creating memorable happiness through personal participation, and trying to make people feel more meaningful, this is "experience". Experience plays a key role in cultural tourism projects. The most important content of cultural tourism project design is to express different characteristics in different projects. Therefore, a good experience design is an effective strategy to improve tourist satisfaction.

Pine and Gilmore (1999) stated that elements that propose experience quality must include: entertainment, participation, beauty, absorption, immersion, suspense and novelty; Corresponding to the needs of tourists and the characteristics of the experience, the participation process of the tourists in the game can be found. Sensory experience can be produced through visual image design, environmental design, sensory design, etc. Emotional experience can be produced through participation and interaction between tourists and cultural tourism content. Thinking experience can be generated through the surprise of cultural tourism characteristic services and innovative interactive design, the mobile experience can be generated by participating in the setting of culture, festivals and interactive attractions, and the related experience can be generated through the sense of belonging and the recognition of the project brought to the tourists by the cultural tourism project. In other words, the play process of cultural tourism projects is an integrated experience design. However, most research on cultural tourism are still based on the perspectives of brand visual image, entertainment design and tourism souvenir design. There are not many research on tourist experience. Therefore, this research is to use the pre-evaluation construction method of charm engineering to explore the attributes of charm experience that cultural tourism projects should have from the perspective of experience.

C. Miryoku Engineering and Evaluation Grid Method

The Japanese version of "attractiveness" is Miryoku, and the English version is Attractiveness. Attractiveness is the embodiment of the user's subjective preferences, mainly through its value judgment system. This judgment system comes from the user's sensory reception, heart decision-making, sociology, artistic evaluation, etc. (Ujigawa, 2000). In 1991, Ujigawa gathered a number of scholars to initiate the research on "Miryoku engineering", with the goal of "creating fascinating products, space technology and knowledge".Miryoku engineering was incorporated as part of Japanese Kansei Engineering in 1998. The term "Magic Engineering" was developed by Sanui and Inui with reference to the "Bed Heart" scientist Kelly (1955) in the book *The Psychology of Personal Constructs*. The research is mainly to capture the general understanding of personal cognition and integrate the research methods (Zeng ludan, 2007).

Sanui (1996) divided the research method of attractive engineering into two steps, the first step is to evaluate the target to answer the like or dislike; the second step is to clarify the meaning of the answer through the additional questions and summarize the respondents' answers to specifically analyze the attractive elements of the product to the user's preferences. Afterwards, the network diagram of the relevant structure is sorted out. This research method is called "Evaluation grid method (EGM)". In the related research of attractive engineering, EGM provides a concrete and theoretically based way of analyzing the attractive factors of things according to the categories under the theme and the in-depth interviews as methods to further understand uses' experience about attractive things. Through the comparison of the preferences of the testees, the testees have obvious feeling differences. The original concept of the subject, and then guide the subject to make a clearer analysis of the original evaluation concept. The original evaluation concept is connected to the upper level abstract concept and the lower level specific description, and then the network structure diagram of the testee and the product is compiled. In the implementation of EGM, first of all, in the evaluation of the target object, the respondent needs to answer whether he likes or dislikes the object. The second step is to clarify the meaning or conditions of the respondent's answer through additional questions. Integrate its answers, specifically analyze the user's charm factors for things, and reorganize its related structure network (Chen and Wu, 2011)

Research Methods

A. Sampling Under Test

In order to clarify the different needs of tourists for cultural tourism and find out the attributes of the city's attractive experience,this study applies the "appraisal structure method" of charm engineering, and selects the famous cultural tourism project-Beijing South Luogu Lane urban cultural district as a sample to explore the charm experience attributes of cultural tourism projects. The evaluation grid method is conducted by using in-depth interviews. The subjects are 8 tourists who have visited South Luogu Lane urban in-depth in person (4 males and 4 females, all of whom have played at least 2 cultural tourism projects of tourists), aged between 20 and 40 years old.

B. Interview Process

(1) Before the start of the interview, share the top five travel notes of South Luogu Lane on the well-known travel app Mafengwo. Ask the interviewees to read the travel notes and recall the visits and feelings at that time.

(2) In this study, the interviewee was contacted by WeChat voice call, and the interview time was determined to be approximately one hour. During the process, the interviewee was agreed to record the whole process for subsequent data compilation.

C. Interview Content

Conduct in-depth interviews with interviewees, mainly about why users like to visit South Luogu Lane. The "EGM" interview method is divided into three aspects: "primitive reasons", "specific matters" and "abstract reasons". After learning the "original reason", ask the "abstract reason" and explain the "specific matters" in sequence.

For example: Ask the respondent: "Why does South Luogu Lane attract you?" The respondent replies: "It is very famous", and extract "reputation" as the original reason. Based on the original reason, I asked from top to bottom: "What makes you think South Luogu Lane is so famous?" Respondents answer: "There are promotions on well-known websites/APPs, and many friends have visited and found them to be very recommended." Extract "media promotion, friend recommendation" as attractive specific items. Finally, I will ask again: "How would you describe the feeling of seeing the promotion in the media?" The respondent replies: "I think it's popular here," and extract "popularity" as the abstract reason for attraction.

Analysis and Discussion

Through the collation of the interview content, the construction of a cultural tourism project—the map of the attractive experience evaluation of Beijing South Luogu Lane urban cultural district, as shown in Figure 2.

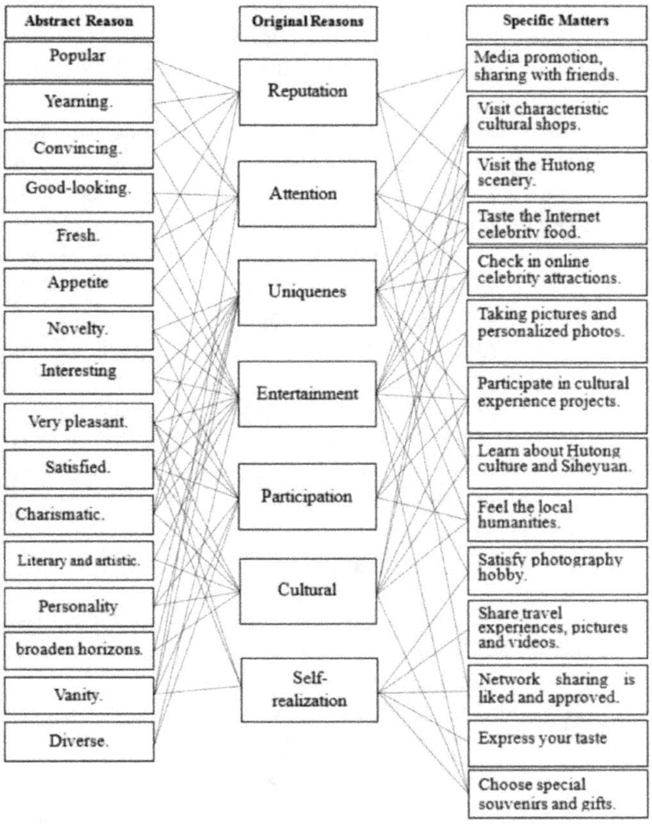

Fig. 2 Evaluation grid Method of cultural tourism projects

According to the interview results, there are seven dimensions as original reasons for tourists participating in cultural tourism projects. Such as reputation, attention, uniqueness, entertainment, participation, self-realization, and cultural, further in-depth interviews with specific matters and abstract reasons, to find out the charm of the cultural tourism project, it is obvious from the structural diagram that tourists have the most direct response to "entertainment" in the experience.

TABLE 1
The relevance of the original reasons, specific matters and abstract reasons

Original reasons	**Specific matters**	**Abstract reasons**
Reputation	(1)Media promotion, sharing with friends; (2) Visit the Hutong scenery; (3)Learn about Hutong culture and Siheyuan	Popular; Yearning; Convincing; Fresh; Charismatic
Attention	(1)Media promotion, sharing with friends; (2) Taste the Internet celebrity food; (3) Check in online celebrity attractions; (4) Network sharing is liked and approved.	Popular; Yearning; Good-looking; Fresh; Appetite; Vanity
Uniquenes	(1)Visit characteristic cultural shops; (2) Visit the Hutong scenery; (3)Taste the Internet celebrity food; (4) Check in online celebrity attractions; (5) Participate in cultural experience projects; (6)Learn about Hutong culture and Siheyuan; (7) Feel the local humanities.	Convincing; Novelty; Interesting; Very pleasant; Satisfied; Charismatic; Personality; broaden horizons; Vanity
Entertain-ment	(1)Visit characteristic cultural shops; (2) Visit the Hutong scenery; (3) Taste the Internet celebrity food; (4) Check in online celebrity attractions; (5)Taking pictures and personalized photos. (6) Participate in cultural experience projects; (7) Satisfy photography hobby; (8) Choose special souvenirs and gifts. Abstract reason.	Good-looking; Fresh; Appetite; Novelty; Interesting; Very pleasant; Satisfied; Charismatic; Literary and artistic; Diverse
Participa-tion	(1)Check in online celebrity attractions; (2) Taking pictures and personalized photos; (3) Participate in cultural experience projects; (4) Feel the local humanities.	Novelty; Interesting; Very pleasant; Satisfied; Personality; Diverse.
Cultural	(1)Visit characteristic cultural shops; (2) Visit the Hutong scenery; (3) Participate in cultural experience projects; (4) Learn about Hutong culture and Siheyuan; (5) Feel the local humanities; (6) Choose special souvenirs and gifts. Abstract reason	Very pleasant; Satisfied; Charismatic; Literary and artistic; Personality; broaden horizons; broaden horizons
Self-realization	(1) Satisfy photography hobby; Share travel experiences, pictures and videos; (2) Network sharing is liked and approved; (3) Express your taste; (4) Choose special souvenirs and gifts. (5) Abstract reason	Very pleasant; Satisfied; Vanity

The following analysis is obtained according to Table 1. Specific items of "Entertainment" (1) Visit characteristic cultural shops. (2) Visit the Hutong scenery. (3) Taste the Internet celebrity food. (4) Check in online celebrity attractions. (5) Taking pictures and personalized photos. (6) Participate in cultural experience projects. (7) Satisfy photography hobby. (8) Choose souvenirs and gifts. Abstract reason (1) It looks good. (2) Fresh. (3) Appetite. (4) Novelty. (5) Interesting. (6) Very pleasant. (7) Satisfied. (8) Charismatic. (9) Literary and artistic. (10) Diverse.

Participants said: rich entertainment and leisure content, for example: delicious food, unique scenery, special attractions, good shopping experience, etc., make travel more exciting and interesting. But if it brings a bad experience, it will reduce the goodwill, so it is very necessary to ensure the quality of the project.

Specific items of "Uniqueness" (1) Visit characteristic cultural shops. (2) Visit the Hutong scenery. (3) Taste the Internet celebrity food. (4) Check in online celebrity attractions. (5) Participate in cultural experience projects. (6) Learn about Hutong culture and Siheyuan. (7) Feel the local humanities. Abstract reason (1) Yearning. (2) Novelty. (3) Interesting. (4) Very pleasant. (5) Satisfied. (6) Attractively. (7) Personality. (8) Broadening horizons. (9) Vanity. Participants said: If you can experience unique projects or services that are not available elsewhere here, such as visiting unique cultural and creative shops, eating unique food, etc., you will be particularly satisfied and pleasant, and will deepen the project impression.

Specific items of "Cultural" (1) Visit characteristic cultural shops. (2) Visit the Hutong scenery. (3) Participate in cultural experience projects. (4) Learn about Hutong culture and Siheyuan. (5) Feel the local humanities. (6) Choose special souvenirs and gifts. Abstract reason (1) Novelty. (2) Very pleasant. (3) Satisfied. (4) Charismatic. (5) Literary and artistic. (6) Personality. (7) Broadening horizons. Participants said: The cultural experience during the trip, such as the hutong cultural scenery, characteristic cultural and creative products, etc., can enable them to understand the local culture, enhance the attraction of the project, and feel novel and joyful.

Specific items of "Participation" (1) Check in online celebrity attractions. (2) Take pictures and take personalized photos. (3) Participate in cultural experience projects. (4) Feel the local humanities. Abstract reason (1) Novelty. (2) Interesting. (3) Satisfied. (4) Very pleasant. (5) Vanity. (6) Personality. Participants said: Checking in the Internet celebrity attractions and taking a rickshaw to visit Hu and other highly interactive content can be greatly satisfied and make a memorable experience.

Specific items of "Self-expression" (1) Satisfy shooting hobbies. (2) Share travel experiences, pictures and videos. (3) Network sharing is liked and approved. (4) Express your taste. (5) Choose special souvenirs and gifts. Abstract reason (1) satisfied. (2) Very pleasant. (3) Vanity. (4) Personality. Participants said: The cultural experience during the trip, such as the hutong cultural scenery, characteristic cultural and creative products, etc., can enable them to understand the local culture, enhance the attraction of the project, and feel novel and joyful.

Specific items of "Reputation" (1) Media promotion, sharing with friends. (2) Visit the Hutong scenery. (3) Learn about Hutong culture and Siheyuan. Abstract reason (1) Popular. (2) Yearning. (3) Convincing. (4) Fresh. (5) Charismatic. Participants said: media and friends' recommendations, historical content is reason for coming.

Specific items of "degree of attention" (1) Media promotion, sharing with friends. (2) Taste the Internet celebrity food. (3) Check-in and internet celebrity attractions (4) Online sharing is liked and approved. Abstract reason (1) Popular. (2) Yearning. (3) Good-looking. (4) Fresh. (5) Appetite. Participants said that they would choose cultural tourism projects because of high-profile content or being followed.

Conclusion

As people's demand for cultural tourism continues to escalate, good experience design is an effective strategy to meet the needs of cultural tourists. In order to solve the prominent problem of the homogeneity of cultural tourism projects, this research explore and study the attractive experience factors/attributes of cultural tourism projects, and aims to provide references for the development and design of cultural tourism projects. This study takes Beijing South Luogu Lane urban cultural district as an example, and applies the evaluation structure method to explore the attractive experience characteristics of cultural tourism projects, including seven factors, such as reputation, attention, uniqueness, entertainment, participation, cultural, and self-realization. An attractive attribute through the analysis of the evaluation structure diagram, it is obvious that entertainment, uniqueness, and culture are more prominent in the experience of cultural tourism projects, which reflects the high demand of tourists for leisure and entertainment and special experience. Self-actualization is also prominent in the seven charm factors. It can be seen from the media era that it enhances external visibility and attention, provides a deeper sense of participation, and promotes the importance of user self-worth realization in design.

References

[1] Ma Minyuan, Hong Jiayong, Zeng Lidan. Research on the Appraisal of the Charm of Taiwan's Local Cultural and Creative Industries-Taking the Festival Industry as an Example. A report on the results of the special research project subsidized by the National Science Council of the Executive Yuan. 2005

[2] Zeng Lidan. Evaluation of the charm of Taiwan's local cultural and creative industries-taking Yilan Children's Play Festival as an example. Proceedings of the 12th Symposium of the Design Society of the Republic of China-Forward-looking Design: Integration of Technology and Humanities (CD-ROM Proceedings), Kaohsiung Normal University, No. 268, 6.May 2007.

[3] Ujigawa, M. The evolution of preference-based design. Research and Development Institute, 46, PP.1-10.2000.

[4] Pine, B. J., & Gilmore, J. H.II. The experience economy: Work is theatre and every business a stage. Boston Massachusetts: Harvard Business School Press. 1999.

[5] Chen Junzhi and Wu Yuying Exploring the Attractive Experience Attributes of Social Network, Journal of Business Design, (15), 2011pp. 133-149.

[6] Feng Yuliang, Chen Junzhi, Wu Shuming. Research on User Experience Charm Factors of "Tikyin APP" [J]. Journal of Jingdezhen University, 2019(3).

[7] Sanui, J. Visualization of users' requirements: Introduction of the Evaluation Grid Method. Proceedings of the 3rd Design & Decision Support Systems in Architecture & Urban Planning Conference, 1. pp. 365-374. April 1996.

[8] Schmitt, Bernd H., Wang Yuying, Liang Xiaoying. Experience marketing. Taipei: Through the point of communication culture. 2000.

[9] Huang Peihua, You Zhangxiong A Preliminary Study on the Application of Experience Design in Cultural Products, 2009.

[10] Zhou Mo. Thoughts on the integrated development of tourism industry and cultural industry, Modern Marketing (late issue), 2020 (07): pp. 156-157.

https://doi.org/10.1142/9789811238727_0038

Exploring the Attractive Attributes of Psychological Healing of Keeping Pets

Chunchih Chen[1*], Yinghsin Chen[2**]

[1] National Kaohsiung Normal University, Kaohsiung 82446, Taiwan
[2] China Agricultural University, Beijing 100083, China
[*]Corresponding Author Email: [*]ccchen@nknu.edu.tw, Phone: 886-930836220
[**]irene1020747@gmail.com, Phone: 886-966223076

Abstract

The research on animal-assisted therapy based on psychological healing has been studied in Taiwan. However the studies for discussing the attractive attributes of psychological healing of keeping pets of cats and dogs are few. This research used the depth-interview and evaluation grid method to summarize the attractive factors, the research result including companionship, responsibility, being depended on, being loved, interaction, cuteness, belonging, and innocence. The emotional attributes and the specific attributes were also identified to well define the therapies and healing of pets-keeping. The results can be applied to the creative industries of pets-keeping and psychotherapy.

Keywords: Animal-assisted therapy, Psychological healing, Evaluation grid method, Emotion

Introduction

The pressures from busy hard work and economic competition make various activities or consumption in the name of "healing". **Psychological healing** has become one of the popular trends of amusement for modern people. On account of the increasing estrangement in modern people's daily life, keeping a pet has become the way to seek comfort for many single men and women. However, animals should not only be seen as mere providers of material value; in fact, they actually enrich humans' lives on an emotional level. Humans have longed for love and attention since the dawn of their existence. To meet the needs of being socially-active and socially-minded, humans need interpersonal contact with persons or groups. If they do not manage to establish these contacts, negative emotions and consequences may arise that will ultimately push them to the brink of extinction. Humans do not naturally look for superficial bonds but rather to appreciate deep relationships that might eventually give rise to friendships. Through the time-intensive process the confidence of people can be built up. Many elderly people simply are not able to establish new social contacts and the subsequent strong bonds when trying to compensate for the loss of their partners or the transition to retirement [1]. However, they long for an intimate and loving companionship. A pet can be such a companion. Some people regard the pet as being just an animal; for a pet-lover, a pet is a friend, true partner, and loyal companion. The companionship between the pets and keeper is underestimated or belittled frequently, even though pets are often intimate companions for many elderly people. They help them fight off loneliness and solitude and continue their activity. To many elderly people, their animal friend means joy and quality of life [2]. Related studies have shown that companion animals can act as catalysts to promote human social interaction [3]. Pets are always the best partner for people, there are more and more people beginning to keep pets in Taiwan, pets also become part of the family, even a commitment to spirit. The conventional concept has always affirmed the value of animals in promoting human health and well-being. Recently, the therapeutic role of keeping pets has become a topic for dedicated research in medicine. Animal assisted interventions (AAI) can be classified as animal-assisted activities, animal-assisted therapy, and service animal programs [4]. The healing function of keeping pets is defined as general and specific functions. The general function includes projection and interaction, and the specific function, especially for the medical field of pet healing, includes psychological and physiologcal functions [5].

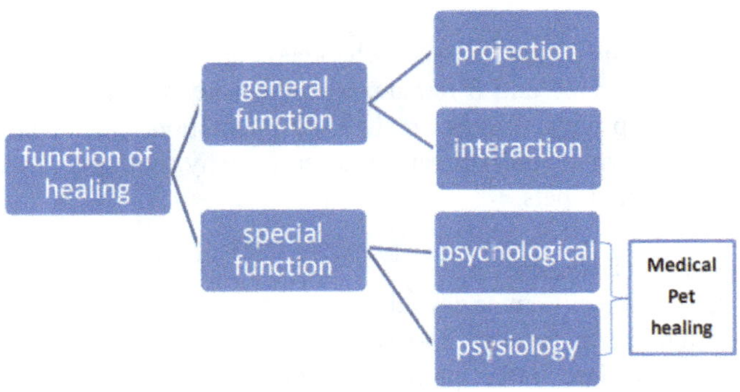

Fig. 1 The healing function of keeping pets

When people interact with the pet, they will release themselves and feel relaxed to project their real thoughts and emotion. Through keeping pets, the whole experience can be a topic to enhance communication abilities and social activities for pet keepers. Pet keeping can heal people. With the coming trend of lower birth rate and aged society, there is a serious gap of relationships among humans. Pets are important and depended on by people. To explore the attractive attributes of psychological healing of keeping pets such as cats and dogs, in-depth interviews were conducted and the interaction between keeper and pet as well as the emotion and feeling of keepers were also discussed. The evaluation grid method

(EGM) is applied to summarize the attractive and important attributes for therapies and healing of pets-keeping.

The Evaluation Grid Method

The evaluation grid method (EGM) is one of the important methods in Miryoku (attractiveness) engineering. EGM was often used as a design aid in architecture as well as the industrial field. Ujigawa and several scholars initiated Miryoku engineering and proposed the evaluation grid method [6]. The primary purpose of the evaluation grid method is to thoroughly explore users' inner feelings to extract details of consumers' cognitive structures and to convert them into real factors of assessment as a basis of design [7]. The application of EGM can obtain customers' preferences and emotions relating to the stimulus through in-depth interviews, which are conducted hierarchically. First, the interviewee is invited to assess the merits and attraction of the stimulus by recognizing similarities and differences to other products and replying to additional questions from the interviewer. Why and what the reasons, specific attributes and feelings of the stimulus attractive to the subject were reported. Therefore, the original reason to attract subject is identified, and then the subject is guided to make a clearer analysis of the original evaluation concept linking between the upper abstract emotion and the lower specific attributes. Further, the whole picture to explain why and what the cognition of subject preference toward the stimulus, the hierarchic structure network of evaluation grid map, can be generated for describing the attractive and important factors [8].

Research Method

Subjects

Among the 13 interviewees who keep dogs and cats mainly, there are 5 male and 8 female, 6 of them keep cats and the others keep dogs. We can realize the interaction and feeling between owners and pets and the reason why they are so in love with their pets.

Research procedure

Each subject is interviewed in a comfortable space without external interference for 20-30 minutes. The interview of EGM is divided into three phases: "original reason", "specific attribute" and "abstract reason". According to the original reason extracted from the interview, the way to go deep into the abstract reason and explain the specific attribute, and the charm of pet healing is constructed.

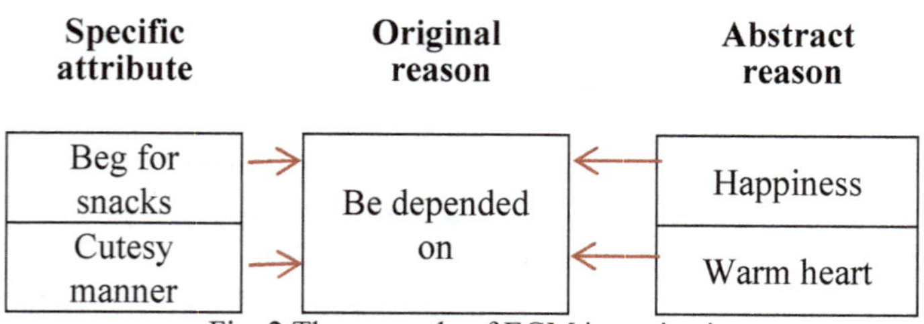

Fig. 2 The example of EGM interviewing

For example the interviewee was asked to report "what's the reason that keeping a pet makes you feel healed?" 'The respondent replied that "I feel that I am in need and am depended on" then "be depended on" will be chosen as the original reason. Then we further ask "What do you feel when you are depended on?", and respondent answered that "I feel happy and warm." Then "happy, warm" will be chosen as abstract reasons. At the same time, asking "Can you describe what specific interactions or actions make you feel happy?", received responses such as "Begging for snacks, showing the cutesy manner". So these attributes will be extracted as a specific attribute. Through in-depth questioning of abstract reasons and the explanation of specific attribute, we can integrate the charm of "pet-healing".

After completing the depth interview, the following questions were also asked the subjects to report:

1. What kind of the role does your pet play for you? friend? family? Or is it just a pet?

2. Do you still want to keep pet whether in the future or now?

3. What is the reason for you to recommend other people if they want to keep pet?

Results and Discussion

According to the interview of 13 owners, the attractive factors and attributes of pet healing for owners, the EGM map was shown in Fig. 3 and Fig. 4.

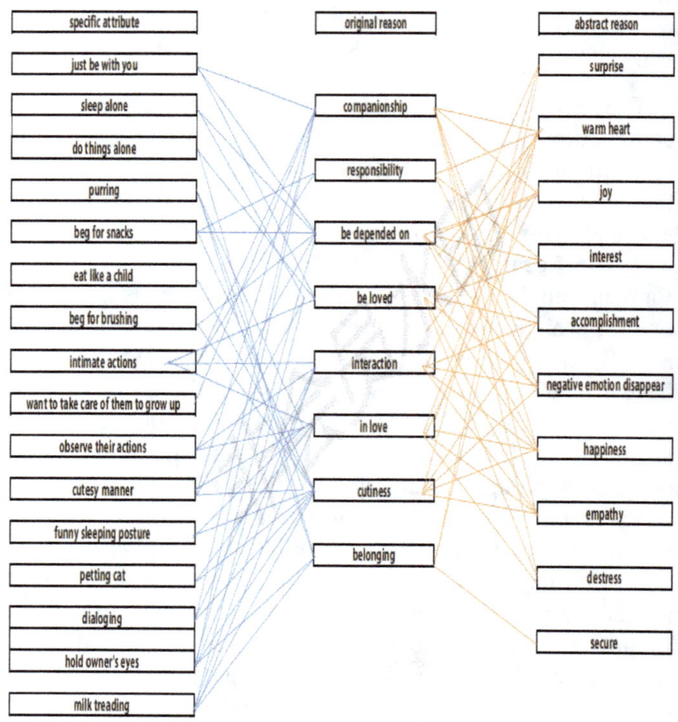

Fig. 3 The EGM map of cat-keepers

As shown in the illustration, there is good consistency of the attractiveness for pet healing on "original reason" between dog and cat keepers, for example: companionship, responsibility, being depended on, being loved, interaction, cuteness, belonging; in addition to dog owners feeling a sense of regaining innocence, cat owners feel empathy. According to the EGM map, we find that while the original reasons for pet healing of cat and dog keepers are similar, the interaction and emotions are different. Take companionship and belonging as examples, dogs have more initiative, following your rear for 24 hours and welcoming you home at the same time every day. There are obvious differences compared to cats which stay quietly and purr, although they also make their owners feel warm and happy.

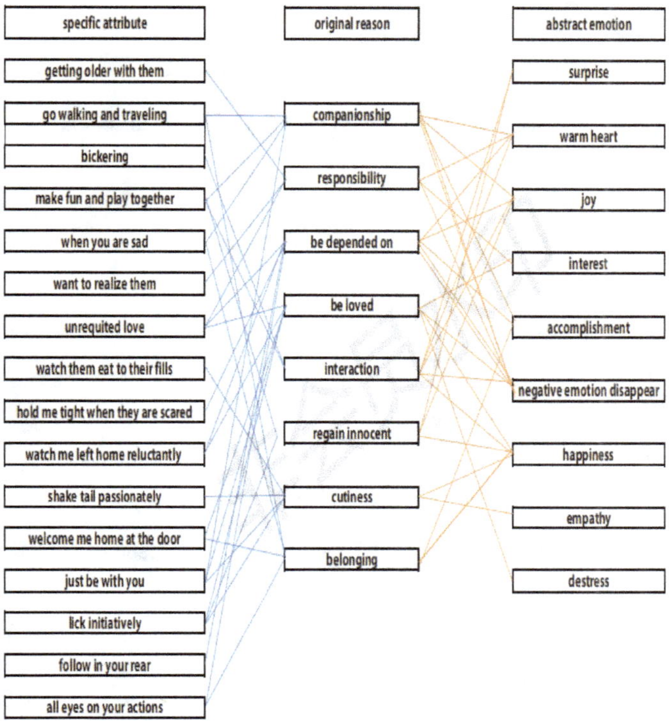

Fig. 4 The EGM map of dog-keepers

The meaning of original reason "interaction" for owners of dogs refers to them feeling happy and healing when playing and interacting with their dogs. The meaning of original reason "interaction" for cat-owners is to observe the funny action and sleeping posture of cats, or to expect feedback by cozying them up. Furthermore, the emotion of surprise and being overwhelmed by cats are so unique for the cat-owners. To compare the owners' emotion of love for pets, dealing with dogs is just like being in a love bubble and dealing with cats is just like flirting with someone who is mysterious.

To identify the meaning of "being depended on", when cats and dogs both come to beg for meal and patting, it always gives the owner a sense of achievement, superiority and satisfaction; Lastly, the link of love between human and pets should not be overlooked. The owner treats a pet as a member of the family and lives together; they are both comfortable and happy because of the existence of each other. Pets love unconditionally without expecting in return and stand beside you through the years whether painful or happy with their owners.

Interviewees said that "He will always be there when I am in a funk."; "All it does is to stay with me until I am ready to face the world."; "Taking care of pet is the source of achievement in my life, getting up early every day to feed it, train him and take him out for a walk and so on. These things give me strong sense of purpose that nothing else can achieve."; "Pets can also know when you are in need and give the best feedback whether to kiss, to lick, or having fun with their owners.", "The deep emotional connection between my pet and myself can't be obtained from friends and family. I can feel that it needs me, and I need it too."; "Pets have the ability to intercommunicate with human emotions, and it is a special quality with healing and charm."

The results indicate that cat-owners are more active than dog-owners. On the contrary, the owner is waiting for the initiative from the dog. The roles of the owner are the servant of cats and the lord of dogs respectively, but the feelings during the process of interaction with dogs and cats are roughly the same. They are sweet, happy, and satisfied.

Fig. 5 The mental difference between owners of cats and dogs

In most cases, pet-owners can be satisfied with the longing for company and the desire for affection. Enthusiasm is the charm point of dogs. People said that: "You won't know what is happiness if you haven't kept dog." It not only adds many sources to our life but also makes us realize many things during the procedure of keeping dogs. Dogs are considered as loyal companions using their whole life to bring happiness and love to their owners.

Have you ever heard that cats are independent, and they don't really care about people? Do some of your friends say that cats only show love to humans because they're hoping for some food? But why are those people still willing to be a servant of cat? The answer is that cats like to play hard to get. Cats might love people more than we think. A new study indicates that many cats prefer interacting with humans more than food, toys, or good smells. Although there was clear individual variability in cat preference, social interaction with humans was the most-preferred stimulus category for the majority of cats, followed by food. This was true for cats in both the pet and shelter population [9]. Some cats don't like to be patted but they like to lay close to people; Even with snacks in hand, they will not move close to you, you still have to send the snack to their face. After they enjoy the benefit, cats will show their white belly to the owner, so that the owners can't help but prepare more delicious snacks for them to see the cute manner again. Cats are a sweet burden for their owners.

To explore the role of pet at home, four interviewees considered that pet plays a role as friend and nine of them considered that it plays a role as family member. For the reasons why you recommend others to keep pets, eight interviewees thought that "We were not alone anymore", five of them thought that "It was a good way to form independent personality and responsibility" and ten of them thought that "It could bring good mood to me every day"; these reasons can explain the healing characters of pet-keeping.

Conclusion

With the trend of lower birth rate and aged society, more and more people keep pets. Not only are pets members of their family but also meat and drink for modern people. Keeping pets has become a popular and effective way for emotion healing. According to the research result, the original reasons of the healing character of attractiveness for owners are quite the same, including: companionship, responsibility, being depended on, being loved, interaction, cuteness and belonging. Dog-owners have other feelings of regaining innocence, while cat-owners have feelings about falling in love. The emotions of healing include: surprise, interest, warm, heart-to-heart, happiness, security, negative emotions disappear, destress, accomplishment and other characteristics. And the different meanings of interaction for the cat-owners and dog-owners were further clarified. The results also indicated that the role of animals was mostly regarded as friend or family, and the important and attractive attributes and emotions of healing characteristics of keeping pets were indicated, as shown in Table 1.

TABLE 1
THE ATTRACTIVE HEALING ATTRIBUTES AND EMOTIONS OF KEEPING-PETS

original reason	abstract reason
companionship	surprise
responsibility	warm heart
be depended on	joy
be loved	interest
interaction	accomplishment
in love	negative emotion disappear
cutiness	happiness
belonging	empathy
regain innocence	destress
yellow: both blue: cats green : dogs	secure

References

[1] R Scheibeck, M Pallauf, C Stellwag, and B Seeberger,Elderly people in many respects benefit from interaction with dogs, Eur J Med Res. 2011

[2] Quine.W.V.A Proof Procedure for Quantification Theory. J. Symb. Log. 1955, 20, 141-149.

[3] Ludwig C: Wenn das Haustier stirbt. Köln: VGS; 2001.3

[4] Otterstedt C, Rosenberger M: Gefährten - Konkurrenten - Verwandte:Die Mensch-Tier-Beziehung im wissenschaftlichen Diskurs.Göttingen: Vandenhoeck und Ruprecht; 2009:184.

[5] Chen, Yinglun, The Study On The Pets Market In Taiwan: Take The Industrial Trend Of The Pets Market In Japan As An Example, Master's Thesis, Department of Applied Japanese, I-Shou University, Taiwan (in Chinese), 2012

[6] Ma,M.Y.; Tseng. L. T. Y. Applying miryoku (attractiveness) engineering for evaluation of festival industry. Adv. Inf.Sci. Seru. Sci. 2012, 4, 1-9

[7] Huang Ying-yu, You Hsiao-chen, Efects of Companion Pets on Interpersonal Interactions. 2018.1(1),

[8] S. Munoz Lasaa, N. Máximo Bocanegra b, R. Valero Alcaidea, M.A. Atín Arratibel a,E. Varela Donosoa, G. Ferrieroc, Animal assisted interventions in neurorehabilitation: a review of the most recent literature, Neurología. 2015, 30(1):1-7.

[9] Kristyn R.Vitale ShreveaLindsay R.Mehrkamb Monique A.R.Udella, Social interaction, food, scent or toys? A formal assessment of domestic pet and shelter cat (Felis silvestris catus) preferences, Behavioural Processe, 141, Part 3, August 2017, 322-328

https://doi.org/10.1142/9789811238727_0039

Exploring the Difference in Horror Movie Execution Modes

Tzu-Han Hung*, and Kuo-Kuang Fan**

National Yunlin University of Science and Technology Graduate School of Design
*Corresponding Author Email: *D10930014@gemail.yuntech.edu.tw, **fankk@yuntech.edu.tw

Abstract

Horror movies are always entertaining people. Therefore, other exciting movies in different genres can be used for psychotherapy. As horror movies induce different levels of pleasure and satisfaction from the audience, this study explores the implementation of various modes through horror movies. There is a difference in the presentations of various categories, the methods of image narration, and the operating mode of horror movies based on the narrations in the literature. The mode of operation in horror movies is generalized as a norm from the perspectives in the literature. Through literature research, the analysis, comparison, collation, and integration are investigated to understand the norm.

Keywords: horror movie, terror element, image narratives analysis

Introduction

In the movie industry, horror movies are popular. In a modern society where information flows extremely fast, watching movies with the development of the movie industry has become one of the popular leisure entertainments. As people pursue various stimulation, movies become a way of treatment in psychology. The rise of online and micro movie service is becoming popular. Micro movies tell complete stories in a short time. Horror movies are highly entertaining by exaggerating and showing bloody scenes and tension. The feeling expresses the compactness and excitement of the story. The horror images are direct portrayals of human anxiety and metaphors the source of fear in society. In response to the needs of the audience, society has produced various horror stories that prove the existence of horror and reflect the phenomenon as popular culture [1]. Therefore, through the literature research on various operating modes of horror movies, analysis, comparison, collation, and synthesis are carried out for a preliminary understanding of the horror movies. This research explores the current operating modes of horror movies through the collection of documents about the production methods of horror movies and the core of the main expressions. Through image narratives, the information expressed by types of horror is found, and the implications of horror movies are explored. Narrative techniques, common elements, and the commonalities in which the elements are used are explored in various horror movies by investigating the movie structure.

Literature Review

A. Literary narration

Narratology is generally the scientific study of explaining the structure of literary works, mainly the narrative theory developed in France. Todorov formally proposed it in 1969 and confirmed that narratology is a theory of narrative structure. Narrative researchers decompose narrative phenomena into many elements and then determine their functions and mutual relationships for helping people further understand the structure of narrative works. Many narrative research results "deepen" the structure of novels. The way of expression or the recognition of aesthetic characteristics opens a way to enter the internal research of narrative works [2]. The narrative structure of the movie is divided into three acts, and a whole story has ten to twenty plot points, major transitions, or key events of dramatic action. At the midpoint of the second act, there should be an unexpected turning point that takes the dramatic action in a new direction [3]. The classical plot is a linear and sequential development, a series of interrelated events or episodes which compose the status quo arrangement and finally lead to a dramatic ending.

B. Definition of "horror movie"

In terms of genre, the term "horror movie" is too general. However, the term "horror movie" covers many movie types that have other elements. A "genre" means that the movie type is equivalent to the language system. In the tradition of movie genres, a movie is equivalent to a sentence or individual words in the genre system [4]. The genre movie contains a single drawing individual speech. There is a relative and interactive relationship between the system and the individual. Furthermore, according to the interpretation of horror movies, a series of works with a wide range of themes and works describe mysterious, abnormal, and supernatural phenomena to arouse the audience's sense of horror. Western critics classify most of these movie products as fantasy works and use the term "terrifying and supernatural fantasy" to distinguish it from science fiction [5].

C. Development of the horror movie genre

The history of the horror shop is as old as the movie. The first horror movie was "The Cabinet of Dr. Caligari" by the German director Robert Wiene (1873-1938) in 1920. In the story, there are strange doctors in black cloaks, sleepwalkers who predict the future, carnivals, murder, escape, and even insanity elements, and scenes full of German expressionism [6]. Paul Wells explained the history of horror movies in

"Thriller Horror Movies" and emphasized the worries of the old world in the Gothic romantic hoop style of anxiety history, fairy tales, and folk legends in the 20th century. Modern horror movies mostly use fear, industry, technology, and economy to describe the characteristics of the new world. Therefore, horror movies are more capable of responding to the formation of social, scientific, and philosophical ideas than other movie genres [7].

D. Short horror movie description

Almost all types of short horror movies are produced in the same mode with various types of monsters, ghosts, creatures, and bloody torture. The story uses conditions that threaten lives. Based on this, a plot that hurts lives easily causes fear. In the psychological suspense and scientific reflection, the "experience" in daily life appears by unusual behaviors, which results in the generation of emotional suspense and fear. The application of various narrative methods is roughly the same with the performance of the lens, the transformation of the character's personality, the rapid editing of the screen, and the setting of the space scene as described in Table 1.

TABLE 1
Narrative Techniques of Various Horror Short Movie Types

literary narration	Types of monsters	Biological type	Psycholog-ical suspense	Scientific reflection type	Bloody killing type
Angle of Shot	POV S/RS PCU/ XCU	POV S/RS PCU/ XCU	POV S/RS PCU/ XCU	POV S/RS PCU/ XCU	POV PCU/ XCU
Personality	Fear to staunch	Scared to Attack	Peaceful to Scared	Exhausted to Greedy	Ruthless to Confused

The short horror movie technique reduces the presentation stage with voyeuristic viewpoints to quickly tell the story, and the use of various viewpoints makes viewers feel the fear of the movie easily. In various short horror movies, the occurrence of direct events is common to explain how the story starts and happens. The content of the story is almost narrated by one action, such as walking, sleeping, and so on. The short horror movie conveys fear to the audience directly from the beginning. Most of the techniques in the production of horror movies are similar. The techniques in the movies almost transmit a daily life model. For example, modern people work overtime and stay up late. Horror movies show the experience of daily life to make viewers integrate the experience with the fear of events [8].

E. Generation of fear in watching movies

Emotion is not spontaneous but is caused by stimuli internally and externally. The internal stimuli refer to the stimulus produced by the individual's organ changes and abnormalities, while the external stimuli refer to those outside the body, such as the warm sunlight, music appreciation, and stage performance. Based on this, an image produces emotional stimulation to viewers and generates fear. The external factors of fear are divided into two types: "experience" and "innate." All lives are afraid of death, and we are afraid and fearful of situations that threaten life. On this basis, if we add a plot that hurts our lives in the process of watching a movie, it easily causes fear. However, in terms of "experience", if an object appears in the movie that once threatened the life in the movie, then the object becomes a signal of fear, and it generates fear when it reappears [9].

Research Method

The research mainly focuses on document analysis and discussion on the topic of fear in short horror movies. Various modes of horror movies were collected. Through document research, the meaning of the movie was analyzed with various viewpoints and arguments. The pattern was found in the frequently used images of horror movies. Through the content analysis method, the relevant documents, materials, and works collected by this research were analyzed by qualitative analysis. The key research literature was analyzed and summarized, and the hidden behind the horror movie techniques were discussed. Finally, we compared the literature in terms of specific standards to determine the similarities and differences.

Horror Movie Execution Mode

The three elements were discussed for the "narrative situation" in different movies. To convey the horror in the shortest time, horror movies often use voyeuristic views and close-up shots. Horror movies usually take the voyeuristic view to shoot the characters with a monitor or at a low angle to make the audience feel like hiding to peep. Therefore, peeping shots in various horror movies is an absolutely important part. It conveys that there is another or an invisible character in the movie, which scares the viewers.

A. Horror source

In the movie layout, each character is explained in detail. However, the horror movie does not explain how and why the event starts but directly states an event. The occurrence of action is to project the viewer's self-impression onto the characters in the movie based on the things, phenomena, or experiences in daily life to increase the shocking effect. The feature movie is presented as a bridge. The subject is often executed in a disguised form unknown in the future and expressed in a certain ideology.

B. Difference between feature and short movies

The performance techniques of horror movies range from objective narratives to the subjective performance of the characters' hearts to see a certain state of affairs through the eyes of the characters and influence the psychology of the audience through the rhythm of the lens movement. In the feature horror movie, it is more concentrated on the stage of presentation, and some of the presentations are less narrative. Based on the story structure in the literature, the story is further divided into four basic structures: background, theme, plot, and result. The method of a movie tells that the events are happening successively by leading the main plot, the successive presentations, and transitions to finally reveal the results. Field mentioned that the beginning is the first ten minutes of the first act. These ten minutes let the audience know who your main character is and what the theme of the story is [10].

Therefore, compared to the production of short movies, the sequence of the narrative content of the feature horror movie follows the rhythm. The narrative structure of the short horror movie is mostly linear and straightforward, and the editing is fast, which makes the viewer psychologically unable to connect and causes confusion and tension. The most common method is showing third-person onlookers, voyeuristic views, and close-ups. In addition to partially explaining the role of the plot, the movie lets the viewer concentrate on the plot and at the same time, conveys the fear of the story in a short time. The differences between the feature and short horror movies are summarized in Table 2.

TABLE 2
Table of Differences in the Performance of Horror Feature Movies and Short Movies

Horror feature movie and Differences in short movies	Horror feature movie	Horror short movies
Performance technique	Rather than following the steps of the plot, the subsequent presentations allow the events to occur one after another.	The quick editing effect is more often used to explain part of the plot and direct events.

The three-act play as a movie's narrative technique is a structure used by many people. Many movie and television screenwriters explain that the focus of a three-act play is to layout, conflict, and resolve. We use a standard structure in a story to understand the process of a complete story with a beginning, middle, and end. The three-act play in many movies lets the viewers understand characters, background ideas, the appearance of things, and people to deepen the conflict, shape the atmosphere, emphasize the main theme, and finally solve the problems. However, it is not possible to use the three-act play structure in a short movie, as the short movie starts the story from the middle section and does not let the viewer know how to open it. Most short horror movies mainly focus on shaping the atmosphere, and the final event occurs. Therefore, the three-act structure is not used in short horror movies.

C. Difference between animation and real shooting

In animated movies, it is easier for people to notice the composition of the animation and the characteristics by visual exaggeration and character design. Animated movies pay more attention to "creativeness". Lasseter (1987) believed that the ultimate purpose is to let people laugh, and there is unlimited creative fantasy in the process of making animated movies. The images in horror animations still do not achieve the most realistic sense of threat and fear, although the characters in the animations and movies are presented as fictional stories. However, horror movies are more authentic. The technological development of computer synthesis or special effects makes unreal pictures realistic. Direct performance allows the techniques to present what makes it easier for viewers to bring emotions. Owing to the role of friends, the viewers are afraid of the characters in the movie, while the animation purely expresses scary horror themes. The reason for the inability to produce shocking effects like live-action movies is the lack of authenticity of cartoons. Therefore, no matter how bloody and horrible scenes are, the animation of monsters and suspenseful performance cannot be as real as a live-action movie. The viewers feel less fear when the movie is known to be a cartoon. When compared to real actors, the images conveyed to the audience are ultimately in a fixed image system even if the animated characters look exquisite and realistic [11].

Conclusion

In the narrative of short horror movies, events occur directly and do not explain the beginning and end of the story. There is less laid-out content, and quick editing is used to scare viewers with the appearance of sudden horror pictures. The narrative stories of feature horror movies are expressed in four basic structures: background, theme, plot, and result. They have a beginning, a middle, and an end, which explain how the story begins and slowly spread out. Most of the techniques used in the production of horror movies are similar. The techniques are used for transmitting a daily life model regardless of the length of movies. horror movies generate fear through the experience of daily life so that viewers integrate and experience the fear of the event. Creating horror movies has still a lot of room for development. With the assistance of current technology, horror movies can have many spectacle shots, which create different expressions for future horror movie creators.

References

[1] Ting-Yu Yu, "The Horror Representation in Japanese Manga", Master's thesis of Shih Hsin University Institute of Communication, 2003.

[2] Cheng Yucheng, Movie Narrative Image Aesthetics-Editing Theory and Demonstration. Wunan Book Publishing Co., Ltd. 2008.

[3] Louis D, Giannett, Understand Movie, 10rd ed., Translated by Jiao Xiongping. Taipei, Yuanliu.

[4] Zheng Shusen, Movie Type and Genre Movie, Taipei, Hong Fan Publishing House, 2005, pp. 6.

[5] Yang Haiming. "World Movie Encyclopedia". Social Science Archives Press, 1993, pp. 2.

[6] Bao Yuheng and Peng Shenli, "On Hollywood Genre Movies: Horror Movies", "Movie Criticism", 18, 2011, pp. 15-40.

[7] Paul Wells, translated by Peng Xiaofen, "Terrorist Movies: Screaming Cinema", Taipei: Shulin Publishing House, 2003.

[8] Tzu-han Hung, Exploring the methods to convey the terror elements in horror movies, Taiwan University of Science and Technology Visual Communication Design Coefficient Contents and Applied Design Master's thesis, 2015.

[9] Zhang Chunxing, Yang Guoshu, "psychology". Taipei City: Sanmin Book Co., Ltd., 1969, pp. 160-161.

[10] Field, S.,Practical movie screenwriting skills Screenplay: the foundation of screenwriting. Taipei: Yuanliu, 2008.

[11] Huang Siru, Use the "Long Night" animation movie to explore the visual and horrifying elements of images, Master's thesis of the Institute of Animation Art andP Video Aesthetics, National Tainan University of the Arts, 2011.

https://doi.org/10.1142/9789811238727_0040

Features and Issues in 3D Facial Animation

Chun-Ming Huang[1]*, Hong-Yi Pai[2]

[1]Department of Visual Communication Design, Chaoyang University of Technology, Taichung, Taiwan
[2]Department of Multimedia Design, National Formosa University
*Corresponding Author Email: [1]jerryhuang151@yahoo.com.tw, [2]hpai@ms38.hinet.net

Abstract

Blend shaping is a type of deformation method that you can use on several target shapes to drive a basic shape. It is a powerful morphing tool. Facial animation is an application of blend shaping, and it brings more life, fun and vibrancy to the subject. There are many advantages and fewer limits in 3D facial animation. We use 3D animation software such as Maya to show its features and check any issues in the 3D facial animation.

Keywords: deformation, blend shape [1], expression, lip synch [2].

Introduction

Deformation is a very important performance technique for animation [3]. Many animations or movies use this technique for performance, such as "Transformers". The transformation behavior of butterflies in the animation transformation process uses in-between techniques to achieve predictable magical deformation effects. The visual deformation of animation has an expotential value. As long as you make good use of the deformation of the deformed elements in space, such as displacement, rotation, zoom, time changes, such as speed, etc., as well as the deformation of objects, you can enhance the illusion of animation and visual spatial changes. Appropriate exaggeration and deformation are complete changes in the visual form, which also affects the mood of the audience, creating a deep impression and can highlight the story content of the animation. It is even exaggerated, funny, and lively, making the animation become tense, achieving the effect of entertainment [4].

Deformation often uses the concept of less control and more to adjustment of the shape, such as a group of vertices or bone joints, and the weight to control the shape. There are many applications of deformation. The most common one used is to transform from one shape to another, such as a person running becoming a cheetah and finally morphing into a car. These are all different shape deformations. These changes will bring the audience magical and fantasy effects. 3D facial expression animation is a very complex technology and art, and it is also highly deformed. Animated expressions are the most challenging aspect of facial animation [2] . This is also the most meaningful. Many 3D facial expression animations are used especially in movies, games and other common applications. The use of motion capture systems can make expressions very realistic and vivid, but the use of motion capture systems seldom cuts into the abstract performance style or the exaggerated characteristics of animation, such as squash, stretch, anticipation [5], exaggeration, etc., This paper aims at such shortcomings and proposes related research to supplement the shortcomings of related 3D facial expression animation.

Fig. 1 Deformation is exaggerated, funny, lively, and transformation, making the animation become tense, to achieve the effect of entertainment.

Literature Review

Common deformation methods include lattices, clusters, deformation, morphing, and soft modification [6]. First, lattices is to simplify a group of vertices or lines. For example, 20*20*20 vertices are simplified into 5*5*5 control points, and fewer points are used to control many vertices, forming a flexible control deformation. Second, a method of using clusters. A cluster is to select a group of vertices to form a cluster. The movement of this cluster will affect these vertices. 3D facial expression animation is very complex and often controlled by clusters. For example, there are several clusters on the eyelids controlling the vertices above and below the eyelid. These clusters form a controller to control the eyelid movement, and finally set the key in the controller to set the animation. Third, deformation method by the use of morphing [7]. Morphing enables one object to assume the shape of another. Morphing is most commonly used in the area of facial animation [8]. Because the face is such a complex shape, it is best to sculpt the many individual poses a character's face may take. A morphing utility enables you to smoothly animate between this shape. Blend shape is a deformer type that lets you use several target shapes to drive a base shape. The tool creates controls for each of the target shapes that can be edited and animated to control the look of the base shape. Facial expression animation is the most common application of blending deformation. There are two common methods for facial expression animation. One is to use the facial controller, the other is to use blend shape for the facial control. Set the controller on the face model to change the shape of the face by displacement, rotation and other methods. The morph method is based on the original face model as the morph base, and then creation of several morph targets, changing the shape of each morph target according to the mouth shape and expression, and finally to mix and deform these morph targets with the morph base [9]. Time given to different morph target settings, continuous broadcast will produce charming animation. 3D facial animation also has its advantages and disadvantages. The following is a comparison with personal operating experience and experiments. Fourth, another deformation method is soft modification. Soft modification is a bit like an extension of a cluster. The selected vertices are used to control the selected transformation by the weight influence range. Compared with the cluster, soft modification sizing is more flexible, the operation is easier, and the deformation is faster. A great help for 3D facial animation is the mainstream tool of modern modeling and character animation.

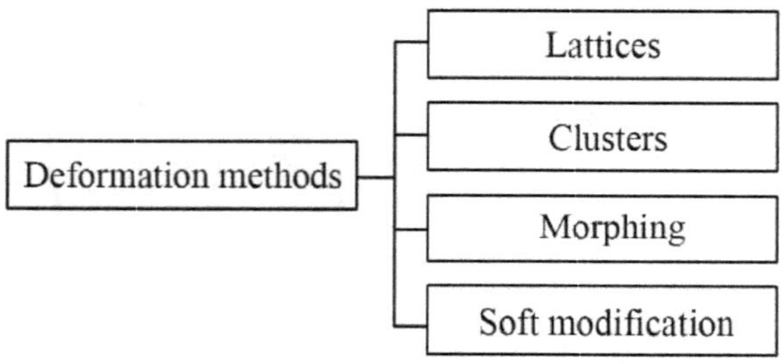

Fig. 2 Main deformation methods include lattices, clusters, morphing, and soft modification.

Animation Creation Teaching Case

This research takes the production of animation-related expressions of a song as an example, and discusses related features and issues, using the 3D animation software Maya. The facial organs of expressions involved in 3D facial animation include mouth, eyes, and eyebrows, among which the eyes and eyebrows are highly connected and almost affect each other. The main steps are roughly as follows. First, evaluate the animation that has an impact on 3D facial animation, and can show the advantages of 3D facial animation. The animation that can best present the characteristics of 3D facial animation is roughly dialogue and singing, because the expression changes as dialogue and singing are more complex. Singing is in line with the current popularity and has the charm of sound penetration. The second choice is a song that is easy to show deformation, especially blend shape, which is attractive and popular. In this example, the English song "Hello" is selected. The main high-pitched part is highly recognizable, and the song is not too fast. The third interception of a popular song part, such as chorus, etc., is easy to express 3D facial Animation. Fourth, look at the different phoneme classifications, and how they're applied to lip synch [10]. The face and voice recognition should be produced in coordination. The voice is mainly vowels and consonants. The vowel has a greater influence because its deformation is relatively large. It is the key to subdivide the key expression shape. The consonant and mouth closure are the details to consider. In addition, the organs that affect the shape of expressions, including mouth, eyes, eyebrows and other facial organs, must be considered, so that 3D facial animation can be perfect. Fifth, make a face model. For the face model, pay attention to the wiring of the face model and UV mapping. In order to make the facial movements more obvious, it is necessary to appropriately color each part of the face, such as coloring the lips. Sixth, create a joint skeleton and bind it with the face model, and let the joint skeleton control the deformed mesh model to make animation. Seventh, the expression model for each important recognition is a mixed deformed mesh model. It is best to use the emotions, sorrows and vowels, and leave the original neutral expressions, that is, the face has no emotions, sorrow, or joy. Eighth, create a blend shape animation, mixing and deforming different expression models with the original neutral. Ninth, use proper mixing and deformation to set the keys in the identification of different phonemes. Check the fine-tuning of the animation, whether the deformation and facial animation are correct or not.

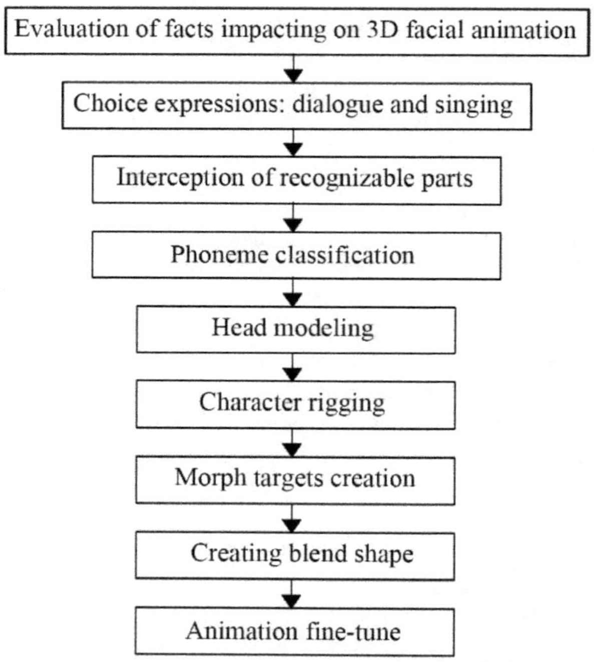

Fig. 3 Pipeline of 3D facial animation process.

Evaluation Result and Discussion

The feature of 3D facial animation is that it has powerful deformation, including blend shape, which provides a kind of change. Second, maintains the movement of the head, the deformation of the eyelids, the eyebrows and the mouth. The rotation and movement of the eyeball, including the muscle changes of the lips, eyes, and eyebrows, such as blinking, smiling, etc., have a strong attraction and charm. Third, 3D facial animation is consistent with the 3D shape of the real space, and can produce realistic animations, and can be combined with real movies. There are also some issues in the process of making 3D facial animation: The first is the typology problem of the 3D facial head shape [11], especially the typology of the mouth and eyes [12]. The corners of the mouth must be a little more lined, and the 3D facial head shape model should also conform. The use of the principle of topology must be used, otherwise there will be some problems with the opening and closing of the mouth and eyes, such as the mouth cannot be completely closed [13], etc. The closed points should be pulled closer, and overlap should be avoided, and all the target shape models should be the same as the base shape neutral mesh model. The vertices, edges, and faces should be consistent. Second, there are some issues with the skeleton controlling the head rotation. The skeleton controlling the face shape must be the priority over the blend shape does, otherwise the head will easily be displaced. Third, the weight of the skeleton affecting the face is not easy to control. In Maya animation software, the greater the weight of the skeleton affecting the mesh model is white, if less it is black. It is not easy to paint the control vertices of the mesh model with the paint skin weight control. The weight is either too large or too small, and it is easy to run away. The auxiliary method is to select the control vertices of the mesh model and enter the values in the Component Editor, but it is not intuitive enough. Fourth, when using blend shape, blend shape can't read your mind [14]. You know the bending tree should move in an arc, but blend shape doesn't know that. When you provide two target shapes to blend shape, all it can do is calculate a straight-line change, or interpolation, in the position of each point relative to its counterpart in the other shape. Fifth, the deformation of 3D facial animation is somewhat limited compared to 2D facial animation. Due to the influence of the skeleton and the typology of the mesh model, it is difficult to completely freely deform to any shape, especially if the cartoon is an extreme exaggeration. Sixth, in terms of animation fine tuning and adjustment, the timing control and modification of each key frame is very time-consuming. Even if there are skeletons, controllers, and blend shapes, it still takes a lot of time to produce, and time is money.

Fig. 4 Keep the movement of the head, the deformation of the eyelids, the eyebrows and the mouth in tune. 3D facial animation has a strong attraction and charm. © Learning Maya 6: Character Rigging and Animation from Maya Press and Sybex Inc.

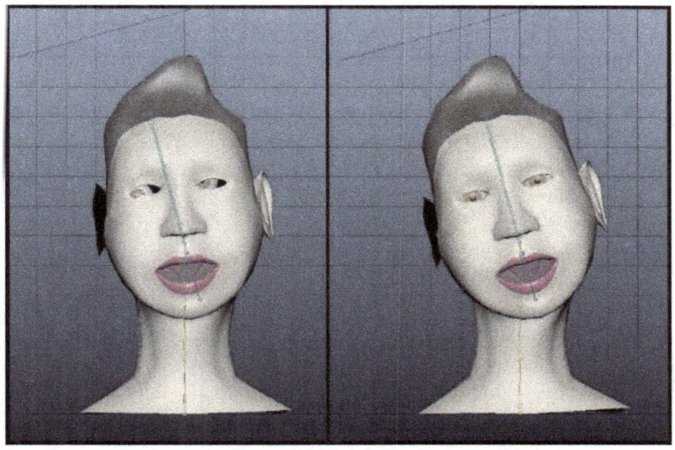

Fig. 5 Skeleton control takes precedence over blend shapes, otherwise the shape will run away. © Learning Maya 6: Character Rigging and Animation from Maya Press and Sybex Inc.

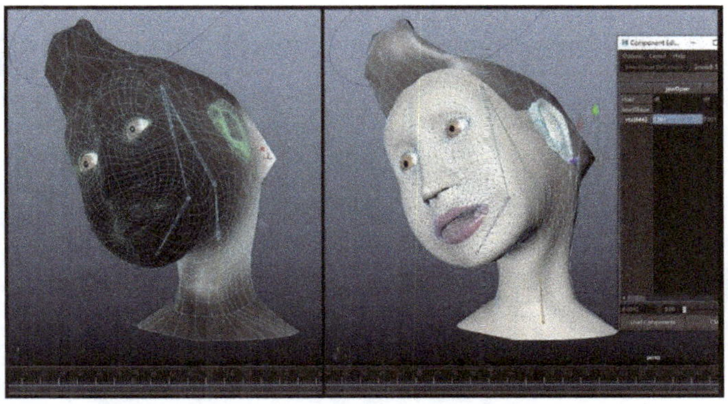

Fig. 6 Paint skin weight is not easy to control, and sometime it will bulge. © Learning Maya 6: Character Rigging and Animation: from Maya Press and Sybex Inc.

Conclusion

3D facial animation has many features and issues. The biggest feature is deformation. With different blend shapes, more deformations are generated to make the animation more vivid and entertaining. Second, keeping the head and eye movement changes, such as blinking and smiling, has a strong attraction and charm. Third, 3D facial animation can be realistic and easy to integrate with real movies. Fourth, the typology of the head shape of the face must conform to the topological rules; the closed vertices must be pulled closer and overlap must be avoided. Fifth, the skeleton control face shape must have priority over the blend shape control face shape, otherwise the head will be easily displaced. Sixth, it is not easy to control the control vertices of the paint skin weight mesh model. Seventh, blend shape cannot calculate the interpolation between two target models. The more target shapes, the smoother the facial animation. Eighth, 3D facial animation still has some limitations for extreme exaggerated deformation. Ninth, although there are many tools to assist 3D facial animation, it still takes a lot of time to make it, and time is money.

References

[1] Niklas Larsson, *Morph targets and bone rigging for 3D facial animation A comparative case study*, pp. 13, 2017.

[2] Bill Fleming and Darris Dobby, *Animating Facial Feature and Expressions*, Charles River Media Press, pp. 97-100, 1999.

[3] Chun-Ming Huang (2003), *Exploring on time and space as the basic elements of animation*, pp. 8, 2003. [*Cross-Straits Technical and Vocational Education Seminar 2005*]

[4] Hao Zhou, *Application of 3D Animation Technique for Chinese Opera,* A thesis I the department of Computer Science at Concordia University, Canada, pp. 18, 2003.

[5] Richard Williams, *The Animator's Survival Kit: A Manual of Methods, Principles and Formulas*, Faber & Faber, pp. 276, 2009

[6] George Maestri, *Digital character animation 2,* Volume 1: Essential Techniques, pp. 140-142, 1999.

[7] Doug Kelly, *Character Animation in Depth,* Creative Professional Press, pp.351, 1998.

[8] Andr´ea Britto Mattos, Jes´us P. Mena-Chalco, Roberto M. Cesar Jr, Luiz Velho, *3D Linear Facial Animation Based on Real Data*, pp. 2, 2010. [*2010 23rd SIBGRAPI - Conference on Graphics, Patterns and Images*]

[9] William Dwelly, "*Learning Maya 6/ Character Rigging and Animation".* Maya Press and Sybex Inc. pp. 265, 2004.

[10] Frederic I. Parke Keith, *Computer Facial Animation*, pp. 8, Waters, 2008.

[11] Chun-Ming Huang, Tzu-Heng Liu, *Abstract Style Analysis of Polygon Models,* pp. 1, 2020. [*3rd Eurasian Conference on Educational Innovation 2020*]

[12] Chun-Ming Huang, *Abstract Style and Case of Digital Creation Teaching,* pp. 1, 2019. [*Ieee International Conference on Knowledge Innovation and Invention 2019 (IEEE ICKII 2019)*]

[13] Chun-Ming Huang (2003), "*Visual style analysis of low-face polygon models*," Taiwan, pp. 1, 2003 [*2003 Design conference*]

[14] Kei Hirose & Tomoyuki Higuchi, *Creating facial animation of characters via MoCap data*, pp. 4, 2012.

https://doi.org/10.1142/9789811238727_0041

Health Measurement Record Tendency Chart Interface with Different Interactive Methods and Information Design

Shih-Chieh Chen*, Jia-Yan Jhuang**

National Yunlin University of Science and Technology, Department of Industrial Design, Yunlin 64002, Taiwan.
*Corresponding Author Email: *chenshih@yuntech.edu.tw, **swallows921@gmail.com

Abstract

This study investigated young people's feelings of operating health measurement records with different interactive designs. With the operation processes observed, they were interviewed. The experiment involved three interactive types (i.e., static, dynamic, and interactive) of tendency chart information design. The participants operated different types individually. After the participants measured and recorded their blood pressure for 14 consecutive days, in-depth interviews and the focus group method were employed. The following suggestions were proposed: (1) The information design of the tendency chart integrates the static and the interactive types. (2) The background of the tendency chart needs different colors for distinction. The design for the display point should be 20 × 20 pixels. Lines need to be in colors or dotted lines for distinction rather than solid lines. The legend is placed above the tendency chart. (3) The tendency chart employs a calendar for data inquiry. (4) When conducting measurement, a reminder mechanism needs to be in place to remind the user whether they show abnormal data.

Keywords: health measurement record interface, information design, interactive interface design, observation method, interview method

Introduction

Through observations and interviews, this study explores the operation of health measurement recording with the interfaces of different designs of an information chart for young subjects. Based on in-depth focus group interviews, the experimental results are analyzed and design is suggested to standardize the information design of physiological data charts. The research results improve interface presentation and design. Therefore, the purpose of this study is as follows:

(1) To explore and improve the acceptable information and health measurement recording interface for young people.
(2) To explore the chart for the health measurement recording and the best presentation and design of different interactive categories in information design.
(3) To improve the visualization chart of health measurement data and propose information design and specifications.

Literature Review

A. Health management records

Under the influence of the new era, the main disease patterns changed from acute diseases such as infectious diseases to chronic diseases. Important health indicators are measured and recorded every day, such as heart rate, blood pressure, and amount of exercise to effectively control important health indicators and reduce and alleviate chronic diseases [10]. In the design of the health measurement recording interface, it is necessary to consider that the text content of the information interface is easy to understand and convey the main health information. Communication and interactive knowledge and skills on the website are necessary so that individuals learn and share. People need to be able to use new information in changing situations, further analyze and judge information through websites, and select available information [5].

B. Information design

Information design is derived from information graphics. The earliest meaning of creative design is to achieve the purpose of communication [2]. It is also a method of integrating graphics and text to illustrate numerical data [3]. International Institute of Information Design (IIID) defines information design as follows: (1) information is the result of processing and integrating data into an organization so that users can absorb it, (2) design is a professional and creative way of presenting solutions through pictures or plans, and (3) information design is the definition, planning, shaping, and carrying of the context in which information is presented to achieve specific objectives and meet the needs of target users [1].

Visual data is easy to view and understand [6]. Reference [7] divided information design into three categories according to its purpose: (1) organized presentation of facts or data, (2) methods to understand the situation or process, and (3) design of the control system. Reference [8] stated that there should be professionals who are responsible for making the information easier to understand. They should be able to design the difficult information to understand as easy one to obtain the required information, thus improving the unbalanced state of information quality and quantity.

C. Interactive definition of infographics

According to different media presentation modes and interactive definitions, infographics have three interactive presentation modes: (1) static infographics: they are applied to newspapers and magazines and is easy to spread through paper and network; (2) motion infographics: they form dynamic charts through images, animations, and sound effects; (3) interactive infographics: they retain dynamic characteristics, increase interactive conditions, and allow users to search and browse specific information by themselves [9].

Materials and Methods

A. Instrument and materials

In this experiment, 6 subjects were invited to test three interactive categories of design information (static, motion, and interactive) of the trend chart, and they were measured for blood pressure. After inputting the blood pressure value, they could see the trend chart. There were three different types of interactive categories of design information for trend charts: (1) static, (2) motion, and (3) interactive.

(1) Static: It is a trend chart without any animation and special effects. The user can see the detailed values by moving the mouse over the display point, but the user cannot click for more information.
(2) Motion: After the user confirms the date and clicks to query, the trend chart curve appears automatically with the curve and each display point. There is an animation play button on the right. The user can choose whether to play it again. The detailed value is displayed when the mouse moves to the display point.
(3) Interactive: It has something in common with the dynamic model. This differs from the dynamic model in that the search can be continued by clicking the display point, and has the same feature of 'Motion'.

B. Methods

The experiment was conducted from May 17, 2020 to May 30, 2020. Blood pressure was measured daily for 6 subjects (3 women and 3 men) with different levels of health awareness. Based on the observational study, the blood pressure values were observed. Daily measurements were taken for 14 days. The interview was divided into two parts. The first part was personal in-depth interview. The second part is the focus group interview. The six subjects discussed the operational process of the health measurement interface and suggestions for improving the information design of the trend chart. The experimental procedure is as follows (Fig. 1, Table 1).

(1) Six subjects were invited to have their blood pressure measured and recorded for two weeks.
(2) The behavior and process of blood pressure recording were observed.
(3) The subjects were invited to conduct a one-to-one in-depth interview.
(4) Six subjects were invited for focus group interviews.
(5) Subjects were interviewed for interface design and improvement suggestions.

Fig. 1 Experimental situation.

TABLE 1
Interface screen

Digital carrier-Laptop (Chinese interface)
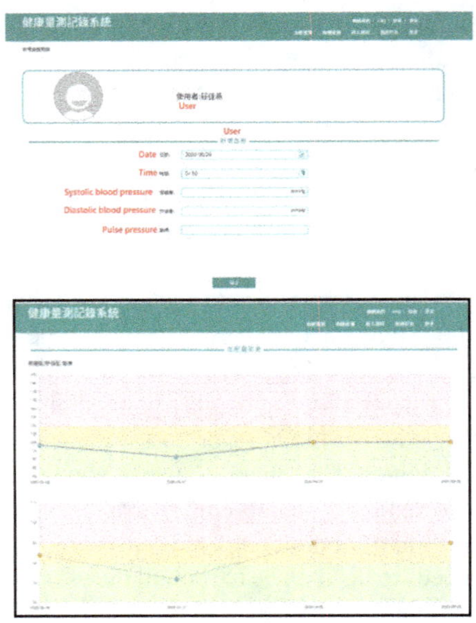

Source: Compiled by this study (Chinese interface)

Results

Three men and three women were invited to participate in the study: 2 males/females × 3 types of information design interaction (static/dynamic/interactive). All aged between 20 and 26 years old with an average age of 22 years (M = 22.13, Sd = 2.23). They were all college or graduate students who were familiar with the operation of 3C products.

A. In-depth interview - content

The first part of this experiment is the one-to-one in-depth interview, which was conducted in the form of a semi-structured questionnaire, including (1) basic questions, (2) trend chart cognition, and (3) viewing the trend chart of blood pressure measurement in two weeks. Ideas and suggestions from different perspectives on a particular topic were collected. With the consent of the interviewee, the interview was recorded and videotaped. The following is the transcript of the interview, with a numbered code indicating the ideas raised by the interviewees.

a. Basic questions

Six subjects (M01, M02, M03, F01, F02, F03) were college or graduate students with an average age of about 22 years. They measured blood pressure only when needed in hospitals and clinics. None of them had used the health measurement APP or system before the experiment, but all had used the exercise APP to measure heart rate and calculate calories. There were five subjects (M01, M02, F01, F02, F03) whose family members had their blood pressure measured at home, but none of them had done it regularly. Three subjects (M02, M03, F01) used paper to record after the measurement and knew the meaning of the values, but they did not see the historical records after the measurement. (Table 2).

b. Trend chart cognition

Only two subjects (M02, F02) knew the interval value criteria for blood pressure. All six subjects (M01, M02, M03, F01, F02, F03) felt that the trend chart helped the user understand the numerical trend over a while and record long-term changes and recent conditions. Two subjects (M02, F03) found the visual information more intuitive.

c. Viewing the trend chart

All six subjects (M01, M02, M03, F01, F02, F03) were able to correctly describe the trend chart of the health measurement records. After two weeks of measuring and recording experiments, the subjects said that if they could continue to measure their blood pressure, they would pay more attention to their health.

B. Focus interview - content

Six subjects were invited to participate in the focus group interview in the form of a semi-structured questionnaire, including (1) interactive presentation of trend chart information design, (2) visual information of the trend chart, (3) overall operation, and suggestions for improvement of information design related to blood pressure and blood sugar trend charts. With the consent of the interviewees, the interview was recorded and videotaped. After the interview, the interview records were sorted out for analysis. The following is the transcript.

a. Trend chart information design interaction category

During the interview, the differences in the trend chart in static, dynamic, and interactive modes were introduced respectively. All subjects observed the difference in the presentation and search of the three modes. Subjects preferred the interactive mode in which they could continue searching and browsing specific information. When clicking on a display point, they could see the value and continue searching by controlling the length of click time or the frequency. The animation play function could be set when needed.

b. Trend chart visual information

During the interview, the subjects suggested the improvement of background color blocks, display points, lines, and the overall trend chart. The background color block could be adjusted to be brighter. It was better to use three to seven colors to distinguish the background color. This conclusion was consistent with the research results of Ref. [4]. The display point section could be resized and reduced to allow the user to accurately read the relationship between display points and values in the trend chart. It was not recommended to use thick and thin lines, but colored and dotted or solid lines could be used. The legend of the overall trend chart was arranged in order of normal, warning and danger, and placed on the top of the trend chart. If there were two values, it was divided into two trend charts with different headlines.

c. Overall operation

In the overall operation, the calendar was set in the search column for an easy query. A knowledge base was inserted into the trend chart so that users instantly understood the different effects of the value. The reminder mechanism was set to remind the user whether the recent value is abnormal (Fig. 2).

C. Interview content

After the personal in-depth interview and focus group interview, the subjects' suggestions on the interview contents related to the trend chart information design were further integrated. Two aspects were listed, respectively for visual design and interactive presentation to provide a reference for the interface design of health measurement records in the future.

TABLE 2
Interview feedback

Item	Content	Suggestions
Trend chart information design	Visual design	1. The display point can be reduced to be more accurate. 2. The color of the background color block can be brighter. 3. Lines can be distinguished by colored and dotted or solid lines. 4. The legend can be placed above the trend chart.
	Interactive presentation	1. It can keep the static state and it doesn't need to play automatically. 2. The display point value can be known directly. 3. When clicking a display point, the view of the value and continuous search can be carried out by controlling the length of clicking time or the frequency of clicking. 4. The reminder mechanism can be set to remind the user whether the recent value is abnormal.

Source: Compiled by this study

Conclusions

According to the observational study, the subjects accepted the one-to-one interview after measuring and recording the blood pressure trend for 14 days. The subjects were not measuring blood pressure before the experiment, and they all agreed that long-term numerical trends could be seen through the trend chart, and the visual information was more intuitive.

All six subjects were able to correctly describe the trend chart of the health measurement records they saw. After two weeks of measuring and recording experiments, the subjects said that if they could continue to measure their blood pressure, they would pay more attention to their health.

The focus group interview focused on the trend chart. The subjects thought that the static and interactive mode of the information interaction of the trend chart could be combined. The values were seen when clicking on the display point, and the interactive mode in which the information was searched further after the clicking was acceptable. For the visual design of the trend chart, the background color block was distinguished with bright colors. The right combination of colors was used to show the information that the user cannot quickly understand. The display point size smaller than the value interval allowed users to read the relationship between the display point and the value of the trend chart more accurately. Lines were distinguished by colored and dotted or solid lines. The legend was placed above the trend chart. In the overall operation, the calendar was set in the search column for an easy query. A knowledge base was inserted into the trend chart so that users instantly understood the different effects of the value. The reminder mechanism reminded the user whether the recent value was abnormal.

Based on the above observations and interviews, the following suggestions and design criteria are proposed.

1. Information design for the interaction of the trend chart: In the design of the trend chart information on health measurement records, the static pictures were used without flash design. They were combined in the interactive mode for further search and mouse click to show the values so that the point value was seen when the user clicked on the display point. When clicking on a display point, the value reading and continuous search were carried out by controlling the length of click time or the frequency of clicking. After clicking, the user searched and browsed specific information and content without the dynamic playback function.
2. The visual design of the trend chart: the background color block was distinguished with bright colors. For example, red (R: 255; G: 0; B: 0), orange means warning (R: 255; G: 153; B: 51), green means safe (R: 153; G: 204; B: 153), and the transparency was 30%. The display points were between 15x15 and 20x20 pixels (the unit of web page, 1 pixel = 0.04cm). Lines were distinguished by colored and dotted or solid lines. The legend was located above the trend chart, as shown in Fig. 1.
3. The overall trend chart search function: the calendar was located in the search column. A knowledge base was inserted into the trend chart so that users can instantly understand the different effects of the value.
4. The function of health measurement records: The reminder mechanism reminded the user whether the recent value was abnormal. The eye-catching text color was used.

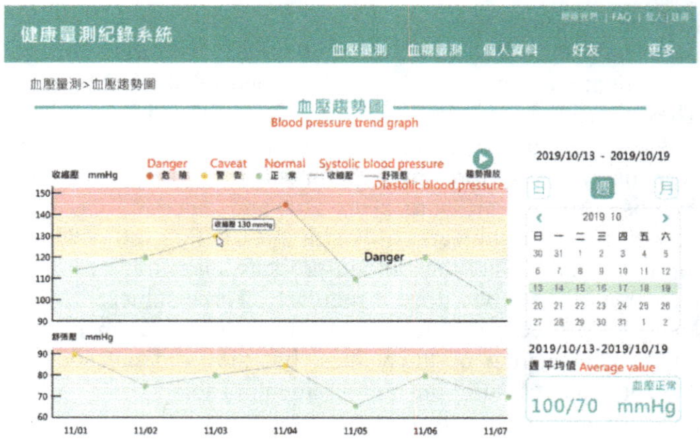

Fig. 2 Improved trend chart based on design suggestions (Chinese interface)

References

[1] International Institute for Information Design (IIID)(2000). About IIID [Online forum comment]. Retrieved from https://www.iiid.net/

[2] Kristof, R., & Satra, A. (1995). *Interactivity by design*. Seattle, Belmont, CA: Adobe Press.

[3] Lester, P. M. (1999). *Visual communication Image with message*. Wadsworth, NY: CRC Press.

[4] Levie, W. H., & Dickie, K. E. (1973). The analysis and application of media. *Second handbook of research on teaching*, *32*(4), 858-882.

[5] Nutbeam, D. (2001). Health literacy as a public health goal: A challenge for contemporary health education and communication strategies into the 21st century. *Health Promotion International*, *15*(3), 259-267.

[6] Roberts, R. & Laramee, R.(2018). Visualising business data: a survey. *Information*, *9*(11).

[7] Wildbur, P., & Burke, M. (1998). *Information graphics*, London, England: Thames & Hudson.

[8] Wurman, R. (1997). *Information architects*. New York, NY: Waston-Guptill.

[9] Hsu, T. F., Wang, S. W., & Fu, M. C. (2017). The study of interactive conceptual model of interactive infographics. *Journal of Design Science*, *20*(2), 1-20.

[10] Lai, S. T. (2016). Strengthen health bracelet to plan and design the seniors health management app. *Journal of Information Communication and Technology Auditing*, *33*, 116-128.

https://doi.org/10.1142/9789811238727_0042

How to Use Camera View Changing and Morphing Technology to Embody the Visual Representation of Metaphor in Augmented Reality

Hong-Yi Pai[1*] and Chun-Ming Huang[2**]

[1]Department of Multimedia Design, National Formosa University
[2]Department of Visual Communication Design, Chaoyang University of Technology
*Corresponding Author Email: *hpai@ms38.hinet.net, **jerryhuang151@yahoo.com.tw

Abstract

Since Lakoff and Johnson (1980) claimed that metaphor is a matter of thought and action, the metaphor has been not only the rhetoric of literature but also an essential conceptual tool for people to understand and remember the physical world. In this research, we concretize the process of mind transformation of a metaphor through augmented reality (AR) technology. The AR interactive system that we create from the concept of Max Black's interaction view of metaphor can display the interaction phenomenon of metaphor from two different domains (rabbit or duck). We use the character of the rabbit–duck illusion as an example of a 3-D virtual model demonstration. This ambiguous 3-D character can be transformed from rabbit to duck with morphing technology. In this system, people can choose their preferences for looking at either rabbit, duck, or rabbit–duck blending. We focus on the morphing visual effect of AR as a metaphor tool and display the blending concept of the pictorial metaphor when the morphing is animated. The AR interactive system combines with an assembly of the gyroscopic motion controller connected to camera movements and morphing parameters. We attempt to prove that changing the camera view can represent the concrete expression of the abstract concept of visual metaphor in the AR system. For example, moving the camera is equivalent to the changing of thoughts and actions of people, and the 3-D morphing is equivalent to a mapping of the hybrid metaphor that people expect to see.

After assessments, this AR system can track the preferences of users by collecting the data of camera raycasting points, and we believe that the system can benefit the developments of museum education and guidebooks in terms of explaining the visual semiotics of artworks.

Keywords: Augmented Reality, Gyroscope, Visual Metaphor, Morphing, Hybrid Metaphor

Introduction

We understand much of our social reality through metaphorical terms, and our comprehension of the physical world is partially metaphorical. Metaphors play a crucial role in determining what we think of this world (Lakoff and Johnson, 1980) [1]. We believe the metaphor is a type of creativity after Black claimed that the metaphor involves the possibilities of novel and non-platitudinous implication-complexes.

Our research explains the context in which the metaphor occurs and elaborates on the creative metaphor (Max Black, 1979) [4] regarding the visual representation of implication-complexes.

The research into metaphorical thinking has developed over many years. People believe that the process of metaphorical thinking comes from sensory experiences. The perception flows from sensory experiences are related in terms of observation, classification, and conceptual thinking (Arnheim, 1969) [4].

Turner claimed that the structure of metaphoric thinking is a conceptual blending that includes frame restructuring (Schon, 1993), conceptual mappings (Gibbs, 1992; Lakoff, 1993; Winner, 1988), and image schema (Efland, 2002, citing Lakoff & Johnson, 1987) [5].

Given the above points, we explore the conceptual thinking of visual metaphors as embodying the representation of pictorial metaphors. We concretize how the mind transforms a metaphor through AR technology. The AR interactive system that we create for mobile devices displays the interaction phenomenon of metaphor from two different domains.

In this experiment, we found that one can regard the AR interactive system as a carrier of metaphorical phenomena. The AR interactive system combines the function of camera change and the morphing effect and fully embodies the figurative features of visual metaphors.

Therefore, we propose the following assumptions and verify their reliability and validity through experiments to prove the relationship between the morphing process and pictorial metaphors.

1. The process of changing metaphorical thinking, corresponding to moving a camera, is equivalent to changes in people's thoughts and actions.
2. A concept map corresponding to 3-D morphing is equivalent to mapping the conceptual metaphors that people expect to see. A texture map corresponding to image schema represents the abstract concept of a metaphor.
3. An AR Frame restructuring corresponding to a 3D object (3-D illusion) contains visual metaphors and is observable.
4. When the user joins certain conditions (camera changing), we can observe the changing process of the whole experiment. This experimental process can be traced back.
5. Morphing has a contextual framework for explaining metaphor.

Pictorial Metaphor

Black (1962) claimed that a metaphor triggers two different domains interactively to emphasize mental mapping in terms of a primary subject and secondary subject. The mapping results in the conversion of the target. Pictorial metaphors have a tentative subdivision: metaphors with one pictorial present term and metaphors with two pictorial present terms.

The duck-rabbit idea comes from the model of American psychologist Joseph Jastrow (1899) [6]. It points out that perception is not just a product of the stimulus but also of mental activity (Kihlstrom 2002).

Using these two perspectives, we make an exploratory contribution to a theory and provide a potential image metaphor for the abstract concept's concrete expression. Therefore, we apply the characteristics of metaphor to the morphing and texture mapping of 3D objects in AR.

Augmented Reality

While real-time camera tracking has found many applications in mobile robotics and augmented reality, vision-based markerless tracking has recently attracted much attention. It aims to estimate camera poses from input images or videos. A markerless AR scene is much more difficult to implement because the AR recognition algorithm has to identify patterns, colors, or some other features that may exist in camera frames. Therefore, there are extensive studies of simultaneous localization and mapping (SLAM) techniques for real-time camera tracking.

In this paper, we aim to build an AR display system that enables accurate and robust motion tracking within ARKit SDK. We employ visual-inertial odometry(VIO) to track the 3D motion of the inertial measurement unit (IMU) body frame in real-time. The overall architecture of the AR morphing system appears in Fig. 1.

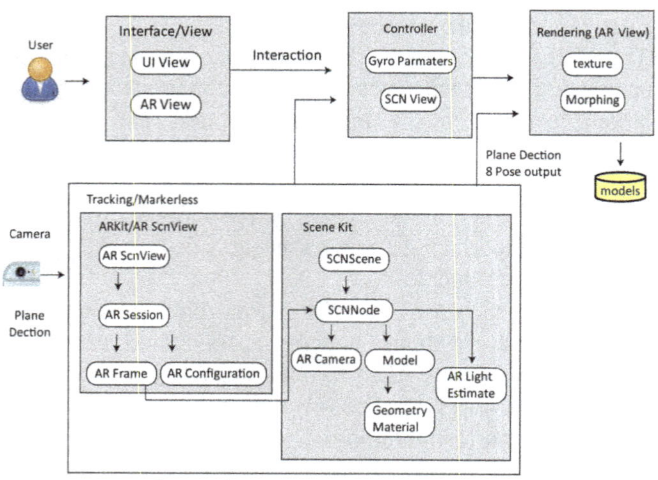

Fig. 1 The AR morphing system frame

The AR system mainly uses the Unity game engine as a 3-D display platform. Unity is an interactive game development tool that supports multi-platform outputs. It contains the most powerful and efficient engine that fully combines all aspects of professional interactive technology and achieves real-time 3-D rendering. The Vuforia engine combines with the iPhone device, and the 360-degree angle view allows users to move simultaneously and experience more on-site effects. The program is compiled with C# and integrates with the 3ds Max software for 3D animation editing and modeling. To coordinate with multi-person collaboration and platform integration, we use SourceTree's free Git GUI, developed by Atlassian, for project control and version synchronization, and finally share it via online services such as GitHub.

This system facilitates the placement of virtual objects in relative positions in physical space. We can observe the changes of virtual objects by moving the mobile device any distance or angle. We can control the effective range of morph by adjusting the program.

For better morphing result, the vertical angle of the lens rotation is within +45 degrees, and the range of the left and right rotation of the lens is within ±45 degrees. The following images show the function of the AR morphing camera view in Fig. 2.

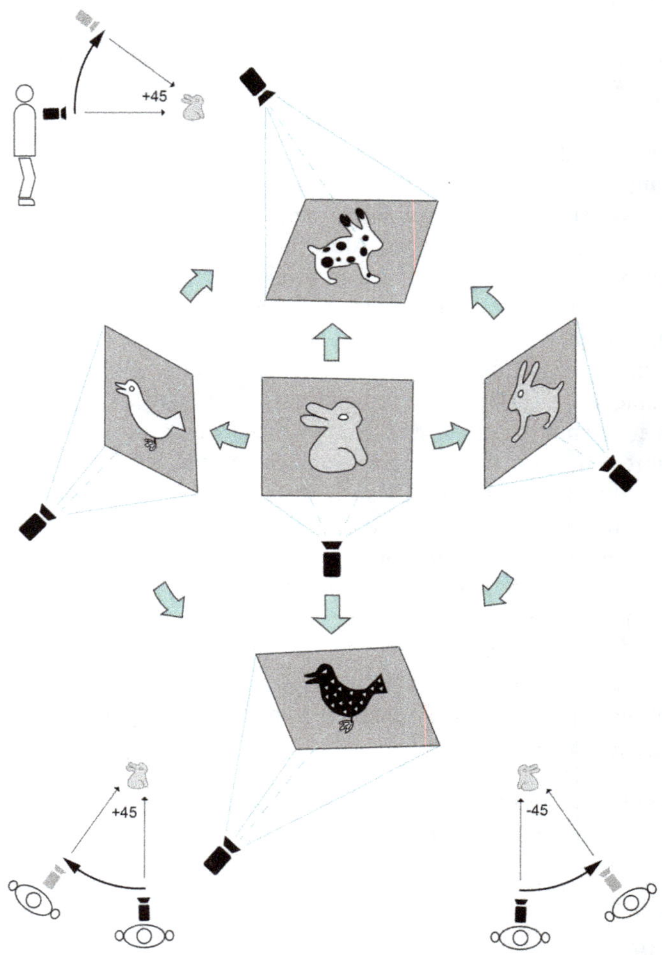

Fig. 2 The function of the AR morphing camera view

Material

I opted for a 3-D illusion model because they usually have a clear-cut purpose, which has proved essential to an initial exploration of the pictorial metaphor's workings.

An interaction phenomenon can be revoked when trying to prove the relationship of reflection mapping across two domains via the rabbits and ducks illusion. The visual case of rabbits and ducks is commonly understood, and it has clear and simple goals that we pursue easily. But, the case is only a change in shape that follows the principle of Gestalt. It is too simple to refer to a shift from A to B or B to A (domain). We could not achieve the experimental expectation of understanding the metaphorical state. At most, the illusion of rabbits and ducks is a kind of explanation of polysemy.

Therefore, we have added some conditions regarding texture changes to explore the metaphorical process that includes abstract concepts of how to map physical objects.

Method

We use several interactive features to achieve the characteristics of the above experiment.

To create the interactive morphing app with AR, we need to integrate AR technology and visual effects using four stages: (1) Develop the plane-detection and pose-output with AR markerless tracking; (2) Construct a virtual 3-D illusion model; (3) Deform morphs, and (4) Gyroscope detection. The interface design conveniently allows users to switch colors and textures when animating the morphing to observe and collect user preferences. The fully-assembled system then illustrates AR's visual morphing effect as a metaphoric tool from two different domains (rabbit or duck). The overall AR-morphing UI appears in Fig. 3.

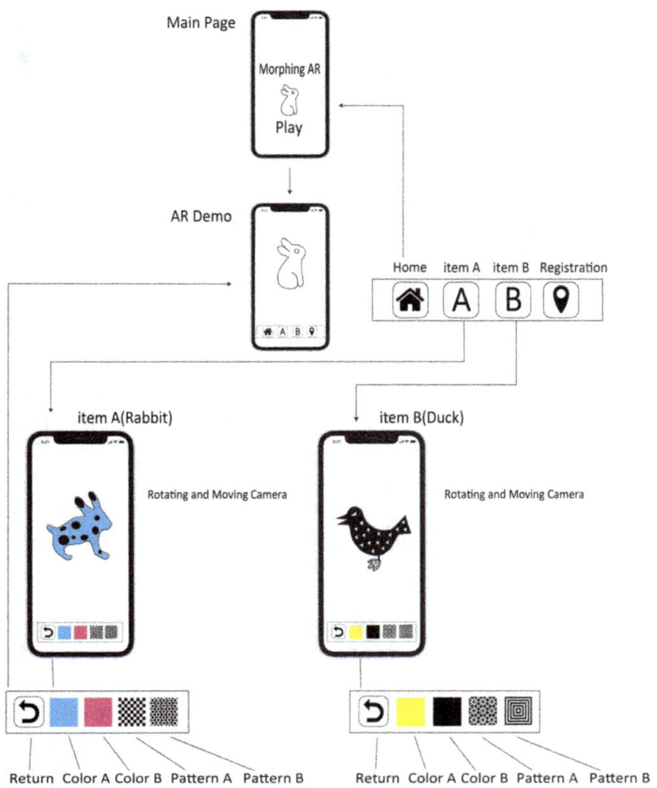

Fig. 3 The AR-morphing UI

1. Develop the plane detection and pose output with AR markerless tracking: After the user defines the target location, the corresponding position of the mobile phone determines the target's morphing. Moving the camera is equivalent to how people change thoughts and actions. The AR system is observable through the mobile phone screen that represents the user's expectations. Users change their location and position to get the full picture of the 3-D object. The process surprises users when the morphing animations change by moving for the first time. They then retrace their preferences again and again.

2. Construct a virtual 3-D illusion model: The viewer's gaze at the 3-D object's position determines their interest. The time and volume of the user's viewpoint become our collection goal. Whether we can achieve the metaphorical concept, our concern is with the morphing animation's consistent performance. The 3-D models must have attractive and rich details and demonstrate textures that show metaphorical symbols.

3. Deform morphs: Morphing combined two objects to reform a new object in several ways: A replaced B, part A connected with part B, and A superimposed B. We used morphing technologies that included A wrap to B, A extruded to B, and A dissolved to B in the procedural animation generation. The morph object becomes a living creature. Therefore, the morphing process must display some simulations of physical phenomena and dynamic effects. We concatenate many morph-animation clips to achieve a morphing sequence similar to the verbal semantics of linear logic.

4. Gyroscope detection: The gyroscope detects the mobile device's changes in location, and the detailed parameter values influence the observed object's degree of the deformation. The gyro has always had the narrator's role, judging the viewer's moving path and carrying out the next explanation. It is a challenge to adjust the camera movement's proper performance and object deformation that resonates with the viewer.

We bring the idea from what you see and what you need. The users do not have interactive control to obtain the information but need observation. Exploration and repeated learning are features of this AR interactive system.

One must precisely define the angle and iterations of the camera's view with the morphing. When the viewer gazes at the object's specific position, they show their point of interest. We must enable this anchor point and analyze special features in nearby areas. Defining a unit of calculation on this object could be an important issue.

Conclusion

From an interactive perspective, the cognitive process of metaphor is a complementary process of dynamic learning (Kozma, 1994) [7]. Therefore, we believe morphing can bridge a relationship between the learner and the medium for constructing representations and performing procedures.

In this experiment, we eliminate the use of text and examine the pictorial metaphor with simple mono-modality. We observe whether changes of texture can symbolize the characteristics of trope figures of speech and if silhouette changes can represent the appearance of symbolic meaning.

We are satisfied with the results and believe that either metaphor or morphing will be vital in people's learning. We hope to achieve the teaching's innovative value through AR interaction and the integration of the two modalities. Furthermore, we believe that the mapping relationships between the two modalities can achieve the following goals.

1. If metaphor is just rhetoric of words, and polysemy is the interpretation of words, a metaphor has no innovative value.
2. Morphing represents viewers' unknown expectations in the demonstration of visual metaphor. So, we give proper incentives and clues from virtual scenes that ignite viewers to chase their point of interest and obtain a sense of identity with a mental domain.
3. Indeterminate form: Following the implementation of staged goals achieves the demonstration of visual metaphor and the verbal semantics of linear logic. Therefore, morphing is not a simple process of in-between. It includes many kinetic energy simulations that are not redundant.
4. From the metaphorical point, morph(hybrid) object itself is a completely novel object (new domain) that does not belong to either source domain or target domain. People are attracted not only by the process of deformation but by the morph object itself.
5. When visual data spread on the virtual space without logical forms, morphing is a better way to connect and organize information easily.

The following image shows the result of performing just this process in Fig. 4.

Our assessments uncovered the characteristics of these different modalities, shown in Table 1:

TABLE I
The characteristics of these different modalities

Item	**Metaphor**	**Morphing**
Dynamic Structure	The cognitive process of metaphor is dynamic learning	Morphing is a media performance, such as animation
Polysemy	Verbal and non-verbal description	Morphing is a process of the description of dynamic semantics through pictorial representation.
Concept thinking	Thinking through non-linear processes	Shape blending through non-linear processes
The emotional states of interaction	The process of metaphorical thinking comes from the sensory experience	The sensory experience of visual interaction
Target	Source domain, target domain	Source object, target object
Causal Mechanism	Causality	Realism
Container	Virtual imagination	Partial reality

Fig. 4 The demonstration of the AR interactive system

References

[1] Lakoff, George, and Mark Johnson. *Metaphors we live by*. University of Chicago press, 2008.

[2] KANEKO, Kosuke; OKADA, Yoshihiro; NIIJIMA, Koichi. 3D model generation by morphing. In: International Conference on Computer Graphics, Imaging and Visualisation (CGIV'06). IEEE, 2006. p. 341-346.

[3] Fauconnier, Gilles, and Mark Turner. "Conceptual blending, form and meaning." Recherches en communication 19 (2003).

[4] Forceville, Charles. "Visual and multimodal metaphor in film: Charting the field." *Embodied metaphors in film, television, and video games*. Routledge, 2015. 17-32.

[5] Serig, Daniel. "A conceptual structure of visual metaphor." Studies in Art Education 47.3 (2006): 229-247.

[6] Gibbs Jr, Raymond W. "Evaluating conceptual metaphor theory." Discourse processes 48.8 (2011): 529-562.

[7] Kihlstrom, John F. "Joseph Jastrow and his duck–or is it a rabbit." University of California, Berkeley. [Online] Available at: http://socrates. berkeley. edu/~ kihlstrm/JastrowDuck. htm [Accessed 12/05/2015] (2004).

[8] Kozma, Robert B. "Will media influence learning? Reframing the debate." *Educational technology research and development* 42.2 (1994): 7-19.

[9] Ziemkiewicz, Caroline, and Robert Kosara. "Preconceptions and individual differences in understanding visual metaphors." Computer Graphics Forum. Vol. 28. No. 3. Oxford, UK: Blackwell Publishing Ltd, 2009.

[10] Lin, Chao-Hung, and Tong-Yee Lee. "Metamorphosis of 3d polyhedral models using progressive connectivity transformations." IEEE Transactions on Visualization and Computer Graphics 11.1 (2005): 2-12.

[11] Forceville, Charles. "Metaphor in pictures and multimodal representations." The Cambridge handbook of metaphor and thought (2008): 462-482.

[12] González, Esther Romero, and Belén Soria Clivillés. "NOVEL METONYMY AND NOVEL METAPHOR AS PRIMARY PRAGMATIC PROCESSES1." Where grammar meets discourse: functional and cognitive perspectives. 2006.

[13] Yan, Han- Bing, Shi- Min Hu, and Ralph Martin. "Morphing based on strain field interpolation." Computer Animation and Virtual Worlds 15.3- 4 (2004): 443-452.

[14] Chien-Wen Chen, Wen-Zheng Chen, Jain-Wei Peng, Bo-Xun Cheng, Tse-Yu Pan, Hsu-Chan Kuo and Min-Chun Hu, "A Real-Time Markerless Augmented Reality Framework Based on SLAM Technique," *2017 14th International Symposium on Pervasive Systems, Algorithms and Networks & 2017 11th International Conference on Frontier of Computer Science and Technology & 2017 Third International Symposium of Creative Computing (ISPAN-FCST-ISCC), UK*, June 2017, pp. 127-132.

[15] Andrew I. Comport, Éric Marchand, and François Chaumette, "A real-time tracker for markerless augmented reality" *ACM/IEEE Int. Symp. Mixed and Augmented Reality, ISMAR'03, Tokyo, Japan*, October 2003, pp. 36-45.

https://doi.org/10.1142/9789811238727_0043

Human Factor and Spatial Information Model of Rescuing

Benson P. C. Liu[1*], Chi-Wei Lee[2], and Chyi-Gang Kuo[1]

[1]Department of Architecture, Chaoyang University of Technology, Taichung, Taiwan
[2]Department of Visual Communication Design, Chaoyang University of Technology, Taichung, Taiwan
*Corresponding Author Email: bensonp.c.liu@gmail.com

Abstract

In an emergency, rescuers cannot find the exit due to insufficient information on the layout of buildings and limited visibility. Based on spatial information, we proposed a model that used theoretical research tools with human factors converted into the spatial model for analyzing and evaluating the internal space of buildings and users' information in the internal space. We analyzed 14 nursing homes to validate the rescuing model with spatial information under different circumstances in a single space.

Keywords: human factor, spatial information, the model of rescuing

Introduction

Visibility graph analysis is a spatial analysis tool that analyzes and evaluates user's spatial information [1], such as spatial visibility of rescuing. It is used as the main research tool of this article. We use quantified data to compare and express the spatial information for rescue in each house. As the elderly would have difficulty escaping, any incident is very serious. The research in this study has been performed in 14 nursing homes.

Research Tool

Recently, visibility graph analysis is becoming a popular tool to analyze the spatial user relationship in buildings [1]. The concept of visibility graph analysis is to cover the spatial layout with grids representing the viewpoint of space. This analysis tool defines the field of each viewpoint and checks the overlapping area. The position of the overlapping area of visual field will be changed when people move in buildings. After calculating the overlapping area of visual field, the result of overlapping area shows spatial visibility. People in the overlapping areas of higher visibility fields have more opportunities to see each other. While users move, the overlapping area of the constant visual field becomes different. In this case, some areas are highly visible. The calculation of the overlapping area in the visual field brings out the visibility value distribution in space [2,3,4,5,6].

Method of Modeling

A. Calculation of model

We tried to measure dangerous situations in the evacuation of an entire building. The target location is safest in the entire space. To the exit, the location is in the deepest part of the entire space configuration. The physical movement in the entire rescuing operation has the longest distance. Therefore, among all rescuing routes, the value of rescuing risk is the highest. When the steering angle at the visual direction decision point in the current action is larger, the visual value is also larger. On the other hand, the model value is considered as accessible with walking steps and rescue routes.

B. Values of models in 14 nursing homes

Table 1 shows the calculation results of the value of the model of 14 nursing homes. The more complicated the space design, the less helpful it is for rescue. However, nursing home 8 and 10 are not the most complicated ones even with the highest calculation results. Even with a relatively simple configuration, its calculated value may still be high. The final results can only be obtained through software analysis and the calculation method proposed by this research.

Findings and Discussions

Curved sidewalks cause too many turns in the rescuing movement route, which result in excessive turn time and visual conversion angle in the rescuing route and loss of the information on spatial locations such as in nursing home 8 and 10. They do not have the most complicated configurations, but their spatial values are the highest. Therefore, for quick escaping of indoor space, the flat and non-winding corridor design is better than the curved type one. Even a good architectural designer, without the help of analysis software, cannot immediately find out the problems of the design plan in rescue in emergency situations [6]. Therefore, it is even more important to make design judgments through the assistance of software analysis.

Funding

This study was funded by the Ministry of Science and Technology (MOST), grant number MOST 108-2221-E-324 -001 -MY3.

References

[1] Lee, C. W., Liu, B. P. C., Kuo, C. G. (2020), "A Computational Model Refinement for Visibility Graph Analysis", *Proceedings of* 2nd IEEE Eurasia Conference on Biomedical Engineering, Healthcare and Sustainability 2020 (ECBIOS), 102-103.

[2] Turner, A. & Penn, A. (1999). Making isovists syntactic: isovist integration analysis, *The 2nd International Symposium on Space Syntax*, Universidad de Brasilia, Brazil.

[3] Liu, P. C. (2018),『From gamification to creation』the dynamic recursion design strategy of gamification – a case study on planning and teaching of an exhibition. *Journal of Design, 23*(1), 19-42.

[4] Liu, P. C. (2018),『Urban Diagnosing』 the Simulation and forecast of city circulation - a Study of urban spatial structure based on segment analysis method of space syntax theory. *Journal of Design, 23*(3), 1-21.

[5] Benson P. C. Liu (2020), "Spatial Intervention Method of Commercial Space Design in Terms of Pedestrian Flow Prediction through Space Syntax–Case Study in Spatial Evaluations of Remodeling a Mall in Taiwan", *Education and Awareness of Sustainability - Proceedings of the 3rd Eurasian Conference on Educational Innovation 2020 (ECEI 2020)*, Singapore：World Scientific Press, pp. 715-718.

[6] Benson P. C. Liu, C. G. Kuo, C. W. Lee (2020). "The Quantitative Research of Applying Visibility Graph Analysis Method of Space Syntax Theory to Visual and Access Cost of Evacuating Buildings", *Education and Awareness of Sustainability - Proceedings of the 3rd Eurasian Conference on Educational Innovation 2020 (ECEI 2020)*, Singapore：World Scientific Press, pp. 913-916.

TABLE 1

The results of the value of model of 14 nursing homes

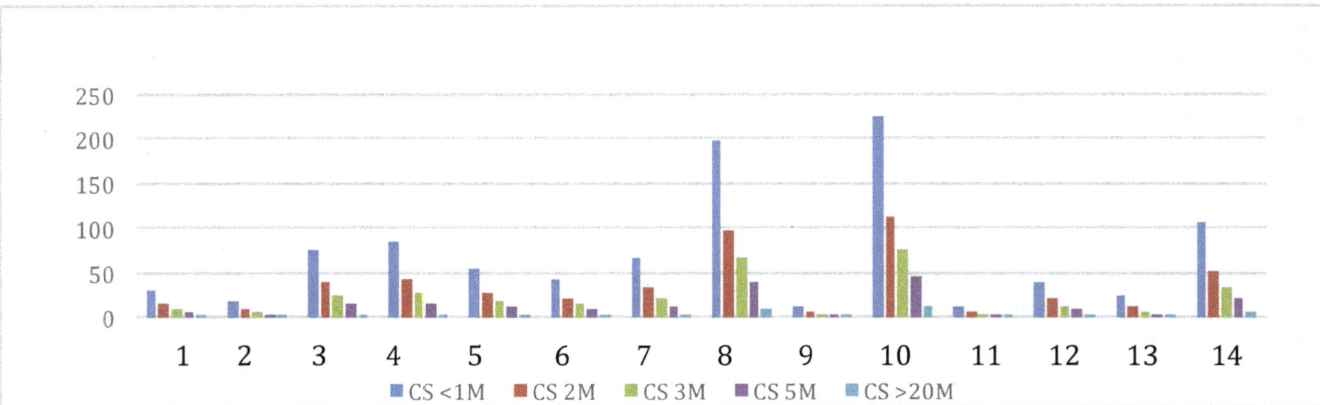

NO.	Routes	Spatial Factors				Value of Model
		θ	A	V	S	VM
1.	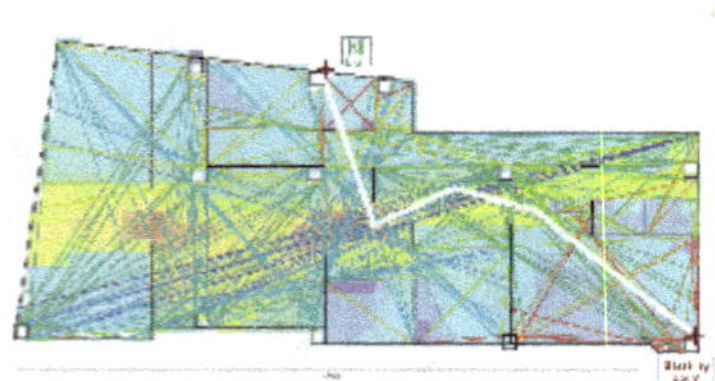	0°	1.7932	5.1249	17.0294	31.9658
		22.53°	1.7418	9.6527	7.2801	
		38.65°	1.4828	9.2306	8.0623	
		96.18°	1.6151	11.2064	13.6015	
2.	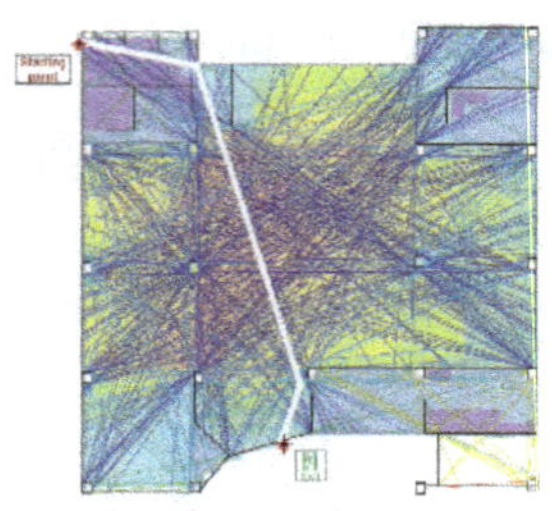	0°	1.9212	4.6598	10.4403	17.8782
		58.74°	1.2093	9.2686	26.5707	

3.	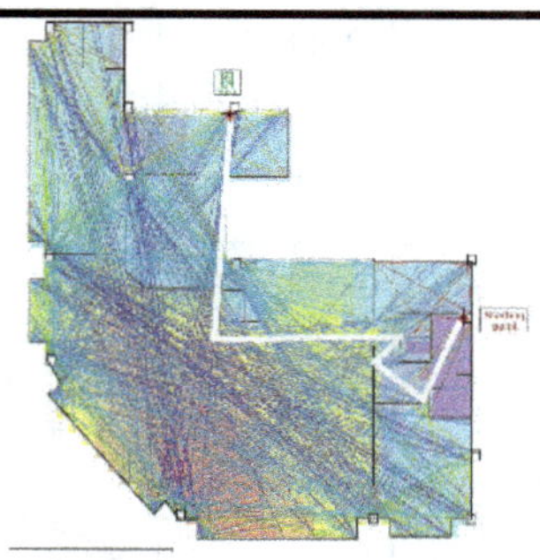	0°	2.0041	2.9664	7.6158	77.7696
		101.39°	1.8057	4.7971	5.6557	
		99.4°	1.4221	4.9314	3.6056	
		136.33°	1.3387	8.3076	15.133	
		95.46°	1.2797	14.747	19.105	
4.	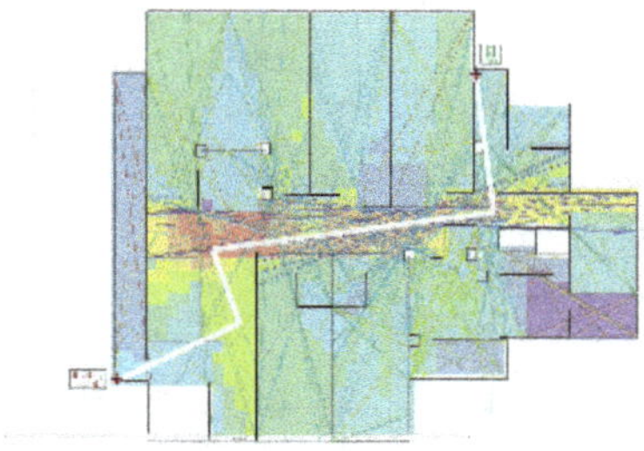	0°	2.4565	3.2898	13.4164	84.4717
		86.79°	2.0192	4.586	7.6158	
		103.67°	1.3744	7.065	26.3059	
		90.11°	1.7484	6.4192	12.1655	
5.	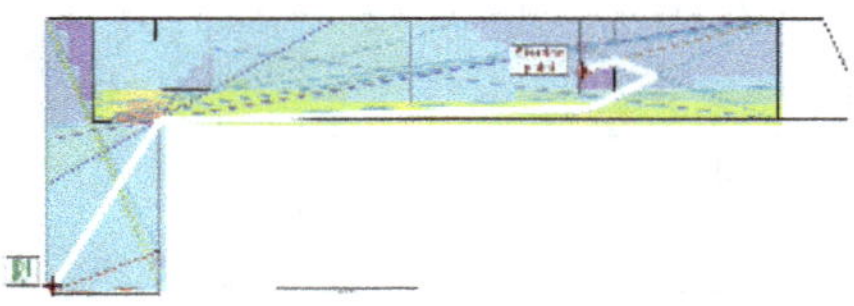	0°	1.8259	2.9943	3.6056	56.0665
		34.37°	1.4086	4.9362	4.4721	
		134.48°	1.4063	5.0851	7.2111	
		23.41°	1.2632	10.0618	36.0555	
		55.52°	1.1078	15.8355	18..0278	
6.	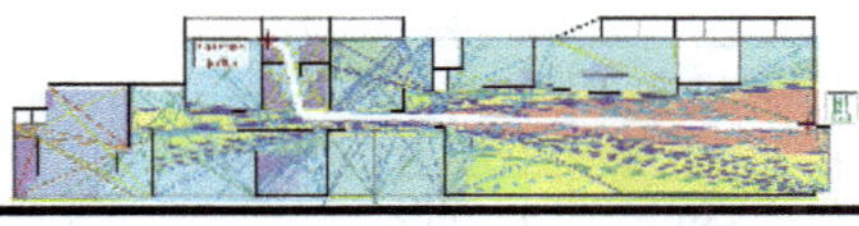	0°	2.4139	2.9074	6.3246	44.418
		56.08°	1.6319	4.2513	8.544	
		74.58°	1.2085	8.3058	59.0169	
7.	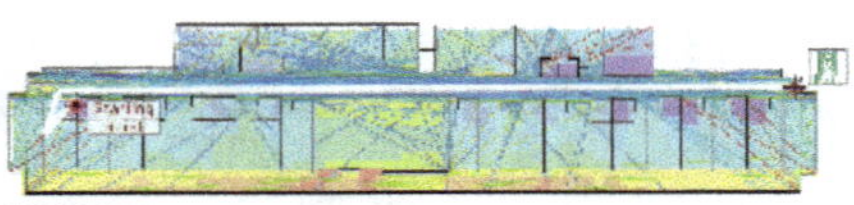	0°	2.411	3.0429	6.4031	67.3603
		156.9°	1.6474	4.8761	5.831	
		71.25°	1.1366	8.0992	84.0238	
8.	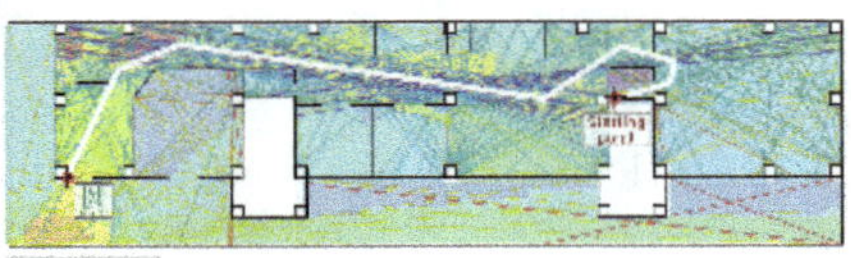	0°	1.9878	3.1846	8.544	198.13
		64.14°	1.9234	3.4737	3.1623	
		83.35°	1.8589	3.5158	7.4162	
		50.75°	1.7417	4.6569	12.2066	
		42.78°	1.5278	6.2462	42.5793	
		30.28°	1.9466	5.7784	9.8489	
		42.82°	1.8465	4.4422	14.3178	

9.	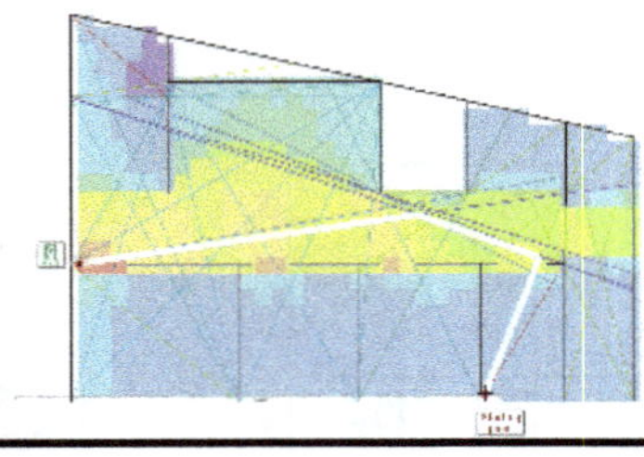	0°	1.5538	4.9152	9.8489	13.2648
		94.08°	0.9912	10.9525	8.9443	
		26.44°	1.0536	10.3127	21.3776	
10.	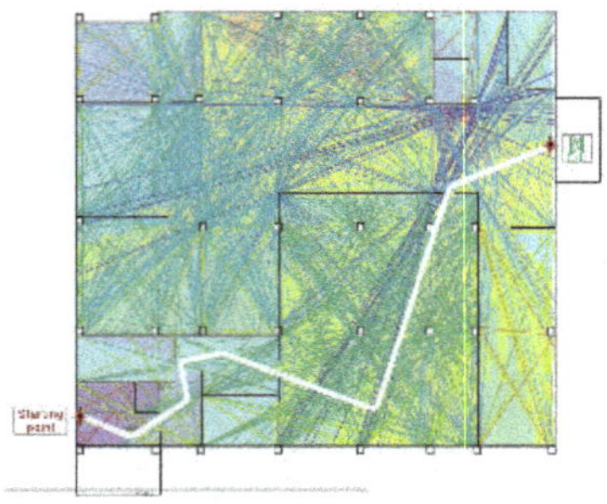	0°	2.3664	2.3537	7.6158	225.41
		54.5°	2.0274	3.2151	8.6023	
		67.36°	2.2056	3.22	6.3246	
		90.58°	2.094	4.7518	6.3246	
		30.63°	2.0611	4.7329	18.9737	
		90.82°	1.582	7.5881	26.5707	
		49.87°	1.8694	7.3706	13	
11.	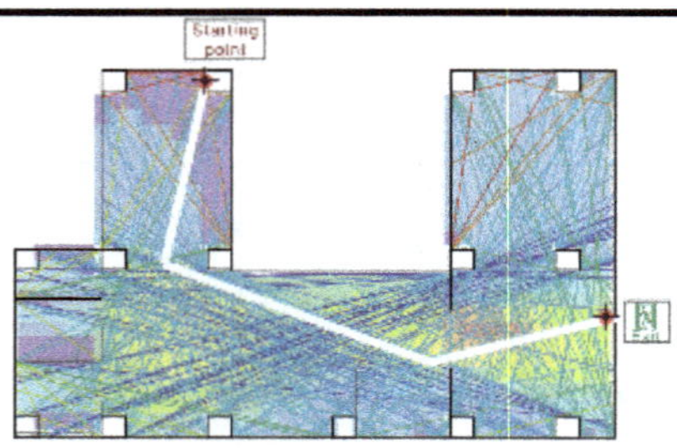	0°	1.3623	6.8289	14.5602	12.1263
		82.93°	1.205	17.4545	20.2485	
		33.54°	1.3209	16.5594	12.6491	
12.	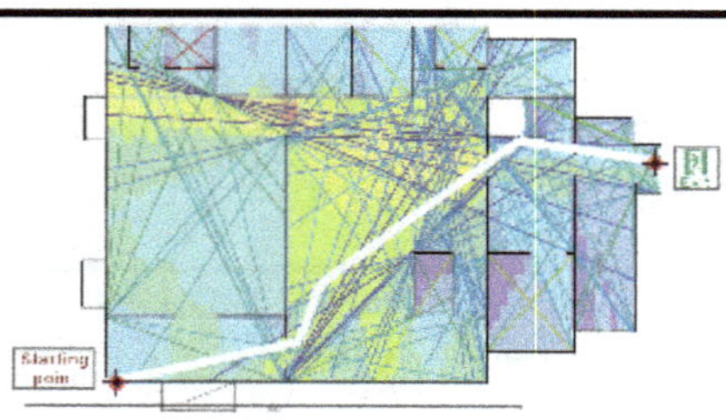	0°	1.6983	7.4758	25.7099	40.5668
		58.58°	1.4286	12.4536	8.544	
		34.74°	1.35	11.2668	33.6006	
		45.05°	1.1386	8.9185	18.4391	
13.	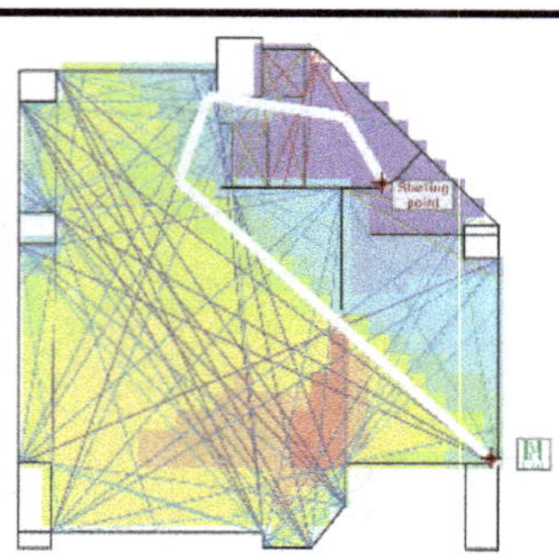	0°	2.4499	3.3061	4.2426	23.7477
		49.71°	1.6533	5.973	8.2462	
		79.47°	1.2272	10.7553	6.3246	
		67.62°	1.2844	20.2301	22.6716	

14.	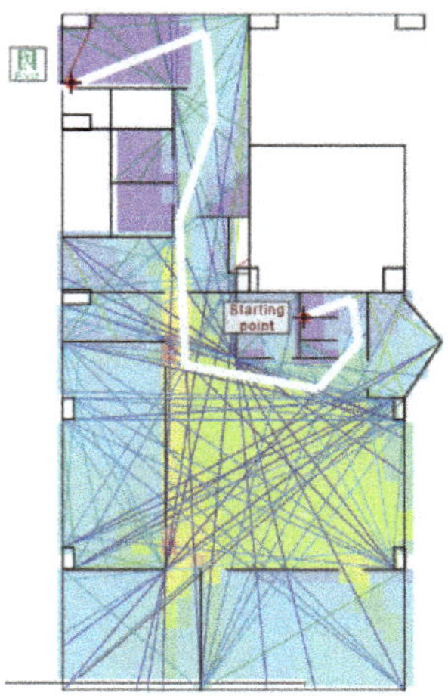	0°	2.2234	3.525	4.4721	105.602
		101.16°	1.5199	5.5444	4.4721	
		49.62°	1.2414	7.6549	5.5657	
		58.48°	1.3431	9.6778	10.198	
		77.21°	1.1469	11.9849	11.0454	
		20.68°	1.6378	8.475	8.544	
		23.74°	1.1725	6.4907	7.0711	
		108.11°	1.8976	7.2084	11.7047	

https://doi.org/10.1142/9789811238727_0044

Indicators for Evaluating the Form of Stress-relief Image: Architecture Buildings as Examples

Yung-Chia Chiu[1*], Ming-Chyuan Ho[2], Li-Chun Huang[3]

[1]Doctoral student, Graduate School of Design, National Yunlin University of Science and Technology, Taiwan; Assistant Professor of Practice, Department of MICE Marketing & Event Management, Shu-Te University, Taiwan
[2]Professor, Department of Industrial Design, National Yunlin University of Science and Technology, Taiwan
[3]Doctoral student, Graduate School of Design, National Yunlin University of Science and Technology, Taiwan
*Corresponding Author Email: mk04271@gmail.com

Abstract

Coping with stress and making appropriate adjustments are important issues in the pressurizing modern environment. The city image is the representation of selection and exhibition and establishes collective memory in society. The city image is the interactions between residents and environments and the reflection of the living quality of a city, which influences the emotion of people. This study aims to characterize the genius loci and investigate the pattern between perceived naturalness, artifacts, and visual stimulation. The architectural buildings are the main part of the city image and influence people's emotions and feelings. Understanding whether the design and index framework of building affect and change the user's feelings trigger deeper psychological responses and stress relief is critical. We investigate the effect of 20 buildings' images (public buildings, condominiums, and townhouses) and performed semi-structured interviews with 50 subjects to understand the stress-relief city image. The Semantic Differential Method with Five Points Image Scale was performed to examine the sensitivity of the collective memory. The evaluation focused on the concept of various styles, the visual of city images, and the Stress-Relief of city building form to obtain the forms of Stress-Relief Building Image. The results reveal the connection between architecture and people's emotions and provide specific and clear references for the architecture designers.

Keywords: Stress-Relief, Image, Indicators for evaluation

Introduction

As part of a modern lifestyle, people are pursuing a better quality of life, resulting in high-pressure environments. Quality of life is based on individual's perception and includes their position in society, the goals, expectations, standards, and concerns in their minds. It is a broad-ranging concept, incorporating the person's physical health, psychological state, level of independence, social relations, personal beliefs, and relationship to salient features of the environment. Therefore, architectural buildings are designed with the main focus of providing communication and interaction between the buildings and people. City image potentially is a means of city governance. For example, Yunlin city is the capital of agriculture, while Taipei is the capital of world design. Therefore, we aim to study how to deliver the city image to citizens through the following.

(1) Taiwan is a community of multiple ethnic groups, which fits into the aspect of design. Does this affect and change the user's feelings about the building?
(2) Does this trigger a deeper psychological response from users?

Owing to the dynamics of the social environment, the problem of communities, and the creation of local culture, we investigated the relationship between Stress-Relief Image and city image using architectural buildings as an example. The purpose of this study includes 1) analyzing the form of architectural buildings in the city and 2) the shape problems in the buildings from the view of Stress-Relief Image.

Study Methods

To understand the Stress-Relief Image, a semi-structured interview was performed to filter the suitable samples for 50 subjects. Then, the stress scale provided by the Ministry of Health and Welfare was used for evaluating the pressure of the interviewees. 10 interviewees with high-pressure were subjected to the K J Method in-depth interview, as displayed in Fig. 1 and Table 1. The result was used to evaluate (1) concepts of styles, (2) city image with different style's visual evaluation, and (3) psychological feeling evaluation. At last, 5 experts were invited for the final discussion on the subject of understanding the Stress-Relief Image atmosphere creation.

Fig. 1 Study procedure.

TABLE 1
THE CODE FOR INTERVIEWERS

code	Personal Profile	code	Personal Profile
A1	Mr. Wu (Kaohsiung) Age:40-45	A6	Mr. Wu (Chiayi) Age:35-40

	Occupation: Firefighter		Occupation: company employee
A2	Mr. Lin (Tainan) Age: 25-30 Occupation: Career soldier	A7	Miss Lin (Chiayi) Age: 25-30 Occupation: Executive assistant
A3	Miss Chiang (Miaoli) Age:30-35 Occupation: public servant	A8	Miss Pai (Taichung) Age:35-40 Occupation: scholar
A4	Miss Lin (Tainan) Age:25-30 Occupation: Executive assistant	A9	Miss Chen (Taipei) Age:30-35 Occupation: Executive assistant
A5	Miss Chen (Taichung) Age:40-45 Occupation: freelancer	A10	Miss Wong (Chiayi) Age:45-50 Occupation: company employee

Rethinking the Stress-Relief Image of Architecture Buildings

The city image influences citizens' place identity. "The meaning of city image is understood after a long period of living, observation, and cognition," K. Lynch said. In "The Evaluation Image of the City", Nasar mentioned that the city image's fundamental characteristic is an emotional connection with people. In addition to the inner emotional connection, the city image also creates a noticeable atmosphere.

A. City's expression: Designing architecture buildings

A spatial area on streets is built up by different functional and public facilities, such as road illuminances, public arts, landmarks, buildings, sign postings, and billboards. However, the design of the form of architectural buildings is often neglected. Thus, under limited time and resources, designers' experience and participation are directly reflected on public facilities that combine local spirits to form the city image. However, the composition of city images is divided into cognition and evaluation. Cognition is the recognition of the environment, while evaluation is the local emotions and values [1]. Successfully designed cities not only raise the image of the city to the glory of local people but increase the competitiveness of cities internationally [2]. Tadao Ando designed four chapels or churches in Japan which are similar to chapel Cappella di Mare (海の教会) (Fig. 2). They are nicknamed the Church of the light, water, wind, and sea, respectively. Chapel Cappella di Mare complex is located in the northern part of the island called Awajishima which connects Honshu main island and Shikoku island by the Akashi Strait Grand Bridge to Kobe in the north and the Naruto Grand Bridge to Naruto in the south. The exterior of this avant-garde and challenging architectural design is low-key peaceful and pure, while the interior is precise and calm. Tadao Ando intends to allow people, art, and nature to meet and have dialog here.

Fig. 2 Chapel Cappella di Mare (海の教会)

B. City image's symbol transformation

A city has the value of gathering the residents and providing space. When the story and city are combined, residents are willing to agree to preserve and widely spread it to create exclusive local memory [3]. This is why designers translate their memories into symbols (Fig. 3). As "Urban Open Space and Urban Aesthetics" [4] mentioned, a landmark is not only the subject for visual experience but also an association as genius loci. A landmark must be able to reflect the characteristics of the surrounding environment, social consciousness, cultural meaning, and vibration of the area or site. As Norberg-Schulz mentioned [5], "both natural environment or manmade space have the spirit (cultural spirit)." A landmark design has to merge local emotional connections that enhance indoor cohesion, which means the design of street furniture requires the display of a city's identification symbol. Ho also mentioned [6] that designers design cities through elements, structure, meaning, and symbols. While citizens often misjudge the meaning of the conveyance with their growing background and the present atmosphere, designers tend to look for the intersection. For example, the famous Dotonbori Glico Sign was designed as an advertisement initially but has now become a landmark of Osaka Shinsaibashi.

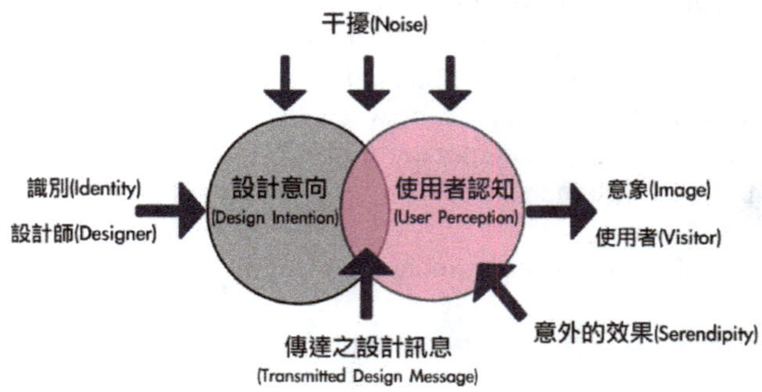

Fig. 3 Conveying design image connotation (Ming-Chyuan Ho, 2019; Compiled by this study)

C. Relationship between elements of image and architecture building restorative perception

The form of an architectural building affects the environment, moving line, and city image. Thus, we have to discuss the form of an architectural building comprehensively. Choue [7] mentioned that the present generation is rich in materials but lacks spirit. When techniques and abilities are superior to humanity, materials turn society inhumane. The ability to detect and interpret the events that are occurring around us allows us to respond to the stimuli appropriately [8]. The fundamental formula of Gestalt theory might be expressed in this way: There is the whole, the behavior of which is not determined by that of their elements, but where the part-processes are themselves determined by the intrinsic nature of the whole. Gestalt theory hopes to determine the nature of such whole [9]. Norman also mentioned in the book *Emotional Design* [10], the purpose of design includes three emotional elements: Instinct (the presentation of city image), Behavior (deliver concept), and reflection (of citizens' feelings and thoughts). In other words, to create an atmosphere of the architectural building image, the design technique must create a certain atmosphere required by the city. Therefore, a stress-relief city image has to integrate the architectural buildings and emotional needs through the fine design.

Stress-Relief Image and Architecture Building

A. Sample analysis

500 images of stress-relief buildings were provided by 50 interviewees. We picked up ten stress-relief public buildings and ten residential buildings as shown in Figs. 4 and 5.

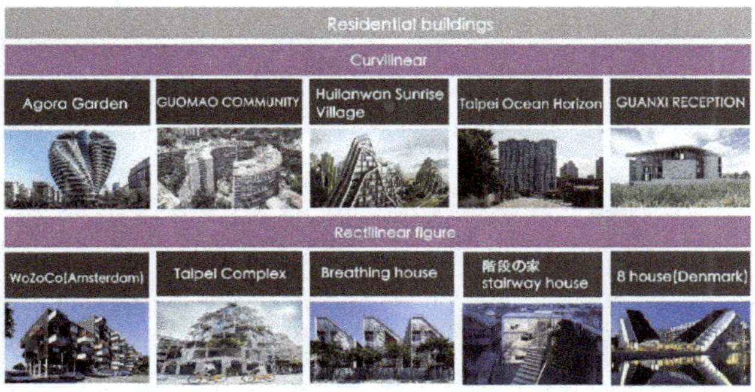

Fig. 4 Public Buildings and residential buildings.

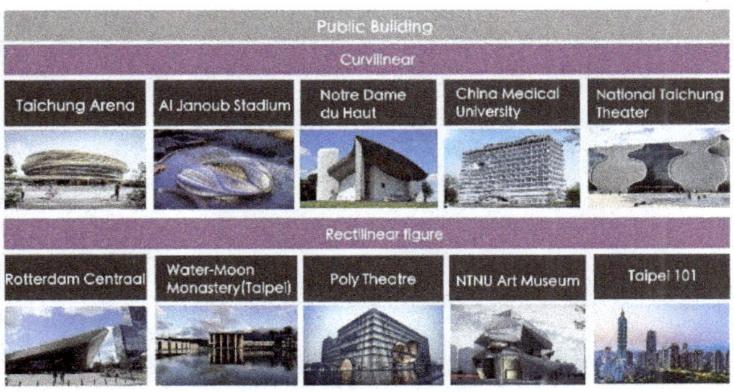

Fig. 5 Residential buildings.

50 interviewees evaluated the buildings with a pressure index scale which was provided by the Health Promotion Administration, the Ministry of Health and Welfare. 10 interviewees with high-pressure scores joined the tests to find important attractive factors by the KJ method. Approximately 521 words were collected and grouped into 17 adjectives. Table 2 shows the top 5 words of "Comfortable", "Kindly", "Friendly", "Amazing", and "Funny".

TABLE 2
THE TOP 5 ATTRACTIVE FEELINGS

Adjective	Votes	Vocabulary related
Comfortable	102	Satisfied, easy, cozy, cheerful
Kindly	80	safety, peaceful, amiable, gentle, benevolent, beneficent
Friendly	73	Nice, kind, heavenly,
Amazing	54	Incredible, Wonderful, Marvelous, Fantastic
Fun	36	Interesting, hilarious, humor, amusing, ludicrous, lively

TABLE 3
THE CODE FOR INTERVIEWERS

code	Personal Profile	code	Personal Profile
B1	Mr. Wu Age:40-45 Occupation: Professor	B6	Mr. Ho Age:55-60 Occupation: Professor
B2	Mr. Guo Age: 45-50 Occupation: Professor	B7	Miss Liu Age: 40-45 Occupation: Assistant researcher
B3	Miss Wu Age:35-40 Occupation: Designer	B8	Miss Pai Age:35-40 Occupation: Professor
B4	Miss Lin Age: 35-40 Occupation: Designer	B9	Miss Liu Age:40-45 Occupation: Designer
B5	Miss Chen Age:40-45 Occupation: Director	B10	Miss Chang Age: 35-40 Occupation: Assistant researcher

B. Filtering of the most representative attractive factors

To filter the most representative attractive factors as the questionnaire items, the selected top 5 abstract feelings and corresponding initial reasons are shown in Table 3.

TABLE 4
THE TOP 5 ATTRACTIVE FEELINGS AND ITS RELATED INITIAL REASONS AND CONCRETE REASONS.

Adjective	Form
Kindly	Pure color, smooth lines
Fun	Curve, unique style, colorful
Amazing	Unique style, curve, color contrast
Comfortable	Smooth lines, simple, pure color
Friendly	Smooth lines, pure color

Discussions

The rectilinear linear patterns exhibit simple line art, whereas curve patterns show changeable curves (Fig. 6). We found that ten high-pressured interviewees agreed that the environment influenced stress generation and simple designs were more stress-relieving.

Comfortable

Fig. 6 Measured sample design.

The Stress-Relief Image and Stress Image are illustrated in Fig. 7. 10 high-pressure interviewees agree that simple and smooth are more stress-relieving than buildings with too many acute angles.

Fig. 7 Corresponding samples.

Conclusion

Today's modern lifestyle is quite competitive. Everyone tries to live well. However, people are always under high pressure. Negative emotions and excessive pressure need to be relieved to avoid mental and physical illness. The relief heals our body and soul so it is called "healing". The study result reveals that the curves of buildings are varying and interesting, but not stress-relief. People with high-pressure consider rectilinear patterns to be more stress-relieving though they are straight and cold. We also found that artwork with simple lines harmonized with landscapes to deliver more stress-relief images.

References

[1] Richards, G. & Wilson, J.C. ,2004, *The Impact of Cultural Events on City Image: Rotterdam Cultural Capital of Europe 2001*, Urban Studies 41 (10), pp. 1931-1951.
[2] Taiwan Cultural Creative Industries, 2012, https://cci.culture.tw.
[3] Chen, Ya-Min, 2015, *Exploring the Relationship between Activities and Affective Bonding in Recreational Sites*, Taipei city: National Taiwan University.
[4] Kuo, Monica, 2006, *Urban Open Space and Urban Aesthetics*, Taipei city, Artist Magazine.
[5] Christian Norberg-Schulz, 1979, *Genius Loci: Towards a Phenomenology of Architecture,* New York: Rizzoli.
[6] Ho, Ming-Chyuan, 2019, *Lecture notes*, Yunlin: National Yunlin University of Science and Technology.
[7] Choue, Young-Seek, Chiou-Shan Lin, 2001, *Oughtopia-Realization of the ideal society*, Taipei city: National Institute for Compilation and Translation.
[8] Gibson, E. J., Pick, A. D. ,2000, *An ecological approach to perceptual learning and development,* New York, NY: Oxford University Press.
[9] Wertheimer, M.,1938, *Gestalt Theory*, New York: Harcourt, Brace and Co.
[10] Norman, Donald A., 2004, *Emotional design: why we love (or hate) everyday things*, New York: Basic Books.

https://doi.org/10.1142/9789811238727_0045

Influence of City Image and Electronic Word of Mouth: A Case Study of Kaohsiung and Chiayi

I-Jen Wu[1*], Yung-Chia Chiu[1], Ming-Chyuan Ho[2]

[1]Assistant Professor, Department of MICE Marketing & Event Management, Shu-Te University, Taiwan
[2]Professor, Department of Industrial Design, National Yunlin University of Science and Technology, Taiwan
*Corresponding Author Email: lawrence@stu.edu.tw

Abstract

A city image is the representation of selection and exhibition by establishing collective memory in society. It also represents the interactions between residents and environments and reflects the living quality of a city which influences the emotion of citizens. The development of Internet technology creates "self-media" that transfers information fast and wide. Using the keyword search for obtaining information has become a part of people's daily life. This study investigated the differences of recognition and emotion between residents and non-residents and the role of designing the spiritual atmosphere by comparison of modern and traditional design in Chiayi and Kaohsiung. To understand the construction of city images in Chiayi and Kaohsiung, an investigation of the role of landmarks (Chiayi Tower, Central Fountain, Fo Guang Shan Buddha Museum, Dome of Light, The Pier-2 Art Center, and Hinoki Village) was conducted with a semi-structured interview of 30 subjects. The changes in keyword search trends were observed in a specific period and region. The change in the search volume of keywords and the prediction of specific fields are both worthy of reference. The evaluation was focused on the concept of various styles, the vision of city images, and the sense of city image. The focus group summarized the design and senses of the landmarks in Chiayi and Kaohsiung City. The form of city images comprises the collection, integration, and exhibition of local specific characteristics. The collective consciousness of the cities consists of recognition, forms, and presentations. The results of this study offer a preliminary foundation for designing the spiritual atmosphere of Chiayi and Kaohsiung City.

Keywords: city image, word of mouth, landmark

Introduction

Along with the popularity of social networking services (SNS), electronic word-of-mouth (E-WOM) evaluation has a significant influence on visitors' preferences. For local reconstruction and identification, the cultural and creative industry narrates the stories of local places more effectively than training, subsidies, and advisements from public sections. The ministry of culture defines and promotes a creative cultural cluster as a special area of creative cultural industries. Design techniques are used to solve social problems, for example, for Sunny Hills of quadrangle house in Nantou County. By thinking of brand management, they narrate Taiwan's local stories that promote local tourism and pineapple marketing. Thus, the combination of design industries, social changes, technology innovations, and policies improves the management of the creative cultural industry, the creation of creative cities and markets as well as planning of creative cultural clusters and city images. In this study, the following are investigated.

(1) Does a design change people's life when it involves social changes? Some designers create their models without thinking about the application of people's life. It is important to consider the effects of the environment, social conditions, and customs as well as infrastructure for daily needs.
(2) Taiwan is a community composed of multiple ethnic groups, which fits into the aspect of design. Thus, the main question is "what images do Chiayi and Kaohsiung have?" and "what is the blueprint when it comes to designing the cites' landmarks?"

With the dynamics of the social environment, the problem of communities and media, or the creation of local culture, we investigated the relationship between city images and E-WOM in the case study of Kaohsiung and Chiayi. The purposes of this study are as follows:

(1) Finding out the differences of recognition and emotion between residents and non-residents and the role of designing the spiritual atmosphere by comparing modern and traditional designs in Kaohsiung and Chiayi
(2) Analysis of the essence of city image and spatial characteristics
(3) The perspective of the public of city images for E-WOM

Methods

This study is based on a discussion of how landmarks and E-WOM influence the development of city images. First of all, to analyze previous studies related to city landmark, E-WOM, and city image, Chiayi Tower, Central Fountain, Fo Guang Shan Buddha Museum, and Dome of Light were chosen. 30 subjects (10 from Chiayi, 10 from Kaohsiung, and 10 from other cities) was invited to conduct an initial semi-structured interview. For the research on the design and formation of images of Chiayi and Kaohsiung, a semantic differential method with Likert Scale was used for 90 subjects (30 from Chiayi, 30 from Kaohsiung, and 30 from other cities) to investigate the subjects' psychological feelings for city images and evaluate the follows: (1) concepts of styles, (2) city image with different style's visual evaluation, and (3) network evaluation. At last, five experts were invited for a final discussion for understanding the creation of an atmosphere for city images.

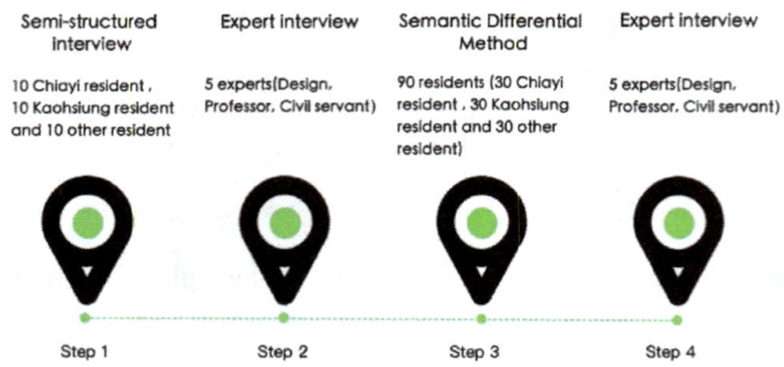

Fig. 1 study procedures

Relation between city image and E-WOM

A. *City Image and Place Marketing*

People care about design and design-thinking. They pursue a better life, products, and services. They also realize excessive consumption causes environmental damage, unbalance in marketing and economy extension, and clashes of different cultural understanding. If these social problems are not solved, our life is full of contradiction and conflict. To solve global and local problems, a city needs to have its specialty through creative and imagination [1].

Governance and marketing have become the new mainstream nowadays. Local governments in Taiwan demonstrate competitive advantages through local governance and marketing to the public. In the process of marketing, the cooperation between the public and private sectors and the awareness of public participation are important. Through the concept and mechanism of governance, the local government integrates the different interests and appeals of participants, improve the transparency and openness of the participation of public policies, and highlight the dynamics of the process of policies communication to implement the marketing strategies smoothly. The goal is to improve the capability of the governance of the local government.

The local development influences local economic activities, employment opportunities, and living quality. The concept of marketing is to remove the difficulties of local development. With appropriate strategies, regional markets boost local industries and economic growth by promoting and revitalizing. The development of local marketing is the main question on the challenge of the local government. In the local marketing, the places are "products" that feature the places to compete with other regions. The city images for the marketing can be found out by using the congenital superiority and nurturing the places. In other words, a local marketing strategy is the main agenda of the local government.

B. *City Image and E-WOM*

The progress of E-WOM begins with the WOM model among consumers [2]. With the emergence of various communication channels, opinion leaders appear among consumers, and consumer experiences are disseminated as references by other consumers [3]. The rise of online and social media platforms decreases the importance of opinion leaders has. Consumers communicate through platforms. Consumer's comments affect other consumers' opinions on products [4]. Americans prefer to be information providers with personal communication, while the Chinese prefer to be information seekers through E-WOM [5]. While Americans prefer to search positive E-WOM, while Japanese prefer negative word-of-mouth (NWOM) [6].

The followings are differences between WOM and E-WOM.

(1) E-WOM is set on an online platform, and the number of audience of E-WOM is larger than that of WOM.
(2) Internet WOM breaks the time limit and provides relevant information to all viewers.
(3) E-WOM has strong continuity. As online information is always posted on the internet, users not only browse but respond to it at any time, thereby generating a topic and discussion block [7].

C. *Influences of Valence and Consistency of E-WOM on Visitors' and Residents' Preference*

The popularity of SNS makes E-WOM more influential on consumer preference than any other means. In tourism, the imagination before a trip is the most important reference. Whether it is positive or negative E-WOM, it affects the impression of a city that travelers choose to travel [8]. Travelers obtain the latest useful information through E-WOM, such as online reviews, blogs, and vlogs from opinion leaders or others. The information to share personal views is posted by anyone including famous reviewers or online celebrities. Residents in the city have an overall perception or impression of their living places, which is based on the estimation or understanding of the city's characteristics [9]. They also spread the impressions on any social media platform and influence visitors and other local people. Therefore, the influence of E-WOM communication also strongly affects the city image [10]. However, the level of the effect of E-WOM and the city image on visitors' or residents' preference has been poorly explored.

Methods

Despite the urban development and industrial changes, people's collective memory remains such as International Band Festival and Stone-carving Monkey Craft. Kaohsiung is trying to develop as a traditional and industrial city, though facing pressure from global competition. As the successful tourism industry allows the improving economy, tourism is considered to make Kaohsiung better. Chiayi's and Kaohsiung's city images are found in the research on landmarks with a semantic differential analysis.

Fig. 2 Related cases.

A. Relative Vocabularies of Kaohsiung's and Chiayi's Landmark

Six famous landmarks were chosen: Fo Guang Shan Buddha Museum, Dome of Light, Pier-2 Art Center in Kaohsiung and Chiayi Tower, Central Fountain, Hinoki Village in Chiayi. Through the interviews with 30 subjects on their opinions of city image, 70 adjectives were collected (Table 1). Five experts (professors and senior designer) selected three adjectives and created a "City image adjectives questionnaire." (Table 2). Six subjects were given for the city images of the two cities and asked to respond to the questionnaire by considering the atmosphere and WOM but not the color and the texture.

TABLE 1
ADJECTIVES

Adjectives	Messy	Ancient	Cute	Mysterious
	Sunny	Serene	Joyful	Cultural
	Bold	Antique	Bright	Quiet
	Prosperous	Plain	Classic	Sacred
	Urban	Solid	Lush	Honest
	Refreshing	Old	Pure	Peaceful
	Modern	Broad	Narrow	Cozy
	Humid	Busy	Delight	Elegant
	Hopeless	Fluent	Funny	Fixed
	Bright	Lonely	Careful	Wild
	Saturate	Tedious	Solemn	Happily
	Relax	Vintage	Majestic	Childish
	Natural	Rare	Serious	Innocent
	Historical	Sublime	Massive	Contrary
	Traditional	Warm	Huge	Carefree
	Crowded	Steady	Glorious	Comfortable
		Simple	Still	

TABLE 2
THE TOP 3 ATTRACTIVE FEELINGS AND CORRESPONDING WOM'S QUESTIONS

Adjective	WOM's question
Comfortable	I frequently gather information from tourists' online travel reviews before I travel to this place (like Chiayi Tower)
Happily	I often read other tourists' online travel reviews to know this place (like Chiayi Tower) make good impressions on others
Sublime	When I travel to this place (like Chiayi Tower), tourists' online travel reviews make me confident in traveling there

B. Landmark Measurement

Three pairs of adjectives and WOM questions were selected to obtain the composition and feeling about the streets of Chiayi's and Kaohsiung's city images from 90 subjects (Table 3).

TABLE 3
SAMPLE STATISTIC

	Project	Number of times	%		Project	Number of times	%
Gender	Male	33	36.2%	Age	20 or below	14	15.5%
	Female	57	63.7%		21-30	8	8.8%
Current residence	Chiayi residents	30	33.3%		31-40	27	29.6%
	Kaohsiung residents	30	33.3%		41-50	23	25.9%
	others	30	33.3%		51 -60	9	10.3%
Occupation	others	28	31.1%		60 or above	9	9.6%
	military personnel, civil servants and teachers	19	21.4%	Highest Education Level	general and vocational high school or below	16	17.7%
	Business	18	20%		Post-secondary school	10	11.1%
	Employee	14	15.5%		University/College	47	52.5%
	Freelance	10	10.3%		Master or above	17	18.5%
	Farming	1	1.4%				

For the experiment, the subjects who have been to the six landmarks were chosen. After the whole evaluation process was explained, the participants selected favored adjectives and preferences which expressed their feelings to each photo and scored with slides shown for 50 s.

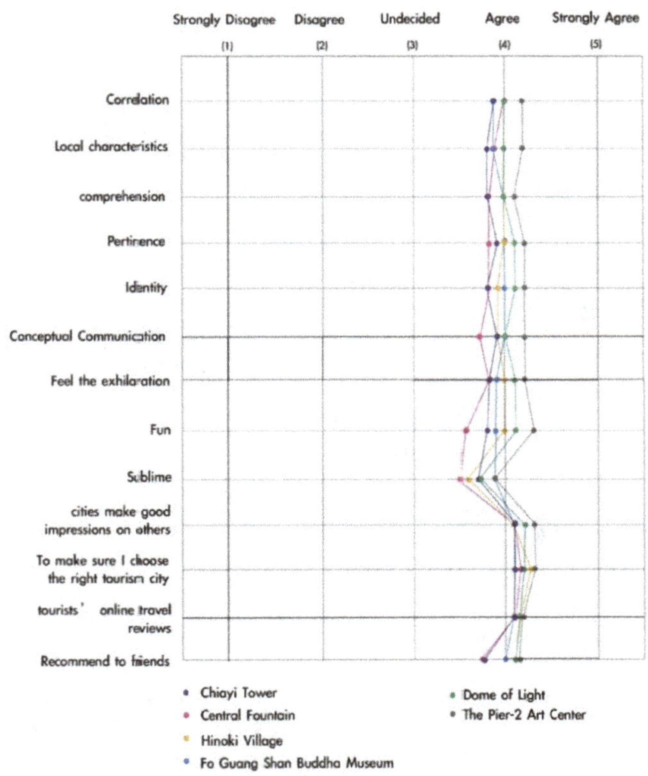

Fig. 3 Measuring point diagram

Discussions

The participants were not necessarily willing to travel although the E-WOM was positive. In the interview before the experiment, the subjects from Kaohsiung did not recommend the Pier-2 Art Center. However, the Art Center was selected as the best landmark among 6 landmarks. The subjects from Kaohsiung had higher positive feedback and recommendation of local landmarks than those from Chiayi. All subjects actively searched for E-WOM as references for opinions of the landmarks regardless of their cities.

Conclusion

With different histories, humanistic, and social conditions, a city has its management strategy. In response to challenges from social changes, a city needs clear guidance to improve efficiency and competitiveness. For improving the city image through E-WOM, the following are needed.

(1) The management pays attention to improve economic activities. They need to introduce creativity into space, but to integrate and share social services and resources.
(2) Visitors would like to know more about the local stories provided by creative economy activities. Elevating the values from economic behaviors without additional social problems is a significant issue in the future.
(3) E-WOM affects the reputation of the city or landmark, which is applied to residents and visitors. For landmarks with a certain degree of popularity and E-WOM, the influence of E-WOM surpasses individual opinions, and recommendations on the internet have the most views.

References

[1] HOSPERS, Gert-Jan. *Creative cities: Breeding places in the knowledge economy.* Knowledge, Technology & Policy, 2003, 16.3: 143-162.

[2] RYAN, Bryce; GROSS, Neal C. *The diffusion of hybrid seed corn in two Iowa communities.* Rural sociology, 1943, 8.1: 15.

[3] FEICK, Lawrence F.; PRICE, Linda L. *The market maven: A diffuser of marketplace information.* Journal of marketing, 1987, 51.1: 83-97.

[4] THOMPSON, Scott A.; SINHA, Rajiv K. *Brand communities and new product adoption: The influence and limits of oppositional loyalty.* Journal of marketing, 2008, 72.6: 65-80.

[5] CHRISTODOULIDES, George; MICHAELIDOU, Nina; ARGYRIOU, Evmorfia. *Cross-national differences in e-WOM influence.* European Journal of Marketing, 2012.

[6] DOBELE, Angela, et al. *Why pass on viral messages? Because they connect emotionally.* Business Horizons, 2007, 50.4: 291-304.

[7] SHEN, Yingtao; LI, Shenyu; DEMOSS, Michelle. *The effect of quantitative electronic word of mouth on consumer perceived product quality.* International Journal of Management and Marketing Research, 2012, 5.2: 19-29.

[8] BEERLI, Asuncion; MARTIN, Josefa D. *Factors influencing destination image.* Annals of tourism research, 2004, 31.3: 657-681.

[9] YE, Qiang, et al. *The influence of user-generated content on traveler behavior: An empirical investigation on the effects of e-word-of-mouth to hotel online bookings.* Computers in Human behavior, 2011, 27.2: 634-639.

[10] GRETZEL, Ulrike, et al. *Analyzing the influence of electronic word of mouth on visit intention: the mediating role of tourists' attitude and city image.* International Journal of Tourism Cities, 2016.

https://doi.org/10.1142/9789811238727_0046

Influence of Visual Field Design on Sense of Pleasure in Dota-Like Games

Yi Qi, Jun He*, Xiaoyan Zhang

Xiamen Academy of Arts & Design FuZhou University, Xiamen, Fujian, China
*Corresponding Author Email: dr.hejun@qq.com

Abstract

DotA-like game is getting popular in recent years, since numerous DotA-like games appeared such as the "DotA", "League of Legends", and "Heroes of the Storm". This study discusses influence of visual field on sense of pleasure in DotA-like Games with three aspects such as normal visual field, special visual field and scaling of visual field. This helps game designers adopt a better vision mechanism when designing DotA-like games.

Keywords: DotA-like, visual field, pleasure

Introduction

In recent years, the most popular game genre in the game market is undoubtedly the DotA-like game. Many manufacturers have released a series of DotA-like games. However, most of the games have been disappeared shortly after entering the market. There are various factors leading to such a situation. For example, as the market has long been divided, it is difficult for the new games to participate. The new works are only imitations without innovation. This paper mainly started from the perspective of game development, to explore the influence of visual field design on the user experience of the entire game, so as to help the developers have better design of the visual field in the process of game development. This enhances user experience, thus taking a great share of spoils from the huge market.

Conceptual Elaboration

A. DotA-like Games

Dota game is a game type that has been developed in recent years (Fig.1). Many people will say that "League of Legends", "Heroes of the Storm" and "DotA" are MOBA games, but I prefer to call them DotA-like games. MOBA is an acronym for Multiplayer Online Battle Arena, which means a massive multiplayer online strategy game. This definition is very broad and does not clearly refer to games like League of Legends, Heroes of the Storm or DotA.

Compared with RTS games, DotA-like games require a lower level of player operation. As entry barrier is relatively low, and these games are more for leisure and entertainment, they have attracted a large number of players. In addition, because this kind of game is played by ten people at the same time, it is more suitable for acquaintances to play together, and it is easy for cross-transmission. In addition, most of these games are free, thus contributing to a large player group.

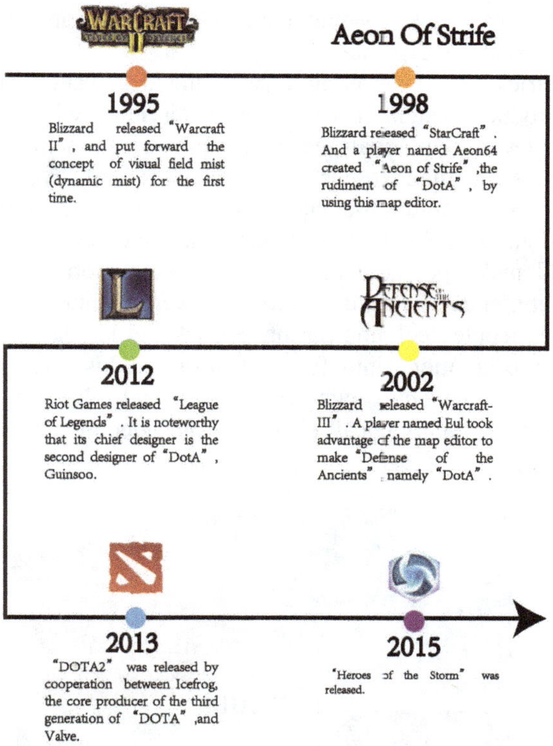

Fig. 1 The history of DotA-like game

B. Visual Field

The visual field refers to the range of space that can be seen when the eyes look at an object in front with the person's head and eyeballs fixed. The earliest adopter of dynamic visual field in the game was "Warcraft II" released by Blizzard in 1998. This design was then used in many games, including "DotA" and subsequent DotA-like games. Dynamic visual field refers to the visual field the player has in the game. It is a circle-like range centering on the player-controlled character. This range is always changing according to the movement of the player-controlled character.

C. Sense of Pleasure

Although psychologists have different classification of emotions, they all agree that happiness is the most basic and primitive emotion of human beings. Because this kind of pleasant psychological feeling is closely related to people's daily life, it has attracted a great number of psychologists to devote themselves to studies of the sense of pleasure, and has caused the attention and thinking of experts and scholars in other fields. However, so far, the scientific community still has no way to give the public a generally accepted authorized definition. Many psychologists define "happiness" from their own perspective. Oxford Dictionary defines "pleasure" as "feel fun, joyful, satisfied, and delighted in a sober or conscious state". The famous American psychologist Donald Norman looked upon pleasure as a kind of positive emotion generated by the interaction between beauty, fun and happiness. From the analysis of some other psychologists' viewpoints, pleasure is a satisfactory experience after goals have been pursued and achieved. It is a kind of enjoyment, with a high hedonistic dimension and confident dimension. And it can make people have a sense of transcendence, freedom and acceptance.

Patrick Jordan earlier put forward the idea to study pleasure in product design. Through the interviews with multiple interviewers, he analyzed and summarized some of the feelings that often arose in the interviewers' daily lives. Finally, he classed emotions, such as security, self-confidence, freedom, excitement, satisfaction, pride, etc., as feelings that could make people feel pleasant, while emotions such as anxiety, anger, being deceived, etc., were feelings that could make people feel unpleasant. Patrick Jordan later divided pleasure emotions into four categories in his book *Design Pleasant Products*, namely physiological pleasure, social pleasure, psychological pleasure, and ideological pleasure (Fig. 2).

Fig. 2 Four categories of pleasure

Physiological pleasure is a category that can directly act on the senses of the human body and produce a sense of pleasure immediately. This category is usually generated without thinking and is an instinct, including vision, hearing, smell, taste, and touch. Social pleasure is simply the pleasure that comes from interactive activities. Psychological pleasure is actually that people's mental activity is influenced by factors like educational level, experience, living customs, regional climate, etc. Ideological pleasure is usually not produced during the use, but after it. It can be obtained through reflection on previous behaviors, with certain hysteretic nature.

However, pleasure is an elusive concept. Therefore, things that make people feel happy are largely determined by the scene at that time. This scene in the game is largely determined by the game mechanism, especially the design of the visual field.

The Influence of Visual Field Design on the Sense of Pleasure in DotA-like Games

In DotA-like games, the characters controlled by the players, as well as the buildings and the minions, have a certain visual field, that is, objects within a certain range are visible, while the map outside the visual field is invisible. It is just like we walk on the road at night. Where there are street lights, we can see very clearly, and places that we cannot see are very dark. The same is true in the games. Once you walk in a place with no visual field, you will always be cautious, and you will feel relieved and happy in a place with wide visual field. It is like a person walking in a place with poor lighting conditions at night. The person will have a sense of insecurity. When there is enough light, such a sense of insecurity will decrease a lot. The visual field is the range that can be felt by human eyes. The pleasure originated by the visual field is actually derived from the physiological characteristics of people, such as fear of darkness and unknown. It belongs to physiological pleasure. However, asymmetries in visual field often occur in DotA-like games. On such occasions, the party with the advantage of visual field will gain more sense of pleasure. This kind of pleasure is first from psychological superiority which is a kind of psychological pleasure. Then the player can take advantage of the visual field to complete some operations, so as to get the pleasure at social level. Finally the player will show off after these behaviors based on the visual field. Eventually they will also get pleasure generated by the player using the visual field to complete the operations, which is a kind of ideological pleasure.

A. Effects on Pleasure under Conditions of Normal Visual Field

The paper will analyze three situations under conditions of normal visual field, i.e., Player A and Player B are invisible to each other, Player A and Player B are mutually visible, and Player A cannot see Player B while Player B can see Player A (Fig. 3).

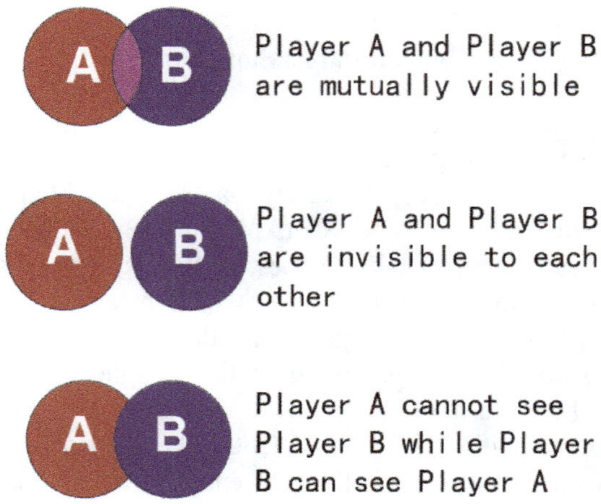

Fig. 3 Three situations under conditions of normal visual field

As shown in Fig. 4, when Player A and Player B are invisible to each other, both players will be in high tension and very careful. In the case where the visual field in the game is not visible, people will have more negative emotions. This is firstly determined by the physiological sense of people. Since the players are under the rules of the game, they know that the opponents will possibly kill them when they cannot see the opponents. This will cause emotions, such as tension, fear, etc., both physically and psychologically.

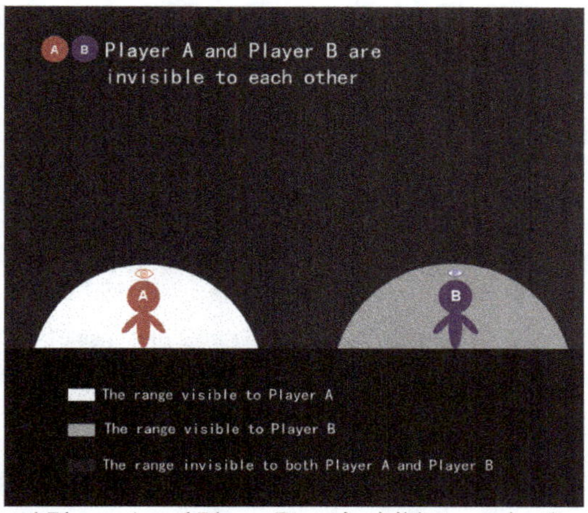

Fig. 4 Player A and Player B are invisible to each other

As shown in Fig. 5, when Player A and Player B are visible to each other, both players will get a relative sense of security in psychology. This sense of security comes from the mastery of information. The reason why the player is most concerned about the blind spot in the game is not the invisibility itself, but that under the established game rules, the player is worried that an opponent will jump out suddenly from the dark to kill him. So when the player masters the position and information of the other players, even if it is not visible in many places on the map, the information is enough for the player.

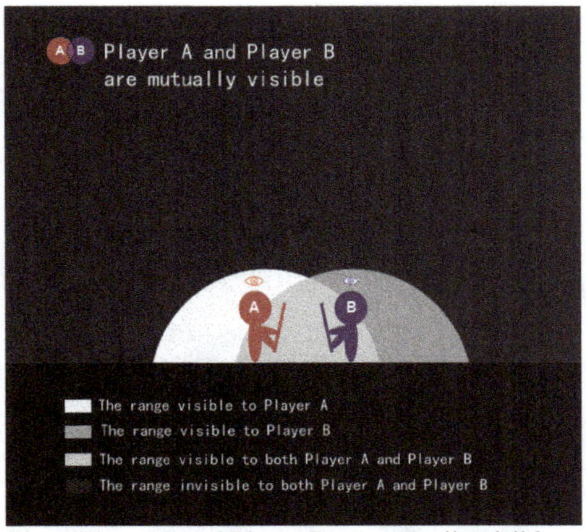

Fig. 5 Player A and Player B are mutually visible

As shown in Fig. 6, when Player B can see Player A but player A can't see player B, Player B will not only have a sense of pleasure due to the sense of security, but more importantly, have a sense of superiority due to the advantage in the visual field, thus getting a sense of psychological pleasure. In this case, Player A often does not know that Player B can see him, and the sudden invisibility of Player B will make Player A nervous and worried. In this case, Player B usually will take advantage of the visual field to take some actions to expand his advantage. The most common action for Player B is to kill Player A in his visual field, so as to obtain more pleasure, including social and psychological pleasure.

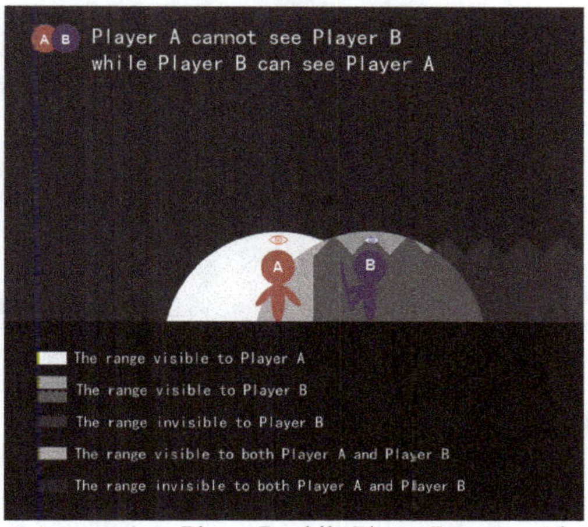

Fig. 6 Player A cannot see Player B while Player B can see Player A

B. Effects on Pleasure under Special Visual Field

In DotA-like games, there are usually some special visual field mechanisms, such as the grass in “Heroes of the Storm” and “League of Legends”, as well as the top and the foot of slope, the day and night, and the woods in “DotA”. The top and the foot of slope in "DotA" is an example. As shown in Fig. 7, the distance between the top and the foot is very close in the game. But Player B at the top of the slope can see player A at the foot of the slope, while Player A can t see Player B. If Player B suddenly kills Player A by taking advantage of the visual field, Player A will have died before he sees Player B, and he does not even know how he has died. At this moment, player B will feel pleasant, and this sense of pleasure belongs to social, psychological and even ideological pleasure. This sense of pleasure comes from the design at behavioral level.

Similarly, due to the design of day and night in “DotA”, the visual field at night is smaller than that in the daytime. As to the design of the woods, the player's visual field will be blocked by the trees, making the player’s visual field very small, resulting in the situation that two people close to each other without seeing each other. These designs allow the player to have more room for operation to achieve a certain purpose, thereby obtaining social pleasure. After these operations, the player often communicates with other people to show off, thereby creating ideological pleasure. This kind of ideological pleasure is not generated when the player performs those operations, but after them. It has a hysteretic nature when compared with physiological and psychological pleasures, and is often accompanied by social behaviors. The physiological and psychological pleasures are feeding back to the player in real time during game play, while social pleasure and ideological pleasure are not exactly like this. Some social pleasure and ideological pleasure will happen in the game, such as the communication with teammates and opponents "Awesome play" and "You too". Some happen after the game, because these behaviors are often remembered by the player. In a long period of time after the game, the player can use it to show off and communicate with others to get pleasure.

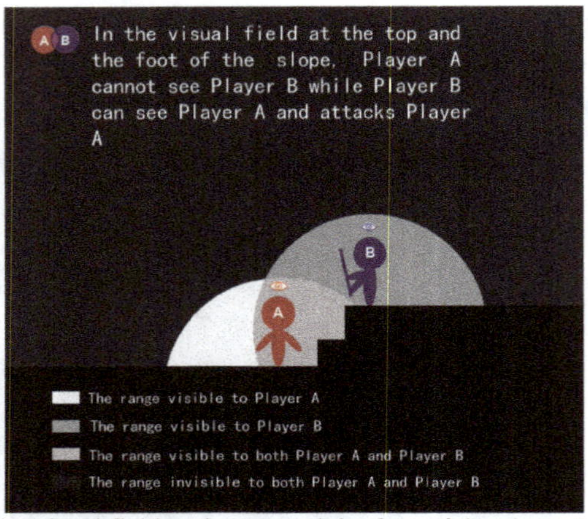

Fig. 7 In the visual field at the top and the foot of the slope. Player A cannot see Player B while Player B can see Player A and attacks Player A

C. Effects of Scaling of Visual Field Range on Sense of Pleasure

The above are analyses of some situations under the premise that the visual field range is a fixed value in the game. This section will analyze the effects of scaling of the player's visual field range on the sense of pleasure (Fig. 8).

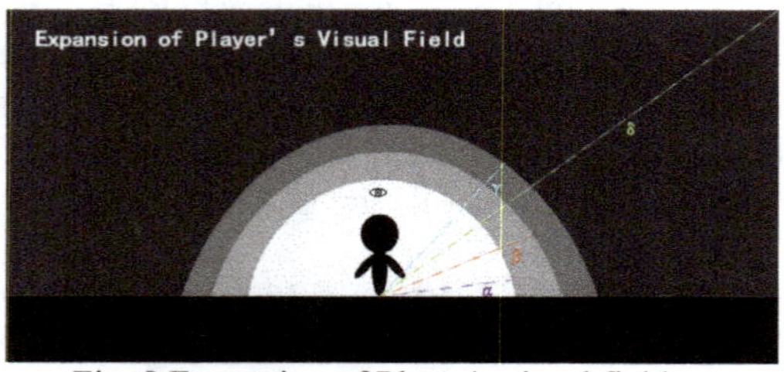

Fig. 8 Expansion of Player's visual field

According to the foregoing discussion, if the player's visual field becomes larger and larger as shown in the figure, the sense of pleasure the player gets seems to be increasing. Indeed, as shown in Fig. 9, when the player's visible range is in the range from ① to ②, the pleasure the player obtains will increase as the visual field expands. It is because in this visual field range, the player's acquisition of physiological pleasure will expand with the increase of the visible range. On the other hand, the unbalanced mastery of visual field and special conditions of visual field will give the player more psychological, social and ideological pleasure. However, when the visible range continues to expand, in the range from ② to ③, the player's sense of pleasure will descend. First of all, for the acquisition of psychological pleasure, one of the main reasons is the asymmetry in two sides' mastery of the visual field. When the range of the visual field of both parties becomes larger and larger, the gap will be smaller and smaller until both sides can see things on the entire map. Then the psychological superiority will disappear. At the same time, as the visual field of both sides continues to expand, both sides finally know what the other side is doing, thus losing the conditions and opportunities to kill the other side through certain operations, which will lead to the decrease of social pleasure and subsequent reflection pleasure and psychological pleasure. And due to the gradual increase in the visual field, the players' behaviors will be seen by the enemy players without reservation, which will also make the players feel they are peeped at and lead to loss of pleasure.

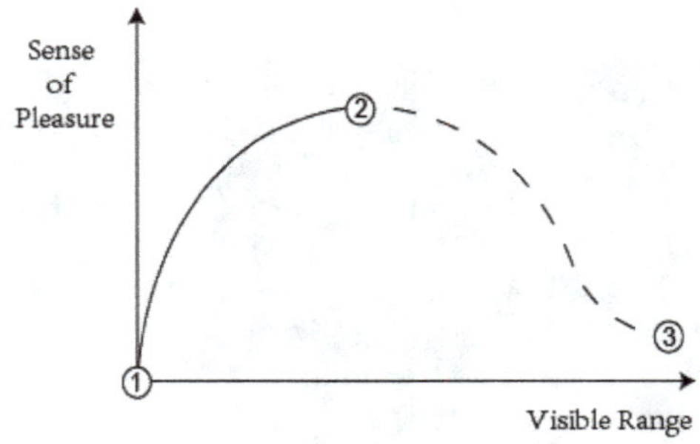

Fig. 9 Effects of scaling of visual field range on sense of pleasure

Conclusion

The fact that games can bring pleasure to people is due to various factors, such as character design, game mechanism design, map design, music composition, art style design, etc. We often feel pleasant and happy when playing games. However, game developers usually do not analyze the reasons for this. Even if there is any analysis, it is just at the gameplay level. There is no analysis of other game elements. This paper, which started from the perspective of visual field, conducted analysis from physiological pleasure, psychological pleasure, social pleasure and reflection pleasure, and has arrived at the conclusion that the visual field design directly or indirectly affects the pleasure in user experience from multiple aspects. So in the map design, when gameplay and balance are fully considered, the visual field design and the formulation of rules need to be paid great attention to. Only in this way can a game which allows the player to enjoy as much as possible be created.

References

[1] Patrick W. Jordan, *Human factors for pleasure in product use*, Phil. Trans. Roy. Soc. London, vol. 29, pp. 25–33, February 1998.

[2] Uriarte. A, Ontañón. S, *Kiting in RTS games using influence maps*, In: Eighth Artificial Intelligence and Interactive Digital Entertainment Conference, Palo Alto, USA, 2012.

[3] Pottinger. D.C, *Terrain analysis for real-time strategy games*, In: Proceedings of Game Developers Conference 2000, San Francisco, USA, 2000.

[4] Hagelbäck. J, Johansson. S.J, *Dealing with fog of war in a real time strategy game environment*, CIG(IEEE), pp.55-62, Perth, Australia, 2008.

[5] Long Zuo, Shuo Xiong, Hiroyuki Iida, *An Analysis of DotA2 Using Game Refinement Measure*, In: Entertainment Computing– ICEC 2017, pp. 270-276, 2017.

[6] Wu Tyan-Yu,Chang Wen-Chih,Hsu Yuan-Hao, "Designing a lighting with pleasure," 1st International Conference on Human Centered Design, HCD 2009.

https://doi.org/10.1142/9789811238727_0047

Inheriting the Intangible Cultural Heritage Handicraft "Huangling Flour Decor" with AR Technology

Jiong Li Shang, Xue Hua Xu*, Ling Jing Zheng

Kongju National University, South Korea
*Corresponding Author Email: seolhua@icloud.com

Abstract

Among the intangible cultural heritage, traditional handicraft "Huangling Flour Decor" has a single form of inheritance. It is particularly vulnerable to the fissile development of the surrounding culture and environment, which consequently causes the Huangling Flour Decor to gradually become unknown to people, and recovery of its inheritance is extremely urgent. At this stage of the market environment, the display and experience of the traditional handicraft cultural focuses more on understanding the surface of the material, while the production process of the product and the search for cultural soul is the core for inheriting the intangible cultural heritage. The application of AR (Augmented Reality) technology can allow the intangible cultural heritage to be visualized and contextualized. Based on basic ideas and process methods of the digital development of AR technology, this paper explores a systematic, AR technology-based theoretical method and practical approach for the digital development and inheritance of the intangible cultural heritage handicraft. This promotes digital interpretation, digital display, digital communication and digital experience of the intangible cultural heritage handicraft. In addition, taking "Huangling Flour Decor" in Yanan as an example, the inheritance of traditional handicraft intangible cultural heritage is researched through AR technology.

Keywords: AR technology, inheritance, the traditional handicraft intangible cultural heritage, the Huangling Flour Decor

Introduction

The experience and technical skill of traditional handmade craftsmanship is an invisible existence. Experience exists in the inheritor's mind, which leads to the achievement of hand-made production, whereas the skill of craftsmanship lies in the hands of inheritors, which contributes to the process of materialized craftsmanship. Traditional handicraft belongs to the category of important intangible cultural heritage, which mainly includes the process of the creation of material carrier, experience and skills in the process of materialization, and even manual craftsmen who master these experiences and skills [1].

The Huangling Flour Decor is a ritual steamed bun of traditional folk custom spread in the rural area of Huangling County, Yanan City, Shanxi Province. It belongs to the intangible cultural heritage and is an indispensable sacrifice for the public offering to the Yellow Emperor, which reflects the good traditions of the Huangling people's simplicity, kindness and their incomparable gratitude for their ancestors. At the same time, it also has deep cultural roots and historical roots.

The Value and Crisis of the Huangling Flour Decor Inheritance

The Huangling Flour Decor is a form of dough art, with wheat flour and edible pigment as main materials, supplemented with sorghum skin, wheat ear, and colored paper as decoration. The Huangling Flour Decor plays a significant role in the local folk custom since it is located in such a unique geographical position, the Yellow River Basin, where the important birthplace of the Chinese nation is. Its development has rich historical and cultural roots, thus forming its unique artistic style and characteristics. The craftsmen who produce the flour decor all have their own special skills. The main tools include scissors, tweezers, combs, spoons, box lids, knives, etc. Using these tools by craftsmen who are skilled, the kneaded dough is squeezed, pulled, wound, knotted, cut, sliced, and tied, (Fig. 1) finally becoming the vivid flour decor artifact of a variety of different forms.

Fig. 1 Making tools of the Huangling Flour Decor.

The Huangling Flour Decor, which is used for sacrificial offering, is dominated by flowers, birds, fish, insects, birds and beasts, and its colors are rich and distinct. Adopting the Chinese traditional five elements concept, there is a sharp contrast simultaneously using the complementarity of red, green, yellow, white, and black. They are harmonious and rich. The Huangling Flour Decor has an exaggerated shape and me ticulous workmanship, such as "Two dragon play pearls" (Fig. 2), "Birds paying homage to the phoenix", "Unicorn delivers sons", "All flowers bloom together", which all contain rich hi storical myths and totem worship [2].

Fig. 2 Two dragon play pearls.

Currently, the inheritance of the Huangling Flour Decor handicraft has the following problems.

In terms of technology, the Huangling Flour Decor requires a large number of continuous steps in the production process, which means that the dough needs to be quickly formed after leavened, whereas large flour decor works are bulky and difficult to be spliced, and are often formed in one body. The consumption of physical strength and mental power is gigantic, and the flour decor has a short preservation time, which is easily weathered, causing seasoning check and deformation. In terms of inheritance, the common problem faced by traditional handicrafts, such as the flour decor, is its low speed and difficulties of inheritance. On one hand, the top art is often mastered by a few artists. On the other hand, the broad masses of the people have access to these arts, but they are not willing to learn and pass on them.

The Feasibility of AR Technology to Protect the Intangible Cultural Heritage

A. The existing application of AR technology

In recent years, with in-depth research of relevant scientific research institutions, experts, scholars, and business organizations in China and foreign countries in the field of AR, and the continuous improvement of the performance of computer hardware and software, the application of AR has gradually moved from the laboratory to the public. Related supporting technologies have gradually developed and matured, providing a powerful technical guarantee for the implementation of digital development in AR in the field of cultural heritage. The development of 3D tracking registration technology has led to a trend that the real scenario of tracking registration becomes diverse. Developed from the traditional marker-based tracking registration techniques to those based on natural image, physical object, real environment and location, it has been possible for AR technology to implement the digital development and the use of intangible cultural heritage in the real environment, like cultural heritage landscape, museums, and cultural and creative products.

Generally, China's practice and research work in the field of intangible cultural heritage protection started relatively late. Digital acquisition, preservation, storage, digital protection technology, digital display, digital communication, and digital development and utilization are all at an exploratory stage.

B. Analysis of advantages of AR technology

The virtual object is the key content when user experiences AR application, and is the bridge and core of emotional communication between the user and the AR. The lack of function of virtual object content, connotation of content creation, creativity and innovation in digital expression will make the AR experience unattractive and miss the desired effect. The abundant content of the Huangling Flour Decor provides a large amount of digital content creation material for the "virtual object" in the development of AR. Through the intervention of digital technology and information technology such as digital animation of AR technology, deep excavating the cultural connotation and spiritual value of traditional culture such as folk crafts and folklore of the Huangling Flour Decor can help develop an AR digital cultural creation product, a combination of interest, education, and entertainment. They can demonstrate traditional culture and provide the experience of virtual-real fusion. However, national cultural spirits such as folk artifacts, folk tales and so on are the core contents and main motives of this kind of product when referring to consumption.

C. The combination of AR technology and traditional handicraft intangible cultural heritage.

The basic principle and three basic features of AR technology includes 1) virtual reality fusion, the combination of virtual object and real environment; 2) three-dimensional registration, the accurate registration of virtual objects in the space and time of the real environment; 3) real-time interaction. All of these represents that the tester can carry out real-time interactive operation with the virtual object and the real scene. According to these, this study proposes a method for digitally embedding traditional cultural content in the form of carriers of traditional handicrafts (Fig. 3) [4].

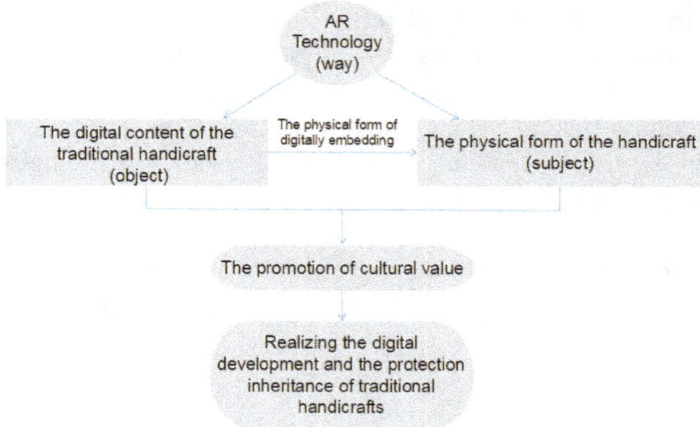

Fig. 3 A method of digitally embedding traditional culture in the form of carriers of traditional handicrafts.

Its basic starting point and foothold is to break the physical space restriction of physical products, and to integrate the rich traditional culture content related to cultural products into physical products and improve the value of traditions. This enables traditional handicraft products to display their cultural connotations in a multifaceted way and to highlight better national characteristics and national brand [5].

The Design Method of Combining AR Technology and the Huangling Flour Decor Handicraft

A. Goals

The design method is mainly implemented on smart phones or tablet computers to complete the digital integration of the content of "Huangling Flour Decor" in the material medium. In the real environment, it provides users with the display and interactive experience of the digital content of Huangling Flour Decor. The digital objects include digital representation formed by contextualized and visualized digital three-dimensional model of historical content of the Huangling Flour Decor, scenarios, digital images, and sounds. The main part of the cultural digital integration is the Huangling Flour Decor model, the virtual scene and the image.

The goal of embedding digital content into the cultural creation product "Huangling Face Flower" is that a three-dimensional and dynamic picture will appear in the mobile phone, when the experiencer recognizes the recognition map or object by the camera of the smart terminal in their hand. According to gestures, display contents can be interacted with, zoomed in or out, and even the content can be deformed, thereby achieving the goal of embedding digital contents into cultural creation products.

B. Process

The design method is to use computer three-dimensional registration method to achieve the superposition and the integration of virtual cultural digital content and real environment. In the development of specific application, corresponding identifiers need to be set, helping the system to complete the real-time tracking registration. In the development process of "Huangling Flour Decor", a cultural tag is used as a tracking target of the system. The Work flow diagram based on the research on development of the traditional handicraft intangible cultural heritage "Huangling Flour Decor" through AR technology is as follows (Fig. 4).

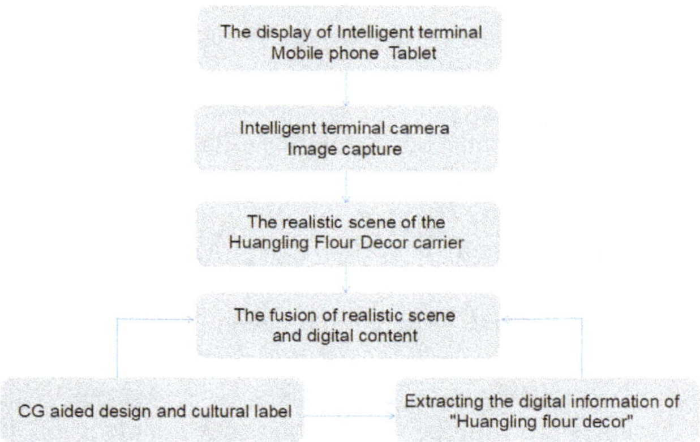

Fig. 4 The Work flow diagram based on the research on the development of the traditional handicraft intangible cultural heritage "Huangling Flour Decor" through AR technology.

The system captures the real scene video and image of the "Huangling Flour Decor" material medium with a cultural tag installed by a camera on the smartphone or tablet computer. In this design, encoding, transmitting, decoding, and processing the video image in the system refers to the camera collecting the "Huangling Flour Decor" model and the image of production scene. The digital culture content required by the system is accomplished through a Computer Graphics (CG) Auxiliary Design System, which mainly includes the three-dimensional model of the Huangling Flour Decor, the three-dimensional scene of the production, and the three-dimensional animation of the storyline. The cultural label is a pattern and figure designed with accordance to the culture content of the Huangling Flour Decor. For instance, the Huangling Flour Decor pattern and souvenir can be used as cultural labels for real-time tracking registration of the real environment. The specification of digital form of the Huangling Flour Decor needs to be designed according to file data format adapted to the Unity and Vuforia SDK integrated development environment. The system can conduct real-time rendering by extracting the cultural data of digital form to generate digital cultural content of the Huangling Flour Decor. Finally, the system strongly pushes the real video image to the display output of smart terminals through virtual reality registration and fusion.

C. Technology implementation

The design and drawing of cultural labels

Culture tags were drawn in the Adobe Photo shop CC, which was mainly used to draw AR real-time tracking objects with the theme of "Huangling Flour Decor" (Fig 5).

Fig. 5 Culture tags were drawn in the Adobe Photo shop CC, which was mainly used to draw AR real-time tracking objects with the theme of "Huangling Flour Decor".

In terms of the digital content design of the Huangling Flour Decor and traditional handicraft intangible cultural heritage, third-party software, 3D max was used for the design and the creation of digital dimensional models and digital animations (Fig. 6) Then digital images were completed on Adobe Premiere Pro CC/After Effects CS6.

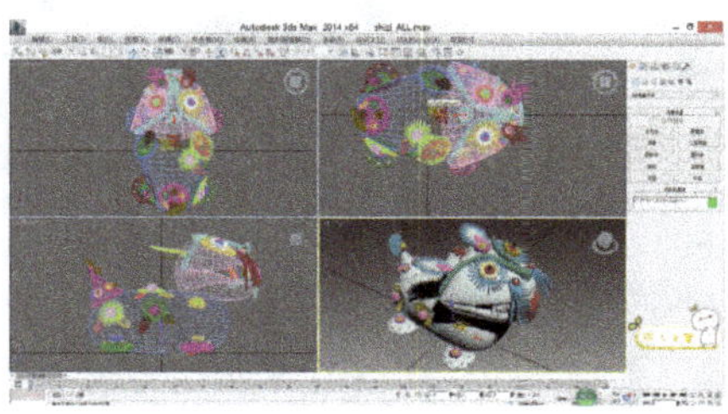

Fig. 6 3D max was used for the design and the creation of digital dimensional models and digital animations.

On the basis of the content of "Huangling Flour Decor", four types of digital content of the Huangling Flour Decor were mainly designed and created in the development of the case: the main character modeling design, three-dimensional scene design, three-dimensional animation of the storyline, and digital imagery design, including a three-dimensional character and plot animation of the flour decor and producer, and a three-dimensional model of the Yellow Emperor Mausoleum. In this experimental test, the Huangling Flour Decor and the digital image of its production process were taken as experimental objects.

AR technology integration

The tool C# was mainly used to integrate the cultural and digital content with its corresponding material medium carrier by virtual-real fusion in the integrated development environment of Uniy 3D and Android SDK (Fig. 7), and finally the tool Android SDK was used to complete compilation and integrate the development environment.

Fig. 7 The tool C# was mainly used to integrate the cultural and digital content with its corresponding material medium carrier by virtual-real fusion in the integrated development environment of Uniy3D and Android SDK.

D. Experimental result

The experimental test of this case was carried out on the mobile phone platform of Android and iPhone. The figure is an augmented reality effect map of the virtual-real fusion in a mobile phone in the on-site test environment where cultural digital integration is implemented in the cultural creation product "Huangling Flour Decor". When the camera on the mobile phone recognizes the cultural tag of the flour decor, the digital content related to cultural tags is superimposed in the real environment and actually output on intelligent terminals. Moreover, the spatial location of cultural labels can be changed by changing camera angles and distances, and interactive operation can be taken through gesture movement, rotation, deformation, etc. (Fig. 8)

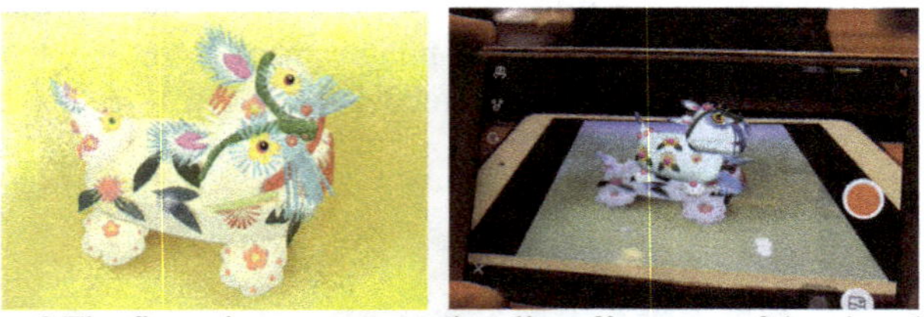

Fig. 8 The figure is an augmented reality effect map of the virtual-real fusion in mobile phone in the on-site test environment where cultural digital integration is implemented in the cultural creation product "Huangling Flour Decor".

The figure shows an on-site testing environment for the implementation of digitally embedding traditional culture in the souvenir "Huangling Flour Decor". When the smart phone's camera recognizes the pattern on the tourist souvenir, the image will be superimposed in the real environment. In the virtual scroll, the process of producing Huangling Flour Decor and the digital three-dimensional animation image of the legendary story will be displayed in real time. When the camera of smart phone recognizes the pattern on the tourist souvenir, the image will be superimposed in the real environment. In addition, the process of producing the Huangling Flour Decor and the digital 3D animation image of the legendary story will be displayed in the virtual scroll in real time. (Fig. 9)

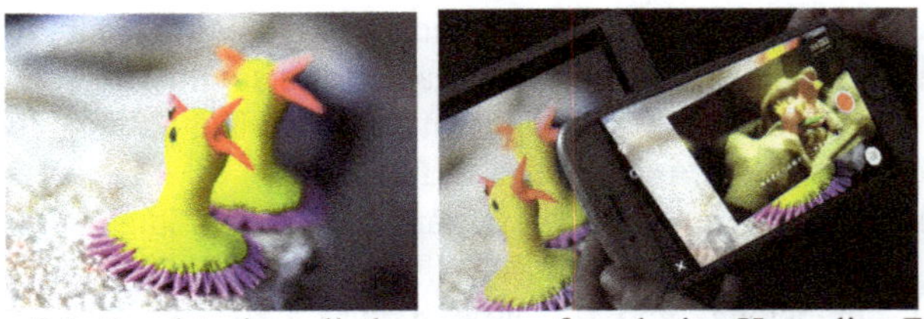

Fig. 9 In the virtual scroll, the process of producing Huangling Flour Decor and the digital three-dimensional animation image of the legendary story will be displayed in real time.

Conclusion

With the advent of the digital era and continuous improvement, the original ecological space which Chinese traditional handicraft intangible cultural heritage extremely rely on, will face serious threats, leading to unprecedented challenges in the traditional protection and the inheritance of traditional handicrafts. It is a trend to make reasonable use of modern technologies such as digital technology and information technology to protect traditional handicraft intangible cultural heritage. However, as the traditional handicraft intangible cultural heritage is a long-term accumulation of knowledge, skill, and spirit stored in people's brains by various ethnic groups, which has a special attribute of "nonmaterial", its production, existence, display, diagnosis, and dissemination should rely on a certain material vector carrier, thus causing many bottlenecks in its protection and development. This study focuses on the status of the digital inheritance of the Huangling Flour Decor and sums up its advantages and existing problems. Based on the basic principle of AR technology, this paper proposes a fundamental thought of digitally embedding traditional culture in Huangling Flour Decor material media carrier and constructs a method for the development of the inheritance of Huangling Flour Decor with AR technology.

Using this method as a guiding ideology and rationally digital technologies such as AR technology, a method of cultural digital integration using AR was carried out, which was oriented for digital application development of the traditional handicraft intangible cultural heritage, the Huangling Flour Decor. Furthermore, the development and the implementation of specific applications were carried out, and the corresponding experimental testing results were given on the mobile intelligent terminal. "Huangling Flour Decor" is only a small part in the intangible cultural heritage. It is precisely the combination of this representative example and augmented reality technology that has contributed to the influence of AR technology in the display of traditional handicraft intangible cultural heritage, its protection, inheritance and the development of national arts and crafts, which seem to form a line. This line can be extended to various types of traditional intangible cultural handicraft heritage to form a new situation for the inheritance and the protection of traditional handicraft intangible cultural heritage.

References

[1] Zhang Suxia. Research on the Evaluation Model Construction and Protection System of Traditional Handicraft Intangible Cultural Heritage Protection Effect Based on Stakeholder Theory[D]. Beijing Jiaotong University, 2014.

[2] Zhang Xinyu; Guo Gengyan; Peng Yule; Yan Yawen; Saying Chinese Stories with Non-faceted Flowers—On the Cultural Implication of Shaanxi Huangling Face Flower[J]; Arts and Technology; 2016-07.

[3] Zhou Dazhao. Design and implementation of experiential teaching demonstration software based on augmented reality. Diss. Guangxi Normal University, 2014. K. Rose, "Title of paper with only first word capitalized," in press.

[4] Xu Fei. Application of 3D Digital Technology in Animation Creation[D]. Southeast University, 2010.

https://doi.org/10.1142/9789811238727_0048

Empirical Analysis of Macao's Traditional Local Brand Souvenirs Innovation Design

Ren Yujie

Faculty of Innovation and Design, City University of Macau, Macau. China
Email: yjren@cityu.mo

Abstract

To support and promote "Made in Macao" merchandise, the SAR government has invested resources for better promotion of "Macau's traditional local brands". The main purpose is to explore business opportunities for enterprises and thereby enhance the development of Macao's traditional enterprises and the city image. Many tourists to Macau would like to bring back local food that is symbolic for the tourist city. Macao's local food is representative of the regional customs of Macao and plays an important role in spreading local culture to improve the image of the tourist city.

Founded in the last century, the traditional brands with a long history used to be the leading brands in the market. In the past few decades, these traditional brands have been very popular among the customers because of their unique processing techniques and the management philosophy being passed down from generation to generation. However, with the changes in the market of the local food, the competition among brands has been getting fiercer. Many traditional brands focus on traditional craftsmanship and promotion for brand images. However, the brands do not respond promptly to the changes in the market, resulting in lagging development. Many traditional brands have gradually declined despite their long history.

According to the existing empirical analysis results, "the brand images of Macau's local food have positive influence on consumers' purchasing intentions and the brands' functional images and reputation images have significant influence on purchase intention." This paper studies how the traditional brands exert their advantages with their brand images and cope with the competition, and then enhance their visual images in the hope of ultimately improving consumers' willingness to purchase.

Keywords: traditional local brand, local food, brand image, innovative design, empirical analysis

Introduction

Souvenirs are the little gifts that are brought for relatives and friends in travel. They usually are small in size and cheap, being bought randomly. The paper studies the local food that is one of the indicators under the category of "tourism shopping" by the Macao Statistics and Census Bureau. Therefore, we consider that Macao's souvenirs have the characteristics of tourist goods that are purchased by many tourists who come to Macau as souvenirs or gifts.

As a tourist city combining Chinese and Western cultures, Macau is rich in cultural resources with strong regional characteristics. In recent years, more tourists visit Macau and many of them buy local food for their friends and families. Thus, Macao's local foods as an important symbol of the tourist city, contain the regional customs of Macao, being one of the purpose of travel. The foods play an important role in spreading the regional culture and enhancing the image as a tourist city. Especially, the traditional local brands are very significant to cultural heritage, but also make an "outdated" and "out of date" impression on the customers because it is easy for them to remind us the past era, which results in decline in brand image [1].

Macau's traditional brands with a long history were founded in the last century. In the past few decades, these traditional brands have been adored by customers owing to their unique processing technology and the business philosophy passing down from generation to generation. However, most of the traditional brands do not make quick response to the changes in the market of the local foods, which results in lagging development, less promotion of brand images and insufficient innovation.

Nowadays, Macau with a pillar industry of gaming and tourism is turning to a center of global tourism and leisure as well as a high-quality tourist city. To support and promote the "Made in Macau", the SAR government invests more resources for the better promotion of "Macau Brand" to provide business opportunities for the enterprises and enhance Macao's overall competitiveness and city image. To cope with the policy strategy, the traditional brands need innovation and development, and it is necessary to enhance their images and inherit their cultures.

Meaning of Brand Image

Park et al. defined a brand image as the "understanding," "perception," or "evaluation" of brand by customers [2]. Some researchers believe that a brand image is the impression or perception, the comprehensive evaluation and perception of brand or product attributes. We have developed a scale for the brand image of Macao's local foods. The empirical research shows that Macao's local food has four brand images: functional, symbolic, reputation and empirical images. Among them, functional images have the most positive influence on purchase intention [3]. The customers come mainly for travel, appearance matters much in the image of local food. The previous study of their functional images revealed that the exquisiteness of their packaging designs have a significant influence on the perception and judgment of brand image in addition to the quality itself [4]. The designer should apply his ideas in design and endow the traditional brands new vitality, retaining the original brand cultures while establishing a better brand image for their sustainable development.

Origin of Macao's Traditional Local Brand "Iun Loi"

Iun Loi, an traditional brand in Macao, with a business history of more than 50 years, has a good reputation. It has inherited excellent processing technology, skills and business characteristics and a distinctive traditional cultural background with Macao characteristics. We take Iun Loi as an example to expound the design innovation strategy for the sustainable development of brands by its innovation design. Formerly known as Iun Loi Tea House, founded in 1920, Iun Loi Bakery is a famous traditional tea house in Macao with a history of nearly one hundred years and was later reformed into a cake house. Its most famous cakes include honey pies, sweetheart pastry, white crisp and traditional wedding cakes. At first, these local foods were for wedding banquets, and become famous for local residents as well as the tourists who travel to Macau. It has become the traditional local food adored by tourists.

Brand Design and Innovation Strategy of Iun Loi

TODOT DESIGN, the designer, was commissioned to update the image of this Macau's century-traditional brand. Lotus is frequently used in its images, and lotus paste has been a common material of its most well-known products. The wedding series is its star product with the image of a combined "Lotus" and "Marriage" embodied in a twin lotus on one stalk. Twin lotus has profound meaning including auspicious, festive, kind, beautiful and unique. For its font, TODOT DESIGN has extracted the most recognizable calligraphy characters from its original old signboards as shown in Fig. 1

Fig. 1 Logo of Iun Loi

We suggest students to innovate the traditional brand souvenirs in his graphic design class. The students studied Iun Loi and then presented designs with further meaning for its logo based on the design concept of TODOT DESIGN with the purpose to combine the lotus and the calligraphy of Iun Loi for a graphics-text logo with more uniform visual effect, as shown in Figs. 2 and 3.

Fig. 2 Draft design of the logo, by Wu Yiqing and Yu Meicheng

Fig. 3 the completed logo design by Wu Yuqing and Yu Meicheng

During the market research, they found that the product packaging bags or packaging boxes placed in the Iun Loi stores were simple and out-dated, and the colors are not matched in a harmonious way, as shown in Figs. 4 and 5.

Fig. 4 Packagings of products of Iun Loi

Fig. 5 Packagings of products of Iun Loi

The visual image of local foods is the carrier delivering the brand image to customers, while packaging is the most important carrier of local food brand. In the previous survey of 450 questionnaires, we found that many of the tourists to Macau are aged from 25-35, accounting for 56% of the total tourists [7]. Therefore, we instructed the students to present an updated design for the packaging for its wedding cake. The design style of local food packaging is positioned as festive and fresh with light warm colors as major as shown in Fig. 6.

Fig. 6 Design for wedding cakes

The opened package is in the shape of small table with a little height, in order to display cakes better. The wedding cakes are usually displayed and shared in Macao and even in

China. Appearance is more important than flavor for the cakes. The visual effect of such a structure is more useful under the background of local customs.

Fig. 7 Package design by Wu Yuqing and Yu Meicheng

Figure 7 shows a simple packaging design with a handle for easy carrying. This package is suitable for the displaying at the door in the traditional wedding banquet. The cakes in this packaging may be given to the relatives and friends to carry conveniently. For tourists, the packaging of these two products is easy for tourists to put in luggage or carry.

In this study, we analyzed the current design of Iun Loi to present an innovative brand design on the basis of the quantitative research results of the questionnaire survey and the market observations. The result is expected to maintain sustainable development of the brand. The design adopts the traditional elements of regional cultures, emphasizing that design innovation not only to preserve the original traditional cultures, but also to present new visually innovative design. New design brings new shopping experience for better brand value for the traditional brand.

References

[1] Xu Yanfeng, Du Hengbo, Zhao Xiaokang (2015). Research on the Influence Mechanism of Brand Extension of Restaurant Brand on Brand Image——Based on the Perspective of Perceived Fit. Journal of Beijing Technology and Business University (Social Science Edition), (05), 99-107.

[2] Park, C. W., Jaworski, B. J., & Maclnnis, D. J. (1986). Strategic brand concept-image management. The Journal of Marketing, 14(2), 135-145.

[3] Ren Yujie, Research on Local Food Industry in Macao, 1rd ed., Beijing: Intellectual Property Rights Press, 2018, pp. 26-27.

[4] Ren Yujie, Research on Local Food Industry in Macao, 1rd ed., Beijing: Intellectual Property Rights Press, 2018, pp. 132.

[5] https://www.facebook.com/275628489499076/posts/600750593653529/

[6] https://www.facebook.com/275628489499076/posts/600750593653529/

[7] Ren Yujie, Research on Local Food Industry in Macao, 1rd ed., Beijing: Intellectual Property Rights Press, 2018, pp. 96.

https://doi.org/10.1142/9789811238727_0049

Innovative Design of Dog Care Equipment Based on Quality Function Deployment

Xi-Hui Jia[*1,a], Jui-Che Tu[1,b], Yu Xiong[2,c]

[1]National Yunlin University of Science and Technology,Taiwan
[2]Guangdong University of Technology, Guangzhou, China
[*]Corresponding Author Email: [b]tujc@yuntech.edu.tw, [a]xavier.cqu@live.com, [c]yasin1006@outlook.com

Abstract

To address the diverse needs of dog owners for the care of their pets, the Quality Function Deployment (QFD) method is applied to the innovative design of dog care products. Taking pet owners as the survey object, a satisfaction questionnaire survey was first conducted to determine how satisfied users were with the functionality of current products on the market, and then a Kano questionnaire survey method was used to prioritize the user's needs according to form, functionality, and human-machine interaction. This was then used to develop the House of Quality matrix. The QFD model was used as the basis for determining key design elements for optimization and establishment of the final design. The application of QFD theory on the design of dog care equipment not only provides reliable and innovative design ideas for the development of dog care products but also provides a reference for the design and development of care products for other types of pets.

Keywords: Industrial design, Quality Function Deployment, Pet equipment, Kano model

Introduction

In an era of increasing consumption, raising pets has become a new option for families, and many consider their pet dogs to be important family members [1]. Thus, daily pet care, especially physical care, has become an important concern for pet owners [2]. Current research on pet care equipment focuses on the specific needs of pets for rest, regular feeding, hygiene, recreation, and so on. However, the market lacks research on equipment that provides integrated care for various pet needs [3-4]. From the perspective of human-machine interaction, Xia *et al.* [5] suggested that the design of pet care equipment should address the problems of large space occupancy and low utilization in pet furniture. Yang [6] verified the feasibility and necessity of different design elements through design practice based on the analysis of canine habits and behaviors. Shen *et al.* [7-9] discussed the design and development process for intelligent pet feeders and pet beds from the perspective of technology. To address the function of pet feeding, the design utilized additional research from Refs. [10-11] to add the functionalities of entertainment and barking reduction. Zhao [12] analyzed the current development in pet hygiene and collated the data. Zhao [13] suggested methods of pet hygiene design.

The QFD method has been widely applied in many fields for user demand mining and priority research and gradually become an important design method in the design process to determine the creative direction based on the calculated priority evaluation [14-19]. The current pet care still lacks systematic analysis and research. Therefore, the QFD method to construct the product demand model and develop the design provides a new solution for the innovative design of dog care equipment.

Principle and application of QFD

Quality Function Deployment (QFD) is a multi-level deductive analysis method proposed by Akao [20]. The House of Quality Matrix plays a key role in QFD through which the direct mapping relationship between user needs and product design elements is established to ensure high consistency in user demands, product design, and production. It has now been widely used in machinery manufacturing, education, product design, software development, and other fields for product research and development. The common denominator in these areas is that they are user-centered, meeting users' needs, and enhancing user satisfaction [21-22]. In the design phase, QFD is mainly used to analyze customers' needs. This includes determining user needs, transforming user needs into design elements, identifying key design elements and objectives, establishing the relationship matrix between user demands and design elements, and prioritizing design demands to determine key design elements. As dog care equipment is designed for pet owners, so the design also needs to be user-centered and reflect their needs. Pet care includes, but is not limited to feeding, hygiene, entertainment, and companionship. Therefore, it is necessary to use a QFD method to analyze the needs of users, especially the prioritization and determination of the key design elements.

Design method of dog care equipment based on QFD

A. Analysis of dog care needs during short periods of pet owner absence.

Dog owners are mostly young people in their 20s and 30s of age. According to the data from the internet, 80% of pet owners in China were born after 1980. The dog care equipment needs designs based on the surveys on dog owners' needs for pet care during short-term absences. After obtaining the survey data, the user needs are sorted and classified to make clear the user needs.

B. Extraction of design elements

Design development needs the guidance of design elements and objectives, so it is necessary to consider user demands from investigation and analysis to identify design elements and to establish design objectives.

C. Prioritization of user needs for dog care equipment

After sorting and classifying the users' needs, they were surveyed based on a scale of satisfied, acceptable, or unsatisfied. The Kano model was used to judge the types of demands and to determine the priority of demands.

D. Construction of House of Quality Matrix for dog care

For the design of dog care equipment, the needs were first sorted and refined into the design elements related to dog care. Then, the design elements were extracted from the user demands to build the House of Quality matrix that consists of user needs and design elements. The research for the innovative design of dog care equipment is shown in Fig. 1.

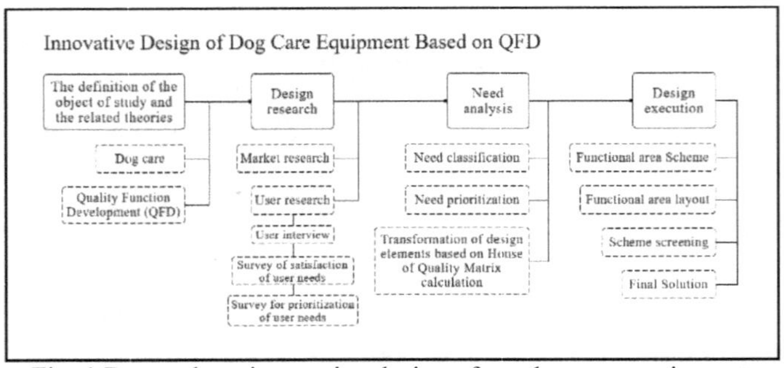

Fig. 1 Research on innovative design of pet dog care equipment.

Construction of House of Quality matrix for dog care equipment design

A. Need analysis of dog care equipment users

Through interviews with dog owners, collection and comparison of existing pet care products on the market, the analysis of the functionality of products was carried out for finding out the corresponding user needs. Preliminary findings included regular and quantitative feeding, drinking water, hygienic excrement collection, entertainment and companionship, remote control, and video monitoring. Then, the process of determining the user's needs and how they correspond to the functions in the product design was refined and sorted according to three aspects: form, function, and human-machine interaction.

At present, there lacks of comprehensive pet care equipment on the market. Most of the products only address a single need in pet care, such as furniture, feeders, and so on. The main users of the products are young people. Therefore, we interviewed users to survey the existing pet-related products according to form, function, and human-machine interaction to summarize user needs and design a satisfaction questionnaire. Through the questionnaire analysis, the actual product experience and the needs of dog owners were studied. The survey results of the questionnaire were scored between 0.0 and 1.0. The degree of satisfaction of users in pet care equipment were used for the analysis and calculation of the House of Quality matrix.

B. Extraction of design elements for dog care equipment

In the survey, 54 of 60 questionnaires were returned. The questionnaire included the criteria of unique form, clean and simple coloring, video monitoring capabilities, entertaining toys, and ease of operation. The respondents of the questionnaire were aged between 18 and 30 years old and pet owners who have used pet care equipment for their dogs when being away from home. The user needs were analyzed to extract design elements to determine product functions as shown in Table 1.

TABLE I
DESIGN ELEMENTS OF DOG CARE EQUIPMENT (PARTIAL DATA)

Number	Design elements
E1	simple styling
E2	rounded, smooth shape
E3	clean, simple colors
E7	faecal disposal
E8	remote control capability
E10	voice communication capability
E11	easy to recognize graphics

C. Prioritization of user needs in dog care equipment

The Kano model divides user needs into five categories: must-be, one-dementional, attrctive, neutral, and contrary needs [14]. Must-be needs are the functions in which the user's satisfaction decreases when not satisfied or is lacking, while it increases when the need is satisfied or the function is provided. One-dimensional needs are the functions in which the user's satisfaction increases with a satisfiable product, while the user's satisfaction decrease when the need is not satisfied or the wanted function not provided. Attractive needs are the functions that improve user satisfaction when the users are attracted by the products. Neutral needs are the functions that do not affect user satisfaction whether the wanted product is provided or not. Contrary needs refer to functions that are contrary to essential needs or any product function that causes user dissatisfaction. The five categories are assigned values from -3 to 5. The larger the number, the greater the importance. The values were 5 for must-be needs, 4 for one-dementional needs, 2 for attractive needs, 0 for neutral needs, and -3 for contrary needs [17]. After the Kano questionnaire survey, the priority of each user need was judged according to the Kano model based on user need categorization. Table 2 shows the types of dog care equipment needs and the values of user need categorization that determine the priority of the user need in the design phase.

TABLE II
NEED CATAGORIZATION AND IMPORTANCE IN DOG CARE EQUIPMENT (PARTIAL DATA)

Num	Demand	Type	Val	Operation
R1	simple styling	one-dementional	4	retain
R2	rounded and smooth form	one-dementional	4	retain
R4	regular ration feeding	must-be	5	retain
R8	pet monitoring	one-dementional	4	retain
R9	rest area	one-dementional	4	retain
R10	pet hygiene	neutral	0	delete

D. Construction of House of Quality matrix for dog care equipment

The design is based on the House of Quality Matrix which reflects the degree of correlation between every two elements in the relationship matrix: the importance of customer need, improvement rate after design, and product characteristics which determine the calculation for the weight of design elements. The weight value of design elements was finally calculated to determine the design objectives [17].

The relationship between the absolute weight of user elements and the importance of customer need, improvement rate, and product characteristics is expressed as

$$W = IRC. \quad (1)$$

Here, *I* represent the priority of all needs judged by the Kano model in Table 2. *R* represents the improvement rate between the quality value of the improved design goals and the current product functions. *C* represents product characteristics, and the assigned values are 1.5, 1.2, and 1. The results of the satisfaction questionnaire were used to determine a value for the quality of the current products on the market. Then, a quality value was ascertained by the designer to reflect the improvements based on the objectives in a newly designed product.

Values are assigned based on the uniqueness and fulfillment of a user's need. The higher the *C* value, the greater the competitive advantage is.

The relative weight of demand quality is calculated as

$$W_i' = W_i \,/\, \sum w_i. \quad (2)$$

Mass factor weight is expressed as

$$W_j = \sum W_j' R_{ij}. \quad (3)$$

Finally, the relative weight of the quality factor is calculated by the weight of the quality factor as Eq. (4).

$$W_j' = W_j \,/\, \sum W_j \quad (4)$$

According to the construction of the House of Quality Matrix, the size of the relative weight represents the design value. The larger the relative weight of the design element, the higher the design value of that element. The primary functions of the dog care equipment are feeding, entertainment, and companionship, while the secondary functions are fecal disposal, video monitoring, and photo documentation.

Case Study Results

A. Design plan of dog care equipment

According to the results of the House of Quality matrix calculation, dog care equipment needs four functional areas: feeding, entertainment, fecal disposal, and rest areas. A scheme design is divided into three stages: hand-drawn, three-dimensional modeling, and rendering.

Sketched plans were designed for three functional areas: feeding, entertainment and companionship, and fecal collection. Three or four sketches were drawn for each functional area. After the screening, spatial layout and integration were carried out for preferred schemes of the three functional areas, and then, several layout models were dawn to select the final scheme.

For scheme selection, the questionnaire survey was again adopted, and the questionnaire consisted of the scheme sketches for various implementation methods of each function. We invited users to give overall ratings for each scheme for form, function, and human-machine interaction. Then, the scheme with the highest rating in each functional area was selected for integration and layout. Again, users were invited to rate in-depth schemes of different layouts to select the final scheme.

B. Functional area design

The design to address the feeding function was mainly based on the consideration of feeding mode and form. It also included different ways of providing entertainment, companionship, and different modes of fecal collection and treatment. The scheme selection of functional areas is shown in Fig. 2.

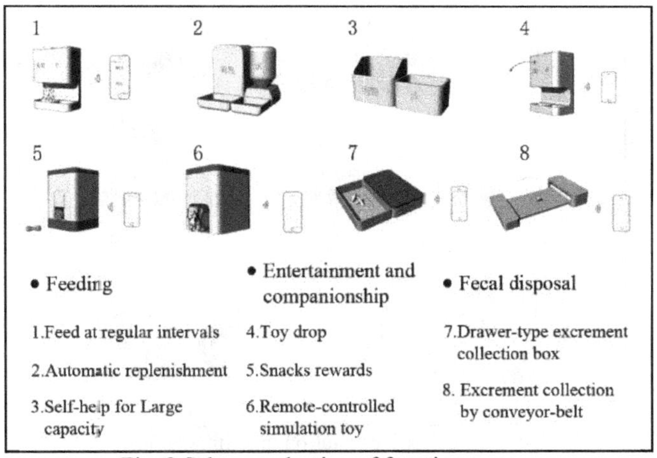

Fig. 2 Scheme selection of function areas.

C. Integration and layout of functional areas

After the first scheme survey of users, the highest rating for feeding function for the design was chosen as shown in Scheme 1 (Fig. 3) which provided regular and measured feeding by remote control through a mobile phone. For entertainment and companionship, Scheme 3 received the highest score. It achieved the purpose of entertainment and companionship through voice interaction and toy delivery. Scheme 2 for collecting and removing feces by a conveyor belt received the highest score for excrement management. After spatial layout and integration of the optimized schemes for each functional area, three layout models were submitted for selection by professional designers. Among the 10 designers who participated in the final scheme selection, 8 of them chose Scheme 1 as superior to Schemes 2 and 3 based on overall usability goals. The main advantages are a compact space layout and the easiness of operation and access when compared to the other two schemes (Fig. 3).

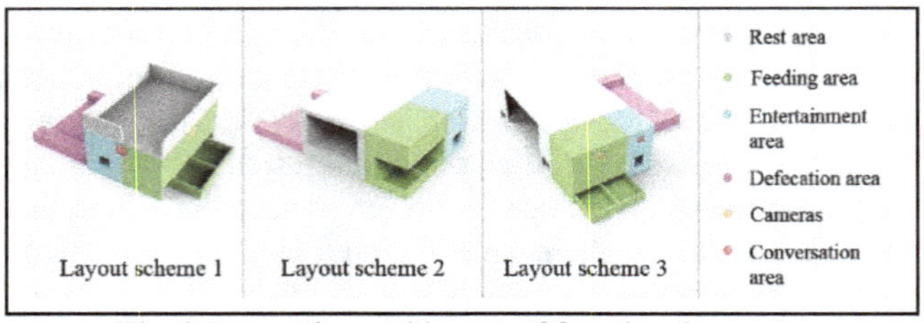

Fig. 3 Integration and layout of functional areas.

D. Final design

The design of dog care equipment also needs to consider the size of the dog. Pet dogs are divided into large, medium, and small body types. This study focused on products for small-sized dogs. The overall size of the device was determined to be 75 cm long, 45 cm wide and 48 cm high. The basic dimensions of the product and design are shown in Fig. 4.

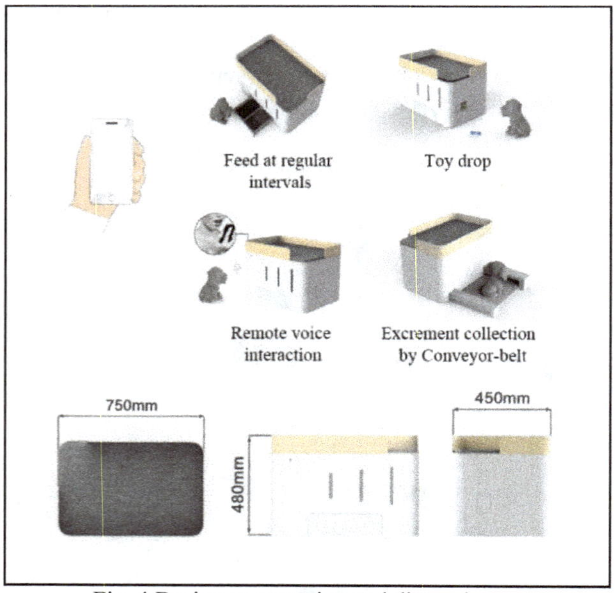

Fig. 4 Design presentation and dimensions.

Conclusion

Dog care equipment is the comprehensive embodiment of integrated innovative design in pet care. In this paper, the QFD method was used to construct the House of Quality matrix for dog care equipment according to user needs and satisfaction surveys from which the priority of design elements was determined. In the design phase, the QFD method sorted the priority of multiple design elements, determine logical relationships between user needs and design elements and ensured the reliability and effectiveness of the design process. QFD addresses the design problems of single function products by integrating multiple functions in a single and simple design to improve the dog care experience and provide diverse choices for the dog care market. Finally, the design of comprehensive dog care equipment products was taken as an example for the development of other design schemes and other size-scaled models to verify the feasibility of the scheme. This design method and process provides a reference for product developers to design for pet care needs in other pet animal markets.

References

[1] Hu Yang, Zhang Yanrong, Yu Jing. Current situation and prospect of pet industry in China [J]. Knowledge Economy, 2018, (10), 50-51.

[2] Zheng Lei,Wu Jiaqi, Ju Le, etc. Problems and Countermeasures of "Empty Nest Pet" Foster Care [J]. Value Engineering, 2017, (10):221-222.

[3] Chen Laihua. Current situation, influencing factors and development trend of pet industry in China [J]. China Animal Health, 2018, 20(8):4-8.

[4] Yang Xia, Xing Yanfei. Study On Furniture Design of Pet [J]. Industrial Design, 2018, (08),60-61.

[5] Xia Xingfei, Gao Yujie. Analysis of interactive pet dog furniture design [J]. Shandong Industrial Technology, 2017, (01), 260.

[6] Yang Danni. Design and research of canis familiars' toy[D]. Zhejiang : Zhejiang Sci-Tech University, 2016.

[7] Shen Yansong. A design of the intelligent pet feeder [J]. Journal of Zhangzhou Institute of Technology, 2018, 20(02), 49-52.

[8] Hu Zhenglian, Wang Qiao, Chen Xu, etc. Automatic pet feeding system for cleaning leftovers [J]. Internet of Things Technologies, 2018, 8(08),92-93.

[9] Chen Siyu, Yu Hao, Michelle Bai, etc. Intelligence Pet House Design Based on SCM Control [J]. Journal of Jiamusi University(Natural Science Edition), 2016,34(02),217-219.

[10] Mou Tiantian. Design and exploration of the feeding-function dog toy——take the leakage toy as an example [J]. Design, 2015, (17):98-99.

[11] Shang Lianhui. Automatic Barking Feeder for pets [J]. Technology Wind,2012,(03),109.

[12] Zhao Xiaojing. Common household cleaning techniques for pet dogs [J].Modern Animal Husbandry Science & Technology, 2013, (02), 51-53.

[13] Zhao Xinzhu. Discussion of the design and application of pet defecator in daily life [J]. Modern Decoration(Theory), 2016,(03),102.

[14] Xi Le, Zhang Hui, Cheng Jianxin. Modeling design of tourist service robot based on Fuzzy-Kano model [J]. Journal of Machine Design, 2017, 34(7):110-113.

[15] Yi Xuefeng, You Yana. Improved Design for Children's Beds Based on QFD and TRIZ [J] Packaging Engineering, 2017. 38(6):246-25.

[16] Li Yongfeng, Xu Yuwen. Design of QFD-based Elderly Smart Phone APP User Interfeface [J]. Packaging Engineering, 2016.37(14):95-99.

[17] Liu Zongming and Ge Bihui. Design of Elderly Household Companion Robot Based on QFD [J]. Journal of Graphics, 2018. 39(4):695-699.

[18] Yang Zhengqiang. Modeling design of friction welding machine based on QFD [J]. Journal of Machine Design, 2015, 32(3):119-122.

[19] Zhou Junjie,Fan Junjie,Shi Yuanwu,etc. Research on Development and Design of Medical Disinfection Products Based on QFD and DOE Model [J]. Machine Design & Research, 2020, 36(04):205-209.

[20] Chen Liang, Dou Hao, Wei Huang, etc. Product Innovation Design Based on QFD, TRIZ and Bionics [J]. China Mechanical Engineering, 2020, 31(11):1285-1295.

[21] Rafat Mahmud Hridoy,Md. Shohel Parvez,Nourin Mohsin. Joining Methods of Analytic Hierarchy Process (AHP), Kano Model and Quality Function Deployment (QFD) to Improve the Tractor's Seat Design for Tractor Drivers in Bangladesh[J]. American Journal of Industrial and Business Management, 2020, 10(05).

[22] Nicolas Haber,Mario Fargnoli,Tomohiko Sakao. Integrating QFD for product-service systems with the Kano model and fuzzy AHP[J]. Total Quality Management & Business Excellence, 2020, 31(9-10).

https://doi.org/10.1142/9789811238727_0050

Innovative Way of Puppet Show Exhibition

Shih-Mo Tseng*, Chao-Ming Wang**

Graduate School of Design Doctoral Program, Associate Professor Dept. of Digital Media Design
National Yunlin University of Science and Technology, Yunlin, Taiwan
*Corresponding Author Email: *mo0321000@yahoo.com.tw, **wangcm@yuntech.edu.tw

Abstract

Puppet show is a popular local opera in Taiwan. The production of puppets is a collection of various folk arts and crafts. The director and screenwriter shape the characters needed in the play according to the needs of different stories. The role of puppets is divided into six categories: sheng, dan, jing, mo, chou and za six categories. In response to the museum's display needs, develop integrated physical interface production, experiential display devices, etc. Participants enhance the role of cognition in puppetry, a better understanding of the characteristics of the memory and the role of cultural content, puppetry and cultural heritage thereby reaching the goal.

Keywords: puppet show, interactive exhibition, interactive experience, tangible user interface

Introduction

Puppet show is a local opera that originated in southern Fujian in China. It was originally a religious performance art with the main function of rewarding gods and removing evil spirits. Following the ancestors who immigrated to Taiwan from southern Fujian, it became the most popular opera performance among the three largest folk puppet shows. In the early days of the immigrant society, not only puppet show played the functions of religion, entertainment, and enlightenment in the daily life of the common people, but also became a potential force for social stability. The development of puppet show has always been closely related to religious beliefs. The use of moving puppets in religious rituals is one of the earliest "performances" of human behaviors [1]. To make the content of the puppet show closer to life, the characters are classified according to gender, age, status, and personality. Therefore, understanding the classification of roles becomes an introductory skill for learning puppet shows. This research focuses on understanding the classification of puppets' roles, and realizes the characteristics of puppets' roles through actual puppetry experience, and finally aims to inherit the puppetry culture.

Literature Review

A. Taiwanese Puppetry Culture

Among the countless local arts in Taiwan, puppet show should be the most familiar one [2]. Puppetry in late Ming and early Qing Dynasty began to develop in southern Fujian, Taiwan passed in the middle of the Qing Dynasty [3]. Before Taiwan's television media developed, watching puppet shows was one of the most important entertainment for the people. With the belief held various folk festivals and temple activities, sponsorship or private funding through the temples have a chance to watch. With the rapid rise of various audio-visual media, traditional puppet shows performances have suffered a major impact, and audience preferences have shifted to movies, TV and the Internet. Although there are still a few loyal audiences supports, but a huge loss of audience and the opportunity to perform significantly reduce the urge troupe gradually decline. Puppet show has undergone many changes in the development process of Taiwan, and suffered many setbacks. During the martial law period, it was unable to gather crowds to perform outdoors. This prompted the change of performance style to internal stage play. The government banned gongs and drums music instead of playing record music. Puppet shows can always be flexibly changed with the political environment and social atmosphere at that time, so that the content of puppet shows must break away from the framework of past historical stories, and the plot must be self-written, self-directed, and self-acted to develop the peak of golden puppet show. The reason why so much fuss troupe, is to let the audience have a sense of shock spot [4], changing appearance puppet show.

B. Interactive design and interactive display

(1) Interactive design

"Interactive" means a two-way communication, both sides will want to convey the message through interactive behavior, helps create awareness and understanding of the message content, and to give each other their reaction and feedback. Winograd is considered to design a variety of interactive design space so that people communicate and exchange [5]. Proposed interactive system plays in people and machinery intermediary role, responsible for data transmission, presentation and storage of information into the form recognizable people, but also to accept, process, respond to human movement [6].

(2) Interactive exhibition

With the development of information technology, digital information can enrich display content, and the integration of video and digital content can increase display attractiveness. If the increase in interactive games and VR display content can be achieved a high rating [7]. Multimedia display can be changed according to demand. Every exhibition content in the digital age requires interaction. Every visitor to the museum is no longer a passive viewer but an actual participant, and will play an important role in the exhibition experience [11].

(3) Tangible user interface

Nielsen believes that a good user interface must try to reduce the complexity of the software operation and use environment, making it simple, efficient and allowing users to enjoy the operation [12]. The physical user interface (Tangible User Interface, TUI for short) was proposed by Ishii and Ullmer [13] of the MIT Media Laboratory Tangible Media Group of the Massachusetts Institute of Technology. Through the proposed TUI theory, the way people interact in the real world and the digital world is introduced into multiple senses and multiple types. The TUI system is a three-dimensional physical interface to explore and imitate what they represent, from different perspectives. Thinking about interactive interface design [14]. In order to solve the shortcomings of GUI and compare the differences between the two, the TUI system has more intuition, and conveys information through the physical interface corresponding to relative spatial objects [15].

C. Interactive exhibition of puppet show

Traditional show with plenty of images, text and lay out a static entity shows a lot of information content, but visitors can only capture part of the content for a limited time. Domestic puppet theater museums still focus on static and physical displays. However, puppets were originally used for performances. If possible, museum visitors must have contact with puppets or even play with puppets [8]. Development of puppetry in different cultures have evolved differently. Eastern puppetry and multi-cultural worship rituals are related; whereas puppetry culture in the West in inclined towards enlightenment as to the nature of entertainment. Puppetry helps people escape from the reality of the role of self-action, puppetry and to replace the chronic child with family or outsiders' interactive experiments. Sick children prefer to use puppet characters to interact with other people [9]. Just as Indians believe that even Iranians, Afghans, Israelis and Americans who dislike each other can sit down and drink and talk about the performance after watching a puppet show [10].

Research Methods

A. Research Design

This research uses information technology to assist in the display of puppet show culture and design an interactive device "role playing". The content of traditional puppet show culture is presented through installation design and production, which can be used as museum experience design and innovation. Firstly, the six characters of Taiwanese traditional puppet show: sheng, dan, jing, mo, chou and za six categories (Fig.1) are classified as the themes of software development. Use each character's narration, background, music and audio content as the display method of puppets, and create devices that can be used for actual puppetry experience for visitors to experience in person, and then use interactive program development as participants to experience puppetry and interactive installation connection manner. The user opens the character environment with sensor cards, and manipulates the puppet's body to match the background music and verbal narration of the character, to understand the various character characteristics and differences of traditional puppet show, and further learn the cultural connotation of traditional puppet show.

Fig. 1 Six roles of puppets

B. Prototyping

To show the puppet scenario, this research designed a set of simple interactive stage as the prototype of the "role playing" system. Set up a projector and a set of RFID Reader on the stage. At the same time, a set of induction cards for various roles are produced, and the induction card is covered with RFID TAG. When the participant puts any character card on the re-induction station, the RFID Reader senses the RFID TAG in the card (Fig.2), and the device instantly turns on the audio and video content of the character, projecting the character's background on the background screen and playing the character's verbal and background music. All audio and video content are made in advance (Fig.3). After operating a character interaction, you can continue to select another character to continue the operation until all characters have been experienced, or you can choose to end the interaction halfway.

Fig. 2 Induction card

Fig. 3 The screen starts to play video

C. Expert interview

The research institute produced and developed "role-playing" installations based on self-edited audio-visual content and self-made interactive installations. After inviting four experts to experience the operation first, they will express their opinions on their respective areas of expertise and work needs. The four experts are university teachers, professional puppet masters, general manager of the puppet culture park and well-known puppet troupe (Table 1). Semi-structured interviews are used to conduct interviews, and the results of expert interviews are used as interactive installations for future improvements in accordance with.

TABLE 1
List of experts

	Employer	Job title	Outline of interview content	Expertise
P1	Department of Digital Content Technology, National University	Associate Professor	Puppet show content learning, teaching media design	New media art, installation art, digital art, technological art, exhibition design, etc.
P2	Puppet carving company	Principal	Store display, digital product catalog	Puppet head carving, puppet painting, puppet show teaching
P3	Puppetry Cultural Center	General manager	Cultural centers show, no autonomous navigation	Puppet show event planning, business marketing, cultural center tour, puppet show product development
P4	Well-known puppet theater	Leader	Learning puppetry, puppetry culture promotion	Puppetry performances even speak, screenwriter, stage design

Research and Analysis

This research uses a "role-playing" device (Fig.4) to first invite f our experts to experience the operation individually, and then use their respective areas of expertise and job requirements as interview content. The four experts are a university teacher, a professional puppet maker, the general manager of the puppet culture park, and the head of a well-known puppet troupe. Because each expert has different areas of expertise, the discussion will be different. According to the experts' suggestions classified as follows:

Fig. 4 Role-playing interaction diagram

A. "Role playing" is helpful to puppet show education and learning

Respondent P1 often leads students to do teaching action research as an educational scholar. Usually, students need to design special courses, and often need to compile textbooks and self-made teaching aids to implement the teaching content of special puppet shows. However, college students who have received teacher training at this stage lack good local culture textbooks, or must collect materials and compile textbooks by themselves. Unless students have professional backgrounds related to puppetry culture, it is difficult to produce complete textbook content. If students can use such teaching materials to do teaching action research, it is believed that there will be very good teaching results, and the taught students will also find it very interesting. This will also make it easier to understand the various character characteristics of puppet shows, and at the same time, it is easy to generate memory, which is very important for learning.

B. "Role playing" helps puppets to choose their roles

Respondent P2 is a professional puppet engraver. He often encounters customers who don't know the role of puppetry clearly and cannot choose the role of puppetry correctly. Role-playing can provide customers with a good reference. Every puppeteer who comes to find a puppet can describe the role of the puppet, and use performances to show the characteristics of the role, which will meet the needs of the troupe. Role-playing can increase the consensus between the puppeteer and the sculptor, and help the puppeteer get the role puppets they really need.

C. "Role-playing" can assist cultural centers to conduct self-directed tours

Respondent P3 is the operator of the puppet show cultural center, she often encountered many visitors in the cultural center at the same time, resulting in insufficient navigation manpower. Role-playing allows visitors to operate interactive installations by themselves, allowing visitors to conduct self-directed viewing, which increases visitors' knowledge of puppet play roles and relieves the pressure of some museum guides. If the number of visitors is small, role-playing can also be used instead of personnel guidance. Through the introduction of audio-visual media, the content is more accurate than the staff guide, and at the same time, you can experience more fun by personally operate puppets.

D. "Role playing" helps promote school puppet show teaching

Respondent P4 is a well-known leader of the troupe, he often needs to provide community and school puppet show teaching. The role-playing content covers every puppet show characters and verbal narratives. It is suitable as a campus teaching experiment teaching material. The content also includes actual puppetry experience. It is very suitable as a local cultural teaching material for students who need teaching practice. In terms of professional puppeteer training, such content is not enough to meet actual performance needs. After all, there are so many roles performed by the troupe that cannot be covered by just six roles, but it is enough for school club teaching.

Conclusions and Discussion

This research uses digital audio and video and digital sensing to create an interactive display system. Participants can learn various role's action and verbal expressions by operating the puppets. After interviews with experts such as educators, professional sculptors, operators of puppet theater museums, and the troupe leader. The following conclusions were reached:

A. *Role-playing can enhance the participants' awareness of the role of puppet show, increase their preference and contribute to the promotion of puppet show culture.*
B. *Role-playing improves the ability to interpret roles through actual puppet experience, and further learns various role classifications and role characteristics.*
C. *In response to the trend of the times, the combination of digital technology and interactive design will increase the sense of technology and interest in traditional puppet show learning experience.*
D. *Role-playing provides a brand-new mode that can be applied to guide introductions of different puppets, increasing the depth and breadth of puppetry learning.*
E. *The interactive display experience has been confirmed by expert experiments, and the interactive display experience can be extended to other cultural promotion activities in the future.*

This system is more attractive than the traditional static display. Aiming at the traditional puppet show culture display, it provides participants with a brand-new exhibition experience. All aspects such as display method, audio-visual content, operation experience, etc. have been carefully designed. The audio-visual content is based on the actual performance situation of the puppeteer on the stage. It can be used as a local cultural teaching material to enhance the participants' cognitive function of the role of the puppet show. Experience operation can deepen the memory of the cultural content of puppet show. After the experience of the experts, they have confirmed that the role-playing display type is more abundant than the static display, and they are satisfied with the video content and experience display type of this installation.

References

[1] Robin Erik Ruizendaal(1999) *Puppet World World Puppetry*: 1999 Yunlin International Festival of Opera Festival album, Yunlin County Cultural Center,(pp. 25-28)

[2] Liu Huanyue (1993). *Fenghua Peerless Hand Art: Taiwan's Puppet Show, updated and reprinted, pages*: 14-79. Taipei: Taiyuan Publishing House.

[3] Zhang Xinan, 2004. *"Study on Huang Haidai and His Handicraft Drama Book"*, pages: 1-29. Taipei: Taiwan Student Bookstore Co., Ltd.

[4] Qiu Wude, & Drama. (2010). Golden Light Revelation: *The Rise of Taiwan Golden Light Art.* The right to speak is published.

[5] Winograd, T. & Wilson, C. (1997) *The usability engineering framework for product design and evaluation.* In M. G. Helander, T. K. Landauer, and P. V. Prabju (eds.) *Handbook of Human-Computer Interaction. Amsterdam*, Holland: Elsevier, pp. 653-688.

[6] David Benyon (2014) *Designing Interactive Systems-A Comprehensive Guide to HCI, UX and interaction design.* 3rd Edition, Pearson, Boston, p10.

[7] Cesário, V., Matos, S., Radeta, M., & Nisi, V. (2017, September). *Designing interactive technologies for interpretive exhibitions: enabling teen participation through user-driven innovation. In IFIP Conference on Human-Computer Interaction* (pp. 232-241). Springer, Cham.

[8] Felicia van Deth, 1999, *Can puppet play and puppet play be represented in a museum environment*, Proceedings of the 1999 International Puppet Show Symposium, Yunlin County Cultural Center, pp. 284~295

[9] Nutting, R. (2015). The Strength of Children Externalizing the Effects of Chronic Illness Through Narrative Puppetry. *Journal of Family Psychotherapy*, 26(1), 9–14.

[10] Skipitares, T. (2013). A new aesthetic in Indian puppetry. *PAJ: A Journal of Performance and Art*, 35(3), 61-68.

[11] Grammenos, D., Zabulis, X., Michel, D., Padeleris, P., Sarmis, T., Georgalis, G., ... & Adam-Veleni, P. (2013). A prototypical interactive exhibition for the archaeological museum of thessaloniki. *International Journal of Heritage in the Digital Era*, 2(1), 75-99.

[12] Nielsen, J., 2003. Usability 101: Introduction to Usability. Nielsen Norman Group.

[13] Ullmer, B., & Ishii, H. (1997, October). The metaDESK: models and prototypes for tangible user interfaces. In Proceedings of the 10th annual *ACM symposium on User interface software and technology* (pp. 223-232).

[14] Schneider, B., Sharma, K., Cuendet, S., Zufferey, G., Dillenbourg, P., & Pea, R. (2016). Using mobile eye-trackers to unpack the perceptual benefits of a tangible user interface for collaborative learning. *ACM Transactions on Computer-Human Interaction (TOCHI)*, 23(6), 1-23.

[15] Macaranas, A., Antle, A. N., & Riecke, B. E. (2012, February). Bridging the gap: attribute and spatial metaphors for tangible interface design. In Proceedings of the *Sixth International Conference on Tangible, Embedded and Embodied Interaction* (pp. 161-168).

https://doi.org/10.1142/9789811238727_0051

Localization of Catholicism through the Study of Religious Images — A Case Study of the Our Lady Queen of China Cathedral Tainan Diocese, Taiwan

Yu-Jyun Chung[1*], Fang-Suey Lin[2]

[1] Graduate School of Design, Doctoral Program, National Yunlin University of Science and Technology, Yunlin, Taiwan
[2] Graduate School of Design, National Yunlin University of Science and Technology, Yunlin, Taiwan
*Corresponding Author Email: fga82129@gmail.com

Abstract

Catholicism, a global religion, has been blended with local cultures and customs over a long period during the spread of the religion. Our Lady of China has become a bridge between Catholicism and local cultures, as faith communities change and integrate with local cultures. The Diocese of Tainan is located in southwestern Taiwan. Features of Chinese and Western cultures have been merged into the architecture of Our Lady Queen of China of Cathedral Tainan Diocese. Its decoration and murals are historical, local, and unique with obvious ethnic features. Historical and field study has been adopted as the method of this study. We also analyzed religious images in an iconological analysis method. Religious images have been analyzed, described, interpreted, and compared in terms of their symbolic meanings by using the Our Lady Queen of China Cathedral Tainan Diocese as the study object. Our analysis reveals that the religious images are a fusion of representative religious images of Chinese and Western culture and presented with decorative themes such as figures, costumes, bible stories, geometrical patterns, and abstract patterns. The Our Lady Queen of China Cathedral Tainan Diocese adopts the local culture to highlight the characteristics of the sacred space of the church. Through the spread of beliefs and the transition between geographic regions and the cultures which were originally in conflict with each other merge and deliver the beliefs of Jesus Christ.

Keywords: Catholicism, localization, Our Lady of China, religious images, Iconology

Introduction

In 1054 A.D., Christianity first split into Roman Catholicism (Catholicism) and Orthodoxy (Eastern Orthodoxy). In 1517, the Reformation took place in Europe and the "Protestant Christianity" [1] broke away from Roman Catholicism (Catholicism). The introduction of Catholicism into the Eastern World began in the late 16th century. Although the missionary process had gone through different periods and regions, it had always been characterized by localization. To bridge the cultural divide and to gain the recognition of the local people, localization is always a fundamental principle of missionary work. In the process of missionary work, the Catholic Church has radicalized and changed the Eastern and Western cultures qualitatively [2]. The forming of Our Lady of China occurred when the Holy See tock the lead in the development of Catholicism in China and established a complete religious system. For Christianity to be accepted by the Chinese people, the spread of the faith must be based on Chinese patterns of thought and apply the materials of Chinese philosophy, religion, literature, and society. In other words, Christianity must adopt Chinese culture as the medium of expression of its beliefs. Rituals, costumes, architecture, and other elements of Christianity should incorporate Chinese culture as much as possible to localize them [3].

As Catholicism is a global religion, it is often blended with local cultures or customs in the long history of spreading the religion. In spreading, a balance has to be reached between Catholicism and local customs to complete its local development in each region. The founding of Our Lady of China was regarded as the representative of Catholicism in China and attracted special attention from church bodies mainly formed by Chinese people. The building of Our Lady Queen of China Cathedral Tainan Diocese has many symbolic images representing some metaphors of both Chinese and Western Catholicism. In this study, we focus on the religious images that are used to decorate the Our Lady Queen of China Cathedral Tainan Diocese to explore the symbolic meanings and cultural values of these images.

The purpose of this study is to understand the symbolic meaning of the religious images of the decoration of the Our Lady Queen of China Cathedral Tainan Diocese. It further aims to find the influence of Our Lady of China on the Catholic faith. This study explores the symbolic and cultural significance of the religious images of the architectural decoration of the Our Lady Queen of China Cathedral Tainan Diocese and applies the methodology of iconography to depict, analyze, and explain the local mechanism of the integration of Chinese culture and Western religious culture.

Literature Reviews

A. Introduction of Catholicism into China

Christianity first entered China in 635 A.D. (the 9th year of the Zhenguan era of the Emperor Taizong of Tang) when the Syrian missionary Alopen arrived at Chang'an (Xi'an City in Shaanxi Province), the capital of the Tang Dynasty, via the Silk Road from Persia and began his missionary work. During the Ming Dynasty, foreigners were forbidden to enter China except for ambassadors who paid tribute and merchants in Guangzhou. It was not until the end of the Ming Dynasty that

Roman Catholic missionaries were permitted to enter China, as the emperors needed cannons and calendars from the Western World. The high-ranking officials of the Ming Dynasty also wanted to enrich the country and strengthen the army with scientific knowledge. As a result of the efforts of Matteo Ricci and many other well-educated missionaries, who endeavored to integrate Catholic doctrines with Confucian culture in China and make friends with celebrities, Catholicism made great progress and development during this period [4].

B. Introduction of Catholicism into Taiwan

In 1632, a Spanish Catholic "Father Esquivel" landed in Huwei (Tamsui) in northern Taiwan and established a church. In 1859, Spanish Fr. Fernando Sainz and some Chinese missionaries arrived in Taogou (Kaohsiung) and established the Holy Spirit Church (now the Minor Basilica-Cathedral of the Holy Rosary, Kaohsiung), which officially introduced Catholicism to Taiwan. Catholicism had been introduced to Taiwan for nearly 400 years. Taiwan has been under the rule of the Dutch Republic, the Spanish Empire, the Qing Dynasty, the Empire of Japan, and the Kuomintang government which relocated from Mainland China to Taiwan. Taiwan's history has also affected the development of Catholicism [5]. Catholicism has been introduced to Taiwan for nearly 400 years. Taiwan has been under the rule of the Dutch Republic, the Spanish Empire, the Qing Dynasty, the Empire of Japan, and the Kuomintang government which relocated from Mainland China to Taiwan. Taiwan's history has also affected the development of Catholicism [5]. In 1949, after the establishment of the Chinese communist regime, Chinese Catholics were persecuted by the government. The persecution caused a large number of Chinese clergy to move from mainland China to Taiwan, becoming the mainstream of the development of Chinese Catholicism in that period [6].

C. Our Lady Queen of China Cathedral Tainan Diocese, Taiwan

Located in Tainan City, Taiwan, with the appearance of a Chinese palace, this building is the Our Lady Queen of China Cathedral Tainan Diocese, commonly known as the Church of Our Lady on Kaishan Road. When Catholicism was introduced into China, it was reformed into a faith suitable for the Chinese society to adapt to the customs of the country and to allow the Chinese culture to be integrated with the Gospel of Jesus Christ. The brief history of the establishment of Our Lady Queen of China Cathedral Tainan Diocese is shown in Table 1.

TABLE 1
Brief History of the Our Lady Queen of China Cathedral Tainan Diocese

Year	Milestone
1963	Bishop Luo Guang, the 1st Bishop of Tainan Diocese, chose the site and the design himself. The cornerstone of the Cathedral was consecrated, and the building was named as the "Our Lady Queen of China Cathedral".
1964	The Cathedral was inaugurated and blessed by Giuseppe Caprio, then the Apostolic Pro-Nuncio to China.
1974	1974 was the 50th anniversary of the consecration of Catholic churches to Our Lady of China in Taiwan. The 2nd Bishop of Tainan Diocese, Bishop Paul Cheng Shi-guang, invites Cardinal Paul Yü Pin, then the President of Chinese Regional Bishops' Conference, to consecrate Our Lady of China once again, and declared the "Our Lady Queen of China Cathedral Tainan Diocese" as a place of pilgrimage.

Research Methods

A. Historical Research

Historical research is a method of studying history and its evolution, by collecting and analyzing related literature and data to categorize religious images. Through the collection of historical documents, we provide the necessary information for our research and then use relevant publications and articles, books, and theses related to Catholicism, Chinese architectural decoration, colorful paintings, patterns, and decorations in China and Taiwan to explore and categorize the collected documents.

B. Field Research

We conducted an on-site investigation and observed the religious images of the building's interior decoration. From direct observation of visual elements such as colors, patterns, lines, and so on, to interpretation of the meaning of the contents, and then deepening into the symbolic meaning of the cultural context, detailed photographs and records were taken.

C. Iconography

Iconography studies the theme and meaning of a work of art as a method of analyzing it. By 1955, Erwin Panofsky had already defined three levels of image interpretation: description, analysis, and interpretation. At the same time, "the interpretation of pictorial hermeneutics" is also used instead of "broad pictorial analysis", and the principles of interpretation are more closely intertwined with each other. The author of the book "*The Meaning and Interpretation of Visual Arts: Iconography*" has merged the two original distinction tables of iconography from Panofsky's books (published in 1939 and 1955) into one table which is shown below.

Analysis of Religious Images: Our Lady Queen of China Cathedral Tainan Diocese, Taiwan

A. Iconographic Analysis

Gabriele Kopp-Schmidt, a contemporary German scholar of iconography, has compiled an outline of the iconography process which is quite effective. She extracted the corresponding wordings from Panofsky's works and proposed a more detailed process than Panofsky's classification table as shown in Table 2.

TABLE 2
Three strata of Iconographic Analysis

Stratum	Description
1st Stratum	Pre-iconographic description: Grasping the phenomenological meanings of an artist's work through the five senses, sense of humanity, and world views.
2nd Stratum	Iconographic analysis: Grasping the connotations of the work
3rd Stratum	Interpretation of hermeneutics: Grasping the meanings of a document: its actual meanings or content. The viewer's interest shifts from the implications of iconography to regarding the works as the records of contemporary perceptions.

B. Caisson

The Our Lady Queen of China Cathedral Tainan Diocese has a caisson above the sanctuary. A caisson was also known as a "Tianjing" in ancient China. It is a kind of decorative ceiling structure in Chinese architecture, which is usually built in the ceiling above the throne of palaces or the Buddhist altar in temples. The patterns on a caisson are square, round, octagonal, etc. Such the structure can make the main hall of the temple look higher and more spacious, presenting a holy space for religious doctrine [9], as shown in Fig. 1.

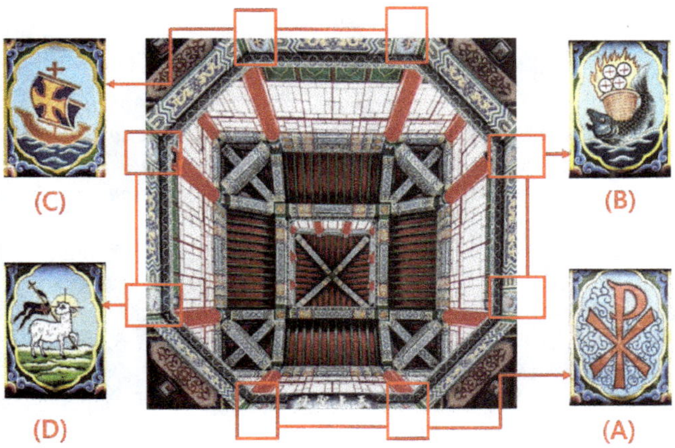

Fig. 1 The Caisson of the Our Lady Queen of China Cathedral Tainan Diocese

The caisson is octagonal, and each side of the caisson has a symbol of Jesus Christ, images of Bible stories, and patterns representing Chinese culture, as shown in Table 3.

TABLE 3
Religious Image Analysis: The Caisson of the Our Lady Queen of China Cathedral Tainan Diocese

(A) Symbol of Jesus Christ	(B) Five Loaves and Two Fish

(C) Calming the Storm	(D) Young Male Goat on Day of Atonement

Iconographic Analysis

Stratum	Description
1st Stratum	(A) The Chi Rho monogram is a symbol for the Greek ΙΗΣΟΥΣΧΡΙΣΤΟΣ (Jesus Christ) constituted by the abbreviation of the first letters of the two words, I and CR (C or chi, and R or rho) respectively [10]. (B) The Bible (John 6:1-14) has the story of a boy with five small barley loaves and two small fish. (C) The Bible (Mark 4:35-41) has the story that Jesus said to the waves, "Quiet! Be still!" (D) The Bible (Leviticus 16:15) has the story that the people would offer a male goat during the Day of Atonement. The four images (A, B, C, and D) are surrounded by a geometric pattern look like a cloud.
2nd Stratum	(A)The Chi-Rho is one of the earliest cross-shaped symbols used in Christianity, and it is not a real cross [11]. (B) When five barley loaves and two fish were given into Jesus' hands, five thousand people were fed and there was plenty of leftovers. It is represented by the image of a carp. It is a symbol of wealth and prosperity in Eastern culture. 魚 (fish) and 餘 (surplus) are homophonic in Chinese, implying a rich and beautiful life [12]. (C)The lake in the Bible, called the Sea of Galilee, is sometimes stormy [13]. After Jesus rebuked the wind, the wind stopped. And the lake became calm. (D) The high priest was to slaughter a male goat for a sin offering to make atonement in the Holy of Holies to remove all the filth of Israelites. The goat was an essential animal in the daily life of Israelites. Goats were clean animals to be used as sacrificial animals in the sacrifices [14]. The Chinese character for "goat" (羊) is the same as "luckiness" (祥) in ancient China. "祥" means "auspicious" in Chinese [15]. The cirrus cloud patterns in four images (A, B, C, and D) are usually S-shaped to form a continuous curl to indicate that the meaning will never end [16].
3rd Stratum	(A)The symbol of Jesus Christ makes people recall Jesus Christ's suffering and symbolizes his status [11]. (B) At the time of the Bible, fish and loaves were the basic food and few people could afford meat. Jesus showed the miracle of increasing the quantity of food to feed the 5,000 people [13]. (C)The miracle that Jesus performed. It is capable of achieving acts that transcend the general natural order [17]. (D) In the Old Testament era, a man had to be cleansed of his sins by offering an animal to die as a scapegoat for his sins [18]. All four images (A, B, C, and D) have cirrus cloud patterns in them. Clouds, the source of rain, moisturize everything and are therefore regarded as a sign of good luck [16].

Analysis and Discussion

The decorative arts in traditional Chinese architecture are often based on human figures, fairy tales, geometric patterns, plants and animals, auspicious animals, and abstract patterns. When Western religions were first introduced into Taiwan, many Taiwanese were not yet ready to accept them, so missionaries had to express their religious connotations in the architecture, while at the same time accommodating local preferences. A Catholic church is a building full of artistic and symbolic symbols. The architectural forms and decorative systems are all closely related to religious doctrines [19]. Traditional Chinese auspicious patterns are usually expressing some auspicious ideas, and those blessings are conveyed through some allegorical, symbolic, and exaggerated ways, which are visualized and illustrated to express people's desire and blessings for good fortune [20]. The religious images above the caisson use patterns representing both Chinese culture and biblical stories. The patterns are the artistic expressions of people's original thinking and consciousness, reflecting their pursuit and desire for a better life. It is found that animal images have opposite or similar meanings in Eastern and Western cultures. The results also reveal the differences between the Eastern and the Western Worlds in terms of faith, culture, life, and conceptual thinking. Those religious images have visual symbolism which is different from that of Western images with the symbolic elements of Chinese culture. However, the connotations of the images are consistent with the Western Catholic faith.

Conclusions and Recommendations

The Catholic Church places great emphasis on adaptation to the society of the time and the place, which can be regarded as a compromise and must be in tune with the local society and culture. In the process of cultural contact and change, the social statuses of the first believer and the first missionary also influenced the degree of integration after acceptance and the preferences to cultural elements, which results in different outcomes such as assimilation, adaptation, or even resistance. At that time, Catholic architecture, religious art, and literature in China were slowly localized by Chinese culture. When the two different cultures came into contact, the foreign and the local culture interacted with each other, until the foreign culture gradually evolved and finally took root in the region as a new local culture [21]. This study takes the religious images of the Our Lady Queen of China Cathedral Tainan Diocese as the main target of the research and conducts a detailed analysis. In this paper, the local religious culture, Our Lady of China is used to highlight the characteristics of the holy space of the church. The process of cultural change resulting from the contact between foreign cultures and the local Chinese culture has led to the development of a localized reform of religion. However, the process of localization must be based on a foundation built on the perspectives of both sides. The Catholic Church, in conformity with the universal spirit of religion, embraces the cultures of different regions and incorporates them into Catholicism for preaching the gospel. The church is not only a holy space but also a living space, fully demonstrating the fusion of the Eastern and Western cultures and the realization of localization, as well as highlighting the importance of religious faith. The special symbolic significance of the Cathedral can be understood through the historical contexts and the religious images that are decorated on the building. The conflicts and fusion of cultures allow us to understand the process of integration of local cultures. The Our Lady Queen of China Cathedral Tainan Diocese was built as a church for making Chinese culture and the Gospel of Jesus Christ blend.

References

[1] Zhao Qiang-Nian, *Jesus in China: The Beauty of Chinese Churches*, Taichung: Jerusalem Studio, 2011, pp. 22.

[2] Zhu Su-Zhen and Li Jian-Ping, *Journal of National Pingtung University of Education: Liberal Arts and Social Sciences*, Pingtung, 39, pp. 93-116, 2012.

[3] Wu Zi-Ming , *Jesus in China: The Beauty of Chinese Churches*, Taipei: Cosmic Light, 2006, pp. 121-127.

[4] Zhao Qiang-Nian, *Christian Universities in China from the Perspective of Global Regionalization*, Taichung: Jerusalem Studio, 2011, pp. 23-27.

[5] Yu Jia-Ling, "A study on the mural paintings in the Yanshui Holy Spirit Catholic Church," unpublished, 2009, pp. 20.

[6] Lin Shu-Zhen, "Wanjin Catholic Church and the change of faith of plains indigenous peoples in Taiwan," unpublished, 2004, pp. 58.

[7] Cui He-Ting and Cui Xuan, *The Art of Wall and Floor Decoration in Traditional Chinese Architecture*, Beijing: China Machine Press, 2009, pp. 140.

[8] Chen Huai-En, *The Meaning and Interpretation of Visual Arts: Iconography*, Taipei: Asif Book, 2008, pp. 235.

[9] Zhang Shu-Xian, *World of Antiquity*, Taiyuan, 6, pp. 35-41, 2003.

[10] Chen Huai-En, *The Meaning and Interpretation of Visual Arts: Iconography*, Taipei: Asif Book, 2008, pp. 52.

[11] China Evangelical Lutheran Church-LC, (2020, October 27), *Christian Symbols and Their Meanings*, China Evangelical Lutheran Church-LC, http://www.celc.org.tw/portal_c2_cnt.php?owner_num=c2_442459&button_num=c2&folder_id=

[12] Tianjin Yangliuqing Art Club, *The Encyclopedia of Chinese Auspicious Patterns*, Taipei: Deeten Publishing, 2006, pp. 123.

[13] Craig S. Keener, *New Testament Background Notes*, Taipei: Campus Books, 2006, pp. 152-153.

[14] En Pei, *TJC Holy Spirit Monthly*, Taichung, 476, pp. 66, 2017.

[15] Li Cang-Yan, *The Encyclopedia of Chinese Auspicious Patterns*, Taipei: SMC Publishing, 1988.

[16] Ancient Culture Research Unit, *Pictorial Dictionary of Classical Chinese Patterns*, New Taipei: Evergreen Publishing, 1997, pp. 167.

[17] Research Center for Liturgy, (2020, October 27), *Christian Symbols and Their Meanings*, Fu Jen Faculty of Theology of St. Robert Bellarmine, https://reurl.cc/Q3Nl50

[18] Yu Jia-Ling, "A study on the mural paintings in the Yanshui Holy Spirit Catholic Church," unpublished, 2009, pp.110.

[19] Lin Shu-Zhen, "Wanjin Catholic Church and the change of faith of plains indigenous peoples in Taiwan," unpublished, 20094, pp.82-123.

[20] Li Jin-Hong, *Chinese Art Patterns: Traditional Patterns*, Taipei: Wen-Guo Publishing, 2000.
[21] Lin Zhi-Ping, *Proceedings of the International Symposium on Christianity and the Chinese Indigenous Church Movement*, Taipei: Cosmic Light, 1990, pp. 637.

https://doi.org/10.1142/9789811238727_0052

Morphological System Study of Tank-Type Character in MOBA Games

LuoXuan Zhou, BaoJun Chu*, Jun He

Xiamen Academy of Arts & Design Fuzhou University, Xiamen, Fujian, China
*Corresponding Author Email: t17075@fzu.edu.cn

Abstract

With the development of e-sports, the market scale of MOBA (Multiplayer Online Battle Arena) games continues to grow. The popularity of MOBA games cannot be separated from its core mechanism. Players use different types of characters to use different tactics in the game process, and the diversified character design enriches the fun of MOBA games. Tank-type character is one of the main character types in MOBA games and plays a very important role in the game process. In this paper, through quantitative analysis, the morphological features of tank-type characters in the mainly popular MBOA game products are analyzed. By comparing the morphological features used in this type of character design, the image of tank-type characters in MOBA games that meet users' needs is studied to provide a theoretical basis for the design method of tank-type characters in MOBA games.

Keywords: MOBA game, computer game, tank-type character battle system

Introduction

The maturity of electronic information technology and the vigorous development of electronic competitive sports have promoted the continuous innovation of technology and playing methods in the game industry, and have produced a series of new types of games. MOBA games are particularly prominent in the diversified categories of electronic competitive games in the market. The vast array of character choices is the soul of MOBA games. In MOBA games, users are provided with diverse and distinctive character choices, which adds infinite possibilities to the development of each round of game and brings richer and more personalized game experience to users.

Tank-type characters are one of the main character types in MOBA games. Based on the diversity of choice of MOBA game characters, how to design the form of the tank-type characters to meet the needs of users is a big problem in the MOBA game design process. The form design of tank-type characters in MOBA games lacks systematic analysis and theoretical basis. In this study, tank-type characters in several popular MOBA games were collected through statistics and comparison of their morphological features, and the morphological features of tank-type character design in MOBA games that meet user needs were analyzed and summarized, providing a theoretical basis for the design methods of tank-type characters in MOBA games.

Tank-type Roles in MOBA Games

A. MOBA Game Overview

MOBA games are derivative categories of character-playing and strategy game. In the process of the game, players are divided into two camps. They choose a single character from various types of characters for control, and use the character attributes to cooperate with the team to use different tactics to compete with each other on the regular map.

MOBA games have become a hot category in the game industry, from the emergence of DOTA to the carnival craze triggered by the 2018 League of Legends global finals. In 2018, global game industry revenue totaled 137. 9 billion dollars and MOBA games accounted for 35% of the market share when the number of games only accounted for 1% of the total market. While the MOBA game market continues to grow, in order to seize the game market, there are many MOBA game products without design thinking. How to balance the roles of different types of morphological system differences, enhance professional design method of character form, make the user experience more in line with the direction of the character design is a form worthy of study.

B. MOBA Game Character Types

With the development of the game industry, when a single type of character design can't meet the user's needs for autonomy and individualization, a richer character system emerges as the times require.

MOBA games typically have six types of characters (tank-type, warrior-type, assassin-type, mage-type, Archer-Type, Support-Type), which provide users with more diverse options while balancing team attributes. Different types of characters have different attributes and play different characters in the team (Fig. 1).

Tank-type: This character type has strong survivability, outstanding defensive ability, and is responsible for absorbing damage in group warfare.

Warrior-type: This type has certain maneuverability, defense and output ability, and is a relatively average character type, which is responsible for fighting against the weak survival ability of the enemy team.

Mage-type: This type usually has deceleration, daze and other control skills, with strong teamwork ability.

Assassin-type: This type has strong mobility, multi displacement skills, can quickly cut into the battlefield to attack enemy teams.

Archer-type: That is, the ADC in the team, with high damage, is the main output of the team.

Support-type: This type has a strong team gain ability and is responsible for healing and gain in the team.

Classification of the Morphological Features of Game Character Design

A. Morphological Features of Game Character Design

The user's understanding of the character starts from identifying the morphological features of the character. The morphological features of the game character design are the epitome of the whole background, attributes and positioning design of the character.

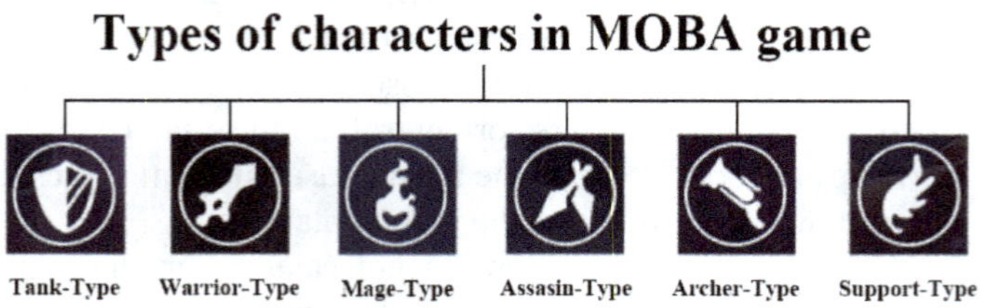

Fig. 1 MOBA game character types.

a. The morphological features of the game character design show the character's identity and personality characteristics to the players. Users can judge the basic information of the character from its image and posture. For example, the strong and upright human image creates a righteous and brave human warrior.

b. The morphological features of the game character design directly describe the numerical attributes of the character. For example, assassin-type characters are characterized by many skills of displacement and strong mobility. Therefore, the form design of assassin-type characters generally highlights the morphological features of "lightness and agility" .

c. The morphological features of game character design highlight the differences of characters. The rich character system in the game enlarges the need for character recognition. Characters need distinct morphological features to differentiate different characters in the same game scene.

B. Design Method of Game Character

The character is the soul of the game, which runs through the whole game and guides the development of the game. An excellent game character design can bring users richer game experience and stronger emotional resonance. Game character design can start from plot planning. The design of game characters depends on the background story of the game. Through the numerical planning and plot planning of the figurative characters, from rationality to sensibility, and through the designers' understanding of the text, the visual image of the characters is shaped and the character characteristics of the characters are explored. Game character design can also start from art. Exaggerated, abstract artistic expression techniques are used to highlight the character of the modeling design. Users are connected to game characters through visual impact, which has a strong appeal. Generally, it is suitable for game products that emphasize game mechanism (Fig. 2).

Morphological Features Analysis of MOBA Game Tank-type Character Design

A. Tank-type Characters in Popular MOBA Games

Through the analysis of the 2019 hot MOBA game ranking list of Sina game product database, Homeless star, 3dm and other game data stations, as well as the reference to the design of major popular MOBA game characters on the market, four MOBA games, which are "League of Legends", "Heroes of the Storm", "Arena of Valor", "Onmyoji Arena" have a huge user base while retaining the traditional MOBA game mechanism. Therefore, the four game products were taken as examples to analyze the demand proportion of their tank-type characters.

As can be seen from the chart, Tank-Type characters are one of the most important types of characters in popular MOBA games, accounting for between 14% and 21% of the total number of game characters (Fig. 3).

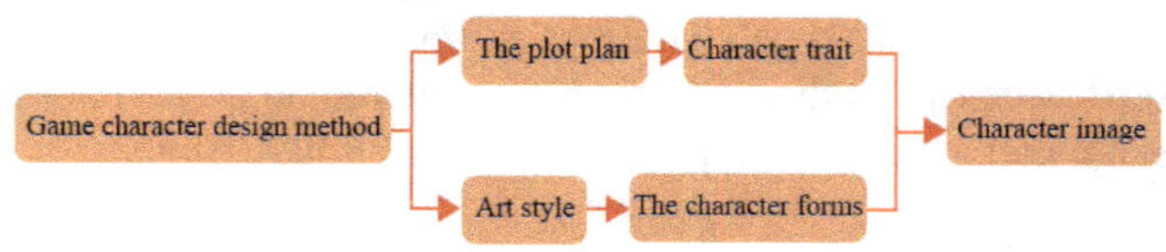

Fig. 2 Design method of game character.

B. Proportion Analysis of Morphological Features of Tank-Type Character Design in MOBA Game

The choice of game characters reflects the user's demand for game characters to a certain extent. In order to materialize users' potential demand for Tank-Type character design, in this study, the four popular MOBA games studied above were statistically analyzed, their morphological features were summarized, and the quantitative differences of each morphological feature were compared (Fig. 4).

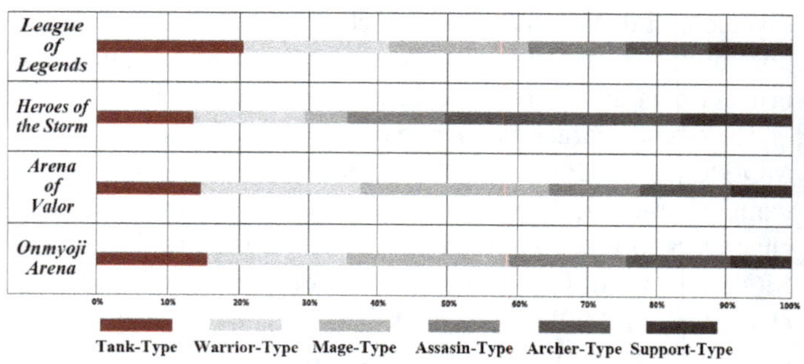

Fig. 3 Analysis of tank-type roles in popular MOBA games.

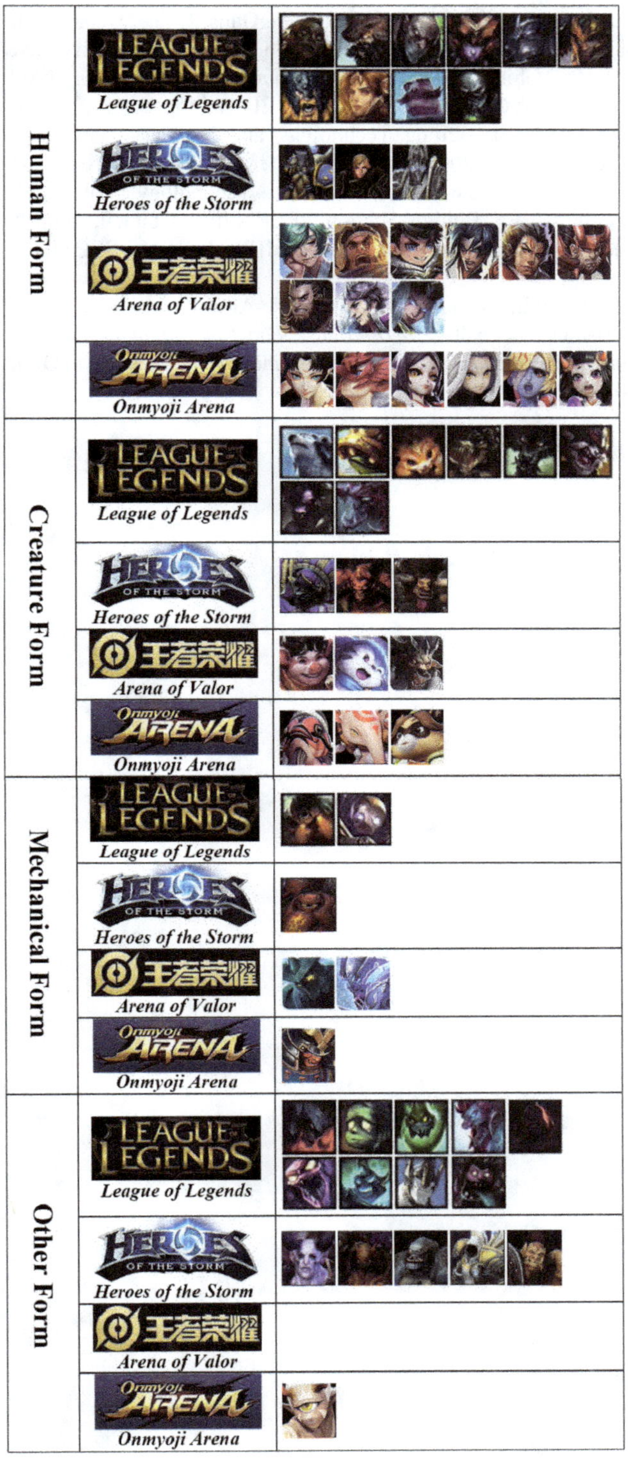

Fig. 4 Classification of morphological features of tank-type characters design in popular MOBA games.

The image of tank-type characters in four popular MOBA games can be divided into four categories according to their morphological features: human form, creature form, mechanical form and other forms. Character images with significant human characteristics are human forms, which retain most of the human skeleton structure and body shape. Tank-type character in creature form refers to character image with other biological characteristics other than human, or human character image combined with other biological characteristics, such as the character "Gnar the Missing Link" in the form of big ear fox in League of Legends and the character "Piggie" in the form of pig man in Arena of Valor. Machine armor, bionic robots and other characters with mechanical sense are classified as mechanical forms, while mythical creatures, ghosts and other forms of character images are classified as other forms.

As can be seen from the chart, among the four morphological features of tank character design in popular MOBA games, human form is the most common one, accounting for between 25% and 64% of the total number of tank characters. The proportion of creature form characters is second only to that of human form, accounting for 22–27% of the total number of tank-type characters. The character of tank-type in mechanical form is relatively small, accounting for 7–14% of the total number of tank-type characters. The character of tank-type in other forms fluctuates greatly, ranging from 0% to 42% of the total number.

C. Analysis and Summary

The proportion of Morphological features of tank-type characters in popular MOBA games reflects the analysis and summary of the potential needs of users in the design of mature MOBA games. Through statistical analysis, the character with human morphological features in MOBA game tank-type characters should account for 25–64% of the total number of tank-type characters. The data shows that in the process of choosing game characters, users tend to choose the character form design with human characteristics, pay more attention to the sense of belonging as a human, and emphasize the power of human. The proportion of creature form tank-type characters should be second only to that of human form characters, accounting for 22% to 27% of the total tank-type characters. The inherent impression of animals should be used to convey the character positioning, which can enhance users' sense of empathy. A part of tank-type characters in mechanical form can be designed (7–14%). The tank-type characters in mechanical form show the popular trend of post-modernist design style among the contemporary user groups. A few other forms of tank-type characters can be designed, which reflects the psychological needs of some users (Fig. 5).

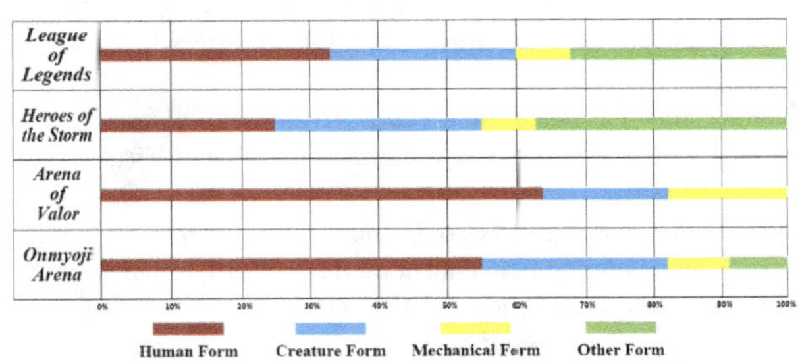

Fig. 5 Analysis on the proportion of morphological features of tank-type characters design in popular MOBA games.

Conclusion

In this study, through the analysis of the proportion of morphological features of tank-type character image design in popular MOBA games, the user's demand for diversified Tank-Type character forms in MOBA games was summarized.

First, when choosing tank-type characters, the user prefers tank-type characters in human form and pays more attention to the sense of belonging as human beings. Second, users have a high demand for tank-type characters in creature form. By using the user's stereotype of a specific creature, the character of the tank-type can be more accurately interpreted. The design of some mechanical tank-type characters reflects the upsurge of postmodern design style, which is popular among teenagers. Other forms of Tank-Type characters enrich the image design of tank-type characters in MOBA games, and satisfy some users' psychology of seeking for differences.

MOBA games provide users with a more diversified and personalized game experience through the selection of various and distinctive characters. In this study, the classification and analysis of tank-type character morphology in MOBA game provides a theoretical design method based on real data for other MOBA games to create more abundant tank-type character morphology. However, in practical applications, the diversity of MOBA games should be paid attention to. Only by taking this data as the theoretical basis for the design of tank-type character morphology and characteristics in MOBA games and using it, can a more flexibly systematic and professional Tank-Type character be created.

References

[1] Xiaoli Yu. *Inheritance and Application of Traditional Culture in Game Clothing under the Background of Digital Art*[A]. Russian State Specialized Academy of Arts(Russia), Institute of Fine Arts, Zhengzhou University(China), International Science and Culture Center for Academic Contacts(Russia), Zhengzhou Yingchun Conference planning Co. Ltd. (China). Proceedings of the 3rd International Conference on Arts, Design and Contemporary Education(ICADCE 2017) (Advances in Social Science, Education and Humanities Research, Vol. 144) [C]. Russian State Specialized Academy of Arts(Russia), Institute of Fine Arts, Zhengzhou University(China), International Science and Culture Center for Academic Contacts(Russia), Zhengzhou Yingchun Conference planning Co. Ltd. (China): International Science and Culture for Academic Contacts, 2017: 4.

[2] Gao Xuemei, Weng Lei, Zhou Yuhong, Yu Hongling. *The Influence of Empathy and Morality of Violent Video Game Characters on Gamers' Aggression.*[J]. Frontiers in psychology, 2017, 8.

[3] Chenlei Wu, Takashi Kanai. *Data-driven detailed hair animation for game characters*[J]. Computer Animation and Virtual Worlds, 2016, 27(3-4).

[4] Andrea Kleinsmith, Marco Gillies. *Customizing by doing for responsive video game characters*[J]. International Journal of Human - Computer Studies, 2013, 71(7-8).

[5] Yang Liuyi. *On Applied Skills of Character Design in Graphic Design*[A]. International Informatization and Engineering Associations, Atlantis Press. Proceedings of 2nd International Conference on Science and Social Research(ICSSR 2013)[C]. International Informatization and Engineering Associations, Atlantis Press: Computer Science and Electronic Technology International Society, 2013:4.

[6] Yanli Wang, Feng Wang, Yun Cheng, Chengling Zhao, Zhongmei Zheng, Department of Educational Science and Technology, HuangGang Normal University, HuangGang, China Department of Information Technology, HuaZhong Normal University, WuHan, China. *The Study of Characters Design in PRG Educational Games*[A]. IACSIT, IEEE Beijing Section, IEEE China Council, Beijing Technology and Business University. Proceedings of 2009 2nd IEEE International Conference on Computer Science and Information Technology Vol. 2[C]. IACSIT, IEEE Beijing Section, IEEE China Council, Beijing Technology and Business University: IEEE BEIJING SECTION, 2009: 4.

[7] Carsten Stoll, Juergen Gall, Edilson de Aguiar, Sebastian Thrun, Christian Theobalt. *Video-based reconstruction of animatable human characters*[J]. ACM Transactions on Graphics (TOG), 2010, 29(6).

https://doi.org/10.1142/9789811238727_0053

Music Genre and Association of Product Form Style

Chi-Meng Liao*, Lan-Ling Huang, Chih-Wei Lin and Li-fen Ke

School of Design, Fujian University of Technology
No.3 Xueyuan Road, University Town, Minhou County
Fuzhou City, Fujian Province, China
*Corresponding Author Email: jameslgm88@sina.com.cn, Tel: +86 152-8040-4658

Abstract

This study aims to explore the association between music type and product form style. During the experiment, the subjects were asked to generate idea sketches when listening to New Age music and Opera music through within-subject design. The results showed that listening to music during design can induce the episodic memory generated by listening to this type of music in the past, induce the subjects to associate the auditory experience related to music, and display its style characteristics in the product's form style, color, material, decoration, and construction mode.

Keywords: Music, Association, Product form style, Sketch.

Introduction

With the rapid development of technology, mobile devices have been widely used to play music in recent years, and ubiquitous music has almost become a part of design activities. Previous studies have shown that most designers listen to music frequently while designing and agree that listening to music has positive benefits [1]. Association is the basis of perception, concept, memory, and imagination. In the creative process, designers often use association to connect existing cognition and knowledge. In this study, music is used as the medium to stimulate the association of product form styles. Based on the association of music type from designers in the process of drawing conceptual sketches, the relationship between music genre and product design style associations is explored through the design mission in the experiment.

A. Music Utility and Association

Previous studies have shown that music played in accordance with the environment has a subtle effect on listeners, indicating that appropriate music can convey specific ideas or influence people's behavior [2]. A study on the influence of music tempo on designer showed that subjects drew faster and had higher fluency and flexibility of creative ideas under the influence of fast tempo music. However, when listening to slow tempo music, the concentration of the subjects increased, showing a better degree of originality [3]. These studies show the effects of music on cognitive behavior.

Listening to music often arouses the listener's mental activities and reminds him/her of musically related matters; this indicates that listening to music awakens people's innermost feelings, and people will have various imaginations based on their experience of listening to similar music. Rock music makes listeners recall more objects with rock characteristics, such as electric guitars, tattoos, and men with long hair. Classical music makes people recall more classical elements, such as cigars, champagne, and pens [4]. Studies have also shown that listening to Hard Rock and Metal music leads to the association of avant-garde style, New Age music leads to the association of minimal style, Rock music leads to the association of vivid style, and Opera music leads to the association of luxurious style [1]. All of these indicate the influence of the music type on associations.

B. Product Form Style

A product is a combination of its external shape and internal function. It is a synthesis of the shape, color, material, and function. Modeling is usually conscious and purposeful; it shapes concepts into concrete forms through certain materials and methods. Remarkably, product form style and product image are important media for designers to communicate with consumers. Through the representation of product form, consumers can better understand the concept and significance of products in addition to the essential functions of products. The designer generates the style attribute of the product and is also the shaper of the product style. In the concept development stage of design process, designers often materialize abstract design concepts through hand-drawn sketches to facilitate communication with their design clients and meet their needs [5]. Therefore, designers have the important responsibility to give appropriate style and image to products according to the design theme and requirements.

Style is composed of multiple units of differentiation, according to these basic units that people can recognize the differences in products, feel the information of products, and distinguish style characteristics. Chang and Van, in their research on design trends and product style of a redesign, expressed product style elements in four aspects: shape, color, material, and detail treatment [6]. A study that explores the minimal design style shows how the shape, color, decoration, component, material, technology, and function are used to elaborate product style [7]. However, technology and function are difficult to be judged from the appearance of product. Therefore, this study explores what specific elements or features designers apply to present the design style in the product's shape, color, material, decoration, and construction mode.

Research Method

A. Experimental Design

The image generated by listening to music is the projection of individual experience and imagination. Each listener may not have the same experience when listening to the same music, and the design ability of the designers involved in the experiment is inevitably different, so this study adopted the method of a within-subject design experiment. Each subject was tested individually, they listened to New Age music and Opera music so that the researchers would understand the product design style differences under these two music genres.

B. Experimental Method

This experiment recruit 16 designers as subjects, they are eight male and eight female. When playing Opera music and New Age music, they assumed that they were lamp designers and that the client hoped that "the lamps could reflect the music style of the restaurant play (New Age music/Opera music)". The conception of lamps was presented in the form of free hand sketches that conform to the music characteristics. The experimental steps as following:

1. Experimental task description: Explain the purpose and process of the experiment, as described above.
2. Warming up: The subjects were asked to warm up 5 minutes before the experiment. They could doodle or sit down to relax.
3. Performing design task: The music was played and the subjects were asked to draw the lamp sketches. The drawing task lasted for 40 minutes.
4. A questionnaire survey of music feelings: After the experiment, the subjects filled in the "Music-induced Design Style Association Scale".

C. Product Form Styles Scale

Music features can evoke a variety of associations among listeners. In this study, we measured the association of the subjects' product form styles caused by experimental music. The Likert 7-point scale was applied. The vocabulary of form style in the scale includes: "soft" and "hard" and "minimal" and "luxurious", "simple", "changeable", "round", "sharp", "curved", "straight", "regular", "chaotic", "delicate" and "rough", with a total of 14 sets of design style vocabulary.

Results

A. Association between Music and Product Form Style

The Music-induced Design Style Association Scale was tested by the Paired Sample T-test. The gender of the subjects ($t=1.73$, $p=0.12$), $p > 0.05$, which not reached significant difference, indicating that there was no significant difference in the views of male subjects and female subjects on the form style association caused by the music. Among the 14 form style adjectives, 9 of them had a significant difference ($p < 0.05$), and 5 of them had no significant difference ($P > 0.05$). Among the 9 design styles with a significant difference, 7 of them had more than 5 points in the intensity of the subject's feelings associated with New Age music. These feelings were: soft ($M=5.56$, $SD=1.06$), minimal ($M=5.37$, $SD=1.31$), simple ($M=5.06$, $SD=1.44$), round ($M=5.56$, $SD=1.11$), and regular ($M=5.56$, $SD=1.25$). Luxurious ($M=6.12$, $SD=0.89$) and changeable ($M=5.56$, $SD=1.12$) were associated with opera.

These results indicate that different types of music lead to different associations of design style. The p values of hard ($t=3.35$, $p=0.01$) and sharp ($t=3.74$, $p=0.00$) were both less than 0.05, showing a significant difference. However, the intensity of the subjects' feelings being less than 4 points showed that the music played in the experiment had little effect on the two lexical items. Among the 5 product form styles not reached significant differences, the intensity of the subjects' feelings on "curved" (New Age $M=5.06$, Opera $M=5.51$, $SD=1.20$) and "delicate" (New Age $M=5.31$, Opera $M=5.25$, $SD=1.34$) was more than 5 points, showing that listening to New Age music and Opera music can strongly stimulate the association of these two form styles.

B. Music Genre and Conceptual Sketch Features

This study deconstructed the lamp sketches drawn by the subjects to understand what specific features the subjects adopted to present the form style into the aspects of product shape, color, material, decoration, and construction mode, so as in line with these music styles. The results showed that the specific features of product shape, surface color, material and decorative application have their own characteristics under two different music conditions. However, in terms of the construction mode, similar unit repetitive design methods were applied, as shown in Table 1.

TABLE I
COMPARISION TABLE OF FORM FEATURES

Music genre Form structure	New Age music	Opera music
Shape	Simple, Large curvature	Luxurious, Small curvature
Color	Natural colors	Black, red, golden
Material	Bamboo, wood	Curtain, metal
Decoration	Less decoration	Tassel, crystal
Construction	Unit repeated	Unit repeated

When listening to New Age music, most of the lamps shape with a large arc that showed a product form style of simple. The surface color was mostly natural colors, such as wood color, grass green. Moreover, bamboo and wood materials were used more. The lamps and did not have too much decorations. Similar units were repeatedly in the construction mode, and the overall style was minimal, as shown in Figure 1.

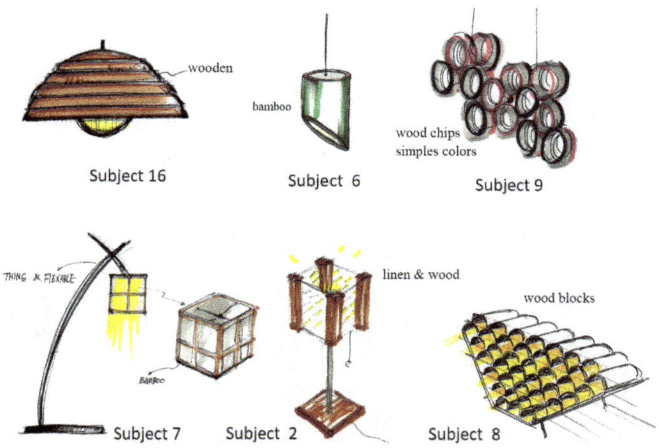

Fig. 1 Sketches of some subjects under New Age music condition.

When listening to the Opera music, most of the lamp sketches showed the following characteristics: most of them had a gorgeous shape with a small arc; the surface color was mostly red, black and golden; cotton curtain and metal were used as the materials; the lamps had many decorations, such as tassels, crystals; similar units were repeatedly in the construction mode, presenting a luxurious style on the whole, as shown in Figure 2.

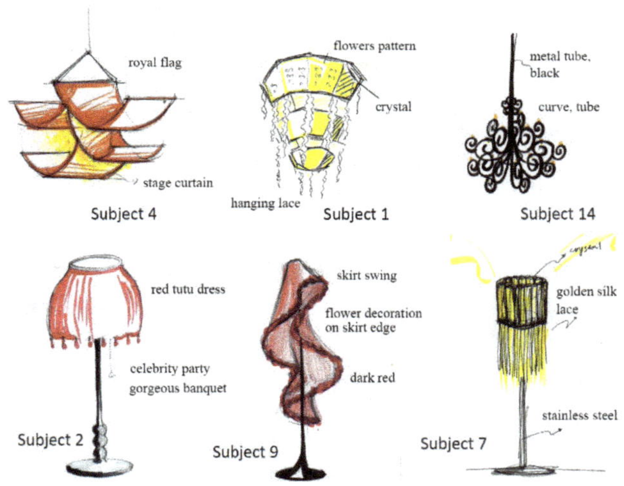

Fig. 2 Sketches of some subjects under Opera music condition.

Discussion and Conclusion

The results show that both New Age music and Opera music can induce the association of specific product form styles from designers. When listening to New Age music, it is easy to associate with soft, minimal, simple, round, and regular product form styles. Moreover, gentle curves, natural materials, simple colors, and fewer decorations are applied to show form features in the sketch design of lamps and lanterns in a minimal style. When listening to Opera music, designers tend to associate luxuriant and changeable product form styles. Therefore, in the sketch of lamps and lanterns, the luxurious style was shown with small changeable curves, artificial materials, rich and bright colors, and many decorations. This result echoes Liao and Chang's study that listening to New Age music may lead to a minimal style association, while listening to Opera music may lead to a luxurious style association [1]. The reason may be that when designers listen to music during their design, the music prompts them to induce the association related to music characteristics [8], recall the episodic memories generated by listening to this type of music in the past, and evoke the projected artistic conception derived from the association generated by the related memories of their lives' experiences [9]. For example, they applied the stage setting of Opera performers wearing gorgeous costumes or full of hanging decorations to the lamp design style. In contrast, the lamp sketch under the condition of listening to the music of the New Age style featured a simple style with natural materials and fewer decorations.

This study explored the impact of listening to music on the development of creative ideas from an auditory perspective. The results show that the stylistic attributes of music can induce similar product form style associations among designers. Therefore, the good application of music may help to stimulate creative ideas and give designers an alternative to improve design ideas.

References

[1] C-M. Liao and W-C. Chang, *A Survey on Effects of Music on Design Association,* Bulletin of JSSD, 61(5), pp. 47-56, 2015.

[2] A. C. North and D. J. Hargreaves, *The Effect of Music on Atmosphere and Purchase Intentions in a Cafeteria*, Journal of Applied Social Psychology, 28(24), pp. 2254-2273, 1998.

[3] C-M. Liao and W-C. Chang, *The Effects of Music Tempo on Designer's Idea Generation*, Journal of Design Science, 19(2), pp. 89-110, 2016.

[4] J. P. S. Yeoh and A. C. North, *The effect of musical fit on consumers' memory*, Psychology of Music, 38(3), pp. 368-378, 2010.

[5] A. T. Purcell and J. S. Gero, *Drawings and the design process: A review of protocol studies in design and other disciplines and related research in cognitive psychology*, Design Studies, 19(4), pp.389-430, 1998.

[6] W-C. Chang and Y-T. Van, *Researching design trends for the redesign of product form*, Design Studies, 24(2), pp.173-180, 2003.

[7] M-H. Lin, *The Characters and Tendencies of Minimalism in Design*, Journal of Design, 17(1), pp. 79-99, 2012.

[8] C. L. Jacob, et al., *Love is in the air: congruence between background music and goods in a florist*, The International Review of Retail Distribution and Consumer Research, 19(1), pp. 75-79, 2009.

[9] J. W. Santrock, *Psychology: Essentials*, New York: McGraw-Hill, 2004, pp. 239-240.

https://doi.org/10.1142/9789811238727_0054

Learning from Performing Voluntary Work or Placement at International Food Bank Organizations: The Student Perspective

Chuan-Ching Hwang

Department of Social Work, Chaoyang University of Technology, Taichung, Taiwan
Email: chuanching.hwang@gmail.com

Abstract

Combining community service and overseas visits makes it possible to explore the culture of a country on more levels. Participating in the regular activities of international food banks is not only easy to arrange, but also likely to broaden one's horizons. Encountering people from different social classes fosters the understanding of different cultures. The author has organized practicum or voluntary work overseas for 28 students at the Department of Social Work at the Chaoyang University of Technology over the last four years. The benefits and difficulties of their experiences are discussed via observation and questionnaires. A questionnaire was sent to 16 students who have been studying in the same class. Foodbank organizations usually welcome international volunteers, as they help to promote their image and gain more support from their society. All of the students are satisfied with what they experienced and learned. These experiences also help them to open their eyes and minds.

Keywords: food banks, international voluntary work, community services, Berliner Tafel, Kechara Soup Kitchen

Introduction

As a Chinese proverb says, "You may learn more by traveling thousands of miles than reading thousands of books". From an educational perspective, traveling to a foreign country is one of the best ways to broaden one's horizons, especially in terms of language, culture, food, religion, and so on. However, traveling as a tourist usually just scratches the surface of society as one usually just visits places of interest without dipping into the stories behind them and the way of life of the society. There is little contact with the locals or people from lower socioeconomic communities. Unless living abroad for a long time, it is not easy to be in contact with different layers of the population. Combining community service and overseas visits explores the culture of a country on different levels. However, there are several obstacles when it comes to committing oneself to community services in foreign countries, such as cost of living, different languages, and social norms. Furthermore, it is also important to find suitable organizations which allow students to participate in their daily work and provide opportunities to contact different population groups. For students, participating in the regular activities of international food banks, even if it is only short-term, is one of the channels more likely to satisfy the above-mentioned goals and is relatively easy to get involved in.

Food Banks, collecting surplus food and delivering to the poor, are normally supported by voluntary workers from different social classes, especially from the middle class. Participants at first gain advantages for understanding a society when working together with volunteers while helping those in need, who are usually regarded as invisible groups in society. Secondly, cooperation with people from a diverse range of backgrounds is required. Thirdly, by evaluating the resources to help those in need, a clearer understanding of how society works and the different lifestyles of people is achieved. Finally, activities such as collecting, sorting, and delivering the surplus food and resources do not require expert knowledge or language ability. Being able to speak a foreign language leads to a better understanding among volunteers, but people can still contribute to the food banks despite a lack of local language ability.

From 2013 to 2019, before the COVID-19 pandemic broke out, 28 students were organized by the author to go to Germany and Malaysia. Two of them went to Germany as exchange students, 16 of them underwent experiences at social institutions in Germany and Malaysia, 10 of them paid a 5-day visit to the Kechara Soup Kitchen (KSK) in Malaysia. All of these outbound placements were either supported by the "overseas internship program" of the Ministry of Education, or by the so-called "thousand people overseas experiences program" of the Chaoyang University of Technology.

As for experience in food bank activities, 7 students participated in a food bank in Berlin, Germany, called "Berliner Tafel". Their daily activities included collecting surplus food from supermarkets, sorting and delivering to social institutions, and providing food directly to those in need in a church [1]. 17 students went to the KSK in Malaysia to participate in collecting food from the Hypermarket Tesco and other supermarkets, delivering food to social institutions, and providing food to households in social housing or homeless people on the street [2]. 10 of them paid a five-day visit, while 7 of them performed their activities for more than a month. Their experiences have been evaluated in this report.

Method

From the 28 students who underwent overseas studies, placements, or short-term visits, 16 were chosen based on being class cohorts of similar age to answer questions and discuss with a focus group to evaluate their experiences. Out of all 16 students, 6 performed a 35-40 day placement at the Kechara Soup Kitchen (KSK) in Kuala Lumpur, Malaysia, in 2018. 4 visited the KSK in December 2017 for five days, and two performed a one-month placement at the Berliner Tafel in 2018. Another three students performed a month-long placement in a nursing home in Germany. Their experiences were compared to other students participating in the activities at food banks.

All of them have been studying in the same class of the Department of Social Work at the Chaoyang University of Technology since 2017 and are in their final year of study. We selected students of matching age who were class cohorts to avoid the impact of background factors such as age and class. They had common friends with whom they could share their experiences. Therefore, we could observe the interaction of these students. This circumstance provided an opportunity to discover why other students from the same class did not take the chance to go abroad and whether they would wish to do the same if they had a second chance. Since the author has been their class teacher for the two or three years since their return, observations of the impact of their experiences have been ongoing.

Evaluating the experiences

In the questionnaire, scales were used to value questions with five options: strongly agree (SA), agree (A), undecided (UND), disagree (DA) and strongly disagree (UDA). 15 questions were asked and respondents were asked whether or not they agreed with the following statements:

1) I am more capable of solving problems independently after the placement/visits.
2) The placement/visits have broadened your international visions.
3) The placement/visits have helped me to further study social work after returning.
4) I understand what social work involves in the country I stayed/visited.
5) I am familiar with eating and drinking habits in the country I stayed/visited?
6) I understand how placement/visit procedures and processes work
7) I understand the social welfare systems of the country.
8) I made many international friends.
9) I have been studying English harder after returning.
10) I have been paying attention to the news of the country I stayed in/visited?
11) I am satisfied with that placement/visit I made.
12) If I could choose again, I would still go abroad on a visit/placement to that country.
13) The institutions organized my learning program efficiently.
14) I would encourage other students to do the same placement/visit.
15) These activities should be promoted and carried on in the future.

As shown in Table 1, almost every statement was answered positively except the following three questions: 1) "I understand what social work involves in the country I stayed/visited." Only the three students who attended a placement in the elderly home reported relatively more positively (67%). This result shows that performing voluntary work or placements at food banks provides chances to contact different people. Furthermore, volunteers do not need a lot of training as the daily activities do not involve much in terms of solving the problems of the poor or making referrals. Therefore, students do not know much about what social work involves in the countries they visit. In addition, social workers are not the key staff at those food banks. The students do not have many chances to experience what social workers do in a country like Taiwan, where social workers have a bigger role to play in food banks. 2) To the statement "I made many international friends", seven of the 15 students answered undecided. Of the seven students, three paid a five-day visit to Malaysia. Due to the time limit and staying mostly in groups, they did not have much chance to make a lot of international friends. Another four students who gave undecided answers were those who attended the placement in Germany. At the KSK in Malaysia, most of the staff speak Chinese, so it is easier for students to make friends. The language barrier and cultural differences in Germany were the main reasons students struggled with making friends, according to a later interview with the students. 3) Another less positively answered question is "I have been studying English harder after returning". Although most of the students claimed English ability is very important if they want to go abroad, six of them (40%) did not report studying English harder after returning.

Food Banks, the KSK and Berliner Tafel

Since the establishment of the first non-profit organization named "Food Bank" in the United States in 1967, food banks have been established all over the world for more than half a century. The USA has the longest-running and largest food banks in the world. For example, there are around 3.7 million people (12% of the total population) who have benefitted from food aid supplied by food banks. In France, Italy, Poland, and other European countries, it is estimated that more than 3 million people use food banks [1]. Today, the United States Food Bank Federation "Feeding America" is one of the top three non-profit organizations (NPOs) in the United States. The German food bank "Die Tafeln" has flourished since its inception in 1993 and is considered one of the most influential social movements since the 1990s.

There are many types of food banks by service in three major categories [2]. The first category is called "business to business" (B2B), also known as the "logistical model". The model is for distributing the collected food to social welfare organizations or food banks. There is a big difference in the size of the organizations. In general, most "Food Banks" in the United States adopt the B2B model, and the size is large. However, in Asia, the size is relatively small. Only a few institutions, such as the "People Food Bank" located in Taichung, tend to operate in a sizable way. The second category is called "business to customers" (B2C), also known as the "Front-line model" in which the collected food is delivered directly to clients at a fixed time. This type is called "Food Pantry" in the United States and "die Tafeln" in Germany. The third category is a hybrid model in which the collected foods are provided either to the client or other social welfare organizations. The KSK can be seen as a hybrid, as the institution not only provide food to the needy directly but also to some social welfare institutions, such as homeless shelter and elderly home.

Learning and valuing from the students

In the questionnaire, a scale was used to value questions with five options: strongly agree (SA), agree (A), undecided (UND), disagree (DA), strongly disagree (UDA). The questions asked include: 1) Do you become more independent after the placement/visits? 2) Did the placement/visits improve your international visions? 3) Did the placement/visits help you to learn your study of the social work after coming back? 4) Did you understand the daily activities of the social workers in the country you stayed/visited? 5) Dis you familiar with the eating and drinking style of the country you stayed/visited? 6) Did you understand the social welfare systems of the country? 7) Did you make a lot of international friends? 8) Have you been learning English more indigently after coming back? 9) Have you been paying attention to the news of the country you stayed/visited? 10) Are you satisfied with that placement/visit you made? 11) Will you make the same decision again? 12) Did the institutions cared about my learning and staying 13) Will you encourage other students to do the same placement/visit you made? 14) Do you agree the teachers should keep promoting these activities?

As shown in Table 1, almost every question was answered positively except the following three questions: 1) Did you understand the daily activities of the social workers in the country you stayed/visited? Only the students undergoing a placement in the elderly home in Germany reported positively. This shows performing voluntary work in the food banks provides chances to contact different people and that social workers are not the key people of the two countries who are involved in helping the needy. For the second question "Did you make a lot of international friends?', seven students answered less positively, especially those who were in Germany. The language barrier and different cultures were the main reasons for this, a later interview with the students revealed. Another question "Have you been learning English more diligently after coming back?" had an interesting answer. As most of the students claim, English ability is very important if students want to go abroad. However, after coming back, six of them did not report studying English harder.

Students picked "strongly agree" in several categories, such as "The placement/visits have helped me to broaden my international visions", "I am satisfied with that placement/visit I made", "If I can choose again, I will go abroad to do the same thing again", "The Institutions arrange well about my learning program", "I will encourage other students to do the same activity?", and "These activities should be promoted and carried on in the future?". Almost all students were highly satisfied with their experiences and learnings. They would make the same decision if they could make it again and encourage other students to do the same.

To know the reasons why other students haven't applied for placement or visits abroad, another questionnaire was sent to 30 students from the same class as the 15 students who went abroad. 20 of them answered the questionnaire. The three most mentioned reasons for not taking the five-day visit to KSK were the cost (61.2%), lack of English fluency (55.6%), and time conflicts due to part-time jobs (44.4%). Although the flight tickets were mostly compensated, students still had to spend around 200 US$ to make the trip. The most common reasons for not applying for a placement longer than one month, were lack of English fluency (77.8), which was the most popular reason, and high cost (66.7%), which was the second most popular. 27.8% of the respondents claimed "a fear of living abroad" as their reason for not applying. Aside from English ability, the cost of living abroad was the most important factor for the students to make the decision. Although all the students who did go abroad mentioned that they would make the same decision again, they would only do so if they received financial support such as compensation for the flight tickets.

TABLE 1
Self-report of the students' experiences

questions	SA	A	UND	DA	SDA
1. Solving problems independently	9	4	2	0	0
2. Broadening my international horizons	12	3	0	0	0
3. Helping further study of Social work	2	10	3	0	0
4. Understanding what social work involves	2	9	3	1	0
5. Be familiar with eating and drinking habits	9	4	2	0	0
6. Understanding placement institution procedures	7	7	1	0	0
7. Understanding social welfare system of the country	4	2	7	2	0
8.Making many International friends	5	3	7	0	0
9. Studying English harder	2	6	6	1	0
10 Caring more about the country after	2	8	3	2	0
11. Satisfied with the placement/visit	12	1	1	0	0
12. Would make the same decision	13	2	0	0	0
13. Felt the learning program was well-organized	13	2	0	0	0
14 Would encourage other students to do the same	12	3	0	0	0
15.These activities should be promoted in the future	12	3	0	0	0

SA= strongly agree, A=Agree, UND=Undecided, DA=Disagree, UDA=strongly disagree

A lot of students in the class needed to take a part-time job in order to participate. Although all the activities are subsidized by the government, students still have to pay some money of their own. It is not surprising that 40% of the respondents would take part in a short-term visit if they could make the decision again, as it costs less. According to their answers, English ability is considered very important if students want to go abroad. The English ability of those who did not go abroad is relatively limited, 70% were in the "beginner-level" and 20% of them have only basic English ability. This suggests that if they improve their English at the time of decision-making, they might decide to apply for placements/visits overseas.

Conclusion

The survey suggests that, according to students' own perspectives, participating in the regular activities of food banks is helpful for students to gain international visions, and to understand foreign societies and different cultures. This can be achieved even if the students do not speak the local languages and lack English fluency. Being able to speak a foreign language leads to a better understanding among volunteers, but people can still contribute to the food banks despite not speaking the local language fluently. Although the students involved were all studying social work, students of other majors could all still have performed these activities.

All the students who attended placements at international food banks or paid a five-day visit to the institutions reported positive feedback in many fields, such as broadening international visions, enhancing their ability to solve problems independently, helping their learning, and so on. Based on experiences gained in the past, food bank organizations usually welcome international volunteers as it helps them promote their image and gain more support from their society. With all this positive feedback, it is clear that financial support for placements and trips is crucial to make these activities possible, such as compensation of flight costs. The results also show that participating in daily activities at international food bank organizations helps students understand the country they visit and allows them to understand society, as it opens their eyes and minds.

References

[1] For more information about the Berliner Tafel, please visit: https://www.berliner-tafel.de/berliner-tafel/

[2] For more information about the Kechara Soup Kitchen, please visit: https://www.kechara.com/soup-kitchen/

https://doi.org/10.1142/9789811238727_0055

Promotion of Aging-friendly Communities through Green Restorative Environments

Tsai Shu-Ying*, Xu Hui-Yun

Taipei Tech Department of Architecture, Taipei, Taiwan
*Corresponding Author Email: tsaishuying0914@gmail.com

Abstract

This paper discusses the use of green restorative environments to promote aging-friendly communities. The Kawakita method was employed to consolidate residents' awareness of aging-friendly communities before they were invited to participate in a workshop that involved various green restorative activities. According to the pre-and post-test analysis, 82.3% of the residents agreed that green restorative environments contribute to the construction of aging-friendly communities. That is, the environment significantly and positively influences older adults in the areas of social skills, logical awareness, participation in hobbies, and gardening knowledge.

Keywords: community, restorative environment, friendly community

Introduction

The World Health Organization published *Global Aging-friendly Cities: A Guide* in 2007 to define eight dimensions for promoting aging-friendly cities. However, each city differs in its availability of resources, administrative system, and development direction. Thus, adjustments must be made to each city's unique conditions when constructing an aging-friendly environment. Governments have begun formulating policies related to aging-friendly society and communities. The goal is to promote an aging-friendly environment and enable the older to live with familiar people in familiar places so that their daily living is satisfied at different stages of life in response to their physiological, psychological, social, and substantial changes. The independence, interdependence, and quality of life of the older need to be reinforced. The provision of social activity sites for the older encourages the exchange with neighbors and helps them discover new purposes in life [1,8].

The concept of healing differs from that of curing. Curing refers to simply satisfying people's physiological or psychological needs, whereas healing alludes to inspiring psychological positivity by using positive external factors, thereby fulfilling not only physiological and psychological needs but also spiritual needs [2]. In contrast to treatment for disease curing, healing refers to the process of eliciting positive feelings in individuals through physiological improvement and positive self-cognition [4]. Studies have employed various healing programs for the various needs and characteristics of participants. Such programs include animal-assisted interventions, horticultural therapy, care farming, green exercise, ecotherapy, nature therapy, and wilderness therapy, all of which exemplify the concept of green care [5]. From a philosophical perspective, horticultural therapy provides people with cognitive, psychological, and social rewards. From a spiritual perspective, it enables enhancing the learning motivation and creativity. In other words, horticultural therapy enables a further understanding of themselves and their surroundings. Owing to its rich and highly variable characteristics, the therapy is suitable for various groups of people [6,7].

A. Research Method and Participants Workshop

This study involved two communities in Da'an, the district with the largest aged population (21.24%) in Taipei City. To elucidate the awareness of aging-friendly communities, residents participated in the design of horticultural activities in a workshop (Fig. 1). The residents' impressions of green restorative environments were investigated through their discussion of horticultural activities. A survey was conducted in August 2020 to examine the residents' awareness of aging-friendly communities by the method of Ref. [9]. 90-min horticultural activities were conducted in September 2020. One month before the activities, research participants were recruited. The participants were 65 years or older. A total of 52 participants participated in the workshop and the questionnaire survey.

B. Questionnaire

The Horticultural Therapy Benefit Evaluation Scale was employed in the quantitative questionnaire. Each item was scored using a 5-point Likert scale from 1 (strongly disagree) to 5 (strongly agree). SPSS was used to evaluate the benefits the participants received from participating in the activity.

Procedure and Results

A. Residents' Environmental Awareness

According to Jiro [9], the participants proposed parks, green alley spaces, and the offices of village chiefs as restorative environments. They stated that green restorative environments contain plants in various colors. The participants suggested urban farms to be introduced to provide residents with congregate meals, which facilitated interactions and reduced their sense of loneliness.

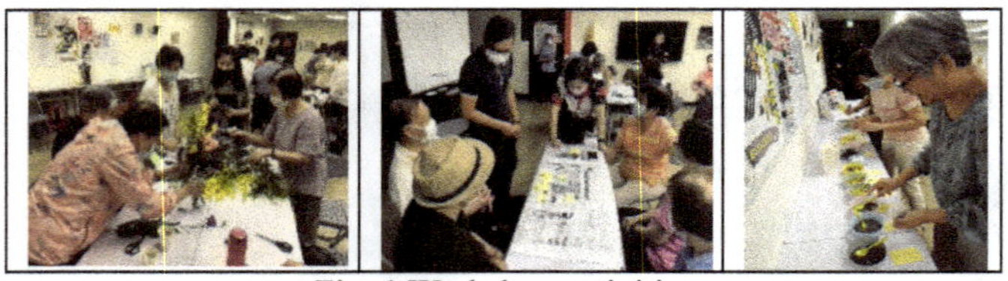
Fig. 1 Workshop activities

B. Evaluating the Benefits of Horticultural Therapy

According to the questionnaire analysis, 82.3% of the participants agreed that a green restorative environment is beneficial for the construction of aging-friendly communities. The Horticultural Therapy Benefit Evaluation Scale was employed to analyze the effectiveness of the green restorative environment. The results revealed that 35.3% (11.8% in the pre-test and 47.1% in the post-test) of the participants agreed on physical activities. 41.2% (from 14.7% to 55.9%) agreed on hobbies, 20.6% (from 17.6% to 38.2%) on relaxation, 29.4% (from 20.6% to 50.0%) on the sense of achievement, 23.5% (from 14.7% to 38.2%) on logical awareness, 23.5% (from 26.5% to 50.0%) on social skill, and 58.9% (from 2.9% to 61.8%) on horticultural knowledge. The changes in the agreement rate on social skills (p<.001), logical awareness, hobbies, and horticultural knowledge (p<.01) were statistically significant. However, the increases in the rate on the sense of achievement, physical activities, and relaxation were not significant. The correlation of age with hobbies and social skills was significant as was that of living status with hobbies, logical awareness, and horticultural knowledge and that of types of residence with logical awareness.

In this study, the seven levels of the benefit evaluation table of horticultural treatment were divided as follows: (1) I can perform demanding physical activities; (2) I have hobbies; (3) I feel relaxed; (4) I have a sense of achievement; (5)I have clear awareness of making decisions; (6) I have good social skills; (7) I am skilled in horticulture (Table 1).

TABLE 1
Results of the Horticultural Therapy Benefit Evaluation Scale

Item		Pretest/ Posttest	Mean	SD	Agreement (%)	Change in percentage of agreement	Percentage of change	P value	Correlation with demographic information		
									Age	Living status	Type of residence
1	Physical activities	Pretest	3.09	0.57	11.8%	35.3%	229%	--	--	--	--
		Posttest	3.59	0.60	47.1%						
2	Hobbies	Pretest	3.24	0.74	14.7%	41.2%	280%	P 0.003**	P0.036*	P0.046*	--
		Posttest	3.97	0.67	55.9%						
3	Relaxation	Pretest	3.21	0.53	17.6%	20.6%	117%	--	--	--	--
		Posttest	4.62	0.49	38.2%						
4	Sense of achievement	Pretest	3.15	0.50	20.6%	29.4%	142%	--	--	--	--
		Posttest	4.50	0.50	50.0%						
5	Logical awareness	Pretest	3.06	0.48	14.7%	23.5%	159%	P0.002***	--	P 0.015*	P0.030*
		Posttest	3.50	0.61	38.2%						
6	Social skills	Pretest	3.35	0.64	26.5%	23.5%	88.6%	P 0.001**	P0.038*	--	--
		Posttest	3.91	0.71	50.0%						
7	Horticultural knowledge	Pretest	2.26	0.82	2.9%	58.9%	203%	P 0.003*	--	P0.011*	--
		Posttest	4.03	0.62	61.8%						

Discussion

The participants were satisfied with the green restorative workshop and activities and expressed that they were helpful to understand the green restorative environments for aging-friendly communities.

Through questionnaire analysis and green restorative workshop, the questionnaire survey of "social skills" turned out to be significant, which was consistent with the research results of Lui *et al.* [1]. An aging-friendly community requires setting up the basis for social activities, maintaining communication with neighbors, and giving the elderly new purposes in life. Increasing interaction among residents reduces loneliness [1,8]. There is a significant difference between logical awareness and hobbies, which is consistent with Relf's conclusion [6]. He stated that gardening activities are rich in nature and highly changeable, so help people understand their interests and hobbies and their surroundings in the process.

Conclusions

This study invited the participants for a green restorative workshop and activities to improve participants' physiological and psychological health. The participants reported an improvement in their welfare after participating in the activities. The activities significantly and positively influenced the participants' social skills, logical awareness, engagement in hobbies, and horticultural knowledge. 82.3% of the participants agreed that green restorative environments were beneficial for the construction of aging-friendly communities. Accordingly, restorative environments that facilitate sensory satisfaction and stimulation need to be introduced in communities to provide physiological, psychological, and spiritual benefits to older adults to create aging-friendly communities.

References

[1] Lui, C., Everingham, J., Warburton, J., Cuthill, M. & Bartlett, H., *What makes a community age friendly: A review of international literature.* Australasian Journal on Ageing, 28, 2009, pp.116-121.

[2] Dethlefsen, T., & Dahlke, R., *The healing power of illness: the meaning of symptoms and how to interpret them: Element Books Ltd,*1997.

[3] Day, C., *Spirit & place: healing our environment, healing environment : Routledge,*2002.

[4] Urich, R. S., Simons, R. F., Losito, B. D., Fiorito, E., Miles, M. A., & Zelson, M., *Stress recovery during exposure to natural and urban environments.* Journal *of Environmental Psychology*, 11(3), 1991, pp. 30.

[5] Masel, E. K., Trinczek, H., Adamidis, F., Schur, S., Unseld, M., Kitta, A., and Watzke, H. H., *Vitamin "G"arden: a qualitative study exploring perception/s of horticultural therapy on a palliative care ward.* Supportive Care in Cancer, 26(6), 2017, pp. 1799–1805.

[6] Relf, PD., *People-plant relationship. Simson. & Straus, M. M. (Eds).* Horticulture As Therapy: Principles and practice: New York: food products press, 1998.

[7] Chen. Y. R., Chen, R. W., Chang, L. R., Tsai, Y. F., Tai, C. Y., and Tsai, W. Y., *Horticultural Therapy: Taichung Agricultural Test Results*, 2010, pp. 198–203.

[8] Huang, Y. R., *Feasibility of Aging in Place and Foundation of Life-time Housing Development.* Taiwan Geriatrics & Gerontology, 1:3, 2006.02, 2006, pp. 138–150.

[9] Kawakita Jiro., *KJ the talking about chaos of legislative*, Central public opinion society, 1996.

https://doi.org/10.1142/9789811238727_0056

PuzzleArt: Interactive Projection System Development to Promote Social Interaction for the Elderly through Painting Activities

Yun-Han Chen* and Chien-Hsu Chen

Department of Industrial Design, National Cheng Kung University, Tainan, Taiwan
*Corresponding Author Email: P36074064@mail.ncku.edu.tw

Abstract

Painting is a common activity in community centers. The artworks of the elderly are displayed on the wall or put into the portfolio collection after they are completed. Unfortunately, few people admire these creations and understand the meaning of the painting. Therefore, the purpose of the research is to display the artworks of the elderly in a new way. Through observation and interview, an interactive projection system suitable for the elderly's painting activity was developed. It allows people to admire and review the artworks. The results proposed a system for the elderly to communicate with others and promote their social interaction.

Keywords: elderly, painting, interactive projection

Introduction

Population aging is an important issue around the world. Governments are focused on boosting elderly care services. To encourage the elderly to keep learning and maintain social connection with other people, many community centers provide social activities. Painting is one of the common activities in community centers as it is suitable for all ages.

In terms of effectiveness, painting has great benefits for mental health. When people engage in artistic activities and appreciate works of art, they can relax their mind and body, regulate their nervous system, and release endorphins in their brains, which results in their feeling of well-being and producing a virtuous cycle for the body and mind [1]. Moreover, painting is used as a form of art therapy. The process of art-making reconciles emotions, improves social skills, and promotes self-transformation and growth [2]. This is widely used in the field of education and psychotherapy in Western countries. However, it is still not popular in Taiwan. It is not effectively promoted in community centers as it is regarded as a general leisure activity.

On the other hand, physical activities have become a major trend for elders. It shows that older adults' mental health tends to be disregarded [3], even though the physical and mental health of the elderly are indispensable. Furthermore, a good psychological adaptation process promotes a healthy lifestyle for the elderly, compensates for the gradual loss of physical functions and social roles, and achieves successful aging [4]. Thus, activities for mental health, such as painting, are important.

There are many ways for older adults to create artworks including painting. The artworks are displayed on the wall or put into the portfolio collection as a painting activity. Although they are displayed in public, few people admire these creations and understand the meaning of the painting. The elderly who are willing to learn need to be affirmed and encouraged. Therefore, essential factors for a painting activity not only focus on painting but also display the artworks effectively for the elderly to express themselves and communicate with others.

As mentioned above, to display the artworks of the elderly differently and provide the opportunity for them to interact with others, the purpose of this research is to design a suitable system for the elderly's painting activity. Through creation review, mutual-sharing, and encouragement, the elderly will be able to promote their social interaction with interactive technology.

Observation and Interview

The observational survey was performed at the Guan Sheng Vil. Community Center in Tainan, as shown in Fig. 1. This center provides various nonphysical activities for the elderly, such as painting, clay cream flower, and zentangle. Healthy people of 65 years and older participate in the activities. There is one caregiver and several volunteers to assist and guide the elderly to complete the activity.

The spiritual art painting class was offered to conduct the observation. The activity was held in cooperation with the program from the Ministry of Health and Welfare for preventing and delaying disability for 12 weeks. During the entire observation process, there was no intervention in the activity. All activities were recorded by photographing and handwriting. The observation aims to understand the process, state, and reaction of the elderly in painting activities, and to explore the elements that motivate the elderly to participate in the activities. The result offers the development basis for the subsequent design.

Fig. 1 The observation survey field.

Methods

The researcher conducted a semi-structured interview to gain a deeper understanding of the reality of the situation and the requirements of the elderly for painting. The interview invited a teacher with many years of experience in teaching art to older adults. There were photographing, sound recording, and key point handwriting recording during the interview. The interview questions were as follows:

- What is the goal of the painting activity?
- What is the participation rate of the elderly in painting activities?
- Why do the elderly want to participate in painting activities?
- What kind of creative content does the elderly prefer?
- Would the elderly share and reviewed their artworks,
- or exchanged their ideas during the event?
- Are they afraid to express their feeling?
- What are the growth and changes of the elderly after the activity?

Based on the semi-structured interview result, three aspects were used as the basis of reference for subsequent design: 1) the condition of the elderly, 2) the course design of painting for the elderly, and 3) feedback from the elderly.

1) The condition of the elderly

- Some elderly do not like to interact with others.
- Some elderly are afraid of expressing themselves in front of a crowd.
- Some elderly do not have confidence in painting and fear being laughed at by others.
- It is difficult for seniors to have a sense of accomplishment in general painting classes, which is why many community centers failed to promote this alternative activity smoothly.

2) The course design of painting for the elderly

- Their painting skills should not be emphasized. Multiple tools and abstract painting can increase their sense of accomplishment.
- Painting tools can be used such as crayons, pastels, tear-off paintings, sandpaper paintings, puzzle paintings, blowing paintings, balloons, lanterns, and windmills.
- Giving praise can increase their sense of identity and confidence.

3) Feedback from the elderly

- *"I am already 70 years old, and I never used a pen to draw before. However, I have a lot of fun here. I am fond of painting now."*
- *"My favorite class is to draw fireworks because it reminds me of my deep memories, the moment I proposed to my wife."*

- After 12-week classes, the elderly appear more confident and happier than before, and they also understand how to apply the methods of painting in life.
- This activity has a high participation rate. 29 participants completed 12-week classes and the attendance rate is 100%. Moreover, many participants want to sign up again, which demonstrates that the elderly think highly of this activity.

System Development

At the beginning of the development, the researcher used the previously collected information as the basis with brainstorming methods to develop solutions to solve problems, as shown in Fig. 2. The participants were instructed for any ideas related to the topic of research, which was recorded for classification and discussion. Through a large number of ideas put forward in a short time, all participants had improved solutions.

During the process of brainstorming, the ideas from all participants were collected, and the participants decided to use puzzle games as an intermedium. Jigsaw puzzles were chosen as the interactive form. It is suitable for multi-person cooperation to improve cognitive ability [5]. Combined with the creations of the elderly, it can achieve effective communication.

Fig. 2 Using brainstorming to categorize the ideas and information.

After brainstorming, the researcher set out to draw sketches and user scenarios, as shown in Figs. 3 and 4. At this stage of conceptual design, the sketch helped to establish the structure quickly. When the design has a bias, it was corrected in time. Based on the results of previous observations, the participants had interviews and discussions on the design criteria and then, were introduced the technology to design. The application of interactive technology has a positive impact on the elderly [6]. Therefore, the application of famous foreign interactive design teams was applied, such as teamLab, TUIO, and interactive forms suitable for the elderly were chosen. Interactive projection technology for the elderly was used to operate with intuitive tangible user interfaces (TUI), and the puzzle pattern with the artworks was combined to create the connection for the elderly. The purpose was to make the elderly conduct self-review of the creations and cooperate to complete the jigsaw puzzles.

Then, the device was developed. The system was developed by Unity and used an infrared camera with OpenCV for object tracking. Each piece of a jigsaw puzzle had a specific marker for a camera to recognize as shown in Fig. 5. To gain better usability, the markers were hidden and only visible by an infrared camera (Fig. 6). A projector showed the images onto the corresponding jigsaw puzzle. When the users moved the puzzles on the wall, the projection images moved accordingly.

Fig. 3 Sketch.

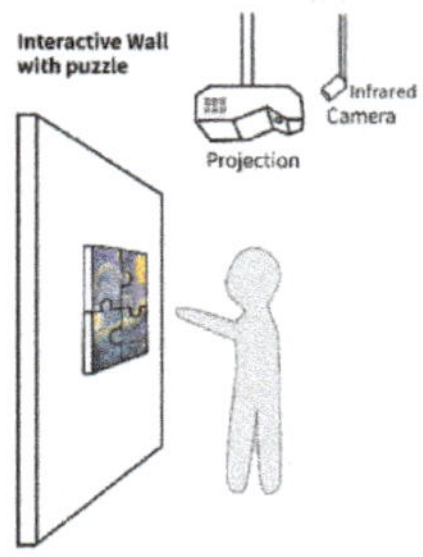

Fig. 4 User scenarios.

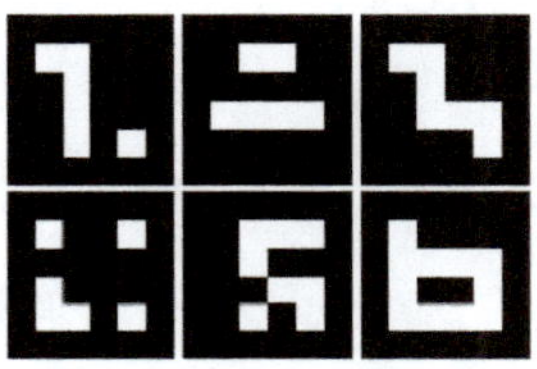

Fig. 5 Marker of each puzzle.

Fig. 6 Hidden marker in puzzle block.

This research developed an interactive system for the painting activity of the elderly by combining painting, jigsaw puzzles, and interactive design. The interactive system of the research is called PuzzleArt as shown in Fig. 7. The system can be improved for the elderly with alternate and suitable activities.

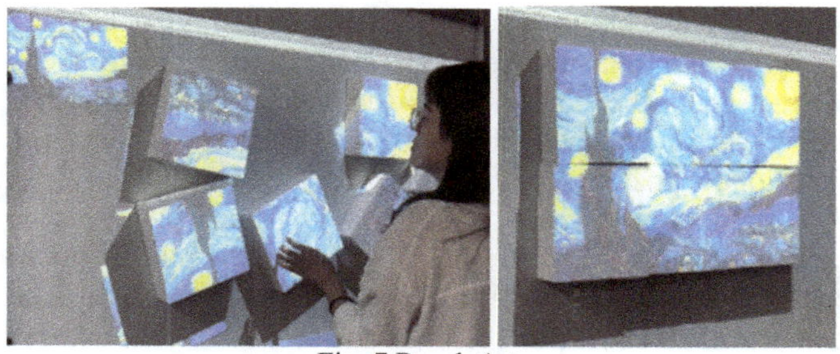

Fig. 7 PuzzleArt.

After scanning the artworks of the elderly from the painting activities, the images of the artworks were divided into six pieces as shown in Fig. 8. The images were then projected onto the six puzzle blocks on the wall. It allowed viewers to see the projection of the painting digitally and in an interesting manner through recalling the feelings and memories of conducting the painting to achieve the effect of creation review.

Fig. 8 Artworks of the elderly.

According to the investigation, the number of jigsaw puzzles designed for the elderly needs to be limited to avoid frustration by the failure to complete the puzzles. The images of the puzzle should not be excessively abstract. During the process of playing jigsaw puzzles, the elderly not only needed the basic visual perception and cognitive ability, mental rotation ability but also hand-eye coordination function. Playing together promoted socialization and cooperation with others, which in turn improved self-affirmation and social value.

With the aid of interactive technology, the elderly displayed their artworks differently from the past, which has changed the original situation in the portfolio which few people saw. The system allowed the elderly to have a new experience of painting activity. Moreover, it promoted social interaction by displaying the creations in an interesting form. It brought new experiences, grabbed more attention, and the artworks of the elderly were admired.

System Testing

The researcher tested the system and invited experts for suggestions and evaluation. After testing the system, it was found that the design of the interactive wall had more restrictions on the operation, and the maximum number of users was three. On the other hand, the puzzles were attracted to the wall by the magnet. Although it was intuitively operated, there were many restrictions on space movement. It was easy to block the recognition of the infrared camera and limit the shape of the puzzles. These are the considerations for further revision. On the other hand, the experts gave positive affirmation and argued that the system helped review learning achievements, enhance self-confidence, and promote social interaction for the elderly. It allowed the elderly to experience a new way of displaying their artworks. For improvement, the shape of the puzzle blocks could be like a real jigsaw puzzle as the original shape made it difficult to recognise the usage method of the system. Besides, the size of the puzzle blocks could be reduced to make it easier for users to pick up. The time to complete the puzzles was considered to set the number of puzzles.

Results and Discussions

The results of the research are as follows:

- All 12-week classes had specific themes (birth, exploration, balance, yin and yang, new life, ocean, aura, release, source of thought, cooperation, ascension, journey) that were related to life experiences.
- The elderly used different mixed materials to paint, which made painting more uncomplicated and more fun.
- The elderly concentrated and had a willingness to learn during the process of creation.
- The elderly admired their artworks and of others.
- Each elderly completed work with a high degree of cooperation and participation rate in class.
- Each elderly had a portfolio of their artworks from 12-week classes.

There is a lack of sharing and communication with creative ideas and stories in an activity. Multiple evaluations and discussions helped many limitations be solved. For example, the system can adopt an interactive desktop instead of a wall, the number of users can be increased to 4–8, the shape of the puzzles can be changeable, and their size reduced. The new system can be easier to use and the recognition of the camera can be improved. This result provides a new direction for the design of interactive painting activities.

This research used the methods of observation and interview to understand the current situation of the painting activity. After analyzing the shortages in painting activities, a system PuzzleArt was developed which was suitable for the elderly's painting activity. It was developed with the aid of design and technology and combined with creation review, jigsaw puzzles, and interactive projection. The purpose was to create a new way to display the creations of the elderly and help them review their learning achievements and promote social interaction.

The results of this research showed that the painting activities of the elderly were improved. Appropriate technology can assist the elderly to have more effective learning and positive influence. This research provides a basis for the system in the future in the field of observation and testing.

References

[1] S. Haruyama, *A great revolution in the brain world.* Taipei City: Third Nature Publishing Co., Ltd., 1999.

[2] "Taiwan Art Therapy Association." [Online]. Available: https://www.arttherapy.org.tw/arttherapy/post/post/data/arttherapy/tw/what_is_art_therapy/. [Accessed: 22-Oct-2020].

[3] C. T. Yao, "Exploring the Mental Health Promotion Strategies of Elderly from the Investigation of their Living Conditions : Viewpoints of Successful Aging," *The Journal of Lifelong Learning of New Taipei City.*, vol. 10, pp. 18-32, 2015.

[4] P. B. Baltes and M. M. Baltes, *Successful aging: Perspectives from the behavioral sciences*, vol. 4. Cambridge University Press, 1993.

[5] M. Linnemeier, et al., "StoryCubes: Connecting elders in independent living through storytelling," *Conf. Hum. Factors Comput. Syst. - Proc.*, pp. 1321–1326, 2012.

[6] P. Khosravi, A. Rezvani, and A. Wiewiora, "The impact of technology on older adults' social isolation," *Comput. Human Behav.*, pp. 594–603, 2016.

https://doi.org/10.1142/9789811238727_0057

Research on Environmental Planning and Space Facilities of Multiple Purpose Complex for Elderly

Shu-Ying Tsai*, Ting-Yueh Chen

National Taipei University of Technology, Taipei, Taiwan
*Corresponding Author Email: tsaishuying0914@gmail.com

Abstract

In Taiwan, 14.05% of the population was over 65 as of 2017. This research aims to build the factors of environmental and space facilities of a multiple purpose complex for the elderly which improve social support for the elderly and define the idea of local aging and successful aging. A questionnaire survey was used to compare index factors to propose a design of a multiple purpose complex for the elderly in Taiwan and explore the planning factors and their needs.

Keywords: local aging, successful aging, social support, multiple purpose complex, elderly

Introduction

A. Literature Review

a. Age-friendly communities

According to the World Health Organization (WHO) definition, the elderly refers to people over 65 years of age. As aging is unavoidable in life, long-term care of the elderly has become an issue in social welfare in all countries. Nowadays, policies for the elderly in major countries have a high priority to maintain their quality of life for independence, self-esteem, and privacy [1]. Aging has positive significance in the physical, psychological, and social aspects of the elderly [2]. The residential satisfaction of the elderly is divided into different environmental factors: (1) satisfaction subscales: aesthetics, safety, and pace of activity, (2) accessibility of stores and services: transportation, proximity, and walkability, (3) social relations with neighbors: positive regard, mutual help, and respect for privacy, and (4) home: pleasant and gracious home [3].

b. Social support

The WHO (World Health Organization, 2017) has proposed a global strategy and action plan for aging and health. In addition to establishing an age-friendly environment, the WHO also proposes to increase intergenerational unity. Social cohesion is also one of the important development goals.

As the elderly grow older, the various functions of the body inevitably degenerate. However, participation in appropriate leisure activities improve physiological functions and delay aging. Social support also significantly increases the quality of life [4]. Leisure activities and social support help people resist stress and reduce the occurrence of diseases, thereby helping and maintaining mental health. Although social interaction is important at any age, it has a greater impact on the elderly [5].

c. Environmental design and activity behavior of senior housing

Recently, the relationship between the ecological theory of the elderly and a healthy aging environment has attracted much attention. Environment and community cohesion are particularly important for the life and well-being of the elderly [6]. Living in walkable green spaces has a positive impact on the life span of urban elderly people [7]. The most common activity that elderly people participate in is walking [8]. After people get old, they usually need to spend more time processing, reflecting, and remembering information although their mental abilities are not damaged, [9].

Environment affects the physical vitality of the elderly. A walkable environment reduces chronic diseases of the elderly and improves public health and the quality of life. Also, increasing accessibility to the physical environment allows the elderly to reach service facilities that provide adequate support which ensures their activity and independence [10]. A survey shows that 40% of the elderly have difficulty going out, 25% have walking disabilities, 23% are worried about falling, 10% feel difficult to cross the road, and 2% worry about getting lost [11]. This implies that walking is the most common physiological activity of the elderly and their activities in daily life need the appropriate space [12].

As the physical functions of the elderly deteriorate, the range of activities is reduced [13]. The distance of the range is in a 10-minute walk and a comfortable distance is 800 meters for normal people [14]. However, the elderly tend to withdraw from society due to physical deterioration, so the daily orbit is usually smaller than normal people. Based on the physical ability of the elderly, the walking distance for 10-15 minutes is about 500m. [15] The physical functions of the elderly are degraded, so the basic commercial facilities, service facilities, health services, and recreational facilities for daily life need to be within a walking radius of about 800 meters. [16].

d. Environmental indicators of multiple purpose complex for elderly

Environmental tools are used to judge and compare the quality of different environmental design and improve the deficiencies in the environment (Table 1). It also improves the quality of the environment [17]. Environmental designs affect people's health and well-being, feelings of safety, security, inclusion, and belonging, and a sense of community cohesion. [18]

Inclusive design has six design principles: familiarity, legibility, uniqueness, accessibility, comfort, and safety. The purpose is to allow all users to use, understand, and enjoy. [11]

Evaluation of Older People's Living Environments (EVOLVE) was developed by Sheffield University in 2010. It is used to evaluate the design of the elderly's residence which contains two major categories: (1) general requirements: personalization and choice, dignity and privacy, comfort and control, personal care, social support in the building, and social support in the outdoor environment, and (2) the support for the elderly: accessibility, support for independence, sensory stimulation, dementia support, health and safety, security, and care for work [19].

The Environmental Audit Tool (EAT) was originally an evaluation tool to examine the environmental indicators of caregiving institutions for the elderly with dementia. It includes safety, the proportion of people, visual visibility, reducing useless stimuli, optimizing beneficial environmental stimuli, supporting action and participation, familiarity, community privacy, community links, and opportunities to participate in ordinary life-autonomy. These help those who use facilities, by promoting healing and care services [20].

The research results showed that an outdoor environment providing an environment and facilities for safe walking allows the elderly to increase physical activity. Environmental barriers for walking including traffic conditions and street design, the quality of sidewalks, personal safety, accessibility to parks and natural landscapes, the availability of shops, and the accessibility and comfortability of seats, trees, and resting areas [8].

There are no evaluation guidelines yet for a multiple purpose complex for the elderly. Therefore, this study compared the design evaluation index from previous research. Then, the questionnaire was created including the five environmental factors as follows:

(1) Security: maximum protection of environmental safety features

(2) Accessibility: reach, enter, use, and walk to the desired service facilities

(3) Comfort: outdoor life and public service facilities

(4) Social support: social activities and psychological support in the environment

(5) Independence/Privacy: the selection of activities in the environment and privacy of spatial fields

Research Methods

A. Questionnaire

As a multiple purpose complex is for all ages of users, the difference in the questionnaire by the different age groups of the respondents needs to be avoided. Therefore, this study divided the groups into youth (18-40 years old), middle-aged (40-64 years old), and elderly (over 65 years old). The responses of the questionnaire were analyzed by using SPSS 20.0.

Results and Discussion

A. Reliability Analysis

Reliability analysis is mainly based on the results obtained by a test survey. The Cronbach alpha was used as the verification value. The higher the analytical verification value, and the more accurate the internal results, and the smaller the error. Cronbach alpha was 0.855, which implies the questionnaire was reliable.

B. Basic Data Analysis

For the question of "Do you know the multiple purpose complex for the elderly?", 60.8% of the respondents said "yes", and 79.2% indicated that they would like to live in. Besides that, 89.2% believed that the living space must be changed when getting older. For the question of "How many elderly do you think is ideal for living in multiple purpose complex?", 47.5% preferred less than 10 people, 28.3% preferred 11 to 15 people, 20% preferred 16-30 people, and only 4.2% preferred more than 30 people.

For the question of "Time from home to most frequently used facilities?", 55.8% answered within 10 minutes, 30.8% answered 10-20 minutes, and 13.4% answered more than 20 minutes away from home.

TABLE 1
Comparative analysis of the environmental indicators for elderly.

Reference	Environmental indicator
EVOLVE, 2010	Safety, Environmental stimulation, Accessibility, Comfort, Independence, social support
EAT, 2003	Identification, Safety, Environmental stimulation, Accessibility, Comfort, Independence, social support
Burton& Mitchell, 2009	Identification, Safety, Accessibility, Comfort, Independence, social support
National Design Guide, 2018	Identification, Safety, Accessibility, Comfort, Independence, social support
Mitra et al. 2015	Safety, Environmental stimulation, Accessibility, Comfort, Independence, social support

C. Frequency Distribution of Environmental Indicators

For safety, the lowest score was given to "environment has simple and good visual aids" as 29.2% were very dissatisfied and dissatisfied.

For social support, the lowest score was for "whether the community nursing and sunshine service center is adequate" as 67.5% were very dissatisfied and dissatisfied.

For privacy, the lowest score was for the privacy and social functions in the community. 30% were very dissatisfied and dissatisfied.

For accessibility, the lowest score was for "Satisfaction with the current distance from residence to service unit and common functional facilities" as 32.5% were very dissatisfied and dissatisfied.

For comfort, the lowest score was for "whether the community provides venues for activities of different sizes." as 42.5% expressed dissatisfaction.

D. Significance

Based on the indicators of a friendly environment for the elderly in previous studies, we investigated the degree of satisfaction of 120 respondents in terms of the differences in personal factors and outdoor environmental indicators (Table 2).

Analysis of Variance (ANOVA) and independent t-tests were used for the analysis.

TABLE 2
The significant differences of environmental indicators.

Environmental indicators	Ages	Living type	Living with people
Safety : Satisfied with sidewalk sign time	F=3.516 P=0.033*	-	-
Safety : Feel safe and secure in the environment	F=3.549 P =0.032*	-	-
Independence/Privacy: space with privacy and social functions	-	F=2.710 P=0.034*	
Independence/Privacy: Independent execution of living areas/facilities	-	-	F=2.838 P=0.019*
Comfort: There are venues of different sizes in the community	-	F=2.537 P=0.044*	

Conclusions

For environmental facilities and needs for multiple purpose complex, the following were found.

Most people maintain a positive attitude towards the housing problems caused by the aging society. Nearly 80% of the respondents expressed their willingness to live in multiple purpose complex, and nearly 90% believed that the living space must be changed as they age. 80% thought that the concept of multiple interactions could be achieved, and 79.2% thought that the physical and mental functions of the elderly were needed. 75.8% chose to share public facilities, and 65.8% thought the quality of life needed to be improved. Outdoor environmental service facilities are important. For the time from home to the most frequently used facility, 55.8% of the respondents preferred less than 10 minutes, while 30.8% and 13.4% preferred 10-20 minutes and 20 minutes, respectively.

The satisfaction with social support items was low. 67% of the respondents were dissatisfied and very dissatisfied, and 81% demanded more day-care services. 49.1% were dissatisfied and very dissatisfied with the environmental design of the residential area and the opportunity to interact with neighbors. Various facilities were used by the elderly: parks and green spaces by 90.8%, shops and supermarkets by 88.3%, clinics by 80.8%, sports area by 76.7%, activity area by 57.5%, community classrooms by 55%, daycare center by 52.5%, community offices by 29.2%, ecological farms by 25%, and hotels by 18.3%. Different living types affect the comfort and privacy of the outdoor environment. Apartment with elevator was favored by 82.3%, apartment without elevator by 68.4%, independent house by 66%, and public house by 40%. Living with others affects independence and privacy, and age affects the sense of security in the outdoor environment. 78.4% wanted to live with spouse and children, 76% with the spouse, 57% with parents, and 53.4 with three generations, while 69.7% wanted to live alone.

In summary, through the analysis and discussion of environmental facilities, this research proposes environmental indicators such as safety, accessibility, comfort, privacy, and social support. The needed facilities need to be established in the distance for the elderly to approach easily: public seats within 100 meters, public toilets in 200 meters, bus stops in 300 meters, playgrounds in 400 meters, elementary schools, health clinics, post offices, banks and shops (food and daily necessities) in 600 meters, medical center, open space, green space and religious facilities in 800 meters, library, leisure facilities in 1,000 meters, community service center and activity center in 1,200 meters, large green spaces, squares, and hospitals in 1,500 meters.

References

[1] Wu, W & Chuang, K, Y, *Aging in Place: The Direction of Taiwan Long-Term Care Policy in the 21st Century.* Taiwan Journal of Public Health, 20(3), 2001, pp.92-201.

[2] Chen, Y, J & Lin, Y, S, *practical experience of community care and care bases-field observation of social workers.* Community Development Quarterly132, 2010, pp.385-403.

[3] Rioux, L & Werner, C, *Residential satisfaction among aging people living in place.* Journal of Environmental Psychology,31(2),2011, pp.158-169.

[4] Godbey, G, *Leisure in Your Life: An Exploration.* State Collage, PA: Venture Publishing,1999.

[5] Campbell, N, *Designing for social needs to support aging in place within continuing care retirement communities.* Journal of Housing and the Built Environment, 30(4), 2015, pp. 645-665.

[6] Cramm, J. M., van Dijk, H. M & Nieboer. A. P, *The Importance of Neighborhood Social Cohesion and Social Capital for the Well Being of Older Adults in the Community.* The Gerontologist, 53(1), 2012, pp.142–152.

[7] Takano, T., Nakamura, K & Watanabe, M, *Urban residential environments and elderly citizens' longevity in megacity areas: The importance of walkable green spaces.* Journal of Epidemiology and Community Health, 56(12), 2002, pp.913-918.

[8] Mitra,R., Siva, H & Kehler, M, *Walk-Friendly Suburbs for Older Adults? Exploring The Enablers and Barriers to Walking in A Large Suburban Municipality in Canada.* Journal of Aging Studies, 35, 2015, pp.10-19.

[9] Patoine & Mattoli, *Staying sharp: current advance on brain research. Memory loss and aging. Washington,* DC: AARP

Andrus foundation, and New York: the dana alliance for Brain initiatives, 2012.

[10] Kerr, J. Rosenberg, D., & Frank, L, *The Role of the Built Environment in Healthy Aging.* Journal of Planning Literature, 27(1), 2012. pp.43–60.

[11] Burton, E & Mitchell, L, *Inclusive urban design: streets for life.* Oxford, UK: Elsevier. (2006).

[12] Jacqueline,K., Dori,R & Lawrece,F, *The Role of the Built Environment in Healthy Aging: Community Design, Physical Activity, and Health among Older Adults.* Journal of Planning Literature.27(1), 2012. pp. 43-60.

[13] Wang.J.P & Qun, T, S*tudy on the Walking Space Design of the Aged People.* Huazhong Architecture, 27, (10), 2009. pp.49-50.

[14] Chen, C. H, *The Concept of Total Planning for Elderly Housing.* Taiwan of Gerontology and Geriatrics,1(3), 2006. pp.122-139.

[15] Lin, W. *Outdoor Space Design of elderly citizens living areas in urban.* Urban plan landscape architecture and virescence. Huazhong Architecture, 2 (3), 2005. pp.77-78.

[16] Ke, S, F & Li, H, *Environmental assessment tools for dementia patients: a review.* Chinese Journal of Nursing. 49(2),2014. pp.211-215.

[17] National Design Guide- *Planning practice guidance for beautiful, enduring and successful places.* 2019. Ministry of Housing, Community and Local Government.

[18] Kerr, J., Rosenberg, D & Frank, L, *The Role of the Built Environment in Healthy Aging.* Journal of Planning Literature, 27(1), 2012. pp.43–60.

[19] Lewis, A., et al., *EVOLVE: A tool for evaluating the design of older people's housing.* Housing Care and Suppot, 13(3), 2010. pp.36-41.

[20] Fleming, R. & Bennett, K, Environmental Assessment Tool-High Care. Handbook. Dementic Training Australia, Desiging for the People with Dementia, 2017.

https://doi.org/10.1142/9789811238727_0058

Research on "Intelligence+" Innovation of Product and Industry Based on the Application of Artificial Intelligence Technology

Xianrong Liang*, Jiangxi Yu, Dong Zheng

Guangdong University of Finance & Economics,
Guangzhou Academy of Fine Arts, Macao University of Science & Technology,
Guangzhou, Guangdong, China
*Corresponding Author Email: 330270210@qq.com

Abstract

With the publication of China's "new generation of artificial intelligence governance principles" in June 17, 2019, the research on the legal, ethical and social problems of artificial intelligence will be strengthened, and the healthy development of the new generation of artificial intelligence will be promoted. It marks a new stage of global artificial intelligence technology. Based on the application of artificial intelligence technology at this stage, especially the innovation concept of "intelligence +" put forward by the Chinese government, this paper takes Foshan City of GBA as an example with the research of multiple application modes of "intelligence +", to clarify the role of "intelligence +" in promoting the innovation of cultural products and industrial transformation, so as to help the development of regional cultural innovation and characteristic cultural industry economy.

Keywords: Artificial Intelligence, Innovation of products, Transformation of industrial, Characteristic cultural, GBA

Text

With the advent of the era of intelligence, people's lives will undergo tremendous changes. We have a mission to make use of the power of the tide of intelligent science and technology, to enable the innovation and development of cultural products with distinctive characteristics, and to do a good job of cultural heritage and innovation.

A. The "intelligence+" era is coming

According to the work report of the Chinese government in 2019, We should persist in innovation leading development and foster new momentum. It mentions that, We should promote the transformation and upgrading of traditional industries. Particularly, it is necessary to build an industrial Internet platform, expand "intelligence+", and empower the transformation and upgrading of manufacturing industry. This is the first time that "intelligence+" appeared in the Prime Minister's report after "Internet +" was written into the government's work report. As a national strategy, AI is gradually merging with industry as an infrastructure to accelerate the optimization and upgrading of economic structure. It will have a far-reaching impact on people's production and lifestyle. This marked the advent of "intelligence+" era. "intelligence+" represents the new stage and new dimension of the development of digital technology. Expanding "intelligence+" is inseparable from promoting the transformation of traditional industries, especially manufacturing industries. The R&D and application of AI, big data and cloud computing will become the key to the development of "intelligence+", and both hardware and software are the support of "intelligence+". "intelligence+" aims to integrate technology with industry, especially manufacturing, and use technology to transform traditional industries, so as to reduce costs and increase efficiency. This is particularly significant in the context of slowing down the growth rate of the external world economy, increasing uncertainties of instability, highlighting the pain of internal economic transformation and increasing downward pressure of the economy.

B. Regional characteristics cultural resources and industry in Foshan

We choose Foshan as a case for analysis and research, because it is a typical city in GBA. On the one hand, Foshan has a profound cultural background and rich cultural resources with characteristics, on the other hand, Foshan has a high-quality industrial foundation, especially the rise of intelligent technology industry. These conditions have laid the foundation for the transformation and innovation of "Intelligent +" cultural products with characteristics.

a. Foshan is a characteristic culture city

Foshan is known for its reputation as the home of ceramics, Cantonese opera, the Wushu, the Canton yarn center, the hometown of South of the Five Ridges medicine, the South foundry center, the hometown of folk art, and the famous tourist and cultural city of Guangdong. The total number of municipal intangible heritage projects has reached 103. There are 163 non-hereditary inheritors at the municipal level and 38 intangible cultural heritages at the national and provincial levels, of which 14 are at the national level. However, with the change of the times, the characteristic cultural products represented by intangible cultural heritage are gradually far away from people's daily necessities, resulting in the low popularity of characteristic cultural products or non-legacy culture and the lack of innovative vitality of characteristic cultural products, resulting in a weak market transformation rate, failing to form a benign economic ecosphere and failing to attract the favor of the younger generation. As a result, it is difficult to inherit intangible cultural heritage and lack of innovation. In addition, the level of development of traditional cultural products manufacturing industry is quite different, and the general understanding of intelligent upgrading is not deep, and the investment in innovation is insufficient.

b. characteristic cultural products innovation ability of Foshan needs to be improved.

Foshan is rich in human tourism resources and characteristic culture. Taking “Lingnan Tiandi” scenic spot as an example, a demonstration scenic spot of cultural reconstruction with Foshan characteristics cultural, 128 historic buildings and 22 cultural relics protection units in the scenic area, through protection, repair and comprehensive utilization of the “three old transformations”, even in the way of integration of Chinese and Western, ancient and modern, make the ancient Lingnan architectural culture shine again, and a large number of cultural and creative supplies, food and ornaments in various formats have emerged in commercial markets. However, more than 90% of the commodities in a wide range of scenic spots have no difference from other scenic spots. A few of the cultural and creative products related to the characteristics of scenic spots have little bright spot, and their consumption attraction is not strong. It is rare to see innovative products that can combine cultural and creative ideas.

At the present stage, the charm of characteristic cultural products is insufficient, resulting in insufficient market transformation vitality and weak innovation and R&D ability of production enterprises. This requires the support of relevant government policies and innovative R&D enterprises, institutions or social institutions to play a leading role in typical demonstrations, set up benchmarks, gather the confidence and determination to promote the transformation and upgrading of cultural products by “intelligence+ innovation”, and use “intelligence+ thinking mode” and scientific and technological means to couple innovation with cultural products with regional characteristics, so as to promote the intelligent upgrading of products. In order to promote the upgrading of traditional cultural industries with characteristics and jointly build an “intelligent + cultural development ecosphere” with characteristics. Then, through demonstration and promotion, the achievements of industrial innovation will be expanded, new sustainable development will be formed, and the transformation from “Foshan Manufacturing” to “Foshan Smart Manufacturing” will be promoted.

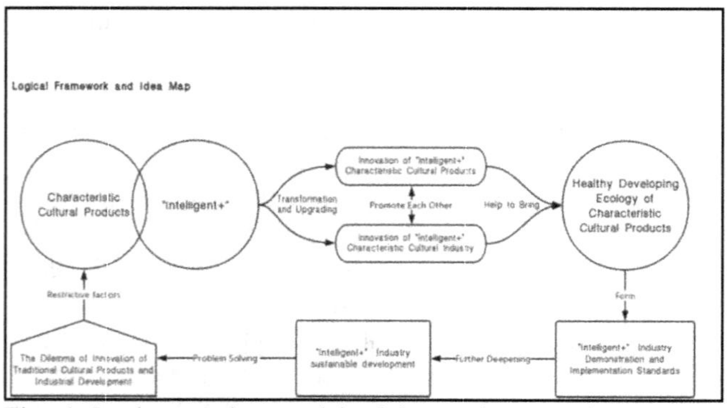

Fig. 1 Implementation model of innovating transformation with "intelligence+" for characteristic cultural products

c. Industry General situation and the Foundation of “intelligent +” Innovation in Foshan

In 2018, the gross domestic product of Foshan was 993.588 billion yuan, ranking third in the province. The added value of the primary industry is 14.445 billion yuan, that of the secondary industry is 56.140 billion yuan and that of the tertiary industry is 41.77 billion yuan. Among them, the dominant traditional industries grew by 7.1%, advanced manufacturing by 7.4%, high-tech manufacturing by 1.7%, and private enterprises by 7.1%. Midea, Country-garden, Jaten and other large leading enterprises have bet on artificial intelligence to seize the industry's commanding heights and promote the transformation from “Made in Foshan” into “Intelligent Creation in Foshan”. In November 2018, China·Foshan Global Artificial Intelligence and Intelligent Manufacturing Summit was successfully held in Foshan. A number of well-known enterprises such as Wasu, LongshenRobot, ClevRobot and Lixunda emerged in Foshan Industrial Robot Industry, becoming the most important ecological builder of Foshan Artificial Intelligence Industry. The traditional manufacturing industry of Foshan has also stepped into the robotics industry, which has strengthened the automation and intellectualization capabilities of industrial production, and laid a solid foundation for the “intelligent + innovation” of Foshan to promote the transformation and upgrading of cultural products.

C. Innovation Needs of Characteristic Cultural Products about “Lingnan Taidi” scenic spot

Traditional characteristic cultural products have strong local characteristic cultural elements, but there are some phenomena, such as the old style of handicraft products, the complex technology and the high cost of making manpower. However, in the design of appearance image of large-scale machine-produced goods, the interpretation of regional culture is relatively superficial, and it falls into the dilemma of “bumping into each other” in the shape of different regional markets, and even appears the dilemma of “mistaken identity” in culture.

According to the author's many investigations and investigations, at present, most of the localcultural products in the domestic cultural scenic spot market have not been able to conduct in-depth research and consumer experience research according to the regional cultural characteristics. It fails to meet the needs of consumers from tourism commemoration, humanistic experience, functional application, consumer care and other aspects. A few characteristic cultural products with innovative concepts are also in a dilemma of applause, failing to form a more benign market economic effect. It is manifested in the following aspects.

a. “intelligence+Design”: Innovative design of product image should pay attention to the symbolic transmission of cultural image.

Cultural products often have strong regional cultural characteristics, can reflect the regional human characteristics and spiritual features, is an important carrier of cultural construction and cultural dissemination. From the visual point of view, the elements related to regional characteristics and culture are deeply studied and refined, combining with the aesthetic style of the times, forming the innovation of visual image symbols. The auditory image needs mainly embody the language culture and music culture with regional characteristics, and combine visual image to achieve the integration of audio-visual cultural communication. Through the cultural transmission of tactile materials, users' three-dimensional tactile sensory experience can be achieved, which is helpful for special groups such as children, the elderly and the disabled to have a thorough understanding of the regional characteristics of cultural products. In some special types of product design, the cultural experience of smell and taste can be formed.

For example, the special food in "Lingnan Tiandi" scenic spot can enhance the cultural experience of vision, smell and hearing in packaging design, make the product meet the multi-dimensional and diversified innovative needs in image symbolic design, make the regional characteristic cultural products bear nostalgia, and become the "cultural hand letter" that can be taken away by the spread of characteristic culture.

b. "intelligence+Material": Innovative application of material technology and development of new processes and functions to meet the needs of consumers.

The functionality of products determines the user selection orientation and the sustainability of product innovation. In the process of product design with characteristic culture, product function design must proceed from the perspective of user needs.

Traditional cultural products with special features, especially some non-heritage products, have gradually been far away from the necessity of daily life in terms of their use functions. More of them exist in the form of handicraft products, forming an embarrassing situation.

The innovation of special cultural products requires the application of material and technological innovation, and the use of scientific and technological innovations and application methods to eliminate some inappropriate materials and processes with new materials and technologies, like "intelligence+IoT (Internet of Things)", to extract the essence of distinctive cultural products and to remove the dross, so as to reduce the production cost, meet the current function and enhance the functionality and cost performance of products after the application of new products and materials. Improve product market transformation capability.

For example, "Shiwan Gongzai" ceramic dolls as a tourist souvenirs selling in "Lingnan Tiandi" scenic spot can only be decorated as handicraft in the corner of daily life as a non-heritage product, which fails to play a substantive role and use. Of course, if we want to endow old and new products with new energy, we must invest a lot of research thinking and innovation costs, vigorously advocate intellectual property protection, actively promote the application of patent for design, utility model or invention related to product innovation, improve the protection of relevant laws and regulations and supervision, and protect innovation can better promote innovation. Sustainable development of innovation of characteristic cultural products through creating environment, legal protection and market economy feedback.

c. "intelligence+Service": In product experience, we need to understand the needs of users better and pay attention to human care.

Characteristic cultural products carry regional characteristic culture and can directly and effectively convey cultural characteristics and folklore feelings. They are often presented to foreign tourists or non-native people as hand letters. Therefore, when faced with the low familiarity of local culture by most tourists and non-native people, the experience of cultural products becomes more important, not only in terms of product quality, but also in terms of product quality. Hard, cost-effective to meet consumers, but also need to pay attention to the effectiveness of the product in cultural communication and the intuition of people's feelings in the use process.

At present, the vast majority of domestic characteristic cultural products fail to pay attention to user experience, especially in the construction of cultural experience mechanism, lack of scientific interaction mechanism and interesting play methods, so they fail to convey emotions to objects and teach to enjoy. Some landmark areas with cultural experience in "Lingnan Tiandi" of Foshan, such as Bell Tower, Longtang Poets' Club, Shiwan Winery, Li-Zhongsheng Chinese Pharmacy and other historical and cultural highlights, have relatively shallow user experience of cultural products, fail to tap deep cultural potential, and fail to bring more profound cultural experience and impression to tourists. In this respect, we can refer to Disneyland's experience of park-style culture and product culture. Through the interaction between scenarios and products, we can enhance the sense of interaction and participation of tourists, form a deeper cultural experience, convey characteristic culture and promote economic growth.

d. "intelligence+Production": The production and mode of production of products need to be innovated, and the allocation of resources needs to be optimized scientifically.

The traditional production technology and mode of production cannot meet the current demand of social productivity. The lack of vitality and adaptability in the application of new materials and the integration of new technologies and innovations results in the overflow of low-end products, waste of production capacity, pollution of the environment, lack of resources allocation, weak innovation and poor market efficiency. Hand-made non-heritage products have low productivity, high human time consumption, market limitations and disproportionate economic returns. At present, it is urgent to use the achievements of scientific and technological revolution to allocate resources and optimize product technology, to reduce the production cost and labor resource cost of cultural products with special characteristics by scientific methods, to promote product innovation by applying scientific and technological achievements, to optimize resource allocation and improve production mode, to enhance product market vitality, to improve enterprise economic efficiency, and to realize industrial growth and sound development.

Foshan is a global high-tech industrial concentration area. The government has made great efforts to support industrial innovation. The famous enterprises such as Midea Group, Foshan Lighting (FSL) and Galanz play a leading role in the innovation reform, and promote the transformation from "Foshan Manufacturing" to "Foshan Intelligent Manufacturing". More enterprises need to devote themselves to product innovation, optimize production capacity, use information technology "intelligence+Allocation" to build a resource allocation platform, integrating the geographic resources advantage of GBA, so that cultural products with special characteristics combined with the achievements of the scientific and technological revolution reflect greater value.

e. "intelligence+Production": Promotion of marketing means and methods needs to be more accurate and effective.

At present, characteristic cultural products are mainly divided into B2C (retail to customers), C2C (retail to customers by individuals), B2B (gift purchasing by merchants).

There are relatively few ways of using O2O (online to offline trading). There are three main reasons: 1) Trading of characteristic cultural products often takes place in tourist attractions or places of cultural experience. 2) Customers do not have a deep understanding of cultural products with regional characteristics, so they have to experience and recognize them before they can form a transaction. 3) At present, there is no brand effect, no systematic framework and introduction of characteristic cultural products. Customers cannot understand the product and cultural connotation information through Internet platform or other channels, nor can they guarantee product quality and after-sales service.

Therefore, it is urgent to establish the brand concept of characteristic cultural products, ensure product quality and service level, establish brand culture and create brand effect. Taking "Lingnan Tiandi" as an example, the establishment of regional brand cultural experience-based shopping business environment for cultural products with characteristics, the construction of a platform for the supply of cultural products with characteristics and the online sales of O2O, relying on the promotion of tourist service centers and visual guidance systems, can realize online trading to offline consumption experience, offline marketing to online trading. From offline marketing to online trading, then to offline consumption experience, online trading or marketing to offline consumption experience, then to online consumption experience, a brand new business model. Through the use of advanced technology such as big data, artificial intelligence and psychological knowledge, the production, circulation and sales process of commodities are upgraded and transformed, and then the industry structure and ecosphere are rebuilt, and a new retail model of deep integration of online service, offline experience and modern logistics is put forward.

f. Creating after-sales and one-stop service platform is an efficient way to promote the sustainable development of product innovation.

Constructing the after-sales service platform and cultural experience extension service of cultural products with brand characteristics will help to enhance customers' trust and feedback on products, increase brand stickiness, promote cultural transmission and extension, and enhance the sustainability of product innovation.

"Lingnan Tiandi" scenic spot currently has a visitor service center and a Wechat service platform online, serving consultation of tourist, cultural orientation and tourism-related management. However, little attention has been paid to the construction of special cultural products, souvenirs promotion and cultural product service platform, especially the social system relying on Wechat public number service platform. The construction of social system is used to satisfy the communication and linkage between tourists and service centers. It is conducive to absorbing a large number of digital network fans, collecting large data information, analyzing customers' personality preferences, realizing the promotion information of precise delivery of cultural products and in-depth interpretation of articles in regional culture, enhancing tourists' sense of participation and interaction in cultural experience, and enhancing the text. The quality of chemical tourism will help the economic growth of tourism and promote the sustainable innovation and development of characteristic cultural products.

D. Conclusion

It is worthwhile to study and promote the innovation and industrial upgrading of cultural products with local characteristics through "intelligence+" innovation. This paper focuses on Foshan's characteristic traditional cultural products. In the era of "intelligence+", we should study how to exert the power of scientific and technological innovation to help transform and upgrade. Learn to make use of the integration of regional culture and modern "intelligent + thinking" to generate tremendous momentum for the transformation and leapfrogging of traditional industries. On the basis of precise classification of traditional cultural products and current human ecology based on regional cultural characteristics, With the scientific and technological means and methods of "intelligence+" innovation such as intellectualization, informationization and systematization, the ecological application of traditional products is redefined in combination with traditional processes. To carry out a series of studies on human ecological environment and social development needs. And summarized them to form certain theoretical results.

The research on innovation of characteristic cultural products in the era of "intelligent +" includes the exploration of the inevitability of innovation of characteristic cultural products, and research on the innovation demand of traditional cultural products transformation, as well as examples of innovation orientation and exploration of cultural products with characteristics enabled by "intelligent +". Through the exploration of "intelligent +" innovation, we can make the cultural products and industries with local characteristics of GBA go higher and farther.

References

[1] Ray Kurzweil. *Future of Artificial Intelligence* [M]. Zhejiang: Zhejiang People's Publishing House, 2016:pp117-170.

[2] Chen Yunhong, He Xia.*Billows: Global Intelligent Revolution Opportunity* [M]. Beijing: Electronic Industry Press, 2016: pp60-126.

[3] Zhou Xibing, *Internet: The Path of Self-Subversion and Reconstruction of Traditional Enterprises* [M]. Zhejiang: Zhejiang University Press, 2016:pp38-90.

[4] Ruan Yonghua. *Internet +: The Way of Intelligent Breakthrough of Traditional Enterprise Products* [M]. Beijing: Machinery Industry Press, 2016:pp141-154.

[5] Wang Jingyan. *Research Report on the Present Situation and Countermeasure of Artificial Intelligence Application in Foshan Manufacturing Industry Chain* [R]. Guangdong: Foshan Association of Social Sciences, 2016:pp2-4.

[6] Song Qi. *Research on the Design of Game-based Social App Products for the Aged in Digital Literature Creation: Taking Sanshui in Foshan as an Example* [J]. Art Science and Technology, 2017, pp07-03:10-11.

[7] Gong Zen, Wu Xumin. *Brief Analysis of User Needs to Promote Product Design Innovation* [J]. Art View, 2017, 2017-10:pp128

[8] Lin Junhong. *Current Situation and Innovative Exploration of Cultural and Creative Products in Guilin* [J]. Intelligence, 2018, 2018-17:pp250

[9] Huang Wei, Yizijuan, Xu Haihao, Wu Jianfeng. *Research on Innovative Design of Household Fitness Products Based on Internet+* [J]. Packaging Engineering, 2017, 38 (22): pp6-10.

[10] Jiang Yan, Cheng Siyuan, Cong Haichen. *Innovative Product Design Method Based on Functional Conversion* [J]. Manufacturing Automation, 2018, 40 (4): pp130

https://doi.org/10.1142/9789811238727_0059

Research on Advertising Visual Design in Style Language

Yisong Chen

Xiamen Academy of Arts and Design, Fuzhou University, Xiamen, China
Email: 645748317@qq.com, TEL: 008618050048446

Abstract

Taking the visual creativity of the International Fashion Brand Dolce&Gabbana as an example, this paper expounds that classicism presents a unique style of luxury image, which contains a high degree of integration of Western culture and brand culture. Under the background of the brand era, the visual benefit of fashion advertising image plays a vital role in the trend direction, which proves that the visual design of advertising must have its own systematic style language The brand image can live forever in the consumer heart.

Keywords: style language, fashion brand, advertising design, visual design

Introduction

Advertising visual design is a set of corporate philosophy and product characteristics as one of the art design. In order to attract consumers, a company or a product needs to show its own characteristics and gain social recognition, so as to establish a Brand loyalty, the visual image of advertising becomes a top priority. The design of advertisement vision should obey the brand idea, and the visual perception of the picture is higher than other visual elements. Most excellent brand vision image promotion can accurately reflect their style personality by the picture performance alone.

A. The formation of artistic concept of style language

As a kind of art concept, the artistic works with different styles have different representational features, and their unique contents and forms are unified with each other, not only having subjective and objective reasons, and it's reflected in the many elements of the work. The works with unique style can produce great artistic appeal and realize the exchange of emotion and aesthetic ideal.

In the colorful world, the works of art with different styles are different from the general artistic characteristics because of the style inside and outside. In different historical conditions, there are different emotional tendencies and aesthetic pursuit, is through the works of art to show an era, a nation, an artist, a brand of internal thinking and aesthetic characteristics.

B. Advertising visual design of fashion clothing brand

Fashion brands lead the world in fashion trends, the industry every year will launch countless fashion advertising visual image, and each season of advertising visual creativity is always the most anticipated after the fashion show highlights. The fashion vision of various styles, various angles and various contents fills our line of sight like snowflakes. Either dazzling luxury, or elegant romantic, fashion brand visual impact has always greatly stimulated people's desire for new product consumption, as well as the construction of Brand loyalty Therefore, it constitutes a visual Feast of fashion advertising design, which is composed of fashion products, brand image and visual design, and forms a unique visual culture direction of modern fashion.

Fashion advertising design is different from the general means of product promotion or promotion, as part of the brand image and visual culture, it is aimed at the spring and summer, Autumn and winter each year after the emergence of new product design, visual Promotion of new product style. Not only to video advertising, but also to occupy the form of photography in the major media, usually by fashion, models, brand image and other combinations of the screen. Includes Photography and fashion style display, as well as the image of the brand often used positioning. The aim is to promote the design style of brand new products, thus achieving further promotion and maintenance of the fashion brand image through extremely powerful images Finally, the concept of fashion products and brands will be deeply rooted in the consumer visual impact produced by the deep touch. Therefore, the visual image of fashion advertising has become not only an important part of the current fashion and luxury areas, but also a graphic visual design art.

The fashion advertisement design of each big brand usually has the story line, the attraction and the shock, pursues the picture the design feeling and the visual impact. Each season of fashion and graphic design style although the theme is different, but there will be some inextricably linked. Thus on the one hand to meet the physiological needs of visual freshness and sensory stimulation, but also to maintain the self-brand image positioning. Fashion brands are often joined by big-name photographers or models, through the creative direction and design of the chief planner and designers, as well as high production costs Although the visual effect that its build comes out is absolute commercialize pursue, but the design work that has originality extremely can call top advertisement The visual impact of a seemingly luxurious fashion advertising idea does not simply depend on the gorgeous appearance of the product or the designer's personality And the visual promotion of International Fashion Advertising has its own unique language and style of cultural design.

C. DOLCE&GABBANA's self-styled language

Dolce&Gabbana, an Italian luxury brand founded in 1985, has a style language around its main inspiration: Sicily. The fashion ads launched every season not only perfectly express the design features of each season, but also always give people the originality of novelty, temptation and eccentric elves, as well as the gorgeous stacking and decoration like Baroque art, which can perfectly interpret the brand positioning of Dolce&Gabbana. What's important is that the design launched in each season not only has its own style, but also has a very iconic image as soon as it appears. It not only brings great visual enjoyment to consumers, but also creates a strong brand identity of Dolce&Gabbana. The Baroque spirit of luxury, grandeur, refinement and decoration creates a great space for the promotion of brand image.

Fig. 1 Dolce&Gabbana Spring / Summer 2009 "Baroque" Advertising Visual Design

a. Dolce&Gabbana Baroque art style design expression

Baroque from Europe in the 17th century, it broke the balance of the characteristics of the renaissance, advocating human luxury, attention to emotional performance, with gripping artistic effect. The combination of Baroque's fashion elements and the aristocratic luxury of the Royal Court is evident in the design of the advertisement.

As shown in Figure 1. On the one hand, from the perspective of the language of the fashion itself, the rich colors of baroque silk brocade and velvet, luxurious and gorgeous hand embroidery at the cost of work, stacked by large jewelry, pearls, gems, etc., and exaggerated round sleeves The angular design of the lower body and the overall flashy decoration show the grandness of Baroque art, like the image of an 18th-century female aristocrat who emerged from Rubens oil painting, giving people a fascinating temptation. On the other hand, those models with classic and luxurious makeup in advertising design play and run in the 18th-century-style rooms with serious expressions of sexy and mysterious; large-scale cameras showing modernity, and full of advertising images The brand font of "Dolce&Gabbana" at the bottom makes the overall picture exaggerated and dramatic. The retro house structure and modern elements constitute a stark contrast, sketching the classic romance from Sicily, Italy, the hometown of the designer Dolce & Gabbana, and also containing a million styles from the south of Italy.

The fantastic design combination of Dolce&Gabbana designers, which combines the classical baroque style with the modern life vividly, reflects the local style of Sicily and the luxury scene of the palace noble life. It not only explains Dolce&Gabbana's 2009 "pigiama Barocco pajamas" spring and summer fashion series, but also creates a very delicate and gorgeous, exquisite and retro Baroque picture It brings endless visual enjoyment to the viewers.

b. Dolce&Gabbana Rococo art style design expression

Rococo's art form is complex, delicate, and exquisite. Its fashion design performance is completely different from the style language of geometric shapes. It discards rigorous style and retains a wide hip design. The intertwined atmosphere of luxury, social enjoyment and desire during the period formed the typical female silhouette effect of the late Baroque.

The advertising visual design of the Dolce&Gabbana 2009 spring and summer series is exactly the cultural information that inherits the characteristics of the brand and the inherent style. as shown in Figure 2. Different from the composition methods of one or two mannequins in other brand advertising designs, Dolce&Gabbana first adopted a combination of multiple people in the composition design to make the two-dimensional plane full of tension. This self-spirit is the most prominent in Rococo art. Large cameras with the same heavy modern feel, and the brand name font at the bottom of the advertising screen make the overall screen not only exaggerated but full and full.

Fig. 2 Dolce&Gabbana Spring / Summer 2009 "Rococo" Advertising Visual Design

c. Dolce&Gabbana advertising visual style expressiveness

The surface of Dolce&Gabbana's fashion advertisements seems to be just the category of clothing design, but it is not. From the advertising design of the new spring and summer 2009, we can see that the language of fashion design is only an element and clue, and the key elements that highlight the visual impact of an ad are not only these, but also the overall atmosphere, composition, font, etc Many ways, as well as leading artistic styles and techniques. Here, as for the overall composition of fashion advertising design, the clothing product itself is only a certain element in the picture, but what you don't see is all the style language that forms the whole, such as storyline, scene atmosphere, screen composition. Dolce&Gabbana Spring-Summer 2009 Baroque-style fashion advertising, no matter from the fullness of composition, rich colors, rich plots, etc., or even exquisite details reflect Baroque luxury, exaggeration, drama, grand, cumbersome details and strong decoration Consciousness and other inner spirits. This requires that the planners and designers of advertising vision should have a solid theoretical framework of artistic design, a solid grasp of artistic style expression skills, and a deep cultivation of Western history and art.

d. The style influence of Dolce&Gabbana advertising visuals

As an important part of the construction of brand image visual arts, fashion advertising plays a vital role in the international language of clothing brands. The visual design of international fashion advertising has its own style language, no matter how exaggerated and luxurious the pictures are, they are highly unified in their respective fashion styles and brand culture. Minimalist art-style CK fashion advertisements and Doir fashion advertisements also perfectly present the connotation of minimalist visual culture and classicism culture. For a long time, Dolce&Gabbana fashion advertisements have a story language, dramatic scene settings, multi-model scene layout and other methods, which not only reflect the classicism and methods of Baroque and Rococo style, but also affect the brand image of similar products.

e. Dolce&Gabbana style language makes timeless classics

After 10 years, Dolce & Gabbana 2019 China Shanghai International Import Expo was held at Shanghai International Exhibition Center from November 5th to 10th, 2019. Dolce & Gabbana is one of the Italian luxury exhibitors with a 400 square meter booth.

As shown in Figure 3. Booth image design is also one of the forms of brand advertising. With classic heritage, superb craftsmanship and attention to detail, Dolce&Gabbana translates these values into aesthetic declarations, improving product quality and proprietary Italian manufacturing technology. The island of ancient tradition and evocative symbols provides countless creative associations for later design, and this information will become the backbone of brand creativity. Dolce&Gabbana's booth was specially arranged around the brand's iconic theme, just like the visual image of an advertisement, continuing its eternal classic with its own style and language characteristics.

Fig. 3 Advertising visual design of Dolce&Gabbana 2019 China Shanghai International Import Expo

Conclusion

Domenico Dolce and Stefano Gabbana, two design masters from Sicily, their wild ideas are not only reflected in the design of clothing, but also in all the visual design of advertising. They shared their love of 17th and 18th century Baroque, Rococo and other classicist artistic styles, interpreted the unique style into the Dolce & Gabbana brand and promoted it to the world. They transformed the concept of fashion design into a visual image to convey the soul of Dolce & Gabbana, and this depends on their understanding and perception of the brand's visual promotion art. With the visual design of advertising in style language, brand image can be rooted in consumers' hearts.

References

[1] Meyer Schapiro, *Theory and Philosophy of Art: Style, Artist, and Society[M]*, Nanjing: Jiangsu Fine Arts Publishing House, 2016.

[2] Li Beilei. He Yun, *Chinese Contemporary Art: Image, Concept, Style[M]*, Jinan: Shandong Education Press, 2019.

[3] Rolf Toman, *Baroque art[M]*, Beijing: Beijing art photography publishing house, 2013.

[4] Vernon Hyde Minor, *Baroque and Rococo[M]*, Guilin: Guangxi Normal University Press, 2004.

[5] McAssey, Buckley, *Fashion Design Elements: Styling and Style[M]*. Beijing: China Textile Press, 2013.

[6] Chen Gen, *Advertising Design[M]*, Beijing: Chemical Industry Press, 2018.

[7] Ye Ping, *Visual Design and Creativity[M]*, Shenyang: Liaoning Fine Arts Publishing House, 2014.

[8] Sarah Bailey, *Brand Visual Marketing[M]*, Beijing: China Textile Press, 2018.

https://doi.org/10.1142/9789811238727_0060

Research on Design of Ceramic Cultural and Creative Products in Macao—Case Study of Macau University of Science and Technology Ceramic Art Laboratory

Xizhi Zhang[1] and Kuo-Hsun Wen[2*]

[1]Faculty of Humanities and Arts, Macau University of Science and Technology, Avenida Wai Long, Taipa, Macau
[2]School of Arts, Macao Polytechnic Institute, R. de Luís Gonzaga Gomes, Macao
*Corresponding Author Email: khwen@ipm.edu.mo

Abstract

Macau is one of the world's tourism and leisure cities, visited by more than 30 million tourists each year, which drives a large demand for cultural and creative products. The Macau government has launched a number of policies on the development and design of cultural and creative products to promote the development of cultural and creative industries in Macao. Therefore, it is imperative to develop cultural and creative products with Macao's cultural characteristics, and the design and development of ceramic cultural and creative products is a blank in the market and needs to be filled. Macao's cultural and creative industries started late, and there are still many shortcomings compared to other cities. The current development strategy of Macao is moderate and pluralistic sustainable development, and the cultural and creative industry is undoubtedly an important one; therefore, the study of cultural and creative industries is of great significance to the development of Macao. Visual art and design is the key to developing cultural creativity. This study is mainly based on the development status of cultural creativity in Macao and conducts in-depth research on the development and design mode of ceramic cultural and creative products.

Keywords: Macao, Culture creative product, Ceramic design, Brand value

Introduction

Macao, with about 30 million tourists a year, is undoubtedly a world-famous tourism and Leisure City. The Macao Special Administrative Region (SAR) government has also issued policies to build Macao into a world leisure center. Therefore, the demand for cultural and creative products related to tourism is increasing day by day. The promotion of cultural and creative industries in Macao is not long, just a decade. Although tourism is one of the main industries in Macao, the concept of cultural creativity to support the sustainable development of tourism industry is relatively immature. Based on this background, it is necessary for the Macao SAR government to think deeply about the cultural and creative products based on Macao's regional characteristics. However, from the perspective of the current development of tourism industry, the development of cultural and creative industries related to tourism is less, and the cultural elements with Macao characteristics are not effectively utilized. Therefore, how to refine and transport the cultural elements of Macao's characteristics is one of the key ways to develop Macao's tourism industry by further exploration in achieving the use of cultural and creative concept to support the development of tourism industry in Macao.

Macao Cultural and Creative Product Research Paths

A. Macao's local culture and status quo of cultural and creative products

Although Macao's geographical space is not large, it has a profound cultural heritage, including the Cantonese culture of the Chinese nation, Minnan culture, and foreign Western culture. Together, these cultures form a special cultural body that coexists in a pluralistic way, directly or indirectly affecting the development of Macao's art culture.

The Macao Cultural Affairs Bureau established the Creative Industry Promotion Office in 2010. In the same year, the Macao Special Administrative Region (SAR) Government also established the Cultural Industry Committee. On October 29, 2013, the Macao SAR Cultural Industry Fund was established, with its main purposes to promote project incubation, industrialization, and scale of cultural industries; to explore cultural and creative projects with distinctive local characteristics; to promote the research and development, design, production, marketing, and promotion of cultural and creative goods; and to promote intellectual property registration [1].

In 2015, the first group of support projects of the Cultural Industry Fund was launched, marking the entry of the cultural industry of Macao into the basic practical stage 1 to provide a better development platform for the cultural industry in Macao. According to the data of the Cultural Industry Fund website, from the launch of the application in 2014 to the end of October 2016, the fund has accepted more than 400 applications for funding with a total funding of more than 138 million patacas. In the first half of 2018, the Cultural Products Fund approved a total of 15 funded projects with a total funding of 33 million patacas and a commercial project investment of 120 million patacas. The products in the creative design category are launched in line with cultural tourism themes, which are sold at tourist spots and airport counters, as well as via the Internet and social media.

At present, Macao cultural and creative products are mostly based on the theme of World Heritage. Macao's local cultural and creative brand has O-Moon (its products are designed with Macao and Portuguese motifs; in addition to general souvenirs, e.g., key chains and notebooks, handbags, jewelry, external chargers, and other products are also offered). Other products are based on the Macau brand Soda Panda with a panda as the main design element; also, the Todot brand has won international awards "its products mainly include four categories, including watches, fashion brands, and stationery products [2]". Owing to the Macao government's emphasis on the development of cultural and creative industries, it is believed that more excellent cultural and creative products will enter the market in the future to enhance the brand image of Macau's cities.

B. Macao cultural and creative product design research ideas

Based on the current situation of Macao's local culture and cultural and creative products market, we conducted systematic research and analysis of Macao's local cultural resources. We sorted out local cultural resources of Macao, established a local cultural resource classification model to assist creative design, analyzed and studied the design attributes of local cultural and creative products, explored the design features presented by the combination of ceramic product design and local culture, and verified the aforementioned using actual design cases, so as to achieve the goal of improving the quality and value of Macao's cultural and creative products. Research ideas are shown in Fig. 1.

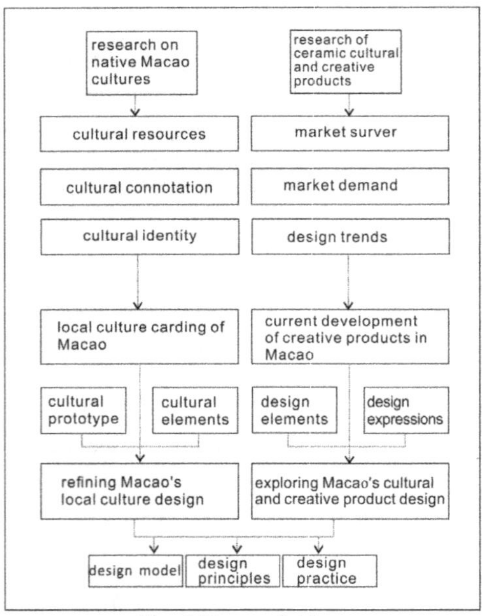

Fig. 1 Research ideas

Macao Ceramic Cultural and Creative Product Design Model

A. Macao's characteristic cultural resources and modal classification

Owing to its diversity, Macao's local culture involves a large amount of cultural content and forms. Therefore, it is necessary to collect, organize, and classify cultural resources, characteristics, connotations, and Macao prototypes and symbols to realize the need to acquire local cultural characteristics (and features), and then assist in the development of creative design. We divided Macao's local culture into three levels, namely physical culture, behavioral culture, and mentality culture, and combined and summarized different types of forms and contents using the method of one-to-one correspondence, and thus obtained the modal classification of Macao's native cultural resources (see Fig. 2).

The physical culture is the various physical substances accumulated in the long history of Macao. It is the integration of local material culture of Macao, which exists objectively in the physical state. It is a unique symbol that records the formation and development of Macao's native culture. Its existence provides designers with a rich and diverse cultural element.

The behavioral culture is the behavioral habits formed by Macao citizens in the process of practice and socialization, including spoken and written language (three written languages - Chinese, Portuguese, and English, and four spoken languages - Mandarin, Cantonese, Portuguese, and English), traditional skills, and the integration of Chinese and Western cultures. It reflects the unique social phenomenon of Macao and the wisdom of the working people, which helps the designer to understand the local culture deeply, and stimulates the design inspiration from the formation, expression, and form of the behavioral culture model itself.

The mentality culture is the unique mental and psychological characteristics and conceptual consciousness formed by the Macao people in social practice and consciousness activities. Designers should thoroughly understand and guide the design to express the deep cultural connotation of the product. The local culture division method involved here is clear in level and conforms to the way of design thinking; in other words, it matches the cognitive level proposed by Donald A. Norman and is convenient for designers to design and translate local cultural information.

In addition, in the process of Macao cultural level induction and modality distribution, based on its cultural characteristic analysis, two design attributes are introduced, namely locality and culture.

Locality means that the design content must be selected with cultural elements, cultural prototypes, and cultural symbols with distinctive local characteristics to assist the design creativity. This approach highlights uniqueness and local characteristics, thus achieving separation from the problem of single and homogenization of cultural and creative products, and achieving the purpose of forming a local brand effect.

Culturality refers to the cultural significance imparted to the product; specifically, a designer should pay attention to the symbolic meaning of culture, refine the cultural prototype of local cultural connotation, embody the symbolic meaning and value of culture in creative design, and better highlight the local characteristics and charm of products. All half-tone illustrations (pictures/ photographs) should be clear black and white prints. Do not use photocopies. These illustrations should be furnished within the copy. Make certain to include a caption in the paper for the illustration as well as to label the illustration on the back.

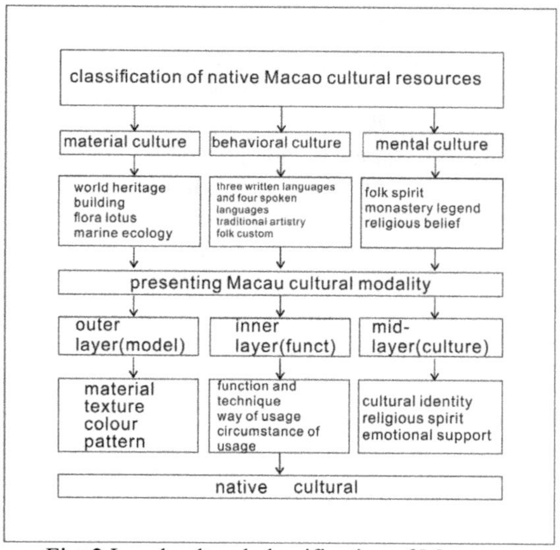

Fig. 2 Local cultural classification of Macao

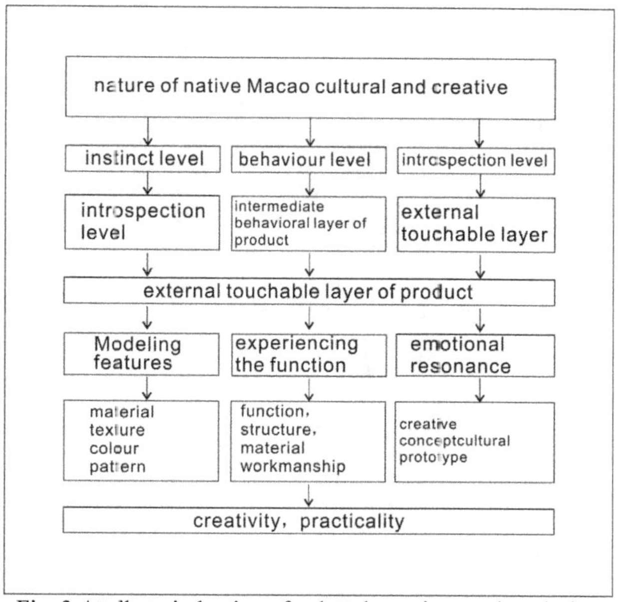

Fig. 3 Attribute induction of cultural creative product design

B. Design elements and characterization of Macao cultural and creative products

The paper starts from the perspective and level of product design, and study, specifically, the shape, form, color, material, texture, and emotional experience. According to Donald A. Norman's three levels of emotional cognition—instinct, behavior and reflection—"instinctive level design is the law of nature," "behavioral level design is related to the use," and "reflective level design covers many fields, and it is closely related to the meaning and use of information, culture and products.[3]" The design attributes and elements of the product can be summarized at a level to form a design element representation framework corresponding to the culture, and then the cultural creative product design attributes can be summarized (Fig. 3). Through this derivation, the design of cultural and creative products is characterized by function, structure, process, shape, color, material, and texture. The level division framework and the structural division of the above-mentioned cultural levels correspond to each other, which is beneficial to the combination of cultural resources in the process of design representation, so as to better interpret the theme. This process, based on the characteristics and requirements of this design, can lead to two attributes, innovation and practicality.

Innovativeness should have the vitality of functional innovation and formal innovation. Designers should properly handle the relationship between design, people, and culture to instantly match products with market demand and consumer demand.

Practicality is paying attention to the principle of practicability while having cultural and artistic characteristics, and also paying attention to the experience and use value of products while having a good form of beauty.

C. Macao ceramic cultural and creative product design model

Based on the above modal type division of Macao's local cultural resources and the division of design and characterization of Macao's cultural and creative products, we sorted out, combined, and classified Macao's local cultural modalities and product characterization elements. We then built a design and development model for the current Macao local cultural and creative ceramic products (Fig. 4), which is used as a reference for the design and development of Macao cultural and creative ceramic products. The principles of locality, culture, innovation, and practicability run through the entire process of productization and branding of Macao's local cultural and creative ceramics. Local culture is the content of cultural and creative products, and the expression of design language is the external expression of cultural and creative products; therefore, creative design means provide a good form of beauty to the product, which is the key to touch consumers' hearts and attract attention. The content and image of local culture is the core value of the product that can meet the needs of consumers and are often more valued by consumers. The cultural attributes and design rules are mutually integrated, and when in design and development phases they should be considered and applied according to the actual situation [4].

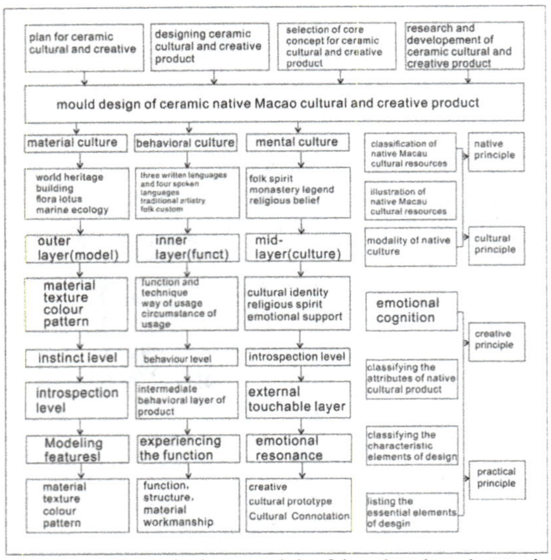

Fig. 4 Ceramic product design model of local cultural creativity of Macao

Macao Ceramic Cultural and Creative Products Design and Application Analysis

This section is based on the research and analysis of Macao's local cultural resources and hierarchical modal induction. The design case presentation and application analysis are based on the local cultural prototypes such as Macao's souvenir culture, marine culture, world heritage, Macao lotus culture, and Portuguese tile culture. First, we consider a ceramic tea set called Cookie, which was designed with souvenir culture as a prototype (Fig. 5). The tourism industry in Macau is well developed, and the tourism industry has also promoted the development of the souvenir (Shou Xin which means gift in Cantonese) industry. Macao's souvenirs used to be seafood, such as crab, oyster sauce, and shrimp paste. Today, there are also almond cookies, lard cakes, egg rolls, and egg tarts. These are typical examples of souvenir culture in Macao's native culture. In the Cookie tea set, the designer extracted the most representative Macao souvenir, the almond cookie, and summarized the shape, pattern, ornamentation, and color in the design, to display the local cultural characteristics. From the perspective of custom culture, guided by the principle of culture, the humanistic feelings of souvenirs also show the unique cultural customs and spiritual features of Macao.

In addition, in the process of deepening the design, the designer should fully consider design trends, boldly innovate in form, combine cultural elements of souvenirs with modern styles of ceramic product design, and strengthen the uniqueness of local culture. These, in turn, bring consumers a pleasant visual sense and fashion sense, and attract consumers' desire to purchase. In terms of the function of the product, the design mainly meets the needs of people in the function of a tea set, in which the overall shape of teapot and teacup is similar to that of an almond cookie, and the pattern of an almond cookie is displayed on the lids of both teapot and teacup; the word in the center of the pattern is converted from the original word "Almond" to the word "Macau" which intuitively reflects the characteristics of Macao's souvenir culture, and also better reflects the characteristics of souvenir culture that fits with Macao's native cultural characteristics. The design of the ceramic product is also uniquely expressed in the material presentation. Through the blending of toner and porcelain clay and via the molding method of plaster mold, the ceramic tea set with the texture effect of an almond cookie is displayed, showing a sense of simplicity and a more innovative product embodying Macao local characteristic.

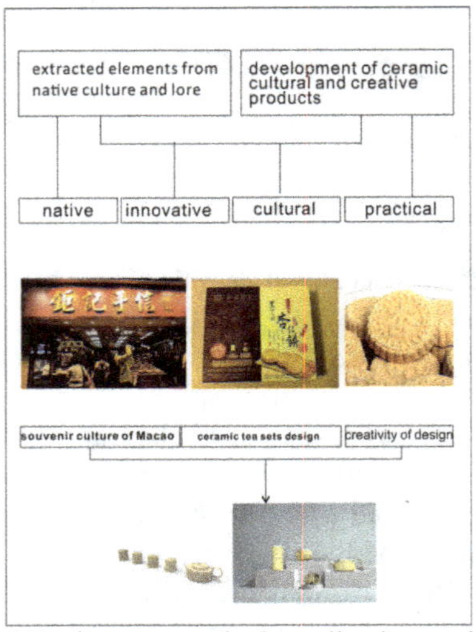

Fig. 5 Design case study & application analyses

Conclusion

The cultural tourism industry is a sunrise industry for the sustainable development of Macao, and the consumption of cultural tourism industry will also become a hot spot for Macao's economic growth. The design and development of cultural and creative products based on Macao's local culture is not only an effective way to enhance the added value of product cultural creativity, but also an important way to spread excellent regional culture. Moreover, it helps establish the image of urban cultural tourism and form a regional brand effect. Through systematic analysis, induction, and integration of Macao's native culture and creative products, we proposed corresponding design principles, established corresponding design models, and displayed and verified them with design examples. The aim is to assist designers in designing and developing more cultural and creative ceramic products embodying Macao's local cultural characteristics and innovative design and practicality, thus providing a feasible method for the design of Macao's local cultural and creative products.

Acknowledgment

Project support: Foundation of Macao University of Science and Technology. Project No.: FRG-19-022-FA

References

[1] Yong Xiang and Shiping Cui, *Regional Synergy and Platform Innovation*, Beijing: Macao Research Report 2015 Social Sciences Academic Press (China), pp. 128

[2] https://www.gov.mo/zh-hans/news/214007/CulturalIndustryFund (FIC)

[3] Donald Arthur Norman, He Xiao (trans.), *Emotional Design*, Beijing: Citic Press, 2012, pp. 58-78.

[4] Kjetil Fallan and Li Zhang, Design History Understanding Theory and Method, Jiangsu Phoenix Fine Arts Publishing, 2016, pp 89-91

https://doi.org/10.1142/9789811238727_0061

Research on Developing Healthy Self-Management Game to Improve College Students' Sub-Health

Shun-Nian Luo[1], Yen-Chang Chen[2*], Tun Kang[3]

[1]School of Information Science and Technology, Sanda University, Shanghai, China
[2]School of Sport and health, SanMing University, SanMing, Fujian, China
[3]Department of Business Administration, China University of Technology, Taipei, Taiwan
*Corresponding Author Email: tokolkk@gmail.com

Abstract

Chronic illness, such as hypertension or diabetes, tends to affect younger patients nowadays with associated suffering sub-health problems. We develop an entertainment-education Unity3D mobile game with which a player improves hypothetical health issues by playing a virtual character. The game is divided into four tasks: health consciousness, healthy diet habits, exercise habits, and the regular lifestyle. In each of these individual modes, the player gains points, as well as broadens knowledge by improving the health of the virtual character. A group of university students was invited to participate in the experiment with the game for over two months. The result of logistic regression analysis shows that all of the four modes of game have statistical significance in carrying out health promotion and disease prevention and keeping themselves in a happy mood, work effectiveness, and achieve academic success. This proves the efficacy of the health promotion game and suggests its business popularity through improving the quality and variety of the game. The games strengthen the healthy behavior of college students in general and achieves the goal of independent health management.

Keywords: Games, health promotion, sub-health, regular life, balanced life

Introduction

Hypertension and diabetes are seeing a trend of patients getting younger and younger, highlighting the seriousness of adolescents' sub-health problems [1,2]. The most common health risk factors are the lack of relaxation and physical activity, frequent work, air, and noise pollution [3]. Modern people generally have sub-health problems. The most common symptoms are fatigue, poor sleep quality, amnesia, fatigue that are not relieved easily after rest, dry throat, dizziness, dry and dry eyes, pain, uncomfortable eyes, early waking, sub-healthy people suffering from shoulder and neck syndrome, lower back pain, metabolic syndrome, and so on [3-5]. It seems that sub-health is the biggest worry about the health of modern people.

College students lack a "health responsibility" (6.5-27.1%) and engage in any form of sports (31.2%) or regular exercise (13.8%). Less than half of them eat fruits (35.2%) and vegetables (48.9%) every day [6]. Students are weak in a sub-health state. Sub-health is a state of mind and body between health and disease which usually manifests in depression, irritability, depression, anxiety, insomnia, lack of energy and easy colds [7].

An effective environment is necessary to maximize the potential of students for the foundation of future health [8]. Healthcare providers need to develop interventions to help students improve healthy lifestyles in their college environment [9]. Research point out that the focus of health intervention programs is to evaluate and improve the health self-efficacy and health value of young people [10]. Schools must provide an important environment for the promotion of health to strengthen health promotion information at the most influenced stage of children's and develop lifelong sustainable attitudes and skills [11]. The guidance of "Health First", vigorously promotes health services with health care effects [7]. It is important to provide an effective environment or conditions to promote the health of students. Therefore, this research uses games to support students' healthy lifestyles and promote healthy lives.

As lifestyle affects human health, promoting healthy activities and healthy lifestyles is the main strategy for promoting and maintaining health [12]. The value and self-efficacy of health significantly predict the degree of participation in promoting a healthy lifestyle [10]. However, with the rapid modernization of lifestyle changes, people do not know much about health-promoting lifestyle and behaviors, although the prominent role of health promotion in medical care is obtaining more attention [13]. "Healthy lifestyle" is is a concept that promotes health and the existence of problem-free behaviors [14]. Though a healthy lifestyle has an impact on health, people don't know what a healthy lifestyle is. This study integrates a healthy lifestyle into games, which allows students to play games, and subtly cultivate a correct healthy lifestyle.

Games and health

Owing to the advancement of science and technology, the development of health games becomes common. INTERACCT games are developed for children of 8–14 years after cancer treatment to promote physical therapy activities and treatment compliance [15]. Through the use of appropriate design and gamification elements, the INTERACCT

(Integrated Entertainment and Response Assessment of Childhood Cancer Treatment) project aims to create a communication tool for pediatric patients suffering from cancer with HSCT (hematopoietic stem cell transplantation) treatment after surgery [16]. Game-based learning (GBL) and gamification improve the education on sexual health, sexual health behaviors and knowledge of young people in areas that have suffered many years of sexual health problems (including HIV/AIDS) [17]. Personalized and adaptive computerized inhibitory control trainings (ICTs) reduce weight by targeting the consumption of sweets and evaluate the feasibility, acceptability and efficacy of gamified and non-gamified. Gamification has a small impact in reducing the impact of ICT [18]. This integration of the immersive AR technology with Internet of Things (IoT) shows its versatile use in health areas of human experience [7] . The calorie battle AR game was developed using mobile AR to solve the childhood obesity problem. Especially, the interaction with AR content and the clarity of the user interface have been improved in the Unity 3D version. This research purposes to have three important contributions: (1) a mobile AR game to motivate children to move, (2) re-implementing the game using Unity 3D, and (3) comparing the usability evaluation results of two versions of games. Game engines such as Unity 3D become an essential part of AR game development in the future [19]. The development of games is beneficial to people's health promotion.

There is also a lot of sutdies on health games. The games emerge with technology and are increasingly important for professional training. They adopt 3D games and game engines to improve the user's real experience. With the advancement of technology and the desire to obtain good health in interesting and pleasant ways, various health games have been proposed in recent years [20]. The impact of the continued development of information and communication technologies influences healthy behavior [18]. We surveyed more than one hundred games for health to propose new classifications by using 15 relevant features, classify all the games under investigation, and propose new classifications in four different aspects. [20].

Many games are beneficial to promote people's health. The research confirms that health games indeed help people maintain their health. The purpose of this research is to develop a game of self-management of health and improve the sub-health of college students.

Game Design

A. Health-Promoting Behavior

There are three types of health behaviors: balanced nutrition, physical activity and regular inspections, and health locus of control (HLC) [21]. Healthy behavior includes physical exercise and nutrition [22], eating habits, exercise, sleep behavior, and stress management. Most patients have low awareness of the disease and low compliance with physical exercise [23]. Health-promoting lifestyle (HPL) is committed to healthy living through lifestyle. Healthy lifestyle includes six dimensions such as "sports activity", "nutrition", "health responsibility", "mental growth", "interpersonal relationship" and "stress management" [24].

This research has compiled documents that promote healthy behaviors through balanced and nutritious eating habits, exercise activities, sleep time, regular lifestyles, health responsibilities, and so on. As an interpersonal relationship and stress management are not easy to design as game contents, they were excluded.

B. Design Healthy Self-Management Game

According to the research on the literature, the health self-management game includes four aspects: health awareness, healthy eating habits, exercise habits, and regular lifestyle.

(1) Health awareness is to have health awareness and responsibility every day. One point is given for each correct answer.

(2) Healthy eating habits is to eat 5 fruits and vegetables in a daily diet with a variety of nutrients. Each food gives one point.

(3) Exercise habit: One minute of exercise a day gives one point.

(4) Regular lifestyle: Three regular meals, early bedtime, and waking up score 10 points.

(5) Scoring method: A user has a virtual character. Health conditions such as fatigue, poor sleep quality, amnesia, pain, eye discomfort deduct 10 points and multiplied by the number of conditions. For example, the degree of pain (1-10 points) multiplied by the number of years of discomfort, is a negative score for health. If a user plays a healthy self-management game every day, a user obtains points. Zero points indicate no illness, and positive points indicate healthy capital. The higher the score, the more healthy capital. The virtual character in the game becomes vigorous and energetic, happy, efficient task-doing with accumulating scores as having good grades in school is the meaning of health.

Research Method

A. Research Design

University students were the research objects and played the game. They were instructed for learning healthy and autonomous methods, and how to promote health according to this game every day from April 20 to June 20, 2020 for two months. After the experiment, the objects filled the questionnaire to assess the achievement of goals of having a good mood, doing things efficiently, and having good grades in reading. If all three items are improved, the health condition has indeed improved, and the experiment is successful. Then, the result is presented by 1. A total of 89 valid questionnaires were collected and analyzed by using a logistic regression model.

B. Hypothesis

According to the four major activities in the health self-management game, the following hypotheses are proposed.

H1 *Health awareness: to have health awareness and responsibility every day to promote health.*

H2 *Healthy eating habits: Having a balanced diet and eating 5 fruits and vegetables every day can promote health.*

H3 *Exercise Habits: Do exercise habits for 30 minutes a day to promote health.*

H4 *Regular lifestyle: A regular life of three meals a day, early to bed and early to rise, can promote health.*

Empirical Analysis and Results

Based on the model, the Cox & Snell R-squared of H1 was 0.168, Nagelkerke *R*-squared was 0.233, and the average explanatory power was 20.05%. The regression coefficient of health awareness was 1.916, which was statistically significant (P=0.000), and the odds ratio is 6.794. Thus, H1 was supported.

The Cox & Snell R-squared of H2 was 0.165, the Nagelkerke R-squared was 0.229, and the average explanatory power is 19.7%. The regression coefficient of healthy eating habits was 1.983, which was statistically significant (P=0.000), and the odds ratio was 7.265. Thus, H2 was supported.

The Cox & Snell R-squared of H3 was 0.075, the Nagelkerke R-squared was 0.104, and the average explanatory power was 8.95%. The regression coefficient of exercise habit was 1.213, which was statistically significant (P=0.010). The odds ratio was 3.634. Thus, H3 was supported.

The Cox & Snell R-squared of H4 was 0.131, the Nagelkerke R-squared was 0.181, and the average explanatory power was 15.6%. The regression coefficient of regular lifestyle was 1.910, which was statistically significant (P=0.001), and the odds ratio was 6.755. Thus, H4 was supported. The results are presented in Table 1.

Conclusion and Suggestion

This research aims to improve the sub-health of college students and develop a healthy self-management game. With the virtual characters in the game and playing the game content of the four main aspects every day, users can exercise and make the virtual characters healthy, finally develop their health consciousness and behavior. To verify whether the actual health status of college students, a total of 89 college students participated in the study. After 2 months of empirical research, the four health behaviors including health awareness, healthy eating habits, exercise habits, and regular lifestyle were assessed whether to improve the health of college students, using logistic regression analysis. These four behaviors effectively helped the college students promote health and prevent the occurrence of disease significantly. They could maintain a happy mood, work efficiently, and study well. It means that the game in this research improved the sub-health of the college students and is worthy of promotion.

A future research needs more research objects including office workers of middle-aged and elderly people and a real-time empirical research again to verify and ensure the effectiveness and reliability of healthy self-management game. The result provides a reference for relevant industry players when developing games and helps to develop more fun and practical games for improving users' health. Then, the game will attract users to improve their health.

TABLE 1
Logistic Regression

IV	Regression coefficients	S.E.	P.	Odds Ration	Confidence Interval
H1	1.916***	.503	.000	6.794	2.535-18.212
H2	1.983***	.517	.000	7.265	2.639-19.996
H3	1.213*	.472	.010	3.634	1.334-8.478
H4	1.910**	.567	.001	6.755	2.224-20.516

References

[1] Mendizábal, B., Urbina, E. M., Mitsnefes, M., et al. (2018). SHIP-AHOY (Study of High Blood Pressure in Pediatrics: Adult Hypertension Onset in Youth). Hypertension, 72(3), 625-631.

[2] Tryggestad, J. B., Shah, R. D., Braffett, B. H., et al. (2020). Circulating adhesion molecules and associations with HbA1c, hypertension, nephropathy, and retinopathy in the Treatment Options for type 2 Diabetes in Adolescent and Youth study. Pediatric Diabetes, 21(6), 923-931.

[3] Xie, Y. M., Liu, B. Y., & Piao, H. Y. (2006). Exploration on the common characters of sub-healthy people based on clinical epidemiology. Zhongguo Zhong Xi Yi Jie He Za Zhi, 26(7), 612-616.

[4] Xie, Y. M., Liu, B. Y., Piao, H. Y. (). Research on the Symptomatic Characters of the Sub-healthy People Based on DME. CHINESE JOURNAL OF INFORMATION ON TRADITIONAL CHINESE MEDICINE. 3(9), 27-27.

[5] Horng, H. C., Chen, Y. T., & Liu, H. H. (2019).Constructing Norm Curves for the Functional Movement Capacity of Sub-healthy Adults via SMARC-a Case Study in Taiwan. MSIE 2019: Proceedings of the 2019 International Conference on Management Science and Industrial Engineering, May 2019, 157-162.

[6] Lee, R. L. T. & Loke, A. J. T. Y. (2005). Health-Promoting Behaviors and Psychosocial Well-Being of University Students in Hong Kong. Public health nursing, 22(3), 209-220.

[7] Pang, J., Tang, H. L., Yang, Y. et al. (2008). Analysis on Sub-healthy Crowd Life Quality Evaluation:Nanjing City. Journal of Liaoning University of Traditional Chinese Medicine, 11.

[8] Kandari, F. A. & Vidal, V. L. (2007). Correlation of the health-promoting lifestyle, enrollment level, and academic performance of College of Nursing students in Kuwait. Nursing & health sciences, 9(2), 112-119.

[9] Wei, C. N., Harada, K., Ueda, K. & Fukumoto, K. et al. (2012) Assessment of health-promoting lifestyle profile in Japanese university students. Environ Health Prev Med,17, 222-227.

[10] Jackson, E. S.,Tucker, C. M. & Herman, K. C.(2007). Health Value, Perceived Social Support, and Health Self-Efficacy as Factors in a Health-Promoting Lifestyle. Journal of American College Health, 56(1), 69-74.

[11] KwanI, S. Y. L., Petersen, P. E., Pine, C. M.; & Borutta, A. (2005). Health-promoting schools: an opportunity for oral health promotion. Bull World Health Organ, 83 (9), 677-685.

[12] Zeidi, I. M., Hajiagha, A. P. & Zeidi, B. M. (2012).Reliability and Validity of Persian Version of the Health-Promoting Lifestyle Profile. Journal of Mazandaran University of Medical Sciences, 21(1), 102-113.

[13] Pinar, R., Celik, R., & Bahcecik, N. (2009). Reliability and Construct Validity of the Health-Promoting Lifestyle Profile II in an Adult Turkish Population. Nursing research, 58(3), 184-193.

[14] [SH8]14. Ebin, V. J., Sneed, C. D., Morisky, D.E., et al.(2001). Acculturation and interrelationships between problem and health-promoting behaviors among Latino adolescents. Journal of Adolescent Health, 28(1), 62-72.

[15] Kayali, F., K Peters, K., Kuczwara, J., et al.(2015). Participatory game design for the INTERACCT serious game for health. Joint International Conference on Serious Games, Serious Games, 13-25.

[16] Peters, K., Kayali, F., Reithofer, A., et al.(2015). Serious game scores as health condition indicator for cancer patients. European Federation for Medical Informatics (EFMI), 892-896.

[17] Haruna, H., Hu, X., Chu, S. K. W., et al. (2018). Improving sexual health education programs for adolescent students through game-based learning and gamification. Int. J. Environ. Res. Public Health 2018, 15(9), 2027-2039.

[18] 18. Forman, E. M., Manasse, S. M., Dallal, D. H., et al. (2019). Computerized neurocognitive training for improving dietary health and facilitating weight loss. Journal of Behavioral Medicine, 42, 1029-1040.

[19] Kim, S.L., Suk, H. J., Kang, J. H., et al. (2014). Using Unity 3D to facilitate mobile augmented reality game development. I.E. World Forum on Internet of Things (WF-IoT), 21-26.

[20] Wattanasoontorn, V., Boada, I., García, R., et al. (2013). Serious games for health. Entertainment Computing, 4(4), 231-247.

[21] Cohen, M. & Azaiza, F. (2007). Health-promoting behaviors and health locus of control from a multicultural perspective. Ethn Dis., 17(4), 636-642.

[22] Wilson, M. (2005). Health-promoting behaviors of sheltered homeless women. Family & Community Health, 28(1), 51-63.

[23] Heydari, A., Ziaee, E. S., & Gazrani, A.(2015). Relationship between awareness of disease and adherence to therapeutic regimen among cardiac patients. Int J Community Based Nursing Midwifery, 3(1), 23-30.

[24] Tol, A., Tavassoli,E., Shariferad, G. R. & Shojaeezadeh, D. (2013). Health-promoting lifestyle and quality of life among undergraduate students at school of health, Isfahan university of medical sciences. J Educ Health Promot., 2:11.

https://doi.org/10.1142/9789811238727_0062

Research on Key Value Factors of Sustainable Development of Taiwan Ceramic Craft

Huang-Chen Lu[1*], Ming-Chyuan Ho[2]

[1]Graduate School of Design, Master & Doctoral Program,
National Yunlin University of Science and Technology, Yunlin, Taiwan
[2]Graduate School of Design, National Yunlin University of Science and Technology, Yunlin, Taiwan
*Corresponding Author Email: kvsvk2001@gmail.com

Abstract

The rise of the maker movement has driven designers to enter the field of ceramic craft production. While ceramic craft products continue to innovate, it has become an important core issue to construct a set of benchmarks for measuring design indicators for the ceramic craft to evaluate the effectiveness of product design. This study constructed the indicators of the innovation design of ceramic craft by collecting data with the document analysis and focus group method and analyzing the data by the KJ method as a qualitative research method. The analyses by the KJ method found 9 evaluative facets and 28 value indicators.

Keywords: ceramic craft, value factors of design, sustainable development

Introduction

The launch of the maker movement gradually changed manufacturing methods and workplaces and inspires the establishment of many maker studios. The equipment and resources of the maker studios allow the designer's product concept to quickly enter the manufacturing stage [1] and promote the vitality of the industry. This development has led ceramic craft products to become more abundant and promote the sustainable development of the ceramic craft industry. A design of view on ceramic craft products does not only focus on functional needs but also beauty, style, pop, culture identity, emotional, social, and oriented thinking. These are important factors to enhance the quality of ceramic craft products. In this way, ceramic manufacturers effectively carry out product design planning and enhance the visibility of ceramic brands to face the ever-changing market environment.

Therefore, it is necessary to provide a set of design reference indicators for sustainable development of ceramic craftsmanship and offer designers opportunities to reflect on their design techniques, skills, and design professional innovation to enhance the value of product design innovation. This study collected experts' opinions on the ceramic process design and proposed an indicator system for sustainable development of the ceramic industry. The result provides design academic researchers and designers with the effectiveness of ceramic product design.

Literature Review

A. Relationship between design intervention and the sustainable development of the craft industry value chain

When designers or artists learn the production process from the ceramic industry, their role turns from creative provider to the product manufacturers who produce ceramic products and conduct marketing logistics activities such as transport and support operations. They also provide products or services for the market, and finally the consumers. This process is in an industry value chain that Porter proposed, and at the same time, constitutes the basis of differentiation [2]. When a design is involved in the value chain, they activate the industry and maintain the sustainable development of society. In David Walker's "Design tree", the craft is regarded as a basic backbone and foundation design and development [3]. It is also the seed of creative inspiration and nourished by the practice of craft making, which is a purposeful and meaningful production activity. Craftsmen bring local knowledge, experience with innovation, skills, bio-regional knowledge, and traditional practices, all of which have a sustainable system approach [4]. Designers are bringing information on the modern market to help craftsmen cope with the post process and consequences of the industrialization process [5]. Specifically, the craft is the basis and connotation of design, whereas design is the manifestation and future of craft [6]. As design has the potential to change the status quo, it contributes to meaningful solutions to multidisciplinary problems [7]. Design helps promote craft as a tool for sustainable development, thus plays a potential role in the process. Innovation-centric collaboration between craft and design, in response to contemporary needs and sustainable development, provides the way for future industrial approaches [8]. Agarwal divides the design and craft cooperation into 7 different scopes in which sustainable development is a process and a design of the most prevalent form of cooperation. By aiming to expand the scope of community production of the product and serve as a tool to achieve sustainable development in economic empowerment, social development themes alleviate poverty and livelihoods [8]. Between craftsmanship and sustainable development, there are developmental aspects of localization, ecological benefits, flexible systems, and contextualized lifestyles. The continuation of traditional crafts and culture can be achieved through the intervention of design. It has the potential to realize cosmopolitanism, solve productivity problems, create value, develop entrepreneurial skills, and improve economic vitality. As such, design contributes to the innovation of products, services, communication, brand, and related methods [9]. This study focuses on the design process involved in the formation of the industrial chain in the creative phase of the sustainable development of ceramic craft product value.

Methodology

This study was conducted using literature analysis, focus group interviews, and the KJ method to find the hierarchy of factors in the value system of Taiwan's ceramic craft industry. The purpose was to provide an assessment model for the sustainable development of the industry.

A. Research subjects

This study first collected background information at two stages. In the first stage, a literature review was carried out to obtain preliminary data for choosing experts. The second stage was the implementation of an expert focus group method. Seven professionals of ceramics (all male, 2 doctors, 1 PhD, and 4 masters) were invited. The experts provided opinions, value factors, discussions on ceramic design to find out the value factors of ceramic design.

B. Research objects

In the early stage, the internal elements of design value were collected based on the evaluation method of product design. Ceramic products belong to the category of general products in general. However, they are different from general products. Therefore, the literature related to product evaluation and the value of ceramic products was searched including 34 articles, 1 design value book, and 22 journals related to design value elements [10]. Based on the design value elements, the factors related to ceramic design value were selected as Table 1.

TABLE 1
Ceramic product value factors.

1	Insight Value	18	True Value
2	Local Emotion Value	19	Technical Value
3	Divine Value	20	Craft Value
4	Memorial Value	21	Social Value
5	Originality Value	22	Political Value
6	Wisdom Value	23	Ethical Value
7	Aesthetic Value	24	Economic Value
8	Beautiful Value	25	Market Value
9	Novelty Value	26	Brand Value
10	Theoretical Value	27	Product Value
11	Sign Value	28	Collection Value
12	Symbolic Value	29	Cultural Value
13	Image Value	30	Religious Value
14	Identity Value	31	Spiritual Value
15	Emotional Value	32	Historical Value
16	Functional Value	33	Environmental Value
17	Experiential Value	34	Artistic Value

In the middle stage, focus group interviews were carried out to obtain a consensus of experts and scholars of ceramics and propose other possible value factors. In the later stage, common factors in the value of sustainable development of ceramic craft level architecture were found.

Early stage

1. Finding problems in ceramic craft product innovation: Ceramic craft industry was assessed for the effectiveness of product design.
2. Literature Review: The definition of the ceramic craft industry, Taiwan's ceramic craft industry, design value, craft industry value chain, and sustainable development of design intervention were studied.
3. Focus on the problem: There was no measurement design indicator for the sustainable development of the ceramic craft industry in Taiwan. Thus, the indicators need to be found.
4. Collecting relevant literature on design value: Collecting literature on the design value and ceramic value for analyzing and sorting out the data.
5. Collecting the indicators related to the value of ceramic design: 34 indicators related to the value of ceramic design were defined.

Middle stage

6. Ceramic design value indicators collected in the early stage were discussed by ceramic experts for pre-examination. 147 value factors associated with ceramic craft products were selected as the basis for screening. After the initial screening by two experts, the factors were reflected in a questionnaire. The experts from Taiwan's pottery association were invited to the focus group method.
7. Refining the ceramic design value indicators: From 34 indicators and 128 sentences, the focus group selected ceramic design value indicators and value points.

Late stage

8. Integration and Narrative: The expert group discussed the cluster wordings and diagrams and refined the narrative description (Fig. 1).
9. Conclusions and Suggestions

Results and Findings

The KJ method summarized the data from the literature research and constructed the value factor of Taiwan's ceramic craft industry. Table 2 shows the value factors that were selected by the expert group.

TABLE 2
The value factors of the ceramic craft industry.

Facets	Value Factor	Grouping coding	Data source
Aesthetic	Inspiration	f	k2-bFD-01-2
	Aesthetics	w-4	k1-lFC-02-1
	Craftsmanship	R-6	k2-bFH-04-1、k2-bFJ-04-2
	Originality	S-4	k1-lFG-03-4、k1-lFC-02-4
	Artistry	Z-2	k2-bFC-03-2
Academic	Theorization	X-7 b-2 j	k2-bFC-07-1、k2-bFD-07-5、k2-bFG-07-1
Emotional	Homesickness	U-6	k1-lFG-05-2、k1-lFL-04-2
	Memorability	i	k2-bFG-08-1
	Novelty	a-2	k2-lFG-06-5
	Happiness	T-5	k1-lFE-06-2、k1-lFJ-06-2
	Experience	V-5	k2-bFG-06-1

Functional	Reliability	K-2	k1-lFE-03-2、k1-lFH-03-1、k1-lFJ-02-2
	Utility	e	k1-lFE-03-3、k1-lFH-03-2
	Problem Solving Ability	I-3	k1-lFD-04-1、k1-lFE-04-2、k1-lFH-05-2、k1-lFJ-03-1
Social	Interpersonal Connections	Y-4	k2-bFC-01-1、k2-bFD-02-3、k2-bFL-01-2
	Status Manifestation	Q-8	k1-1FC-01-2、k1-1FD-02-2
	Ethical Morality	c P-2	k1-mFJ-07-2
Economic	Brand Power	L-7 N-2 O-2 M-3 d	k1-bFD-07-2
	Marketability	A-5 D-4	k2-bFD-07-5
	Collectability	B-4	k2-bFD-07-4、k2-bFG-04-2
Cultural	Local Specialty	C-5	k2-bFG-02-2
	National Specialty and Adherence	F-4	k1-lFL-02-2
	Historical Linkage	E-4	k2-bFJ-08-4
Divine	Solemnity	G-6	k2-bFE-08-2
	Spiritual Sustenance	H-7	k1-lFE-07-2
Ecological	Materials with Environmental Certification	J-3	k2-bFE-09-5
	Treasure	h	k2-bFF-09-6、k2-bFI-02-2、k2-bFJ-09-2
	Low Carbon Technology	g	k2-bFE-09-3

The experts believed that academics have become an essential element of the sustainable development of the ceramic crafts industry. They thought that the creation of works by ordinary ceramic craftsmen was inadequate as they cannot highlight the deep meaning of the work. The ceramic makers can not explain their design or creative ideas in detail but manufacture the product of aesthetic appearance or functions to express the value. However, consumers want to know more about the products. When a product lacks the background value, it does not obtain the empirical value of academic certification. The academia examines the ceramic craft products and discusses the creative value. Function, ecology, aesthetics, culture, economy, society, emotion, and sacred are explored by academia.

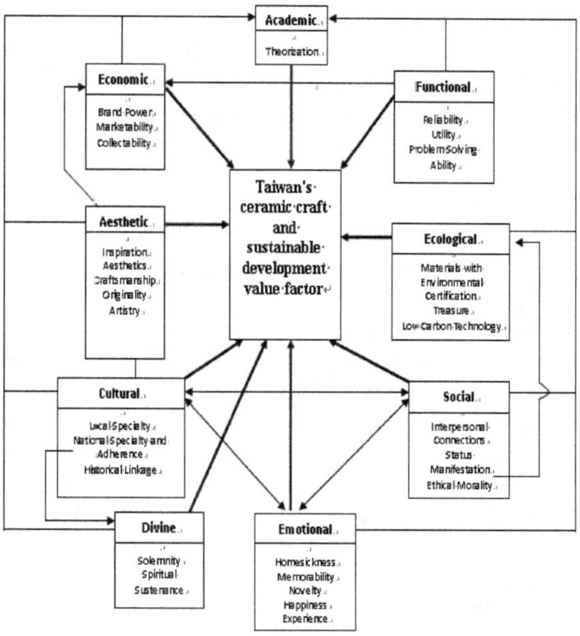

Fig. 1 Graphical explanation of the relationship between indicators

The aesthetics of ceramic crafts arouse consumers' attention to sell. Many studies suggested that aesthetics has a relationship with market trading, collection value, and the construction of personal or company branding, and interacts with the economic level. On the other hand, culture and aesthetics are closely related to each other. Whether it is a national or local culture, the historical context can be traced, and various factors in aesthetics have become the creative factors of craftsmen. Cultural influences have diversified many typical craft products. Recently, craft products with local culture have the characteristics of product differentiation influenced by globalization, which highlights product characteristics and a design strategy by designers.

In Taiwan's folk culture, since the land is the center of faith, clay has been often used to create sacred objects. It has been passed down for more than 300 years and has never been interrupted. It belongs to the local special cultural beliefs.

Culture, emotion, and society have mutual influences on each other. In addition to artistic exquisiteness, ceramic craft products carry the historical culture of various places. Until today, in addition to antiques in art collections, innovative ceramics become folk gifts as a maintainer of interpersonal emotions. The works of famous ceramic brands or potters have become a symbol for consumers to highlight their social status. There are many ceramic dolls in Taiwanese temples that matched landscapes and architectural backgrounds. They are mainly used to promote the ethical and moral meaning of benevolence, righteousness, and etiquette to educate the world and become part of the representative of folk beliefs. The ceramic craft categories involve economic issues in the trading process.

The moral value in the social dimension is related to environmental ecology. From design to production of ceramic craft products, it is necessary to consider the minimal impact on the ecology not to cause environmental burden or damage. Therefore, environmentally certified, cherished materials, and low-carbon methods are important factors that need to be considered when designing ceramic processes.

Conclusion and Suggestion

This study constructed the indicators of ceramic value innovation design with the KJ method. 9 evaluation factors, 28 value indicators, and a description of 30 values were selected. The 9 factors are aesthetic value, academic value, emotional value, functional value, social value, economic value, cultural value, divine value, and ecological value. These factors affect the value of sustainable development of the ceramic craft industry through the value indicators in design innovation.

This study could not determine each value quantitatively. Thus, the following study needs to find weights to provide designers with a reference for ranking the value indicators to apply the indicators to the value innovation of the ceramic craft industry comprehensively.

References

[1] F.W. Tung and Y.F. Chang, *From Co-Creation to Entrepreneurialism- KAMARO'AN,* Vol.23(2), Journal of Design, 2018, pp.49-70.

[2] Michael E Porter Competitive Advantage—Creating and Sustaining Superior Performance, (M.G Li, R.M. Chiou, Trans.), Taipei:Commonwealth Publishing, 2010.

[3] M.C. Ho, From design studies to design disciplines, sicence development 453, 2010, pp.6-11.

[4] Ihatsu, A., Making sense of contemporary American craft(Publications in Education No.73).Savonlinna:University of Joensuu,2002.

[5] Craft Revival Trust, Designers meet artisans. New Delhi: Grass Root Publications Pvt. Ltd, 2006.

[6] W.T. Li, M.C. Ho, C. Yang, A Design Thinking-Based Study of the Prospect of the Sustainable Development of Traditional Handicrafts, Sustainability, 11, 4823, 2019.

[7] T. Irwin, Transition Design: A Proposal for a New Area of Design Practice, Study, and Research, Design and Culture, 7(2), 2015, pp.229-246.

[8] R. Reubens, Holistic Sustainability Through Craft-Design Collaboration, Publications Routledge, 2019.

[9] Zhan, X.; Walker, S.; Hernandez-Pardo, R.; Evan, M., Craft and Sustainability: Potential for Design Intervention in Crafts in the Yangtze River Delta, China, The Design Journal, 2017, doi: 10.1080/14606925.2017.1352802, s2919-2934

[10] X. CHEN, Redefinition of Evaluation Benchmark of Product Design Value. Hundred Schools in Arts, 3,2013, pp.215-217.

https://doi.org/10.1142/9789811238727_0063

Research on Service Innovation Courses of Music Culture Industry

Luo-Xiao Zhang[1*], Min-Tsai Lai[2]

[1]Ph.D. Program in Business and Management, Southern Taiwan University of Science and Technology, Tainan, Taiwan
School of Music, Changchun University, China
[2]Department of Business Administration, Southern Taiwan University of Science and Technology, Tainan, Taiwan
*Corresponding Author Email: zhangluoxiao.ccu@gmail.com

Abstract

Music creation needs different educational models, policy mechanisms, and environmental openness for implementation. Simultaneously, the differences in creative protection are derived from the integration of foreign cultures, and the environment that is inclusive in the music culture industry. This paper uses literature analysis, a questionnaire, and interviews to survey and explore music creation to provide references for developing the music culture industry. There are music culture industry education and training methods, music culture industry management mechanism, music culture industry marketing model, and music culture industry's creative environment.

Keywords: music culture, creative environment, culture industry, and service innovation.

Introduction

Confucian culture started in China more than two thousand years ago, along with the so-called "Ceremony and Music" in Confucian culture. Among them, the "Ceremony" is for rituals or norms, and "Music" is the general term for poetry, music, and dance as the collective name of culture [1]. The "Music" is the alternative business model currently formed globally. The use of cultural methods and packaging to implement commercial promotion is named "Cultural and Creative Industry" [2]. Recently, due to Western capitalism and culture, the "cultural creative industry" commercializes culture, art, and creation to form chimneyless industry and innovation. A large amount of transmission or invasion and penetration into developing or undeveloped countries. To transform culture and creativity into industries, industrial development policies need implementation.

The creative industry was promoted by the British Blair cabinet in 1997 for the first time [3]. Then, in 2002, Adorno and Horkheimer [4] stated that the cultural industry was a set of standardized production and consumption models. Therefore, the concept of "cultural industry" was used by the Frankfurt School Adorno and others as a negative concept to highlight the anti-function of popular culture. The cultural industry ideology is based on consumers and acting as social control and cultural dominance. The ideal state of culture is art that is a special and outstanding form of human creativity [5].

This paper focuses on the service innovation of the music creation industry on both sides of the Taiwan Strait. It also discusses the management and protection mechanism of the music industry policy, the creation of the music industry and creative environment, and the protection of the intellectual property rights of music creation works. The discussion on the related literature firstly deals with the current situation of the music culture industry and the tools and management of the music culture industry development by exploring the relationship between the music culture industry and social responsibility.

This paper introduces previous research, and then research methods and steps including research framework and process, research analysis tools and platforms, and the status of research question analysis and questionnaire design. The results of the research is explained by comparing the education and training methods of the music culture industry, the management mechanism of the music culture industry, the marketing model of the music culture industry, and the influence of the creative environment of the music culture industry. The conclusions of this research and future development suggestions are described for the reference of policy development and formulation.

Background Survey

The music culture includes the creation and innovation of songs and works, the organization of live concerts and performances, audio and video recording, composition and sheet music, and companies that assist and represent music creators' organizations and associations to make money, or independent artists [6,7]. Since it is classified as an industry, the goal of music culture needs to be essentially economic. All music culture production and creation efforts are focused on economic success.

Individuals and organizations engaged in the music industry are grouped into the following: (1) songwriters and composers who create new songs and musical works; (2) singers, musicians, conductors, and band leaders who perform music (3) Companies and professionals who create and sell recorded music and/or scores (for example, music distributors, music producers, recording studios, engineers, record companies, retail and online music stores, performance rights organizations); and (4) Personnel who assist in organizing and displaying live music performances (sound engineers, booking agents, promoters, music venues, road administrators) [8,9,10].

The types of music are divided into traditional music, classical music (Classical), folk/country songs, electronic music (Electronic Dance Music, EDM), hip-hop/rap (Hip), indie music, rhythm and blues/soul, and rock music. The basic forms of all music are similar as they complete the record and transmission of culture [1,12].

Motivation and Structure

According to the different time and space factors such as the personal thinking of the music creator and the environment, the music has different purposes and functions: inspiring, invigorating, calming, or depressing. In the prerequisite of industrialization, there are an inherent danger and the cultivation of false psychological needs, as it is a product package by economic considerations in the capital market. Therefore, these popular music cultures through mass production methods pose a threat to technically and intellectually difficult and high-end music, such as classical court music.

The new generation (post-war tide) after the Second World War in Taiwan and Mainland China, has been nurtured by Chinese culture and influenced and eroded by the Western music industry. Nowadays, all countries in the world are aware of the importance as it is also related to the preservation and inheritance of traditional music, and the centripetal and gathering of nations. At the same time, music culture is also an invisible tool of aggression. Therefore, countries have begun to emphasize the creation and development of the music industry in a process that is mixed with strong national and populist awareness.

This research explores different educational methods, environmental constructions, and political factors in different places, the impact on individuals (music cultural creators, performers, consumers), the society, and the country's views, implementation, management, and management of music culture and the music industry at the two sides of the Taiwan Strait under the same Chinese culture. Within a race, ethnicity, or country, many people are not literate in education. There are ways of cultural transmissions such as music, dance, or patterns, and music is a combination of language (sometimes combined with dance). All countries have considerable ideas and intuitions. Music production and creation, one of the cultural industries, is an emerging industry with marketability, future, and hope. However, in recent years, not many students have a vision for music production and creation. The music creation industry market does not provide them with sufficient opportunities to perform, which results in a difficult job situation and even the provision of resources during the learning process.

With the importance of the music industry and the continuous emergence of new products with new entrepreneurial patterns and new models, the demand for creative students with management and marketing knowledge in the music industry continues to grow. The overall employment prospects of the music industry and the market still have room for growth. As a new professional industry, as music industry management is not well-known in the job market as traditional management majors, it is needed to improve the training model of professionals in the music industry and enhance practical ability training. The expectations of society and industry require such human resources.

Based on the above-mentioned needs and goals, this paper will compare the following research through the different music industry strategies of Taiwan and China.

Research comparison:

1. Comparison of music culture industry education and training methods.
2. Comparison of management mechanism of the music culture industry.
3. Comparison of marketing models in the music culture industry.
4. Comparison of creative environment of the music culture industry.

Research recommendations:

1. The management and protection mechanism of music industry policy.
2. Music industry and creative environment creation.
3. The protection of intellectual property rights of music creation works.

The progress and schedule of the questionnaires are shown in Table 1.

TABLE 1
The progress and schedule of questionnaires.

Jobs	Date
Experts and scholars meeting	2020/09/20，09/28
Prototype questionnaire completed	2020/10/04
First version revision	2020/1010/06
Revise the first draft	2020/10/08
Pre-test implementation	2020/10/11~2020/10/17

The pre-test of questionnaires was carried out by 6 participants from 2020/10/11 to 2020/10/17. According to the feedback from the pre-test and opinions of the experts and scholars, the questionnaire was revised. The final version of the questionnaire is listed as Table 2. After that, the second pretest with the revised questionnaire was performed. The final questionnaire was distributed and returned by using the platform of Wechat and KingData mini Web software.

TABLE 2
The contents of questionnaires.

Items	Numbers
Personal background information	13
Music culture industry education and training methods	12
Management Mechanism of Music Culture Industry	13
Marketing Model of Music Culture Industry	11
Creative environment of music culture industry	12

The questionnaire consists of the following five items: personal background information, music culture industry education and training methods, management mechanism of the music culture industry, marketing model of the music culture industry, and creative environment of the music culture industry, and the numbers are 13,12,13,11, and 12, respectively.

Conclusions

Due to the rapid development of the music industry and a new profession that has emerged in recent years, many countries have invested manpower, finances, and resources in the music industry. However, they are still trying to adjust, such as the cognition, understanding, and policies of the music industry, as well as the goals, teachers, and equipment of music talent education. There are differences between Taiwan and China in terms of cultural characteristics, writing, language, and customs in the music industry. As the music industry is an emerging industry in both Taiwan and China, the related policies, laws, social and public acceptance need to be explored and adjusted. Thus, the research process and the restrictions are suggested as follows.

1. There are intellectual property rights involved in music creation and business models, and in-depth information cannot be obtained based on the principle of protection.
2. The resources provided by Taiwan and China for creators are different from open standards, which results in inaccurate information acquisition.

The questionnaire of this research is randomly distributed online. The online questionnaire platforms of Wechat and KingData mini Web software are selected to implement service innovation for the cross-strait music and cultural industry by the people of Taiwan and China. The questionnaire includes questions about analysis, management, and policy cognition.

References

[1] A. Adriana et al., *Presented at the AOIR Conference*, Milwaukee, Wisconsin, 2009.
[2] N. K. Baym, *Participations* 9, no. 2 (2012): 286–316.
[3] D. Pastukhov, January 7, 2019, Soundchart.
[4] D. George, et al. SPSS for Windows step by step: A simple guide and reference. 11.0 update (4th ed.), Boston: Allyn & Bacon.
[5] H. Mcdonald, The Music Industry Facts Every Musician Needs to Know," Updated November 24, 2019.
[6] L. M. Grobman, Music and Social Work: The Connection," The new social career magazine, 2018.
[7] R. Lagueux, Music Business Research Methods, Kerklee online, September 28, 2019.
[8] P. Wikström, The Music Industry in an Age of Digital Distribution. HUMANITIES, 2015.
[9] S. Cole, The impact of technology and social media on the music industry," September 9th 2019.
[10] S. Moulton and J. Clayton, what is the Music Industry? - Definition & Facts," Music Lesson Plans & Activities/ Humanities Courses, Study.com.
[11] W. Tucker, How To Make It In The Music Industry," Feb 13, 2019. Forbes.
[12] P. Wikström, The Music Industry: Music in the Cloud. 2nd ed. Cambridge, UK: Polity Press, 2013.

https://doi.org/10.1142/9789811238727_0064

Research on the Application of New Media Technology in Traditional Folk Art Teaching — Dongyang Bamboo Weaving Technology as Example

Zhu Qingqin* and Li Jingping**

Yiwu Industrial and Commercial College, Yiwu City, Zhejiang Province, China
*Corresponding Author Email: *793083199@qq.com, **741931822@qq.com

Abstract

This paper studies effective methods for improving the classroom teaching of traditional folk art through information-based teaching technology in the new media context. It aims to reach the teaching goal of integrating new media technology and teaching traditional folk art. By studying the application of new media technology to inheriting and teaching folk art, the paper puts forward thoughts for applying new media technology to teaching traditional folk art. Citing the teaching of Dongyang bamboo weaving techniques as an example, it redesigns teaching traditional folk art through new media technology following the thought of course integration. Specifically speaking, new media technology can be applied to expand the platform of teaching resources for traditional folk art, which helps to achieve the goal of sharing, co-building, and public utilization of such resources.

Keywords: new media technology, folk art teaching, Dongyang bamboo weaving, curriculum integration

Introduction

As an indispensable part of humans' cultural heritages, traditional folk art affects the lifeblood of the development and progress of human society. With social progress and technological iteration, the environment where traditional folk art relies on is changing. Correspondingly, traditional modes of inheritance no longer meet the needs of transmitting and teaching traditional folk art in the new context. As new media technology develops, there arises the call for integrating with modern teaching designs. How to ensure sustainable development for the cultural connotations of traditional folk art in the new media era becomes a hotspot problem for current design education.

Status Quo of Inheriting Dongyang Traditional Bamboo Weaving

A. History and Values of Dongyang Bamboo Weaving

Dongyang bamboo weaving is a traditional local folk art originated from Dongyang County, Jinhua City, Zhejiang Province. It has a history of more than 1,200 years. Regarding technological characteristics, it has unique weaving techniques and processes local fish-scale bamboo, golden bamboo, and Gui bamboo through complicated handicraft art. Detailed historical materials about bamboo weaving techniques and products in Dongyang can be found in the Records of the Jinhua Government Office and Annals of Dongyang County, two books respectively complied in the Wanli period of the Ming Dynasty and Kangxi period of the Qing Dynasty. According to existing knowledge, there are more than one hundred weaving techniques for Dongyang bamboo weaving. Nowadays, these techniques are in continuous innovation and perfection [1].

B. Status Quo of Inheriting and Developing Dongyang Bamboo Weaving

As early as the early 21st century, the bamboo weaving industry in Dongyang showed signs of decline and downsizing under the impact of the modern industry and the Internet economy. At present, less than one thousand personnel are still engaged in bamboo weaving, including one national-level intangible cultural heritage inheritor, two national-level craft masters[2], two Chinese bamboo craft masters, one intangible cultural heritage inheritor of Zhejiang Province, and four provincial-level craft masters. In the meantime, great changes have taken place in the employment structure of the traditional bamboo industry. At present, Dongfeng Bamboo Weaving Handicraft Factory is the only enterprise engaged in bamboo weaving and decoration in Dongyang City. Currently, the government mainly protects the traditional craft by two means. Firstly, it is passed on to and promoted by intangible cultural heritage inheritors. Secondly, arts and crafts studios are set up to promote the traditional craft. Although traditional bamboo weaving artists have high bamboo weaving techniques, they lack innovations. Moreover, their artworks can hardly be manufactured through large-scale industrialization and do not match modern consumption habits and demands. To some extent, the decline in the economic benefits of traditional bamboo weaving craft results from complex production techniques and a longer production cycle. Meanwhile, the craftsmen engaged in the bamboo weaving art are aging and decreasing annually. Therefore, Dongyang's bamboo weaving industry faces the crisis of inheritance discontinuity.

Thoughts of Applying New Media Technology to Teaching Traditional Folk Art

The traditional handicraft represents the cultural essence of a nation and accentuates the regional cultural context and aesthetical characteristics. With changes in the modes of life, young people rarely have opportunities to contact such techniques. With time, the folk art eventually declines. Local universities form the backbone for inheriting and developing the local intangible cultural heritages. The young may take courses at such universities to learn knowledge about intangible cultural heritages. Such education enhances young people's identity with and enthusiasm for the local traditional culture. Also, it plays a vital role in assisting the young with protecting, innovating in, and transmitting relevant cultural heritages.

The advantages of new media technology provide a systematic theoretical foundation for applying information technology to teaching traditional folk art. Currently, such an application is mainly achieved by implementing practical projects in relevant courses. This paper explored specific application methods through Dongyang bamboo weaving, traditional art with a local industrial background, and advantageous characteristics. It aimed to solve three difficulties facing the inheritance education of Dongyang's bamboo weaving. Firstly, there is no digitalized protection for the traditional bamboo weaving art, so its techniques, methods, and inheritors are disappearing. Secondly, traditional Dongyang bamboo weaving has complicated techniques, which makes inheriting the art inefficient. The art is mainly inherited through the traditional apprentice system, namely face-to-face teaching and oral instructions. Thirdly, there are inadequate efforts for transmission and promotion. As a result, Dongyang's bamboo weaving art is not recognized by the young, which leads to decreasing inheritors.

New Media Technology Related to Teaching Traditional Folk Art

A Application of Virtual Reality Technology to Teaching Traditional Folk Art

Currently, virtual reality technology is mainly used for repairing, restoring, and protecting traditional folk artworks. Secondly, the technology achieves virtual realization of folk artworks that have disappeared and whose appearances can hardly be restored. This mode not only restores the classical glory of destroyed folk artworks through information technology but also displays the inner structure and detailed characteristics of artworks through digitalized models. The virtual restoration of the Old Summer Palace is the most classic example of all cases for restoring intangible cultural heritages through virtual reality technology.

The documentary entitled The Old Summer Palace restored the prosperous scene of the king garden of all gardens through 3-D special effects and the virtual reality technology. Presented through digital images, it enables modern people to appreciate the beauty of classical gardens and salutes to classical gardens in China. By this means, viewers study it more immersive. Thanks to the application of technology, the image-based study in teaching traditional folk art is changed into an immersive study.

B Application of 3D Printing Technology to Teaching Traditional Folk Art

3D printing technology is currently the most widely used rapid prototyping technology. It is used for reconstructing traditional folk works through digitalized models and constructing objects through layered printing. 3-D printing technology is applied to restoring and redesigning folk artworks. It is characterized by low processing costs, high efficiency, high precision, and material-saving. It is suitable for objects with a complex structure. Also, the 3D printing technology is of high significance for shifting traditional folk artworks to shift towards industrial design objects and achieving innovative transition for traditional industries.

Information Technology for Exhibition and Communication of Achievements in Teaching Traditional Folk Art

A. Application to Classroom Teaching Exhibition

To some extent, the new media technology can be used to diversify the means of classroom organization during the exhibition of teaching traditional folk art and enhance the interactive experience in classrooms. Technological speaking, a new media exhibition consists of the ring-screen projection, virtual showcase, automatic page-turning, and digital desk, which jointly diversify the effects of the dynamic exhibition. Unlike traditional paper media and image media, the new media technology can be used to break the misunderstandings of traditional folk art learning and is applicable to the situation-based experiential teaching.

B. Application to Constructing a Teaching Resource Library

Constructing the teaching resource library for traditional folk art is the most fundamental and one of the most important means of digitalized protection for traditional folk art teaching. It is the process of collecting, classifying, and arranging effective information for teaching traditional folk art through various new media technologies. Meanwhile, such information is stored by the computer and the Internet. It eventually sets up the digitalized teaching platform and resource platform for traditional folk art where students can study and take reference.

C. Application to Exhibition for Mobile Internet Teaching

The most common exhibition mode for mobile Internet teaching is to display diverse online open courses through Internet technology. It is basically characterized by open, interactive, and convenient participation anytime and anywhere. It has a strong ability of social application, high convenience, fast and convenient application, and high privacy, which makes it suitable for the application habits of contemporary young people. Also, such a display makes it convenient for students to have fragmented study and automatic management and learning practice. In conclusion, it is an important means of displaying and transmitting traditional folk art.

Reconstruction of Traditional Folk Art Courses under New Media Context

Currently, the research on course integration has shifted from subject-centered curricular theory to experience-centered course theory and knowledge-centered course theory, and eventually to the humanism-centered course theory. Correspondingly, the teaching technology is being iterated. In the 20th century, the revolution of information technology brought earthshaking changes to current information teaching technology. The integration between diverse new media technologies and curricular teaching gradually formed the research and practice fields concerning modern education technology, opening up the era when new media technology and courses are integrated.

A. Case Analysis of Design Reconstruction for Combining New Media Technology and Teaching Traditional Folk Art

The design reconstruction for combining new media technology and teaching traditional folk art is generally achieved by two technologic means. Specifically, classroom projection technology and relevant online resources are used to assist with teaching traditional folk art. Firstly, it assists with the online exploratory study in the classroom. Secondly, classical techniques and works of traditional folk art are reappeared to guide students' observation and study. The author's research case mainly aims to solve the low efficiency of learning Dongyang bamboo weaving in traditional teaching and make technique-based teaching procedures more institutional. Thus the teaching priority places an emphasis on activating intangible cultural heritages and guiding innovative thinking

In the information-based teaching case of Craft and Techniques for Porcelain Covered by Bamboo Filaments, the cloud classroom of the online course platform is first used to guide students to complete tasks before the class. The process can be completed through mobile interaction terminals, such as mobile phones. Students study and repeatedly watch coursework in fragmented spare time after class. It divides the complex techniques of traditional bamboo weaving craft classrooms into dynamic tasks, which enhances the efficiency of classrooms. Secondly, live-streaming platforms such as the Internet breaks the time-space distance for students to communicate with craft artists. Thus the traditional teaching of skills is turned into interest guidance with higher human interest. Lastly, online courses guide students to study independently and divide the original time spent on classrooms into the fragmented time before and after the class. It provides adequate opportunities and time for classroom sharing and expands innovative thinking. Also, teaching traditional folk art is guided into the path of thinking training with more innovative design logic.

Implementation process: the willingness for intervention and internalized creation; combine expressions and deepen meanings; display works, evaluate, and appreciate beauty; expand and increase values. All links are connected with each other, achieving the inner connection and development for three monomers: from cognitive experience to method learning; from form cognition to emotional experience; from innovative design to connotation understanding. This process is centered on developing students' intuition from beginning to end. These three links are combined, which fully reflect the humanity and workmanship in the course of craft art. Based on guiding students to learn the craft technology, it expands new thinking in the humanistic materials of the craft art, which meets the requirement on cultivating comprehensive design talents in the current era.

B. Stereoscopic Reconstruction of Combining New Media Technology and Teaching Traditional Folk Art

With the rapid development of new media technology, art design becomes a highly comprehensive subject. The Techniques of Making Porcelains Covered by Bamboo Filaments has one teaching priority: teaching and promoting the techniques of making porcelains covered by bamboo filaments, which has wide application and high operation difficulty. This course is centered on activating and redesigning intangible cultural heritages, with an emphasis on general improvement in students' vocational qualities and professional skills.

This course guides students to explore the background culture of porcelains covered by bamboo filaments through group work. Next, the appreciation of master's works attracts students to learn about weaving technology. Lastly, on-the-spot teaching enables students to have manual practice and grasp techniques and common procedures for this art.

The first step is task-oriented guidance on learning. Students practice the weaving technique of "pressing and take-up" according to micro-course in the cloud classroom. Next, students study the background and development status of porcelains covered by bamboo filaments. Lastly, students complete the trial exploration and upload the micro-video of weaving onto the cloud classroom. Afterward, a survey report is formulated through group work (such as PPT and videos).

The second step is question-oriented guidance on learning. Students and teachers discuss problems in the "pressing and take-up technique". Meanwhile, students appreciate the works of craft artists. Next, students display the homework of before-class survey and analyze its technological characteristics. In this project, students need to discuss pre-class homework in the cloud classroom and exchange doubts in the practice process. Afterward, group representatives report the survey task in the classroom and discuss technological characteristics combining with masters' works.

The third step is the situation creation. In this link, teachers guide students to analyze the techniques of porcelain covered by bamboo filaments and displays operating procedures. The chrysanthemum method and the pressing-and-take-up technique are shown in Fig. 1. Next, classroom tasks are assigned—taking the project of porcelain covered by bamboo filaments as an example. Students learn weaving techniques by watching the video. Afterward, students are required to record the common procedures of making porcelain covered by bamboo filaments, watch teaching animations, abstract laws from weaving hand gestures. They can also learn the technique from masters through online videos. Students are required to communicate with masters about the essence and feelings of making bamboo filaments online. Lastly, students are required to practice weaving techniques for porcelains covered by bamboo filaments and fill out the task form.

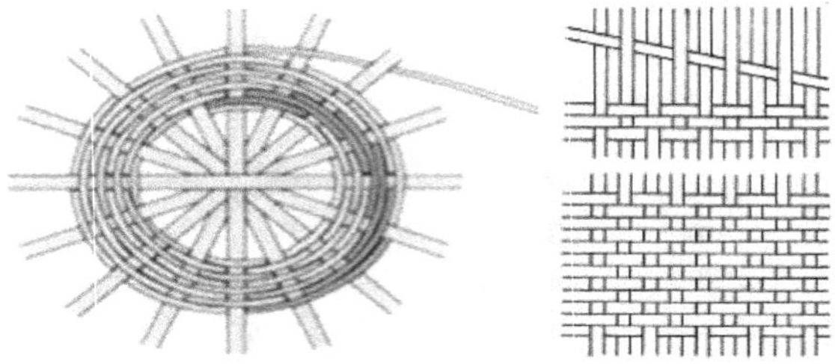

Fig. 1 Chrysanthemum weaving techniques and "pressing and take-up" technique

The fourth step is translation and reconstruction. In this link, teachers guide students to discuss difficulties and priorities of porcelains covered by bamboo filaments and know about the characteristics of bamboo materials. Owing to the texture characteristics of bamboo filaments, porcelains covered by bamboo filaments are resistant to dryness, non-deformed, pest-proof, water-proof, and washable. Besides, the bright patterns do not fade after being used for decades of years. It can not only be used as objects for appreciation and collection but are also practical. Students can be taught relevant materials and methods for processing, including selecting materials→ scrape off the green shell →splitting bamboo strips→ blow all bamboo strips dry →split bamboo strips into bamboo filaments.

In the last step, achievements are displayed in the cloud classroom. Meanwhile, measures can be taken to apply and promote porcelains covered by bamboo filaments as articles of daily use in modern homes. Afterward, the artworks made by students are exhibited, helping students to find the laws in graphic weaving techniques. Besides, the application and promotion are achieved through the Internet. Eventually, the survey report is completed after the application and promoting of porcelains covered by bamboo filaments in modern home life.

C. Achieve Community of Virtuality and Reality of Traditional Folk Art Learning

The integration of information technology and teaching traditional folk art refers to combining different types of media in teaching traditional folk art. With the quality change, it creates a new form of media, such as new teaching materials for traditional folk art.

The application of new media technology to teaching traditional folk art includes s the online restoration of traditional folk artworks through the new media technology. As a technological process, it reflects the integration of traditional crafts and new technology. As the quality change of the traditional folk art in the new media era, it is the collision between innovative thinking and traditional cultures and stems from the demand for constructing a new ecologic environment for developing traditional bamboo weaving techniques.

References

[1] N Danwei L. & Xiesheng L. Dongyang bamboo weaving: prosperity and vitality. Dongyang Daily, 2009-12-14 (No. 5)

[2] J Jun H. Status of cultivating inheritors for intangible heritages in central Zhejiang Province and construction of the inheritance environment, Identification and Appreciation to Cultural Relics, 2018 (06): 113-115

[3] J Xueying W. An analysis of development and prospects of the printing technology and industry, China High-tech Enterprises, 2012 (26): 3-5

[4] D Chengxin L. Integration and reconstruction: an analysis of interactions between technology and course teaching, Nanjing Normal University, 2006

https://doi.org/10.1142/9789811238727_0065

Research on the Design of Juicy Feedback in Educational Applications for Children

Nan Zhang, Jun He*, Jing Lin

Xiamen Academy of Arts & Design, Fuzhou University, Xiamen, China
*Corresponding Author Email: dr.hejun@qq.com

Abstract

Due to the particularity of their users, a number of details should be paid attention to in the design of educational applications for children, and the effective feedback design can be a positive reinforcement on their educational effect. When using the applications, the real-time feedback to every motion of children will play an incentive role continuously, thus improving the initiative and efficiency of learning. For the sake of improving the user experience through feedback design of educational applications for children, this paper, based on the status quo of existing feedback designs of educational applications for children and the characteristics of users, probes into the feasibility of applying juicy feedback in game design to educational applications, studies its impact on the feedback effect, and puts forward ideas and suggestions for feedback design in such applications.

Keywords: educational application for children, juicy feedback, user experience

Introduction

With the development of the "Internet+ education", application software as a new form of education running on the mobile terminals, has increasing drawing attention of educational researchers and is widely used in children's educational practice. Children's educational applications has been started late, which are mostly based on adults' applications as the reference for development and evolution. On such a basis, visual elements favored by children, such as cartoon patterns and interesting animations, are added to the interface of the products, but there is little change in terms of interactive mode. Thereby, the utility level of the products to children is low, which leads to the problems of low interest of children users and low retention rate of users. Feedback design as one of the interactive ways, setting a rational feedback mechanism in the interactive design of application products will affect the fluency of communication and interaction between children users and application products, and plays an important guiding role in children's operating habits [1]. Therefore, it is of great significance to design an effective and rational feedback mechanism in children's educational applications. In game design, whenever feedback is needed, designers would set their sights on juicy effect, and to fulfil juicy feedback in their designs that can make players have pleasurable sensations in a natural way, so as to maintain the players' generation of mental flow and retention of happiness in the game. In this paper, from the perspective of feedback design elements in children's educational applications, the characteristics of juicy feedback in games are applied to children's educational applications, and by using the characteristics of juicy feedback can improve players' experience in games, improvement suggestions are put forward on the details of feedback design from visual, auditory and comprehensive feedback to improve feedback effect in children's educational applications.

Design elements of a feedback system for children's educational applications

A. User characteristics

Children nowadays are a generation growing up with the rapid development of the mobile Internet. All kinds of electronic products and mobile applications have been around children since their birth, creating a diversified educational and living environment for them. These days, children have become an important consumer group of the mobile Internet. According to survey statistics, 52 % of children aged 2 - 14 in the United States have the experience of using mobile applications, while 70 % of children under the age of 12 in Chinese households equipped with tablets have the experience of using tablets [2]. Children are not having mature psychological cognition of things in the early stage of growth; therefore, when designing products, it is necessary to fully consider their cognitive level and habits, and to grasp children's comprehension capacity and acceptance ability [3]. Children are full of curiosity and desire to explore the world, to which designers should provide guidance and encouragement in their design [4]. In the settings of daily life and educational environment, it is difficult for preschool children to concentrate for as long as adults. In the initial stage of memorizing, things with distinctive features, vivid color, conflicts and changes in the content would attract children's attention and are easier for them to remember. Children are used to comprehend the world through making contact with the world. In the process of using application products, children tend to get to know the contents in the application products and the rules for using the products through touch and pointing; therefore, for every behavior of children users, timely and effective feedback mechanisms should be designed to help and guide children to quickly understand the characteristics of things or comprehend the results of the current operation. If children users fail to get timely feedback during their operation, they may be confused and unable to judge the correctness of the current operation result, resulting in the inability to proceed to the next operation, thereby affecting their user experience, and causing termination of using a product. Although the basic feedback design principles are also applicable to children's educational applications, due to the particularity of children users, more attention should be paid to the detailed design of the feedback mechanism. (Fig. 1)

Fig. 1 Characteristics of children user

B.Product features

Children's educational applications are targeting children as the user group, with education as the major purpose, and mobile phones, iPads and other mobile devices as the carrier of the applications. Based on the characteristics of the carrier of Children's educational applications, information output can be implemented by visual, auditory and tactile sensations of the human body, and could be not subject to the limitations of space and time, that the users can proceed to learn at any time. Due to the particularity of the users, in terms of visual design, a rich variety of vivid and brilliant colors should be based on, and according to the content, there could be a rational arrangement of cartoon characters, animation and other interesting elements. In the interaction of the product and information transfer of its content, a simplified process is applied, with the level and process of the application being simplified, visually emphasizing effective, touch-sensitive information, expanding the hot zone of touch-sensitive information, improving fault tolerance of the product. As children are active in thinking, in terms of sound design, it is advisable to add background music, character dialogue, operation sound etc. that are consistent with the content of the application product, so as to attract the attention of children users, increase their curiosity and concentration. Most children's educational applications are developing toward the direction of gamification, so that a product would have playability, increase interestingness of educational applications, and some applications can be personalized for children's education, in which children's favored content can be chosen for their learning, so as to achieve the effect of teaching through lively activities [5]. (Fig. 2)

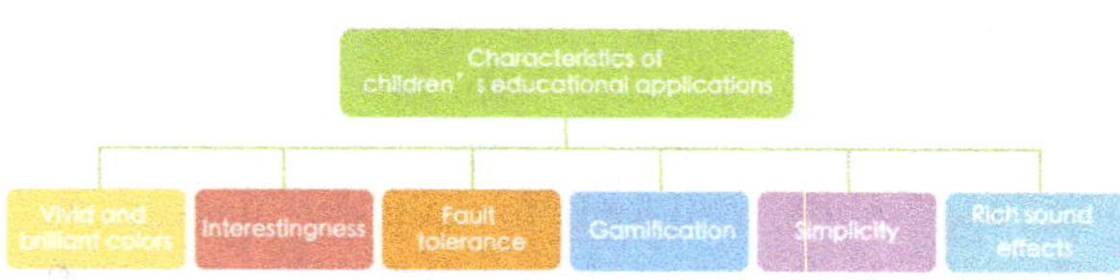

Fig. 2 Characteristics of children's educational applications

The introducing of juicy feedback in children's educational applications

A.The concept of juicy feedback

Jakob Nielsen's 10 general principles for interaction design are important reference standards for product design and user experience design. The first principle of which is the visibility of system status, that is, the system should always keep users informed about what is going on, through appropriate feedback within reasonable time. Therefore, feedback is always an important part in product design. Feedback is almost ubiquitous in a game, in which any operation of the player in the game is naturally presented to the player through visual and data feedback, such as the remaining life value, available time, position and even the state of other players. Game designers often use "juicy" to describe effective, exciting and fascinating feedback, and whenever the opportunity for feedback comes, designers would strive to achieve a "juicy" effect of feedback [6]. According to the description of juicy feedback characteristic by game designer Robin Hunicke, juicy feedback can be summarized as: a logical and rational feedback mode that meets the expectations of players, makes players feel delighted and surprised.

B.Characteristics of juicy feedback

In the description of the characteristics of juicy feedback by game designer Robin Hunicke, it is mentioned that juicy feedback has eight characteristics: haptic, expectant, consistent, smooth, natural, iterative, moderate and novel.

a. Haptic

Once feedback appears in a game, the player could almost instantly perceive its arrival. While in the process of playing a game, feedback is not mechanically presented, but in a natural way. For example, in a shooting game, the mobile phone will have a haptic vibration when the player shoots, just like the recoil after shooting, which would enable the player have the sense of presence, and enhancing the illusion of immersion in the playing process.

b. Expectant

Players are eager for feedback in their interactions with a game, expecting their effort to pay off, which should be positive feedback. This creates an intrinsic dynamic that constantly motivates players to continue to be involved in the game.

c. Consistent

Feedback should be implemented in the way that it is integrated into the background of the game. Great majority of games would have a story setting before unfolding themselves, so that special characters, things, or environments can exist reasonably in the game. Therefore, the content and means of feedback should not only be consistent with the actions and events in the game, but should also respond to the storyline unfolded.

d. Smooth

The emergence of feedback should have fluency, that a sense of waiting from the players is not advisable. In RPG games, when the character being played is upgraded, it should be under transition with special effects or animations, rather than directly changing from one state to another.

e. Natural

Feedback should be presented naturally in a well-organized and orderly manner. The naturalness and smoothness of feedback are complementary. Feedback exists in the background of a game, and its presence should be logical and rational.

f. Iterative and moderate

If targets, challenges, or obstacles arise many times during a game, feedback can be repeated. However, when a player accepts the feedback and takes the corresponding action, or the player has regarded the feedback as a subconscious reaction of the body, the timing and frequency of feedback should be moderate, that the amount should not be excessive, otherwise the player will be at a loss about what to do.

g. Novel

Feedback needs to have variation to allow players to find unexpected surprises, which would be both fascinating and enjoyable. Surprise would win acceptance of players and should be coordinated with the smoothness of feedback.

The characteristics of juicy feedback can improve the experience effects of feedback and satisfy the psychological and behavioral characteristics of children's users. It will give children a sense of pleasure and immersion, and make them feel positive when it be used to children's educational applications. There is a close relation between the characteristics of juicy feedback and the characteristics of children's users. Children will get a sense of satisfaction through juicy feedback, which also can give children more fun and a sense of participation in the application. As a result, it forms a good feedback loop and encourages children to continue to try and experience.(Fig. 3)

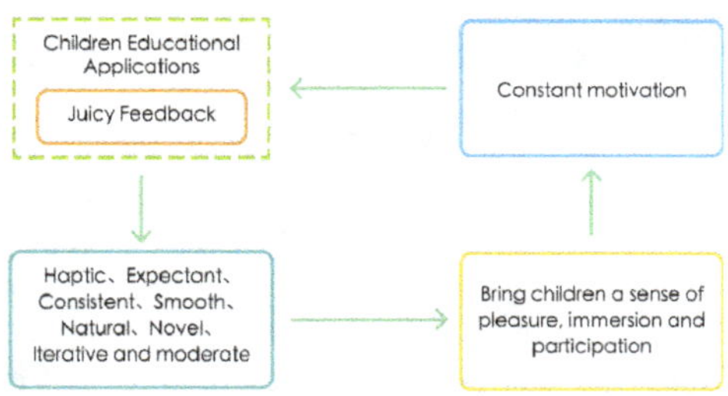

Fig. 3 The effect of Juicy feedback on the feedback effect of educational applications in children

C. Application of juicy feedback

Incorporating the concept of juicy feedback into children's educational applications will not only facilitate children to have a correct perception of the information in the application products and have a better interaction with the products, but can also increase the interestingness of the products and enhance emotional experience of children users. Children's educational applications should be based on the characteristics of its carrier to interact and communicate with children from three aspects: sight, hearing and their integration with the sense of touch, so as to introduce an effective and rational feedback mechanism.

a. Visual feedback

When children interact with application products, visual graphics, animation and coloring are the key contents of design in an interactive interface. Australian psychologist Werner's experiment proves that children's perception, discrimination and choice of things are mostly based on colors that have strong visual appeal [4]. Children are often attracted by colorful graphic elements, when children touching graphic elements and acquire visual feedback that is consistent with graphics, it would be in line with children's expectations. Visual elements in an interface should have a sequence of priority, that the functional and indicative elements should be emphasized with graphic patterns with brilliant colors, and the decorative elements should be diluted. Functional attributes should be assigned to colors in feedback design in a way that children could be attracted by the elements emphasized by color, who would touch the elements to produce alteration of colors, or the elements themselves with brilliant colors would become a kind of indicative feedback, which would prompt children to touch here in the interface. In some picture book reading applications, children tend to touch the graphic elements in a picture book (Fig. 4); however, taking account of children's immersion in the reading process, in many picture books, there will be no feedback upon touching on graphic elements, for which an interactive widget should be added to the interactive operation area, such as the elements of icons or page-turning animations that have a strong contrast to the screen color to emphasize, so as to guide children to operate.

Fig. 4 A picture book reading application

In children's educational applications, interesting cartoons or animations are often used to create a story setting for children and pass knowledge on to children in the process of telling stories. In such applications, feedback should be based on story-telling and logicality, which should be in line with the setting of the story established in the application, and presented in a rational way.

Reward mechanism is a common form of feedback in children's educational applications. According to B. F. Skinner's theory of Operant Conditioning, children's learning behaviors depend on external reinforcement or encouragement to some extent [5]. For children of different ages, the visual content and form presented through reward mechanisms will be different. For children of early school age, decorative items or collection item such as medals, cards, etc. would be more attractive. Sometimes a reward can also be an emotional feedback during interaction, not necessarily visual items. For example, cartoon characters' laugh or applaud can also be used as a simple feedback of reward.

When children users need to practice the same skill over and over again, the visual reward they receive should have variation, while repeated and stereotyped rewards can also get children bored. For example, in the Baby Paradise application (Fig.5), children have to find the same letter several times for penguins to eat. This exercise has to be repeated three times, and the application lights up a different card reward at the end of each exercise to motivate the children users to have the persistence to complete the exercise.

Fig. 5 Reward feedback in Baby Paradise

b. Auditory feedback

When children do not yet have a mature understanding of graphic images, the addition of auditory feedback in the design of children's products would make the presence of feedback more natural and smoother. Adding sound effects imitating different objects and encouraging voice feedback to children's educational applications can improve children's cognition of things and enthusiasm in using an application, thereby enable them experience the fun of learning. On the other hand, the sound effect of an application product can also promote the development of children's auditory senses to some extent.

In the English educational application "Ji Li Gua La" (Fig. 6), in order to help the ants to cross the river, children should click on the ants to send them to the wooden bridge. At this point, the ants will make a cry of "ant", showing a happy expression while moving forward. Here, the sound effect of "ant" would convey the pronunciation of words to children users while expressing the happy voice of ants. This application makes use of auditory feedback, which not only conforms to the story setting of the application, but also produces interesting and rational sound effects at this point. Finally, the information is transmitted and fed back by way of auditory sensation, which can easily attract children's attention and interest.

Fig. 6 English Education application "Ji Li Gua La"

c. Comprehensive feedback

In the process of perceiving things, children usually comprehensively use visual, auditory, tactile and other sensory organs at the same time, and the various senses will interact. A single way of feedback may be affected by time, distance and other factors, resulting in incompleteness or inaccuracy of children's cognition. Therefore, in the design of children's products, a variety of feedback methods can be used at the same time to make up for children's cognitive deficiencies, so that children users and a product would realize better communication and interaction. In a nurturance game, when a fish gets a nibble on the hook, the mobile terminal device would vibrate, simulates the feeling of pulling the rod with effort, and the intensity of the vibration indicates the size of the creature being caught, accompanied by the sound effect of splash. When the fish is out of water, the type of the fish is introduced in detail. (Fig. 7) The application provides children with a holistic understanding of the fishing process, enhances users' presence in the experience, and applies an interesting approach to introduce knowledge about fish to children. In daily interaction of application products, children have been used to feedback through visual and auditory means; when a tactile experience is introduced, it will bring children users more sense of participation and freshness. Under the action of such diversified stereoscopic feedback, the learning process would become vivid and more interesting, and also, use experience of children users would be enhanced.

Fig. 7 Simulates the feeling of pulling the rod with effort

Conclusion

In order to meet market demand, more and more companies and individuals are engaged in the development of children's educational applications, that children's educational applications of various types emerge in an endless stream. While providing children with diversified applications, more attention should be paid to children's sense of experience in using products. By using juicy feedback, users' sense of participation and enjoyment can be improved. In the details of feedback design in children's educational applications, by improving the multi-sensory feedback forms of visual, auditory, haptic etc., children users would receive continuous motivation, and their emotional needs of engagement in the use of products would be satisfied, which is conducive to improving user experience of the products and improving children's activeness in their learning.

References

[1] Wei Yongxia. Analysis on the Application of Feedback Mechanism in Children Products [J]. Journal of Baoji University of Arts and Sciences (Natural Science Edition), 2015, 35 (03) : 45 – 47

[2] Research Report on Supply and Demand Forecast and Investment Strategy of Chinese Children's Education Software Market From 2018 to 2024. Zhiyan Consulting Group. 2018

[3] Zhou Li. Analysis of the Design and Development Principles of Children Products [J]. Qun Wen Tian Di, 2011 (10) : 104 - 106

[4] Sun Qinghua. Children's Physiological and Psychological Characteristics of Design [J]. Contention of Literature and Art, 2011 (10) : 81 - 82

[5] Fu Yu, Huang Beixuan, Wen Ying. A Review on the Current Situation and Suggestions of Children's Educational Applications [J]. Chinese and Foreign Entrepreneurs, 2019 (08) : 164 - 165

[6] Karl M. Kapp. The Gamification of learning and Instruction [[M] Translated by Chen Zhen, China Machine Press, 2015

https://doi.org/10.1142/9789811238727_0066

Research on the Development Trend of Digital Intelligent Advertising

Liang Wang*[1], JoonYoung Hur[2]

[1]QiLu University of Technology, Jinan, Shandong, China
[2]Hoseo University
*Corresponding Author Email: 12990486@qq.com, Tel: +86 150-6909-9517

Abstract

Aiming at the development trend of digital intelligent advertising, this paper explores various forms of advertising communication. It puts forward several aspects of "taking digital intelligence as a means, taking the survival form, industrial form and concept form of advertising as the leading, and taking the traditional advertising communication form as an effective supplement". It discusses the problems of the survival and future development of digital intelligent advertising. It explores the multi-level, eco intelligent advertising communication form and the development strategy of "Internet plus advertising".

Keywords: new communication ecology, advertising industry, internet +, communication form

Introduction

In 2016, the State Administration for Industry and Commerce officially issued the "13th Five-Year Plan for the Development of Advertising Industry". The plan clearly stated that during the "13th Five-Year Plan" period, China's advertising industry faced a major strategic opportunity for innovation and development. China's market economic system is perfect, the national economy maintains steady growth, the income level of residents rises, and the country's comprehensive strength enhances the solid economic and social foundation for the development of the advertising industry. The strategic adjustment of the national economic structure and economic development has entered a new normal, the continuous growth of social consumption demand and the supply-side structural reform have enhanced the internal motivation of the development of the advertising industry. The state promotes the implementation of a series of major development strategies to provide a broader space for the development of the advertising industry. Economic globalization and the implementation of the "One Belt, One Road" development strategy by the state have increased the opportunities for international development of the advertising industry.

It also proposes to optimize the industrial structure further, explore the new mode of advertising business, and form the media linkage development between different natures and fields through the innovative media form of "Internet + advertising". It supports the integrated development of the advertising industry and the Internet industry, standardizes the programmatic transaction management of digital advertising, and establishes a new digital advertising ecosystem. So, it encourages the advertising industry to realize cross-media, cross-platform and cross-terminal integrated services with "Internet + advertising" as the core. Thus, today's advertising industry is facing new opportunities, new development and new challenges under the new communication ecology.

Newly Spread Ecological Environment

According to David L. Altheide, a professor at the University of Arizona Law School, the ecology of communication refers to the structure, organization, and accessibility of various forums, media, and information channels. The challenge of studying the dissemination ecology is to find a perspective that connects information technology, communication (media) forms, and communication actions (activities) [1].

A. The multi-layered advertising market under the new economic normal.

The era of artificial intelligence and big data is coming. Simple marketing methods and means of communication are no longer able to function effectively, and traditional marketing or communication methods are becoming more and more incapable. Therefore, companies are increasingly inclined to use integrated marketing communication as a new way of marketing communication. The so-called multi-layered and eco-friendly advertising industry has emerged as the result of market operation and continuous optimization of industrial structure. The multi-level is the comprehensive integration and construction activities of the advertising industry, which is aimed at adapting to the new environment, and the final integration of the industry on this basis.

B. The market environment in which digital technology and new media integrate marketing communication.

With the development of digital technology, various digital new media have sprung up. Emerging media, represented by the Internet and mobile APP, play an increasingly important role in our daily lives. The development of new technologies has had an irreversible impact on the traditional advertising industry. It has a profound impact on the spread of advertising. The sustainable development of the new dissemination of the ecological environment aims to promote the sound development of the advertising industry. It has played a powerful role in promoting the long-term development of the Chinese advertising industry in a constructive manner.

Promoting The Development of the Advertising Industry is an Accurate Way to Develop "Internet + Advertising."

A. Promoting the integration and development of the internal factors of the advertising industry is to encourage and support the integration and development of advertising enterprises and e-commerce, new logistics and other economic formats

1. Under the impact of new technologies, the traditional form of advertising communication faces an unprecedented predicament. The four traditional media, former dominant newspapers, magazines, radio and television, are facing unprecedented crises and challenges. However, we are more pleased to see the growing maturity and development of the Internet and digital media technologies. Digital technology shortens the distance between people in time and space, and achieves efficient communication that traditional media cannot achieve.

2. The newspaper industry, which has been in the mainstream media status, is struggling in the straits of the integration of traditional media and new media. In the 1980s and 1990s, there was still a saying that "a cup of tea and a pack of cigarettes, a newspaper for half a day". Nowadays, it has already withdrawn from the historical stage at a rapid speed, as a brilliant mark of that era. Today, people are more likely to use the Internet and mobile phones and digital products as a way to touch the world and understand the world. People are enjoying the convenience and dependence of high-tech digital technology, and the application and popularization of the Internet have enabled more and more people to communicate by using the Internet and mobile phones.

3. The deep integration of traditional media and emerging media in the advertising industry is an effective way to build a flexible advertising, new technology and competitive new media.

To achieve cross-border and integration, it is necessary to promote the innovation and development of the advertising industry with "creative, innovative, and entrepreneurial" as the core, create a platform for advertising, crowdsourcing, public support, crowdfunding, and build a demonstration base for advertising industry and innovation in advertising industry. The R&D base and the business incubator build a new type of entrepreneurial innovation mechanism that is coordinated by advertising companies, universities, scientific research institutions, and multi-party.

B. The advertising industry and the Internet industry are integrated and developed, standardizing digital advertising programmatic transaction management, and establishing a new digital advertising ecosystem. Encourage the advertising industry to focus on "Internet + Advertising" to achieve cross-media, cross-platform and cross-terminal integration services.

The digital communication method will be the main mode of communication under the new communication ecology. Advertising in the traditional media environment is one-way communication, and media and media are independent. In the era when traditional media dominates, advertising exists in the form of combined delivery, that is, advertising is placed in different media and time periods. It is coordinated with the overall advertising and promotion effect of the advertisement. In the new media environment, the communication channels have developed into multiple levels and diversified. New media has changed the limited distribution of traditional media information. Internet+ and big data are changing people's thinking patterns and expanding audiences' information reception initiatives and adapt to the diversification of demand and market segmentation.

C. Supporting the integration of the advertising industry with other modern service industries and cultural industries, promoting the cross-industry and cross-sector industry integration of the advertising industry, and building a new advertising industry ecosystem.

The integration of advertising and equipment manufacturing, consumer goods industry, construction industry, information industry, tourism industry, agriculture and sports industry has been further strengthened. All industries work together to develop together and seek long-term benefits. In the future, the advertising industry will pay more attention to cross-sectoral industry integration, optimization and adjustment, and move forward in the process of integration and innovation [2].

The Era of Advertising in the New Communication Ecology Under the Internet of Everything

The Internet+ era has arrived. Only by adapting to the changing development of new technologies can we maintain the sustainable and healthy development of the advertising industry. New technologies have gradually made the way of life intelligent. In the context of the interconnection of all things and the interconnection of personal life, the advertising industry is required to further transform and integrate.

The development of the advertising industry should be considered from the chain of communication. It is necessary to think from the context of the crowd. To think from the mode of media communication, we can find the way of innovation and development from the root.

A. The development of VR virtual reality has unlimited possibilities for the future of the advertising industry.

Virtual reality technology (VR) mainly includes simulation environment, perception, natural skills and sensing equipment. The simulation environment is a computer-generated, real-time, dynamic, three-dimensional, realistic image. Perception means that the ideal VR should have the perception that everyone has. In addition to the visual perception generated by computer graphics technology, there are also perceptions such as hearing, touch, force, and motion, and even smell and taste, also known as multi-perception.

For example, people in the future can use VR technology to achieve an immersive shopping experience without going to the mall in person; they can experience face-to-face sensory communication without visiting a friend's house.

The emergence of VR games, VR movies and other forms shows that virtual reality technology is no longer far away from our lives, which means that when we come into contact with an advertisement in the future, we seem to try it for ourselves. This development is just a matter of thought. It's exciting to think about it. Therefore, virtual reality (VR), as a new economic growth point of the advertising industry, has caused widespread concern in the advertising industry.

B. Digital and artificial intelligence will be applied to every detail of life.

Every "item" in the future life is no longer isolated, such as a table, an electrical appliance, etc. Each of them will probably have the Internet life endowed by artificial intelligence, which will make the "articles" in the traditional sense, an agent that can communicate so interactions between people and devices will become simpler. After the Internet of Everything, a new business ecosystem will be established, and a new form of advertising industry will be formed.

Conclusion

The integration of advertising industry is the trend of the times. Throughout the development of the current advertising industry, industrial integration has penetrated into many aspects and multiple disciplines in the market and research fields. It is accompanied by the growing maturity and perfection of technological innovation, the driving force of economic and market demand, and the technological integration that occurs at the boundaries or intersections of relevant industries.

Technological innovation is the intrinsic driving force for the phenomenon of convergence. Digital technology provides a platform for symbol conversion and resource integration for different media, and also provides new conditions for the integration of different forms of media, such as television, newspapers and mobile phones, and mobile phones or other smart devices. With the impetus of technological development, the new media industry has become the frontier of industrial integration. As the medium of advertising activities, its integration has broken the existing communication form of the advertising industry, and inevitably triggered the all-round transformation and integration of the advertising industry.

References

[1] Yan Ziyan, *Analysis of the Dissemination of China's Advertising Industry from the Perspective of New Environment*, The Press, China, 2009.2.

[2] Ma Erwei, *On the Transformation of Advertising Communication Subjects in the New Ecological Environment. J.China*, Friends of Editing, 2013.7.

https://doi.org/10.1142/9789811238727_0067

Research on the Relationship between Form and Function in Information Graphic Design— Example of Haze Information Visualization Case

Pei Ling Xuan[1*], Huang Wen Tsong[2], Zhu Jing[3]

[1]Ph.D. Program in Design, Chung Yuan Christian University
[2]Department of Commercial Design, Chung Yuan Christian University
[3]MA, Graphic Design and Visualisation, Loughborough University
[*]Corresponding Author Email: lingxuanpei@gmail.com

Abstract

The research of Infographic has attracted much attention in recent years as it reflects the trend of interdisciplinary times. This study explores the relationship between form and function from the perspective of literary theory and the visualization process of information visualization in the case of Haze Information Design created by the researchers of Loughborough University. The purpose is to find out how the relationship affects design practice. The research methods include a questionnaire survey, case analysis, and data collection and analysis on the Datacenter.com platform. The conclusion is as follows: (1) Infographic must be based on information display rather than personal preference. Visual form affects the target audience's understanding of data. (2) In the process of Infographic, consideration must be given to how to present infinite information in a beautiful, concise, and orderly way, which requires the combination of the principles of information cognition and communication as well as the consideration of functions. The focus on function in the creative process also verified that different functions require different forms of expression so the form of expression of the research object is limited to a certain extent by function. (3) Based on the information readability function, text layout design, grid structure, graphic distribution, color representation, and other forms help the viewer find the relevance and hierarchy of information. It is necessary to create an emotional bond with the audience to deliver information quickly and effectively.

Keywords: Infographic, Information Visualization, Form and Function, Haze.

Introduction

A graphic is understood more easily and quickly by the human brain than numbers and letters [1]. A language as one of the ways to convey information is single. Its form of expression and delivery efficiency may not be able to meet the demand for acquiring knowledge and information from large quantities of information. Fortunately, this problem can be solved by information design that uses graphics to improve people's perception of information and increase the ability of the human visual system to notice patterns and trends [2,3]. Haze issue in China is more complicated than that of London and Los Angeles, which makes researchers profoundly reflect and study how to make people pay attention to this problem.

A. Research Process

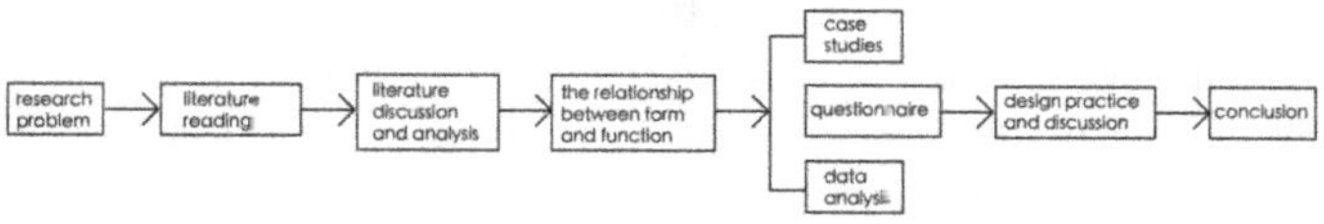

Fig. 1 Research flowchart (Compiled by this research).

B. Research problem and purpose

The research problems are "what is the relationship between function and form in infographic design?" and "does the relationship between form and function in theory have new inspiration through the design process?". The purpose of the research is to explore the relationship between the function and form of infographic design.

Literature Review

A. Information design

Information design includes data visualisation, information graphics, knowledge visualisation and so on. Its purpose is to communicate and provide information in a fast and well-defined way that enable the target audience to observe, explore, and immediately understand a sizeable amount of information. It requires the ability of designers of observation, thought, and imagination to gather information and then express it in a visual form. Its essence demands the designer to refer to content and understanding of information combined with multi-disciplinary and use graphics to convey the information [4]. Research from Smiciklas *et al.* indicated that the first impression of infographic is the attraction that is mainly based on color and visual complexity. Through research, "understandable", "simple", "visual", "color", "easy to read" were found to achieve a high attention rate by people. Not all information are equal. Some information is more valuable than others [5]. Consistency means the difference between great and mediocre designs. It conveys the logic or language of design. With a consistent format, location, and elements, a designer can add hidden information so that the target audience understand what they are trying to convey and keep it in the form. For example, fonts, shapes, rules, and colours are relevant or the same as size, bold, italic, and so on. A good designer creates a fantastic infographic by using an excellent format [6].

B. Information visualisation

The traditional definition of information visualization is "As one of the means and tools supporting people to analyze and understand large and complex information" [7]. The other definition is the visualization of data and ideas which conveys the complex information and knowledge quickly and clearly to the target audience [8]. Information visualization is combined with text, graphics, and visual diagrams. Three different functions are communicating the information and data to the audience as an information description, providing different visual explorations, and using the data as self-expression.

C. Function and Form

Cairo held the view that "Functions restraint and abide by the form". Information design is not a means by which artists show their inner worlds and feelings. Therefore, the information visualization has conflicts in the function, objectivity, accuracy, and aesthetics [9]. Kirk considered that the final work must be attractive and functional in aesthetics. Good aesthetics can produce critical emotions and psychological reactions [10]. During the information visualization, the form must be concerned, not just the support of the function. The researcher believed that if the design cannot represent the information accurately, or the form is not suitable, it shall not be considered as a high-quality work regardless that it has aesthetic appeal or not (Fig. 2). The researcher agreed with Moere *et al.* and Tufte [11] that infographic is functional art that combines art and information to convey precise information. And hold the same view as Lankow *et al.* The design must focus on the target audience and information display rather than personal preference to specify the applicability and effectiveness. Sometimes, the forms affect the target audience's understanding of the data. The function depends on the design purpose and cannot be ignored or too much emphasized [12].

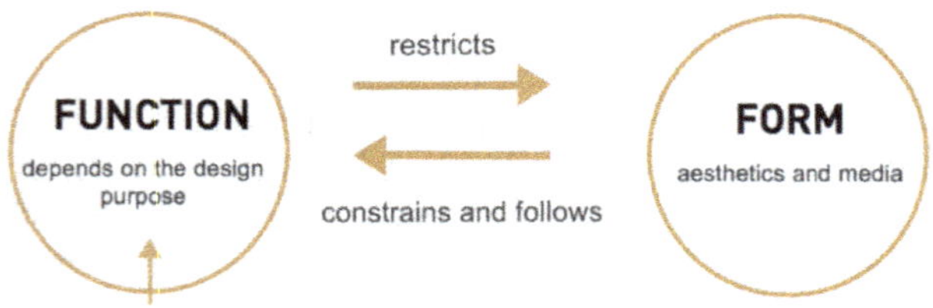

Fig. 2 The Relationship of Function and Form (compiled by this research).

Research Methodology

This study uses a questionnaire survey and case analysis. The data is collected from the official platform HTTP://datacenter.mep.gov.cn/index. From the collection of the haze data on the platform, analysis in the actual creation process was performed, and the relationship between form and content was verified and explored through information visualization.

Research result

A. Results of questionnaire survey

The questionnaire survey was carried out offline with 30 subjects. The questionnaire contained questions about the haze. The answers with the highest proportion of the questionnaire results were used as references for the subsequent creation of a questionnaire. The tested subjects were selected randomly regardless of age, occupation, and gender. The main questions of the questionnaire were as follows: (1) how do you think the haze has changed in recent years? (2) what is the first impression of haze? (3) choose a color to represent the impression of haze. The findings are summarized as follows: The smog was denser in winter and spring, which was a comparative reference for data analysis and visualization design to observe the relationship between people's sensory perception and data. 82.5% of the respondents felt that smog rendered a dull and depressing feeling. 30% chose black as the basic impression, while 65% chose gray and soil color. The answers of the remaining people were not included in the final design. The finding was used for the subsequent creations. A human-centered design approach is intended to provide tools for improving the interaction between design objects and their use by designers [13].

B. Case studies

The first case was from works called "Dear data" designed by Giorgia Lupi and Stefanie Posavec (Fig. 3). The designers recorded, collected, and drawn personal data. Then, they made them into infographic and sent them to each other by postcards. Designers tried to design the information in an interesting, free, and logical way by hand painting. The second case was the design "Organism" by Stefanie Posavec (Fig. 4). She designed the same flower structure which was divided into subcodes according to Darwin's original text that split them into paragraphs "leaflet". The small wedge of "leaflet" stands for the sentence. She said, "I like the design that's fundamentally meaningful, and everything is for some reason. Also, visualization must work for some reason". The method she used is the same as the method for the final project. Kirk thought the method was based on a designer's judgment. It is a personal interpretation of the experience. The key is to identify important design goals. As the function of this design is to convey information and self-expression, a designer sets colors and rules based on personal experience and preferences. The third case study is from "The Potato Lifecycle" (Fig. 5). This work showed the importance of the designer's self-definition of rules and colors. The data must be presented in a logical and meaningful way, and the interpretation section needs to be clearly described in the poster.

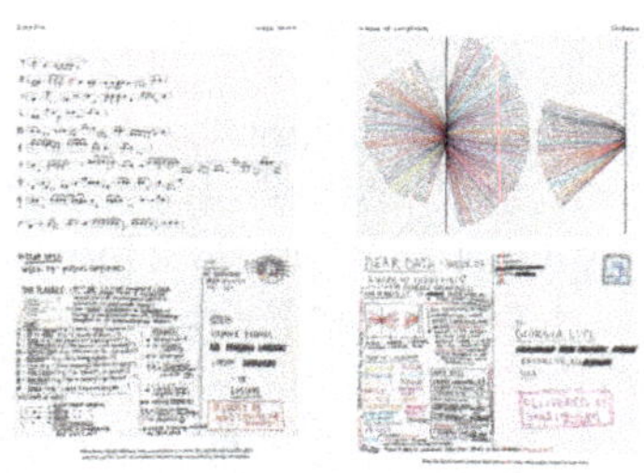

Fig. 3 Dear Data (2015), Giorgia Lupi and Stefanie Posavec.

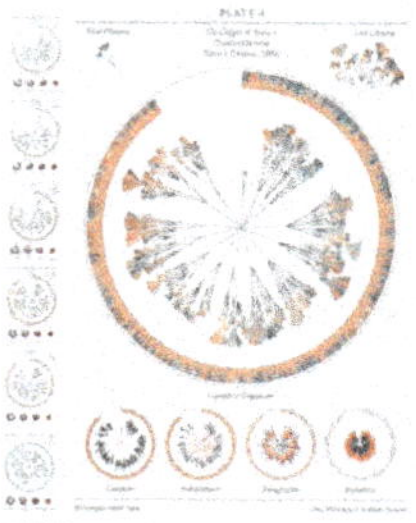

Fig. 4 Organism, Stefanie Posavec.

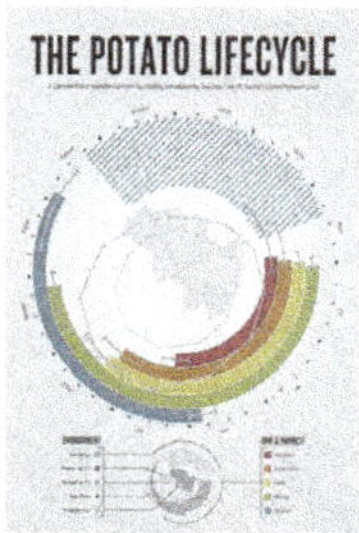

Fig. 5 The Potato Lifecycle, August Miller.

Research discussion and analysis

A. Three main methods of design practice

There are three main methods of infographic design.

(1) Deliberate design: Kirk thought each mark and design features have reasons. The designer ensures that the contents are adequately planned, understood, and reasoned. Shapes, colors, the location of labels, or interactive usage options are needed to be considered.

(2) Visual metaphor: It means that the visual form of expression and theme. A design has a special meaning.

(3) Network layout: Nodes are organized around a central node, with their position related to the number of hops to reach. To present the complete information objectively, the design must respect the facts and reflect the information accurately and coherently. The design process follows the guides to design from Dalton: (a) set a clear goal, (b) choose one form, (c) consider the target audience, (d) make some special meaning, (e) ensure well designed, and (f) use reliable resources [14].

B. Creation process and analysis

The most important thing is the management of data. Designers stress that data mining is necessary as an important part of the design process. When creating a visualization, most of the time must be used to deal with data, rather than do the form [15]. This point of view is fully revealed in the creative process that uses three main methods and combines the results of the previous questionnaire to inspire reference and advance.

(1) Collection, screening, and data analysis

The haze data of the required year (2014.01-2017.04) was collected from the official website, then filtered out for the average, the maximum, and the minimum value of each of monthly data, and showed the trend of total values by the visualization of data to the target audience.

(2) Data visualization

In the outermost circle of the main chart, the designer filled each area in different colors according to the data for indicating different air levels. Different transparency of the same color is used to distinguish data, which means different degrees of meaning. Metaphor design combined with previous questionnaire results inspired choosing colors and styles. It presents a smoggy feeling, like countless particles floating in the air. Sub-Poster (Fig. 6) also used different visualization methods, designed by the principle of numerical distinction, and placed circles with different color levels on the corresponding numerical positions.

(3) Infographic part and analysis

In the main part of the infographic (Fig. 7), designer classified the objects that need to be designed and drew a simplified diagram. Next, the designer used the same rounded corners, inclination, and standardized the overall chart style to obtain a complete design. Research and analysis found that the entire visual chart layout is the interaction between the target audience and the information in information visualization. This layout requires the sorting and extraction of information before it is understood by users. It includes the charts, colors, texts, and the proportion and positioning of the elements.

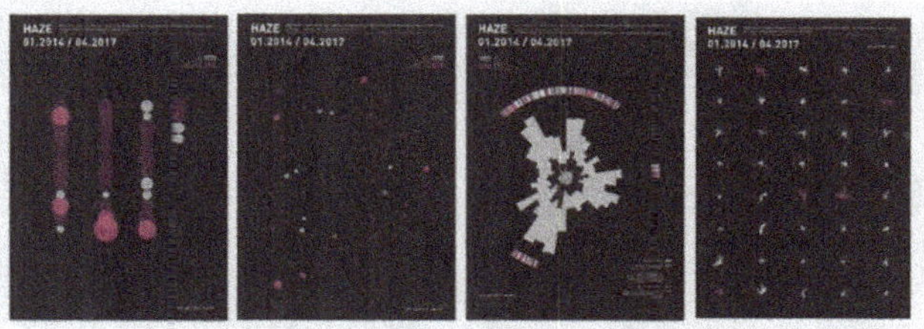

Fig. 6 Sub-Poster - Sub-Poster - Main-Poster- Sub-Poster.

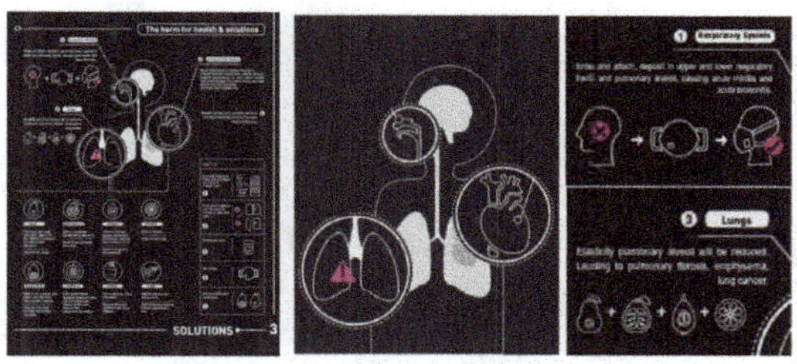

Fig. 7 Infographic part.

Conclusions and recommendations

This report introduced three important methods of design, visual metaphor, and network layout. Through the design process of infographic of haze, various forms of expression were proposed, and the form and function of the infographic design were further discussed.

The research conclusions are as follows:

(1) Infographic must be based on goals and information display, rather than personal preference. Visual form sometimes affects the target audience's understanding of data.

(2) In the process of Infographic, more consideration must be given to how to present infinite information in a beautiful, concise, and orderly way. This requires the combination of the principles of information cognition and communication as well as the consideration of functions. The focus on function in the creative process also verifies that different functions require different forms of expression so the form of expression of the research object is limited by function.
(3) Based on the information readability function, text layout design, grid structure, graphic distribution, color representation, and other forms further help the viewer find the relevance and hierarchy of information. It is necessary to create an emotional bond with the audience to deliver information quickly and effectively.

The methods of questionnaire and focus group shall be used in the following research. This research took the created case of "haze information design" as a sample to carry out cognitive survey statistics of the respondents. Further exploration of the influential relationship between form and function of an infographic needs combining with the SPSS quantitative statistical software.

References

[1] Alazmi, A. R. (2012). Data mining and visualization of large□databases. International Journal of Computer Science and Security, 6(5), 295-314.
[2] Heer, J, Bostock, M., & Ogievetskey, V. (2010). A tour through the visualization zoo. Communications of the ACM, 53(6), 59-67.
[3] Card, S., Mackinlay, J. D., & Shneiderman, B. (2009). Information visualization. Human-computer interaction: design issues, solutions, and applications, 181.
[4] Smiciklas, M. (2012). The power of infographic: Using pictures to communicate and connect with your audiences. Que Publishing.
[5] Harrison, L., Reinecke, K., & Chang, R. (2015, April). Infographic aesthetics: Designing for the first impression. In Proceedings of the 33rd Annual ACM Conference on Human Factors in Computing Systems (pp. 1187-1190). ACM.
[6] Morris, C., & Wocknitz, S. (2013). Teaching an old dog new tricks How data visualisation & design can be used by everyone. Southern African Marketing Research Association Conference.
[7] Moere, A. V., & Purchase, H. (2011). On the role of design in information visualization. Information Visualization, 10(4), 356-371.
[8] Lankow, J., Ritchie, J., & Crooks, R. (2012). Infographic: The power of visual storytelling.
[9] Cairo, A. (2012). The Functional Art: An introduction to information graphics and visualization. New Riders.
[10] Kirk, A. (2012). Data Visualization: a successful design process. Packt Publishing Ltd.
[11] Tufte, E. (1997). Visual explanation: Image and quantities, evidence and narrative. Graphics Press. Cheshire, CT .
[12] Jing, Z (2017). Literature review [Information design of haze and smog (data visualization)]. Loughborough University.
[13] Mejía, G. M. (2013). Visual intelligence and mood in visual communication design. Information Design Journal, 20(1), 47-57.
[14] Dalton, J., & Design, W. (2014). A Brief Guide to Producing Compelling Infographic. London School of Public Relations.
[15] Bigelow, A., Drucker, S., Fisher, D., & Meyer, M. (2014, May). Reflections on how designers design with data. In Proceedings of the 2014 International Working Conference on Advanced Visual Interfaces (pp. 17-24). ACM.

https://doi.org/10.1142/9789811238727_0068

Research on Visual Image Symbols in Dynamic Context

Qingyue Lin, Yisong Chen*

Xiamen Academy of Arts and Design, Fuzhou University, Xiamen, Fujian
*Corresponding Author Email: 645748317@qq.com, Tel: 008618050048446

Abstract

With the diversification of information media, the visual image symbol has more possibilities for extension and application in the Visual Identity System. Especially when entering the information age, digital technology makes dynamic visual images possible, and dynamic visual design has become an emerging trend. This article will summarize the dynamic extension of visual symbols in image design, and discuss the design and innovation of visual image symbols in the dynamic context in the new era with specific cases.

Keywords: visual image symbol, dynamic context, identity design, image extension

"Dynamic in static"

A. Rich application methods

"Dynamic in static", that is, although the visual symbol does not change in the time dimension, it gives the overall visual image a sense of change through its various ways of application. The visual symbols in the identity design can be logos, colors, or auxiliary graphics. The logo is usually easily restricted when changing from static to dynamic with its strong fixity. In contrast, the auxiliary graphics have a higher degree of flexibility and more extension methods, and a reasonable design can make the brand image richer. It is worth noting that many companies have begun to pay attention to creating a rich brand image, and dynamically extend the visual symbols which represents their own image and apply them to products. Their design methods are also varied [1]. As Fig. 1 shows, the auxiliary graphics of Target Supermarket are formed by cutting and magnifying different parts of its logo. The patterns are different but the overall style is consistent. While ensuring the recognizability, it also adds flexibility, achieving the purpose of improving its brand recognition.

Fig. 1 Flexible application of Target Supermarket auxiliary graphics

B. Multi-environment and multi-cultural needs to adapt

The dynamic design of visual image should take cultural elements into account and make adjustments according to different market environments. Under the premise of basic recognition, companies can appropriately change a visual symbol to meet the cultural adaptation needs in different environments. In order to meet the local people's environmental awareness, McDonald's changes the theme color of some European stores from red to dark green to shape a green corporate image, which is shown in Fig. 2. In addition, it also incorporates the current design trend style into the design to cater to the current cultural upsurge. Through various forms of display such as illustrations, McDonald's image becomes "dynamic".

Fig. 2 Cultural adaptation of some McDonald's stores

C. Cultural adaptation of some McDonald's stores

Multi-series use requirements also prompt the dynamic development of image design. Driven by the growing enterprise scale, the brand image needs a more diverse way of expression to distinguish different categories. Setting different colors, different graphic symbols for different categories, or deconstructing and reorganizing existing visual elements to form new symbols are more common processing methods. As shown in Fig. 3 the logo of Unilever is a "U" letter composed of 25 small patterns. The designer deconstructs the logo and recomposes it, then forms a new auxiliary pattern, such as waves, blocks, bands, etc. according to different application requirements. In this way, a unified and varied series of visual effect can be created.

Fig. 3 Unilever's serial application of graphics

The development of any brand or industry is inseparable from the detailed and serialized management of functional departments. With the increasing use requirements, the performance of such "dynamic" visual images is gradually enriching. It is worth mentioning that the updated dynamic logo design and image extension of Bulgarian just as Fig. 4 shows. Its logo adopts the shape of roses and the sun, and the interior is composed of graphic symbols such as lakes, mountains, and beaches that are rich in natural symbolism. At the level of image extension, they maintain the overall rose-shaped outline and the central sun pattern unchanged, other elements can be combined to form a varied design with different application requirements. When applying, different parts of the logo are selected according to the size and shape of the visual media layout to be enlarged. The style is unified but the details are different, so that the sense of dynamic arises spontaneously. Reasonable deployment of the relationship between "static" and "dynamic" can make the overall visual image take into account both recognition and diversity.

Fig. 4 Serialized application of Bulgarian Tourist logo graphics

"Dynamic in dynamic"

A. Changes in performance requirements based on media changes

"Dynamic in dynamic", that is, based on the static visual image at a certain point in time, the visual symbol has a dynamic change in form, color or position within a certain time dimension, thus presenting a dynamic visual effect. With the advent of the Internet era, such dynamic visual symbols appear more and more frequently in front of people. Compared with static, dynamic visual image design has a "timeline" element [2]. Dynamic visual design needs to consider the trajectory of the visual image symbol on the time axis. Its dynamicity is mainly reflected in the control of key frames, that is, the start and end points of the animation. Based on a static visual symbol at a certain time point, the fixed form is broken in the time dimension to form a dynamic design with dynamic and vitality [3].

In the age of multimedia and the Internet, due to the changing needs of new expression media, the visual symbol image design has begun to incorporate the attributes of dynamic design. Such as the fixed beginnings and endings of video images, dynamic display of corporate logos, dynamic interactive design of web pages or APP interfaces, etc. All of these can be grouped into dynamic design categories. There are various methods for dynamic visual design. Color changes, graphic changes, material changes, and audio-visual integration are all feasible design points[4]. Compared with static visual image, dynamic effects can make people's attention to the visual symbols themselves more easily, and arouse people's interest in further observation. The famous art theorist Rudolf Arnheim once said: "Motion is the most likely phenomenon to attract strong visual attention"[5]. Seizing this visual feature for design will have a considerable bonus effect on the presentation of visual images and the improvement of recognition.

Fig. 5 shows a part of Youku's dynamic design. Through the transformation of the red, blue and black circular symbols and the Youku logo, the relationship between the two is established. Its visual image is full of recognition and brand culture. In addition, this kind of motion effect design used for the beginning or end of videos is often used in conjunction with unique tones or slogans and other auditory symbols to break the barriers of the senses. In the context of multimedia, the dynamic performance of visual images is more abundant, with huge creative space.

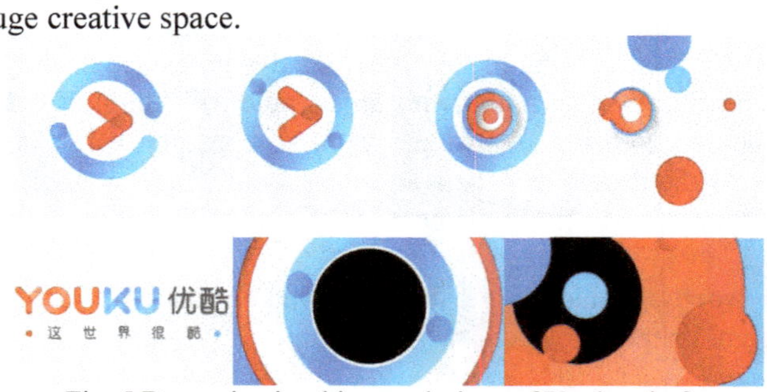

Fig. 5 Dynamic visual image designs of Youku platform

B. Design innovation based on media changes

After the popularity of multimedia visual media, new technologies and Internet media have also broadened the designer's design ideas. Taking NORDKYN's visual image design as an example, which is shown in Fig. 6, the shape and color of the logo will change with the change of wind direction and temperature data. The logo reflects the weather data at every moment and is updated every five minutes [6]. From the perspective of time, the visual symbols are dynamic. Starting from nature and combining data processed by new technologies, the dynamic creativity of the entire visual image can be realized. In addition to providing designers with a display platform, designers can also draw inspiration from new media technologies and integrate them into the design.

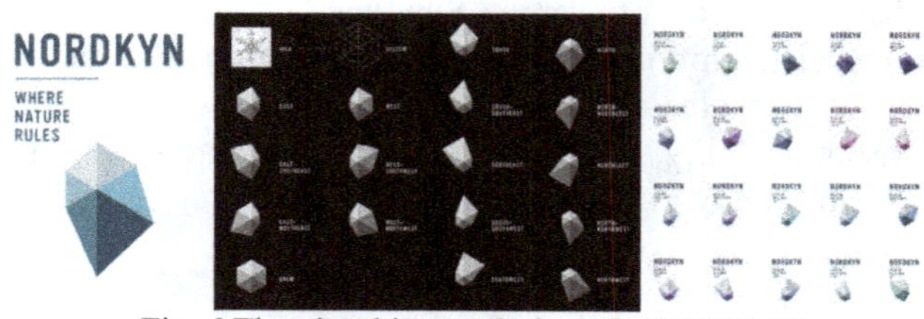

Fig. 6 The visual image design of NORDKYN

C. Design requirements of dynamic Visual Identity System

Compared with the static design, the dynamic visual recognition system is more suitable for presentation in digital media, and is more flexible in practical applications. As shown in Fig. 7, the logo of the Hannover World Expo incorporates dynamic elements, which makes the visual effect quite different from previous static designs. The shape is no longer regular, and the animation is also quite flexible. It uses design elements such as virtual-real relationships, dense relationships, special textures or the light and shadow changes. The characteristics of digital technology are well integrated into the design of visual images, which is full of a sense of future. It can be said to be a milestone in the dynamic design of visual image recognition.

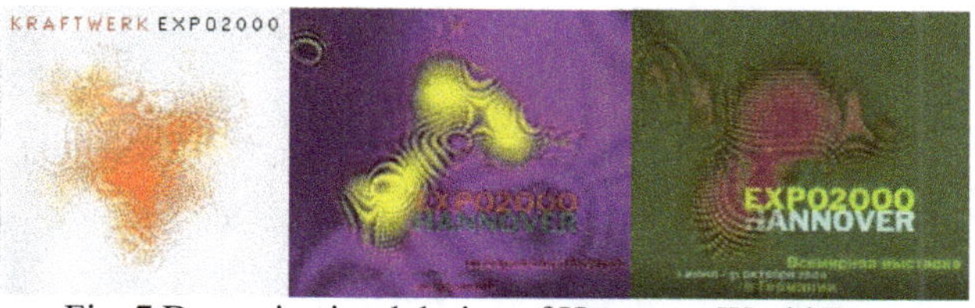

Fig. 7 Dynamic visual design of Hannover World Expo

The visual image proposal designed by Kenya Hara for the 2020 Tokyo Olympics also uses the form of dynamic logos, and the auxiliary graphics derived from the dynamic signs also have various forms of expression. As Fig. 8 shows, the design of the auxiliary graphics is based on the spherical outline and the curved shape in the logo, and also has a flexible application space in the three-dimensional space.

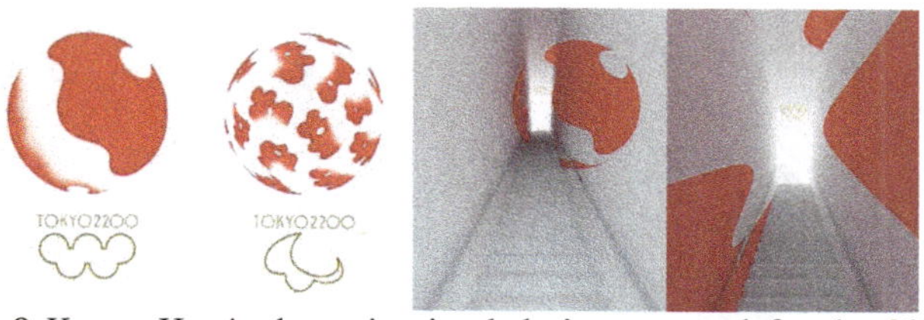

Fig. 8 Kenya Hara's dynamic visual design proposal for the 2020 Tokyo Olympics

The 2016 World Cup's visual identity design is also presented in an animated form, with moving lines, hexagons, football patterns, diverse colors or other changing visual symbols. Figure 9 shows its specific applications. It extracts these dynamic visual symbols from the logo one by one and applies them to all visual media such as illustration design, IP image, background shading, et al., which makes the design have a sense of series and recognition.

Fig. 9 Dynamic visual design of the 2016 World Cup

Because the dynamic visual image gives people a stronger sense of interactive experience and better effects of publicity, many companies that originally used static images have also begun to try dynamic expressions to cater to the trend of the times. Google, as a large Internet company, has a close relationship with new media, and has begun to have a try in this field very early. As shown in Fig. 10, in some festivals, based on the original logo, google often combines the characteristics of festivals for secondary creation. This type of logo is often presented in a dynamic visual way to enhance the interaction and the fun of the logo.

Fig. 10 Dynamic visual design of Google logo in special festivals

Development trend of dynamic design of visual symbols

Nowadays, the dynamic application of visual symbols has become a strong development trend. “Dynamic in static” refers to more meeting the actual use of visual symbols and presenting various visual images with flexible applications. “Dynamic in dynamic” is a dynamic design in the true sense. It is a brand-new artistic expression emerged as the technology advances, which is adapted to multimedia platforms such as TVs, computers, and networks. Over these years, we have witnessed the progress and development from the “first media” represented by newspapers to the “fifth media” represented by digital technology. People's aesthetic needs and consumption ideas have gradually changed accordingly. Compared with the static, dynamic visual image design can help companies establish their image more efficiently, which is conducive to the improvement of brand value [7]. In terms of information carrying capacity, timeliness of information transmission, visual expression, et al., dynamic design occupies a large advantage. Therefore, more and more companies are willing to try to use dynamic methods to shape the visual image in the new era, so as to better convey the required information [8].

Problems that should be paid attention to in the dynamic design of visual symbols

A. Stay systematic

Variability and flexibility are the key elements of the dynamic design of visual symbols, but when developing dynamic design around the visual image, it is necessary to maintain the unity of the overall visual image. In dynamic vision, many visual symbols appear to be moving and changing, but such changes are often followed by rules. How to maintain the sense of unity and regularity of the overall dynamic image through the control of dynamic visual elements, is also a design issue worth considering [9].

B. Avoid formalization

Dynamic visual effect is a useful expression carrier in the process of information dissemination. The ultimate goal of dynamic visual images should be mainly to convey visual information. It should not just focus on the design of dynamic effects, and lose the original intention of information transmission, which is counterproductive. In the dynamic design of visual symbols, in addition to exploring the various feasible performance methods of dynamic design, it is also necessary to avoid formalization, not to let dynamic design become a formal burden and hinder the control of the overall design.

Conclusion

With the development of today's technology and the need for diversified visual performance, the dynamic visual expression is getting closer to the public's vision. Compared with the traditional static visual performance, dynamic visual symbols are more flexible, giving people a stronger visual impact and experience. Whether it is "dynamic in static" or "dynamic in dynamic", the core of both is a dynamic design thinking. So far, dynamic visual design has shown us its infinite development space. As an expressive visual design method, how to properly integrate this changing form into the design and give full play to its value is worth further discussion.

References

[1] Zhang Mingli, Xiong Ying, *Design and Application of Supporting Graphics in Visual Identity System [J]*, Packaging engineering, 2016.

[2] Liu Jia, *On the Dynamic Logo Design under the Background of Digital Media Development [D]*, Qingdao University of Science and Technology, 2017.

[3] Liu Lin, Xu Min, *Analysis of Design Form of Dynamic Logo in New Media Environment [J]*, Drama House, 2016.

[4] Ke Wenyan, *Dynamic Symbol Design Exploration [J]*, Art and Design (Theory), 2009.

[5] Rudolf Arnheim, *Art and Visual Perception [M]*, Sichuan: Sichuan People's Publishing House, 1998.

[6] Hu Songyong, *Discuss the Design Method of Dynamic Visual Extension of Logo Design [J]*, Public Communication of Science & Technology, 2019.

[7] Jin Yinhui, *Research on Dynamic VI Design Creation in the Context of New Media [D]*, Tianjin Polytechnic University, 2019.

[8] Yang Huijuan, *Research on the Extensibility of VI Design in Dynamic Visual Communication [D]*, Northwest University, 2007.

[9] Zhang Baoxiang, *The New Dimensions of Dynamic Logos in the Digital Age [D]*, China Art College, 2018.

https://doi.org/10.1142/9789811238727_0069

Rural Community Interaction Behavior and Environmental Sustainability Based on Happiness Index

Feng Di

[1]Graduate School of Design, National Yunlin University of Science & Technology, Yunlin 64002, Taiwan
[2]School of Art, Huaiyin Normal University, Huaian 223001, Jiangsu, China
Email: 305995850@qq.com

Abstract

Although modernization drives move into cities, villagers retain nostalgia after leaving their hometown. Rural communities are likely to live happily owing to the harmonious relationship between people and the environment. Good interpersonal relationship promotes the interactive behavior and communication among villagers, which is beneficial to the sustainable development of the community. Based on the interacting behavior and happiness index of residents in rural communities, this paper discusses the degree of willingness to promote the sustainability of the community environment. The interaction behavior, happiness index, and the intention of sustainable development of the community environment in Yugou village, Huaian, China were also investigated by a questionnaire survey. The results show that there are significant correlations between the factors. Interpersonal relationship and community interaction behavior in the community is one of the important factors for people to pursue happiness. It is important to support and promote sustainable development at the level of community interpersonal relationships.

Keywords: community interaction behavior, interpersonal relationship, environmental sustainability, the happiness index

Introduction

The United Nations declared that the pursuit of happiness and well-being is the universal goal and expectation of human life, and decided to set March 20 as the "International Day of Happiness" (NEWS ABC, 2012). Happiness is not only personal but also communal in a community since rural communities are familiar and attached to the basic unit of life [8]. This connection is between individuals and the community, between the members, and related to the well-being of the residents of the community. Happiness is a positive emotion that produces joy when spiritual needs are met (Diner, 1985). Sustainable development in the community environment is what makes people happy and extends to future generations. It needs community members' participation, maintenance, and support. Based on this, this paper discusses the interaction between residents in rural communities and the improvement of their happiness for a happy, harmonious, and sustainable rural community.

Background of Problem

In daily life, the atmosphere of a community has a direct impact on the well-being of residents. The English word "community" comes from the Latin word communis that means common feeling or relationship. Leyden found that people who often walked are more likely to get acquainted with neighbors and had a stronger sense of community than those who drove in Galway, Ireland. When compared to the increase in family income, a sense of belonging has a greater impact on life satisfaction [12]. Neighbors cooperate and talk often to achieve happiness [3]. Therefore, the community relationship is an important source of happiness [9].

Good interpersonal relationship creates a harmonious atmosphere in a community and is the source of villagers' happiness. It is not only a social connection or interaction between people but also a manifestation of behavior. As a producer of community social action, individual behavior improves individual happiness when it praises others. Members of a community have a close relationship, mutual respect, and friendship which form a common "atmosphere" and "cultural" collective sense and act for the good of the community. Sharing in social conversations has an important impact on social structure and group behavior [13]. Therefore, the development model of a rural community promotes and publicizes the sustainable development of the community environment by the close interpersonal relationship of the villagers.

Yugou Town is located in the northwest of Huai 'an Huai Yin District, Jiangsu Province, China. It has an area of about 7km^2 with a population of about 50,000. The town has a long history and rich resources. There are still "Linchuan Academy", "Octagonal glass well", "Guan Di Temple" and other historical relics in the rural. Yugou s' villagers are proud of their cultural heritage. In urban modernization, villages around Huaian flooded into southern Jiangsu where Wuxi, Suzhou, Shanghai, are located for opportunities [1]. As the development faces transformation, the boundary between urban and rural areas is blurring. The rural areas are also seeking development but the countryside offers more development opportunities. Due to the homesickness of those who left their hometowns, some villagers choose to return. Therefore, we chose Yugou as the investigation site to explore the interactive behavior, happiness index, and environmental sustainability of residents in the community.

Problem Solving

To evaluate the happiness generated by community interaction, this paper conducted a questionnaire survey in the rural community of Yugou by considering demographic variables: gender, age, and education level. Simple random sampling was used to issue the questionnaire.

The questionnaire contained questions about people's well-being scale and green environment by adopting Argyle's social adaptive self-assessment scale (SASS) [3]. It consisted of community interaction, community happiness, and community environment maintenance. The respondents scored from "strongly agree" (5) to "strongly disagree" (1).

Results and Discussion

150 questionnaires were distributed and 126 valid ones were returned. 44.4% of the respondents were males. 7.1% of respondents were under the age of 20, 54% from 20 to 40, 21.4% from 40 to 60, and 17.5% over 60 (Table 1).

TABLE 1
GENERAL INFORMATION

Characteristic	Contents	Number	Percentage
Gender	Male	56	44.4
	Female	70	55.6
	Total	126	100
Age	Under 20	9	7.1
	20-40	68	54
	40-60	27	21.4
	More than 60	22	17.5
	Total	126	100
Educational background	Under high school	39	31
	undergraduate	45	35.7
	graduate student	15	11.9
	Graduate or above	27	21.4
	Total	126	100

A. Community interaction behavior analysis

The results for the interaction behavior showed that 72.5% of the residents in the community had neighborhood interaction, 75.6% participated in community activities, 76.2% cared about their friends, 71.6% agreed with behavioral cooperation in the community, and 75.8% thought it was necessary to communicate with people in the community. Generally, residents in communities of the caring environment were more willing to participate, carry out cooperative behaviors on some issues in the community, and contribute to the community and environment (Table 2).

TABLE 2
RESIDENTS' COGINITION OF SOCIAL INTERACTION BEHAVIOR

Problem	options	Number	Percentage
Neighbors help each other	not important at all	1	0.8
	not important	4	3.1
	neutral	29	22.8
	important	49	38.6
	very important	43	33.9
		126	99.2
Activities participate	not important at all	0	0
	not important	2	1.6
	neutral	28	22.2
	important	53	41.7
	very important	43	33.9
		126	99.2
Care Between friends	not important at all	1	0.8
	not important	5	3.9
	neutral	36	28.3
	important	50	39.4
	Very important	34	26.8
		126	99.2
Behavior cooperation	not important at all	2	1.6
	not important	5	3.9
	neutral	28	22.0
	important	45	35.4
	Very important	46	36.2
		126	99.2
communication	not important at all	0	0
	not important	5	3.9
	neutral	26	20.5
	important	54	42.5
	Very important	41	32.3
		126	99.2

B. Analysis of community happiness Index

As for the interaction behavior, the results showed that 72.4% of the residents were satisfied with the current community interaction, 61.4% thought the life of the community had a collective sense, 74.8% thought the relationship was good, 79.5% regarded chat with people to be happy, and 74.8% were satisfied with the interaction with people. Those who have positive mental and emotion have good health and help the overall improvement of the community well-being. The residents of mutual help and concern are more willing to participate by carrying the cooperative behavior and to create good atmosphere and environment. (Table 3).

TABLE 3
RESIDENTS' PERCEPTION OF COMMUNITY HAPPINESS INDEX

Problem	Options	Number	Percentage
Life satisfaction	not important at all	0	0
	not important	3	2.4
	Neutral	31	24.4
	Important	47	37.0
	very important	45	35.4
		126	99.2
Sense of community	not important at all	2	1.6
	not important	6	4.7
	neutral	40	31.5
	important	45	35.4
	very important	33	26.0
		126	99.2
Community relationship	not important at all	0	0
	not important	5	3.9
	neutral	26	20.5
	important	49	38.6

	Very important	46	36.2
		126	99.2
Friendship needs	not important at all	0	0
	not important	4	3.1
	neutral	21	16.5
	important	62	48.8
	Very important	39	30.7
		126	99.2
Interaction satisfaction	not important at all	1	0.8
	not important	4	3.1
	neutral	26	20.5
	important	56	44.1
	Very important	39	30.7
		126	99.2

C. Analysis on the intention of sustainable development of community environment

As for the interaction behavior, the results showed that 92.6% of residents were willing to maintain the community environment for the healthy growth of children, 74.5% were willing to share the water, 84.2% regarded a green environment and related activities to be important, 85.8% exchanged recycling methods, and 75.6% shared the community identity.

Planting trees improves the community environment, enhances the quality of living, and at the same time, contributes to the healthy growth of children. This indicates that the residents in the community are willing to actively maintain the community environment for the younger generation in the community. The residents together tried to recycle wastes and save energy to achieve the environmental sustainability of the community (Table 4).

TABLE 4
RESIDENTS' DESIRE FOR SUSTAINABLE DEVELOPMENT OF THE COMMUNITY

Problem	options	Number	Percentage
Environment maintenance	not important at all	0	0
	not important	0	0
	neutral	8	6.3
	important	44	34.6
	very important	74	58.3
		126	99.2
Energy saving	not important at all	2	1.6
	not important	12	9.4
	neutral	30	23.6
	important	44	34.6
	very important	38	29.9
		126	99.2
Green environmental quality	not important at all	0	0
	not important	1	0.8
	neutral	18	14.2
	important	53	41.7
	Very important	54	42.5
		126	99.2
Waste reuse	not important at all	0	0
	not important	1	0.8
	neutral	16	12.6
	important	60	47.2
	Very important	49	38.6
		126	99.2
Community identity	not important at all	0	0.8
	not important	4	3.1
	neutral	26	20.5
	important	49	44.1
	Very important	47	30.7
		126	99.2

D. Community interaction behavior Community happiness Index -- the relationship between the community's desire for sustainable environment

The correlation between the variables of community interaction behavior, community happiness index, and sustainable cognition of community environment was studied through correlation analysis. As shown in Fig.1, the correlation coefficient between the community happiness index and the community interaction behavior was 0.772, the correlation coefficient between the community interaction behavior and the community environment sustainable cognition was 0.762, and the correlation coefficient between the community happiness index and the community environment sustainable cognition was 0.761. The increase in age improved community interaction behavior, happiness, and environmental sustainability.

Therefore, the interaction among residents promotes the residents' happiness index to share "environment maintenance", "energy-saving", "green building", "recycling" and "maintenance and construction of good community environment".

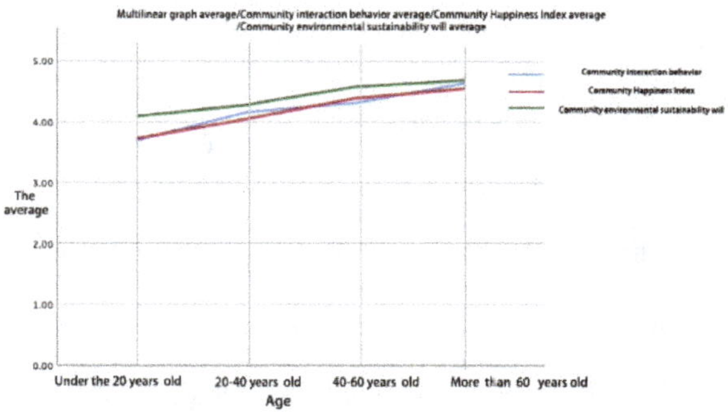

Fig. 1 The correlation between community interaction behavior, community happiness index, and community intention to maintain the sustainable environment in different age groups.

Conclusion

The pursuit of community happiness is both an individual and a common goal of a community. The sense of belonging changes the behavior significantly [11]. For example, people living in pedestrian communities are more likely to walk to work, which reduces air pollution. People feel happy when interacting with others in an environment of mutual. Through voluntary and spontaneous behavior, they solve the problems of the community, but also improve the living environment for a life of quality and happiness [7]. Therefore, a good community interaction provides a friendly social space for community residents, creates a win-win situation for happiness, reduces environmental pressure, and increases the social connection of happiness for the sustainable development of the community [11]. The development of a community depends on its interpersonal relationship. The rural social structure affects the community's interpersonal relationships. In the community environment, the community members live together, and the pursuit of a happy life is the common goal. By promoting community interpersonal relations, the sustainable development of the community becomes a common goal. To meet the needs of the community members and consider the survival of future generations, the community members need to share common interests, maintain the community environment, and have a common goal. Therefore, the interpersonal relationship and interaction behavior of a community are important factors to pursue happiness and promote sustainable development at the level of the community interpersonal relationship.

Acknowledgment

Project: Phased achievements of Jiangsu Social Science Foundation Youth Project in 2019 (19YSC005).
Project: The phased achievements of the project approved by Hunan Social Science Achievements
Review Committee in 2020 (XSP20TBC052)
Project: Phased achievements of National Natural Science Youth Fund Project Approval in 2018 (No. 51808249)

References

[1] Bu Min (2018). Rural population Migration and Intergenerational income Mobility. Contemporary Economy (23),108-111.
[2] Song, Zhenzhao (2004). Sociological theory, Taiwan: Wunan Book Publishing Co., LTD., ISBN957-11-1420-0.
[3] Argyle, Michael (2001), Shih Chien-bin, Lu Lu-yi (1997), The Psychology of Happiness, Taiwan: Big Stream Books, ISBN: 9577320740.
[4] Seligman (2002), trans. Hong Lan, (2003), True Happiness, Taipei: Far Flow, ISBN: 957-32-5002-0.
[5] Cai Hongjin (1989), rural sociology, Taiwan: SAN Min Book Co., ISBN: 907-14-0015-7
[6] Lu Luo (1998). The connotation, measurement and related factors of Chinese people's happiness. Journal of NSC Research: Humanities and Social Sciences, 8 (1), 115-137.
[7] Lin Mingzhen (2011A), intermediary organizations: problems of community development and operation in Taiwan and alternative choices. Journal of social policy and work, 15,1, 137-166
[8] Francis T. Andrew, Trans. Wei Zhifen (1995), environmental Psychology, Taiwan: Wu-nan Book Publishing Co., ISBN: 957-11-0982-7.
[9] Diener, E., Emmons, R. A., Larsen, R. J., & Griffin, S. (1985). The Satisfaction With Life Scale. J Pers Assess, 49(1), 71-75. doi:10.1207/s15327752jpa4901_13
[10] Dunbar, R.(1998), Social brain hypothesis, Evolutionary anthropology 6 (5): 178–190.
[11] Helliwell, J. F. (2017). Social norms, happiness, and the environment: closing the circle. Sustainability: Science, Practice and Policy, 10(1), 78-84. doi:10.1080/15487733.2014.11908126
[12] Helliwell, J., R. Layard, & J. Sachs (Eds.). 2012. World Happiness Report. New York: Columbia University, Earth Institute.
[13] Rimé.B, Bouchat. P, Paquot. L, Giglio. L,(2020), Intrapersonal, interpersonal, and social outcomes of the social sharing of emotion,Current Opinion in Psychology, Volume 31, February 2020, Pages 127-134
[14] Min Jee Nikki Han, Mi Jeong Kim(2019), Green Environments and Happiness Level in Housing Areas toward a Sustainable Life, Sustainability 2019, 11(17), 4768; https://doi.org/10.3390/su11174768
[15] NOTE: Division of Rural Social and Economic Survey, National Bureau of Statistics. China County Statistical Yearbook. 2018 (Township Volume) [M]. Beijing: China Statistics Press, 2019.05: page 168.

https://doi.org/10.1142/9789811238727_0070

Sociocultural Perspectives of a Blended Learning Model to Reading Instruction

Xianghu Liu[1*] and Yaxin Deng [2]

[1]College of Foreign Languages, Bohai University, China
[2]Bohai University, China
[*]Corresponding Author Email: liuxianghuinchina66@hotmail.com

Abstract

As has recently been noted, the field of education has been affected by the technological and communications revolution. Blended learning has been introduced into the field of education as well. The growing popularity of blended learning is indisputable because it is set to transform education. Until today, the learning model, which combines online courses with classroom teaching, has been explored and evaluated. Many blended learning curricula in today's academic environment are built around traditional curricula, which now enrich online content and functions.

Keywords: blended learning, social-affective strategy, sociocultural theory

Introduction

In the socio-cultural paradigm, education and awareness is cultivated through situational activities for more effective use of strategies. These situational activities allow learners to develop and improve their individual abilities. In the blended learning model, this means that programs must provide a context based on a series of strategic tasks and the purpose of those tasks so as to help develop the learners' higher mental processes. This encourages self-reflection and new strategic orientation in learner behaviors. In other words, socio-cultural theory supports the application of blended learning in educational activities, which means learning in an authentic environment and meets the needs of the learning context.

Literature Review

A. Sociocultural theories

Sociocultural theories from the work of Vygotsky advocate that gaining knowledge is an energetic procedure and that the environment performs a very crucial function in learning [1]. He pointed out that gaining knowledge is an individual issue as well as the improvement of the social environment. According to sociocultural theory, the social environment has been placed at the core of learning [2]. Without social-cultural theory, the improvement of ideas is impossible [3]. The reason is that learning is intervened. Vygotsky recommended that in the learning procedure, specialists use tools to find out about the mediation. Others interact with learners, using agent equipment to increase the gaining knowledge of procedure. Improvements in cognition can happen as well. The equipment is naturally psychological, as the tools are employed to assert specific thoughts together with language, symbols, texts and reminiscence skills [4]. The most significant sociocultural tool is language, because of the use as a teaching tool and the importance in terms of mental function development in higher education [5]. In the process of internalization, when learners start to utilize the advanced tools to convey their thoughts, these tools will modify and change their thinking process. Therefore, social environments can influence learners on learning obviously in the way that they express ideas [6].

B. Blended learning

Blended learning has many advantages, which make it more popular among teachers and students. Some of them are listed below:

1. By combining different educational models and means, blended learning can improve students' academic performance [7].
2. Learning can be applied to students with different learning styles and levels [8].
3. Blended learning can save costs and reduce the cost of general education.
4. The use of various educational technologies has attracted more students' attention to the subject of the course.
5. By combining traditional education with other educational technologies, students can acquire knowledge from anywhere until they communicate face-to-face with their teachers.

Language courses that mix face-to-face instruction can promote language learning. In addition, blended learning models with face-to-face education improve students' empowerment, which indicates that learners actively interact with the materials. This engagement with interactive applications can reduce poor associations with language learning because learners do more than just passively obtain information. As a consequence, it can lead to mobilizing student enthusiasm for reading [9].

C. Blended learning with reading

Behjat [10] investigated the results of blended learning on student reading and learning attitudes. The participants in the control group were allocated to obtain printed texts out of class while those in the experimental group were required to go to a weblog after class to discover their reading homework. The reading materials on an e-tool like wikis were reported to encourage leaners to read as the materials had hyperlinks and were editable, and learners could get entry to them just through ticking on the underscored term or phrase to enter a new webpage, consequently they accessed more reading resources. It was concluded that blended learning inspired learner autonomy in reading more materials independently in terms of what was provided in class, which causes students to increase their interests in reading.

Schechter, Macaruso, Kazakoff and Brooke [11] explore a blended learning approach in reading training for students in early fundamental grades. This research project investigates the possible advantages of a blended learning model in terms of the reading abilities of students in Grades 1 and 2. Results demonstrated significantly more pre-test/post-test gains in a standardized reading evaluation for the experimental students in contrast to the control students, and also indicated that a blended learning model can be advantageous in improving the students' reading abilities, which has been proven by the other researchers. Yang [12] explored blended learning for the university students with English reading difficulties in order to check how they blend their conceptions and employ blended learning approaches to improve their reading proficiency. Of 108 participants, 54 students were allocated to the experimental group by using blended learning and the rest were the control group with on-site instruction solely. The research results indicated that the blended learning was advantageous in improving students' reading proficiency in the experimental group. Alebaikan and Troudi [13] researched the outcomes of blended learning on college students, showing that reading levels in the experimental group measured by a post-test have been significantly improved because of online instruction in comparison with the control class. This also implies that using online instruction is an advantageous tool to enhance learners' reading abilities.

When learning supporters such as the teacher, the reading activity, or the automated system in the learning environment, are not properly combined, this can raise nonessential or inefficient cognitive overload in the students' learning procedure [14]. All the questions suggest that classroom courses solely turned into blended formats do not certainly guarantee the efficiency of blended learning in reading teaching. The shortage of teaching ability in the teacher might be why students in online learning may not perform well reading tasks.

Taken as a whole, the positive effect on learners' attitudes and reading strategy is obvious, while the effect on learners' ability is worth studying. Moreover, very little research has examined the results of blended learning on learners' English reading comprehension, especially at junior high school level.

D. The relationship between sociocultural theory and blended learning

In the process of learning, learners should learn behaviors, skills and strategies, focus on the learning itself, try to complete challenging tasks and to supply learning content. Ames [15] found that some learning situations are more conducive to learning and students' adaptation, and he also pointed out that the learning environment is related to the theory of standard orientation. Anderman [16] found that the learning situation can affect the student's goal orientation. Stone and Lopez [17] claims that strategical activity is seen as inherently goal embedded.

Learners who use this new model choose learning tasks that suit them, based on the information provided and their own language learning goals. This option regulates their interaction with the learning contents. This view of strategic development helps learners to adopt more active task-oriented learning models. The design of a blended learning model allows learners to participate in activities or ask them to complete certain tasks, according to the basic ideas of the teaching theory, in which they must use a second language. This prompts them to complete the task. Furthermore, it regards tasks or activities as an important way to learn a language, and considers the learning process to be more important than the results of that learning [18] (Nunan, 1999).

E. Reading strategies

In the area of teaching reading, gaining knowledge of some reading strategies has favorable effect on reading learning [19]. Grabe [20] claims that reading strategies allow students to modify the speed of reading, anticipate information, and so on. In reading classes, students need to cultivate strategic reading in L1 fields [21]. L1 researchers agree that teaching reading strategies is good for reading comprehension [22]. Furthermore, reading strategies have the potential effect to promote English reading courses [21].

Different scholars divided reading strategies into different types. Grabe and Stoller [23] divided reading strategies into two types: cognitive as well as meta-cognitive reading strategies. Besides, Anderson [24] claims that reading strategies should include three types: cognitive and meta-cognitive as well as socio-affective reading strategies respectively. Mokhtari [25] conducts a study that is designed to assess students' strategies using on the aspects of reading educational materials. Reading strategies consist of three types: (1) Global reading strategies used to set the phase for reading. (2) As the problem-solving strategies, it is used to do with reading troubles. (3) Support reading strategies, which are used to keep reading through assisted tools. These three types of strategies contribute to scholars understanding what kind of strategies learners are using in reading.

The findings of Yang [26] revealed that students could use blended learning to choose suitable reading strategies to satisfy their own reading speed, style, and level. In other words, learners could control their own reading, and decide on what, how, when and why to read. Hinkelman [27] claims that a blended learning model can improve reading strategies. In addition, blended learning enhances learner use of reading strategies, such as listing, enforcing, and reviewing.

Research Design

In order to explore the effectiveness of blended learning, the study emphasized on only one research question: to what extent can blended learning improve the high students' reading achievements?

A test study helps researchers to be clear by how much capability and performance has been improved among learners [28]. The test aims to measure student reading ability about what to be improved by using the blended learning model of teaching.

The participants taking part in the study were 86 high school students whose average age was 13 years old. Class One with

44 students was randomly selected as the Experimental Class (EC) and Class Four with 42 students as the Control Class (CC). Both classes were given the same teaching tasks and taught by the same teacher over four months. Students of the EC received the blended learning, while the CC used the traditional teaching.

The CC and the EC were tested twice during the study. The first test was to see whether there is a difference between the EC and the CC before the blended model teaching. The second test was to see whether there was a significant difference between the EC and the CC in the performance of the two classes after the blended learning teaching, so as to infer the influence of the blended learning model on middle school students' reading ability.

Results and Discussion

The pre-test was conducted in the reading section of a high school entrance examination. The total score of the reading test was 25. After the reading course was completed, the pre-test and post-test scores of each student in EC and CC was collected.

TABLE 1
THE RESULTS OF THE PRE-TEST AND POST-TEST

	pre-test		post-test	
Group	EC	CC	EC	CC
Number	44	42	44	42
Mean	9.82	9.62	12.41	10.26
Std. Deviation	4.19	3.35	2.18	2.05
Std. Error Mean	.63	.52	.33	.32

Table 1 shows that students from EC were not significantly different from students from CC about scores in pre-test. It is obvious that the two groups have the same level before the experiment. The difference between the means is 0.2 points.

In post-test, students from EC were significantly from those in CC about scores. Inspections of the two groups means show that the average of EC is significantly higher than the score of CC. The difference between the means is 2.15 points.

Conclusion

By evaluating the scores of the two groups of students in the pre-test and post-test, it can be safely seen that the post-test scores of students in Experimental Class are better than those in the pre-test. In comparison with the results of paired sample T-test, the enhancement of students' reading scores is significant. In addition, the answers from the interview also show that with the help of the blended learning model, students become more confident in completing reading tasks and their reading ability has been significantly improved.

The analysis and main research results provide some teaching significance for high school reading teaching.

First of all, blended learning model can be used in junior high school students' reading teaching. This method enables students to develop the ability of cooperative learning, which is totally different from the traditional method such as isolated reading method. From this point of view, this advanced learning model is of great help to students' reading.

Secondly, teachers should realize the importance of reading strategies and concentrate on the training of reading strategies. Blended learning model is a necessary condition for students to improve their reading ability. The investigation showed that many students did not fully understand reading strategies, and some students even knew nothing about the reading strategies before the experiment. Therefore, teachers should help students learn how to use reading strategies and design relevant training activities.

Finally, the results of this study also show that reading teaching based on blended learning model does not mean that teachers are redundant. On the contrary, teachers are required to be more strict. On the one hand, teachers still play a critical part in organizing classroom activities. That is to say, teachers should master the skills of using computers and multimedia. A good courseware designed by teachers can stimulate students' interest in learning. Teachers should make good use of multimedia technology to guide students to study efficiently and effectively.

References

[1] Vygotsky, L. (1978). Mind in society: *The development of higher psychological processes.* Cambridge: Harvard University Press.

[2] Karpov, Y. (2003). Vygotsky's doctrine of scientific concepts: Its role for contemporary education. In A. Kozulin, B. Gindis, V. Ageyev & S. Miller (Eds.), *Vygotsky's educational theory in cultural context* (pp. 138-155). Cambridge: Cambridge University Press.

[3] Cole, M., & Wertsch, J. V. (1996). Beyond the individual-social antinomy in discussions of Piaget and Vygotsky. Human Development, 39(5), 250-256.

[4] Rogoff, B. (1990). *Apprenticeship in thinking: Cognitive development in social context.* New York: Oxford University Press.

[5] Sutherland, R., Armstrong, V., Barnes, S., Brawn, R., Breeze, N., Gall, M., et al. (2004). Transforming teaching and learning: Embedding ict into everyday classroom practices. *Journal of Computer Assisted Learning*, 20(6), 413- 429.

[6] John-Steiner, V. & Mahn, H. (1996). Sociocultural models to learning and development: A vygotskian framework. *Educational Psychologist*, 31(3), 191- 206.

[7] Sharpe, R., Benfield, G., Roberts, G., & Francis, R. (2006). The undergraduate experience of blended e-learning: a review of UK literature and practice. *The Higher Education Academy,* 4 (2) 24-250.

[8] Marsh, J. (2002). *How to design effective blended learning.* Atlanta: Brandon-hall.

[9] Bueno-Alastuey, M.C. & López Pérez, M.V. (2014). Evaluation of a blended learning language course: students' perceptions of appropriateness for the development of skills and language areas, *Computer Assisted Language Learning*, 27(6), 509-527.

[10] Behjat, F. & M. Yamini and M. S. Bagheri. (2011). Blended Learning: A Ubiquitous Learning Environment for Reading Comprehension, *International Journal of English Linguistics*, 2(1), 97-106.

[11] Schechter, R., Macaruso, P., Kazakoff, E.R., & Brooke, E. (2015) Exploration of a Blended Learning Approach to Reading Instruction for Low SES Students in Early Elementary Grades, *Computers in the Schools*, 32:3-4, 183-200.

[12] Yang, Y. F. (2010). Development a reciprocal teaching/learning system for college remedial reading instruction. *Computers & Education,* 27, 78-102.

[13] Alebaikan, R. & Troudi, S. (2010). Blended learning in Saudi universities: challenges and perspectives, *ALT-J,* 18:1, 49-59.

[14] Leacock, T. L., & Nesbit, J, C. (2007). A framework for evaluating the quality of multimedia learning resources. *Educational Technology & Society*. 60(3), 22-232.

[15] Ames, C. (1992). Classrooms: Goals, structures, and student motivation. *Journal of Educational Psychology,* 27, 78-102.

[16] Anderman, L. H. (1999). Classroom goal orientation, school belonging, and social goals as predictors of students' positive and negative affect following transition to middle school. *Journal of Research and Development in Education,* 32, 89–103.

[17] Stone, K.W. & Lopez, C.W. (1989). Evaluation of the Solar One Track Alignment Methodology. *Solar Engineering,* 1(1), 521-523.

[18] Nunan, D. (1999). *Second language teaching and learning.* Boston, MA: Heinle & Heinle Publishers.

[19] Niakaris, C. I. & Kiely, R. (2015). Reading comprehension in test preparation classes: An analysis of teachers' pedagogical content knowledge in TESOL. *TESOL Quarterly*, 49(2), 369-392.

[20] Grabe, W. (1991). Current developments in second language reading research. *TESOL Quarterly,* (25), 375–406.

[21] Grabe, W. (2004). Research on teaching reading. *Annual Review of Applied Linguistics*, 24, 44–69.

[22] Pressley, M. (2002). Metacognition and self-regulated comprehension. In: Farstrup, A. & Samuels, S. (eds.) *What Research Has to Say About Reading Instruction*. Newark, DE: International Reading Association, 291–309.

[23] Grabe, W. & Stoller, F. (2002). *Teaching and researching reading.* Harlow, Essex: Pearson Education.

[24] Anderson, N. J. (2004). *Exploring second language and reading: Issues and strategies.* Beijing: Foreign Language Teaching and Research Press.

[25] Mokhtari, K., Sheorey, R., & Reichard, C. (2008) Measuring reading strategies of first-and second-language readers. In Mokhtari K, Sheorey R (eds). *Reading Strategies of First- and Second-Language Learners: See How They Read.* Norwood, MA: Christopher-Gordon Publishers, 43–65.

[26] Yang, Y. F. (2010). Development a reciprocal teaching/learning system for college remedial reading instruction. *Computers & Education,* 27, 78-102.

[27] Hinkelman, D. (2018). Strategies for Blended language learning. *Blending Technologies in Second Language Classrooms.* Japan: Sapporo Gakuin University.

[28] Cohen, L., Manion, L. & Morrison, K. (2018). *Research Methods in Education. (8th Edition)* [M]. London and New York: Routledge.

https://doi.org/10.1142/9789811238727_0071

Study of the Influence of Spatial Elements on Tourist Behavior in Macau Historic District

Chenyu Wang

Faculty of Innovation and Design, City University of Macau, Macau, China
Email: U19092105078@cityu.mo

Abstract

Based on the objective fact that spatial elements have an impact on human behavior, this study aims to examine the impact of the difference in the spatial form of various streets on tourists' behavior through quantitative analysis by using the spatial syntax theory. The internal relationship was explored between Macau's historic district and tourist behavior to provide a comfortable experience in Macau tourism and the renovation of the streets. The result provides a basis for the planning and design of Macau's historic district to promote the construction and development of Macau tourism as a leisure center.

Keywords: Macau, historic district, spatial elements, tourists' behaviors, spatial syntax

Introduction

With the rapid development of society, urban street space has undergone tremendous changes. In 1961, Jacobs emphasized the importance of street space design in *The Death and Life of Great American Cities* [1]. At the same time, many researchers began to explore the physical elements of the street environment and the characteristics of pedestrians' behaviors [2]. For example, Gehl found that the spatial form of a street has an important impact on the behaviors of pedestrians on the street. He summarized the behavior categories of users and summed up a series of elements for user requirements and high-quality places. The elements include street spatial form, the density of stores, greening rate, and the relationship between spatial vitality and architectural interface [3]. Fang *et al* studied the size of urban street space from the proximity size based on Yoshinobu-Ishihara's space theory in *The Aesthetic Townscape* [4]. The theory controlled the absolute and relative size of street space through people's perceptions. Human is the main element of a street. Human behaviors determine the spatial form of a street. However, a street space with a sense of belonging can also be created by analyzing human psychology [5]. For developing related researches, the research method covers from literature discussion and summary to mathematical model and statistical analysis. Chen and Zhao analyzed the influence of various variables of a street space interface on pedestrian behavior through data collection and model establishment [6].

Based on the above discussion, this study took the Macau historic district as an example, explored the influence mechanism of spatial elements of the district on tourists' behaviors and their relationship based on the spatial syntax theory in three aspects: spatial form, spatial composition (physical space, business form elements), and facility environment. It provides a reference for the creation of a tourist environment and the construction of a historic district and promotes the efficient and rational utilization of spaces in the district.

Materials and methods

A. Research scope

In 2002, the Macau Special Administrative Region Government submitted the declaration of 'Macau Historic District' to the UNESCO World Heritage Centre in Paris to introduce the treasures and cultural characteristics of Macau to the world. On July 5, 2005, the 'Macau Historic District' was officially included in the World Heritage List by UNESCO and became the 31st World Heritage Site in China. After more than 400-year nourishment of eastern and western cultures, Macau's historic district reflects the collision and reflection of different cultures. From eastern temples to western churches and from the mansion of the rich to streets and the alleys, the district retains ancient streets, residences, religions, and public buildings in Portuguese and Chinese styles and has witnessed the blending of aesthetic, cultural, religious beliefs, architectural and technological influences between the East and the West. Based on the vigorous development of international trade, the district has witnessed the earliest exchanges and sustainable development between China and the West [7,8]. The core area of the 'Macau Historic District' is composed of 8 squares and streets which connect each square and historic buildings. The middle zone is located in the periphery of the core area (Fig. 1). The area of the color zone is about 1.23km^2, of which that of the blue and red zone (middle) is 0.16 and 1.07km^2, respectively [9].

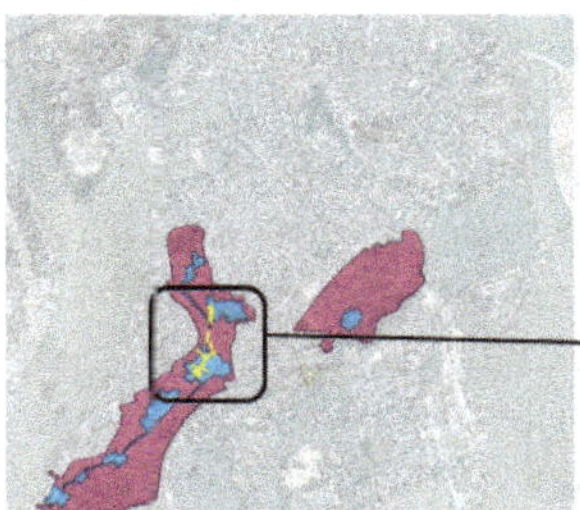

Fig. 1 Scope of Macau Island and Historic District

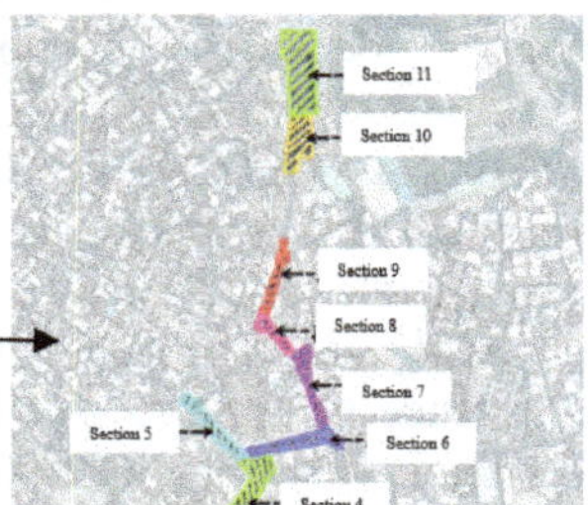

Fig. 2 Diagram of the Studied Historic District

Due to the complicated roads and the diversified street forms in Macau's historic district, the main axis of the historic district of Macau Ruins of the Cathedral of Saint Paul was selected as the research object to weaken the influence of non-block spatial variables. Figure 2 shows the locations of the blocks, and the road traffic conditions are good. Moreover, most of the historic blocks with a long history are not easy to change. To facilitate measurement and calculation, the road of the district was divided into 11 sections: Largo do Senado, the South Street of Gongju Xinshi, Right Lane of the Holy House of Mercy, Front Ground of Our Lady of the Rosary Church, Micao Lane, Our Lady of the Rosary Church Street, Maicaodi Street, the Ruins of the Cathedral of Saint Paul Street, Largo da Companhia de Jesus, the Ruins of the Cathedral of Saint Paul Lane, the Ruins of the Cathedral of Saint Paul.

B. Research content

The historic district is mainly a space for pedestrians. The research was composed of three parts.

(1) Description and quantification of spatial elements

The spatial elements are grouped into three: spatial form, spatial composition, and facility environment. Then, five morphological variables were discussed through spatial syntax: connectivity, control, depth, integration, and choice. The spatial composition includes environmental and business form elements. The environmental elements are perimeter, area, length, and the widths of streets, while the business form elements are the density of shops. The facility environment mainly includes a density of chairs and a green rate.

(2) Statistics and research on tourist behavior

Tourists' behaviors (Y_1) refer to a series of behaviors of tourists which are divided into commercial (Y_2) and social behavior (Y_3). There are two main types of commercial behaviors: commercial observation (Y_4) and stop (Y_5). Commercial stop refers to staying in interesting shops. Commercial observation refers to the slow-down or returning to see interesting businesses along the street during a visit. Social behavior is mainly divided into three categories: social wait-and-see (Y_6, greeting, avoiding pedestrians, and watching road signs), social stop (Y_7, waiting for people, smoking, talking, rest, sitting, and so on), and other behaviors (Y_8, waiting for cars, taking pictures and so on).

(3) Relevance between spatial elements and tourist behavior

To see if there are correlations between the elements of historic blocks and tourists' behaviors, the elements in the data were analyzed with regression analysis by SPSS. The regression method used maximum likelihood with the walking behavior as dependent variables: business stop, business observation, social stop, social observation, and other stops(a_1, a_2, a_3, a_4 and a_5, respectively). The total number of tourists with stay behaviors was set as a_0, and $a_0 = a_1 + a_2 + a_3 + a_4 + a_5$. The spatial elements were taken as covariates: connectivity (C_i), control ($Ctrl_i$), depth (D_i), integration (I_i), choice (R^2), street circumference (C), street area (S), street distance (d), street width (W), density of stores (D_s), greening rate (G), density of chairs (D_c), and z_i was for the parameter estimation. Thus, the model was established as

$$a_i = \int z_{1i}C_i\,; z_{2i}\mathrm{Ctrl}_i; z_{3i}D_i; z_{4i}I_i; z_{5i}R^2; z_{6i}C; z_{7i}S; z_{8i}d; \quad (1)$$
$$z_{9i}W; z_{10i}D_s; z_{11i}G; z_{12i}D_c.$$

Results and discussion

A. Analysis of spatial elements of Macau's historic district

Street width is an important form of describing or creating a street shape for constructors and residents. In Kevin Lynch's urban design study based on environmental perception and human behavior, the street width, as a spatial feature of streets, strengthens the image of the road in the minds of users. He pointed out "whether streets are wide or narrow, they can attract people's attention" [10].

Jacobs mentioned and demonstrated the relationship between a street size and urban vitality [11]. Although Jacobs did not directly explain the relationship between a neighborhood size and urban space, a large number of case studies showed that the size does affect people's spatial cognition and use behavior, and there was a relationship between them.

Table 1 shows that the maximum area of the sections is section 1 (Largo do Senado) with an area of 2,749.03m^2, followed by section 11 with an area of 1,470.21m^2 (the Ruins of the Cathedral of Saint Paul). Their functions are similar to those of a square where the distributing spaces exist at the beginning or the end of a road. The section with the highest store density is section 9 where the souvenir shops are gathered in the narrow street. Section 11, the Ruins of the Cathedral of Saint Paul and Underground Cathedral Cemetery has a surrounding greening environment and the green rate is the highest.

TABLE 1
Statistics of the spatial composition of the studied sections.

Section	C(m)	S(m^2)	d(m)	W(m)	D_S(%)	D_C(%)	G(%)
1	242.5	2749.03	71.6	29.26	61.5	95.5	12.5
2	108.75	383.48	46.59	8.89	87.3	0	0
3	122.03	212.32	56.85	3.72	4.9	0	5
4	190.68	925.52	74.88	9.14	90	18	5.6
5	154.7	556.38	69.51	8.04	81.7	0	0
6	175.73	636.07	74.48	8.5	62	0	0
7	148.64	445.38	70.02	3.71	88.7	40.1	11.4
8	100.55	207.86	39.99	4	84	0	0
9	141.34	278.54	64.67	3.19	90.2	0	0
10	127.82	749.64	44.19	19.29	73.7	60.1	1
11	178.5	1470.21	63.01	14.64	0	0	19.3

In addition to the description of space composition, the street space also includes the description of a space form. This research had five main aspects: connectivity, control, depth, integration, and choice. The quantitative values of the spatial morphology of the studied area are summarized in Table 2.

TABLE 2
Statistical data of spatial morphology of the studied. sections

Section	1	2	3	4	5	6	7	8	9	10	11
C_i	6	4	1	5	4	4	5	5	5	4	3
Ctrli	2.02681	1.33333	1.66667	1.11667	0.825	0.9	1.95	1.98333	1.48333	1.14286	1
D_i	8.27494	9.26739	9.2741	9.15004	9.12406	9.74686	9.61442	10.2121	9.84493	10.4535	10.9522
I_i	1.05104	0.924872	0.924122	0.938189	0.94119	0.874175	0.887614	0.830028	0.864482	0.808832	0.768299
R2	10023	1413	0	1624	880	1103	10595	11501	11569	7533	1760

The depth and integration (Fig. 3) had a negative correlation. The higher the depth, the lower the integration, and vice versa. Integration is used in the spatial syntax theory. Generally, areas with high integration are likely to generate human traffic aggregation. The integration is highest in Largo do Senado connected with Avenida de Almeida Ribeiro (section 1). In scenic area planning, section 1 is the most convenient place for people to gather, which urban builders pay much attention to.

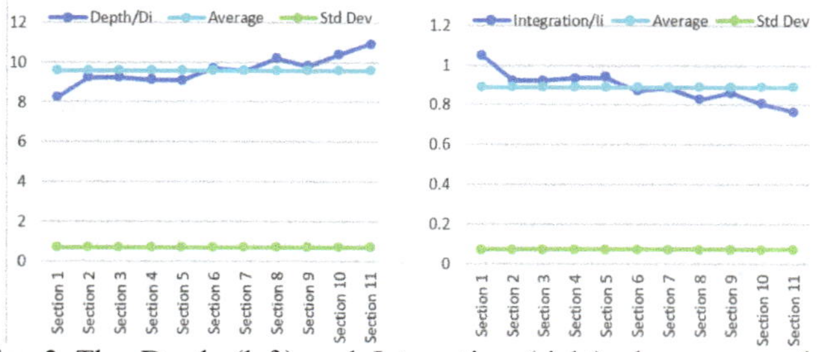

Fig. 3 The Depth (left) and Integration (right) show a negative correlation

B. *Statistics of tourist behavior methods in Macau historic district*

To summarize the behaviors of tourists, this study set 11 sections and collected the data on random dates and times from November 2018 to January 2019. The results are shown in Table 3.

TABLE 3

Statistics of tourist behavior in the studies sections.

Section	Y1	Y2	Y3	Y4	Y5	Y6	Y7	Y8
1	788	380	408	243	137	102	276	30
2	612	422	190	266	156	40	114	36
3	58	27	31	2	25	0	7	24
4	714	380	334	272	108	14	284	36
5	470	334	136	216	118	14	90	32
6	956	534	422	454	80	216	174	32
7	710	428	282	272	156	4	250	28
8	800	712	88	538	174	14	64	10
9	1174	984	190	578	406	78	90	22
10	814	262	552	146	116	28	220	304
11	614	0	614	0	0	16	158	440

The Ruins of the Cathedral of Saint Paul historic district is composed of old streets for commerce and residence. Most of the buildings are low-storied. Section 9 has the highest number of total behaviors, which is related to its geographical location. As it is the only way to the Ruins of the Cathedral of Saint Paul and there are many shops, the total and commercial behaviors are the highest. Section 11 is the section with the Ruins of the Cathedral of Saint Paul. It is popular for taking pictures, waiting, and taking rests, so has the highest social behaviors. Section 1 is a square in an open space with evenly distributed shops and rest seats. As section 3 has few shops and leisure facilities, it has the lowest behavior values. There are many commercial streets in this historic district. People come here mainly for commercial activities. Only in the Ruins of the Cathedral of Saint Paul, the commercial behaviors are changed into social behaviors, such as taking pictures, gathering tourists, and so on.

C. *Interpretation of the relevance between spatial elements and tourist behavior in Macau historic district*

Figure 4 shows a matrix of 20 x 20 which comprises the spatial elements and tourists' behaviors of Macau's historic district. The matrix reveals all the correlations between the 20 urban district elements and tourists' behaviors. The black letters show a linear trend map, the blue letters show a logarithmic trend map, and the green letters show a polynomial trend map in an order of 3. The scatter plots represent the trend maps of 190 correlation coefficients, and the numbers are correlation coefficients. The trend maps and values are diagonally symmetrical. The correlation values in the graphs are maximum *R* or adjusted R^2 corresponding to the best fitting curves.

There are 25 negative correlations (the lowest R=-0.01, the highest R=-0.11) and 165 positive correlations (the lowest R^2=0, the highest R^2=1) in the scatter plot matrix. There are 96 correlations between spatial elements of the historic district and tourists' behaviors and 16 negative correlations (the lowest R=-0.03, the highest R=-0.11) and 80 positive correlations (the lowest R^2=0, the highest R^2=0.91). Among them, R^2=0.91 is the relationship between D_s and Y_4. D_s and Y_4 are for the density of stores and the business wait-and-see behavior, respectively. The density of stores is positively correlated with business wait-and-see behavior, which indicates that more stores in the block contribute to more tourists' behaviors and business observations. D_s and Y_2, D_s and Y_5 have R^2 of 0.87. As Y_2 is the commercial behavior of tourists and Y_5 is the commercial stop behavior, the higher commercial density enables more tourists to stop. However, it is also related to the density of stores. The correlation between Y_2, Y_5 and D_s is less than that of Y_4 and D_s, which means that most tourists' behaviors are mainly for observation. To attract more tourists to shop, commercial stores need to be attractive.

The R^2 between I_i and Y_8 is 0.84. This implies that high integration causes more social behaviors. The visual has a memorable place where tourists have other social activities. Therefore, the streets with high integration should not be narrow. Otherwise, congestion is easy to happen and other phenomena. The correlation of D_i and Y_8 is R^2=0.83, which is second highest to that between I_i and Y_8. The greater the depth is, the farther the distance between the place and other space of the block, and the more difficult it is for visitors to reach. Most of the spaces are quiet rest areas as they are far away from the crowd. Thus, they are not easily disturbed by the crowd with a relatively quiet environment. S and Y_3, W and Y_8, S and W have R^2 = 0.71. When the area of the street increases, social behavior such as rest, sitting, waiting, and taking pictures also increases, as tourists feel more relaxed owing to the ample space. At the same time, their social behaviors do not cause traffic congestion.

The correlation between D_c and Y_7 is 0.66. This indicates that the higher the density of chairs in a street, the more social stopping behaviors occur. Therefore, in the future street construction, the number of chairs around a commercial block needs to be reduced, while that in open areas to be increased to guide visitors' behaviors. R^2 between C_i and Y_7 is 0.65. The street space with higher connectivity has better permeability. However, higher connectivity causes higher probability of going wrong. Thus, the social stop behaviors increases with the higher connectivity. As pedestrians wait around at the intersection to find the right road, the space with higher connectivity require more signboards to prevent pedestrians from getting lost or congestion by too many social stop behaviors of tourists.

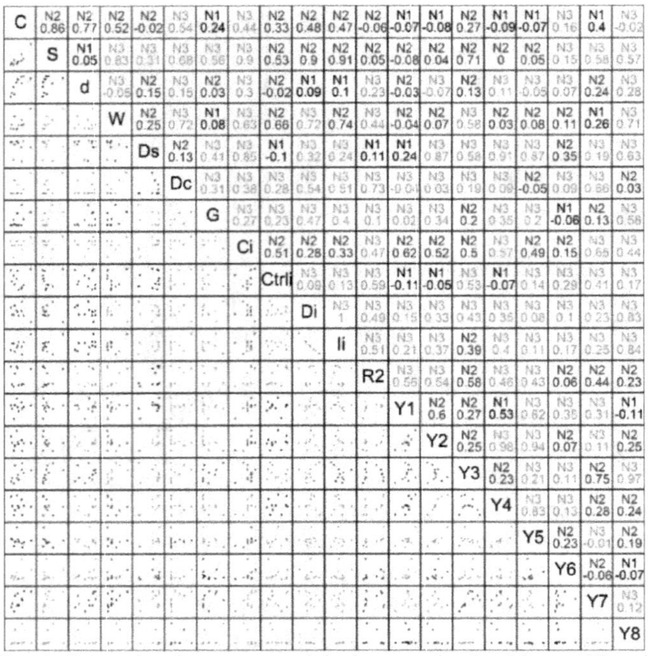

Fig. 4 Correction between spatial elements in the Macau Historic District and Tourist Behavior

Conclusion

For the historical district of Macau as an example, the external connection and internal interaction between spatial form and tourists' behaviors were investigated. The difference in the size of a space and orientation creates different environments. The spatial elements have an inseparable influence on the relationship between human's inner influence and behavioral activities. Spatial syntax plays an essential role in the analysis of block morphology through which the corresponding parameters are obtained by the analysis of similar spaces. The overall characteristics of the street space are easy to be understood with graphic expression. This study applies the spatial syntax to analyze the structural characteristics of Macau's historic district systematically, and draw the following conclusions through the field research and literature review.

The layout of streets and lanes of the Ruins of the Cathedral of Saint Paul is integrated, tortuous, and multi-directional. The integrity is mainly reflected in the layout of roads and spaces formed by the buildings, while its twists and turns are mainly reflected in the internal space structure. Since most of the streets are narrow and crowded, the space is flexible and rich in layering with different sizes of squares. The buildings on both sides of the street have different sizes, changeable styles, and rich details, all of which form the interesting and characteristic street to weaken the feeling of depression by the crowded narrow space.

The change of spatial factors in Macau's historic district has an impact on the behavior of tourists. The density of stores is positively correlated with the wait-and-see behavior of the business. The greater the commercial density, the more often visitors stop, while the tourists' wait-and-see behaviors are more than stopping behaviors at the same commercial density. It is essential to enhance the attractiveness of stores to attract more visitors. Social behavior increases with the increase of the areas of streets and the density of chairs. Consequently, the chair density around the commercial block can be reduced, and that in the open area increased to guide the tourists' behaviors in street construction.

A space with high connectivity in street indicates that it is connected to multiple roads. The higher the connectivity, the better the permeability. However, it may cause a higher probability of getting lost. The higher the connectivity is, the more the social stop behaviors. Thus, the space with high connectivity needs more obvious road signboards to prevent pedestrians from going wrong or creating road congestion by many social stops.

References

[1] J. Jacobs. *The Death and Life of Great American Cities*. Ihome, 2012.

[2] Likun Liu, Jixiang Zhang. *Research on the correlation between street space variables and pedestrian activities: Taking Jinan Yaotou Road as an example*, 60 years of planning: achievements and challenges-Proceedings of the 2016 China Urban Planning Annual Conference, 06.

[3] Gehl, J., *Life Between Buildings: Using Public Space*, 1987.

[4] Zhiguo Fang, Kun Song, Qing Ye. *Rethinking the theory of the street aspect ratio of Yoshinobu Awara-Research on street space based on the perspective of "near human scale"*, New Architecture, 2014 (5).

[5] Guojie Zhao, Li Chen. *Research on Behavioral Psychology of Traditional Commercial Street Space——Taking Nanhou Street of "Three Lanes and Seven Alleys" as an example*, Chinese and Foreign Architecture, 2015, 000(008):44-46.

[6] Yong Chen, Xinghua Zhao. *Research on the street bottom interface from the perspective of pedestrians: A case study of Huaihai Road in Shanghai*, Urban Planning, 2014, 000(006): 24-31.

[7] Xianjue Liu, Feng Xuan. *An Introduction to the Development of Macau City*, Overview of Macau City Development, Huazhong Architecture, 2002, 020(006):92-96.

[8] Weiren Wang. *Research on the Urban Texture of Historic Districts in Macau: Architectural Investigation and Workshops "Enclosed" by the Catalyst Space*, World Architecture, 2009(12):112-117.

[9] The Cultural Affairs Bureau of the Macao Special Administrative Region Government, *the framework for the protection and management of the historical urban area of Macao*. Macao: Cultural Affairs Bureau of the Macao Special Administrative Region Government, 2014.

[10] Lynch K . *Reconsidering The Image of the City*, Cities of the Mind. Springer US, 1984.

[11] Litscher, M., Jane Jacobs, *The Death and Life of Great American Cities*, 2017.

https://doi.org/10.1142/9789811238727_0072

Study on the Evolution of Main External Styles of Mazu Temple — A Case Study of Fujian, Guangdong and Macau

Shengzhen Wu

Faculty of Innovation and Design, City University of Macau, Macau, China
Email: U19092105153@cityu.mo

Abstract

As the carrier of Mazu culture, Mazu temples have evolved several times in the process of propagation, either inheriting traditions or integrating local characteristics. In this study, the age, region, and style of Mazu temples were selected, and the architectural pattern, roof, and gable were compared and analyzed for Mazu Temple at Meizhou, Lao-Ma Temple in Shantou, and A-Ma Temple in Macau. It was found that the architectural shape and style of Mazu temples had changed in the process of development.

Keywords: Mazu cultural, architectural style, Macau A-Ma Temple

Introduction

Mazu culture originated from Meizhou Island in Putian City, Fujian Province. It is the general name of the material and spiritual wealth which have been left and inherited by the Chinese ancestors in the process of worshiping and believing in Mazu for thousands of years [1]. During the Song and Yuan dynasties, the Mazu belief was introduced to Guangdong province via Fujian Province. Up to now, there are 35 Mazu temples in eastern Guangdong, among which Shantou Lao-Ma Temple is the most famous [2]. There are 25 Mazu temples in Central Guangdong, among which Chiwan Tianhou Temple in Xin'an County plays an important role. There are 88 Mazu temples in western Guangdong, among which Leizhou Tianhou Temple is the most famous. In the north of Qujiang city, the Tianhou Temple of Fengchijiao has been built and occupies an important position in the local religious belief.

Fujian, Guangdong and Macau Mazu Temples

The Mazu Temple on Meizhou Island is the starting point and the Mazu Temple in Macau is the endpoint. There are many Mazu temples, among which representative ones are Shantou Lao-Ma Temple and Nansha Tianhou Temple. Shantou Lao-Ma Temple is the oldest, while the Nansha temple was built later and "integrates the style of the Imperial Palace in Beijing and the imposing manner of Zhongshan Mausoleum in Nanjing" [4]. The Mazu temple on Meizhou Island and the A-Ma Temple in Macau has quite, different architectural style. Therefore, this paper takes the Mazu temple in Meizhou, Lao-Ma Temple in Shantou, and A-Ma Temple in Macau as the main objects to carry out the research, and aims to find the relationship between the three buildings of the same vein.

Mazu Ancestral Temple in Meizhou

The Mazu Ancestral Temple in Meizhou Island (hereinafter referred to as "Ancestral Temple") is located in Meizhou Island, Putian City, Fujian Province. It was built in the early Song Dynasty. At first, it started as a small "goddess Temple" [5]. Later, it was funded by the imperial court and spontaneously donated by local believers. After many times of construction and expansion, it became the origin of Mazu belief all over the world.

Today's Ancestral Temple complex mainly includes the old and the new hall built in the 1980s. The following focuses on the old hall as the research object.

The Mountain Gate of the old hall is shaped like a royal palace since Mazu has been canonized by the highest imperial court as "Tianhou" in dynasties. The main ridge on the mountain gate is "Swallow tail ridge". The main ridge is inlaid with porcelain of Shuanglongxizhu shape. The four diagonal ridges are decorated in traditional Southern Fujian grass and flowers pattern, and the beams and arches are decorated with colorful paintings. Up the Mountain Gate, there is a granite archway. The gable-on-hip roof is the combination of the traditional "Sanchuan ridge" and "Swallow tail ridge" in Southern Fujian with the green glazed tile. The ridge block is decorated with clay sculptures and paintings, the ridge lips and ridge hips are inlaid with porcelain in the double dragon pagoda shape and in traditional Southern Fujian grass & flowers pattern, respectively (Fig. 1).

Fig. 1 From left to right is: The Mountain Gate of Ancestral Temple, granite archway. (Photo: http://www.mzmz.org.cn).

The bell tower was rebuilt in 1989 and has a three-story building with antique style and pyramid hip roof. The Taizi hall was a Chaotian pavilion: 3 bays and 1 depth, post and lintel construction, double eaves gable-on-hip roof, covered with brick red glazed tiles, decorated with swallow tail ridge and inlay porcelain. Two round window openings are in the front wall and decorated with granite carving, columns in the middle bay are Huian stone carving with dragon shape. The wall is simple and elegant and made of white granite. Chaotian pavilion is a 3-story octagonal tower building that has the painted wood carvings on the roof and eaves as the key decoration parts (Fig. 2).

Fig. 2 From left to right is The bell tower of Ancestral Temple, the Taizi hall, The Chaotian pavilion. (Photo: http://www.mzmz.org.cn).

The main hall is the bedroom hall behind the left side of the Taizi hall, also known as Tianhou Temple (Fig. 3). It is a typical traditional religious building in Southern Fujian. It was built in the Song Dynasty (AD 987), and it is the first Mazu temple in the world. In 1374, it was rebuilt by Zhou Zuo, the commander of Quanzhou Prefecture. The bedroom hall was rebuilt in 1431 by Zheng He, in 1683 by governor Yao QiSheng and in 1684 by marquis Shi Lang [6]. The present buildings were kept the layout of the Ming Dynasty and the style of the Qing Dynasty. It consists of a gate hall, main hall, and side porches. The main hall is with a single eave gable-on-hip roof, 3 bays and 5 depths, post, and lintel construction building. The bedroom hall roof has the “swallow tail ridge” shape and is covered with red brick glazed tiles. On the main ridge is porcelain inlaid with Shuanglongxizhu shape. The ridge hips are inlaid with porcelain in traditional Southern Fujian grass and flowers pattern. The beams and arches are made of white carved granite. The facade is concave in shape, and the wall block is made of granite decorated with carvings and paintings. Each column of the bedroom hall is one granite stone from base to body and shows a double octagonal style with no painting.

A new group of imitation complex (New Hall) has been built on the south axis side of the Ancestral Temple. Among them, a “Tianhou Square” has been used as the main venue for worship and festivals.

Fig. 3 The bedroom hall of Ancestral Temple. (Photo: https://touch.travel.qunar.com)

Shantou Lao-Ma Temple

Lao-Ma Tample is located at the end of Wai Ma Road in Shantou City Guangdong Province, was one of the earliest building in Shantou City, same as the Guandi Temple next to it [7]. Chaoshan is adjacent to Fujian and the sea route is interlinked. As the first stop for Fujian people to enter Guangdong, besides trade and economic exchanges, religious beliefs are also introduced into Guangdong along with immigrants.

Fig. 4 Shantou Lao-Ma Temple. (Photo: https://touch.travel.qunar.com)

As facing southwest, Lao-Ma Temple is a typical arcade architectural style, and has a fixed stage building (Fig. 4). Lao-Ma Temple is a typical Chaoshan “4 point gold” layout, which is a 3 Bay 2 depth building with a worship hall. The courtyard is in the center and surrounded by wing rooms and small halls. The roof is “Sanchuan ridge” covered with green glazed tiles. The center is raised and added with ridge hips in the edges to form a simple gable-on-hip roof. The decoration is porcelain inlaid for beauty in form and the narrative of religious belief (Fig. 5).

The exterior walls are mainly decorated with carved granite. The main hall gate sides and the surrounding external walls are inlaid with large stone carving plates most of which are reliefs with no painting. Each column is a granite stone from base to body and has a double octagonal style, no painting.

The top of the gablets is arranged by following the “five elements”, with arrays of concave-convex lines repeatedly to form a rich level. Below it, a dark gray belt clay sculpture decorates to highlight the 3D outline of the building. Although the color on the sculpture has been peeling off, the style of the time can still be seen.

Fig. 5 From left to right is: The gablet of Lao-Ma Temple, the gate of Lao-Ma Temple, porcelain roof decoration, the plinth of Lao-Ma Temple. (Photo: https://map.baidu.com/).

Macau A-Ma Temple

Fig. 6 From left to right is: The Mountain Gate of A-Ma Temple, Bogoulong, granite archway, "The First Palace of the Holy Mountain".

According to reliable info, A-Ma Temple in Macao was built in the first year of Hongzhi of the Ming Dynasty (1488), which is derived from the Ancestral Temple. Its architectural style is not only influenced by the traditional religious buildings in Southern Fujian, but also related to those in

Lingnan, and even influenced by the Portuguese culture in Macao (Fig. 6).

As situated halfway up the western slope of Barra Hill and facing southwest to the sea, it is the oldest temple and building in Macao [8]. It was called "Niangma Temple", "Tianfei Temple" or "Haijue Temple" before. It consists of "The First Palace of the Holy Mountain", the Zhengjiao Chanlin, the Hall of Benevolence, the Hall of Guanyin and other buildings.

"The First Palace of the Holy Mountain" is for the prayer hall and stone hall in 2 depths. The main building materials are granites and bricks and adopt rolled ridge roof in the front hall and a double eave roof in the rear hall. Eave columns on the front hall are covered by cap blocks. The natural grottoes are cut out from the shrines in the rear hall, as enclosed by columns and walls. The whole building is covered with a green glazed tile roof and decorated with exaggerated upturned ridges with sculpture. Square glazed tile windows are set on both sides of the wall. The gablets of the front hall are decorated with a dark gray sculpture belt. Each column is a granite stone column from base to body in the 3-layer square with no painting. The center of the main ridge of the rear hall is decorated with jewels.

Zhengjiao Chanlin belongs to a group of Buddhist buildings with typical Lingnan style, which was built in 1828 (the 8th year of the Daoguang period of the Qing Dynasty) and destroyed in a fire in 1988. The present one is a reconstruction of a reinforced concrete structure. The roof of the archway and the mountain gate are covered with green glazed tiles. The eaves are decorated with sculpture upturned ridges and a porcelain bead on top. Except for the center room, all roofs are decorated with "bogoulong" and decorated with a large area of sculpture inlaid. There are rows of decorative arches between the center and the side rooms. The building is made of granites, Each column is a granite stone column from base to body, in the 3-layer square form with no painting. The main entrance is located on the left side of the archway. The green glazed tiles are decorated with "bogoulong", and the walls under the eaves with exquisite sculptures. The round shape gablets on the side are typical Lingnan traditional architectural style (Fig. 7).

Fig. 7 From left to right is: The entrance of Zhengjiao Chanlin, the archway of Zhengjiao Chanlin.

The Hall of Benevolence is the smallest in scale and dated back to 1488 in the Ming Dynasty. It's a 3 square meter stone hall [9] with the Chinese name carved on the beam at the entrance, next to the name written as the 8th Daoguang Qing Dynasty (1828). The back wall is the rock on the mountain, and the double eaves roof and two sides of the wall body were made of granite. On the sidewalls, there are reliefs of the maid of the Tianhou and the God warriors. On the stone roof, there are green glazed tiles and upturned ridges decoration, and the center of the roof was decorated with porcelain beads.

The hall of Guanyin is located in the highest part. It was jointly built in 1605 by the imperial court and merchants. The hall of Guanyin is located in the highest part. From the Hall of Benevolence to it, cliff stone carvings along the way are seen with the word "Taiyi" written on it, which show the cultural connection to Taoist. It is made of plain bricks, roofed in the "Yingshan" (flush-gable) tradition. Different from other buildings, there are arch elements on the gablets, which is a typical western architectural element.

Barra Square is in front of the A-Ma Temple, which is mainly used as a temporary stage for religious Mazu worship activities. The pavement is a typical Portuguese style with irregular stones of different sizes. The sea wave patterns are patched by different colors of stones. It symbolizes the Portuguese maritime culture. On the other hand, it also contains the special identity of Mazu culture originated from the sea, and Mazu is the "goddess of the sea". See Fig. 8.

Fig. 8 From left to right is: The Hall of Benevolence, the hall of Guanyin, Barra Square.

Study on Style Evolution

According to the records of Mazu in Meizhou book, Shantou Lao-Ma Temple and Macao A-Ma Temple were separated from Ancestral Temples in the Jiaqing period of the Qing Dynasty and the Tianqi period of the Ming Dynasty respectively. However, as generally accepted in academia, the A-Ma Temple along with the Mazu religion was brought to Macao by Yan Qisheng of Zhangzhou. As Zhangzhou and Putian belong to southern Fujian, Mazu culture was introduced to Shantou and Macao from Meizhou Island of Putian in different periods when Macao has been a part of Guangdong since ancient times. Thus, there is a certain connection in architectural style.

Ancestral Temple has been restored and constructed several times and has formed a large scale owing to the particularity of its geographical location and the richness of land resources. Therefore, its architectural complex includes mountain gate, archway, bell tower, main hall, and annex. Even to carry on worship activities, a new complex was built on the side of the Ancestral Temple under the old system. Among them, Tianhou square was the main venue for religious activities. The architectural style is the most primitive in the early Qing Dynasty with a strong traditional religious style in Southern Fujian. Shantou Lao-Ma Temple was built at a later age with limited space, so the architectural structure is simplest. The main hall in the building is usually used as a stage for worship the gods. Macao's A-Ma Temple complex is built along the mountain. There are a mountain gate, an archway, a main hall, an annex, and the Barra sqaure as the temporary stage in front. The architectural style is mainly the traditional Lingnan religious style, and there are obvious western elements in the gablets of the Hall of Guanyin as well. Figure 9 shows the building layouts of Ancestral Temple, Shantou Lao-Ma Temple and Macau A-Ma Temple.

Fig. 9 From left to right is: The building layouts of Ancestral Temple, Shantou Lao-Ma Temple, Macau A-Ma Temple.

The roof of Ancestral Temple is a single eave gable-on-hip roof, which is made of large timber covered with glazed tiles. On the main ridge, there are porcelain inlaid in Shuanglongxizhu shape and porcelain beads. The ridge block is covered with clay sculpture, and the hip ridges are inlaid with porcelain in traditional grass and flowers pattern. Shantou Lao-Ma Temple is roofed with "Yingshan" (flush-gable) and Sanchuan ridge style, and the other decorative features are consistent with Ancestral Temple in materials and style. A-Ma Temple in Macao is slightly different, roofed with double eaves upturned ridges. The ridge is decorated with bogoulong components, and the roof is made of stone. The main ridge is only decorated with porcelain beads, and the decoration on the upturned ridges is a simple clay sculpture.

Most of the roofs in Ancestral Temple are gable-on-hip roofs, and the pattern on the gablet is partially decorated with colorful paintings. The wall is made of granite and decorated with stone carvings and murals. The top of the wall on Shantou Lao-Ma Temple is made of multi-layer concave-convex lines to highlight the 3D outline and decorated with clay sculptures. The body and wall block are decorated with large stone carvings. The gables of Zhengjue Chanlin in A-Ma Temple are round shapes and unique in Guangdong Province. There is a dark gray belt on the top of the wall. The wall is granite and decorated with red paint except for white granite stone columns. The gablets of the Hall of Guanyin are Y shaped with a dark gray belt on the top with sculpture. Different from traditional Chinese temples, the eave edge of the front hall has a Roman arch structure. The wall is made of granite and bricks and decorated with green paint except for a white granite column.

Conclusion

Obviously, after the spread of Mazu culture, the architectural forms of the temples change with the region. In terms of space, Shantou is closer to Meizhou Island than Macao. Therefore, Shantou Lao-Ma Temple continues the architectural style and construction techniques of Mazu temple in Southern Fujian, and even the same decoration. Both of them emphasize the architectural layout on the central axis, and the decoration of granite relief, roof, and eaves. The ridges are complex and gorgeous. In terms of period, A-Ma Temple was built earlier and geographically more remote than Shantou's Lao-Ma Temple. Moreover, it was built on the mountain and near the sea (the Barra Square was built by sea reclamation in the later period). Therefore, its architectural decoration follows the traditional style of Guangdong with a restaint. Due to the influence of Portuguese culture in Macao, many new temples built in the later period were simplified and even integrated with western elements. Therefore, the main external style of Tianhou temple is intertwined with the evolution of time and region. We did not study a certain dimension in isolation, but explore in multiple directions. The following research continues to expand the field investigation of Tianhou temple in different areas for updating research results.

References

[1] Zou Zhaoxia, Liu Qijuan, Lin Nanjing. Academic Analysis of Mazu Culture and Sports circle. *Young Science: Teacher edition*, 2014, 35(007):375.

[2] Xin Xiuqin. On mazu Belief in Chaoshan Region . *Journal of Mudanjiang Normal University (Philosophy and Social Science Edition)*, 2011(04):59-61.

[3] Yi Y Li, Luo Yi Y. A preliminary study of The rental beliefs and changes of Guangdong moms. *Journal of Putian College*, 2011, 18(006):1-8.

[4] Hu Yufu. Investigation on the rejuvenation mechanism of Xunliao Tianhou Palace in Huidong. *Journal of Putian College*, 2017, 024(003):13-18.

[5] Xie Yingju. Xie Xiangxi.Xie Hongwei xie Xiaofeng.Doubts on the Report on The Achievements of the Xia-Shang-Zhou Chronology Project during 1996-2000. *Learning theory*. 8, 2011:P78-P102.

[6] Liu Xiong. Communication between Eastern Fujian and Taiwan in the Qing Dynasty. *Journal of Ningde Normal University: Philosophy and Social Science edition*, 2019, 000(001):75-80.

[7] Yu Yang. Multi-god worship in shantou folk belief. *Chinese National Review*. 20, 2015:P50-P52,54.

[8] Anonymous. Macao, a famous tourist city built on the world cultural Heritage. *Splendid*, 2011, 000(008):154-158.

[9] Xiao Dongfa. Earthly Heavenly Palace: The Mazu Temple of extraordinary attainments. *Earthly Heavenly Palace: the Mazu Temple of extraordinary attainments. Modern Press*, 2015.

https://doi.org/10.1142/9789811238727_0073

Sustainability and Value-Add of Culture-Constructing Religious Brand Design Strategy Model from Service Design Perspective

Tsen-Yao Chang, Yu-Ju Chuang*

Department of Creative Design, National Yunlin University of Science and Technology, Yunlin, Taiwan
*Corresponding Author Email: juyuchuang@gmail.com

Abstract

Among all the cultural features and resources of Taiwan, aspects relevant to the local religions have become a focus of the local government for promoting tourism. In this research, students went through the stages of learning at the course for serving as the facilitators for the course and making proposals from the designer's perspective. They learned to detect problems, narrow down the issue, and offer solutions. The constructed design strategy model of the religious brand helps local sustainable management and development.

Keywords: service design, experience design, religious culture, branding

Introduction

Taiwan's diverse and religious culture has enriched the local features and boosted tourism development. Since religion is integrated into daily life of Taiwanese people, the religious culture is one of the essential elements for tourists to know the local culture. The statistics from the Ministry of Interior Affairs in 2019 showed that there were 12,279 temples around Taiwan, many of which were historical heritages. An official religious and cultural map of government-certified religious-cultural assets can be found on taiwangods.com that was established by the Ministry of Interior Affairs. Under the classification of Buddhism, Taoism, and folk beliefs, a total of 217 temples are listed as heritage sites or historical buildings. The website helps people to learn about Taiwanese religious-cultural assets by providing information about religious events in Taiwan. On the other hand, it presents the current development of religious tourism in Taiwan from the industrial perspective such as the management of religious cultural fields, the transmission of ideas, and the process of praying for blessings from the perspective of service design. Thus, visitors can perceive the value and connect themselves to local people to create a journey experience, which is important for the interaction between customers and services. The "touchpoints" refer to physical facilities, indicators, brochures and merchandise sold in the field, and so on. These "experiences" are constantly generated through different service touchpoints that are scattered in every connection in the experience process [10]. The management of religious branding creates interactive touchpoints through the development, sales, gifts of merchandise. Thus, the characteristics of the religious can be propagated effectively. With the historical context as well as the laws and regulations in Taiwan, most temples are managed by committees. The operation methods and the service provided in the field are different. The cultural values in the religious field include tangible buildings, Buddha statues, utensils as well as intangible values such as sacrificial rituals, traditional customs, and united local people. Many religious buildings are historical sites, and it is necessary to preserve and inherit their culture, delicate craftsmanship, and historical meaning. For the administrators of the temple, it is also an irreplaceable asset in the process of branding religious beliefs.

Literature Review

A. Cultural Sustainability- tourism benefits of religious culture

According to the official statistics from the Ministry of the Interior in 2018, there were more than registered 12,000 temples. Many of them have become internationally renowned tourist destinations. There are also distinctive religious events that attract a large number of tourists and create a lot of business opportunities and additional effects. Religious tourism is a form of cultural tourism with a close relationship between them to develop religious tourism as an inevitable trend. Rinschede believed that religious tourism is a type of tourism as the participants are mainly or partially motivated by religion [12]. The types of tourism vary by changes in lifestyle and consumer preferences. The tourism committee of OECD (Organization for Economic Cooperation and Development) has published a report in 2009, which analyzed the relationship between "tourism", "culture" and the "attraction and competitiveness of tourist destinations". The forms of tourism change from heritage and cultural tourism in the past to creative tourism that reflects changes in consumer consumption patterns and the development of the experience economy.

Many religious buildings display superb construction techniques that are regarded as historical and artistic assets. Temples are usually the place where local people gather. They boost the development of industries in the community. A study by Hong and Hsieh pointed out that religious culture not only has an impact on the facilities of the surroundings but also demands the improvement in management services such as understanding religion and culture [5]. Appropriate understanding and application of religious culture play a significant role in the service experience related to religious events.

B. Brand added value- integrated design thinking of religious culture

The modern social structure regards "service" as the standard. Keeping good product quality, technology, or sales capabilities is no longer essential for dominating the consumer market. Service providers must identify the needs of customers and cater to their needs [13]. Jensen proposed that consumers seek the hidden story behind the products and the emotional experience connection through shopping behavior [9]. Consumers not only shop for practical functions but psychological satisfaction [17]. Therefore, designers tend to use design methods to make products a medium of cultural transmission.

In addition to making the design for users and the market through design thinking, it is also necessary to further consider the value and necessity of branding. Brand image has long been regarded as an important concept in marketing as well as an important basis for gaining competitive advantage, distinguishing, and managing brands [9]. It is also a way to create differentiation [1,3]. Brand image drives brand equity and builds brand value. It is also one of the sources to create brand loyalty [6]. Tsai pointed out that brands use related images and symbols to differentiate themselves from competitors as an expression of commitment and assurance of quality [16]. There are three functions: explicit recognition, implicit cohesion, and market orientation. The items contained in the three functions include cross-domain professional knowledge connotation. It requires an integrated strategy operation to construct the brand from identity strategy and spiritual value to market value. The systematic thinking of service design provides an entry point for brand construction.

C. Service Experience- the service design perspective of religious culture

Service design is decided by people's needs and feelings by using system and design thinking to form a complete design method [14]. Service design is not a new method and belongs to a holistic, cross-domain, and integrated academic field. In the process, professional design procedures are introduced into service design to achieve service innovation. It is a service innovation that satisfies the needs of the "service recipient" and "service provider" [11]. The observation and user-oriented thinking that service design emphasizes are used in various topics and fields. It organizes the touchpoints and stakeholders of each stage to create different perspectives and thinking directions.

In sightseeing, MacCannell proposed that a tourist attraction comes from the empirical relationship among tourist, sight, and marker. The "marker" refers to mediums such as propaganda, leaflet, and travel book that convey travel information [18]. Common touchpoints in the religious field (Taiwan's main Buddhist and Taoist fields such as Buddhist temples and palace temples, for example) include brochures, free distributions, and sales of related merchandise. Chang pointed out that religious souvenirs not only a transaction between purchaser and temple but also a gift-exchanging between people and gods [2]. Therefore, the purpose of merchandising is not just about profit, but importantly about the religious meaning, attitude in life, and value that the merchandise symbolized. It has the value that combines commercial considerations and religious beliefs.

D. Summary

The skill of brand shaping gives the religious field a unique identity. Through a well-positioned brand, it brings consumers attractive and intense associations and further develops the design of related touchpoints [7]. The practice of brand shaping gives the religious field the design thinking of branding management.

Research Design

The study was based on a one-year teaching experiment and design practice. It takes the representative religious culture field in Yunlin – "Kongfan Temple" as the design practice subject. The course was taught in junior year in the first semester and emphasized the application and practice of service design tools. Then, it was taught in the freshmen year in the second semester. It emphasized creative thinking and involved students with design experience to obtain different design ideas. At the end of the one-year course, students in the course joined the design project and made design proposals to complete the project based on the actual needs of the Kongfan Temple. A guidebook and merchandise packaging for the temple were proposed as the practice of service design application.

The overall research process focused on action and cycles through plans, actions, observations, and reflections. In the planning part, literature analysis was carried out to provide a theoretical basis and then plan the teaching process. Through teaching implementation and content analysis, the students' learning status and the adequacy of the teaching materials were observed. Finally, the overall strengths and weaknesses of the process as the future course design revision and improvement direction were described. The first-stage curriculum design allowed the students to conduct on-site field surveys, used the non-participant observation method, and analyzed with service design tools to define the insufficiency in the field. Then, with the first-hand information obtained in the process, it combined the comprehensive analysis of literature reference to make design and practice for completing the first semester. In the second stage, six students course in the first semester were selected as the mentors in the new semester to help freshmen make a design in the new semester in purposive sampling. In the third stage, three students made actual design proposals with the temple committee to participate in the religious branding process (Table 1).

TABLE 1
Three Stages Of The Course Planning

Content	The First Stage	The Second Stage	The Third Stage
Key Teaching Points	Field study Application of service design tool Design method	Creative thinking Design method Communication	Industrial practice Design proposal

Key Design Practice	Creative culture merchandise	Design thinking and creative	Design marketability

Discussion

There is a cycle composed of three stages in the course implementation of the study which allows junior, freshman, and senior students to participate in the design of Kongfan Temple's service touchpoints in sequence. The design process included concept proposals, model making, and the final proposal which involved the overall process of Kongfan Temple's branding strategy service. The discussion of the results can be divided into two categories with four dimensions: "design implementation" - "service design application", "design element exploration", and "participant role" - "student" and "service recipient".

A. Service design application: transform insufficiency into design performance

We used a field study to discover the insufficiency in the Kongfan Temple and found customary items in the religious and cultural fields. Since most of the visitors are residents and believers, they do not need additional guidance and instruction. Thus, Kongfan Temple does not provide services or create experiences in the field. However, with the changes in consumer experience habits, tourism is developed towards in-depth experience. As a national monument, Kongfan Temple has a large number of historical, architectural, and cultural assets all of which present economical development and characteristics of religious cultural tourism.

Therefore, this research investigated the field of the case with observation methods by using a customer journey map. The purpose was to observe the stages and problems which were encountered by the worshippers in the journey from entering to leaving. The solution showed through design practice by proposing a guidebook for Kongfan Temple. It re-designed the Buddha statues in the temple and highlighted the appearance of the statues with simple color blocks to explain the meaning and background story represented by each god. It also explained the sequence of visits and the worshipping steps. Through the visual presentation of information, the problem of unclear information encountered by tourists in the field was solved.

Most of the religious-cultural heritages have background stories with rich culture and art and create artistic background stories. The stories and knowledge must be effectively transmitted to travelers for creating emotional memories that emphasize the characteristic of travelers. Therefore, the development of a brochure introduces the history and the beauty of the architecture of Kongfan Temple with information-based graphics and text to enhance tourists' understanding of Kongfan Temple. It allows Kongfan Temple's history, culture, and the beauty of craftsmanship to be spread and seen.

B. Study of design element: Interpretation and recreation of traditional code

In the process of the design for Kongfan Temple (as shown in Fig. 1), the confirmation of the design implementation was needed from the Kongfan Temple temple administrators. The designer responded to their opinions and thoughts. At this stage, students obtained a large number of elements and images in the religious and cultural field through a field study and collection of textual materials to summarize and develop ideas. In the process of design, it is necessary to understand the meaning of cultural elements, analyze and apply design conversion, and combine color plans, modeling, code application, and so on to complete the design application of religious cultural elements.

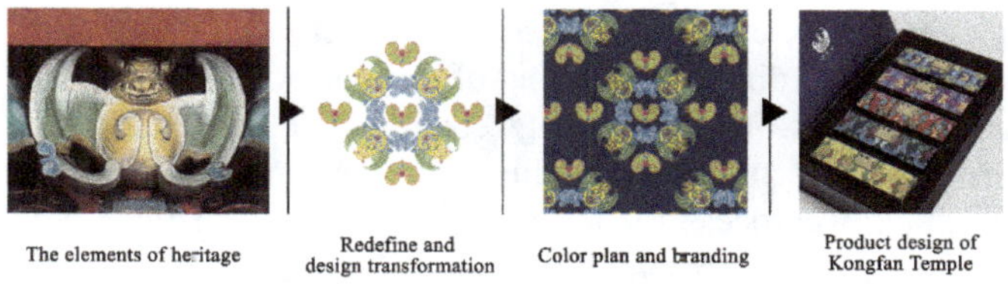

Fig. 1 The design application and transformation of the element in the religious field

In the third stage, students participated in the design proposal for the finished product. Safety rice was chosen in the design. Kongfan Temple contains rich craftsmanship. All the carved beams and painted buildings on the beams, pillars, and stone walls are meaningful. They are also rich in the cultural assets of the temple. The patterns carved on the cylinders and walls have symbolic meanings. Five of them were selected and used the representative patterns to design. The meanings represented by these five designs were childbirth, longevity, fortune, safety, and academic work (as shown in Fig. 2). Applying these five meanings to packaging in different colors to create the richness of visual packaging strengthens the connection between the product and the field. In the color application, the relevant background story was reflected in the unique design of the historical Kongfan Temple.

Fig. 2 Design packaging for safety rice with the concept of the Five Elements.

This research involved teaching into the local religious field and led students to consider local cultural issues and traditional culture for analyzing its meaning in various application possibilities of cultural elements. The field study observation method allowed students to interact with the regional culture. It was an important process for cultivating the observation and communication skills of the students. The time length for the students to observe in the field affected the student's ability to analyze local cultural characteristics. Therefore, the student's analysis context and the ability of information collection and transformation were observed through the operation of different groups. If the students interact with the local people or related workers for a long time, it helps to improve their analysis and integration ability.

Conclusion

The various designs in branding Kongfan Temple revealed that the students have developed the designs broadly and deeply. There were field tours and design applications that help crafts transformed into merchandise. The merchandise design was proposed with the "people-oriented" idea. A large amount of information was obtained from field observations, relevant interviews, and research on historical literature and performed by diffusive thinking of religious culture and local characteristics. They gradually converged in the process of design and discussion to combine "culture" and "localized" in the thinking process for the concept, draft, simulations, and finished product presentation. Finally, product designs were proposed for cultural value and local characteristics.

The religious-cultural field has rich values in culture, history, and art. It is also a living circle of beliefs closely connected with the local area. It is recommended to adopt a phased approach and gradually adjustment and change according to how well the locals receive it in creating a brand. There are three developments in the future: (1) temple brand rebuilding for the culture and history of Kongfan Temple to create a new image with contemporary life and local characteristics, (2) creating a new image and meaning for improving the existing merchandise and packaging design of Kongfan Temple and adding value for the old culture and tradition, and (3) creating sustainable tourism and cultural value with sustainable business space and value for local culture and tourism through design planning.

In the status quo of the development of Taiwan's religious culture through this research, the field of religious culture has diverse historical culture, craft backgrounds, and cultural characteristics. All of them have the potential to develop and promote cultural tourism. There are problems in the field management through the service design process. However, a religious-cultural branding with design gradually is built and executed. This creates a win-win opportunity for local operation and cultural inheritance to maximize the value.

References

[1] Aaker, D.A. (1996). Building Strong Brands. The Free Press, New York.

[2] Chang, Y. C. (2011). Religious Tourism and Research in Taiwan: An Approach of Essentialism and Methodology. Yu Da Academic Journal, 27, 65-84.

[3] Hankinson, P. (2001). Brand Orientation in the Charity Sector: A Framework for Discussion and Research. International Journal of Nonprofit and Voluntary Sector Marketing, 6(3), 231-242.

[4] Ho, S. S., & Sung, T. T. (2014). The Development of Academic Research in Service Design: A Meta-Analysis. Journal of Design, 19(2), 45-66.

[5] Hong, S. H. and Hsieh, D. W. (2010). Discussion on the Cultural and Tourism Value of Religions. Buddhism and Science, 11(1), 11-20.

[6] Huang, S. M. (2017). Exploring a Missing Link for the Brand Image Effect on Brand Loyalty: The Mediated Path of the CAC Extending Model. Journal of Management, 34(1), 1-29.

[7] Janonis, V. & Virvilaitė, R. (2007). Brand image formation. Engineering economics, 2(52), 78-90

[8] Jensen, R. (1999). The dream society: The coming shift from information to imagination. London: McGraw-Hill.

[9] Keller, K. L. (1993). Conceptualizing, measuring, and managing customer-based brand equity. Journal of Marketing, 57(1), 1–22.

[10] Lovile, L., Downs, C., and Reason, B. (2008). Bottom-line experiences: measuring the value of design in ser vice. Design Management Review, 19(1), 73-79.

[11] Moritz, Stefan. (2005). Service Design: Practical Access to an Evolving Field. Unpublished master's thesis, Köln International School of Design, Cologne, Germany.

[12] Rinschede, G.(1992).Forms of religious tourism.Annals of Tourism Research,19(1),51-67.

[13] Saco, R. M., & Goncalves, A. P. (2008). Service Design: An Appraisal, Design Management Review, Winter 2008, 19, 1, pp. 10-19.

[14] Sangiorgi, D. (2011). Transformative services and transformation design. International Journal of Design, 5(2), 29-40.

[15] Sung, T. T. (2014). Preface-the essence of service design and process tools. Journal of Design, 19(2), 1-8.

[16] Tsai, C. T. (2009). Exploring School Brand Building and Marketing Management. Journal of Research on Elementary and Secondary Education, 23, 139-160.

[17] Verganti, R. (2009). Design-Driven Innovation-Changing the Rules of Competition by Radically Innovating What Things Mean, Harvard Business Press

[18] Yin, P. N. (2011). Historic Cities, Representation of Architecture and Cultural Tourism: A Case Study on Tang Paradise in Xian City, China. Journal of Design, 16(2), 23-43.

https://doi.org/10.1142/9789811238727_0074

Technology and the Change of Hip Hop Creative Culture in Taiwan

Kang-Sheng Mo

Department of Applied English, Chihlee University of Technology, New Taipei City 22050, Taiwan
Email: kangshengmo@mail.chihlee.edu.tw, TEL: (02)2257-6167 ext. 2379

Abstract

As times pass by, new technologies have been invented, and new approaches have been applied to the spread of information in this age of globalization—and they are obvious specifically in music. While the transformation of how musicians produce music and make themselves heard differ from the early days, the process of the transformation is often overlooked and viewed as inevitable. In fact, the users of these new, modern tools need time for adaption. The most noticeable change in musical production is how it shifts from analog to digital. This includes change of ways to create, quickly, and almost simultaneously the musical works in terms of content, length, how they are marketed and presented, and so on. Thus, the change actually goes deep—technology has changed the ways artists create, and the artists who adapt to these new approaches have changed music. In this paper, I will choose hip hop as the musical genre to elaborate on how it grows and develops in Taiwan in relation to the external factors.

Keywords: Hip Hop, music, digital, culture

Introduction

Music has long been existent in human history, and it serves an important role for numerous reasons. Such a form of art is useful for entertainment, education, propaganda, and so on. However, it is fleeting as it is being played or sang—meaning it cannot be saved and replayed. The invention of new technology such as the Phonograph by Thomas Alva Edison in 1877, or the more recent carriers such as vinyl, cassette tapes, CDs, and MP3 files, have all chronologically changed the production and marketing of music. In the evolution of the medium for music, one is able to see each of these transitions moving toward the convenience for consumption. The appearance of a new, popular vehicle for music usually means it is more accessible for people—the new medium tends to be cheaper, easier to carry, and presented in higher quality. Starting from the mass production of vinyl and turntables, people are able to purchase and "own" music they like with affordable prices, and it is the beginning of the music business model that people are familiar with nowadays. Thus, the demand for new artists and music become the drive for record companies to find new talents and produce new music to sell. Other than classical music, people are also in favor of rock-n-roll, jazz, disco, funk, or more recently, hip hop.

Discussion

Hip hop, unlike the other genres mentioned, did not solely start based on formal musical training or the skills of musicians; instead, the musical genre is actually formed by African Americans and Latin Americans who were mainly in the lower class. With limited financial ability, most of the hip hop artists were not musicians who knew how to play musical instruments. In the book *The Concise Guide to Hip-Hop Music* by Paul Edwards, a definition of hip hop music is defined: "[t]he two main elements that make up hip-hop music are rapping and beatmaking. These are sometimes referred to as simply *beats and rhymes*, where rhymes refer to rapping, while beats are the instrumental tracks that are rapped over." [1] However, these so-called instrumental tracks did not come out of nowhere.

Hip hop music was born from the technique called sampling. Essentially, it is to dissect portions of original songs and take these parts as samples by using a sampler (or a computer software), and then use the sample as the foundation to create a new song. This technique is common to hip hop music producers specifically in the early days of hip hop, because most of the producers are unable to build an entire song due to their financial limitation and/or lack of skills to play musical instruments. Thus, a sampler gives the producers the power to manipulate musical parts from others' sonic creation, and to use them as elements to make a new song. Even if the hip hop producer is unable to read sheet music, he is still able to create by applying these musical samples, adding or subtracting these materials along with other sounds to complete a new song. And because of its crucial role to the development of hip hop music, Tricia Rose explained how hip hop producers innovated the application of sampler in her work *Black Noise*. She states:

> . . . . sampling remains a tactical priority. More precisely, samplers are the quintessential rap production tool. Although rappers did not invent drum machine or sampling, they have revolutionized their use. Prior to rap music's redefinition of the role samplers play in musical creativity, samplers were used almost exclusively as time- and moneysaving devices for producers, engineers, and composers. Samplers were used as short cuts; sometimes a horn section, a bass drum, or background vocals would be lifted from a record easily and quickly, limiting the expense and effort to locate and compensate studio musicians. Although famous rock musicians have used recognizable sampled from other prominent musicians as part of their album material, for the most part, sampled were used to 'flesh out' or accent a musical piece, not to build a new one. In fact, prior to rap, the most desirable use of a sample was

to mask the sample and its origin; to bury its identity. Rap producers have inverted the logic, using samples as a point of reference, as a means by which the process or repetition and recontextualization can be highlighted and privileged. [2]

The creative application and the nature of samplers are differentiated by hip hop producers. And the same logic of highlighting/emphasizing the sample has become a norm in hip hop music. In other words, even when a hip hop producer is making beats from his DAW[1], he/she would tend to center the sample instead of hiding it. And the reason behind such a choice is possibly to arouse memory of nostalgia of the audience. When the audience hear a new song which contains a certain part or element of an old song that was previously released, it is more likely to be remembered. This does not guarantee the song will become a hit; however, it allows the audience to (re)connect the song beyond its original territory.

The popularity of DAW started to rise in the millennium for hip hop producers, because it is mostly cheaper to purchase a software than hardware such as the sampler or turntable. More and more songs were starting to be made from computers instead of hard disks. At first, people had doubts about how it violated the original way to make hip hop music, questioning the authenticity of its sound. However, as technology advances, it becomes less and less of a problem for producers. Nowadays, one can barely tell whether the song is made from a sampler or DAW because even the static sound can be mimicked through DAW processing, and it is able to provide a larger range of sounds than hardware, which is why DAW has become the mainstream music production tool.

However, as more musicians started to apply DAW instead of hardware, it also affects the speed of growth or decline of the companies that produce hardware. Other than instruments such as guitars, basses, pianos and so on, the drum machines and samplers were desperately producing new products with more digital expansions and functions. And as technology advances, old prestigious brands that produce classic samplers such as Akai would start to compete against Machines by Native Instruments, and the consumers would start to notice how the classic MPC machine by Akai decided to update and catch up with the time—adding larger sensible monitor and digital sound library in its new models. While the fundamentalists despised the change, it was the only way for Akai to go—to go forward.

Under globalization, hip hop music has become international through the help of media such as radio, television, and the internet. And as the internet bandwidth started to grows larger, the internet service also becomes much cheaper and more popular among the mass. Thus, it becomes way easier for people from across the world to learn about things from far away almost simultaneously (or to be influenced by these things). Moreover, the influence of hip hop spread throughout the world, and start to localize as people internalize these influences. And inevitably, Taiwan is among many countries that started to make its own hip hop music.

During its initial stage, Taiwan had a few attempts of infusing hip hop elements into pop music in the 1990s; however, the first authentic hip hop artist would be MC HotDog, who released his first single in 2001 via Magic Stone Records.

The time period is very interesting for the rise of MC HotDog. The record sales were started to decrease globally because of illegal online downloading, the cassette tapes were disappearing, and CDs were the main music products, collectors and DJs mostly purchased vinyl. At the same time, it was the time period when music producers started to familiarize with the DAWs. Even though online piracy hurt record sales, MC HotDog's demos were circulating online before his official release, and it was the best advertising campaign for it built him a fan base without going through the old promotional tours hosted by record companies. Here, we are able to see how technology comes into play and have concrete influence on multiple aspects of record production, promotion (strategies), and the transition from analog to digital age.

Starting from then now, the total sales of physical copies of music products including vinyl, cassette tapes, and CDs have all went down drastically. One can see from [3] that the traditional audience is facing a huge change to buy and listen to music. And fast forward to year 2020. The dominance of digital streaming services such as Spotify, Apple Music, Tidal (or KKBOX in Taiwan) is obvious. The sales of physical copies are no longer the most important; instead, online hits and streaming charts have taken over. This has also reflected on the length of the songs—they are all shorter than before. Many songs are barely longer than two minutes in length, and it tells a lot about the current atmosphere. All these new, convenient technological devices/gadgets easily distract people, and the concentration level is at all time low. Record companies and the digital streaming platforms all encourage the artists to make more music, with attention spans so low, artists are expected to catch the ears of the audience at the first five to ten seconds of the song, and the lack of patience completed changed the ways musicians make the songs.

Conclusion

Most of the Mandarin music audience in Taiwan use KKBOX as their choice of streaming service, and for those who listen to western music, Spotify is their top choice. As for the hip hop artists in Taiwan, to market themselves online become the first priority for most of them. They would interact with fans through social media such as Facebook or Instagram, announce upcoming shows and music releases, share personal lives or new music video on the internet. Nowadays, it seems as if one is disappeared if he/she is not active on social media, and it is especially important for artists and musicians to participate in order to stay relevant. Though new technology is refreshing and helpful in aspects such as music production and advertisement, both the artists and audiences must find ways to apply time more efficiently and not to be controlled and/or manipulated by these new inventions. After all, the technology is invented to serve the people, not the other way around

[1] A digital audio workstation (DAW) is an electronic device or application software used recording, editing, and producing audio files.

References

[1] P. Edwards, *The Concise Guide to Hip-Hop Music,* 1st ed., New York: St. Martin's Griffin, 2015, pp. 5.

[2] T. Rose, *Black Noise: Rap Music and Black Culture in Contemporary America,* Middletown, CT: Wesleyan University Press, 1994, pp. 73.

[3] H. Harris, "The day the music shop died," The Guardian, Dec. 7, 2003. Accessed on Aug. 13, 2020. [Online]. Available: http://theguardian.com/music/2003/dec/07/popandrock.netmusic

https://doi.org/10.1142/9789811238727_0075

The Amis Innovation Products Design of Hammered Leaf and Flower Prints

Kai-Siang Chen[1], Chin-Jung Chao[1], Po-Hsiang Liu[2*]

[1]Department of Industrial and Systems Engineering, Chung Yuan Christian University, Taoyuan 32023, Taiwan
[2]Department of Industrial Management, St. John's University, New Taipei 25135, Taiwan
[*]Corresponding Author Email: bsliu@mail.sju.edu.tw

Abstract

Taiwanese indigenous peoples (e.g. Amis) applied the juice of Shoulang yam (i.e. *Dioscorea matsudae Hayata*) to dyeing on fishing nets and reducing the erosion by sea. In this study, the cold dyeing method of the natural pigment is extracted directly by hammering the leaf and flower. This study conducted a survey on consumer behaviors of innovation products in the hammered leaf and flower prints and preferences and willingness to purchase the cultural merchandises of Taiwanese indigenous people. A total of 1000 questionnaires were dispatched, with a response rate of 87.3 % (n = 873). Results of analysis showed that 48% of consumers are very interested in cultural merchandises of indigenous people. Consumers are most interested in merchandises of hammered the leaf and flower products for T-shirts (28%), followed by notebooks (22%), handbags (18%) and backpacks (14%), respectively. 43% of consumers want to DIY (Do It Yourself) their unique products of hammered the leaf and flower prints. Further, The analysis of 4P (Product, Price, Place, Promotion) and SWOT provided the information to enhance and promote cultural and creative industries of indigenous peoples.

Keywords: hammered leaf and flower prints, indigenous people of Taiwan, innovation products, consumer behavior

Introduction

Recently, the development of Taiwan's cultural and creative industries has been enthusiastic and related products have sprung up in the market. However, we need to know what kind of cultural and creative products can be favored by consumers, in order to create differentiated products in the competitive market. Su et al. [1] adopted the three emotional design elements of Visceral, Behavioral and Reflective design proposed by Norman [2]. After statistical analysis, the conclusion is that the reflective design of the three elements of emotional design of cultural and creative products can best influence consumers' willingness to purchase.

Ko [3] explored into the design aspect and business strategy for a unique product of cultural creative products designed (i.e. Fortune Bags). As to the business operations strategy, the following key areas have been thoroughly investigated and planned. In terms of marketing 4P, in addition to adopting innovative strategies, the products will provide "customized" tailor-made personal specialties.

The Amis are an Austronesian ethnic group native to Taiwan, and are one of the sixteen officially recognized groups of Taiwanese indigenous peoples. The traditional territory of the Amis includes the long, narrow valley between the Central Mountains and the Coastal Mountains (Huatung Valley), the Pacific coastal plain eastern to the Coastal Mountains and the Hengchun Peninsula (Council of Indigenous Peoples, Taiwan). Amis people applied the plants in the natural environment to develop various living utensils with handicraft techniques. Chang and Hsiao [4] applied the totem of Amis' cloth and accessory to create arts, in order to acquit different styles. Making clothes are made use of draping to make the style which can conform to a certain style, and then use the quality of material to show the beauty from combination of totem and modern clothes.

Lee et al. [5] focused on how indigenous traditional wisdom can be incorporated into school science and what students learned as a result. The wisdom of indigenous knowledge is based on a sacred respect of nature, due mostly to indigenous peoples' relationships and responsibilities toward nature [6]. Thus, learning indigenous knowledge may help children recognize this intimate connection between humans and nature.

This study conducted a survey on consumer behaviors for innovation products in the hammered left and flower prints and preferences and willingness to purchase the cultural and creative merchandises of Taiwanese indigenous people.

Methods

A. Hammered leaf and flower prints

Taiwanese indigenous peoples (e.g. Amis) applied the juice of Shoulang yam (i.e. Dioscorea matsudae Hayata) to dyeing on fishing nets and reducing the erosion of fishing nets by sea. In this study, the cold dyeing method of the natural pigment is directly extracted by hammered the leaf and flower.

The steps of hammered leaf and flower prints followed (Fig. 1): (1) finding a piece of cotton cloth or sackcloth; (2) finding leaves and flowers to work with and looking for things with bright colors that aren't too juicy or too dry; (3) trimming the flowers/leaf and paste with scotch tape; (4) sticking the leaves and cloth; (5) starting by making small, even taps using the flat side of one of the hammers. This will set the flowers or leaves in place. Then go carefully over the entire area with a ball- or cross-peen hammer; (6) peeling back the cloth to check the progress. If the pattern on the cloth is filled in, it is probably done. If not, the step is repeated.

Fig. 2 The brand story of Milahci Company (mother's eyes and indicated that mother is guarding her children to grow up)

B. Innovation products of hammered leaf and flower prints

Milahci Company (Amis language meaning of dreams) was established in 2000. The brand story is about mother's eyes and indicated that mother is guarding her children to grow up. The Logo of Milahci Company consists of fulfilling dreams, mother's eyes, indigenous totems, leaf prints, guardianship and inheritance (Fig. 2).

The innovation products design of hammered leaf and flower prints involved bags, cosmetic bag, coins bag, mobile bag, key case, wallet, pencil box, notebook, pillow, and scarf etc. For example, some innovative products showed in Table I.

The characteristics of these products are nature, handmade and unique. The original woven creative products are made of undyed natural fiber cotton, hemp, silk and other fabrics. From the beginning of the process of desizing, refining, coloring and fixing, products do not use any chemical dyes. Therefore, the cloth products dyed from original leaf and flower. It is the best gift that nature brings us.

C. Questionnaire survey

The questionnaire was designed to determine the design factors of innovation products design of hammered leaf and flower prints. Questionnaire involved background of participants, consumer behaviors of innovation products in the hammered leaf and flower prints with preferences and willingness to purchase the cultural merchandises of Taiwanese indigenous people. Rating of the design attributes was accomplished via 5-point Likert-type scale: (1) strongly disagree, (2) disagree, (3) neither agree nor disagree, (4) agree, and (5) strongly agree. A total of 1000 questionnaires were dispatched, with a response rate of 87.3 % (n = 873). All data were coded and analyzed using SPSS 21.0 software for Windows.

D. 4Ps-SWOT analysis

The 4Ps marketing mix that is a foundation model refers to four broad levels of marketing decision, namely: product, price, promotion, and place. This has been defined as the "set of marketing tools that the firm uses to pursue its marketing objectives in the target market" [7].

SWOT analysis (or SWOT matrix) is a strategic planning technique used to help a person or organization identify strengths, weaknesses, opportunities, and threats related to business competition or project planning. It is intended to specify the objectives of the business venture or project and identify the internal and external factors that are favorable and unfavorable to achieving those objectives. SWOT has been described as the tried-and-true tool of strategic analysis [8].

Present study applied the 4Ps-SWOT analysis to generate meaningful information for each category to make the useful and identify competitive advantages.

Results

A. Questionnaire survey

A total of 1000 questionnaires were dispatched, with a response rate of 87.3 % (n = 873). Results of analysis showed that 48% of consumers are very interested in cultural merchandises of indigenous people. Consumers are most interested in cultural and creative merchandises of hammered the leaf and flower products for T-shirts (28%), followed by notebooks (22%), handbags (18%) and backpacks (14%) respectively. The 43% of consumers want to DIY their most exclusive products of hammered the leaf and flower.

B. 4Ps analysis

Products: the products of hammered leaf and flower prints should add the fun from DIY (Do It Yourself) and integrate into indigenous culture. The products of this study combine indigenous culture and creativity to promote more people who like indigenous style. The development of products could be divided into short, medium and long term.

The short-term products are mainly experience packages. In the future, we will develop products with design and uniqueness, so that the originality of products will be deepened and differentiated. In the surrounding products, we will develop towards the story, so that each product has its own personality.

The medium-term product is an online customization platform where consumers can make their own products on the Internet. The in-depth experience of indigenous culture can be made more realistic. It is not only on-site experience, but also on the Internet design experience. Thus many consumers who can not experience the scene can feel this move.

Furthermore, it is necessary to set up a sightseeing farm to cooperate with the government policy. The local ecological park in Hualien also allows consumers to enjoy DIY dyeing and weaving, and also experience rural areas, and provide indigenous lunch and dinner, while outside is a different business. Cooperation to create business opportunities is need as symbiosis.

<u>Price</u>: handicrafts have a long production time and retain the concept of creativity and art. However, the current apparel market and fierce price competition have resulted in no place for handicrafts. Thus, we will continue to develop the innovative marketing models and enhance product value.

In order to respond to the market demand price strategy, design and information elements are included, especially in design, to increase product items through design elements.

<u>Place</u>: in order to increase the exposure of indigenous products, we will actively participate in cultural-related markets and exhibitions in addition to local cultural promotion. In the medium term, it will be combined with travel operators to increase the crowds and promote the products to the Internet through the promotion of the Internet platform. In addition, a design platform is set up to allow consumers to design their own styles.

<u>Promotion</u>: the development of the Internet allows products to be exposed more quickly, and the promotion of services is set up in blogs, microblogs, and the recently popular Facebook community platform. The promotion includes free distribution of special festivals, promotion of remote tribes and charity sales. Examples are participating in relevant cultural markets, school leaf fall promotion (graduation ceremony), online free experience platform, advertising board or windows of airport and MRT stations, and actively participating in related competitions and cultural exhibitions to increase visibility and exposure. These activities accumulate business experience and make sense of advertising-free marketing.

C. SWOT analysis

The SWOT analysis for innovation products of hammered leaf and flower prints showed in Table II.

<u>Strengths</u>:

Consumer experience and customization: Provide a network virtual platform, allowing customers to freely match different styles, so that customers have a different feeling.

High product quality: The products are presented by professional personnel with pure handwork, and the quality has a certain level.

<u>Weaknesses</u>:

Time-consuming production of weaving products: Since the products are all handmade, the time of the manual will inevitably take a long time. The price positioning of handicrafts is relatively high: purely handmade, it will cost a lot of manpower, so based on cost considerations, and the price positioning will be relatively high.

Publicity requires a lot of money: because customers don't fully understand the product, and it is not widely available on the market. Handmade production is insufficient.

TABLE I
SOME INNOVATION PRODUCTS OF HAMMERED LEAF AND FLOWER PRINTS

Products	Photo
Bags	
Cosmetic bag	
Coins bag	
Pillow	
Scarf	
Notebooks	
Phone bag	
Key cases	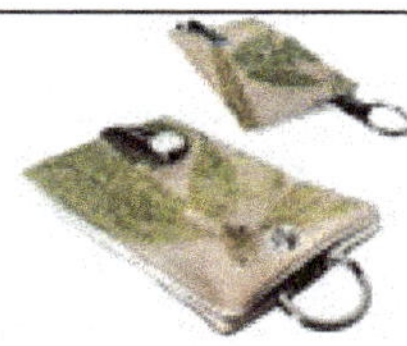

<u>Opportunities</u>:

The government promotes the policy of cultural and creative industries: The government is committed to promote the development of cultural and creative industries. With the cultivation of the government, the speed and recognition of the circulation of this product in the market has been promoted.

Internet marketing booms: As Internet usage increases year after year, sales on the Internet can also provide customers with a convenient platform for customers to choose.

Threats:

The rise of various workshops: With the investigation of the Internet, due to the low cost of opening and the low barriers to entry, many workshops for weaving and dyeing fabrics have emerged.

The low cost of foundry in Southeast Asia: the large number of manufacturers, resulting in confusion in the market, so that customers are at a loss when they choose.

The impact of traditional culture and popular goods: the colors and patterns of many Indigenous products are too bright or too much to compete with today's popular products.

TABLE II
SWOT ANALYSIS FOR INNOVATION PRODUCTS OF HAMMERED LEAF AND FLOWER PRINTS

	Helpful to achieving the objective	Harmful to achieving the objective
Internal Attributes of organization	Strengths ● Consumer experience ● Customization ● High product quality	Weaknesses ● Time-consuming production of weaving products ● The price positioning of handicrafts is relatively high ● Insufficient capacity
External Attributes of environment	Opportunities ● Indigenous people cultures ● The government promotes the policy of cultural and creative industries ● Internet marketing and e-commerce development	Threats ● The rise of various workshops ● The low cost of foundry in Southeast Asia ● The impact of traditional culture and popular goods

Discussion and Conclusion

In recent years, the government or non-government organizations have poured financial supports to assist indigenous people in developing cultural creativity industries. In the past, traditional handicrafts were developed for daily uses, especial ceremonial ones. Nowadays, tribal handicrafts might not only carry and transmit cultural traditions but also constitute cultural creative industry by transforming indigenous knowledge into knowledge economy [9-11]. Lin [12] reported that Taiwan's indigenous cultures offer great potential for enhancing design value and becoming recognized in the global market with their beautiful and primitive visual arts and crafts. The study was to collect visual icons from three tribes (Paiwan, Rukai, and Tau) and to identify the characteristic of form and its meaning among collected visual icons, and to organize the information in a table format (including tribe, name of object, type, image, material, color, appearance, usability, pattern, form grammar, form structure, inner content, cultural meaning, and original resource etc.). This unique art form enhances the significance of the localized culture among the global market [13].

Lai and Liu [14] investigated the critical design factors of consumers concern with innovative DIY products. After analysis of Analytic Hierarchy Process indicated that the rectangular shape is more popular DIY products. The “added value”, “practicality” and “operating convenience” are the most important factors of dimensions for critical design factors. These factors let consumers experience the product process, and let consumers have a deeper understanding of nature and the original culture. In each product design, there added different stories to make the product more commemorative, and original and sense of accomplishment. For DIY (Do It Yourself) practices, customers could make couples suits or family suits together, and add the original story to the design of the surrounding goods, bringing more touch. Target market is locked in consumers who are willing to calm down, happy to live, and interested in culture, to have an in-depth experience of cultural products.

Acknowledgement

Thanks for the assistance of the Milahci Company and Mr. Muhu Dawa, Mrs. Dawa Lisin.

References

[1] W.Z. Su, et al., The Study of Cultural and Creative Products' Emotional Design and Customer Purchase Intention, Journal of CAGST, pp. 213-224, 2018.

[2] D.A. *Norman, Emotional Design: Why We Love (or Hate) Everyday Things*, New York: Basic Books, 2004.

[3] Y.H. Ko, An Innovative Design of Cultural Creative Product and Business Strategic Planning of Starting an Enterprise: A Case Study of Fortune-Bags, Journal of Innovation and Management, 12, pp. 39-75, 2016.

[4] Y.W. Chang and M.L. Hsiao, Fashion Design of Amis's Totem Art, Journal of the Hwa Gang Textile, 12(2), pp. 172-178, 2005.

[5] H. Lee, et al., Indigenous Elementary Students' Science Instruction in Taiwan: Indigenous Knowledge and Western Science, Research in Science Education, 42, 1183, 2012. https://doi.org/10.1007/s11165-011-9240-7

[6] P. Knudtson, and D. Suzuki, Wisdom of the elders. Toronto: Stoddart, 1992.

[7] C. Grönroos, From marketing mix to relationship marketing: towards a paradigm shift in marketing, Management decision, 32(2), pp. 4-20, 1994.

[8] G. Dess, (2018). Strategic Management. New York: McGraw-Hill.

[9] Y.H. Wang, The Revitalization of Kavalan Banana Weaving, Journal of the Taiwan Indigenous Studies Association, 5(1), pp. 105-116, 2015.

[10] K. Yair, et al., A. Crafting competitive advantage: Crafts knowledge as a strategic resource. Design Studies, 22(4), 377-394, 2001.

[11] K. Yair et al., Design through marking: Crafts knowledge as facilitator to collaborative new product development. Design Studies, 20(6), 495-515, 1999.

[12] R.T. Lin, Transforming Taiwan Aboriginal Cultural Features into Modern Product Design: A Case Study of a Cross-cultural Product Design Model, International Journal of Design, 1(2), pp. 45-53, 2007.
[13] T. Y. Wu et al., The study of Taiwan aboriginal culture on product design. In Proceedings of Design Research Society International Conference. Paper (Vol. 238, pp. 377-394), 2004.
[14] H.H. Lai and B. S. Liu, The study of critical design factors of innovative DIY products. In Proceedings of Design Research Society International Conference Cross-Straits Conference on Economics and Management (2013 CSCEM), Dalian, Liaoning, China, 2013.

https://doi.org/10.1142/9789811238727_0076

Analysis of Crucial Abilities of Different Design Majors in Taiwan

Shu-Ping Chiu[1], Jui-Che Tu[2], Li-Wen Chuang[1*], Wei-Cheng Chu[3]

[1]School of Fine Arts & Design, Lingnan Normal University, Zhanjiang, China
[2]Graduate School of Design, National Yunlin University of Science and Technology, Yunlin, Taiwan
[3]Graduate School of Applied Design, Shu-Te University, Kaohsiung, Taiwan
*Corresponding Author Email: sphill200406@163.com

Abstract

In recent years, university enrollment rate has increased substantially but unemployment rate of university graduates has also gone up. In order to adapt to trends of globalization and the knowledge economy as well as rapid change of labor market and surrounding environment, this generation of young people should possess not only professional skills but also core employment ability that meets new economic requirements when entering the workforce. With this context, this study aims at developing a set of evaluation indicators applicable to core competences of design students in our country. This will function as criteria for assessing students' competitive advantages in order to implement development of pragmatic and practical curriculum in vocational and technical colleges as well as provide courses in conformity with industrial requirements. This will also favor the increase in TVET (Technical and Vocational Education and Training), students' career competitiveness and provide a reference for relevant education units to carry out instruction effect assessment as well as course progress and content planning and adjusting. Students will be assisted in pre-service diagnosis, and the learning-practice gap to meet demands on industry talents will be narrowed. Definite evaluation indicators developed here can be used as standards for related education units to assess students' competences, as well as bases for the industry to choose talents and make appraisal in the future.

Keywords: TVET, crucial abilities, design education

Introduction

Taiwan has strong cultural power and abundant creative talents. Long-term continuous cross-disciplinary, cross-industrial cultivation and development has established and formed the humanistic foundation of cultural and creative industry. In recent years, Taiwanese spontaneous creative energy has been accumulating and radiating, and Taiwan has made impressive achievements in movie, design, workmanship and pop music [1]. Since 2005, Taiwan government has been promoting students of vocational and technological colleges and universities to actively take part in international technology and skill contests, as well as assisting enterprises in attending four major international design competitions: Germany iF and reddot, USA IDEA and Japan Good Design Award. Recently, the design industry has repeatedly created new high in quantity of awards won in four major international design competitions. Domestic vocational and technological colleges and universities have rich innovation and invention energy, and encourage students to actively be involved in and devoted to patented and innovative invention, in order to present fruitful achievements of vocational and technological education as well as shine on the international stage frequently. Such strong power is an important impetus for industrial and economic innovation. Under the major trend of globalization, in consideration of Taiwan's current advantage sources, there are two mainstreams of future economic development- continuous development of high technology and design & service industries, both vigorously supported by the government recently.

Therefore, it is significant to consider how to cultivate the industry-required talents with innovation and integration competency, cross-disciplinary competency, internationalized experience and view, overseas marketing competency and other internationalization competency to follow the trend of international cooperation and competition. Driven by "knowledge-based economy" and "creative industry", such developmental trend will contribute to more prominent necessity of ensuring national competitiveness by higher design education, change ecological model of the industry, and also influence development and revolution of educational system. In response to this trend, colleges and universities have successively established many emerging departments recently, especially design and cultural innovation related departments. The Ministry of Education divides the design discipline into five classes: space design, product design, visual communication design, integrated design and other design. Due to social change and rapid development of medical technology, the trend of population ageing and shrinking has formed. Furthermore, in the overall environment, factors like economic recession exert influences. Consequently, since 1990s, employability has become a youth policy issue highly valued by advanced countries. Enhancing employability of university graduate has become one of the major driving forces for European and American higher education reform [2]. This study analyzes teaching objectives, core competency indicators or curriculum maps of design groups of the entire Taiwan and finds that all concepts are generalized and non-specific and that indicators are independent and lack consistency between schools. As a result, no definite and measurable indicator is available for pre-employment diagnosis or core competency evaluation of students, which easily leads to cognitive standard difference or fuzzy zone.

This study is aimed to construct a set of evaluation indicators which will be accepted by most design departments, can evaluate student's core competency and competitive advantage and will develop into questionnaire. Questionnaire survey is used to further find out whether design department students possess competitive advantage. This study mainly investigates the differences in key vocational competencies between students of different design specialty backgrounds, so as to assist students in conducting pre-employment self- analysis and knowing own shortcomings as well as strengthen students' competency in vocational requirements.

Literature Review

With regard to definition of competency, Zhen-Rong Tian (2002) pointed out that, many academic researchers tried to unify the name and definition of "competency" but no consensus has been reached due to heterogeneity in different countries' explanations of the name [3]. "Competency" usually represents a person's talent in an aspect. As proposed in study of Weinert (1999), competency is a kind of specific expression of cognition, leaning and behavior [4]. Competency refers to personal the knowledge, skills and attitudes formed through leaning or experience accumulation, and can be applied to different fields of life. Therefore, competency has many different meanings such as externally-expressed talent and skill, knowledge and skill in certain field, etc. Based on research over the past 20 years, European Commission develops eight competency groups including basic competence, living competence, social civic competence, broad competence, key competence, employability, entrepreneurial competence and management competence. Each competency group includes several sub-groups of competencies, and is divided into two dimensions according to competency attribute: life and work [5]. The job competence model proposed by Mansfield & Mitchell (1996) integrates common competence and professional competence, and can enhance completeness and comprehensiveness of competence indicators [6]. Therefore, this study develops concepts of competence and standard as proposed in the British job competence model of Mansfield & Mitchell (1996). However, different countries and different research institutions adopt different names. Therefore, to avoid confusion, this study uses the name proposed by American National Standards Institute and calls the common workplace competences "Crucial Abilities"; the competences necessary for specific field of specialized occupation are called "professional competences" to maintain the consistency.

Research Methodology

This study adopts Meta-Analysis to know relevant researchers' research process and method appropriateness, in order to provide the most accurate method selection and objective reference of theory. It also applies content analysis method to summarize teaching objectives of design academic groups of the whole Taiwan and uses conceptualized method to classify teaching objectives into key competency and professional competency according to the attribute. Furthermore, these objectives are included in expert Delphi questionnaire in the form of structural items. This study also proposes "Crucial Abilities" indicator items of core competency through summarizing related research and survey reports from Britain, Australia, USA, Common Wealth Magazine, Cheers Magazine, National Youth Commission Executive Yuan, Taiwan University, Jian-Du Lai (2002), Ying-Yao Zheng et al (2011), Xi-Hui He (2009) and UCAN platform [7,8,9], and includes these items into expert Delphi questionnaire [10]. As pointed out by, content validity can be constructed by virtue of collective expert decision-making. This method is advantageous in that it is economical and can rapidly construct competency model through expert's knowledge and insight. The benchmark developed through such method can act as a reference for organizational learning.

Therefore, this study integrates advantages of traditional Delphi method and makes use of convenience of modified Delphi method. Through implementation of modified Delphi method and exchange of expert opinions, it guides experts to propose constructive viewpoints, and uses them as research variable model and hypothesis of formal questionnaire. Through two rounds of Delphi questionnaire survey and collection, the mean (M) is between 8.00 and 9.69 ($\geqq 8$); the standard deviation (SD) is between 0.48 and 1.405 ($\leqq 2$); the CV% is 4.96%-16.58% < 25%. All of the items conform to the standards recommended by scholars.

Some scholars (Jun-Yan,Lin 2002; Wen-Kui Xie, Guang-Di Cai, 2002; Xin-Xian Chen 2005) put forward that, in terms of research method, no quantitative survey is added to verify appropriateness of indicator[11, 12]. Therefore, according to these scholars' advice, this study further uses quantitative questionnaire to conduct survey and verification. The questionnaire is designed as structural quantitative questionnaire. Likert 5-point scale is used as research tool, with 5 points as the standard, 5-1 respectively represents: (5) strongly agree; (4) agree; (3) no opinion; (2) disagree; (1) strongly disagree.

Four components of Crucial Abilities are: attitude ethics, creative thinking, self-management, and analytical application. Each component contains 4 indicators at least. Research hypotheses are proposed.

H1: regarding key competency, different demographic variables have significant differences in attitude ethics.

H2: regarding crucial abilities, different demographic variables have significant differences in creative thinking.

H3: regarding crucial abilities, different demographic variables have significant differences in self-management.

H4: regarding crucial abilities, different demographic variables have significant differences in analytical application

Result and Discussion

Analysis of "crucial abilities" of core competency indicators shows, the mean of its items is between 3.24 and 4.01, reaching middle and upper level. Dimensional analysis

TABLE 1
AVERAGE ANALYSIS OF CRUCIAL ABILITIES OF CORE COMPETENCY

Dimension	Indicator item	average	standard deviation
Attitude ethics	I have good personality and citizen quality	4.01	0.70
	I follow professional ethics and moral rule of service	3.98	0.69
	I have ability of group cooperation	3.92	0.74
	I have responsible working attitude and discipline	3.87	0.72
	I have positive attitude towards thinking	3.85	0.77
	I can develop self-plan that matches the company development	3.84	0.68
	I have personality trait that guarantees high employment stability	3.84	0.76
	I have active and positive independent learning attitude	3.81	0.73
	I have good interpersonal communication ability and social skill	3.80	0.74
	average of dimension	**3.88**	**0.56**
Creative thinking	I have ability of independent thinking	3.84	0.74
	I can properly express creativity to be understood by others	3.76	0.72
	I have systemic ability of understanding things	3.76	0.71
	I have thinking ability of drawing inferences	3.67	0.76
	I'm familiar with method for inspiring creativity	3.66	0.72
	I have massive novel design ideas	3.64	0.75
	average of dimension	**3.72**	**0.58**
Self- management	have highly-flexible environmental adaptive ability	3.77	0.74
	I have high plasticity	3.75	0.79
	I have high resistance to pressure	3.74	0.77
	I have competency of handling crisis	3.72	0.80
	I have career developing and planning ability	3.66	0.75
	I have competency of leading a team	3.56	0.81
	I have self-marketing ability	3.54	0.85
	I have good emotional management ability	3.48	0.83
	I have global perspective and foreign language ability	3.24	0.93
	average of dimension	**3.61**	**0.60**
Analytical application	I have ability of archives management	3.82	0.71
	I have ability of summarizing and analyzing data	3.77	0.69
	I have decision-making and judgment ability	3.66	0.83
	I have ability of mining and solving problems	3.64	0.75
	I have ability of applying information technology	3.62	0.77
	I have ability of combining theory with practice	3.53	0.74
	I have number concept and computational ability	3.44	0.89
	average of dimension	**3.64**	**0.58**

TABLE 2
ANALYSIS OF CRUCIAL ABILITIES DIMENSION OF DIFFERENT GENDERS

	Dimension	gender	average	standard deviation	t value	significance
Crucial Abilities	Self-management	male	3.68	0.60	2.095*	0.036
		female	3.58	0.60		
	Analytical application	male	3.71	0.57	2.065*	0.039
		female	3.62	0.59		

$^{*}p<0.05$ $^{**}p<0.01$ $^{***}p<0.001$

indicates attitude ethics 3.88 > creative thinking3.72 > analytical application3.64 > self-management (Table 1), so mean score of each dimension is close. The score of item 1 of attitude ethics is up to 4.01, suggesting most testees think they own good morality and citizen quality, can follow professional ethics and moral rules of services, have team spirit and professional dedication, hold responsible work attitude, observe workplace disciplines, take positive attitude toward thinking, as well as are capable of keeping pace with company development and own career plan, actively learning, possessing stable employment attitude, establishing interactions with others and expanding interpersonal relationships and social skills. Research results demonstrate the tested samples have attitudes and characteristics beneficial for employment and conform to the good core employability proposed by UK officials.

Two dimensions of Crucial Abilities- "self-management" and "analytical application" have p value of 0.036 and 0.039 respectively, both < 0.05, which represents significant difference. Further analysis of the mean shows that males (M=3.68) are significantly superior to females (M=3.58) in "self-management"; males (M=3.71) are also significantly superior to females (M=3.62) in "analytical application" (Table 2). Compared with females, males have significantly

TABLE 3
ANALYSIS OF CRUCIAL ABILITIES DIMENSION OF NATIONAL/PRIVATE UNIVERSITY

	Dimension	National/ private	average	standard deviation	t value	significance
Crucial Abilities	Attitude ethics	national	3.95	0.52	2.783**	0.006
		private	3.84	0.57		
	Creative thinking	national	3.78	0.54	2.386*	0.017
		private	3.68	0.59		

*$p<0.05$ **$p<0.01$ ***$p<0.001$

better resistance to pressure, stronger concept of career planning, and significantly higher number computation ability. Besides, males are more competent in mining and solving problems than females. Research demonstrates that male students of design departments have competitive advantage in workplace compared with female students.

In terms of above four dimensions, National universities are superior to private universities in the mean of each dimension, and significantly better in "attitude ethics" and "creative thinking". Results show that students of national universities have better workplace competency than private universities (Table 3). However, private schools are advantageous in "design application". From perspective of work attribute, national university belongs to originality research and development while private university focuses on practical design. Analysis of technician skill evaluation specifications of our country shows that, current skill evaluation only focuses on test of professional abilities but doesn't include Crucial Abilities (common workplace competences). Scholars (ANTA, 2001; Down, 2000) pointed out that, in countries such as Britain, USA and Australia, more and more competency indicators have moved forward the integration of "professional abilities" with "crucial abilities" [12].

The circle of vocational and technical education and related government units of Taiwan should think and consider whether the existing Taiwanese technician skill evaluation should include Crucial Abilities into the test items as a response to such trend so as to ensure perceptiveness and internationalization of education.

Acknowledgment

The work was supported by the Special Taiwan Talent fund of Lingnan Normal University (ZW2008 and ZW2009).

References

[1] 101 years of government policy report. Ministry of Culture of the Executive Yuan, 2012.

[2] Jia-Chun Xiao & Wen-Hui Chen, 2012. Longitudinal Analysis of University Students' Employability: an Investigation into Interdisciplinary Program.

[3] Tian Zhen-Rong Tian, Li Jichang, Kang Fengmei, Yang Shaoqiu, Rao Daqin and Song Xiude (2002); Construction of professional competence standard of higher vocational school students in our country (II); National Science Council, Executive Yuan, achievement report of special-topic research plan; plan number: NSC89-2511-S-003-089-X03

[4] Weinert, F.E., Definition and selection of competencies : Concepts of Competence. Organization for Economic Co-operation and Development, 1999.

[5] Zhen-Rong Tian, 2006. Research of Constructing Professional Competency Indicators for Academic Groups of Higher Vocational Schools; Monographic study and program outcomes report; Technical and Vocational Education Division of Ministry of Education.

[6] Mansfield, B., & Mitchell, L. (1996). Towards a competent workforce. Gower Publishing: UK.

[7] Jian-Du Lai (2002), Design education trends and evolution in Taiwan (initial edition), Taipei City: Longchen.

[8] Ying-Yao Guo, Li-Zhen Ye, Kun-Xia Liu, and Mu-Zhen Mo (2011); Construction of basic competence indicators of university students; Journal of Test, 58(3), 531-558.

[9] Xi-Hui He (2009), Constructing student learning ability indicators: an example of student e-portfolio in Soochow University; Criticism, bimonthly; No. 19.

[10] Dubois, D. (1993). Readings in fuzzy sets for intelligent systems.

[11] Jun-Yan Lin (2002), Construction of professional competence indicators of technical and vocational schools; National Science Council plan number: NSC 91-MOE-S-027-006-X3.

[12] Wen-Kui Xie, Guang-Di Cai (2002), Construction and application of professional abilities of financial department students under structural change- predominantly banking and insurance departments; National Science Council plan number: NSC 91-2511-S-237-001-X3.[13] ANTA (2001). Training Package Development Handbook. Retrieved from http://www.anta.gov.au/publication.asp, July 20, 2002.

https://doi.org/10.1142/9789811238727_0077

The Characteristics of Cartoon IP Images in the New Media Context

Qiao Liang Li, Xiao Yu Huang*, Jian Ling Xu

Xiamen Academy of Arts & Design Fuzhou University, Xiamen, China
*Corresponding Author Email: 20769210@qq.com

Abstract

Cartoon IP images combine content and intellectual property, serving as the core element of the entire industry chain. As they are visual, simple and easy to understand, cartoon IP images play an active role in various cultural fields and have greater impacts on today's society. With the rapid development of new media technology, cartoon IP images break through the limitations of the traditional media context, and there emerge some of their new features. This paper compares the different ways of presentation of cartoon IP images in traditional media and new media contexts, and analyzes the expression and interactivity of cartoon IP images in the new media context in terms of virtual presentation, interactive display and fragmentation.

Keywords: New media context, Cartoon IP images, Interactivity

Introduction

Nowadays, amid the increasingly diversified and personalized mass consumption, there arises a growing demand for the IP images of cartoon. With the external image at the core to be supplemented by the internal contents, and the infinite potential for image application and expansion, the IP images are exerting a growing influence in the society. Different from cartoon IP images in traditional media environment, the IP images in new media environment come in more forms with a variety of features.

Overview of IP images of cartoon

The word "cartoon" is originally an Italian word that emerged in Europe in the 19th century. At that time, it mainly took the form of paper media and appeared in journals and news. Writers created humorous and ironic illustrations to express their thoughts. Since then, the artistic form has been popular among readers. In response to the changes of times, artists have made use of the special characteristics of cartoons to create diversified artistic works, including cartoon comics, cartoon movies and TV programs. As a result, cartoon has enjoyed popularity among a growing number of audiences.

As a diversified means of expression born in the Internet era, IP image takes the original contents at the core. That means it can be a true celebrity, or a fictional character. According to professor Yin Hong of Tsinghua University, though IP originally stood for intellectual property, the IP nowadays refers to not only the IP in its traditional sense, but holder's property right to the intellectual works created by him. IP image, in a good position to meet the market demand, not only embodies the spiritual culture of entertainment and leisure, but communicate its unique values and worldview. Winning the recognition and empathy from the public with different forms of trans-boundary adaptation, it has the ability for wide dissemination and derivation.

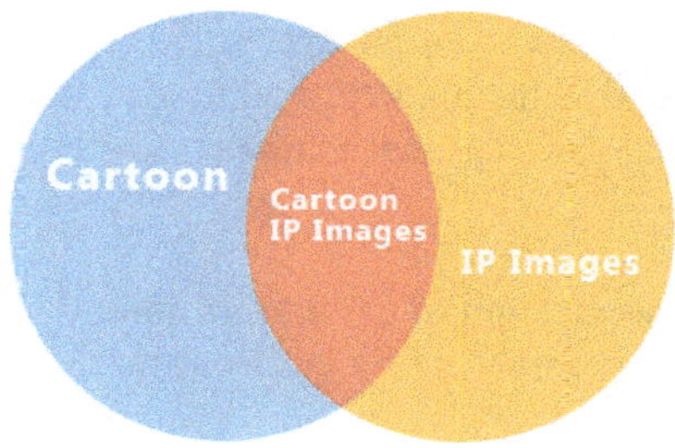

Fig. 1 Cartoon IP image illustration

Cartoon IP Image Type	Animation, Cartoon Characters	Monomer image	Network Derivative Modeling
Cartoon IP Image	 Baymax, Elsa	 Kumamon, Fuwa	 Line friends, Sad frog

Fig. 2 Cartoon IP image type

"Cartoon IP image" is an intellectual property with cartoon characteristics on which the businesses can build up a gigantic industry chain (Fig. 1). It can trace back to such images as Mickey Mouse and Doraemon. The growth of Internet has led to more types of such images. By sources, there are three categories, namely animation, cartoon characters, single image and network derivative modeling (Fig. 2). Cartoon IP images of animation and cartoon characters come from excellent animation and cartoon characters, whose characteristics and personality are portrayed though the story lines, as evidenced by Baymax of Big Hero 6 and Elsa of Froze. Single image cartoon IP image springs from some kind of activity or mascot design demanded by individuals, such as Kumamon launched by Kumamoto prefecture, Japan, and Fuwa, the mascot of the 2008 Beijing Olympic Games. The image of online derivative modeling stems from cartoon characters that spread and become popular on online platforms, like Line friends and Sad frog. Cartoon IP image can be attached to the products and derive the whole industry chain, of which the IP image operates as the soul. Such images project the writer's multiple emotions, which in turn make the characters more vivid and lively. Once characters are successfully portrayed, their role in the entire IP is irreplaceable. Cartoon IP image is gradually growing into a cultural symbol, and the story contents of them are constantly updated and enriched in combination with the times, appealing to a growing number of new audiences.

Now the most successful classic cartoon IP image is Mickey Mouse, a small black rat with a round head, round ears, and pipe-like limbs. The globally popular Mickey Mouse is so lively, optimistic, interesting, and amazing that it has long become the brand and soul of the Walt Disney Company, bringing huge profit to the Group by delivering visitors an amazing experience of animation and theme parks. Starting from Mickey, IP images have been brought to the audience one after another by Disney's designers. As mass consumption turns more diversified and personalized, such IP images as Mickey are exerting a growing influence on the society. They are active in various cultural fronts, playing a growing commercial role. It is the market trend to give the IP image a three-dimensional shaping and combine it with products for added value.

Presentation of cartoon IP image in the new media environment

A. Characteristics of the new media environment

New media here refers to the media form emerging in the context of the new technical support, covering all forms of digital media like digital traditional media, network media, mobile media, and digital TV. A mass communication as opposed to online media emerging in recent years, traditional media regularly release information to the public or provide them with education and entertainment, mainly including newspapers, radio, television, etc. The development of new media has a great impact on traditional media. The new media environment has changed our daily life, behavior and aesthetic habits.

B. Advantages of cartoon IP image in the new media environment

In the era of traditional media, cartoon IP images are mostly presented in the form of TV, movies, newspapers, books and pictures. Take the Doraemon created in 1970 by Fujiko F. Fujio, a Japanese cartoonist. Doraemon, a cat robot IP image, can take out lots of amazing props out of his pocket. Coming mainly in the form of comics, play, movie, or drawing, Doraemon is as popular around the world as Mickey.

However, the traditional media only allow the cartoon IP images some limited forms, and it is impossible for the audience to engage in interaction. In the traditional media environment, these cartoon IP images are limited in presentation, interaction, and dissemination. As the time advances, especially after the industrial revolution when the modernism and postmodernism aesthetics exerted quite a clout, the contemporary generation has accepted more concise, contracted design style in the subconsciousness. Further, the large amount of information also leads to unconsciously shifting through information among people. Cartoon image gives a visual sense of simplicity. It is easy to spread with great influence. All these features are in line with the new media landscape. New media, free from the limitations facing traditional media, enjoys great advantages over the latter. Wide audience, fast communication speed, and diversified forms of communication have greatly enhanced the communication effect of cartoon IP images. For example, Doraemon, Mickey Mouse and other traditional classic cartoon IP characters are more vibrant as they are updated by the new media environment. Today, new media digital technology has served as the main means of communication. Cartoon IP images in the new media environment have more forms of expression than in the traditional media circumstance, amazing the audience with a host of features.

Characteristics of cartoon IP images in the new media environment

A. Virtual presentation characteristics

Thanks to technological advance, virtual characters are not confined to the screen, but reach our reality through new means. As early as 1988, Who Framed Roger Rabbit, an animated movie by Warner Bros, made it a success to have actors and cartoon IP characters performing together. That is a milestone in the history of cartoon film. Hero Eddie Wallint played by a true star interacted with cartoon Roger Rabbit on the screen. The film is about Roger Rabbit, a cartoon star, who, after accidentally involved in a homicide case, worked with the private detective Eddie to locate the killer so as to prove himself innocent. The film, by involving true players and cartoon images, brought back audiences who had stayed away from cartoon films. In Gallery Invasion, a dynamic stereoscopic projection by a French company SkullMapping in 2016, a monkey jumped out of the scene into the real world by means of reality-augment techniques. It chased the red plane and shot it down (Fig. 3). In 2017 Gorillaz hosted a vocal concert where an audio-visual feast was offered by using the same techniques to combine true players and IP images of Gorillaz (Fig. 4). By projecting virtual characters in real life using the technology, as was the case of Gallery Invasion and Gorillaz, a sense of reality was created that is quite different from the virtual expression of traditional media. The cartoon IP images presented by virtual presentation technology are binary and mixed, more vivid and intuitive. With its visualization and interactivity, virtual presentation technology is better to impress audience with the IP images than that appearing on screen.

Fig. 3 Gallery Invasion

Fig. 4 Gorillaz vocal concert

B. Interactive presentation features

Amid the development of modern information technology and network technology, Flash cartoon with certain interactivity appeared in 1990s. With the support of digital processing, computer network, modern communication and multimedia technologies, Flash cartoon has been used more and more widely, and the interactivity of Cartoon IP image began to emerge. In the Flash cartoon, the audience can use the mouse or keyboard to control the cartoon IP images to some extent, while the images can response differently to different choice of the audience, thus shaping the plot. Xiaoxiao, a Flash role created by Zhi Qiang Zhu is an example. It is a match man in the form of a small black image. It can perform according to the audience's choice to determine the development of the story. By doing so, the author endows the cartoon IP image with a brand-new charm, wining himself a group of fans who are fascinated by Xiaoxiao. With the continuous development of the new media environment, cartoon IP image also becomes more interactive. For example, in Stitch Encounter (Fig. 5), an entertainment work launched by Disneyland in 2016, the audience could communicate and interact with the cartoon IP image, namely the Stitch on the screen, on which Stitch moves not in pre-designed patterns, but in accordance with audiences' behaviors. In Lilo & Stitch, a 2002 animation, however, there were only interaction between pre-designed Stitch with the other characters, and the audience had no chance for any changes or interactions (Fig. 6). Compared with the traditional media allowing only unilaterally appreciation of cartoon IP images, this interactive presentation process delivers a better dynamic and interactive experience to people.

Fig. 5 Stitch Encounter

The interactive presentation features of cartoon IP images enable the audience to interact with cartoon IP images while appreciating cartoons, or even allowing for independent setting of cartoon situation independently and control over plot development. In short, the audiences are in a better position to engage in interaction. When interacting with Cartoon IP images, the audience is no longer the "others" independent of the cartoon, but participants in the creation of the cartoon. As now an active actor in the construction of artistic works, the audience has an unprecedented powerful subjective initiative in beauty-appreciation. Cartoon IP image is no longer an unchanged aesthetic object, nor does the audience treat cartoon IP image as an external object to appreciate. Rather, they expand their life by a full absorption in the external objects and tap into the potential for growing a truer self through the interaction with the outer world. In this manner, an improvement is achieved on the aesthetic experience, which featured one-way and passive aesthetic subjects' extremely limited scope.

Fig. 6 Lilo & Stitch

C. *Features of fragmented demonstration*

By fragmentation of information, we mean the information coming in greater amount with fragmented contents, as people turn to network media of data. Complete information is decomposed into fragments by various classifications, and that is the cause and significant embodiment of the current information explosion. Currently, the fragmented Internet information includes short video, emoji, microblog, WeChat public account, and Facebook, all products of the era.

Emoji is an example for a way of using pictures to express feelings. In the era of information fragmentation, most people tend to reject excessive written information, while hailing quick expression of visual images. To cater to people's habit of new media audience's "fast-food" and "fragmented" reading, the rapid expression of visual images must catch the attention of the audience in a short time and convey the information intensively and efficiently. Due to its simple visual images, Cartoon IP image can be well expressed in the form of emoji, which are more vivid than those rigid words. In written communication, the addition of emoji will add a lot of fun, ease the awkward atmosphere, and at the right time can also be a good expression of emotion. It makes up for the drawbacks of boring written communication and inaccurate attitude expression, while effectively improving the efficiency of communication. It reminds us of the great mime Chaplin who, even without sound or words, could present a wonderful performance just by actions and expressions.

In this new media environment, emojis have become the new favorite of the communication circle. With the lowering of the threshold for making emojis, it is more and more convenient for users to produce them. The Kumamon, for example (Fig. 7), rouses in users' emotions during the production and dissemination of popular works, and then covey their feelings through IP images. In this way, value identification of this cartoon IP image is achieved. Also, the process attracts other users to follow suit, thus greatly expanding the spread of cartoon IP images. Emojis not only meet the needs of people's fast-paced life, but put an end to the boring way of delivering information in the past. In this sense, it is a popular culture formed after social software became active. This kind of pictures, bearing emotional expression and involving the various forms of application on the network, provide a better communication mode and presentation form for cartoon IP image than the traditional media.

Fig. 7 Kumamon emojis

Conclusion

Cartoon IP image face greatl restrictions in traditional media environment, both spatially and temporally. Further, due to the uni-directionality of media communication, little regard was paid to audience's psychological feelings aroused by cartoon IP images, along with lack of interaction with the audience. The development of new media environment has created more opportunities for cartoon IP image, greatly shaping its forms and contents. New media environment also brings a new way of communication for cartoon IP image. As compared with the traditional media, the new media environment is free from the obstacles, under which cartoon IP image is better able to meet the needs of audiences for interactive expression, entertainment and visual experience, thus catering to their demand for fragmented entertainment.

First, in the new media environment, the audio-visual language of cartoon IP image has infinite expression space. It is far more attractive and stimulating to the audience than that in the traditional media environment. Further, it is far more inclusive, adaptive and interactive than the traditional media environment. Second, Cartoon IP image has great potential creativity in the new media environment, as it frees itself from the limitations of live shooting and performance, and is no longer limited to the cartoon IP image performance and story-telling mode. The continuous development of new media technology may result in a variety of abstract, exaggerated, and composite creative works. In the future, cartoon IP image, as an eye-catching and increasingly popular cultural symbol, has infinite potential for development in the new media environment.

References

[1] Ying Fei He, On the Transformation and Development Strategy of Animation Industry from the Perspective of Animation IP Upgrade: A Case Study of Shanghai Fine Arts Film Studio, Film Review, 2017.

[2] Yuanyuan Hu, Cartoon Art creation and Aesthetic Evolution in the New Media Era, Art and Design, 2017.

[3] Zhi Ying Chen and Yue Yang, Exploration of Illustration's Dynamic and Fun Based on Digital Media Communication, Packaging Engineering, 2017.

[4] Hu Xiang Zhang, Industrial Upgrading and the Advent of Independent Innovation: A Case of the Chinese Cartoon Industry, China: An International Journal, Volume 14, Number 1, PP. 112-129, February 2016

https://doi.org/10.1142/9789811238727_0078

The Cognition of Local Cultural Heritage under the Background of Landscape Narrative Analysis: A Case Study of Qing-yan Yuan in China

Di Feng[1,2*], Shang-chia Chiou[1], and Feng Wang[2]

[1]Graduate School of Design, National Yunlin University of Science and Technology, Yunlin 64002, Taiwan
[2]College of Fine Arts Huaiyin Normal University, Huai'an 223001, Jiangsu, China
*Corresponding Author Email: fengdi165@gmail.com

Abstract

As a cultural heritage with local characteristics, ancient Chinese government buildings have the function of landscape sightseeing. However, further research is needed on how to enhance the residents' awareness of traditional government buildings through the attractiveness of the landscape. This article uses the method of landscape narrative analysis to explore the perceptions of the residents and cultural workers on traditional government offices. The site of the Huai'an Government Office（Qing-yan Yuan）in the Qing Dynasty in China was selected for the case study. In-depth interviews with residents and cultural workers were conducted, and then by using content analysis methods, information from the Internet, news, and periodicals for decoding was collected and analyzed. Through the analysis of the aggregated landscape narrative data, three categories of local government architectural cognition were summarized: (1) originality metaphorical cognition, (2) functional metaphorical cognition, (3) meaning metaphorical cognition. The result allows the establishment of the image and positioning of traditional government office buildings in the perception of the residents.

Keywords: Landscape narrative analysis, traditional government office buildings, heritage management, heritage value, local public.

Introduction

The government office building is an important building type in ancient China. Since the Tang and Song dynasties, its construction is usually combined with plants and flowers for decoration, forming a small-scale garden and a complex of government buildings in the combination of "government", "house", and "garden" [1,2]. This is a mixture of the two functions of ancient Chinese architecture and gardens. Based on the architectural space, the garden has expanded its leisure and recreational functions. However, the existing number is limited due to historical changes [3–5]. The only remaining government buildings were destroyed or incomplete, and some were converted into local tourist attractions. As the garden landscape is the main attraction for leisure and travel, Chinese traditional gardens have cultural connotations, environmental thoughts, architectural regulations, and local historical memories [5, 6]. They are important environmental sites for residents to understand local history and culture. On the other hand, the residents enjoy the fun of the landscape through the experience of the garden and establish feelings with the place, thereby understanding its past and listening to its stories. Reference [7] stated that the landscape is the common value of the entire society, meeting the current social needs, architectural intelligence and aesthetic interest, and fusing the sound of the past with the sound of the "present". However, as a combination of architecture and landscape, the traditional Chinese government office has been seldom analyzed for the preservation of the heritage from the perspective of the government office garden. By using narrative analysis, this article aims to discover how experiencers use metaphors in daily communication and vocabulary for the value cognition of the government office building and to promote the local development of architectural cultural heritage value.

Literature Review

A. The heritage value of ancient office building

The ancient office building was mainly used for the work and life of Chinese officials in the Ming and Qing Dynasties. "Ya「衙」" 「舊時官署之稱」in Cihai is interpreted as "the name of the old government office". The "Kangxi Dictionary" interprets "department「署」" as: "「部署有所罔屬,廨署,署位之表也」deployment has a non-proprietary, department, a table of signs." It shows that the government office is the old name for the office of ancient Chinese officials. As a product of the ancient Chinese government management system, the government office building was a symbol of state power in local governance. Its layout has clear levels and obvious partitions. For example, the main building is often located on the central axis and symmetrical from left to right, which symbolized the authority of feudal rule [2,8]. As a local authority, construction regulations are restricted by etiquette, clan system, and hierarchy. Generally, the ancient office buildings follow the traditional characteristics of the front and the back, the left and the right, and a three-coating [3,6,9]. Therefore, the traditional government office building served as office space for local officials to protect the local economy and people's livelihood, and at the same time connect the central government. It is an important form of Chinese traditional cultural heritage.

The ancient government office buildings have important values in terms of style, history and culture, and local folk customs. For example, in terms of architectural style, different officials transformed the living environment to cater to their tastes, and finally form the characteristics of combining southern and northern styles [3, 9]. On the other hand, the government building has witnessed the historical changes and development of the place and has high social, cultural, artistic, historical, economic, and scientific values [4,5,8,9]. At the same time, it records local customs, aesthetic characteristics, official culture, and etiquette thought [2,10]. After it lost its original historical function, it has brought economic values such as cultural tourism and commercial display. Reference [8] suggested that reasonable protection and development of the ancient government office buildings help to continue the urban texture of historical and cultural cities and evoke the memory of the city. Therefore, it is necessary to arouse the residents' awareness of the value of heritage so that the building sites of the government office form a trend of sustainable preservation, thereby continuing its spiritual connotation.

B. The rhetorical form of landscape narration

"Narrative" is derived from the Latin "qnarus" and the Indo-European root "qna", which means "to know". This refers to the knowledge gained through language and the understanding of the world [11,12]. It is a memory after understanding, which helps people build a better cognitive system. The landscape narrative is to establish a connection between the landscape and the narrative. The place in the landscape constitutes the narrative frame, and the landscape is the process by which important images and stories in the place are generated [13]. Landscape narration combines literary theory, human geography, visual art, involving social identity, history, and the nature of places. It becomes historical protection, heritage protection, public art, and sustainable development planning. Therefore, exploring the cognition of cultural heritage value with landscape narrative contributes to people's understanding.

In the process of landscape narration, it is necessary to portray narration and landscape as a meaningful cultural system for making people realize the importance of context. Rhetoric is the basic means of constructing in language, narration, and landscape [13]. As rhetoric is defined as a means of persuasion, the use of language to form an attitude or cause others to take action [16,17]. As a form of rhetoric analysis, metaphor analysis emphasizes how to influence the listener's thoughts through rhetoric, and then establishes a personal knowledge system. Moreover, using metaphor to analyze the artistic conception and themes of classical gardens is a common technique for research. For example, metaphorical thinking, as observation and image acquisition, expands the time and space, connotation, artistic conception of gardens, and allows garden experiencers to obtain rich spiritual enjoyment [18]. Reference [19] interpreted the expression of "stone" from the concept of metonymy and metaphor in cognitive linguistics and discovered how people understand irrelevant language phenomena. Reference [20] analyzed the application and expression form of metaphor design from garden decoration, color, plant, sketch, and material. The knowledge that the experiencer encounters in daily life, the meaning of the heritage conveyed through the use of associations and metaphors contribute to the construction of personal cognition [21]. Therefore, there is a strong connection between metaphor and cognition, which makes abstract imagination and content concrete and easy to understand.

C. Metaphorical rhetoric and heritage value recognition

Narrative analysis is affluent in gardens and architecture, but it has received little attention in recent years. A landscape is an individual's perception and observation of a certain scene which are appreciated by people [22]. In narrative research, garden stories are a key to understanding spaces and places, and subjective concepts are formed through the process of description [23]. Using landscape thinking to protect cultural heritage is linked to memories and is the shaping of place identity and place spirit [24, 25]. Especially in the study of historical heritage protection, since the language between viewers defines the common landscape, researchers examine the dynamics of the transition process of the garden and produce cultural self-evidence and a sense of identity, not just the aesthetics of the garden features [26, 27]. When discussing the protection of cultural heritage, people use stories and historical facts to explain the places where they live. When these are integrated into the landscape, the place becomes real and natural [13]. The experience of cultural heritage emphasizes the human perception of the background of the heritage story, the ability to understand the hidden meanings and stories in the heritage and to understand the knowledge of the past [21]. Besides, the buildings, plaques, mountains and stones, and inscriptions in the gardens of the government offices are the main appreciation content, and at the same time constitute the narrative framework of the heritage site. Based on their social and cultural connotations, the experiencers transform traditional cultural places into learning spaces through the appreciation of the government's gardens and play the educational significance of heritage values [28, 29]. On the other hand, in psychology, cognitive operations are usually understood in terms of how a certain activity responds to the needs of humans to interact with the world, which has an identifiable effect [30]. Cognition is the process of reasoning from the semantics of language expression or other symbols. The development of cognitive linguistics has made people realize that the figurative practice in traditional rhetoric not only enhances the effect of language expression, but also has an important cognitive effect [31].

This article uses the perspective of metaphor analysis to explore the degree of the residents' interpretation of cultural sites and discover how residents establish the process of heritage value recognition to promote the sustainable inheritance and development of the local government's architectural cultural heritage.

Discussion

Qing-yan Yuan (also known as the Governor's Court of the River Course), as the largest government agency garden in the history of water transport in the Ming and Qing Dynasties in China, exhibits a garden art style with unique local characteristics. It was originally an office place for river management established during the Kangxi period of the Qing Dynasty to solve the flooding of the Yellow River [32, 33]. The overall structure of the whole park is complete, the ancient style still exists, and it is rich in era characteristics and local style. It was once called "the first garden in Jianghuai" [34]. Later, it was abolished during the Guangxu reign of the Qing Dynasty and changed to a local park. It attracted residents and tourists with the image of a garden. However, when viewing the landscape of Qingyan Garden, different experiencers realized that it had different identities at different times, and use some metaphors to express personal opinions.

In the process of understanding the objective world, human beings communicate and inherit the culture accumulated by humans through language [35]. When residents visit the garden, they see a common "landscape", which triggers an understanding of the government's garden background. They communicate their thoughts through language, and with the accumulation of time and frequent exchanges, a common understanding arises [36]. In the process of cognitive mapping, individuals can obtain information about the relative positions and attributes of phenomena in daily spatial environments. The metaphorical analysis emphasizes that it is an imperceptible tool of persuasion that influences the listener's thoughts and builds cognition through rhetoric. Therefore, using the metaphorical perspective of landscape narrative to explore the residents' cognition of the local government office buildings promotes the experiencer's understanding of the value of architectural sites.

This article uses content analysis to sort out four types of experiencers, including journals, travel websites, news reports, and interview objects. The narrative data of Qing-yan Yuan, and then the coding analysis of the language data content are summed up as the language main axis of different experiencers' perceptions of the government office building and explored the protection and protection of the government office building in the language description of various visitors.

As an important form of Chinese classical gardens, the government office gardens have humanistic and historical value. They often induce the association of visitors through architecture, plaques, inscriptions, stories, and so on.[37,38]. The visitors turn the landscape into a language that they understand and build a legacy story of personal cognition. Vocabulary becomes a cognitive method in this process, especially the description of originally complex concepts into concepts within the scope of experience through comparison and simulation [39]. In this article, the visitors use metaphorical vocabulary to simplify the ins and outs of the story, establish the basic concept of the value of the garden site, and construct a personal cognitive situation. For example, through the local social status of the garden site, the visitors told others why Qing-yan Yuan was located in Huai'an, China, and expressed the function, value and significance of the site with the metaphor of "water transport official garden". From the selection of Qing-yan Yuan in Huai'an, its special position in the waterway of the Beijing Grand Canal as the key to flood control was found. On the whole, the garden integrates landscapes, flowers and trees, lakes and stones, inscriptions, pavilions and pavilions. The landscape is rich in content as it served as the office and living place of local officials during the Ming and Qing Dynasties and invisibly reflected the social status of Canal Governor-general. These significant functions of the place also enhance the symbolic significance of the water transport culture in Qing-yan Yuan. Therefore, landscape metaphor is a tool for people to express their personal thoughts. The public realizes the reasons for its construction from site selection and then to observation of the buildings and rocks in Qing-yan Yuan, and gradually form the value concept of cultural relics and establish personal cognition.

Conclusion

After summarizing, coding, and decoding landscape metaphors, different metaphors were found in personal interpretation of local cultural heritage. There are "originality metaphorical cognition", "functional metaphorical cognition" and "meaning metaphorical cognition". First of all, "originality metaphorical cognition" is the visitors' interpretation of the reasons for the construction of the Qing-yan Yuan. For example, "Huai'an Cao-yun Throat" represents the criticality of Qing-yan Yuan's geographical location, "Water Control Center" represents the background of the establishment of the Office of Government, "The Predecessor of Qing-yan Yuan" is the visitors' comprehensive understanding of the multiple identities of the ancient office building, " Canal Governor-general Designer" is a metaphor for officials' enthusiasm for garden construction. Secondly, "functional metaphorical cognition" is an understanding of the historical function of Qing-yan Yuan's space and place. For example, " Canal Governor-general Garden" symbolizes the leisure and relaxation of officials in the space, "Identity Level" is the architectural form and style of Qing-yan Yuan. It is a metaphorical expression of official social status, "Xing-gong Academy" not only expresses Qing-yan Yuan's reception of the emperor but also represents their sense of pride in Qing-yan Yuan in history, "Inscriptions on the merits" conveys the historical contribution of the Governor of the Canal and Taoism, "Famous Aspirations" is a method of expressing personal mood implicitly with the aid of landscape elements. Finally, "significant metaphorical cognition" is a vocabulary used by the visitors in the process of conveying the value of Qing-yan Yuan to others. For example, "connotation of Qing-yan Yuan" is a symbol that the experiencer gives to local culture and modernizes Qing-yan Yuan. "Water Control Museum" "Citizen Learning Garden" is an abstract concept formed by the experiencers after understanding the landscape elements, historical and cultural background in the garden, and the image of the site established for them. These metaphorical vocabularies, through the experiencer's continuous interpretation and use, as well as the interaction with other experiencers, provide a reasonable explanation for the existence of the ancient office building.

In short, in this study, the visitors communicated in the language during the process of observing and understanding the gardens of the government office, and used figurative vocabulary to obtain the story of the garden's past, and established a basic understanding of the value of personal cultural heritage. However, the research of this article is limited to the analysis of metaphorical vocabulary. In the future, it shall be possible to explore the preservation and reuse of heritage buildings from other theories, such as spatial symbols and experience economy to have a deeper understanding of the application of the relationship with the building.

References

[1] Zhao, M. Zhang, J. On the ancient Chinese government office gardens, Chinese Gardens, 2003, 4, pp. 73-76.

[2] Li, X. W. The Ming and Qing Government Buildings under the Hierarchical System. Anhui Architecture, 2012, 4, pp.12-38.

[3] Niu, S. J. Research on the Building System of the Office of the Government in the Ming and Qing Dynasties, Xi'an University of Architecture and Technology, 2003.M. Smith, "Title of paper optional here," unpublished.

[4] Zhao, X.P., Zhao, X. F., Zhang, H. Research on the characteristics of the architectural culture and protection strategy of the Northern Government Office. Innovation, Development and Harmony-Special Papers of the Second Annual Conference of Social Sciences of Hebei Province, 2008.

[5] Liu, D. Z. History of Ancient Chinese Architecture. China Construction Industry Press, 1984, p.423.

[6] Chen, L. Architectural Space and Etiquette Culture: An Interpretation of the Symbolic Function of the Song Dynasty Local Government Office. Journal of Southwest University: Social Science Edition, 2016, 42(5), pp.182-188.

[7] Antrop M. The concept of traditional landscapes as a base for landscape evaluation and planning. The example of Flanders Region，Landscape Urban Plan, 1997,38, pp.105-117

[8] Ma, X. B.; Cai J. W. The protection and renovation of Nanyang Government Office, 2005.

[9] Fan Y. J.; Chen J. Y. Discussion on the Preservation and Utilization of the Central Government Buildings in Beijing's Ancient Capital Style District. Collection, 2019, 6.

[10] Tian, L., Zhang, X. X. A Study on the Architectural and Cultural Implications of Taoist Office in the Qing Dynasty: Taking Qinghe Road Office as an example. Ancient Architecture and Garden Technology, 2016, 3.

[11] Turner, V., Mitchell, W. J. T. (1981). On Narrative.

[12] Polkinghorne, D. E. Narrative knowing and the human sciences. Suny Press,1988.

[13] Potteiger, M., Purinton, J. Landscape Narratives Design Practices for Telling Stories. J. Wiley & Sons, New York, 1998.

[14] Johnstone, B. 32 Discourse Analysis and Narrative. The handbook of discourse analysis, p. 635.

[15] Bakhtin, M. M. 1981, The Dialogic Imagination, 2001, p.250.

[16] Aristotle, W. R., Roberts, I., Bywater, F. Aristotle Rhetoric. Psychological Review, 1954, pp.224-253.

[17] Burke, K. A. Rhetoric of Motives, Berkeley and Los Angeles: University of California Press, 1969.

[18] Zhang, J. N.; Chi, Q. Y. Metaphorical Thinking and Chinese Classical Gardens. Guangdong Gardens, 2009, 31(2), pp.5-9.

[19] Luo, Y. M.; Song, X. L. Ingenious brush painting of gardens, poetry, history, beauty and god-Reading Hu Jialuan's "Renaissance English Poetry and Garden Tradition". Foreign Languages and Literatures, 2010, 27(3), pp.209-211.

[20] Jia, Y. Y. Piao, Y. J. Analysis of Metaphorical Design in Landscape Architecture. Agricultural Technology and Information (Modern Gardens), 2012, 3.

[21] Papathanasiou-Zuhrt, D. The Know-How Booklet for Cultural Heritage Operators, Ciberespacio, Madrid, 2012, p.36.

[22] Sauer, C. O. The morphology of landscape, Berkeley: University of California press,1925, Vol. 2, pp. 19-54.

[23] Feng, W. Landscape Narrative and Narrative Landscape—Reading "Landscape Narrative: The Design Practice of Storytelling", China: Landscape Architecture, 2008, (2), pp.116-118.

[24] UNESCO, Introducing cultural heritage into the sustainable development agenda， 2013. Accessed 30 November 2020. http://www.unesco.org/new/fileadmin/MULTIM

[25] Xia, J., Chiou, S. C. On the Preservation of Cultural Heritage from the Perspective of" Landscape". Architecture Science, 2016, (14), pp.29-53.

[26] Holtorf, C.; Williams, H. Landscapes and memories, 2006, p.235.

[27] van der Laarse, R. Gazing at Places We Have Never Been: Landscape, Heritage and Identity. The Cultural Landscape and Heritage Paradox, 2010, pp.321-328.

[28] Waxman, S. Correlative Neuroanatomy, Appleton and Lange, Stamford, CA, 1996.

[29] Sweller, J. Human cognitive architecture. Handbook of research on educational communications and technology, 2008, 35, pp.369-381.

[30] de Mendoza Ibafiez, F. J. R. Metonymy and cognitive operations. Defining metonymy in cognitive linguistics: Towards a consensus view, 2011, 28, p.103.

[31] Zhang, T. Translation and sublimation of metaphorical design in garden vocabulary. Young writer, 2015, 12.

[32] Zhu, Y. S. The West Garden of the Cao Canal Governor-generals in the Ming and Qing Dynasties, Chinese Landscape Ar- 1180 chitecture, 1994, No.1.

[33] Jia, J. Huai'an Qing-yan Yuan. History of Architecture, 2011, p.11.

[34] Cai, W. G. The Garden of Ming and Qing Dynasties and Its Compatible with North and South Cultures -- An Analysis of 1164 Qing-yan Yuan Garden Art in Huai'an City, China: Landscape Architecture,2019, No.6, pp40-44.

[35] Hu Z. L. Language, Cognition and Metaphor. Modern Foreign Languages, 1997, 4, pp.50-57.

[36] Downs, R. M., Stea, D. Cognitive maps and spatial behavior: Process and products, 1973, pp. 8-26.

[37] Wang, F. X. On the Expression of Artistic Conception in Chinese Classical Garden, Chinese Landscape Architecture,2004,20 1187 (6), pp.43-44.

[38] Wang, X. H. Nomenclature and Taoist Meaning of Jiangnan Landscape Architecture, Journal of University of Science and 1194 Technology Beijing, China (Social Science Edition), Vol.24 (3),2008, pp.164-168.

[39] Lakoff, G., Kövecses, Z. The cognitive model of anger inherent in American English. Cultural models in language and thought, 1987, pp.195-221.

Funding

This research was supported by the Program of Jiangsu Social Science Foundation Youth Project in 2019(No. 19YSC005), China. This research was supported by the project Program of Philosophy and Social Science Research in Jiangsu Universities in 2020(No. 2020SJA1765), China. This research was also supported by the Program of National Natural Science Youth Fund Project Approval in 2018(No. 51808249), China. This research was also supported by Chinese Ministry of Education Project Approval in 2019(No. 19YJA760055), China.

https://doi.org/10.1142/9789811238727_0079

The Construction of Traditional Non-Heritage Culture in Art Design Education — A Case Study of Fujian-Zhejiang Wooden Arch Gallery Bridge

Zhang Ke Yong

Xiamen Institute of Arts and Crafts, Fuzhou University
852 Ligong Road, Jimei District, Xiamen City, Fujian Province, China
Email: 513225630@qq.com

Abstract

As an intangible cultural heritage, Fujian-Zhejiang wooden arch bridge is an excellent example of the comprehensive embodiment of human settlements in mountainous areas of China. It positions itself as a traditional cultural symbol. We study the integration of traditional culture and design to enhance the theoretical and cultural emotions of the design works and understand the cultural characteristics and connotation of the design. The result helps the non-relic culture of the wooden crafts survive. In design teaching, a new attempt is proposed to train students with rich design ideas and strong practical operation ability, and a reference method and training method are provided for exploring the innovative way of art design education.

Keywords: Non-Heritage Culture, Wooden arch gallery, bridge, Art design, teaching

Introduction

Fujian and Zhejiang Province are located on the southeast coast. In the long-term historical development process, a large number of intangible cultural heritages and ecological folk cultures have been created and preserved as forming a spectacular and colorful cultural landscape of Fujian and Zhejiang. As a world intangible cultural heritage, Fujian Zhejiang wooden arch bridge was built by using exquisite technology as it is rooted in a mountainous area of about 200 kilometers from the south to the north. The way to properly combine the inheritance and development of traditional culture with modern design, technology, and business enhances the theoretical depth and cultural emotion of design works and makes the design more cultural characteristics and connotation. It also enables the intangible cultural heritage of the wooden arch bridge to inherit and the traditional intangible cultural heritage to glow with new vitality. From the perspective of design teaching, the teaching space teaching resources expand as the heritage allows the teaching to explore the combination of the art design and culture. Teaching activates the tradition with design innovation, ensures the interesting innovation of design teaching, and improves the traditional culture inheritance of art design, which can be described as "two birds with one stone".

Application of "intangible cultural heritage" in art design teaching

Intangible cultural heritage has been handed down for hundreds of years and recorded folk arts which are closely related to people's production and life. It is a cultural memory of "living" from generation to generation. In art and design, by understanding the rich historical themes, modeling features, technological processes, typical patterns, and other elements in intangible cultural heritage, teachers and students of different majors can open a window to Chinese traditional culture and art. This strengthens their confidence in the nation and culture and inspires their interest and love in Chinese traditional culture. The integration of intangible cultural heritage into the curriculum of design is beneficial to the existing teaching content and practice. It is important to inspire students to use different cultural elements and design symbols to express their design ideas. The development of the course of "intangible cultural heritage" project expands the teaching space, enriches the teaching content, and allows the teaching to "go out". The students purposefully use some traditional cultural symbols in their design works to express their understanding of design through recognition of traditional culture. The students rediscover, recombine and innovate the cultural symbols in traditional Chinese art to generate new inspiration in the collision of modern culture and traditional culture and to improve professional ability. At the same time, as the change of social environment impacts economic and technological development, intangible culture has become increasingly difficult. There is no time to delay the protection and inheritance. The traditional intangible cultural heritage needs to be integrated into the art and design teaching for establishing the basis for the inheritance of the "intangible cultural heritage" culture. The wisdom of the ancestors and the brilliant cultural heritage continues to remain as playing an important role. At present, the teaching course in the art design major of colleges and universities combines the basic theory and practice of intangible cultural heritage to which innovation workshops are added.

First of all, teachers lead students to design practices for intangible cultural heritage culture. By starting from regional culture through field investigation and data analysis, we comb out the most distinctive design methods for carrying out targeted design practice and eventually providing design majors. For example, students majoring in visual communication can refine, reorganize and innovate typical carving patterns and colors of traditional buildings to build a visual identification system for traditional buildings and develop cultural and creative souvenirs. Students majoring in the environment and architectural landscape design can apply it to their design and planning by analyzing and interpreting the structural process and layout of traditional buildings. Students majoring in product design can improve or develop new products with traditional cultural connotations through research on traditional building components and traditional appliances. The design innovation with regional intangible cultural connotation promotes the inheritance and development of intangible cultural heritage in the process of artistic design practice such as "teaching" and "learning".[1] Therefore, intangible cultural heritage is extended to the construction of urban architecture.

Summary of intangible cultural heritage of the wooden arch bridge in Fujian and Zhejiang

The wooden arch bridge in Fujian and Zhejiang belongs to a group of "the same historical and cultural group" in a series of heritages of "the same type with the same region". (Fig.1) The construction history of the wooden arch bridge in the region has been distributed from the Song, Yuan, Ming, and Qing Dynasties to the present. The arch bridge is made up of hundreds of straight trees, weaving, pressing, and biting. The process of building includes selecting a bridge site, building abutment, erecting arch frame, laying bridge deck, building Gallery House, and so on. The arch structure of the bridge body is the only one in the world. The arch frame includes the upper three seedlings, the general column, the large bent frame, the upper five seedlings, and the upper scissor seedlings. In the process of grasshopper leg and bridge plate seedling, all wood components are connected by mortise and tenon for "intersecting vertically and horizontally, inserting and pressing, supporting each other, and bearing the force evenly". On the bridge deck, an ancient and unique public building is formed by erecting a wooden structure corridor or a house or pavilion. It is characterized by "erecting a bridge on the river, building a corridor on the bridge, protecting the bridge with the corridor, and integrating the bridge and corridor". It is not only the living fossil of the Chinese wooden structure bridge but also shows the unique construction technology of wooden structure bridge in the history of the world. It is mainly distributed in the mountainous area at the junction of Fujian and Zhejiang provinces. Up to now, there are only over 100 historical heritages left in China. They are the cultural creations of regional production and living tradition. In the process of history, they have gradually absorbed and eliminated different cultural forms, and finally formed a building product with regional cultural characteristics. The unique style of the Langqiao building sets off the rich folk culture and the struggle history of farming life in Fujian and Zhejiang mountainous areas. It is a miracle of mountain residential buildings and an important heritage of the farming building. [2] In 2009, the "traditional construction technology of Chinese wooden arch bridge" represented by Fujian Zhejiang wooden arch bridge was selected into the first batch of UNESCO World Intangible Cultural Heritage list with the urgent need of protection. In 2012, 22 wooden arcade bridges in Fujian and Zhejiang provinces were included in the preparatory list for China's application for world heritage. (Fig.2)

Fig. 1 The structure of the wooden bridge.

Fig. 2 The picture of Shouning Luanfeng bridge.

Exploration of the Elements of "Fujian Zhejiang Wooden Arch Bridge" In Practice Teachinghelpful Hints

The traditional culture and technology of the wooden arch bridge are huge treasures. Combining modern technology and design as well as inheriting the technology and culture of the wooden arch is important. At this stage, the teaching course can be adopted in the art design major of colleges and universities. That is, the basic theory and practices of the intangible cultural heritage are integrated into the basic design course and the innovation of the intangible cultural heritage. In this way, students are encouraged to study "intangible cultural heritage". Among them, Professor Wang Shu of China Academy of fine arts, who won the Pritzker Prize, explored the practice module of the architectural basic design.

3.1 Practice I"Super light village project - temporary residential unit". (Fig. 3)

The goal of the project is to solve the housing shortage after the earthquake. It requires light and quick design. Wang Shu found the wood arch bridge technology to originate from the Northern Song Dynasty. Its light and efficiency have become a structure that facilitates the disaster victims to carry out their construction work. At the beginning of the course, through learning the development history, structural principle, construction technology, modeling characteristics, and other theoretical knowledge of "Fujian Zhejiang wood arch bridge intangible cultural heritage culture", students learn the traditional "mortise and tenon" structure. Students are divided into different groups to discuss the design plan. They need to explore and understand the mechanical structure of various materials by themselves. They are required to understand how the technical principle of the wooden arch bridge is combined with the construction technology of weaving, wearing, and bridging platform, which is applied to the student design course "super light village project".

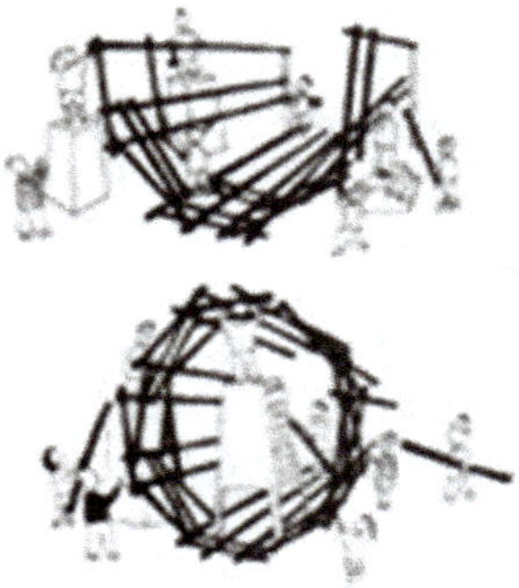

Fig. 3 The design sketch using the structure of the bridges.

At last, the connection of a considerable span is realized through small-size wood lapping, which is easy to disassemble and reuse. With a simple masonry method mixed with simple wood and steel structure, each temporary house is a "temporary building" that is composed of about 400 wooden bars, rivets, and wind hooks. The transparent organic board on the top floor protects the wind and rain. A unit is used for the life of four families. (Fig. 4)

Fig. 4 Completed residential unit.

3.2. Practice II;expert reception center of Xiangshan Campus of China Academy of Fine Arts (Fig. 4)

In 2013, the Xiangshan Campus expert reception center was completed. The roof of the whole building is covered by a large wooden frame roof. However, the large-scale wooden beams are not used but only the pinewood square of 60mm square, which presents the wood arch technology. The big roof of Xiangshan Campus, with a small wood section (Fig. 6), has realized a huge span. The bridge-building technology in the ancient painting "Qingming Riverside painting" (Fig. 5) a thousand years ago still plays a role in the modern architectural design, which makes people wonder about the huge potential of the traditional wood structure technology. When compared with the imitation of ancient buildings to the "shape" of ancient Chinese roof (Fig. 7), the inheritance and application of this combination of modern technology to the ancient wooden arch construction technology is an essential philosophical blood connection, which makes the ancient technology have new vitality in modern times. [3]

Fig. 5 Qingming Riverside painting.

Fig. 6 The big roof of Xiangshan campus made by using small wooden boards.

Fig. 7 A wooden roof.

In the course of Intangible Cultural Heritage Construction of the wooden arch bridge and the basic product design course, the students are required to observe, analyze, and understand the principle, material, structure, technology, technology and shape of the wooden arch bridge from different angles. The different connection ways of mortise structure of the wooden structure, refine, process are summarized and found. According to the mechanical properties and structural mechanics of the wood arch bridge, the structural connection law of the bridge needs understanding the material, material, structure, configuration, technology, technology, and shape for perfect unity. The designed structure supports people's expectations by using the old corrugated paper to create a new way of connection and a chair or bridge with a load-bearing structure.

3.3. Practice topic I: Corrugated "bridge" design, design and manufacture a certain span of "bridge"(Fig. 8)

This topic requires observing, analyzing, and summarizing the connection structure of the wooden arch bridge and expressing it in the form of a chart. The new connection mode effectively uses the law of wooden arch bridge with a clear connection purpose, proper material selection, and firm structure. Less paperboard is processed and formed, and the structure with a span of 50cm is designed to bear the weight of multiple bricks. The operation must meet the requirements of the subject, with novel creativity, beautiful shape, and excellent processing.

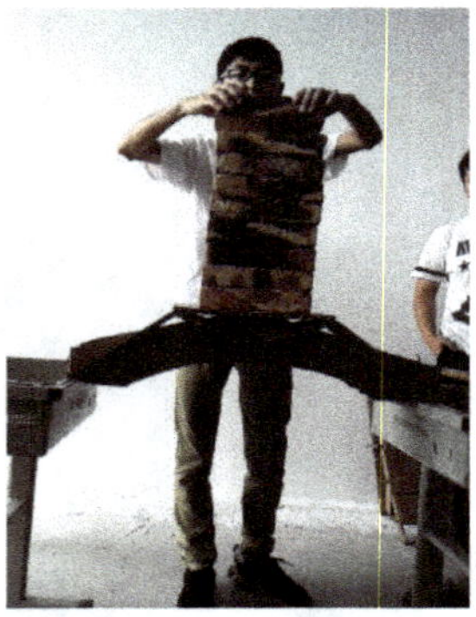

Fig. 8 Load bearing test of the paper bridge.

3.3. Practice topic II: cardboard seat design (Fig. 9)

The requirement of the topic is observing and analyzing the principle, structure, and technology of the wooden arch bridge. Its new structure combination is needed to be found after summarizing. The seat allows people to sit, lean, recline and rest. It should be easy to fold, carry and save space.

Fig. 9 A cardboard seat.

The above practical topics not only absorb and digest the experience of nature and predecessors, but also the nutrition of intangible cultural heritage by learning to create "other mountains and stones can be used to attack jade" instead of becoming a simple imitation and plagiarism. The concern and interest in traditional culture are maintained as the basic design with innovative significance and cultural connotation is the essence of the culture.

Conclusions

Colleges and universities are important to carry forward and spread Chinese traditional culture, and also the fertile soil to cultivate the survival of intangible cultural heritage. Through the research on the teaching of the cultural heritage of Fujian Zhejiang wooden arch bridge in art design major, this research provides the exploration for the innovative application and development as well as the inheritance and future of the cultural heritage of Fujian Zhejiang wooden arch bridge. Through the teaching of the "intangible cultural heritage", we fully inherit and carry forward the traditional Chinese culture. We also provide art design education of new connotations and forms. The ultimate goal of inheriting intangible cultural heritage is to integrate traditional culture into the design and help students rediscover and innovate the elements of traditional Chinese art and culture. This enables creative works as the new era concept. It is an effective means to cultivate excellent designers with artistic accomplishments, artistic potential, and artistic skills. Although there are some deficiencies in the teaching practice of Chinese traditional cultural symbols, we need to see the possibility of using traditional cultural symbols to spread the charm of the new era, as well as the valuable inheritance and continuation of intangible cultural heritage in the teaching of art design education in colleges and universities.

References

[1] The inheritance of art design education in Colleges and universities to Shanxi traditional architectural culture Huo Wen's sea of art, No. 12, 2017, pp116-117

[2] The cultural ecology of the wooden arch bridge in East Fujian from the perspective of regional culture zhangke yong Journal of Fuzhou University (PHILOSOPHY AND SOCIAL SCIENCES EDITION) 2017 issue 4 pp17-21

[3] The past and present life of timber arch structure technology Wang Guanyi, construction technology, 2017, issue 8 pp28-31

Fund Project

Fujian Social Science Planning Project in 2019, spatial environmental memory and cultural heritage and development of Fujian and Zhejiang wooden arch bridge, fj2019b120

https://doi.org/10.1142/9789811238727_0080

The Effect of Sustainability on Firms' Performance in the Fujian Garment Industry

Qian Yang[1,2*], Ming Li[3]

[1]Fujian Key Laboratory of Novel Functional Textile Fibers and Materials, Fuzhou, China
[2]Faculty of Clothing and Design, Minjiang University, Fuzhou, China
[3]College of Business, San Francisco State University, San Francisco, USA
[*]Corresponding Author Email: girlnox511@gmail.com

Abstract

Based on a six-area framework of competitiveness of GEM model, we surveyed 78 garment firms in Fujian (China) to rank environmental sustainability with a questionnaire of 36 questions. The findings from the statistical analysis show that environmental investments in surrounding infrastructure and green marketing (whether locally or externally) improves profitability in terms of cash flows among the competitive areas of GEM, while developing green products harms the profitability, at least within three years.

Keywords: sustainability, garment industry, GEM

Introduction

Sustainability has become a growing concern for society. The "short-term goals" of corporate are inconsistent with the environmental and social welfare of the public. Corporate sustainability means 'meeting the needs of a firm's direct and indirect stakeholders, without compromising its ability to meet the needs of future stakeholders as well' [1]. Sustainability comprises three dimensions: economic, environmental, and social. In this paper, we concentrate on the environmental sustainability issue that concerns the public mostly in the garment industry. Management strategies are different between companies. However, there are basic theories of strategic management. Porter [2,3] proposed a market-based-view framework of six areas to develop competitive strategies of a company. The success of management is measured based on the performance of a company on profitability and related accounting measures. We examine the relationship between sustainable investments and profitability based on these areas. Sustainability in all the GEM areas (Table I) suffices to provide a perfect framework to study how sustainability impacts the financial performance of a firm. In a survey, we embed environmental or sustainable issues around the GEM areas. Data collected in these areas are instrumental in analyzing the impact. We believe the approach is the first for the specific adoption of GEM areas in a sustainability study.

Environmental sustainability and Performance

A. Data

The data was collected through a survey on managers of 78 companies in the Fujian Province, China. Fujian is a major manufacturing hub of the clothing industry in China. These companies scatter around three major clothing clusters: Fuzhou, Quanzhou, and Xiamen in the province.

TABLE I
GEM MODEL OF FIRM COMPETITIVENESS

GEM Dimension	Area of Competitiveness	Code Number	Sustainable Theme of Questions
Groundings	Resources	1	Human and Financial Capital
	Infrastructure	2	Communication and Transportation
Enterprise	Suppliers and Supported Business	3	Supply Chain of Green Products
	Strategic Goals of Enterprise	4	Development of Green Products
Markets	Local Markets	5	Fashion Marketing
	External Markets	6	Fashion Marketing

The responders were asked to evaluate the status of environmental sustainability by answering 36 questions on the financial, statistical, and profile of firms. Each of the 36 questions represents one specific aspect of competitive areas in GEM. They cover six areas of the competitive advantages of a firm: resources, infrastructure, suppliers and supporting business, firm structure and strategic goals, local markets, and international markets. On each question, the responders were asked to rank the environmental or sustainable efforts from 1 to 10. Descriptive statistics were obtained upon the responses. Efforts of developing green products were surveyed in the fourth group, Strategic goals of Enterprise, while green fashion marketing is asked in the fifth and sixth group (Table I).

The survey also collected the financial performance of the firms, such as growth rates of sales and free cash flow (as profitability measurement). We investigate the impact of those environmental measures on the free cash flow (hence fore cash flow) of the firms. Free cash flow was defined as the sum of net income and depreciation minus the sum of the change in the net working capital and capital expense. Table II shows the basic statistics of the firms in the sample.

TABLE II
DESCRIPTIVE STATISTICS OF FIRMS (2016-2019)

	Number of Firm	Mean**	Standard Error**
Sales (millions of Chinese yuan*)	71	95.10%	11.90%
Average sales growth rate in past three years	71	8.66%	1.47%
Average profit growth rate in past three years	71	8.59%	1.43%
Average cash-flow growth rate in past three years	71	5.77%	1.45%

* In local currency, Chinese Yuan.
** Mean and standard error are estimated based on categorical ranges

B. Dimension reduction with factor analysis

We looked for the potential determinants among the surveyed variables of the performance of the firms. In the large set of survey questions, if there were overlapping concepts among the 36 survey questions, a reliable regression analysis would be impossible especially with a small sample size. Thus, we decided to reduce the number of survey questions to a smaller number of factors. We performed dimension reduction on each of the six groups with the principal component analysis to extract the factors out of the original survey questions. We selected a component as a factor variable when its eigenvalue was larger than 1. Table III summarizes the number of factors in each group and the explanatory power of the factors. Each of the extracted factors has a linear combination of the survey questions.

TABLE III
CHARACTERISTICS OF EXTRACTED FACTORS

Competitive Area of GEM	No.	Notation	Variance Explained	Survey Questions Represented
1.Resources	1	FAC1_1	86.99%	1-4
2.Innfrastructure	4	FAC1_2 FAC2_2 FAC3_2 FAC4_2	89.83%	5-11
3. Suppliers	1	FAC1_3	90.42%	12-16
4. Strategic goals of enterprise	2	FAC1_4 FAC2_4	78.69%	17-24
5. Local Markets	2	FAC1_5 FAC2_5	85.10%	25-31
6. External Markets	2	FAC1_6 FAC2_6	79.03%	32-36

C. Regression model

To understand how environmental measures impact the performance, we used regression analysis on the performance variables on the extracted factors. Since the performance variables (cash-flow growth rate) are categorical in design, it is appropriate to use an ordered logistic regression in which the dependent variable Y is modeled as the odds of probability falls into different categories with an ordered outcome of Z in N categories. We defined probability Pi as the cumulative probability of a dependent variable in a specific interval $i=1,\ldots,N$ where $P_i = P(Z \leq i)$ for $i = 1,\ldots,N$.

We modeled the log of the odds as the dependent variable of interest.

$$-y_i = log\frac{P(Z>i)}{P(Z\leq i)} = -\beta_{i0} + \beta_1 x_1 + \beta_2 x_2 + \cdots + \beta_k x_k, \quad (1)$$

where the dependent variable $-y$ represents the odds of increasing performance if Z is the measure of firm performance, such as cash flow. The independent variables include the extracted factors of survey questions on the GEM areas of competitiveness. To control for the effect of size, we added the size of the firm as an independent variable.

D. Regression of cash-flow growth

We ran the regression analysis of the growth rates of the cash flow as a measure of profitability. The growth rates were divided into the following three intervals: (-∞,-0), [0,20%], and (20%,∞). These intervals were presented in the questionnaires when we designed the survey.

A regression of the cash flow growth rate on the environmental sustainability of six GEM areas was conducted. Extracted factors were identified by the second subscript number, which corresponded to the GEM area number. According to the regression results (Table IV), some factors had a strong (positive or negative) impact on the cash-flow growth rate.

In the first set of factors from a GEM area- resources, the factors' impact on cash flows was undetermined since the estimate of its coefficient was statistically insignificant. Among the second group of GEM factors, two factors were statistically significant but with contradicting signs. One of the two factors, FAC2_2, corresponds to survey questions 6 and 8, while the other factor corresponds to FAC3_2 survey question 10. The coefficients imply that more green communication methods and more efforts of association in sustainability improve the firms' cash flow, while governmental regulations in environmental issues had a negative effect. The third group of GEM factor had only one factor. The impact of the factor on cash flow was negative as the factor was related to suppliers. The negative impact comes from higher costs to suppliers, which in turn passed onto the firms. In the fourth group, two factors contributed negatively to the cash flow. Since this group was mainly about developing green products and sales in the market, the investment in green products did not help cash flow increase. In the fifth and sixth group of GEM factors, all the significant extracted factors, FAC1_5, FAC2_5 and FAC2_6, had positive impacts on the cash flow. These factors were derived from the survey questions of the market size of green products and green marketing. They contributed to the cash flow increase.

TABLE IV (a)
LOGISTIC REGRESSION ANALYSIS OF CASH-FLOW GROWTH RATES ON EXTRACTED FACTORS(a)

		Estimate	Std. Error	Wald
Threshold	(-∞,-0)	-6.793	1.860	13.342
	[0,20%]	-2.320	1.507	2.370
Location	Size	-0.617	0.243	6.458

FAC1_1	-0.642	0.707	0.824
FAC1_2	0.635	0.611	1.080
FAC2_2	2.473	0.917	7.272
FAC3_2	-1.996	0.740	7.264
FAC4_2	-0.362	0.496	0.533
FAC1_3	-2.807	0.933	9.053
FAC1_4	-2.611	1.261	4.286
FAC2_4	-2.467	0.861	8.218
FAC1_5	1.886	0.870	4.702
FAC2_5	4.069	1.229	10.956
FAC1_6	-0.348	0.559	0.387
FAC2_6	3.367	0.991	11.538

TABLE IV (b)
LOGISTIC REGRESSION ANALYSIS OF CASH-FLOW GROWTH RATES ON EXTRACTED FACTORS

		df	Sig.	95% Upper Bound*	95% Lower Bound*
Threshold	(-∞,-0)	1	0.000	-10.438	-3.148
	[0,20%]	1	0.124	-5.273	0.634
Location	Size	1	0.011	-1.093	-0.141
	FAC1_1	1	0.364	-2.028	0.744
	FAC1_2	1	0.299	-0.563	1.832
	FAC2_2	1	0.007	0.676	4.271
	FAC3_2	1	0.007	-3.447	-0.544
	FAC4_2	1	0.466	-1.334	0.610
	FAC1_3	1	0.003	-4.636	-0.979
	FAC1_4	1	0.038	-5.082	-0.139
	FAC2_4	1	0.004	-4.154	-0.780
	FAC1_5	1	0.030	0.181	3.590
	FAC2_5	1	0.001	1.660	6.478
	FAC1_6	1	0.534	-1.442	0.747
	FAC2_6	1	0.001	1.424	5.309

*Confidence interval

Conclusion

We studied the implication of environment-friendly policies to the corporate profit among clothing companies. We adopted an ordered logistic regression to examine the statistical relationship between them. An environment-friendly infrastructure is beneficial to the sales and cash flow of the firms. Of course, the firms cannot accomplish such infrastructure. It needs either governmental support or large investment. The result indicates that green marketing improves profitability while developing green products as a strategic goal negatively impacts it. This leads to further study to find out a reasonable explanation.

Acknowledgments

The department of Fuzhou Science and Technology Bureau of Fujian Province supported this research: Research on 3D garment display technology based on human point cloud data and hololens (2019-G-58).

References

[1] Dyllick, T. and Hockerts, K. (2002), Beyond the business case for corporate sustainability. Bus. Strat. ssseszEnv., 11: 130-141. doi:10.1002/bse.323

[2] Porter, M.E., 1979. How competitive forces shape strategy. Harv. Bus. Rev. 57 (2), 137-145.

[3] Porter, M.E., 1980. Competitive Strategy. Free Press, New York.

https://doi.org/10.1142/9789811238727_0081

The Effects of Digital Board Game on the Social Sciences Learning Outcomes of Indigenous Fifth and Sixth Grade Students in Taiwan

Jen-Yi Chao*, Yin-Sen Chang, Yi-Hsin Yeh

Graduate School of Curriculum and Instructional Communications and Technology,
National Taipei University of Education, Taipei 106, Taiwan
Tel: +886 2 2732 1104 Ext. 55532, +886 918 2-53896 Fax: +886 2 2739-4270
*Corresponding Author Email: jychao@tea.ntue.edu.tw

Abstract

In general, indigenous students in Taiwan have worse learning results than regular students, especially in History. Indigenous students prefer dynamic, visual and situated learning, which can be designed as game-based learning. Therefore, this study aims to develop a digital board game to improve their learning results. "Brave across the Taiwan Strait" is a memory digital board game, which matches the historical events of the Qing Dynasty with Taiwan place name cards. We interviewed 7 experts to set up the appropriate instructive object and game mechanism. This game also references from the "Ziche Zocke" and includes a website, Augmented Reality (AR) and 3D printing technology.

This study was designed based on the pre- and post- test of single target group under the quasi-experimental standard. The target group was 40 indigenous students from two indigenous elementary schools in Yilan. Students had to complete the learning achievement test and learning attitude performance pre-test three days before, and take the post- test after the game. The results showed that through the evaluation of the learning achievement test and learning attitude performance in the post-test, the students showed significant learning improvement and learning effectiveness in understanding the Qing Dynasty playing this digital board game.

Keywords: Indigenous students, Game-based learning, Digital board game, Augmented reality, Learning effect

Introduction

This study comprises the partial research outcomes of the "Development and Implementation of a Teaching Platform for Indigenous Student CPS Spatial Conceptualization Learning Courses and Assessments--Main Project" funded by the Ministry of Science and Technology, Taiwan.

The aim of this study was to develop a digital board game on Taiwanese history for fifth and sixth grade elementary students, and to understand the effects digital board games have on the learning outcomes of fifth and sixth grade indigenous elementary students regarding the history of Taiwan under Qing rule.

Literature

A. The learning outcomes and learning styles of indigenous students

The learning outcome of indigenous students is one of the major focuses of education research in Taiwan [1]. Currently, Han culture dominates the domestic learning environment, whereas the differences between Han and indigenous cultures tend to lead to a number of issues, including the lessening of indigenous student learning motivation, thus resulting in poor learning outcomes, and ultimately lowering their opportunity to enroll in higher education and their competitiveness in the job market. Many complex factors may have contributed to the learning gap between indigenous and non-indigenous students, therefore it is difficult to discern the primary factors that have resulted in the differences in learning outcomes [2-3].

In order to effectively improve the learning outcomes of indigenous students and mitigate the learning gap between indigenous and non-indigenous students, the most urgent task was to understand the learning characteristics of indigenous students. According to domestic studies on the learning styles of indigenous students, five learning characteristics were deduced and summarized: (A) Indigenous students enjoy group work and less competitive learning environments, and are happy to share with their peers; (B) they prefer hands-on experiences and investigations or activity-based teaching rather than the mainstream instruction methods involving symbolic and abstract teaching; (C) they prefer utilizing their sensory abilities for learning, especially visual, auditory, and corporeal aided learning; (D) they prefer an informal and lively learning atmosphere; (E) they tend toward right-brain rather than left-brain thinking [4-5].

Gaps between the learning characteristics of indigenous students and the traditional instruction methods and Han culture-oriented education do exist, and oftentimes it is these gaps that have resulted in the poor learning performance of indigenous students. Therefore, research experts have suggested that when designing a teaching strategy for indigenous education, the learning characteristics of students should be taken into account [6], and teaching methods should be formulated based on how they learn best. Current literature on the learning outcome of indigenous students mostly concern subjects like languages, mathematics, physics and chemistry; the social sciences have on the other hand been less studied. Among existing literature of indigenous student social science education, it was found that Mei-Hue Lin [7] incorporated issues related to Atayal culture into the process of teaching the social sciences, and that teaching methods were formulated based on the students' learning styles and habitual modes of communication. It was furthermore discovered in this research that utilizing the action research of culturally responsive teaching could increase students' learning motivation for the social sciences and change their learning style; however, relevant learning outcomes were not specified in the study.

B. Game-based learning

Game-based learning is an innovative design method for teaching, the objective of which is to enable student learning through games. Professor James Paul Gee of the University of Wisconsin-Madison [8] proposed the concept of "gaming as learning," and suggested that aspects of learning hidden in games can serve to stimulate internal motivation for learning, which in turn generates pleasure during the learning process. When immersed in diverse and interesting gaming contexts, players are able to actively solve various challenges and problems encountered in the process of interacting with the game. New information is eagerly absorbed, thus achieving the effect of "edutainment" (education through entertainment) [9]. Western scholars refer to all game-based learning that combines digital technology as "Digital game-based learning (DGBL)," through which learners may acquire the specialized knowledge and fundamental skills in demand today [10].

Game-based learning can be utilized in a diverse number of applications. Judging from recent research publications, students' abilities to focus, acceptance levels, learning motivation, and learning outcomes were among the most common research variables in studies of game-based learning [11]. This also demonstrated that actual usage, mastery through practice, cooperative learning, and feedback immediacy were all factors that directly influenced whether learning outcomes showed improvement or not [12].

Game-based learning has the capacity to improve students' ability to focus as well as their cooperative learning and problem-solving abilities. Positive effects on elementary and middle school students' learning of languages, mathematics, and the natural sciences have also been observed, while the needs of special education have moreover been satisfied [13]. It was additionally found that the greatest level of improvement was exhibited in the learning outcome of social sciences. In comparison with the outcomes generated using general teaching methods, both the students' ability to focus and their learning motivation showed significant improvement. Students also acquired enhanced understandings of the theoretical and practical aspects of social sciences and could better distinguish historical events through improved capacities for logical thinking [14-16].

C. Incorporating digital technology with board games

"Chou shan you shi" (literally, "tabletop game") is abbreviated as "Chou you" (literally, "table game"). In English, it is commonly referred to as "table game" or "board game," and in Taiwan, "Chou shan you shi" refers generally to various types of games that have internal mechanisms and rules and can be played on a flat surface. Common board games include backgammon, Chinese chess, Monopoly, and poker. Nowadays, however, "board games" refer mostly to games from America and Europe, the majority of which are from Germany. As such, board games are also called "German-style board games."

In recent years, board games have been increasingly incorporated into flipped classrooms both domestically and abroad. Students are given the opportunity to engage in "heads on and hands on learning," thereby strengthening their learning motivation and facilitating their knowledge comprehension, memorization, and application [17]. Studies on the application of board games in educational design have discovered that in comparison with game "theme" or "art and accessories," the characteristic of "internal mechanism" carries higher learning potential [18] and make the game more entertaining and challenging. Players become fully immersed in the game and undergo a flow experience [19]. Therefore, the internal mechanisms of board games currently available on the market were referenced in this study and re-designed into a board game compatible with the social science learning content of sixth grader indigenous students.

Technological developments have brought more possibilities into board game design and plenty of board games on the market have already incorporated digital technology. Even though a wide range of innovative digital technologies are available for application, considering the scope and limitations of the study as well as the popularity of mobile devices (smartphones, tablets) and the convenience of their portability, mobile devices, in combination with websites, Augmented Reality (AR) and 3D printing technology, were selected as the basic components of game design. The game's information was delivered via multimedia on websites. Studies of the application of Augmented Reality in teaching have already been conducted, through which it has been found that AR does indeed help to achieve satisfactory learning outcomes while increasing student interaction and inspiring learning interest [20-22]. On the other hand, 3D printing has also been effective for the materialization of game accessories.

Research method

This study was a design-based research conducted using one-group pretest-posttest experimental outcomes and the collection of quantified data (including the "Learning Outcome Assessment" and "Learning Attitude Scale"). Two-sample t-tests for paired data analyses were carried out using the statistics software SPSS. The game and learning assessment developed during the study were examined, pre-tested, and tested for reliability by experts so as to increase the reliability for this digital board game and learning assessment.

A. Game content and method of implementation

A brief description of the conceptualization, content planning, and implementation of digital board game "Brave across the Taiwan Strait" is as follows:

(A) Game conceptualization: The gaming mechanism for "Brave across the Taiwan Strait" was modified after "Zicke Zacke" made by German's Swan Panasia, a memory-based game. Inspired by the mechanism of the hair-pulling sport, important historical events and historic concepts of Taiwan in the era under Qing rule were incorporated into the background structure of the game.

(B) Game content: “Brave across the Taiwan Strait” requires 2-5 players and about 30 minutes to play. The game design covers the historical developments of Taiwan’s early periods under Qing rule, including social infrastructure, the economy, developments in the liberal arts, and historic events. The game content include a map , historical event cards, geographic name cards , three kinds of resource cards, and four kinds of prop cards. Players can choose to play as one of the three ethnic groups: Zhangzhou Hokkien, Quanzhou Hokkien, or Hakka. The boats that represent the players are placed at equal distances and going clockwise starting from the youngest player, each player would pair each event card with a geographic name card. Players download the Aurasma APP onto their phones, which is then used to scan the event cards, and once the card is identified, players are shown a video on the event’s history and the geographic name. This enables players to verify whether they have made a successful pairing with a geographic name card.

If the paring was successful, then the player could move 1 block forward, turn the event card back to faced-down, and continue to turn the next event card. If the pairing failed, then the geographic name card was to be turned to faced-down and the round would be over, and the next player may make a move. The player who obtains all of the figures in the game is the ultimate winner. For more game rules and content, please refer to the website the digital board game developed in this study: chang3301.wixsite.com/mysite-1.

(C) Method of implementation: “Brave across the Taiwan Strait” was completed after six tests and modifications. An accompanying teaching flowchart was also created. (a) Introducing the digital board game and the game's background story. (b) Playing the tutorial explaining game rules. (c) Teaching how to scan event cards with tablets. (d) Start game (e) End game (f) Final review of historical knowledge. In particular, background information and the explanation of the rules were introduced through the digital board game’s website. Scanned game cards were created in conjunction with the Augmented Reality application, Aurasma.

B. Research subject

The main research subjects of this study were two tribal schools located in Nan’ao Township, Yilan County. Unlike other regions with mixed populations of both indigenous and Han peoples or those with significant levels of outward emigration [23], Nan’ao Township is one of the two only highland tribal regions in Yilan County with a settlement pattern more typical of highland tribes [24]. The subjects enrolled in School A and School B, respectively, and included a total of 45 fifth and sixth grade students. However, as School A and School B each had two students who were absent and did not participate in the post-test, and as there was one non-indigenous student in School A, five invalid samples were excluded. The total number of valid samples was 40, out of which 14 were from School A and 26 from School B respectively.

C. Research tools

The data collected for this study include that derived from: the "Learning Outcome Assessment Test" and "Learning Attitude Scale," the contents of which are briefly described below.

(A) Learning Outcome Assessment Test: The content of the digital board game developed for this study was designed based on analyses of textbook units on Taiwan under Qing rule sourced from various versions of social science teaching materials. During the designing process, course content and teaching goals were considered, and teachers were interviewed to discover potential difficulties and problems in their teaching experience. An assessment test with twelve questions was formulated, four of which are true-false questions and eight are multiple choice questions. Each question was worth 5 points, and the full mark was 60.

(B) Learning Attitude Scale: The three aspects of "Learning Attitude," "Effectiveness," and "Accessibility" from the "Post-game survey for game-style learning of history" compiled by Chen, Chin-Hung [25] were adopted. Without changing their meaning, the questions were adjusted to accommodate the content of the digital board game. The survey content was examined for expert validity by two social science teachers. After adjustments for expert validity, a formal scale was devised.Eight questions on "learning attitude toward history" (Cronbach's alpha = 0.92), five questions on "effectiveness" (Cronbrach's alpha = 0.82) and six questions on "accessibility" (Cronbrach's alpha = 0.85) were included for a total of nineteen questions in the Scale. The Scale was calculated according to the six-point Likert's scale for quantifying student learning attitude.The higher the total points, the more active and positive the student’s learning attitude was toward the social sciences.

Research result

Pre-test and post-test questions were identical for the "Social Science Learning Outcome Assessment Test." The pre- and post-tests were conducted at least three days apart to eliminate the influence of memory. By conducting sample t-test analysis, it was found that in the "Social Science Learning Outcome Assessment Tests" (Table 1), a difference of t-value 6.686 was exhibited between the students' pre- and post-test learning outcomes (p= 0.000<0.001), demonstrating a significant influence upon their capacities in social science learning.

TABLE 1
LEARNING OUTCOMES IN THE SOCIAL SCIENCES: COMPARISON OF PRE- AND POST-TESTS

Sample number	Mean value	Standard deviation	Standard error	t-value	p-value
pre-test (40)	24.38	8.857	2.374	6.686	.000***
post-test (40)	40.25	12.401			

***p<.001

Through analysis of the answers given for each test question, it was found that true-false questions were answered with higher accuracy than multiple choice questions in the pre-test, but after the implementation of digital board games, the accuracy rate for answering multiple choice questions increased significantly; in particular, the accuracy rates for answering questions 1, 4, and 5 increased to greater than 50%. Since multiple choice questions are considered to be appropriate for evaluating any social science knowledge objectively, these results demonstrate that the students did indeed learn the correct historical knowledge from the digital board game, and is therefore regarded as one of the indicators for assessing learning outcomes in this study.

Two-sample t-test for paired data was used to examine the pre- and post-test results in "Scale of Learning Attitude toward the Social Sciences," and a t-value of 2.594 was obtained for the pre- and post-test difference in students' learning attitude toward the social sciences (Table 2). There was a significant difference in their learning attitudes toward the social sciences between pre- and post-tests ($p= 0.015 < 0.05$).

TABLE 2
PRE- AND POST-TEST COMPARISON CHART FOR LEARNING ATTITUDE TOWARD THE SOCIAL SCIENCES

Sample number	Mean value	Standard deviation	Standard error	t-value	p-value
pre-test (40)	5.319	.693	.110	2.549	0.015*
post-test (40)	5.6	.515			

*p<.05

From the data above, it was discovered that "Brave across the Taiwan Strait" had immediate effect on the learning outcomes of indigenous fifth and sixth grade students in terms of mastering Taiwanese history.

Conclusion and suggestion

A. Conclusion

According to the statistics of the pre- and post-tests of "Learning Outcome Assessment Test" and "Learning Attitude Scale," the following can be concluded:

(A) Learning outcome: According to experiment results, it was found that use of the digital board game an immediate effect on the learning outcome of indigenous fifth and sixth grade students in terms of mastering the history of Taiwan under Qing rule. There was a significant difference in in their post-test grades for the "Learning Outcome Assessment Test." Since students' memorization and recognition of Taiwanese history and their learning of geographic names could indeed be strengthened, it can be inferred that digital board games can actually improve indigenous student learning of history as a social science.

(B) Learning attitude: As the experiment results show, the learning attitudes of all indigenous fifth and sixth grade students were improved after playing digital board games and achieved a significant difference.

B. Suggestion

This study recommends that those who are interested in conducting similar studies in the future divide indigenous students into experiment and control groups for their study and investigate if the learning outcomes of digital board game and traditional teaching methods differ in any way. The effect of digital board games on the learning attitudes of indigenous and Han students and whether the outcomes differ is also worthy of further exploration.

"Brave across the Taiwan Strait" is a social science-oriented digital board game designed according to the history of Taiwan in the era under Qing rule. We suggest that, in the future, researchers developing the application of digital board games in learning can apply the gaming mode of digital board games to other forms of social science content or other learning subjects.

References

[1] Y.C. Chen and T.M. Liu, "Educational Attainment and Urban/Rural Discrepancy: An Analysis of Spatial Cluster," *Journal of Population Studies*, Vol. 37, pp.1-43, 2008.

[2] K.T. Tan et al., *Multicultural Education*, Taipei, Taiwan: Higher Education, 2008.

[3] Y.S. Chou et al., "The Influences of the Application of Animation Teaching toward Aboriginal Students' Aesthetic Experience," *Educational Technology & Learning*, vol. 3, no. 1, pp. 1-24, 2015.

[4] M.H. Su, "Applying indigenous students' learning style on edu cation," *Journal of Internet Sociology and Communications*, n 0. 40. [Online]. Available: http://mail.nhu.edu.tw/~society/e-j/ 40/40-11.htm.

[5] H.Y. Chi and H.L. Liu, "The Learning World of Atayal Children in Elementary Schools," *Journal of National Hualien Teachers College,* vol. 10, pp. 65-100, 2000

[6] Y.S. Chou et al., "The Influences of the Application of Animation Teaching toward Aboriginal Students' Aesthetic Experience," *Educational Technology & Learning*, vol. 3, no. 1, pp. 1-24, 2015.

[7] N. R. LeMoine, "Language variation and literacy acquisition in African American students," In *Literacy in African American communities,* J. L. Garris et al., Eds. Mahwah, NJ: Hampton Press. 2001, pp. 169-194.

[8] J.P. Gee, *What video games have to teach us about learning and literacy.* NY, US: Palgrave Macmillan, 2003.

[9] K.C. Huang et al., "Design of Scientific Education Activities Based Upon the Game-Based Learning Platform," *International Journal on Digital Learning Technology*, Vol. 01, pp. 56-71, 2008.

[10] M. Prensky, *Digital Game-based Learning*. St. Paul, MN: Paragon House, 2007.

[11] L.W. Shih, "A Study of the Situation, Achievements and Issues in Game-Based Learning," M.S. thesis, Dept. Technology Application and Human Resource Development, National Taiwan Normal Univ., Taipei, Taiwan, 2013.

[12] Y.C. Lan, "The Design-based Research of Applying Game to Mathematics Remedial Instruction," M.S. thesis, Dept. Curriculum and Instruction Communication Technology, National Taipei Univ. of Education, Taipei, Taiwan, 2012.

[13] Y.S. Chang, "A design-based research on the effect of digital board game on the learning outcome of indigenous fifth and sixth grade students: using Taiwan under Qing rule as an example," M.S. thesis, Dept. Curriculum and Instruction Communication Technology, National Taipei Univ. of Education, Taipei, Taiwan, 2016.

[14] X.Q. Zhao, "Digital game-based learning study of learning history, attitudes and learning on junior high school students branches," M.S. thesis, Dept. Education, National Chung Cheng Univ., Chiayi County, Taiwan, 2011.

[15] J.H. Chen, "Development of A Time Scale-based Concept Map Historical Game-Based Learning--The Taiwan's Recovery History by Zheng Chenggong," M.S. thesis, Dept. Computer Science & Information Management, Soochow Univ., Taipei, Taiwan, 2013.

[16] C.F. Huang, and C.Y. Shen, "A Research of the Effect of Contest-Based Digital Games on Fifth Graders' Social Studies," Dept. Educational Technology, Tamkang Univ., New Taipei City, Taiwan, 2012.

[17] Yo Its 5 Pigs-European Board Game Workshop. "What is a 'bo ard game?" Accessed on: Dec. 12, 2011. [Online]. Available: h ttp://yoits5pigs.pixnet.net/blog/post/8930375

[18] C.Y. Liu, "A guide and mentra on board games for teachers." A ccessed on: Apr. 8, 2015. [Online]. Available: http://board-gam ification.blogspot.tw/2015/04/blog-post.html

[19] H.T. Hou, "Increase learning interest with play: expert advice on how to choose 'board games," *Parenting*, Vol. 60, pp. 208-211, 2014.

[20] Y.Y. Su, "Designing a Board Game for Elementary Science Teaching: A Case Study on the Learning Unit of "The Life of an Insect," M.S. thesis, Dept. Digital Technology Design, National Taipei Univ. of Education, Taipei, Taiwan, 2013.

[21] C.C Hsiao, "Designing Learning-Oriented Board Games: A Case Study on Disaster Precaution Education," M.S. thesis, Dept. Digital Technology Design, National Taipei Univ. of Education, Taipei, Taiwan, 2014.

[22] Y.C. Chen, "Designing a Board Game on the Endangered Wild Animals of Taiwan," M.S. thesis, Dept. Digital Technology Design, National Taipei Univ. of Education, Taipei, Taiwan, 2013.

[23] Council of Indigenous Peoples, *Report on Indigenous Education*, Taipei, Taiwan: Council of Indigenous Peoples, 2011.

[24] J.Y. Chao, "On the Development of Creativity and Cooperation Skills in Indigenous Elementary School Students during a LEGO Mindstorms NXT Course," *Journal of Educational Practice and Research*, Vol. 26, No. 1, pp. 33-62, 2013. doi: 10.6300/JNTNU.2003.48(2).03

[25] J.H. Chen, "Development of A Time Scale-based Concept Map Historical Game-Based Learning--The Taiwan's Recovery History by Zheng Chenggong," M.S. thesis, Dept. Computer Science & Information Management, Soochow Univ., Taipei, Taiwan, 2013.

https://doi.org/10.1142/9789811238727_0082

The Expressions of Design Inquiry

Wang Ye

Ph.D. Candidate in Tongji University, College of Design and Innovation, Shanghai, China
Email: 1710628@tongji.edu.cn, Tel: +86-136-818-09377

Abstract

In a field of design that is constantly being expanded and gradually involved in all areas of human experience. A strategy of inquiry will become a critical direction for the discipline of finding the problems instead of answering. The method is varied, but the outcome is the same. Through the discussion of the "reality" category, this paper analyzes the similarities and differences between the understanding of the design's inquiry method and the research methods. Combining Mckeon and Buchanan's research on the design of the inquiries, a deeper understanding of the inquiry method should be seen as a unified whole. Provide a certain path reference for design method research and practice.

Keywords: dialectic, art of persuasion, rhetorical inquiry, grammar, methods

Introduction

In a field of design that is constantly being expanded and gradually involved in all areas of human experience. A strategy of inquiry plays will become a critical direction for the discipline of finding problems instead of answering. The method is varied, but the outcome is the same.

The history of inquiry is the history of reforming the understanding of the term *Reality* (Fig. 1). Trees, rivers, mountains, buildings, vehicles that we can see, touch and recognize, this earth and the entire cosmos. That is the Reality of *Entitativity, as a pure entity*, the world we live in, to construct knowledge from the elements of the knowable [1]. All physical activity manufacturing takes place here, but not all the problems. As a Humanity, cognitive evolution determines the formula for acquiring and understanding the world. "Naturally", the process of knowing the Entity was segmented by cognitive limitations. Understanding is the first step when confronting complex objects, and the method of inquiry becomes critical. Resolve the problems encountered in the known in theory practice, and production to reconstitute the known in a new form [1]. In the reality of thought, the world we identify, every entity has a set of attributes that are necessary to its identity and function [2]. Epistemic, built on the limited understanding of perception and inquiry, present the known as products of the discrimination and activity of the knower [3]. That is *Existential* in the reality of thought. The "existence" comes from the *Latin* word *exsistere* meaning "to appear", "to arise", "to become", or "to be", the world we know. The forming process of an idea of *Existence* is meriting research, not to reinforce the shape but try to expand and dilute it.

Fig. 1 Category framework of the concept of "reality"

The complex objects from inquiry and cognition are not only a natural reality but also cultural complexes must have a real existence. That is Ontology in the reality of thought, the world we seek, assimilate the knowable to knowledge [1]. The word "*Ontology*" in Dictionary means a branch of metaphysics concerned with the nature and relations of being or a particular theory about the nature of being or the kinds of things that have existence[1].

In the inquiry of reality, practice and production are the main problems in the design of embryonic, and the solution led to further limited by the understanding of the elements of objects in the Entity word. The real problem has not shown yet.

The fragility of the design ability takes place in the world of imagination, where one invents and manipulates ideas and concepts instead of the real thing[4]. In such an inquiry, the problem comes from the design itself, considering that the understanding of the entity is from the elements of the knowable, but also in the experience of the designer's research of the physical world and the communication with the user. In The Liberal Arts is *Rhetoric*, a structure of Facts, art of persuasion and communication [5]. In the strategy of inquiry, that is Rhetorical Inquiry[4].

We must not forget that as the depth of inquiry becomes vast and sophisticated, Rhetoric faces a problem, provided disciplines applicable to facts by isolating structures of facts; those structures do not become more complex and challenging as facts become numerous. Examines inventions in the humanities and discoveries in the sciences are needed, an new Rhetoric [5]. In the Liberal Arts is *Grammar*, an art of interpreting language, experience, actual verbal usages. However, with problems, Use of footnotes to recover meanings familiar to the artist does not always contribute directly to uncovering of values in his art [5]. In the strategy of inquiry is *Design Science*, seeking the basic elements combined and synthesized to yield the world of experience and the cognitive processes of designing and decision making[4]. Provide the discipline for interpreting the structure of statements and experiences in arts, sciences, and societies are needed, an new Grammar [5]. In the Liberal Arts is Logic, a Structure of Methods of Inquiry and Proof the achievements of men in appreciation. However, the problems of the social sciences and the humanities may not easily become intelligible and solvable when the scientific method is applied to them [5]. In the strategy of inquiry, that is *Productive Science*, focuses on the discipline of making, within the framework of products and their use, or Poetics—from "*poeisis*" the ancient *Greek* word for all activities of human making, and from *Aristotle's* specific use of the term for the science of made -things or the artificial [6].

Fig. 2 The Strategy of Design Inquiry form Buchanan

A new Logic is needed, provide the discipline for examining the structure of consequences in processes and discourse, a Structure of Systems of Knowledge and Action individuality. In the Liberal Arts is *Dialectic*, the art of systematization. But degraded to an ideological and schismatic, often expressed as a need for a common frame of reference for all men, all cultures, or all knowledge, no preserve the pluralism of frames that made possible the advances in knowledge, in culture, and in community which have constituted mankind a common frame of reference [5]. In the strategy of inquiry, that is Dialectic, explain design and the products of design within a larger whole or system (Fig. 2) [6].

The Essentialist intuition

Moholy Nagy discusses the nature of design in the reality of Essentialist, to resolve the problems encountered in the known and reconstitute in a new form, define it as Complex Objects. In the article Design Potentialities, published in Design in Motion, the inquiry begins with Louis Sullivan the statement of Form Follows Function as a Principle. Apply one to the phenomenon in nature, every process has its necessary form, which always results in functional forms [7]. The Nature principle when translated into human technology seem falls very far short of the optimum. The reason may come from the knowledge and practice, and the ability to reason and grasp [7]. However, the inquiry was not extended to the process of cognition (or reasoning) and the ability to choose, but the essence of the problem. By explore the influence of materials, tools, and techniques on the form of artifacts while also pointing to another problem that new production technologies, such as assembly lines, was not created a new age that may change the status. The pretentious goal of the novel form Materials and Manner rotates around the creation of the resulting alternatives, rather than finding new features, new meanings, or new possibilities.

Further conclusions show that the answers are not always easily described or rationalized. The emergence of alternatives might bring difficulties to appear before the design is complete and loss of choice. When after finding the problem and attempting to decompose logically inferring, Nagy synthesizes the elements that have been analyzed and perceive the interrelationship to finding the Functional Elements. The answer comes from the intuition of the designer, The Artist`s Role [7]. The word "intuition" that Nagy used means insight, sensitivity, the guides for structure, proportion and form. However, it will take a long time for such new ideas to be accepted.

Although, discover the form, manner, material, and function of the cause, take the logic strategy to understand the phenomena to integrate and find the functional elements. That is the method of Problematic, the art of Poetics, the strategy of Productive Science, inquiry by resolution and questions dependent on discoverable causes. It also has problems from the strategy which mistakenly believes that the scientific method will make the social sciences and the humanities intelligible and solvable, thus ignoring the functional elements of society and humanity, especially those that are illogic [1].

One remedy against this is the conscientious training of a new generation of producers, consumers and designers who have grasped the importance of the basic relationship of "form and function."[7]

The one that the conscientious training must have a process from the search for design activities or the search for physical objects. The reason why designers being limited by knowledge and practice, as well as the ability of reason and grasp and the social implication in the process, was not considered to be the locus of the Essence inquiry.

Existential Combination

Herbert Simon discusses the nature of design in the interpretation of *Existential*. We must be clear that the interpretations of Existential and Essentialist are *Phenomenal*. The latter resolve problems by seeking properties and cause which are natural functions or acquired conditioning, the former discriminate statements and meanings which may be used to produce knowledge or attitudes or satisfactions [1]. We may see the different methods, *Logistic* in the strategy of Grammar and *Problematic* in the strategic of Poetics, the common require methodological procedures for different problems or subject-matters, each with Its own indemonstrable first principles and univocal definitions, this is *Particular* methods [1]. Similar to Nagy, Simon recognizes products and processes as an intricate component and having the potential to be influenced by the elements that underline. In the article *Problem Forming, Problem Finding, and Problem Solving in Design*, Simon scientifically examines underline elements that shape design and the methods in which the selected ideas, processes, and objects that can exist. He focuses on fining and forming the properties and implications that behind those issues.

At the beginning of it, Simon made a subjective review of the design by identifying Terminology. He perceives the value of analysis and synthesis in design action as Nagy, both aware of the impact of design choices on design conclusions. Although, He noticed the design action is trying to *find an acceptable solution* that *can be realized.* Also, the difficulty of design experience in choosing alternatives, one always starts with some components that *can be produced.*

Though Darwin's research, Simon found the underline elements in the design active: *Combinatorics* [8]. However, there always are unexpected alternatives that be foreseen. The problem lies with the designer's choice in the analysis and synthesis from the process of gathering and processing information in the brain.

By combining the index of cognitive science, Simon finding others underline elements that influenced design action: *limited information, limited memory,* and *limited computing power*. Moreover, the design is the game of Combinatorics those *Primitives*[9]. Further analyzing the structure of these signals that have found forming a critical conclusion. While the process of giving meaning base on what could be known, then not only do alternatives emerge in the course of the design process, but the design goals emerge also [8].

The "logic" is presented in terms of Language and Experience. Simon interpreting actual verbal explains keywords, such as synthesis, analysis, choice, alternatives, primitives, combinatorics, with strong subjective expressions. He is "talking" to the audience alternately tracing consequences in statements, thoughts, and processes like the art of Poetics/Logic in Nagy`s, the inquiry by resolution and questions dependent on discoverable causes. With the help of these signs and symbols, Simon drawing a map of the designer`s cognitive process and forming and finding the underlying elements of the problem. These constitute meaningful conclusions. That is the art of interpretation knowledge, a strategy of *Grammar*, a *Science*, use *Logistic*, proof by construction and decomposition dependent on indivisible elements. It also has problems from the strategy which mistakenly believes that using *footnotes* is the best way to recover meanings familiar, thus deviating from the values behind signs.

Synthesis symbols of limitation and causes of cognitive processes, those limited by the knowledge, practice, and the ability to reason and grasp, seem Design issue is powerless. Even so, however banal the primitives, novelty - even admirable novelty - can emerge out of this combinatorial process [8]. Still, the impact of the alternatives produced and the choice active in the process of design inquiry, as well as the perceived flexibility of such seemingly inevitable crises, is determined to be the inquiry focus and does not explore the meaning of these novelties.

The Entitativity Imaginative act

Horst Rittel discusses the nature of design in the reality of *Entitativity*. In the article *the Reasoning of Designer*, he saw the widespread dissatisfaction with our ability to design *the worlds we live in.* Moreover, by interpreting the scope of the entities design, one seems to get deeper into all the field of human experience and seems to be unmanageable. What Rittel tries to make an opinion that the future of design can only be seen in this series of actions by studying the specific commonalities that may exist.

Those are Facts, and Rittel at the beginning of the article explains the conditions, behaviors, and problems that arise in the design and physical world. In the search for specific commonality, we can easily find the performances of designers in think before act. Those are Situations or Phenomenon. Based on them, Rittel tried to convince and pass on the understanding and perception of those facts. Design is plan making that takes place in the world of imagination, in order to create ideas and concepts for the upcoming reality and to be prepared [4]. To explore the possibility that in the case of intentional, purposive, and goal-seeking actions called *disorder*, the effective and only way that Rittel *relies on Reasoning*. Those are *Opinions*, induce by arguments that lead to agreement, but not Submission or Hypnosis.

Unlike Nagy and Simon, "logic" in there is not the sense of a formal logic, but as a certain way of reasoning, a "philosophy" guiding mode of conduct [4]. Rittel explains the special meaning of "Reasoning" and the description of its process phenomena and thus the renewed meaning.

The situation that Rittel depicts an idea of the "whole" resolution that the designer has at the beginning of the design process is another perspective trying to portray this problem. He focuses on the Functional Elements that have "an idea", intuition in synthesis; unlike Simon, Rittel focuses on the "an idea" formed in the combinatorial process. Rittel was converging on "an idea" that *already have* and the one communication with the entity world which will probably re-adjust it.

Those Facts are aware of difficulties and instability in the selection process. Also show that all deliberations terminate with judgments, a "Cognitive Style". Must be clear that it is different from the Existentialistic. For the former, the entity does not change, the individual and the way of interpretation is changed; the latter, the result of the feeling is the entity that is combined after analysis, a subjective existence. Rittel tried to introduce a new argument that the persuaded or convinced may be the key under the situation of Design action that happens in the world of imagination, a more representative example to convince understanding.

To clarify this Opinion, he analyzed the elements of the complicated. The search has not been turned into process and structure, but a state evaluation of essential factors behind it and a speech for new possibilities. Though, unlike Simon's "talking", *an art of Persuasion* attempting to prove new arguments using arguments adapted to existing opinions. That is methods of *Operational*, a strategy of *Rhetorical Inquiry*, one focuses on communication and the imaginative power of the designer [6].

It has problems from the strategy which to isolating structures of facts to become more numerous, somehow, which avoids the multiple influence factors and ignores the more comprehensive whole and details. Rittel explored the way of reasoning through facts in the presentation clues of the impact between the entity and the design. Yet, the concerns of Nagy and Simon about the problems that arise during the reasoning process may reform the idea. A Holistic Systems view is needed.

The Ontological Dialectic

Raymond Williams discusses the nature of Design in the reality of *Ontological*. In the article *Dominant, Residual, and Emergent* included in *Marxism and Literature* in 1977, Williams is devoted to the discussion of culture and systems to points out the common problem of disconnection of reality. Culture discussion should not be reckless into Epochal analysis and Static but *Staged* in historical[10].

Social impact and Novelty also appear in the inquiries of Rittel, Simon, and Nagy, but the difference is that Rittel discusses Culture and Novelty only in the reality of Entitativity and Facts of Persuasive Communication. Nagy discusses Culture and Novelty only in the reality of Essentialist and intuition in the design action.

Simon discusses the Culture and Novelty in the reality of Existential and interpretation knowledge. Similar to Williams' analysis of culture, Simon sees the design process as a temporal flow, a continuous sequence of decisions with a past, a present, and a future [8, p. 255], It is not a static functional element but a historical internal connection. Moreover, in some design objects, there seem to be more possibilities for action, like buildings, cities, and institutions that have long lives. The same situation also occurs in the inquiry for novelty.

Although there is no honest discussion on the Nature of Design, Williams' attempt to explore the Culture and Novelty also affect design as an essential element while reflecting the lack of design exploration in a new perspective in the context of Culture and Novelty. Williams began experimenting with culture as a larger whole or system by breaking it down into elements of alternative or oppositional relationships.

Culture on the path of the times must have the current *Dominant* power, effectively seized the ruling definition of the social, leading and producing certain forms, meanings, and values [10]; *Residual*, an element of the past may alternative or oppositional form Dominant, as effectively formed in the past, but it is still active in the cultural process and an active element of the present [10]. A future continues to be created: *Emergent*, new meanings and values, new practices, new relationships and kinds of relationship are continually being created, and Emergent in the strict sense, rather than merely novel [10].

Those are Elements (or Moments). Williams seeks Holistic Systems through individual exhibitions and dialogues between them. However, the focus of inquiry is different from Simon or Nagy in the process and specific issues, but trying to see the meaning of the culture itself produced by the relationship, the Unifying Ideas. And we can see through it to the nature of Design, see an idea that was co-founded by Moholy Nagy, Herbert Simon, and Horst Rittel. This is a method of *Dialectical*, the art of *Systematization*. The system it sought was not merely an ordering of things in a universe, but an ordering of things, thoughts, and symbols in a cosmos [5], a strategy of *Dialectic*, one focuses to explain design and the products of design within a larger whole or system [6]. It has problems from the strategy which has been easily *graduated*.

With its help, we can now compare and analyze the reasons for the separation and the necessity of existence. More importantly, the mutual support and supplement generated by the exchange of independent contexts makes the Strategy of Design inquiry an idea of whole.

Conclusion

We are aware of the strategies of analysis and inquiry from different contexts in the discussion of the field related to the nature of Design. While this should be seen in the problems revealed, we may not merely attribute the inquiry strategy and the problems faced to a unique scientific method or principle; we should see that the knowledge of the Entitative world that design expressions should be decomposed into multiple dimensions, not merely split and remain independent, not one-sided but whole, through it, inquiry will be able to respond from biological, psychophysical and sociological requirements. We cannot separate the inquiry strategy into disciplines, but try to see the mutual complementation and opposition of the standard extensions behind the differences and the continuous evolution of the goals. We must see the true meaning of form follows function.

The only way to inquire complex objects is to start from a further comprehensive imagination of the structure, to improve and change the analysis and synthesis of specific problems. Only then, in the flexible thinking of the inquiry can get the "right choice" in the seeking of complex objects in the Emergent of many alternative and new goals, not just novel.

References

[1] H. A. Simon, "Problem Forming, Problem Finding, and Problem Solving in Design," in *Design & Systems: General Applications of Methodology*, 1995, pp. 245–257.

[2] H. W. J. Rittel, "The Reasoning of Designers," in *The Universe of Design: Horst Rittel's Theories of Design and Planning*, 2010, vol. 9780203851, pp. 171–179.

[3] M. Nagy, "Design Potentialities," in *New Architeclure and City Planning*, Paul Zucker, Ed. New York: Philosophical Library, 1944, pp. 675–87.

[4] R. Buchanan, "Strategies of Design Research: Productive Science and Rhetorical Inquiry," in *Design Research Now*, R. M. Zurich, Ed. Birkhäuser Verlag AG, 2007, pp. 55–66.

[5] R. McKeon, "Future of the Liberal Arts," in *Freedom and History and Other Essays: An Introduction to the Thought of Richard McKeon*, Chicago: The University of Chicago, 1990, pp.273-282.

[6] R. McKeon, "Philosophic Semantics & Philosophic Inquiry," in *Freedom and History and Other Essays: An Introduction to the Thought of Richard McKeon*, Z. McKeon, Ed. Chicago: The University of Chicago, 1990, pp. 242–56.

[7] R. McKeon, "Rhetoric and Poetic in the Philosophy of Aristotle," in *Aristotle's Poetics and English Literature,* E. Olson (comp.), Chicago, 1965, pp. 201-236.
[8] R. Williams, "Dominant, Residual, and Emergent," in *Marxism and Literature*, Oxford University Press, 1977, pp. 121–127.

https://doi.org/10.1142/9789811238727_0083

The Ideals and Predicaments of Promoting Regional Revitalization Through Temple Cultural And Creative Industry — Case Study of the Sihu Haicing Temple

Chi-Chen Ho[1], Shyh-Huei Hwang[*2]

Graduate School of Design, National Yunlin University of Science and Technology, Douliu, Taiwan
[*]Corresponding Author: Email: [1]hocc@yuntech.edu.tw, [2]hwangsh@yuntech.edu.tw

Abstract

From the discussion and writing of the local creation and development plan of Sihu Township in the past year, it has been discovered that local economic and social problems have become increasingly serious due to industrial decline and population aging. How to co-create value with localities and develop a sustainable circular economy in economic and cultural capital is full of problems and difficulties. However, local temples still have a rich value to society. With the Yunlin Sihu Haiqing Palace as the case study object, cultural and creative development models of palaces and temples were to promote local creation in cultural and creative industries. This study uses document analysis, case study, in-depth interviews, and a focus group method to (1) analyze the content and characteristics of the cultural and creative industries of palaces and temples, (2) explore the role of cultural and creative industries of palaces and temples on local creation, and (3) explore the types of difficulties encountered when working with palaces and temples to promote local creation. The results showed as follows: (1) the characteristics of the cultural and creative industries of palaces and temples on the foundation of religious beliefs are closely related to folk prayers and serve the believers while making profits with a tendency to develop land; (2) the investment helps local creation but has the risk in business ability and style; (3) the dilemmas faced by the self-investment of Gongmiao and the ideal of local creation include the management committee's unclear mission recognition with limited vision and ability, and local politics network.

Keywords: palace and temple culture, cultural and creative industries, regional revitalization

Introduction

According to statistics from the Ministry of the Interior, the number of temples in Taiwan reached more than 12,000 in 2013, a record high over the years, and even more than the number of supermarkets. This shows that the religion of the folk beliefs in Taiwan affects the people significantly. The degree of influence, the effectiveness of the temple, the number of faithfulness, and the prosperous incense, have become a part of the cultural life circle that cannot be ignored. If it attracts more believers to worship, it also has considerable human and financial resources.

Through belief and cultural life circle, consumer behavior is understood in the life circle. The cultural image of the place increases the number of local tourist visitors of Four Lakes, completes a local cultural brand, and uses cultural marketing as the promotion of cultural characteristics..The purpose of this study is as follows:

(1) Analyzing the content and characteristics of the palace and temple cultural and creative industry.

(2) Discussing the role of palace and temple cultural and creative industries on local creation.

(3) Exploring the types of difficulties encountered when working with palaces and temples to promote local creation.

Literature

The relevant documents related to this research were searched and analyzed to understand the connotation of cultural creation of palaces and temples, explain the process of localization of cultural creations of palaces and temples, and analyze related cultural industries and local creation strategies and models.

A. Temple culture

Folk beliefs are transmitted from past beliefs and cultures as having temple beliefs as a part. In the definition of folk beliefs, Feng proposed that folk belief is a system of ideas from generation to generation, a spiritual phenomenon that has been practiced for a long time, and a spiritual activity derived from social activities [1]. For example, Taiwan's folk beliefs have been influenced by the three most important religions, Buddhism, Taoism, and Confucianism as the basic forms. Zheng proposed that the folk beliefs accumulated in the lives of the people belong to the spiritual activities of the people in the field of beliefs [2]. They provide spiritual support and activity guides for interpersonal activities on which their lives are based. Activities are formed in free development. Folk beliefs are indeed related to people's living habits. For example, Taiwan's folk beliefs and traditional industries are closely related. The past agricultural customs and beliefs cannot be separated from each other. As Taiwan has moved towards an industrial and commercial society in recent years, agricultural customs are not as complicated as in the past, but folk belief organizations and activities have stayed as they have been.

B. Definition of temple culture

Religious belief is still a controversial issue. People with beliefs hold different positions and perspectives. When comparing different religious beliefs and behaviors and spreading out the different developmental histories of human beings and social culture, it is not difficult to find the basic similarities and differences in human religion and learn the difference between beliefs and social culture. Folk beliefs are the result of continuous evolution and the gradual integration of believers and culture. Faith reveals a lot of artistic beauty. The architecture and sculptures of building temples, traditional performing arts, and sacrificial acts are full of the inheritance of beliefs and culture. Culture and society are interdependent. With the continuous evolution of social development, folk beliefs constantly adapt to society. Folk beliefs changes with the development of society.

C. *Locality of the temple culture*

As the folk belief culture has been passed down from ancient times to the present, it needs to be preserved and continued through cultural inheritance. Cavalli-Sforza and Feldman defined cultural inheritance as a universal model of human behavior in Cultural Transmission and Evolution [3]. Behavior and its related things are manifested in the inheritance and accumulated thoughts of the previous generation, and then through the transmission of knowledge and value all of which affect the thoughts and behaviors of future generations. Culture changes with time and background. The culture at present is not immutable and copied from the past. Through the accumulated culture, transmission from the ancestors let life unintentionally integrate into society. The elements are more related to folk beliefs in three perspectives that communicate and influence each other: folk beliefs, life, and culture. They influence society and gradually merge, and a balance is achieved in them.

D. *Cultural and creative industries*

Definition of cultural and creative industries

The cultural and creative industry is mainly based on cultural marketing for cultural and creative products, historical and cultural knowledge, and so on. Different forms and services are needed for cultural marketing and promotion. The term "cultural marketing" is the conceptualization, pricing, promotion, and sales of goods or services based on the American Marketing Association's definition of marketing. Through various procedures, it creates a way to satisfy individuals and organizations [4]. When compared to commercial marketing, social marketing is a method of marketing principles and strategies that have influenced the target masses to change social policies and accept rejections [5]. Social marketing based on marketing principles tries to change the opinions and ideas of the public and promote social development through marketing strategies. Cultural marketing is based on the concept of commercial marketing that is positioned as a marketing technique of art or cultural creation products.

Relevance of cultural and creative industries and temple culture

The cultural industry and the temple culture jointly developed the religious creative industry and extended the cultural creative industry. The religious-cultural creative industry is based on the cultural creative industry. Su defined that the cultural industry should have two characteristics in a broad sense to appeal and be profitable [6]. The religious-cultural creative industry based on religious consciousness creates economic value and has an economic scale industry by religious culture. Li stated that the concept of religious cultural creative industries should include four different categories: religion, culture, creativity, and industry. The concept of each has different connotations and objects from the perspective of religious education [7].

E. *Local creation*

Definition of local creation

The local creation was originated in Japan. It is based on three perspectives such as production, region, and people. Through the combination of geographical characteristics and cultural customs, suitable industries can be developed in various regions. According to the definition of the National Development Commission of Taiwan, the rural areas in Taiwan have cultural connotations with their unique cultural landscapes, industrial history, and inheritance craftsmanship. They promote the characteristics of local resources through innovation and creativity and other planning. The industrial method is used to add value to create an atmosphere different from the past but retains the traditional things of the former stockholders and the landscape aesthetics shapes the local image.

Relevance of local creation and cultural creation of palaces and temples

Li and Cai defined the religious-cultural creative industry as "Based on the content of religious culture, it is a cultural industry that can be created, produced, economically performed, cultural trade and sustainable operation, and protected by intellectual property rights." [8]. Lu proposed the development of cultural industry under the brand vision as thinking based on low-carbon transformation which cultural consumption requires consumers to have higher cultural literacy based on the higher spiritual culture of consumers [9]. The cultural and creative industry has still room for growth and has changed the type of traditional industries. If the content of religious culture is combined with the cultural and creative industries, it becomes a comprehensive industry that integrates traditional culture, reverses traditional industries, and changes the traditional industry type, but retains the traditional religious culture. Through the innovation and creativity of cultural development, it continues to develop in the cultural and creative industry.

Belief and culture are not limited to spiritual values. Combining religious beliefs and culture with creative business models transforms them into goods or services with economic value as a part of the cultural and creative industry. Zhu *et al.* believed that the cultural industry is emerging with creativity as its core, and has the characteristics of originality, integration, and high relevance to the industry [10]. It should be promoted through the integration of the cultural industry. Relevant religious industries such as the business circle extended by the temple culture can be integrated into the cultural creative industry, and the value and cultural creativity in the cultural creative industry can be established.

Methods

A. Document analysis

To understand the connection between local creation and the cultural and creative business model of palaces and temples, the literature analysis method was used to explore the factors of the connection between the two, and to analyze and sort out the necessary conditions for a successful business model. Through the collection, analysis, and research of the literature, the required information was collected from an objective perspective and systematic description of folk belief culture, cultural marketing, and palace culture creative business models. Related books, master and doctoral dissertations, journal papers, and other materials were used to analyze the successful business model of palace cultural creativity.

B. Focus interview

To conduct an in-depth and clear interview for the successful cultural and creative business model of the temple, respondents were invited to an equal and non-pressured environment. Through interviews, they proposed the successful model of the palace cultural and creative industry and the conditions and factors as reference materials for the research.

C. Case study

The creation plan for four lakes in Sanjolun was a case to clarify the problem to explore feasible solutions. The key factors as the basis of this research were found in the cultural and creative industries of palaces and temples and local creation.

Results and Discussion

A. Case analysis and problem

<u>Origin of the plan</u>

Su Junhao, the deputy chairperson of Yunlin County, was a native of Sihu. He felt that the local population was aging and the industry was declining. He hoped to inject vitality into the locality and revive the industry through a group of enthusiastic seaside youths and young farmers. It was an urgent task for young farmers and entrepreneurs to find a suitable sales platform.

In June 2020 together with Li Mingyue, Director of the Planning Office, Su Jinzhi, Chairman of the Haiqing Palace, and Su Guolong, the mayor of Sihu Township, held a local creation work coordination meeting in Haiqing Palace. At the same time, they visited the area around the Haiqing Palace to find a platform for sales of young farmers in the area. After the inspection, it was decided to use the Lunnan Lunbei Activity Center to plan and build a beautiful rest station on Highway 61, and at the same time let young farmers enter for sales.

During the second visit to the coordination meeting, it was learned that Haiqing Palace was to invest 300 million yuan to build a five-star pilgrim building. Director Li Mingyue said that there were local industries to invest in to promote the surrounding revitalization, which was in line with the spirit of the local livelihood plan.

At the same time that the Yunguan Office also began to repair and renovate the Santiaolun Beach, the Planning Office imported the resources of the international kite surfing school to solve the problem of excessive wind and waves on the West Yun coast from October to February each year.

The third meeting was convened by Vice Speaker Su Junhao and Haixian Qingnong at the Lunnan Lunbei Activity Center to discuss the needs of the sales platform and conduct consensus discussions. For the fourth time, the chairman of the Haiqing Palace served as the chairman, and the chief secretary of the Sihu Township Office jointly convened to listen to the planning briefing of the Yunke University team and conduct consensus discussions. At the fifth meeting, a formal plan was filed to obtain funding from the central government. At this time, the township chief notified that the development of plans in the Lunnan Lunbei Activity Center and surrounding spaces were not allowed, and the local livelihood plan was temporarily suspended.

<u>Project content</u>

This plan upgrades the existing Lunnan Village Activity Center into the Sanjolun Visitor Center by introducing a national tourist information area, combining local agricultural and fishery specialty sales areas and catering areas, and adding bicycle rental services to make up for the lack of outdoor and international tourism and recreation services. This becomes the starting point for tourists to enter Sanjolun. At the same time, this base extended and integrated the resources of nearby scenic spots by connecting the three Lunhai waters, bicycle trails, and the Haiqing Palace's faith and cultural creation, Haiqing Cultural Tourism and Haiqing Market and expanding into the "Haiqing Cultural Life Circle". It has become a local brand with outdoor sports, marine ecology, local industries, and the humanistic charm of faith. The rate of visits and return of tourists meets the economic needs of local employment and entrepreneurship.

Therefore, this project upgraded Santiaolun's existing sightseeing and recreational service facilities and expanded the connection of important attractions such as the Haiqing Palace, Santiaolun Water Field. Bicycle trails jointly created the Santiaolun area into a "Haiqing Cultural Life Circle" (Fig. 1). The local creative brand that combined outdoor sports, marine ecology, local industry, and humanistic beliefs has become the most interesting happiness highlight of Taiwan Route 61.

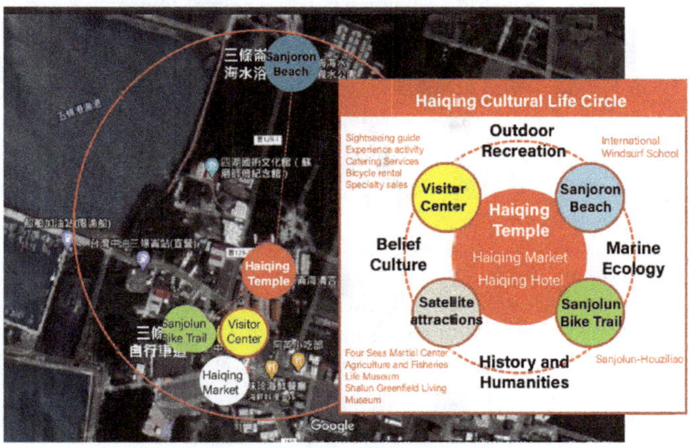

Fig. 1 Haiqing Cultural Life Circle Model

Conclusions

Since we observed discussions on the local creation and development plan of Sihu township in the past year, it has been found that economic and social problems had become increasingly serious due to industrial decline and population aging. At the same time, although the local temples are rich with China's social, economic, and cultural capital, how to co-create value with local governments and develop a sustainable circular economy was full of problems and difficulties.

There are many predicaments in the process of revitalizing the temple culture for the value and importance of the culture according to whether the relevant stakeholders have the willingness to support and the limited resources cause the exclusivity of cultural resources. The research results indicated the following: (1) the characteristics of the temple culture and creative industry included the foundation of religious beliefs that were closely related to the prayers of local people which collected donations for land development; (2) the land development and service expansion of the palace was an investment in the local economy, which contributed to local creation with management capabilities; (3) the difficulties faced by the self-investment of palaces and temples and the ideal local creation included the understanding of the mission of the management committee, limited vision capabilities, and pull of local political networks.

References

[1] Feng Tiance (1992), Introduction to Faith, Nanning, Guangxi People's Publishing House.

[2] Zheng Zhiming (1998), The Origin of Gods: Taiwan, Nanhua School of Management.

[3] Luigi Luca Cavalli-Sforza & Marcus W. Feldman(1981), Cultural Transmission and Evolution: A Quantitative Approach, Princeton University Press, Princeton, New Jersey.

[4] Wu Mingqing (2003). Knowing changes, adapting to changes, seeking changes: the marketing and response strategies of educational reform policies. Taiwan Education, 620, 2-12.

[5] Kotler, P., Roberto, N., & Lee, N. (2002) Social Marketing: Improving the Quality of Life (2nd edition). CA: Sage.

[6] Su Mingru (2004). Deconstruction of Cultural Industry-Research on Ecological Travel of Island Cultural Creative Industry. Kaohsiung City: Chunhui Publishing House.

[7] Li Maorong (2015), Reflections on "Religious Cultural Creative Industries" from the Perspective of Religious Education, Fu Jen Religious Research Issue 30, pp. 111-132

[8] Li Shengli, Cai Youxin (2009). A preliminary exploration of religious cultural creative industry. Proceedings of the International Symposium on Xuantian God Belief, Culture and Art, 4, 661-678.

[9] Lu Xiaocheng (2017). The development of cultural industry from the perspective of brand-based thinking on low-carbon transformation. New Taipei City: Songbo Publishing Co., Ltd.

[10] Zhu Xinyue, Li Shimei, Zhang Qian (2013). "The Composition and Expansion of the Cultural Industry Value Chain" "Economic Aspects".

[11] Li Yiyuan (1987), Faith and Culture, Taipei, Huayi Publishing House.

[12] Li Yiyuan (1996), Culture and Accomplishment, Guangxi Normal University Press.

[13] Li Mingzong (2002). The appearance of contemporary Taiwanese festivals-the formulation of the interpretation of leisure sociology. Institute of Physical Education, Taiwan Normal University, PhD thesis.

[14] Zhang Xun (2014), "Religion and Cultural Creative Industries: Xingang Fengtian Palace and "Xiangyi Cultural Park", periodical paper, Department of Family Affairs, Fu Jen Catholic University.

[15] Lin Meili (2008), Sacrifice Circle and Local Society, Taipei, Boyang Culture.

[16] Ke Guangren (2018), The Religious and Cultural Creative Industry and Operation Mode of Fuxing Palace in Xiluo, Journal Literature Information Network.

[17] Ma Qunjie, Chen Tinghui (2010), Local Cultural Creative Industries and Regional Cultural Marketing-Taking Tainan City as an Example, Journal of Marine Culture.

[18] Huang Yunxi (2009), "From Cultural Creative Industry to Religious Creative Culture", other types, Department of Religion, Xuanzang University.

[19] Yang Minzhi (2002). Research on the Interactive Model of Local Cultural Industry and Regional Revitalization-Taking Puli's Nine Cultural Industries as an Example. Institute of Urban Planning, Taipei University, PhD thesis.

[20] Liao Shizhang (2016), Local Cultural Industry Research, Juliu Book Company.

https://doi.org/10.1142/9789811238727_0084

The Impact of Virtual Reality, Augmented Reality and Mixed Reality on the Marketing of Film and Television Creation Industry

Honglin Yang[1], Tsung-Chih Hsiao[2*], Rui Ge[1], Chih-Cheng Chen[3**]

[1]College of Computer Science and Technology, Huaqiao University, Fujian, China
[2]School of Arts, Southeast University, Nanjing, China
[3]Department of Aeronautical Engineering, Chaoyang University of Technology, Taichung, Taiwan
Email: *108109061@seu.edu.cn, **ccc@gm.cyut.edu.tw

Abstract

Realistic contents are now in steady development and have achieved good results in all sectors, but in the film and television industry, their development direction is very narrow, with most applications focusing on improving sensory experiences such as VR movies, unlike the comfort that Parallax and Motion 3D movies bring to us, VR movies allow viewers to walk into a movie scene to see their surroundings at 360°. However, there are far more applications of realistic contents in the film and television industry. This paper would like to solve these problems by putting forward existing problems and providing some direction to the film and television industry practitioners to better use this technology.

Keywords: Virtual reality, Augmented reality, Mixed reality, Film and television creation, Film clips

Introduction

What are realistic contents? Virtual reality blocks the real world and creates a fully digital, immersive experience for users. Augmented reality overlays digital creation content in the user's real world. Mixed reality, including augmented reality and augmented virtuality, is a new visual environment that combines reality and virtual worlds (see Fig. 1).

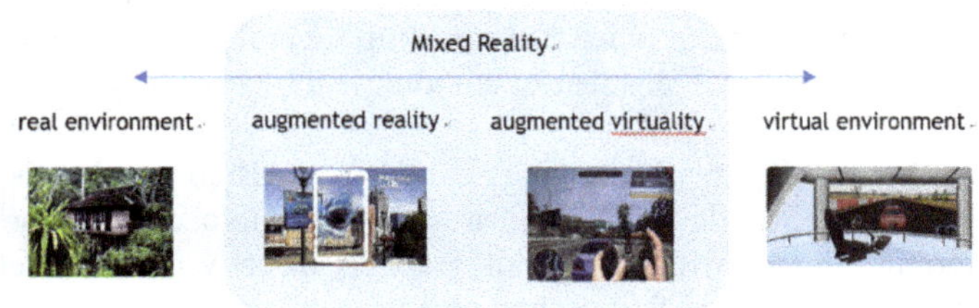

Fig. 1 Reality-virtuality continuum.

Here are some examples of the fields these realistic contents have been applied to.

(1) The first example is the VR glove, an open source textile data glove which is designed to facilitate detailed manipulation of 3D objects in VR, enabling scientists to accomplish a range of spatially complicated molecular manipulation tasks [1].

(2) The second example is also about VR. VR can be used by athletes to prepare for the Olympics. Skiers, for example, can wear VR helmets to simulate a run on the mountain, while ski-shaped balance boards provide some tactile feedback. What is more, it can also be applied in court where witnesses use it to recall the scene, in education [2-4] and so on.

(3) The third example is AR mask. Oster out Design Group, a well-known AR smart glasses manufacturer, has developed a product that uses AR-technology masks that will allow pilots to clearly see other scenes in a smoke-filled cockpit. Designed to help pilots land safely in an emergency, such as in smoke. There are other AR applications. For instance, AR also can enhance awareness on green consumption of electronic devices [5], be applied to sports entertainment [6] and advance designers' understanding of the fabrication equipment as a platform [7].

(4) The fourth example is the application of MR in aviation. Microsoft partnered with Western Michigan University to integrate MR technologies such as Microsoft HoloLens into aviation education. Currently, there are two ways to use it. One is a new simulation that can help pilots prepare for changes in the weather. Another application is an interactive MR application that allows students to explore the various components of an airplane.

We will see a significant downward trend in VR in the market. From this line graph, we can see that the figure reached the highest in 2017, but after that, it suddenly went down (see Fig. 2). This clearly reflects that VR does have many problems that limits its development.

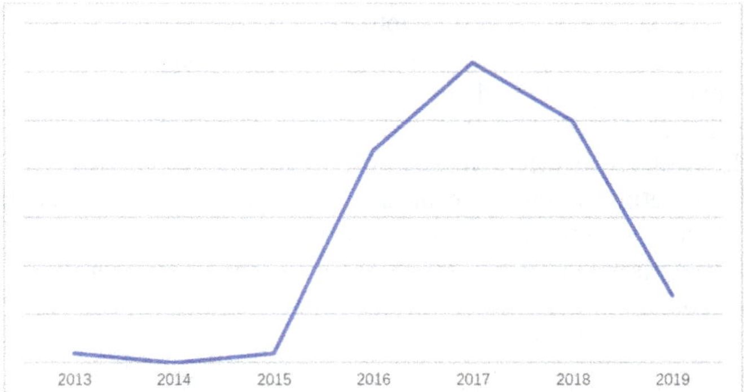

Fig. 2 General trend of the number of related articles posted.

Methodology

A. Screenwriters

When writing a script, screenwriters often encounter the difficulty that they are not familiar with the background of the subject matter to be written and cannot fully realize the interaction between actors and set scenes, because after all, it is impossible to write a script in the scene.

As an example, now a screenwriter needs to write an aviation-themed TV series, but he certainly did not have a pilot background, does not know the pilot's work process, and also does not have aviation-related knowledge, then to solve this problem, he can use realistic contents to experience the scene, help to complete the work. What is more, in Harry Potter and the Chamber of Secrets, in the scene where Dobby appeared in Harry's home, there are three parts of interaction: (i) Harry and Dobby, (ii) Dobby and items and (iii) Harry and the objects. In this case, if the screenwriter cannot see the layout of the home it will increase the pressure of the director and props group, so in order to improve efficiency, more natural interaction, the participation of realistic contents is needed.

Another example is when a story completely occurrs in a villa, then the screenwriter can use realistic contents to be in that villa, and write the script at home. This method saves time and effort, greatly improves efficiency, and is suitable for achieving the effect of one shot.

B. Directors, anyone who wants to make a movie (especially movie that requires fertile imagination)

Many young people who love movies will have a dream to become a big director like Christopher Nolan and James Cameron, but even if they have great ideas but cannot find a way to achieve, because even though they have learned how to tell stories, even formed their own genres [8], without the help of an ambitious production team, it simply cannot be achieved. For example, the Lord of the Rings could not have been completed by one person. However, now times are different, with the advent of realistic contents, they can create their own movie world, where they can have unlimited imagination, make their own scenes, actors and so on. This does provide a way for people who don't have a behind-the-scenes team to solve the problems.

C. Film and television theme park

As we all know, film and television are inspiring, it would want you to try, to do something. For example, watching documentary films may cause you to be concerned about climate change [9], then watching movies with beautiful scenery, you will want to go to the location to see. Film and television are an effective way of tourism promotion. This kind of marketing method can attract people to places they have seen on the screen to travel, not only because of the attraction of the natural landscape. In fact, the most important factor is its symbolism, storyline, character relationship, star, thrilling scenes and exciting endings, and even some cartoons without exterior view, such as "Beauty and the Beast", "The Lion King" and "Notre Dame" also attract many visitors to the scene of the cartoon.

This has also led a large number of scholars to research, to find out the different forms and motivations of film and television tourism, and in more than a decade of research, found that most of the film and television cities and theme parks have these problems. First, the sensory nature of environmental experience is too single. Many buildings are only on the level of having pictures taken by tourists, lacking a sense of participation and integration with the real environment. And also the device experience is not interactive.

But if you can show all the film clips taken there at the corresponding shooting venue, then allow visitors to pick and choose their favorite clips, wear glasses, so that fans can actually enter the shooting scene to feel. Such transmission has more effect on people's emotional transmission [10, 11]. This form will greatly enhance their visiting experience and participation, and also let them pay attention to all aspects of the scene, they can choose to pay attention to the main character, or his favorite supporting role, in order to avoid the film shooting's disadvantages of only focusing on the main characters. Moreover, some directors may be very attentive to details but this cannot be tshowed in the film, such as some costume drama. In fact, each of the main character's clothing are perfectly restored to the scene at that time, but the film may not reflect this, then this form of visiting will greatly enhance the audience's favorability, so that the audience feel their intentions.

In fact, the film and television theme parks can also be completely virtual, like a game, and let fans go into the virtual world playing a role [12].

D. Actors

With the development of technology, now making a film requires actors to use their imagination more and more. Actors have to rely on their performance experience of many years and act with no actual objects. However, it would not have been a problem to actors who already have a wealth of performance experience. But if the main character is a child, then inexperience is going to be a problem. The filming process can be very complicated because the director has to constantly correct his movements and tell him where to look. For example, in the process of shooting the film called "The Jungle Book", the whole film only has one real actor, others are all made by data. All scenes are in the shed, using green curtains to complete all the action, you can see the whole forest scene only from the camera. Then he can perform more naturally, and the interaction with the surrounding items will be more natural.

For example, in a scene of the movie where he needs to interact with a huge snake that can wrap several people, then if he can actually see, his fear of emotion will be expressed more real.

On the other hand, allowing actors to use AR contact lenses to perform, while importing virtual objects into cameras or mobile phones will make photographers directly capture the interactive scenes of actors and objects.

Realistic contents can be used not only during filming, but also for better practice. For example, if you need to perform as a pilot, you can wear VR glasses to simulate the real circumstance of flying a plane. Wearing glasses, the actor can choose to enter the shooting venue for a practice, making it easier for the actor to get into the state faster when shooting. What is more, they can also choose to practice their other upcoming movie scenes in their spare time without actually reaching the shooting site, which greatly improves shooting efficiency.

E. Casting directors

The process of choosing corners has evolved. In the studio days of Hollywood, a production company's bunch of signed actors waiting in line auditioned to see who could stand out every time. Then in the era of independent production, the cornering process formed a mature commercial system, including the implementation of assembly line operation, the establishment of various types of actors database and value assessment files. But no matter how developed, this step of trial cannot be avoided.

Actors need to face the camera separately to complete the performance title given by the crew. So at the beginning of the trial, the casting directors need to compare personal information. This can be done by scanning the actor, and then use AR to show all the information, such as height, weight, and college background and so on. The advantage of on-the-spot scanning is that there is no problem of information interleaving and also saves paper. Actors can wear glasses and perform in a specified scene or with a specified item, which give actors more room to play.

In the selection phase, it can also be combined with artificial intelligence, before the interview, they could use algorithms to compare and match the role requirements and artist information, screening out more actors that are suitable for the role as an alternative, and then use realistic contents for further screening.

AR can provide an unlimited screen that allows you to work with multiple resumes at the same time, greatly improving screening efficiency.

In addition, in terms of appearance-matching they can also use AR technology. Let each actor stand next to the shape of its role, can be more intuitive.

Conclusion and Discussion

According to the current development situation, the combination of realistic contents and the film and television industry is far from enough.

Contact lenses are not replacing current devices for the time being. And helmets pose a lot of problems. A team of researchers at the University of Leeds in the UK conducted a study. To test the health effects of VR headsets, they studied children ages 8 to 12 playing games with VR headsets after 20 minutes. They found that the use of VR helmets could cause serious health problems. "In virtual reality devices, a virtual 3D world appear on a 2D screen, which puts pressure on human vision systems," Mark Mon-Williams, a professor of cognitive psychology at the University of Leeds, wrote in an article discussing the new study. "In adults, this can lead to headaches and eye pain. For children, the long-term consequences are unknown."

It may reduce the revenue that star effect could have brought us, but we can create our own star virtual characters, once the virtual characters are set up, there may be less contradictions between brokerage companies and production companies. We can always use this character, which means the benefits are indefinite.

For example, when we take a taxi, before the virtual city map of Beijing was available, we had to look for experienced drivers, we had to ask for directions, and could not predict what time to come, as we may encounter traffic jams. But when we set up a virtual city model, such as Google or Baidu, the virtual map allows us to set the start and end points. The path we take can be optimized, by choosing the best path through the virtual, such as the Google navigation map, and with real driving data, can correct the deviation in real time. Optimization can be achieved after many iterations.

Acknowledgments

This work was supported by the Science & Technology Planning Fund of Quanzhou (Nos. 2016T009) and the Natural Science Foundation of Fujian Province of China (Nos. 2017J01109).

References

[1] Glowacki, Becca.Rose.; Freire Rachel.; Thomas, Lisa.May.; O'Connor, Michael.; Jamieson-Binnie, Alexander.; Glowacki, David.R. An open source Etextile VR glove for real-time manipulation of molecular simulations. **2019**.

[2] Merchant, Z.; Goetz, E.T.; Cifuentes,L.; Keeney-Kennicutt,W.; & Davis,T.J. Effectiveness of virtual reality-based instruction on students' learning outcomes in K12 and higher education: Ameta-analysis. *Computers. Education.* **2014**, *70*, 29–40.

[3] Lee, Jang. Hee.; Shvetsova, Olga. A.; The Impact of VR Application on Student's Competency Development: A Comparative Study of Regular and VR Engineering Classes with Similar Competency Scopes. *Sustainability* **2019**, *11*, 2221.

[4] Manuel Sanchez-Garcia, Jose.; Toledo-Morales, Purificacion. Converging technologies for teaching: Augmented Reality, BYOD, Flipped Classroom. *Red-Revista De Educacion a Distancia.* **2017**, *issue.55.*

[5] Bekaroo, Girish.; Sungkur, Roopesh.; Ramsamy, Priscilla.; Okoloa, Alexander.; Moedeena, Waseemah. Enhancing awareness on green consumption of electronic devices: The application of Augmented Reality. *Sustainable Energy Technologies and Assessments.* **2018**, *30*, 279-291.

[6] Mahmood, Zahid.; Ali, Tauseef.; Muhammad, Nazeer.; Bibi, Nargis.; Shahzad, Imran.; Azmat, Shoaib. EAR: Enhanced Augmented Reality System for Sports Entertainment Applications. *KSII Transactions on Internet and Information Systems.* **2017**, *11(12)*, 6069-6091.

[7] Poustinchi, Ebrahim.; Subtractive digital fabrication with actual robot and virtual material using a MARI platform. *International Journal of Architectural Computing. SI.***2018**, *16(4)*, 281-294.

[8] Tseng, Chiao-I. Beyond the media boundaries: Analysing how dominant genre devices shape our narrative knowledge. *Discourse Context & Media.* **2017**, *20*,227-238.

[9] Bieniek-Tobasco, Ashley.; McCormick, Sabrina.; Rimal, Rajiv.N.; Harrington, Cherise.B.; Shafer, Madelyn.; Shaikh, Hina. Communicating climate change through documentary film: imagery, emotion, and efficacy. *Climatic Change.* **2019**, *154(1-2)*, 1-18.

[10] Fikkers, Karin.M.; Piotrowski, Jessica.Taylor. Content and person effects in media research: Studying differences in cognitive, emotional, and arousal responses to media content. Media Psychology. **2019**. Available online: https://doi.org/10.1080/15213269.2019.1608257 (accessed on 30 Apr **2019**).

[11] Castle, Jeremiah.J.; Stepp, Kyla. Silver screen sorting: Social identity and selective exposure in popular film viewing. *The Social Science Journal.* **2018**, *55(4)*, 487-499.
[12] Timplalexi, Eleni. Shakespeare in Digital Games and Virtual Worlds. *Multicultural Shakespeare-Translation Appropriation and Performance.* **2018**, *18(1)*, 129-144.

https://doi.org/10.1142/9789811238727_0085

Research on the Aestheticization of Digital Culture in Modern Life from the Popularity of Hatsune Miku

Jiadai Li

Sanda University of Shanghai, NO. 2727 Jinhai Road, Pudong District, Shanghai, China
Email: jiadai91@163.com

Abstract

Under the environment of modern life in cities nowadays, we are living with digital culture that develops at a fast speed. In the digital culture of mass media, Hatsune Miku exists in a metaphysical sense, belonging to the subculture of Japan anime. Her great success pushes us into a new century of how we interact and expect. Some inklings could be told from this phenomenon through the aesthetic changes in everyday life.

Keywords: Hatsune Miku, aesthetic, digital culture, digital aestheticization

Introduction

In this age of samples and techno-park, we've already heard what machines can sound like. But why stop there? "Night Flight" predicts that in the future, all rock stars will be computer generated.

These candid evaluations show no emphasis on culture differences from countries. Likewise, there are also almost no voices online that have considered the culture differences between regions and races. We could think this as the new values of globalization in culture, under the influence of multiculturalism in the modern society. These new values should belong to a culture which is based on a different system, the digital culture. Being produced and driven by digital devices, she is a resident of the digital world. The world of its own aesthetic and working system. People provide data to create the world in which they are also influenced in return.

Hatsune Miku is a humanoid persona voiced by a singing synthesizer which belongs to an application of Cryption Future Media. She was released on August 31, 2007, as "an android diva in the near-future world where songs are lost." Miku was promoted by the public since 2008, based on her original use for professional musicians. Before Miku, there were another two characters who worked the same way but were not as successful as her. Her first step of booming into the public sight was the mass sales of all her brand goods up to one billion JPY. The great success in market directly shows her priority in the area of the virtual character. She is the best example of a virtual idol for current conditions about the public's aesthetic orientation. After the great success of her sales in Japan, the company began to open the Western market. Surprisingly, she also got a top 10 position in the US iTunes' singer on the first week of sales. From this time, the company decided to make her open as a flexible singer who could perform the audience's songs in order to enlarge the market. This is her present job. Looking back to her history, it is not hard to find that she was not predicted to be so successful, which means the creators are still to explore this area without a complete aim of how this should look like and what would this do. The consumption of the situations now about such digital culture background production are creating a new century of such related areas. Actually, the experiment of a virtual singer is not a new creation, but it has become mainstream recently. The market for this kind of product is much more mature under the context of today's background. Apparently, her great success results in the huge consumer culture impact in the world, the digital culture with Japanese culture background, high-tech background and anime culture background, under the big picture of the world wide postmodernity in current mass culture. Even by the standards of a pop star, she must be the most eccentric and protean one, which has a unique characteristic of mystique elusive. She has more than 100,000 original (crowd sourced) songs, 2 million likes on Facebook, even has been the face for Google, Toyota, and Louis Vuitton, the paper reports. With the help of the hologram, she uses the digitally synthesized voice to hold sold-out concerts around the world. She is no longer a software character or an animation pop star in the computer screen, she now is trying to occupy the real world as a real human idol could.

Aesthetic in Visual and Digital culture

Koten has discussed realism, the shifting from real to imaginary as the main drivers of the consumption of their production. [3] He gave out a famous example of McLuhan, as an export in electronic enlightenment. The basic principle to distinguish a hot medium is whether it contains more senses than others. Thus, to make the medium more attractive and interesting, the better senses count. Also, he had proved that people model themselves on what they see from the media. Thus the content will influence the social value which manifest by attitude or practice in culture value, daily taste, consumption and so on. The dynamic relations between social and culture performance are mainly made by the market force. Therefore, the consumption of what's popular is the phenomena of what to research. Many people addicted to the virtual world now indicate a question of realism, why the digital media are trying their best to make it immersive as the reality, or why people are so immersed in the virtual reality? The constant process of making the best possibility of realism in 2D is now reaching its hand to 3D and VR, leading the market in a new direction. According to Lacan, we are still in the imposed socialization process, which is our pleasure principle and the Oedipus complex. We are still addicted to the desire of have the primordial unity of wholeness, through the tramps between imaginary and symbolic, which the digital environment could provide.[5]

The early cinemas and amusement parks were the fundamental aesthetic that led to the direct spectacle and sensation properties of popular entertainment at the end of the nineteenth century. For the amusement park, it was the mechanised rides that provided the attraction, while the moving graphic displays of the cinema allowed the fascination with technologies of spectacle. In the visual aesthetic sphere, the profound impact of modern culture was basically given by Baudrillard's work, whose thinking was influenced by Walter Benjamin and Marshall McLuhan. Under the history background of the consumer culture, Baudrillard took the term media in its own and argued that "technically reproduced work increasingly becomes the work designed for reproducibility".[1] He endorses the idea that the way media communicates is more important than the contents, the mediating power of technique structures the modern world directly. In the culture aspect, this implies the theory which "privileges the particularities of a technological form and how it induces certain relation, experiences and effects, over, say, looking at the content or meanings contained in its various mediations"[1], the broad aesthetic values in every culture. The desire of making it more "real" has the reason of its own aesthetic because the mass media produce a new form of world connecting to the reality via a screen. Thus the dissolution of the subject-object distinction, the distinction between public and private, which blurred the interior and exterior, substituted with the hyperreal in digital world. [1]

Actually, people are used to the aesthetic of digitalized comic style from the early times with medias. "By the 1920s, comics such as Outcault's famous Buster Brown in the *New York Herald* were read by millions, becoming part of everyday American life. Through newspapers and magazines, comics became the new icons of national culture, visual symbols that America's "imagined community" shared".[7] The kind of aesthetic in Japanese anime was rooted from manga culture, the basic artwork form of current popular cartoon aesthetics. From the time this culture entering into the academic sphere, this started the career in pop culture around the year of 1990 in the world market. Manga and anime attract young people from all over the world, the charm seems irresistible. Not because of the eastern mystical sense of art beauty, but owing to their aesthetic of exaggerate, breakthrough, freedom of willing. They are especially appealing since they are the kind of inexpensive forms of entertainment to be enjoyed, the "pure pleasure commodities". [7] "They are mediascapes of dreamscapes, where stressed-out modern urbanites daily work out their neuroses frustrations". [2] This culture also has the same character as the consumer culture, which could be owned to the background of the time period. The widespread use of the internet accelerated the unified world as a whole, thus the digital visual culture in anime are cultural hybrids with Japan and the modern West. As a form of contemporary art, it dissolves the line between high and low art, as it is not right to say this is inferior to the fine arts. It is the mixture of medias which constitutes an important marketing niche in the globalized culture industry.

Back to the history of the aesthetic in 2 dimensional works, the primary work of using the computer to mimic the humanity with a character is the start of combining technology with art. Mostly these are classified as cartoons, with the other forms of work such as manga, the stationary pictures; illustration, digital paintings; or animation, the derivatives of the computer art. "Digital entertainment, from video games to simulation rides, is now a central feature of popular culture." [4] The computer based art has been changing from the traditional production of the aesthetic in the culture value, to a new form of spectatorship. Darley has argued that "contemporary culture is far more nuanced or differentiated at the aesthetic level" despite the "extraordinary regularities operating across its different forms".[4] The popular and mass culture belong to the social phenomenon as the wider acknowledgement of art. The art of digital is commonly refered to as computer generated image, such as graphic displays, animated cinema, arcade games, music videos. These are the various forms where the technological link with the contemporary culture aesthetic. Visual simulation of the real object in the computer graphic begins from dots and lines, and this is their basic aesthetic style. We saw the computer as the instrument which has great potential in the development of the aesthetic form. As digital visual culture was used for science in the area of medical, military, aircraft, and so on, the aesthetic is focused on the functional terms, unlike our popular taste for mass culture entertainment. But it is not proper to say there was no aesthetic impulse in connection to these early centres of computer art. Later on, the computer image became image manipulation, simulation, animation and realistic synthesis, in a two dimensional screen around 1980s in the art works of computer games, special effects cinema and simulation interactive activities.

Analysis

As a singer, she was created in a similar way to a real singer, a young idol with immature body at a really young age. From the research data, the author provides some reasons why people like her. Firstly, she looks pretty, with white skin and a slim body, is fashionable and has a cute face. Actually her look is mostly based on the aesthetic of Asian people's public standard of the beauty. But this standard also has to be in line with the background of globalization. Combined with Western cultures to fit in their taste right now, as long as she is not a real human, she could change the imperfect part as much as the audiences wish. It seems obvious that they prefer pure, cute, young and naïve type. Good looks are a fundamental requirement of a pop star, so there is no doubt few people will regard her as ugly. Secondly, as a pop star, she will not have negative news which a real star would to break their fans' hearts. She won't get old; she will change into any appearance with the ideal shape; she won't have gossip, which means no immoral affairs. She has the ability which a real star could not have and may never reach as she is as clean as an infant, could be accompanied with each one, and belongs to every single fun! Thirdly, as the young in Asian have much pressure on study and less entertainment activities, they put most of their passion online, within the world on the internet. But the productions for the young are not as much as for adults, especially in reality. They prefer a younger star who is similar to their age and could share their unique language which the adults may not understand. Miku has filled the blank of this market in their life which is the completion of their immature world. Finally, Miku is a production of the representative of high-tech, the closest new creation which a public can get close to, and enjoy the advanced experience. She also attracts a number of the adults as well, because it is fashionable to know about her stuff as a proof of keeping with the times. She will become better and better, with the help of her audiences. This is an investment does not lead to depreciation worry of a star. Her potential is much greater with the diversification of possibilities.

From my research, the majority audiences are from the younger group, who are students and have the time and interest in the digital cartoon culture. Anime was basically made for children and adolescents; they were designed to entertain them. Back to the model of Miku, she could be considered as a doll, which could sing and dance as young people's favourite, the simulation of real human character, who is more beautiful and vivid. She represents the desire of everyone who was a child to wish the toy has its real intelligence, like a real creature. It is not a peculiar thing to see a child talking to his/her toy even with just a word of its given name. We have the sympathy to treat the toy as if it is alive. We use Miku in the computer to treat her as an advanced toy and we are happy for her to come into the real world. That is another reason why she is so popular among all ages since she is a virtual toy for everyone on earth. Children could see the reproduction of her audios and videos which was made by the adults, and themselves; adults could enjoy the process of making her as what they want to be and play the harder mood "game" of the toy. The communication is advanced, better than the old way of just being a receiver. There is more fun with timely interactions and the beautiful aesthetic pleasure in the multiple sense of entertainment. The traditional toys are changing their shape in the evolution of the new century, digital culture bring not only the technology but also the way of being for many things. It has moved from the traditional physical form, to the digital mechanical control, to the virtual form in mobile-media, to the combination of virtual and reality to-date.

The cultural taste and lifestyle directly appeal to how people see themselves, the character socially constructed with their preferences and tastes. While today's cultural taste is on the trends of globalization, it is a mixture of diverse cultures. Our everyday life is combined with different cultures especially in a big city, the wild usage of the Internet makes a huge influence and reproduces in our daily lives. Back to the case study, the avatar girl Miku is a creature "living" in "cyberspace". Under the environment of the virtual field, her physical behaviour, the performance, could be considered as a mode of communicative behaviour, as the avatar is actually operated by human, the performance of her should be based on the conception of her culture. What she does could represent the aesthetic of the digital cultural characteristics which both combined with people's wish and the limitation of the digital media. The performance of an avatar is the expression of an emotion communicating aesthetic, thus some people in the reality try to imitate them as well. The professional impersonation is the action of doing "cosplay". During the research of collecting the graphic of Miku, her cosplay formed a majority. Girls are dressing like her, put their make up as similarly as her face, and wear green hair to make themselves look sas much as Miku. Also, their pose and facial emotion try to estimate the animate-like of Miku, which seems unnatural in reality. This is the way people could be neoliberal subjective to be what they want to be, making their aesthetic freely expressed. The neoliberal postfeminist subjectivity, as Evans has claimed that the "aesthetic labour" work is the continuation of the social commodity, which under the cultural and contextual changes in the developing of technology could compromise social mobility. So, the group of people who are doing the cosplay of Miku could be considered as the derivatives that belong to the object commodities of Miku's culture. The objectification of the aesthetic of Miku is more and more apparent to show that under the background of consumer culture, values could also be commercialized to be consumed.

Firstly, in the instance of Miku, girls at a young age make her a real idol and learn her ways of acting and singing. They try to look cute when they are representing or performing. Actually, most girls in Japanese anime share the same quality of cuteness, which appears to be naïve, sweet, and silly. Thus this leads to the influence in many Asian countries that girls are changing their looks to approach the aesthetic of the digital character. They perform cute postures, kawaii emotions, and silly actions. There are also some videos recording them singing or dancing as Miku, which is popular among the younger group nowadays. There are many real changes influenced by the digital visual aesthetic of this kind of anime beauty, not only in cosplay. As self-consciousness apply in the subjectivity of modern people, they tend to make it the same way as used in characterizing Miku. They are trying to make themselves look young, white and slim. Photoshop their pictures and selfies match the aesthetic of the digital pictures. In the younger generation in China, some school girls are found wearing cosmetic contact lenses, to make their eyes in an unusual colour and enlarge the pupils in order to look big and shining. They also buy a lot of accessories to look more kawaii, decorating nails and so on. Women who are older would choose plastic surgery to make their face smaller, and some other similar aesthetics for looking more "perfect" similar to the digital picture in the 2 dimensional way.

This culture aesthetic is the most obvious culture phenomenon in Japan, which is really successful in high-technology and anime industry. How popular is it? Another example is "pokemon go", released in July 2016, which is the most modish phone game among young in the Western country now (because they did not open the market in Asia right now). The story is about a group of teenagers who are aiming to be the digital monster's trainer and collector, taking on a journey in the world. The game is based on the story and makes the player the protagonist to take a trip in the real world and collect creatures in animation. Players will walk in the real world and find monsters in the real position on screen which are set by the GPS with google map. This way of creating a relationship with people in the physical world, while putting their mind in the spiritual world shortens the distance of communication between 2-dimensional and 3-dimensional reality world. The mass population playing this game severely exposed the desire to break the wall between the virtual and reality that has been developing for years, as another good proof of the trend. From another aspect, the great success has also confirmed the truth that the aesthetic of the digital culture is accepted by all regions and are becoming the leader in this area. Because of the uniqueness of digital art, it has no borders and does not completely belong to any country's cultures. It is the product of the postmodern times, which is a new century with a powerful tolerance of difference such as globalisation, postmaterialization, hybridity and multiculturalism. The digital aesthetic of art with reality is coming from reality but higher than reality, filled with the wishes of utopia romanticism and evolutionary fantasy. There are also some good examples in this aspect under Western culture, for instance, the superhero series, Ninja Turtles, Terminals and Zootopia. These are all in the process of making them come true, in the history of making the 2D into 3D then into VR.

The popularity among the young is not only because they are easily interested in anything, but because they are the representation of the future. Creation is the theory to make the unbelievable become true, so this is the dream the old have had, and they make them into reality now. Miku is changeable with her potential of changing styles by will, as she is more than a real singer, and can keep on living by having infinite development spaces. She emphasizes positive values and with the whole spirit of her audiences would live long and prosper. The aesthetic for Utopia is mostly used on the younger group, such as children's advertisement and products. All of them are designed to be beautiful, cute, friendly with some uncommon characters which are already unreal in the reality. One of the reasons why adults always like to make utopian products for young is because young children are more likely to believe in it and enjoy it. That is the reason they more likely to accept and love the virtual as not considered unreal. No one can be sure to guarantee that the things we have dreamed of could not come true one day in the future.

Conclusion

In conclusion, the aesthetic of digital culture has influenced our life in a way of taking the market and immersing in our daily activities of entertainment. The spectacle of using high-technology is a form of composing art performance, which is the expression for our own emotions. The desire for having more communication with mechanical tools, such as computer, is a trend to make them more human-like with some emotions connection. The interaction of making this kind of aesthetic in a digital world started from the virtual character, to use medias with technology to achieve. The culture is constantly changing to become closer o our real life. In the aestheticization process, the community of the digital visual culture trying to break the "dimension wall" of the digital world and the real world. As for Miku the example, they make her visual physical body "real" and actions more close to reality. But that is not to say they want to make her totally real. She has to have her own characteristics which make her different as a virtual singer with her cultural aesthetic – the digital style. Our modern city life blurs the line of art and life, with the influence of the digital visual culture. This provides a prospect of the living concept in our future life and aesthetic in a broad sense of reality.

References

[1] A. Darley, *Visual digital culture- surface play and spectacle in new media genres,* London: Routledge, 2000.

[2] F. L. Schodt, *Dreamland Japan: Writings on modern manga*, Berkeley, CA: Stone bridge Press, 2006.

[3] H. V. Koten, *"The digital image and the pleasure principle: the consumption of realism in the age of simulation,"* Digital visual culture: Theory and Practice, A. H. Gardiner and T. Cashen, Eds., Malta: Gutenberg Press, 2009, pp.89-98.

[4] J. Baudrillard, *For a critique of the political economy of the sign,* St Louis: Telos Press, 1981.

[5] J. Lacan, *The Mirror Stage*, In Ecrits, a selection, A. Sheriain, Eds., London: Tavistock, 1966.

[6] J. M. Bouissou, *"Japan's growing culture power: Manga in France,"* Reading manga: Local and global perceptions of Japanese comics, J. Berndt and S. Richter, Eds., Leipzig: Leipzig University, 2006, pp. 149-165.

[7] M. W. MacWilliams, *Japanese visual culture: explorations in the world of Manga and Anime,* New York: An East Gate Book, 2008.

https://doi.org/10.1142/9789811238727_0086

The Study on Eye Movement and Induced Movement of Discontinuous Line Graphic in Motion Forms

Guang-Dah Chen[1], Chih-Chao Chang*[2], Chao-Ming Wang[3]

[1]National Taiwan University of Arts, Associate Professor, Taipei, Taiwan
[2]National Yunlin University of Science and Technology, Graduate School of Design, Doctoral Program, Yunlin, Taiwan
[3]National Yunlin University of Science and Technology, Associate Professor, Yunlin, Taiwan
*Corresponding Author: Email: [1]gd196478@yahoo.com.tw, [2]s650415@yahoo.com.tw

Abstract

This study extended the project of "The Study on Rotational Motion Perception and Eye Tracking in Motion Forms". By using eye-tracking equipment and technology, the visual movement and eye tracking change of perception were investigated, and the relationship between motion illusion perception and eye movement was analyzed. The related studies on motion perception of a column of rotational motion illusion in kinetic art are classified into "forms change" and "continuous line graphic on the form". However, as the graphic on the surface is focused on "continued line graphic", it is not extended to "discontinued line graphic." This study focused on the "discontinued line graphic" and combined eye-tracking with vision tracking. With the standard of the best geometric form of induced movement of motion illusion perception, different types of discontinued line graphics were observed and compared for finding the difference.

Keywords: Motion illusion, Induced movement, dis-continuous line graphic, eye movement, eye tracking

Introduction

The visual representation of kinetic art and the various motion perception have great research value. Currently, the studies on dynamic shape are divided into two fields: the change of the shape such as cylinder, cone, sphere, and the change of continuous line segment of graphics of shape bodies such as parallel lines, spirals, curves, and so on. The contours are based on continuous lines. However, there is a lack of studies related to "discontinuous line graph". Therefore, this study explored the different patterns of "discontinuous line graph" through the perspective of geometric shape based upon the basic theory of kinematic contour and focused on the dynamic effect of the shape surface graph dominated by discontinuous line in the next stage.

Literature Review

A. Expression of the Dynamic Illusion Effect of Prisms

The "Barber-pole illusion," a dynamic model integrating actual motion and perceived motion [1] with the rotational motion of a geometric prism (cylinder) is used for studying dynamic illusion effects. The "Barber-pole illusion" refers to the dynamic illusion generated by a rotating cylindrical signboard such as a traditional one at barbershops. Although the cylindrical signboard rotates around its vertical axis, the stripes that are parallel to each other on the surface appear to be moving upward along the vertical axis. These stripes are perceived to be moving rather than rotating (Fig. 1). The actual direction of the movement of the stripes on the boundary of the cylinder is perpendicular to the length of the cylinder, but the stripes are perceived to be moving in the same direction as the cylinder [2]. When watching an object, people have various visual reactions according to the distance from the object. In particular, watching a static object differs from watching a dynamic object. For example, people watch and observe a static object with clear identification. When people watch a moving object, the movement speed of the object affects the reflection of visual effects such as model characteristics, graphic settings, viewing distance, and other factors as the crystallographic regulation and interpupillary distance correctly express the relative distance. However, the distance is considered to be longer by the retina than the real distance [3]. Therefore, when people observe graphics at various distances, the smaller the distance is, the larger the graphics appear and the viewing angle is. Correspondingly, the further the distance is, the smaller the graphics are and the viewing angle is. As such, the distances relate to the sizes of the objects. If the size of an object remains unchanged, the appropriate viewing distance for the specimen can be tested for various distances (Fig. 2).

Fig. 1 Barber pole illusion.

B. Studies on Eye-Movement Data of Illusion

Few experimental studies have been conducted on eye-movement data for illusions. Some experiments have been conducted on the relationship between the generation of an illusion and eye movement. For example, Fu and Sun [5] observed and measured changes in the scan paths of Muller-Lyer illusion graphics by assessing the eye movements for Muller-Lyer illusion graphics to understand whether the generation of illusions affects the eyes' pursuit movements. Festinger *et al.* [6] examined eye movements for Muller-Lyer illusion graphics, too. Coren and Hoenig [7] investigated eye movements for Oppel–Kundt illusion graphics. They observed and measured the scan-path changes of the movement for the curve illusion formed by Hering and Wundt illusion graphics and the area of illusion formed by Ebbinghaus illusion graphics to understand whether the pursuit movement of the eye is affected by the illusion graphics [8,9]. Studies have demonstrated that the eye movements are significantly affected by illusion graphics, which cause differences in scan-path distribution. The findings have validated relevant visual theories. Henderson and Hollingworth [10] stated that people's complicated visual cognitive processes can be effectively obtained in real-time observation of eye movements. Therefore, to observe people's visual data processing, the analysis must be undertaken with observation indicators for the eye movement for understanding the significance of eye movement processes. As discussed, no certain criteria exist for observation indicators of the eye-movement. According to Megaw and Richardson [11], different observation indicators should be used in response to different study topics, purposes, participants, experimental materials, and scenarios, as well as other factors. However, the visual analysis should be conducted using certain key observation indicators for observing eye movement, including fixation times or duration, saccade amplitudes, the number of fixations or "fixation count," sequence of fixation points, and pupil size.

(1) $\theta = 2\arctan(l/2d)$ (2) $\tan(\theta/2) = l/2d$

θ : view d : distance l : object watched

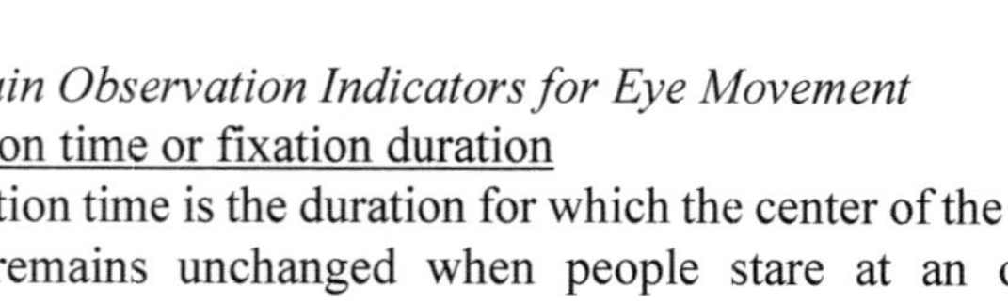

Fig. 2 Formula for viewing angle [4].

C. Main Observation Indicators for Eye Movement

Fixation time or fixation duration

Fixation time is the duration for which the center of the visual axis remains unchanged when people stare at an object, namely the time from the end of one saccade movement of the eyes to the start of the next saccade movement (in ms). Rayner [14] stated that, in visual searches, people's average fixation time per fixation point is approximately 275ms, whereas the time increases to 330ms in sense-perception. The length of fixation time is related to the richness of image detail.

Saccade amplitude

This refers to the displacement of the viewing angle of the eyes from one to the next fixation point. The distance between fixation points represents the effective range of observation for each fixation point. Henderson and Hollingworth [12] stated that the saccade amplitudes reflected by eye-movement positions are significantly and directly related to the content of the image when people observe an image. The more meaningful the content of an image is, the higher the saccade amplitude is. Thus, eyes are attracted to objects at longer distances. In particular, when people watch a target object with both images and text, a significant difference occurs in saccade amplitudes of the eyes.

Number of fixations or fixation count

The number of saccade movements occurs when eyes are staring at an object. Buswell indicated that visual fixation points were not distributed at random but regionally centralized or scattered in various positions [15]. Therefore, the focus points of viewing an image can be understood by analyzing the density of fixation point distribution with the number of fixation points in each area of the image.

Sequence of fixation points or sequence pointer

The sequence of fixation is a time sequence. A scan path can be obtained by combining a continuous fixation sequence with saccades [16,17,18], that is, overall vision consisting of perceptions obtained by eye movements. Scan paths can specifically, intuitively, and comprehensively reflect the temporospatial features of eye movements as well as the scan paths and differences according to various stimuli, experimental conditions, and experimental participants.

Pupil size

In terms of visual mechanisms, pupil size is a physiological indicator for measuring the sensitivity of mental activities [19]. Changes in pupil size reflect the mental load. The greater the mental load is, the larger the pupil size is [20,21,22].

This study aimed primarily to measure eye movement with perceptual reactions to dynamic illusory motion perceptions induced by dynamic models, to observe the distribution and scan-path states of perceptual reactions to three types of the dynamic illusory motion perceptions with different geometric prisms, to understand visual movement direction and the eye-movement state presented by the three dynamic illusory motion perceptions, and to assess whether there is a difference in the distribution and area of their scan paths. Therefore, to analyze the perceptual process of the dynamic illusory motion perception, various studies on eye-tracking movement were implemented in the experiment based on the basic form of eye movement. Measurement of the observation indicator and the scan path for eye movement was carried out for visual analysis of perceptual reactions to understand how the vision is affected by perception and eye movement. The relationship between dynamic illusory motion perception and eye-movement was also explored.

Research Method

The previous studies discussed induced eye-tracking movements with various phenomena and relations between dynamic models and dynamic illusory motion perception by applying psychophysical, adjustment, and scan-path measurement methods in visual psychology. Intrasubject design was adopted for the experiments, and three types were arranged in a random order for the experiments (Fig. 3). To avoid ordering effects, participants in the experiments were selected according to the purposes and conditions of the experiments. A total of 20 subjects between ages 23 and 25 years (10 women and 10 men) were enrolled in the experiments, and they all passed color-blindness testing. An EyeLink® II headset eye-movement tracker (Fig. 4) was used in this study for analyzing eye-movement data. A digital variable-frequency control system was applied for rotating the object that was fixed by a multifunctional disc holder. The main purposes of the study are as follows: (1) obtaining the saccade amplitudes, the number of fixation, and the distribution and state of the trajectory, (2) finding out differences in the individual eye movements, and (3) exploring the reaction between the induced motion perception and the eye movement for dynamic illusion.

Graphic	Triangle	Square	Circle
Cone No.	**I1**	**I2**	**I3**
Specimen	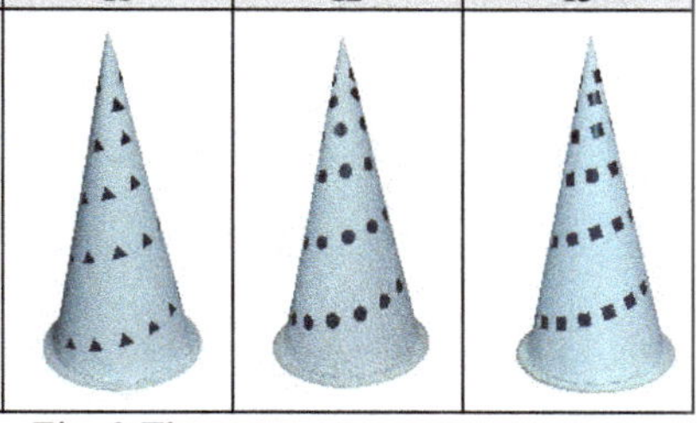		

Fig. 3 Three cone types.

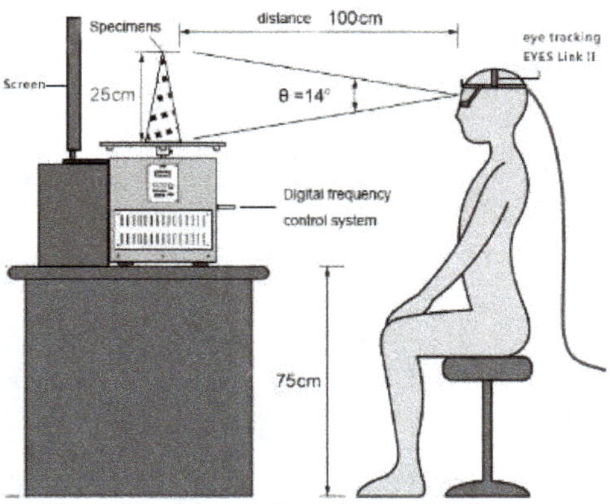

Fig. 4 Experimental environment diagram.

Experimental Results

As the discontinuous lines of the cones changed, the saccade amplitude of the sensory movement of the eyes became different. At the lower saccade amplitudes, the discontinuous lines of the cones were seen as squares. The saccade amplitudes at the upper threshold also gradually increased. Different discontinuous lines of the cones changed the saccade amplitudes of motion-induced eye-movement. For I1 type, the average saccade amplitudes at the lower and upper absolute thresholds were 76.350 and 84.50 pixels. For I2 types, the average saccade amplitudes at the lower and upper absolute thresholds were 66.49 and 75.54 pixels. For I3 types, the average saccade amplitudes at the lower and upper absolute thresholds were 77.77 and 88.83 pixels (Fig. 5). Therefore, regarding the dynamic illusion and motion-induced eye-movement, I3 showed the highest saccade amplitude.

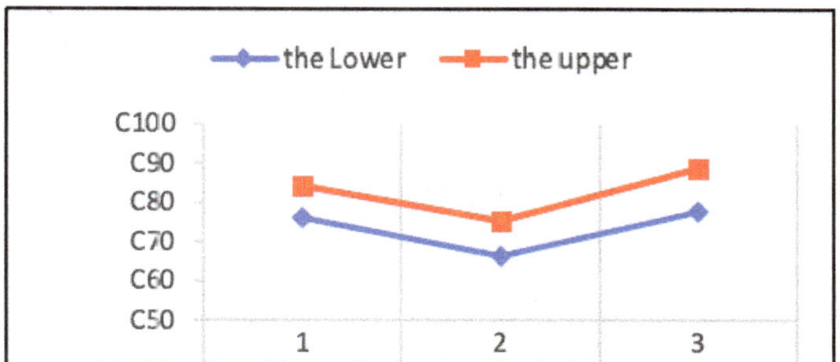

	1	2	3
the Lower	76.35	66.49	77.77
the upper	84.50	75.54	88.83

Fig. 5 Three discontinuous line Graphic types for induced motion; average saccade amplitudes (unit: pixel)

Conclusions

By using the dynamic illusion perception model, the measurements of changes and distribution states for scan paths of dynamic illusory motion perception were carried out. The measurement of eye-movement scan paths was also performed. The results helped to understand the dynamic illusory motion perception and its effects on people's visual motion. Comparison and analysis of various visual and perceptual processes demonstrated that the cones with different discontinuous lines and rotation speeds affected the formation and intensity of eye-movement and the upper and lower thresholds of saccade amplitudes and the number of fixations or fixation count directly affects. Different discontinuous lines and thresholds of rotational speed affected the formation of the eye-movement scan path of motion-induced perceptions and participants' reactions and judgments that influenced the saccade amplitudes. The saccade amplitudes for I3 type were the highest, while those for I2 type were the lowest. The results provide a reference for artistic creativity.

Acknowledgments

We are profoundly grateful to the Ministry of Science and Technology, Executive Yuan for partial budget subsidy under project number MOST 108-2410-H-144-005-

References

[1] Chen, G.D. (2008), The Study of Kinetic Art Dynamic Optical Illusion on Column with Spiral Pattern, Ph. Tech, Design Institute, National Taiwan University of Science and Technology, Unpublished.

[2] Palmer, S.E. (1999). Vision science. MIT Press, Cambridge, MA.
[3] Wallach, H., & Frey, K.F. (1972). Adaptation in distance perception based on oculomotor cues. Perception and Psychophysics, 11, 23-28.
[4] Oyama, T., Imaii, S., Wataru, K. (2000). New Sensory Perception Psychology Manual. Tokyo: Seishin Books.
[5] Fu, M.C., Sun, C.W. (2010), Pursuing Eye Motions on Müller-Lyer Illusions, Journal of National Taiwan College of Arts, 6 (2), 125-141.
[6] Festinger L., White C. W., & Allyn M. R. (1968). Eye movements and decrement in the Muller-Lyer illusion. Perception and Psychophysics, 8, 35-42.
[7] Coren, S. K., & Hoenig, P. (1972). Eye movements and decrement in the Oppel-Kundt illusion. Perception & Psychophysics, 12, 224-225.
[8] Fu, M.C. (2009), Pursuit Eye Motions on Visual Illusions, doctorate dissertation, Chung Yuan Christian University, unpublished.
[9] Fu, M.C., Sun, C.W., Lin, P.C. (2010), Eye Pursuing on Hering and Wundt Illusions, Study on Design Science, 13 (1), 63-78.
[10] Henderson, J. M., & Hollingworth, A. (1998). Eye movement during scene viewing: An overview, in eye guidance in reading and scene perception, G. underwood, ed. elsevier science ltd., 269-293.
[11] Megaw, E. D., & Richardson, J. (1979). Target uncertainty and visual scanning strategies. Human Factors, 21, 302-315.
[12] Henderson, J. M., & Hollingworth, A. (1998). Eye movement during scene viewing: An overview, in eye guidance in reading and scene perception, G. underwood, ed. elsevier science ltd., 269-293.
[13] Megaw, E. D., & Richardson, J. (1979). Target uncertainty and visual scanning strategies. Human Factors, 21, 302-315.
[14] Rayner, K. (1998). Eye Movements in Reading and Information Processing: 20 years of Research. Psychological Bulletin, Vol.124, No.3, 372-422.
[15] Loftus, G. R. & Mackworth, N. H. (1978). Cognitive determinants of fixation location during picture viewing. Journal of Experimental Psychology: Human Perception and Performance, 4(4), 565-572.
[16] Norton, D., & Stark, L. (1971a). Eye movements and visual perception. Scientific American, 224, 34-43.
[17] Norton, D., & Stark, L. (1971b). Scanpaths in eye movements during pattern perception. Science, 171, 308-311.
[18] Norton, D., & Stark, L. (1971c). Scanpaths in saccadic eye movements while viewing and recognizing patterns.
[19] Backs, R. W., & Walrath, L. C. (1992). Eye movement and pupillary response indices of mental workload during visual search of symbolic displays. Applied Ergonomics, 23, 243-254.
[20] Kahneman, D., & Beatty, J. (1966). Pupil diameter and load on memory. Science, 154(3756), 1583-1585.
[21] Kahneman, D., & Wright, P. (1971). Changes of pupil size and rehearsal strategies in a short-term memory task. Quarterly Journal of Experimental Psychology, 23(2), 187-196.
[22] Granholm, E., Asarnow, R. F., Sarkin, A. J., & Dykes, K. L. (1996). Pupillary responses index cognitive resource limitations. Psychophysiology, 33(4), 457-461.

https://doi.org/10.1142/9789811238727_0087

Tangible Interactive Space Design to Relieve Children's Preoperative Stress by Storytelling

Hongjiang Wang*, Thomas Mical

Shanghai Institute of Visual Arts, Shanghai, China
*Corresponding Author Email: We2design@163.com

Abstract

Based on a comparative study on the operation waiting area of Shanghai Children's Medical Center before and after renovation, Post-Occupancy Evaluation (POE) toolkit for Built Environment was used to track the interactive mural of "beach rainbow" and "mini-submarine" parent-child reading space for a year. Fear is a common cause of children's psychological stress before surgery, and the stress of children will be transmitted to family members and medical staff, which has a negative impact on the degree of preoperative cooperation and medical experience. The narrative space based on tangible interaction is more immersive and has a sense of storytelling compared with pure virtual interface interaction. It can effectively reduce the crying rate of preschool children and the anxiety of older children by positive distraction, and improve the degree of preoperative cooperation and user satisfaction with medical treatment. In the future, with the wider application of 5G and IoT, tangible interactive narrative space will become a more effective means to relieve stress used in children's healing environment.

Keywords: interactive, children, stress, storytelling

Background

The Operation Waiting Area is a special space in children's hospitals. According to the data of 2 years' follow-up investigation in the waiting area of Shanghai Children's Medical Center, the main causes of preoperative stress include: separation from parents, fear of unfamiliar environment, fear of pain and danger of surgery. The primary fear of preschool children aged 2-4 is fear of separation from their parents, while children aged 5-6 are most afraid of the unfamiliar environment after the separation. The biggest fear for children aged 7-14 is the fear of pain and the dangers that surgeries may bring. The stress generated by children's pre-operative fear will be transmitted to parents and the medical staff, which has an adverse impact on preoperative cooperation and medical experience. Therefore, relieving the preoperative stress of the children is the key to this problem, and the entry point for relieving the stress is to relieve the preoperative fear.

Related Theories

As one of the postmodern psychotherapeutics schools, "Narrative Therapy" was founded and represented by Australian psychologist Michael White and New Zealand psychologist David Epston. The theory of Narrative Therapy was firstly proposed by them in the 1980s. The co-authored book of Narrative Means to Therapeutic Ends in 1990 is a classic work of the Narrative Therapy. Children's narrative therapy includes reading stories and writing stories. Free writing and telling stories can effectively stimulate children's self-healing ability. Literary anthropology believes that healing is one of the most fundamental functions of literature, and that "the language of stories can create a sacred therapeutic space."[1] Children's narrative therapy emphasizes understanding children rather than evaluating them. "We should separate the problem from the person, and reconstruct the story of life by externalizing the problem, dissecting the right of speech behind the story, and looking for missing pieces of the story." [2] The best key to open the door of a child's heart is the "story". A child's perception and mind will be opened and understood through a good story. But as each individual has unique experiences and knowledge, each child has kept his or her own precious life stories in their heart. Children's narrative-oriented therapy emphasizes the discovery of children's talents and good qualities, supports children to become their own masters, and empowers them with respect and strength. Narrative therapy is like the hot springs healing the souls, surrounding children with warm goodwill when they are faced with illness, trauma and other life difficulties,

The spatial narrative puts the stories into the space and provides an immersive interactive environment for children's narrative therapy, creating a more friendly environment for the healing process of children (Fig.1). The child healing environment refers to an environment that can induce the child's body to self-heal and can stimulate the child's positive transformative abilities to enhance his or her physical, mental and spiritual health. Different from a purely functional medical environment, the healing environment emphasizes the reduction and the positive shift of negative factors in the environment, such as fear, stress, depression, and despair.

Tangible interaction combines both the features of timeliness and gameplay, which make it one of the best methods for spatial narrative. It uses the physical space and the content facilities as the information input and output carriers respectively. Through digital technology, a bridge of mixed reality can be built between the virtual digital world and the real physical world. When the tangible interaction in space appears as a public art, it uses the tangible objects as the interactive media, the physical space as the interactive container. It conveys the artistic concepts and constructs the spirit of the place through the human-object-information-space interaction. Compared with the literal narrative, spatial narrative is congenitally deficient in dealing with the time order of narratives, but the procedural characteristics of the tangible interaction make up for this deficiency to a certain extent. Thus, it is ideal for hospital's waiting areas and rehabilitation areas, especially the operation waiting areas, since it can have a positive distraction effect on preoperative fear and anxiety. Preoperative fear is largely due to the lack of understanding of the surgery. Therefore, the spatial narrative that integrates with preoperative medical education, and targets at different preoperative fears of children of different age groups is particularly important.

Hypothesis

The design of the tangible interactive spatial narrative plays a positive role in relieving the preoperative stress of child patients and can significantly improve the emotional conditions dominated by negative feelings such as anxiety and fear.

Methods and Process

Using empirical design and Post-Occupancy Evaluation toolkits, we applied the tangible interactive design to the renovation of the operation waiting area of Shanghai Children's Medical Center, and conducted data collection and comparative analysis among the users of the built environment.

Data collection methods include questionnaires, semi-structured interviews, unobtrusive observation methods. Data analysis includes environmental behavior map and APOEM(Action-People-Objects-Enviroment-Messages) table

A. Pre-design Survey

Before the design, the team conducted a questionnaire survey on the narrative picture content preferences of children in the Yangtze River Delta region. The number of samples: n=814. The average age was 8.1 years old. Among them, 396 were girls aged 2–14 and 418 were boys aged 2–14. The results of the survey show that the most popular among all age groups is the nature theme as 61.2%, followed by the technology theme while the abstract theme is not welcome.

The design team also conducted a questionnaire survey among the medical staff in the operation area and collected 62 valid questionnaires from 4 children's hospitals through an online questionnaire survey powered by www.wjx.cn. The data shows that for children under 6 years old, 88.7% of medical staff believe that they are afraid of strange environment after separation from their parents; for children aged 6–14, 77.4% of medical staff think that they are afraid of the surgery itself. In addition, up to 71% of medical staff believe that it is necessary to include interactive public art containing storytelling in the surgery waiting area.

B. Case Design

Based on the results of the previous surveys, in the space reconstruction of the operation waiting area of the Children's Medical Center, the design team selected the nature theme of ocean and used the design of the tangible interactive spatial narrative to alleviate the preoperative stress of the children patients. The team has combined the interactive mural of the beach rainbow, the entrance corridor of the submarine tunnel, the lifeboat nurse station, the lighthouse door, and the mini-submarine calming cabin shared by the parents and children together to form a spatial narrative with the theme of "Hope". The functionalized furniture and facilities embedded in the space in an interactive way are used as carriers, and the two modes of intelligent interaction and non-intelligent physical interaction are integrated (Fig.4,5,6,7).

C. Post Occupancy Evaluation for the Built Environment

In January 2017, the renovated children's operation waiting area was put into use. The evaluation team of Shanghai Children's Medical Center used observation and questionnaire to conduct a comparative study on the satisfaction of the selected 200 child patients and 200 family members using the surgery waiting area 5 months before and after the reconstruction. The data showed that after the reconstruction, the preoperative comfort level of the children (n=200) increased from 63.2% to 89.5%, and the crying rate was reduced from 36.8% to 10.2%. After the reconstruction, the satisfaction degree of the family members (n=200) rose from 68.8% to 92.7% (Fig.2).

The environmental behavior maps captured two time periods, namely, weekends and working days before and after the renovation. They mainly focus on the location and frequency of the interactiven activities, sampling for 2 hours each time; and in the meantime, use APOEM unobtrusive observation method to evaluate the users experience in the built environment (Fig.3).

Conclusion

Through the comparative study on users' experience before and after the reconstruction in this case, it can be seen that the interactive narrative space design has significantly reduced the anxiety and fear of the child patients waiting before surgeries, and has alleviated the psychological stress of the children. The narrative space based on tangible interaction is more immersive and has a sense of storytelling scene compared with the pure virtual interface interaction. It can effectively reduce the preschool children's crying rate and the anxiety of older children by positive distraction, and improve the degree of preoperative cooperation and user satisfaction with medical treatment. In the future, with the wider application of 5G and IoT, tangible interactive narrative space will become an more effective means to relieve stress used in children's healing environment.

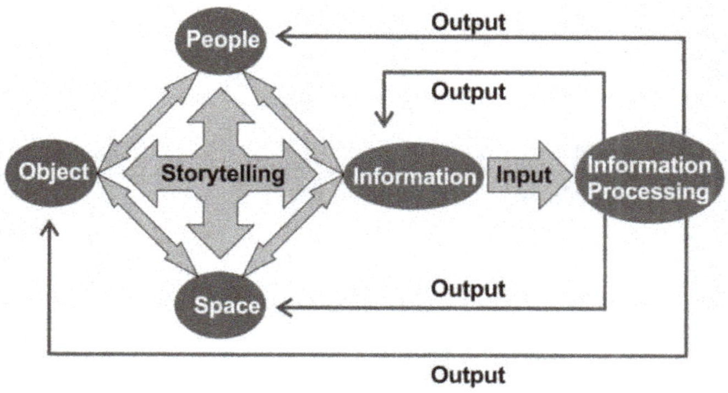

Fig. 1 The Elements in Tangible Interactive Narrative Space

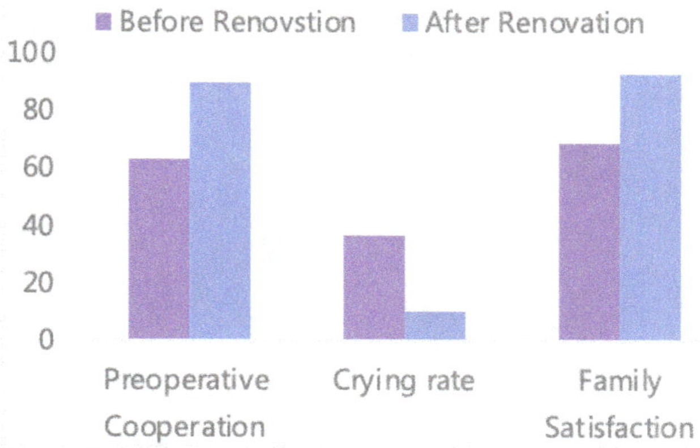

Fig. 2 Comparison of User Experience before and after the Operation Waiting Area's Reconstruction n=200

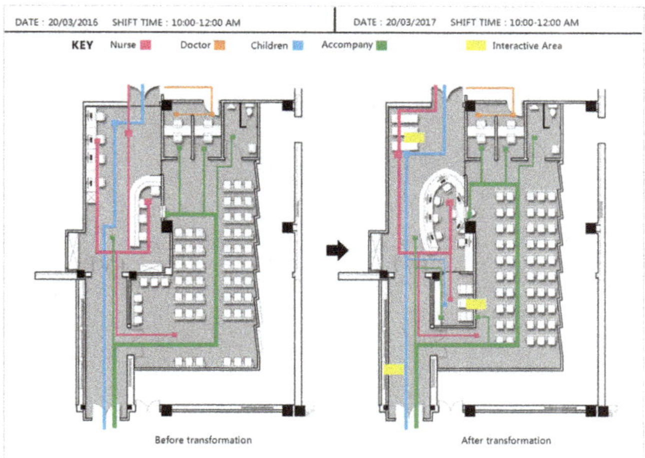

Fig. 3 Comparison of Environmental Behavior Map before and after the Reconstruction

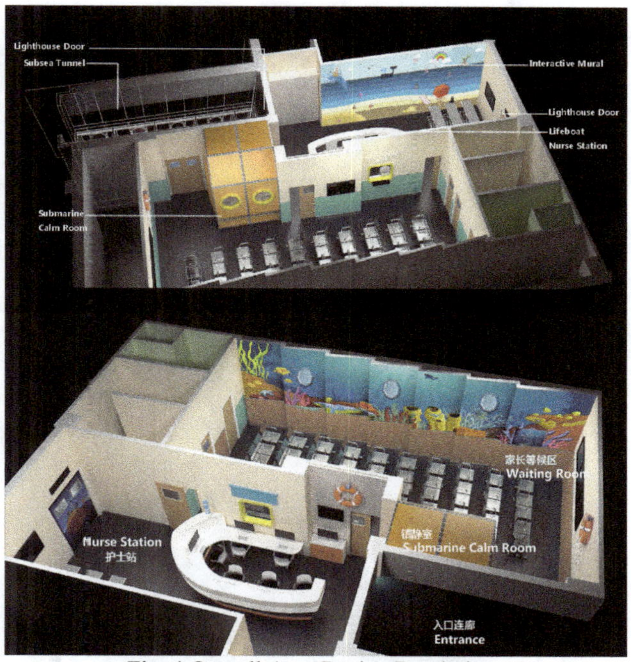

Fig. 4 Overall Area Design Renderings

Fig. 5 Comparison of Nurse Station before and after Reconstruction

Fig. 6 Comparison of rest area for accompanying members before and after Reconstruction

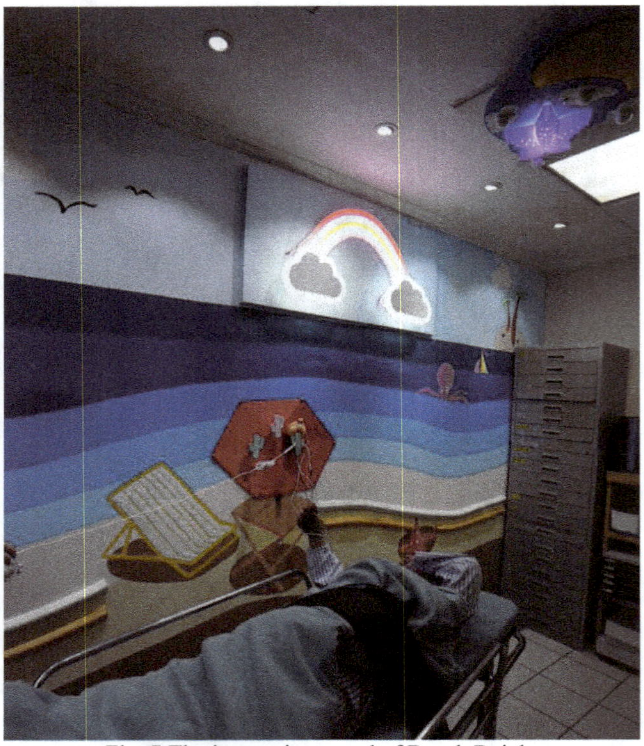

Fig. 7 The interactive mural of Beach Rainbow

References

[1] Long,Xiaomei, *Marlow's Healing Narration and Conrad's Spiritual Salvation in 'Heart of Darkness'*[C], Contemporary Foreign Language Education, 2016, issue 1.

[2] Zhong,Yaolin, *Rewrite the Life Story: Narrative Analysis of Self Healing Action Program*[J], Journal of Guangdong University of Technology(Social Sciences Edition), 2015, 15(4): 42-49, 90.

https://doi.org/10.1142/9789811238727_0088

Research and Practice on the Transmission of Chinese Traditional Culture in the Digital Age: Taking the Artistic Digital Communication from "Book of Songs" as Example

Liu Chang*, Chen Wei

Century College, Beijing University of Posts and Telecommunications, Beijing 102101, China
*Corresponding Author Email: 2574097338@qq.com, Tel: +8613720049663

Abstract

This paper takes the artistic digital communication experiment of the "Book of Songs" as a case study. It effectively extracts the traditional cultural characteristics and collects the symbols of traditional cultural elements based on the digital standard. It then further constructs the requirements that meet the needs of contemporary users on the cultural communication and evolution model of the Book of Songs and proposes a transmission and dissemination strategy of Chinese traditional culture in the digital age.

Keywords: poetry art, digital communication, traditional culture, digital standard, cultural study

Introduction

Chinese traditional culture contains the unique spiritual values, ways of thinking, and imagination of the Chinese nation. It embodies the vitality and creativity of the Chinese nation. It is the crystallization of the wisdom of all nations and the treasure of all human civilization.

With the development of digital technology, the digital dissemination of China's excellent traditional culture has become an irreversible trend. In the digital age, the spread of Chinese traditional culture faces the problem of "difficult conversion of traditional culture and digital technology, lack of cultural communication strategies adapted to contemporary contexts".

Based on the digital dissemination of the art of the Book of Songs, this thesis attempts to explore the innovation and transformation of Chinese traditional culture communication in the digital age.

The Cultural Status and Communication Value of The Book of Songs

The Book of Songs is a classic work of the Four Books and Five Classics. Western sinologists have commented that "The Book of Songs and Homer's epic, Shakespeare's plays stand in full swing, and have great value in the history of world culture." The cultural connotation of the spirit of heaven and man, the spirit of social harmony, the spirit of moral self-discipline, etc. The content in the Book of Songs can resonate with the world.

The internationalization of the Book of Songs has a long history. The Book of Han, Book of Tang, and related historical books have been recorded. From the Western Han Dynasty, the Book of Songs was passed through the Silk Road to West Asia, Rome, Indochina, North Korea, South Korea, and Japan. Since the 16th century, the Book of Songs has been introduced to Europe, North America, Russia, Poland, the Czech Republic, Romania, Hungary, and other countries.

The Digital Communication of the Art of The Book of Songs: Standards, Models, Paths, Methods

The digital communication of the Book of Songs adheres to the theme of learning the Book of Songs, enjoying art, understanding the history, integrating science and technology, cultivating culture, and reinterprets the original meaning and extension of the art of the Book of Songs in a digital way. The poems with strong artistic charm in The Book of Songs are presented in the form of new media and multi-platform.

Construction logic of digital standard system

From a practical perspective, the first problem is that traditional culture and digital technology are difficult to transform, and the new media era lacks an operational cross-media digital standard.

In the research practice, the author tries to construct the standard system of the digitalization of the Book of Songs from the planning and production aspects, guided by the ITU-T.621 framework, the first international technical standard in the field of Chinese culture, from file format and interactive animation (Fig. 1). Content provision, future platform operation, user rights, and other aspects, forming an overall specification.

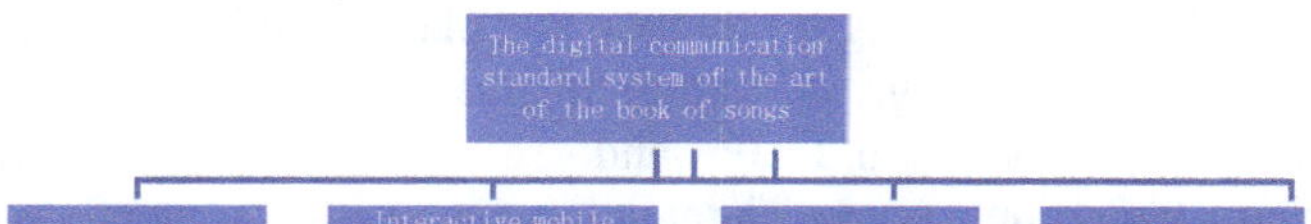

Fig. 1 The Digital Standard Construction Logic Diagram of the Book of Songs

The library of related content in the project planning stage is mainly for the support of the visualization of the art of the Book of Songs. It involves pictures of poems in the museums and exhibitions, and a library of poems and essays (a total of 6 sub-libraries: rituals, costumes, weapons, chariots and horses, daily-use sundry, buildings), and a collection of books on the study of the Book of Songs. Among them, the pre-Qin architecture can be adjusted to the pre-Qin period and the Qin and Han dynasties.

The interactive mobile animation content file structure of the Book of Songs: The content source file, technical parameters, specific specifications, storage structure, metadata, and content quality requirements are all defined.

The cross-media products of the Book of Songs include development documents based on AR technology, digital music, interactive animation, picture book albums, etc. Different documents face different media platforms for grafting, and the project standardizes the relevant requirements for file formats.

The poetry cross-media product operation service specification is intended for future operations. It will stipulate that the project product operators provide user service manuals, service methods, service channels, and user rights protection for animation product services for mobile terminal users.

The formulation of digital standards is to spread the cultural connotation of the Book of Songs and to reveal the complex and tacit knowledge of the Book of Songs. It has laid a certain logical foundation for its visualization and digital modeling, which is close to the originality of traditional culture. Adapt to the dissemination and display of the modern information environment and promote the best integration of technology and art.

The digital communication mode of the art of The Book of Songs

In the digital age, the spread of the art of the Book of Songs must focus not only on the transformation of content, the diversification of forms but also on the effective integration of new media art and new media technologies.

The new media is characterized by mobility, socialization, and intelligence. Considering the media environment, text, pictures, music, and audio make all kinds of information forms that need to rely on the production and dissemination of different carriers to be integrated into the new media platform. At the same time, multi-sensory design methods such as touch, hearing, and vision can be used to build new users. Cognition and expressing infinitely rich content with a limited specific image, and it provides users a full range of aesthetic and emotional experiences.

In the process of digital creation and planning of the content of the Book of Songs, the author advocates the concept of the Book of Songs and IP and selects the content of characterization, scene, interaction, interest, culture, and education from 305 pieces of poetry. Pluralistic thinking and creative thinking is once again planned and produced, and it becomes a three-dimensional communication content. This process is the process of inheriting and innovating the content of the Book of Songs (Fig. 2). The content of the post-innovation poetry is transformed according to the contemporary context of communication, taking full account of the audience's experience in different media platforms such as mobile phones and IPADs, and developing a cross-media narrative and cross-form communication of traditional cultures that are relatively independent but the same mainline.

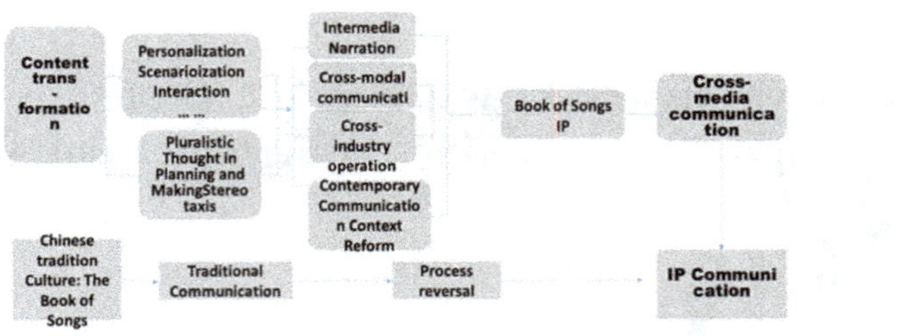

Fig. 2 Traditional Culture Communication: The Digitalization Mode of the Book of Songs

The path of digitalization communication of the Book of Songs

The digital dissemination of the art of the Book of Songs aims to reflect the life picture in the Book of Songs in the form of new media art expressions. Taking "poetry theme, regional culture, application frequency, and aesthetic value" as the composite standard to make selection of the contents of Feng, Ya, and Song from The Book of Songs. Selected to include more than 30 first "Book of Songs" essence, forming the "Book of Songs" art collection database (Fig. 3).

At the same time, using interactive animation, dynamic graphics, 3D images, music elements and other means of expression to reconstruct the expression of the "Book of Songs" art, to convey the aesthetic value and educational significance of the art of the Book of Songs, to present a cross-media new media poetry artworks to the audience.

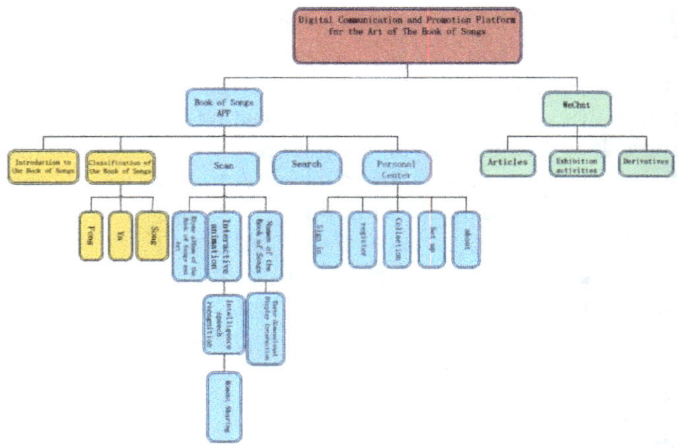

Fig. 3 The functional structure diagram of the digital promotion platform of the Book of Songs

The digital realization process of the art of The Book of Songs

1) Firstly, the content data and classification index standards of the Book of Songs are established, and the content of the poems is screened by combining the composite standards. The data content of the complete poems is formed, and the script planning, creative scheme, music sound selection, and technical support scheme of the poetry art digital products are determined, and so on.

2) The architecture design and functional design of the digital platform, using PS, AE, and other software for the interface design of the digital platform to create a database model for data storage.

3) Use two-dimensional animation software such as flash to create scene animation, and use Unity3D engine to display

interactive animation, content classification, and search functions.

4) Using a variety of electronic devices to digitally display the new media art symbols of the Book of Songs to present the beauty of the art and the educational significance of the Book of Songs.

The Transformation and Communication Strategy of Chinese Traditional Culture in the Digital Age

The digitization of the art of The Book of Songs is a representative exploration of traditional culture communication in the new media era. The project is devoted to innovatively telling the Chinese story. In the long run, it is conducive to the promotion of China's traditional cultural digital industry upgrade, helping China's outstanding traditional culture to meet domestic demand. At the same time, the audience can go out and walk in the cultural consumption demand, and actively contribute to the global communication context.

Inspired by the transformation and dissemination of Chinese traditional culture: In the digital age, the combination of culture, science and technology, and art is close to the originality of traditional culture and adapt to the communication requirements of the modern information environment, whether from content or performance. The tactics and the digital communication of traditional culture have formed a new aesthetic experience, which is conducive to the realization of cultural inheritance and innovation.

References

[1] Gao Weihua, Jia Mengmeng. "Several problems to be solved in digital communication of traditional culture" [J]. Media Review, February 2016

[2] Xia Chuan Cai, "Briefly describe the development of the study of the book of songs abroad", Journal of Hebei normal university (social science edition) [J], April 15, 1997: pp 71

[3] Mobile phone (mobile terminal) animation standards editorial board. Mobile terminal animation standard analysis [M]. Beijing: Beijing university of posts and telecommunications press, November 2014: pp 18

[4] Shi Ke, "The Study on the Problems and Countermeasures Existing in the Current Traditional Chinese Cultural Dissemination", Shandong normal university[D], 2018: pp 68-69

https://doi.org/10.1142/9789811238727_0089

Thinking of the Development of Design Education to the Future Space Design

Xing Ji[1,2*], Mingming Zong[1**]

[1]Beijing Technology Institute, Zhuhai, China
[2]Studying school for doctor's degree, Bangkok Thonburi University, Thailand
Corresponding Author Email: *54619184@qq.com, **Zmm77800@126.com

Abstract

Education for the future has arrived. The future is not destined but created by humans. Education not only creates its future but also breeds the creators of the future world. Modern design education needs to keep pace with the development of the times and constantly innovate. This article analyzes the development trend of modern design education and the "change" and "unchanged" of future design education. In the rapid development of scientific and technological information technology, the traditional education model requires thoughts on future space design.

Keywords: Design Education, Future, Space Design

Introduction

In the 21st century, we have to face a series of objective issues: the rapid development of information technology and intelligent technology, the crisis of energy and resources, the deterioration of the environment, the rapid increase of the population aging phenomenon, and the unprecedented expansion of human demand upgrade and construction. What people choose for survival and for the spatial conditions of life is far from the ecological needs of the environment as the future human settlement environment will be greatly challenged. The design discipline, with its unique artistic characteristics and social functions, must meet the use of space under the premise of function and aesthetic needs. It is design educators' responsibility and obligation to take advantage of its industry in the process of promoting social progress, explore the future of space design, and train students who adapt to these developments.

Modern Design Education

In recent years, China's design education has developed rapidly and made great contributions to the construction of the country and the improvement of people's living standards. However, China's design education falls far behind developed countries.

Nowadays we observe the increasing maturity of internet technology, the emergence of new business models, and the new types of social needs. This phenomenon has not only provided new opportunities for design professionals but on the other hand, it has brought challenges to design education. The original foundation of design education is not enough to support today's complicated one. This is an important problem encountered in the development of the curriculum. Design education must be combined with a wide range of social needs, macroeconomic conditions, technological development trends, and research results in related disciplines. This also must be understood when thinking about design issues.

Nowadays, with the substantial increase in the world's population, life expectancy, and economic aggregate, environmental problems, food safety, population aging, human health, fair education, cultural conflicts, and other social issues are gradually replacing the issue of food and clothing. They become a major global concern. Recently, the rapid development of green and sustainable design, service design, and universal design has been reflected in the design field. The country is also vigorously enhancing its soft power and industrial competitiveness by developing an innovative economy and promoting the economy. The structural adjustment and the transformation of the development method to accelerate the realization of the internal demand from "Made in China" to "Created in China" are important to improve people's quality of life.

The education concept of modern design education also changes in content according to the needs of social development. Changes in the demand for talent inevitably affect the development direction of design education. Either it is to meet the needs of the industry or lead the development of the industry, design education must understand and study the development trend of the industry, as the development of the industry is also an intuitive manifestation of the wide demand of the society.

Interdisciplinarity and common practice have always been important in design education while finding commonalities is also a process of design education. No matter how the goal of education is set, the acquired skills, the mastered knowledge, the innovation of thinking, and the expression of concepts need to be effectively linked together. Therefore, design education is not only a simple knowledge transferring but practice, teaching, coaching, nurturing, digging, inspiring, and ultimately training talented people. These have positive values and outstanding personalities.

The current design education needs to be reformed. Regardless it is taking advantage of the trend or responding passively, understanding the context of the times and the concept of new disciplines is the basis for repositioning the training goals, training content, and training model.

The "Change" and "Unchanged" in the Future Design Education

The discipline of design has now guided the healthy work and life in China with its unique artistic characteristics, social functions, and on the premise of fully satisfying the use function and aesthetic needs. It also has played a major role in promoting social development. Today, design education is facing major challenges. The wave of new technologies is accelerating the development of society. At the same time, ecological problems appear. Design education is far behind the pace of social change. Design education in the future is closely linked to the theme of the times and cultivates human resources with innovative capabilities. Integrating art and technology to promote sustainable ecological design is an important issue for the design education industry. Therefore, it is necessary to adjust and reform the teaching concepts, methods, and management of design education.

A. Unchanged in the Future Design Education—Human ecology

The boundaries of design are becoming increasingly blurry, as the knowledge, skills, and qualities required by new innovative talents are changing. Design education is not only on the level of knowledge but on the deeper level of spirit and soul.

First, education makes people seek the truth. "True" is to explore the essence of things and educate people to understand the relationship between nature and the world. Its significance is to make everyone learn to understand the nature of things by exploring, being inspired and enlightened, and ultimately harmonizing people and nature. At the same time, education makes people good. "Goodness" is friendship and kindness. Educating people on the relationship between people and society promotes human moral conscience, cares for others and society, and thus benefits mankind. Furthermore, education makes people beautiful. "Beauty" is in the spiritual world. It is not an external expression. Educating people must pay attention to the value of human life, let them discover beauty from the inside out, and understand and create beauty.

The ultimate goal of design education is to cultivate people to pursue truth, goodness, and beauty eternally. This is the highest mission of design education in the future. In brief, discovering the problems of social, natural, ecological, and people's livelihood for truth, goodness, and beauty is an insurmountable essence in any design field in the future of education. This is the foundation of design and design education.

B. "Change" of Future and Design—Technology

In the era of artificial intelligence and Industry 4.0, technology has extended in the military and medical fields. To a certain extent, high and new technologies are controlling our lives and monopolizing cultures. Does the technology in the Future Design Education still serve humanity? Will the advent of technology serve humanity or control it? When artificial intelligence, big data, cloud computing, and even more sophisticated technologies are changing rapidly, what will be the performance if the technology is fully penetrated future design education?

New technologies are constantly changing the way we think, and we are constantly redefining what we learn. The use of artificial intelligence technology in future design education provides students with precise learning solutions and content. It makes people believe that the learning content provided by technology is suitable for knowledge. In many learning resources, such a training way is separated from the student's ontology, as everyone is a different individual. Using big data to pass the information and knowledge will not achieve the concept of teaching owing to students' aptitude.

The use of educational information technology can solve the problem of uneven global high-quality resources in education. It achieves the internationalization of education and enhances the richness of the classroom. In the future, design education will use new technologies to enhance the effectiveness of the classroom and the efficiency of student learning. However, to improve learning efficiency, the school often ignores the learning itself. The students learn things instead of being used by technology to achieve a certain purpose. All in all, technology must serve education and humanity. In the context of the new era, what remains unchanged is the essence of education, while what is changed is the technical method. How to apply advanced technology to design education reasonably is also a problem that contemporary educators need to ponder.

Developing Direction of Future Space Design

With the rapid deterioration of the environment and the rapid aging, what will happen to our future lives? Nobel Prize winners from all over the world have gathered in Paris to discuss the new challenges in our humanity. The winner of the Peace Award, the conference host, Wesser, pointed out the plight of mankind after discussing the great achievements of mankind in the 20th century: "Human beings are already walking on the moon, but they are not close to their own kind; human beings are exploring the depth of the ocean and the limit of the universe, but neighbors living in the same corridor are still strangers to them; people's lifespan is prolonging, but longevity is becoming a burden and doom." Therefore, by taking humanistic care as the premise, future design education starts from the essence of design and scientific and technological means to achieve the sustainable development of the ecological environment.

The future space design must integrate human nature and technology with the ideas on life and survival. Taking human-nature-space as an indivisible whole, the concentration of wisdom needs to build a better space environment for human survival to achieve the harmonious and effective communion, explore the culture, and to design ecologically.

A. Humanity Space

The essence of design is to care for human nature, which is the basic starting point of sustainable ecological design. The future space design must meet people's psychological needs. Especially for special groups, in addition to protecting and satisfying the basic functions of their living space, they must respect their feelings, and people's spiritual needs are rich and diverse. In dealing with the division of space functions and the enclosing of new spaces, it is not to give people loneliness and indifference, but to create a warm and more appropriate atmosphere for the body and mind than before.

The communication between people and nature, people and objects, people and people is the sustenance and fusion of people's emotions and the landing and placement of people's hearts. The future space design must be humanized and cultural, based on the design of function, color, shape, and even light. Taking people's living habits, cultural levels, and consumption patterns as design ideas and constructing a reasonable humanistic space allow people not only to live healthily and comfortably but also to live spiritually happy. Thus, people's desire for humanistic ecology will be realized.

Good design is always for people with a people-oriented foundation. A dignified life is a necessary condition for the survival of people.

B. Technology Space

Science and technology are the primary productive forces and the driving force of social progress. Big data and artificial intelligence are the most common terms in the field of science and technology in recent years. In the era of data science and space perception technology, people begin to rely on data to confirm the logic behind things, rather than just to explain the spatial phenomena in life through assumptions.

The intelligent system brings a more convenient life for human beings than before. Future space design includes smart home, AR, VR, and even MR, to guide more people to interact with the design, solve the design gap, and make the design adapt to the needs of people. Technology is used for an unpredictable future.

C. Formats

Another development direction of future space design is a natural ecological design. Fundamentally speaking, ecological design can ultimately be attributed to the harmonious coexistence of man and nature. It is based on nature and combined with nature. From living space to living space, it restores the mutual respect between man and the natural environment. Based on what human beings already have, it completes the saving and recycling of resources. It is accustomed to enduring design to create a living environment where people and natural design symbios mutually.

The division and enclosure of space are not artificially to separate man from natural space but to integrate with nature as much as possible. Natural resources are the main content of the interaction between space and nature. How to use natural resources effectively rather than relying on technical intervention or even destroying them is also the main problem that space design needs to face and solve in the future.

Future ecological design must consider the use of materials and energy. The reason for the long-living future of the design is to let the design materials return to nature, try to avoid non-renewable resources as reasonably as possible, and try to recycle the material infinitely based on its nature. Foreseeing the physical and chemical impact on design products is brought by the future overall planning of the space and the special geographical environment. To avoid the multiple demolition and construction of the economy and waste of resources, the following are demanded: saving energy, reducing carbon emissions, making full use of renewable resources, using local materials as much as possible, and reducing the waste of resources caused by material transportation.

Conclusion

Nowadays, with the rapid development of technology, artificial intelligence has replaced many designers' work. Designers must return to their most important role, which is to design for the most fundamental interests of mankind. Achieving the sustainability of ecological civilization is the desire of all human beings, and it is also the desire and concern of the design teachers and students. We must have human empathy. Design is responsible for the mission of saving the planet. By integrating human empathy, the truth, the goodness, and the beauty of mankind into the development of new technologies, design always serves our humanity.

References

[1] Xin, Xiangyang.(2019). Redesign of Design Education. *Design Studies*, 2019:213-225.

[2] Zhou, Xiaojie, & Huang, Jian.(2019). Brief talk about the current situation of design education in China. *Modern decoration (Theory), 2017*(01): 281.

[3] Liang, Shumin, & Zhong, Le, & Peng, Xiaopeng.(2019). Research and development Suggestions on art design education in Colleges and universities in China.*Research on Art Education, 2019*(21): 146-147.

[4] Liu, Yanyan, & Lan, Ruile. (2019). Analysis of the research status of design thinking in the field of education in China.*Modernization of education, 2019*, 6(88): 252-256.

[5] Sang, Xinmin, & Zhu, Dequan, & Lv, Linhai, & Li, Yan, & Zheng, Xudong, & Jiang, Fengguang, & Yang, Lei, & Liu, Yanqiu, & He, Ying. (2020). Study science and future Education. *Teaching and research, 2020*, 43(01): 1-22.

[6] Yuan, Chengzhi. (2018). Talk about the future of design education reform. *Shanxi Building, 2018*, 44(25): 236-239.

[7] Wang, Yu, & Li, Mingzhu. (2016) The future of Design education in China from a multi-dimensional perspective. *Art education, 2016*(12): 22-27.

[8] Liu, Guanzhong. (2014). Design- The third wisdom for preserving the future. *Creativity and Design, 2014*(05): 4-8.

[9] Wang, Lirui, & Cao, Yue. (2014). Design for the Future of Mankind- On the importance of green design Education. *Design, 2014*(07): 149-150.

[10] Chen, Xiaoyan. (2019). Research on the development of smart home in the future living space design. *Housing and Real Estate, 2019*(31): 56.

[11] Wang, Guobin. (2020). The future has come!-- research on the design of virtualized living environment in the information age. *Design, 2020*, 33(11): 112-114.

[12] Zhao, Meihong, & Lu, Jie, & Ye, Tong. (2018). Future Space Environment Design. *Building Materials and Decoration, 2018*(22): 68-69.

[13] Ma, Mingjun. (2017). On the Future Development Direction of Environmental Design Major. *Art Education Research, 2017*(12): 83.

[14] Ning, xiaoli. (2014). Ecological space- future path of environmental design. *Art & technology, 2014*, 27(12): 152.

https://doi.org/10.1142/9789811238727_0090

To Believe or Not to Believe: The Impact of Dual-Route Factors on Individuals' Perception of False News on Social Media

Shuhui Sophy Cheng[1], Shao-Liang Chang[2], Chi-Ying Chen[2*]

[1]Chaoyang University of Technology, Taichung, 41349, Taiwan
[2]Asia University, Taichung, 41354, Taiwan
[*]Corresponding Author Email: megcychen@asia.edu.tw, Phone: 886-4-23323456 #1823

Abstract

Because of the threat of fake news, numerous efforts or activities have been initiated in terms of algorithm, fact-checking, platform scheme, and policy changes. However, the volume of fake contents distributed on social media has not decreased. Regardless of many discourses on the subject, we know little about what makes people susceptible to believing false news in an online context. This study examines the impact of central and peripheral cues to determine how each cue impacts on user's belief or disbelief in false news on social media from the perspective of the elaboration likelihood model. Besides, the moderating effect of information literacy on the cues is investigated. Results indicate that users' identification of the falsehood of messages is related with argument quality, however, topical relevance contributes to their susceptibility to believing in false news (BFN). Regarding the peripheral cues, source trustworthiness tends to make users vulnerable to BFN, nevertheless, no influence is found by image appeal and homophily. Information literacy has neither direct effect on BFN, nor moderating effect on any cues.

Keywords: fake news, misinformation, information literacy, elaboration likelihood model

Introduction

Fake news is nothing new, while in fact the problem has been existing since the development of the earliest writing systems [1]. This form of false information has become prominent recently due to its global implications. The widespread dissemination of false information can have negative consequences at both individual and societal levels; such as can be seen in stock price fluctuations [2], health emergencies and crises during an outbreak of Ebola [3], and political ramifications during the 2016 US presidential election[4]. Misinformation and fake news are often used interchangeably. More specifically, misinformation is defined as false contents that are not supported by clear evidence and expert opinion[5]. Fake news is further defined with two key features; authenticity and misleading intent[4]. That is, fake news contains false contents that is manipulated with some deceptive intent to mislead readers in order to gain an ideological or financial benefit [6]. Due to a global concern about the damage caused by false stories, various arguments of how to fight against arouse.

Executives of Google, Facebook, and Twitter have been requested by congressional committees to confirm their pains to battle against false contents due to social media being criticized as a potentially fertile ground for the dissemination of misinformation [7–8]. Mark Zuckerberg, the CEO of Facebook, told Senators that Facebook would use artificial intelligence to distinguish fakes. He also acknowledge that AI currently activates at the "keyword" level, labeling text structures and calculating statistical correlations between the structures and their sources [9]. However, applying AI technology to combat fake news has been criticized for putting technology into an arms race with itself, because abusers will not just stay where they are. They often search for strategies with the intention of manipulating the fake content to make it appear more authentic. Moreover, they find new ways to outwit detection. Sooner or later, it turns out to be technological cat-and-mouse games recurring on the Internet [10].

Besides, a network of fact checking organizations has been established in many countries as concerns grow about the damage caused by false information. According to the Duke Reporters' Lab, there are presently 168 active fact-checking groups all over the world. The process of fact-checking is time consuming, intellectually demanding, and greatly dependent on human effort to investigate and establish the veracity of data or documents. Consequently, the efficiency and scalability is limited. In addition, it has been found that online false stories spreads much quicker and more largely than real news [11] and, by 2022, people in developed countries could be coming across more fakes than real information[10]. The contributions of fact checkers, hard-working though they are, would not be sufficient to meet an urgent demand, and thus much (perhaps most) false information will never get marked. An untagged false story may actually increase the belief in its truthfulness due to the "implied truth effect", that is, the absence of a warning may be perceived as verification of the story [12].

Both solutions, AI algorithms and fact checking, are less than satisfactory. It is, therefore, argued that individuals should be at the center of efforts to cope with the threats of fake contents, given that humans are more often than robots to spread misinformation [13–14]. A large-scale misinformation cascade can become viral within minutes when individuals share and retweet. To make things worse, it has been found that people often spread information without verification [15] or even without reading the whole article [14]. From the perspective of information literacy, a literate individual is less likely to be misled because they are used to thinking critically and often try to distinguish false information from accurate information [16]. Thus, information literacy is suggested as a major counterweight to the rising challenge of fake news.

Regardless of many discourses on how to combat the dissemination of false stories, we know little about what makes people susceptible to believing false news in an online context, and whether information literacy can leverage their vulnerability. To unveil such questions, the current research investigates and compares the impacts of factors associated with user's belief and recognition of misinformation and the moderating role of information literacy, based on the Elaboration Likelihood Model (ELM). Developed by Petty and Cacioppo, the ELM is a dual process theory of attitude formation and change resulting in persuasion outcomes [17]. This model has often been used in IT persuasion research, such as consumer reactions to online advertising [18]. The assumption is that persuasion may be incurred through a central route grounded on the strength of arguments existing in information, or a peripheral route based on cues such as credibility of the message source, image appeal, homophily, etc. The extent to which individuals inspect the information delivered from each route depends on their state of "elaboration likelihood." Individuals in states of high elaboration likelihood tend to engage in a cognitive processing of messages and be persuaded by argument quality. On the other hand, people in states of low elaboration likelihood are tending to be motivated by peripheral cues. Based on the foregoing discussion, the research model is illustrated in Figure 1. We proposed the following hypotheses:

H1. Belief in False News (BFN) is associated with the intent to disseminate.

H2. Argument Quality influences BFN.

H3. Topical Relevance is associated with BFN.

H4. Image Appeal has an impact on BFN.

H5. Source Trustworthiness is related with BFN.

H6. Homophily influences BFN.

H7. Information Literacy has an impact on BFN.

H8. Information Literacy has a moderating effect on the relationships of Argument Quality (H8a), Topical Relevance (H8b), Image Appeal (H8c), Source Trustworthiness (H8d), and Homophily (H8e) with BFN.

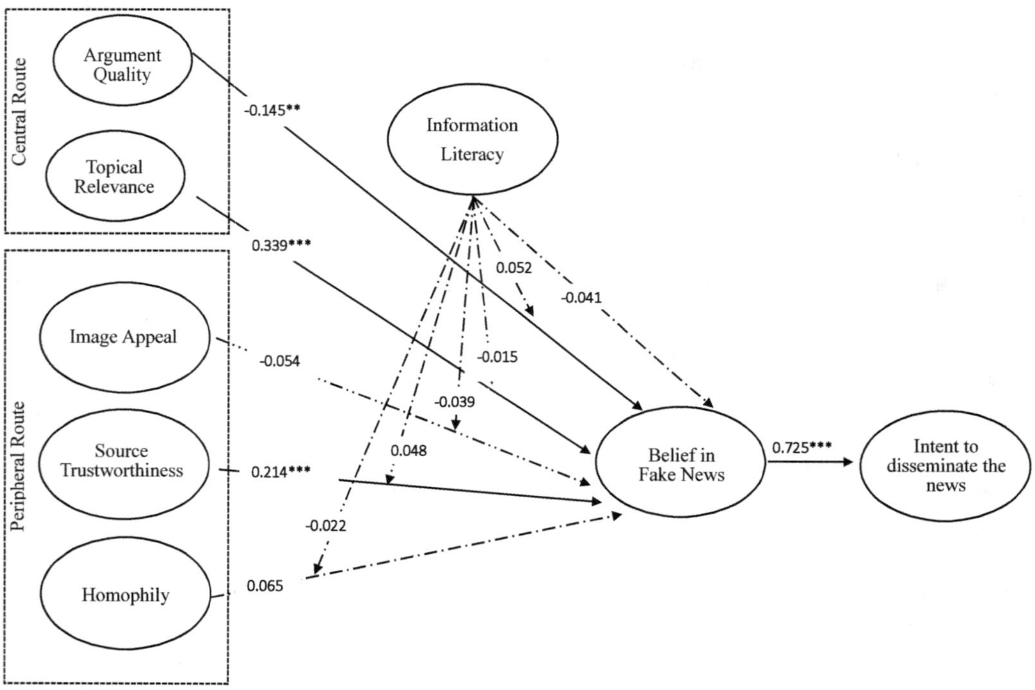

Fig. 1 Research Model

Method

Participants and Procedure

Participants were recruited from students from Asia University, with a sample age around the 20s, and students from Taichung community colleges, with a sample age above 30. Participants encountered a false news message in an online context, and then completed an online measurement. We reviewed over 100 fact-checking reports by Taiwan Fact-Check Center and selected two news messages judged false from Facebook and LINE. Participants from randomly selected classes in Asia University and in Taichung community colleges were presented with one of the two false news items and then asked to complete an on-line survey. In study A, 227 participants were asked to read a policy-related false news; in study B, 236 participants were presented with life-related misinformation. Data of the two groups was combined to analyze the modeling structure of believing in false news on social media. A total of 463 participants completed the questionnaire. Of these 463 participants, male accounted for 42.5% and 57.5% were female, and, their ages ranged from 18 to 73 years [mean = 36.69, standard deviation = 16.96].

Measurement

For the purpose of this research an online survey, adapted from previously validated constructs in the literature, was developed with measurements of: central cues (argument quality and topical relevance), peripheral cues (image appeal, source trustworthiness, and homophily), information literacy, belief in fake news, and the intent to disseminate. Except for belief in fake news, all items in the survey were constructed as "highly disagree–highly agree" statements on a five-point Likert scale.

For the item of belief in fake news, samples were instructed to rate their perceived accuracy of the news messages on the degree to which they believed them to be true on a five-point scale (1 = Not at all accurate, 5 = Very accurate).

Analysis

Structural Equation Modeling (SEM) was conducted to verify the hypotheses by using SmartPLS. Partial least squares (PLS) path modeling method is an appropriate technique for testing models/theories in the initial phase of development [19]. Due to the absence of research concerning a user's information processing model in facing false messages, as well as the interaction effect of information literacy, we deem PLS to be a good analyzing method. A positive association value between a central/peripheral cue and BFN implies the specific cue influences users to be susceptible to believing false news. Alternatively, if the association is negative, the implication is that the cue foster user's recognition of misinformation.

Result

Confirmatory factor analysis (CFA) was employed to calculate discriminant validity. It is recommended that the factorial loadings of measurement items on their respective latent constructs should be larger than their loadings on other constructs [20]. Further assessment of interconstruct correlations were also examined. It is advocated that the reliability is ideally higher than 0.7, or at least higher than 0.5. The criterion measurements for the data sets was satisfied.

Figure 2 depicts the analysis of the model (n=463). The R2 value for BFN is 0.318, and the R2 value for disseminating intent is 0.525. Based on the results in Figure 2, Hypotheses H1, H2, H3, and H5 are supported, while H4, H6, H7, and H8 are not supported. BFN is highly associated with Disseminating Intent. In addition, Argument Quality negatively influences BFN, while Topical Relevance, and Source Trustworthiness influence in a positive way. Information Literacy is not related with BFN and neither moderates any of the central and peripheral cues.

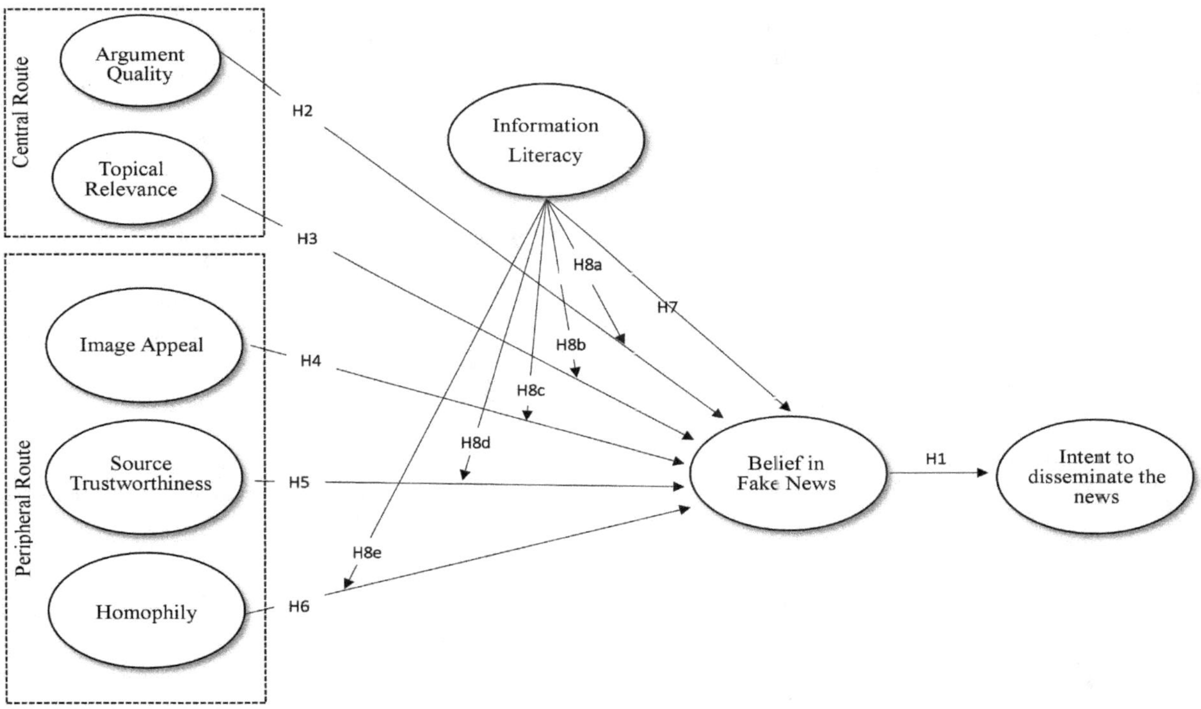

Fig. 2 Result from Structural Model Analysis

Conclusion

This study examines the impact of central cues (argument quality and topical relevance) compared with multiple peripheral cues (image appeal, source trustworthiness, and homophily) to determine the relative influence of each cue on a user's belief in, or disbelief of, false information, and to investigate whether information literacy acts as a moderator to both type of cues. The literature in this regard is rare. According to the analytical results, several insights are derived from this work:

1. The model indicates that user's news disseminating intent is highly associated with their belief in the message. It is somewhat contradictory to the finding that the majority of Tweets were shared by users without even reading the contents[14].
2. The Argument Quality of the central route plays a critical role for the information processing of false news. The negative relationship between Argument Quality and BFN indicates that users depend on the argument quality to recognize the falsehood of the information. Alternatively, the other central cue, Topical Relevance, contributes to user's susceptibility to BFN.
3. Source Trustworthiness of the peripheral route is positively associated with the perception of false news. It demonstrates that users tend to believe in false news if they read the messages from their trusted social media. Thus, social context of AI detection methodology is necessary as a complementary tool to leverage the damage of false stories on social media.
4. Information Literacy does not moderate the relationship between central/peripheral cues and BFN, and has no direct effect on BFN either. Since an individual play an essential role as media gatekeepers for social media information, information literacy education in this regard is urgent.

References

[1] Joyce Marcus. 1993. Mesoamerican Writing Systems: Propaganda, Myth, and History in Four Ancient Civilizations. Princeton University Press, Princeton, NJ.

[2] Kenneth Rapoza. 2017. Can 'fake news' impact the stock market? Forbes. Retrieved from: https://www.forbes.com/sites/kenrapoza/2017/02/26/can-fake-news-impact-the-stock-market/#743c0ed42fac

[3] Sunday Oluwafemi Oyeyemi, Elia Gabarron, and Rolf Wynn. 2014. Ebola, Twitter, and misinformation: a dangerous combination? BMJ, 349.

[4] Hunt Allcott and Matthew Gentzkow. 2017. Social media and fake news in the 2016 Election. Journal of Economic Perspectives, 31(2):211–236.

[5] Brendan Nyhan and Jason Reifler. 2010. When corrections fail: The persistence of political misperceptions. Political Behavior, 32(2):303-330.

[6] David M. J. Lazer, Matthew Baum, Yochai Benkler, Adam J. Berinsky, Kelly M. Greenhill, Filippo Menczer … and Jonathan L. Zittrain. 2018. The science of fake news. *Science*, 359(6380):1094–1096.

[7] Ben Popken. 2018. Apologies and promises: Facebook and Twitter tell senators they will do more to combat misinformation. NBC News. https://www.nbcnews.com/tech/tech-news/apologies-promises-facebook-twitter-tell-senators-they-will-do-more-n906731, last accessed 2019/03/28.

[8] Hamza Shaban, Craig Timberg and Elizabeth Dwoskin. 2017. Facebook, Google and Twitter testified on Capitol Hill. Here's what they said. The Washington Post. https://www.washingtonpost.com/news/the-switch/wp/2017/10/31/facebook-google-and-twitter-are-set-to-testify-on-capitol-hill-heres-what-to-expect, last accessed 2019/03/28.

[9] Gary Marcus and Ernest Davis.2018. No, A.I. won't solve the fake news problem. The New York Times. https://www.nytimes.com/2018/10/20/opinion/sunday/ai-fake-news-disinformation-campaigns.html

[10] Anjana Susarla. 2018. How artificial intelligence can detect – and create – fake news. MSU Today. https://msutoday.msu.edu/news/2018/how-artificial-intelligence-can-detect-and-create-fake-news/

[11] Soroush Vosoughi, Deb Roy and Sinan Aral. 2018. The spread of true and false news online. *Science*, 359(6380):1146-1151.

[12] Gordon Pennycook, Adam Bear, Evan Collins and David G. Rand. 2019. The implied truth effect: Attaching warnings to a subset of fake news stories increases perceived accuracy of stories without warnings. Available at SSRN: https://ssrn.com/abstract=3035384 or http://dx.doi.org/10.2139/ssrn.3035384

[13] M. Laeeq Khan, and Ika Karlina. 2019. Recognize misinformation and verify before sharing: a reasoned action and information literacy perspective. Behaviour & Information Technology, Online first version.

[14] Maksym Gabielkov, Arthi Ramachandran, Augustin Chaintreau, and Arnaud Legout. 2016. Social clicks: What and who gets read on Twitter? ACM SIGMETRICS / IFIP Performance 2016. Retrieved from: https://hal.inria.fr/hal-01281190/document

[15] Arkaitz Zubiaga and Heng Ji. 2013. Tweet, but verify: Epistemic study of information verification on twitter. Social Network Analysis and Mining. Retrieved from: https://arxiv.org/abs/1312.5297.

[16] Don Fallis & Dennis Whitcomb. Epistemic Values and Information Management. 2009. *The Information Society*, 25 (3):175-189. Retrieved from *SSRN*: https://ssrn.com/abstract=1509163

[17] Richard E Petty and John T Cacioppo.1984. Source factors and the elaboration likelihood model of persuasion. *Advances in Consumer Research*, 11:668–672.

[18] Dianne Cyr, Milena Head, Eric Lim and Agnis Stibe. 2018. Using the elaboration likelihood model to examine online persuasion through website design. *Information & Management*, 55 (7):807-821.

[19] Nils Urbach and Frederik Ahlemann. 2010. Structural Equation Modeling in Information Systems Research Using Partial Least Squares. Journal of Information Technology Theory and Application (JITTA). 11(2), Article 2. Available at: https://aisel.aisnet.org/jitta/vol11/iss2/2

[20] David Gefen & Detmar Straub. A practical guide to factorial validity using PLS-Graph: tutorial and annotated example, 2005. Commun. Assoc. Inf. Syst, 16:91–109, 2005. Available at: https://aisel.aisnet.org/cais/vol16/iss1/5

https://doi.org/10.1142/9789811238727_0091

Traceability Design Based on Folk Custom and Folk Art Culture: Example of Sanshui Longevity Cultural Image Design

Song Qi

School of Art and Design, Guangdong University of Finance and Economics, Guangzhou, GZ 510320, China
Email: 19484622@qq.com, Fax: (86)84096580

Abstract

All parts of the Pearl River Delta are developing cultural tourism undertakings of "beautiful countryside" and "characteristic towns". Sanshui District of Foshan City is a region with strong folk customs, folk arts and cultural characteristics. This paper attempts to innovate the image design of Sanshui Longevity Culture in the course of teaching design in Colleges and universities. Combining visual style with modern art design, we can inject the fresh flavor and young style of the times into the cognitive impression of traditional longevity culture. Several design ideas are summarized in the teaching practice.

Keywords: Folklore and Folk Art, Traceability Design, Sanshui Longevity Cultural, Image Design

Traceability of Sanshui and Development Trend of Design

Sanshui District is located in the northwest of Foshan City, located in the central part of Guangdong Province and the northwest end of the Pearl River Delta. The terrain inclines from northwest to southeast, with high hills in Northwest and alluvial plains and low hills in southeast. In the fifth year of Jiajing in Ming Dynasty (1526), Sanshui was named for the confluence of Beijiang, Xijiang and Suijiang rivers. The Baini town Yinzhou Beiqiu site in Sanshui proves that as early as the Neolithic Age more than 4000 years ago, there were human activities on this land.

Corresponding to the long history, Sanshui District of Foshan City is the "longevity town" selected by the Gerontological Society of China and the only wealthy longevity town in Guangdong Province. But like other common phenomena, Sanshui's unique regional characteristics are weak in the process of modern media dissemination. Its local longevity characteristics, related folklore and folk arts, native agricultural products and other high-quality elements are mostly presented in simple forms such as catering snacks and table bread, and there are generally uneven quality, blurred grade, confused image, impossible to break out of the limitation of regional location and other issues. Sanshui's local image lacks cultural brand, can't form a cross-border integration of industrialization ideas, does not meet the needs of the development of the times image planning and product design, so it can not resonate with consumers, lack of identity.

In the process of modern information dissemination, visual elements are often the first source of information perceived by the audience. The Pearl River Delta is in the background of rapid development of transportation and tourism industry. Everywhere has put the "beautiful countryside" and "characteristic towns" into full play. As a region rich in folklore, folk art and cultural characteristics, Sanshui District of Foshan City should seize the historical opportunity and publicize its good image. From the perspective of visual communication, we can trace its origin from its long history (the Neolithic period has already been inherited) and geographical characteristics (the hinterland of Lingnan, Sanjiang confluence), and combine the reasoning and derivative techniques in modern design thinking, with the inheritance of Sanshui folk customs (the Star Tune of Guangdong Opera and the Xingshi Long Quan, etc.), folk crafts (the silk of Scotch and the bamboo weaving of Lu bud), and humanistic characteristics (traditional overseas Chinese, traditional villages, and bamboo weaving, etc.). Longevity people and other elements are deduced together to extract and strengthen the cultural brand of "Longevity Fudi", which is then transformed into a specific visual image design effect, and then integrated with Sanshui's own tourism ecological scenes such as Nandanshan Scenic Area, Xujiang Zumiao, Daqi Tou Ancient Village, Lotus World, etc.

Application Case of Traceability Design Based on Sanshui Folklore and Folklore Culture

On the basis of the above, the author tries to design an innovative image of Sanshui Longevity Culture in the university classroom where he teaches, guided by the design thinking of regional traceability. Considering the cultural composition and age level of the audience groups of tourism consumption, the author integrates the overall visual orientation with the modern cartoon animation style, and injects fresh era spirit into the old Longevity Culture in the traditional cognition. The main cases in teaching practice are presented as follows:

A. Spiritual Lion Dancer: Black-skinned Wax Gourd Boy

a. Traceability Background

Awakening lion belongs to the southern lion in Chinese lion dance, which was born out of the court lion dance in Tang Dynasty. On May 20, 2006, Guangdong Awakening lion was listed in the first batch of national intangible cultural heritage list approved by the State Council, and was included in Sanshui District intangible cultural heritage list in January, 2009. Awakening lion pays great attention to the head, has a godly image, and is full of drum joy, which is the auspicious mascot of physical health. Black-skinned Wax Gourd is the most characteristic agricultural product of Sanshui, which is produced on selenium-rich land and has dense meat, good quality and durable storage and transportation. It is the first certification trademark of vegetable category in Guangdong Province approved by the State Trademark Administration in November 2006. Baini Town of Baiqiu site in Yinzhou is found to be the wholesale center of wax gourd in the Pearl River Delta.

b. Design Thought Orientation

Based on the Black-skin Wax Gourd, the anthropomorphic boy image is created, and the role is placed in the context of the family inheritance of the awakening lion. The visual effect of dynamic and affinity is used to present the cultural connotation of "simple, healthy, historical and inheritance" of longevity.

c. Key Points for Programme Implementation

In this case, the implementation of the program focuses mainly on the integration of agricultural products and personified images. The difficulty is the integration of role dynamics with local folklore and the connotation of longevity culture.

B. The Inheritors of Cantonese Opera Star Tune: Grass Sparrows Girl

a. Traceability Background

Cantonese opera is the largest local opera in Guangdong Province. Star tune is the most popular genre of Cantonese opera. It was created by the famous actress named Little Star (formerly Dunn Manwei) of Sanshui nationality in the 1920s and 1930s. Star tune extensively absorbs the strengths of Cantonese folk wooden fish, dragon boat, Nanyin rap, and pays attention to absorbing Cantonese and Man tune, blind public tune and other singing methods, which can better integrate foreign music elements. Integrating the tone and rhythm, forming a distinctive singing characteristics, in terms of vocal luck, voicing and turning board tone and rhyme, etc., all have their own; with the solid style of work and broad creative spirit. Little Star has formed a unique style of legendary singing in her short life, and later generations are honored as "Star Tune" by her artistic name. Grass sparrow used to be a gourmet business card in Sanshui, but now it has been listed as a national bird for protection because of the sharp decrease in its number. The Market Supervision Bureau often carries out special law enforcement inspections with the departments of industry, commerce, public security and so on. It needs more people's understanding, support and cooperation.

b. Design Thought Orientation

Based on the anthropomorphic creation of the image of a girl with grounding air, the role is placed in the context of inheritance and singing of the Cantonese opera star tune, and the cultural connotation of longevity is presented with aesthetic and affinity visual effects, which are "steadfast, auspicious, cultural and developmental".

c. Key Points for Programme Implementation

In this case, the implementation of the program focuses mainly on the integration of animal characteristics and anthropomorphic images of grass sparrows. The difficulty is the integration of role modeling, costume and local folk art, as well as the connotation of longevity culture.

C. Come from Gaoming but don't want to return: White Deer Little Knight

a. Traceability Background

Located in the central part of Gaoming District, Foshan City, Guangdong Province, Ludong Mountain is 4.5 kilometers southwest of Ming Town. Its name comes from a folklore that Zhao Tuo, king of South Vietnam, met white deer occasionally in Gaoming territory more than 2000 years ago. In the "Development Plan of Culture, Tourism and Sports Industry in Gaoming District (2011-2020)", it was clearly put forward that "White Deer" should be taken as the core symbol to make "Gaoming White Deer" to Cultural IP. Sanshui Lotus World is currently the largest lotus ornamental tourist attraction in the world with the richest variety resources. There are not only innumerable aquatic plants co-breeding ecological culture in the region, but also South China Sea embroidery and other folk arts and crafts handed down since the Tang Dynasty.

b. Design Thought Orientation

Gao Ming is located in the south of Sanshui and has a close geographical location. It can create a human-like image based on the legend of the Gaoming White Deer. Put the role in the traveling situation of Sanshui Lotus World and embodies the longevity cultural connotation of "richness, beauty, communication and inheritance" with attractive visual effects.

c. Programme Implementation Priorities

In this case, the implementation of the program focuses mainly on the integration of animal characteristics and personified images of white deer. The difficulty is the integration of local specialties and role clothing, dynamics and cultural connotations of longevity.

D. Hardworking and Benevolent Lucky Grandma: Grandma of Paper-cut

a. Traceability Background

Foshan paper-cut originated in Song Dynasty and became a commodity production between Song and Yuan Dynasty. It was the most prosperous in Qianlong Period of Qing Dynasty. Its products were sold to provinces in central and southern China and southwest China, and exported to other countries in South China. Foshan paper-cut has two types: paper-cut and carving. They generally used Foshan famous specialty copper foil and colored paper as the main raw materials, with rich color and vigorous bold and unrestrained. In terms of subject matter, most of them are lucky flowers, birds, fish and beasts loved by the working people, as well as popular opera characters and folk stories such as "dragon", "phoenix", "carp", "four seasons melon and fruit", "luck and longevity", "dragon boat race", etc. The color is mainly orange-red, pink, Sophora yellow, mustard yellow, purple, dark green and light blue, and the picture is bright and harmonious; the colorful folk customs of Foshan promote the development of paper-cutting, and the development of paper-cutting technology also makes Foshan more attractive. Sanshui was named "China's Longevity Town" by the Chinese Gerontological Society in June 2008. It is the fifth longevity town in China and the first "wealthy" longevity town in China. According to the latest statistical list of 72 centenarians in Sanshui in August 2014, there are 69 women, accounting for more than 95%.

b. Design Thought Orientation

Choose a higher proportion of women among centenarians as the role prototype, based on Foshan paper-cut folk art to create the image of grounding spirit, and embodies the longevity cultural connotation of "ingenuity, diligence, longevity and fortune" with the visual effect of affinity and craftsmanship.

c. Programme Implementation Priorities

In this case, the implementation of the program focuses mainly on the integration of paper-cut folk art and female image of the elderly. The difficulty is the integration of role dress and local folk art as well as the connotation of longevity culture.

E. God of Vegetables and Fruits: God of Snow Pear Melon

a. Traceability Background

Leping is a town in Sanshui District, where there is a folk allusion to Snow Pear Melon and the famous historical and cultural village of China, Daqitou Ancient Village (Shangshutitle of Qing Guangxu Military Department, former residence of Zheng Shaozhong and his four sons and his family), which is said to be fragrant after being cut, the whole house is refreshed, the food is cool, sweet as honey juice, and the wine is dispelled; and it is cool and warm, so it is difficult to treat the food. Leping Snow Pear Melon is the second agricultural product certification trademark after Sanshui Black-skinned Wax Gourd. It has rich aroma, more sweet juice, less fiber and good flavor. The sugar content of seven-ripe Sydney Melon reaches 15 degrees, and that of fully ripe Sydney Melon exceeds 18 degrees.

b. Design Thought Orientation

Based on Snow Pear Melon, the anthropomorphic image of elderly men is created, which complements the female roles. The roles are placed in the context of folklore and farm produce. The visual effects of affinity and labor temperament are used to embody the cultural connotation of longevity of warmth, diligence, health and inheritance.

c. Programme Implementation Priorities

The key point of this case is the fusion degree of Snow Pear Melon temperament and personified image. The difficulty is the fusion of simple role modeling and costume with folklore and the connotation of longevity culture.

F. Natural and Abundant Good Luck Spirit: Lotus Budding Sister

a. Traceability Background

The world of Sanshui lotus has been traced back briefly. 480 rare lotus varieties can be seen in the lotus ecological area. There are rare varieties such as "space lotus" cultivated in the sky and "ancient lotus" unearthed in Liaoning Province. There are dozens of water lily varieties. Among them, there are some introduced from Taiwan with high medicinal value. There are Wanglian with a diameter of 1.98 meters, which can bear 40 kg, and hundreds of aquatic flower varieties. Lotus fragrance is refreshing all over the country, the best ornamental flowering season is May to October in spring and summer in Guangdong. Likewise, the old village of Daqitou mentioned above has another folk food sign, Leping Big Steamed bun, which weighs up to 0.5 kg each and is well-made. The fillings in it include chicken, pork, half an egg, mushroom, shage and other fillings. It is soft and delicious, white and tender and beautiful. It is the food representative pursued by the people of Guangdong Province, and also carries the memory of countless people in the Pearl River Delta.

b. Design Thought Orientation

Taking Sanshui lotus and Leping steamed bun as the prototype, this paper carries out the personification of the grounding atmosphere of the image creation of young people. Put the role in the situation of leisure and laughter, and embodies the longevity cultural connotation of "rich, beautiful, lively and healthy" with lovely and dynamic visual effects.

c. Programme Implementation Priorities

In this case, the emphasis is mainly on the integration of physical characteristics such as lotus, bags and personified images. The difficulty is the integration of role modeling, costume, color matching and local specialties as well as the connotation of longevity culture.

G. The Secret of Longevity of Selenium-rich Land: Uncle Straw Hat

a. Traceability Background

Bamboo knitting has a long history in China, and Sanshui bamboo knitting has been flourishing for a while. Today, bamboo basket is still an auspicious item for weddings in the Lubo area. Folk craftsmen have created their own "eight birds go home, chatter, basket with wine to their mother's home". This kind of basket is woven with bamboo sticks, which has the characteristics of lucky face, Dragon Ridge top and eight feet. It implies festivity, simplicity and practicality. and is widely used in Sanshui Lubao Town. Bamboo weaving is fine, such as basket, hat, straw hat, grain basket, rice basket, rice basket, vegetable basket, needle basket, etc. Rough weaving such as pig cage, mud basket, grass basket, bamboo chair, etc. are the life memory of many Sanshui people; Sanshui bamboo weaving, which is well-known far and near, has been included in the third batch of intangible cultural heritage protection in Sanshui District.

b. Design Thought Orientation

Taking the three-water bamboo braided articles as the character clue, combining with the production and working situation, the middle-aged male image creation of grounding gas is carried out, and the long-life cultural connotation of "industrious, simple and healthy" is embodied by the affinity visual effect.

c. Programme Implementation Priorities

In this case, the implementation of the program focuses mainly on the integration logic of bamboo knitting supplies and character images. The difficulty is the integration of role modeling, supplies and local folk goods, as well as the connotation of longevity culture.

H. Optimistic and Open-minded Elders: The Immortal of Longevity

a. Traceability Background

There are many supporting conditions for Sanshui's longevity cultural phenomenon, including the geographical advantages of Sanjiang confluence, the good ecological environment rich in agricultural products, the open-minded Lingnan life attitude, and the industrious and simple working style, which are all excellent local characteristics.

b. Design Thought Orientation

Integrate the excellent elements mentioned above, create a human-like image of grounding air, place the characters in the context of both historical inheritance and fantastic legends, and embody the comprehensive cultural connotation of longevity with imaginative and fantastic visual effects.

c. Programme Implementation Priorities

The key point of this case is the integration of multiple elements. The difficulty is the integration of the overall image of the role and the connotation of longevity culture.

Summary and Prospect

Based on the elements of longevity culture, folk crafts, folklore inheritance, stories and legends, and local agricultural specialties in Sanshui District of Foshan City, this paper carries out modern image design under the guidance of the thought of retrospective design, aiming at better publicity and promotion of local fine elements, which can not only help the development of local tourism, agricultural e-commerce and other economic industries, but also hope to play a more important role of protecting and inheriting intangible cultural heritage.

Starting from the visual communication design based on local culture and folklore, we can further develop derivatives. In terms of materials and technology, we can choose plastics and metals commonly used in modern industrial products and combine them with the local characteristic fabrics of Foshan, such as scoop silk, paper-cut, ceramics and woodcut New Year pictures, as the carrier of inheritance and mass production, so as to play a role in the development of Lingnan Fortune Land in the new era, bring a solid material and spiritual cultural foundation.

Acknowledgements

This article is a research achievement of Guangdong Social Science "Thirteenth Five-Year Plan" 2016 project "Research on Aging Allocation of Urban Community Public Facilities" (GD16XYS17); Guangdong University of Finance and Economics 2019 Undergraduate Teaching Quality and Teaching Reform Project (professional ideological and political demonstration major) "Product Design"; Guangdong University of Finance and Economics 2020 School Level Degree and Graduate Education Reform Research Project "Ideological and Political Practice and Exploration under the Guidance of Morality and Talent Cultivation".

References

[1] Zhou Yan, Design synthesis and abductive reasoning. *Journal of South China University of Technology (Social Science Edition). China*, July 2017, pp. 1-7.

[2] Tengteng, Bama Village Health-preserving Tourism Longevity Cultural Image and Cultivation. *Jiangsu Commerce, China*, August 2011, pp. 115-117.

[3] Wang Hua, Lu Chen Gang, Research on Longevity Culture of Zhongxiang, Hubei. *Hubei Social Sciences, China*, July 2011, pp. 189-192.

[4] Li Jingmo, Deng Lili, Reflections on building a longevity cultural brand in Dongxing Binhai. *Guangxi Economy, China*, July 2012, pp. 56-58.

[5] Wang Xingkui, Research on the cultural image design of place names in the marketing of new countryside. *Modern Commerce and Trade Industry, China*, June 2010, pp. 155-156.

[6] Wu Qiong, et al., Research on the development and design process of cultural derivatives based on product system design theory. *Hundred Schools in Arts, China*, June 2013, pp. 211-214.

[7] Xiao Jing, Teaching Research on Visual Design for Reshaping the Historical and Cultural Image of the Old Revolutionary Areas: Taking the Visual Image Design of "Interesting Soviet Area" in the Soviet Town of Zijin County as an example. *Art & Design, China*, February 2017, pp. 121-123.

https://doi.org/10.1142/9789811238727_0092

Use of Cartoon Characters in City Public Commercial Space

Jian Ling Xu, Ling Xuan Wang*, Miao Lian Chen

Xiamen Academy of Arts & Design Fuzhou University, Xiamen, China
*Corresponding Author Email: zellwlx@sina.com

Abstract

We conducted comparison and summary of WeChat article contents in order to classify and collect statistics of the types and sources of cartoon characters involved. For this, we used articles recommended by WeChat public numbers of Xiamen large business community as sample sources and selected the WeChat articles containing cartoon characters of the last three years as research data. The result showed that commercial brands mainly use two-dimensional cartoon characters for display and propaganda with a much smaller proportion of real cartoon objects. At the same time, it is the overseas cartoon models that occupy the dominant position in quantity rather than the domestic ones which are less often seen. Such results can be due to the high investment cost, high market risk of real cartoon character objects and less influential power of local cartoon characters to the public, etc. With this result, we hope to deliver information about what influence the public space display of cartoon characters can make on itself and commercial brand impact, as well as what innovations can be made for the local cartoon characters so that they become more attractive. In addition, this study can be a reference for those industries which have just set foot on the use of cartoon models in actual business operations.

Keywords: cartoon characters, public space, localization

Introduction

The recent years have witnessed the development of social spiritual civilization, and the higher aesthetic taste and life quality of the public, which account for the rapid development of the animation industry. Through the analysis of the articles of WeChat Official Account, this study finds that more and more cartoon styles are used in urban public commercial space to display its image. The rich and various cartoon styles have brought more promotion and sales opportunities to a company and at the same time, will create publicity for the cartoon and promote the development of the animation industry. The research reveals that with more displays of cartoon character, most of the companies will choose the theme based on the current trends, yet, there are relatively few styles with strong personal consciousness.

Research Design

A. Research object and methods

The paper uses the content analysis method to contrast and analyze the articles of the WeChat Account of two major central business district (CBD) in Xiamen. The analysis aims to study the status quo and summarize the expected status of the research problem.

Content analysis is a method of investigation that provides an objective, systematic and quantitative description of the content of an explicit communication. The method aims to sort out and understand the essential facts and development trend of the research object, so as to reveal and explore the deeper layer of the object, and predict and grasp its development trend. The implementation of content analysis is usually divided into the following steps:

Firstly, the scope of the target population is defined according to the research problem, then screens the over range of the targets to sort out the research samples. After that, we select the analysis unit of the study, determine the research coding system, encode and collect the literature samples, and finally analyze the statistical data to obtain the research results. This article will be structured in this order.

B. Times and frequency of using the cartoon characters

The research object of this study is the articles that use cartoon characters as a display, mainly from the WeChat articles of shopping malls in publicity promotions and activity forecasting. The selected time range is from January 2016 to May 2019, and we analyze the theme and sources of the cartoon characters, the form of display, and the influence on both sides.

The author reviewed the articles posted by two major shopping malls in Xiamen between January 2016 and May 2019. In terms of the total volume, Shoe Mart (SM) shopping mall posted three articles in 2016, and eight, seven, and one in 2017, 2018 and 2019 (until May) respectively. China City shopping mall posted ten in 2016, nine each in 2017 and 2018, and two in 2019 (until May). As for the development trends, both malls are in a stable state in three years. Compared with SM, China City has more stable frequency. From the data of 2019, SM may have a downward trend.

Secondly, to learn about the frequency of application of cartoon characters, the research focuses on the months when the cartoon characters are displayed. The application cases of cartoon characters in urban commercial public space during the period of January 2016 to May 2019 were studied, which is shown in Table 1.

TABLE 1
APPLICAAAATION FREQUENCY BY MONTH

Table1 refers that the number of cartoons exhibited by SM (Shoe Mart) is relatively stable, mostly in May and July. There are more events in spring and summer compared to that in winter. On the contrary, the exhibition frequency in China City fluctuates greatly, with the most in January, followed by June and September, and no data available in March and August. China City has three peak values, and the overall number is larger than that of SM, while the overall number of SM is more than average. From the data, there may be competition between SM and China City and to compete for more customers, the two are less likely to display cartoon characters in the same month.

This shows that the display of cartoon characters usually lasts for a long time, probably for 1-2 months. In the month with holidays, the display of cartoon characters is held more frequently and the duration of the display will increase. The following reasons can account for this phenomenon as, 1) the display of cartoon character is promotion event features creativity and usually require large capital investment in the design and display. Such investment usually has a large market risk and needs a long time to recover the cost 2) Displaying the cartoon character during holidays can help avoid the loss caused by insufficient customer flow. If the exhibition fails to bring expected customer flow, maybe due to the less-attractive characters or other cooperation problems, it will be difficult to recover the initial investment.

Research Result and Analysis

A. Analysis of the resources of cartoon characters

Through the articles posted by shopping malls, the author studies the resources of the cartoon character displayed in the malls to learn about the public's preference, popular trend and so on.

The author firstly classified and counted the resources of the cartoon characters and plotted Table 2.

TABLE 2
RESOURCES AND NUMBER OF CARTOON CHARACTERS

	International	Domestic	Local
SM (Shoe Mart)	9	5	5
China City	16	12	9

Table 2 reveals that in the recent three years, both SM and China City prefer international cartoon characters in their promotion events. The percentage of domestic and local cartoon characters used is relatively small.

Fig. 1 Local, domestic and international Cartoon character exhibition

From Table 2, it can be learnt that when selecting a partner, companies usually give priority to international cartoon images and brands. (Fig. 1) Therefore, there is still a long way for domestic and local cartoon images to improve publicity, increase popularity, increase the opportunities for cooperation with business and achieve a positive cycle.

In addition, to study whether the cartoon source has a film foundation, the author re-classifies the source of the images according to whether or not they have an original image basis and the result is plotted in Table 3.

TABLE 3
NUMBERS OF IMAGES WITH OR WITHOUT ORIGINAL IMAGE BASIS

	With original image basis	Without original image basis
SM(Shoe Mart)	9	9
China City	11	17

As shown in Table 3, during the time from January 2016 to May 2019, when merchants are choosing the cartoon images to display and cooperate, they don't pay much attention to whether or not the image has an original basis. From January 2016 to April 2019, SM chooses the same number of images with and without an image basis, which is in a balanced state.

Moreover, Table 4 is derived to analyze the proportional relationship between the classic and original image displayed in the business place.

TABLE 4
NUMBER OF CLASSIC AND ORIGINAL CARTOON IMAGES

	Classic	Original
SM(Shoe Mart)	6	7
China City	12	13

As shown in Table 4, the proportion of classic and original cartoon images exhibited in both shopping malls is relatively close to the average. Original and classic cartoon images are used in public spaces as a combination, due to two reasons. Firstly, classic cartoon images will not fade out of the public over time and lose its commercial value, and secondly, the original cartoon images can refresh the animation industry and add new vitality and keep pace with the times.

B. Display form

In the application of cartoon styles in the urban commercial space, the display form is different. To study the display form of cartoon images, the author analyzes the display forms of cartoon characters in the two shopping malls and plotted Table 5.

TABLE 5
NUMBER OF DISPLAY FORM

	SM(Shoe Mart)	China City
Theme landscaping	9	16
Brand cooperation	6	6
Artist Sharing	6	4
Interactive display	1	5
Promotional film and performance	2	3

It can be seen from Table 5 that the two shopping malls both pay more attention to the theme landscaping in the mall (Fig. 2). Also, they pay attention to the cooperation with brands and artist sharing as well.

There will also be overlapping parts in the form of display. For example, theme shaping is always included in the cooperation with brands, and in the artist sharing meetings, theme landscaping is sometimes included, as well as cooperation with brands. In general, theme landscaping is a useful and traditional display form. The application of interactive display and parent-children interaction is relatively less. If there is a brand outlet store or theme store of the cartoon in the mall, then it is necessary to display the cartoon images for a long time and hold promotion or exhibition events regularly.

Fig. 2 Theme design exhibition

Consideration and Suggestion

After being exposed to animation and new media, the author has recognized that as a new cultural industry, the animation will have a powerful impact on the future. The analysis of the articles of WeChat Official Account demonstrates that the application of cartoon characters for display is increasing and the choices are various. In the display form, theme landscaping is the main form used. Animation itself has unlimited possibilities to serve any field and can be integrated into any form of art. Displaying cartoon character in commercial public space is beneficial to both the image itself and the brands. In the future, there will be more shopping malls and even supermarkets and convenience stores adopting this marking model, which integrate the cartoon images with business brands. Overall, the research on the application of cartoon character in urban commercial public space not only has important practical significance but also has great explorative and practical value.

References

[1] Alexander B Barker, Content analysis of tobacco in UK television, Tobacco Control, 2018

[2] Molly E Waring, Content analysis of Twitter chatter about indoor tanning, Translational Behavioral Medicine, 2019

[3] Zhang, HX, Industrial Upgrading and the Advent of Independent Innovation: A Case of the Chinese Cartoon Industry, China-An International Journal, 2016

[4] Wangzeng, Analysis of application of animation elements in environmental public art design, Intelligence Journal, 2016

[5] Curcio Claudio, The Italian cartoon industry. Companies and resources of the international and global markets, Economia della Cultura, 2016

https://doi.org/10.1142/9789811238727_0093

Using Service Design to Enrich the Visiting Experience in Kinmen Houpu District for Youths

Hai-Ping Jao, Ting-Yu Yang, Chun-Di Chen*

Department of Arts & Design, National Taipei University of Education, Taipei, Taiwan
*Corresponding Author Email: cdcvic@tea.ntue.edu.tw

Abstract

This study aims to identify users' requirements on information platforms in mobile devices to enhance the youth's tour experience by combining the characteristics of the Kinmen Houpu district and the application of augmented reality. The youth's preference in visiting monuments at the district and developing service design guidelines of the online information platform are explored. The main method for collecting data was interviewing 12 college students who are familiar with the Houpu historic site in varying degrees and 4 experts who come from the tourism-related fields by applying the service design principle. The questionnaire of the interview primarily considered the youth's motivation in visiting Houpu, their visiting mode, sources of the tour information, and the problems during visiting. The results from the analysis of the interview indicated that most of the visitors stayed at the historic sites for about 2 hours and they started from the historic site in the entire Houpu district, then the stores, restaurants, and the feature spots around the historic site. The problems during the visits more likely came from finding the routes and the attractions. Overall, the information on the platform should provide the route of the area, the location of the historic site, the surrounding attractions and stores, and the public amenities. This information on the platform provides a better experience for the visitors in terms of

1. Providing the introduction of the tour route
2. Offering information about the surroundings
3. Presenting the routes and introducing the attractions in terms of panoramic photos
4. Enabling the interactive guides for the historic sites and attractions
5. Allowing selfies using AR

Keywords: Kinmen historic site, young group, service design, augmented reality

Introduction

Despite the business and land development in Kinmen by long-term military rule, the historic sites were reserved for over half a century. Houpu, the political and business center of Kinmen, attracts many tourists and becomes the major district for tour promotion.

To improve the youth's understanding of the local culture, the information is becoming increasingly important. Nowadays, a lot of information is offered on websites or apps. The information reads easily but also triggers the willingness for visiting. However, the style of the information in the current official tour websites seems transformed from a textbook with only a few photos. Moreover, the information of the historic sites is not presented by interactive operation, which is less interesting to youths. Based on the value of the user experience, it is important to make the information interesting, playful, and impressive.

Augmented reality (AR) has been widely used to enrich the tour experience in historic sites by combining historical photos, modern buildings or landform, and the introduction to the site, which makes the visitors easily understand the historic site.

This study aims to suggest a design guide on mobile information platforms in terms of a service design principle for historic sites in Houpu for youths.

The purposes of this study are (1) to analyze the tour needs of youths as they visit the historic sites, (2) to explore the painful points and sweet points during the tour over Houpu historic sites with service design principles, (3) to develop the customer journey map, and (4) to propose the design requirement of the digital information platform.

Service Design

Satisfying customers is the key point in the present business. The satisfaction comes from both design and service expertise and makes the emergence of service design. Indeed, many businesses have expanded their merchandise from physical products to service consumption as Apple's development of applications. Also, Disney considers the value of the user's experience.

The service design pays attention to the identification of the customer's experience and the provision of service value. By taking the space-time as a whole, service design focuses on the touchpoint during the customer's journey from both physical and immaterial objects or systems. These touchpoints are analyzed to find out the pain points of the customers. The pain points further implicate the service gap and the ways of service improvement from the whole system (Brown, 2009; Norman, 2010).

Augmented Reality

At present, the studies and applications of augmented reality (AR) enrich users' experience and offer information on the exhibits in museums and historic sites. Hong *et al.* [3] indicated that digital technology could initiate the users' attention and provide access to the information as the digital space could offer flexible ways of presentation and transmission of the information in historic sites. The use of digital technology combines GPS, google map, and street view to impress the users in historical sites, and animations and 3D images to improve the visual perception and experience. Digital technology becomes a supplement to physical objects.

In 2010, the Museum of London created a downloadable AR application with the pictures of old London so that the visitors could see the old images on the modern physical buildings (Fig. 1). This application led to increasing visitors at the Museum of London. The various ways of providing information increase the visitors' interest in the museums and promote willingness to visit museums.

Fig. 1 AR in the Museum of London.
https://petapixel.com/2010/05/24/museum-of-london-releases-augmented-reality-app-for-historical-photos/

To promote the historic site or old street culture, the availability of digital technology is studied. However, the current technology mainly employs the transformation of format from paper and audio to digital (Chen, Lu., 2007). Few studies addressed the extent to which digital information could be recognized, welcomed, and appropriately used to encourage the visiting of historic sites. This study, therefore, proposes the design guides of information platforms in the mobile device by focusing on the youth's needs in visiting historical sites.

Discover Stage

Service design considers physical objects, immaterial systems, information offering, interface design, and customers' satisfaction with received service. Houpu was the target site for the study that focused on the exploration of the youth's needs and problems in visiting the historic sites of the area. In the discovery stage, as Ussai (2015) proposed, the study to "when" and "why" was the key point in terms of observation and in-site retrospective interview surveys to generate empathy and dialogue between the researcher and the visitors. Therefore, according to the service design principle [4], the main research method in this stage was the semi-opened interview with 12 youths between 18 to 25 years old and four experts.

The information on the interviewees is shown in Table 1. All interviewees have visited Houpu, and half of them were students of Kinmen University. The information on four expert interviewees is shown in Table 2. All of them were familiar to Houpu, and two of them were professors at Kinmen University. One of them was a local tour guide, and the other one was in charge of the training course for tour guides in Houpu.

TABLE 1
The information on the interviewees.

Coding	The Dept & School	Type of experience
AS	Tour study, KU	Visiting Houpu several times due to class need
BS	Tour study, KU	Visiting Houpu several times due to class need
CS	Tour study, KU	Visiting Houpu several times due to class need
DS	Tour study, KU	Visiting Houpu several times due to class need
ES	Tour study, KU	Visiting Houpu several times due to class need
FS	Tour study, KU	Visiting Houpu several times due to class need
GS	Nursing, MKE	Visiting Houpu several times for personal reason
HS	Diplomacy, NCCU	Visiting Houpu several times due to class need
IS	Arts & Design, NTUE	Touch this area because of need of expertise
JS	Law, NTPU	Born in and be familiar to Houpu
KS	Future studies & LOHAS industry, FGU	Transferring, staying in Houpu shortly
LS	Creative product design, TNU	Transferring, staying in Houpu shortly

KU: Kinmen University
MKE: Mackay Junior College of Medicine, Nursing and Management
NCCU: National Chengchi University
NTUE: National Taipei University of Education
NTPU: National Taipei University
FGU: Fo Guang University
TNU: Tungnan University

TABLE 2
The expert interviewees

Coding	Title
AT	Prof. Dept of Architecture, Kinmen University
BT	Prof, Dept of Tour Study, Kinmen University
CT	Senior local tour guide
DT	Chairman, Association of Kinmen Tour Guide

We firstly developed the interview questions and acquired the confirmation from the interviewees. After the interview survey, the results were analyzed with the focus on the pain point for drawing out the customer journey map and the design needs of the information platform.

Semi-structured interview survey

The interview survey was conducted by using a semi-structured interview. The interviewees were encouraged to respond in openness. The questions for the expert interview survey included the following.

1) What are the features in Houpu to attract the young?
2) What is the problem and suggestion to promote Houpu historic site to the young?
3) What is the suggestion to have fun in Houpu for the young?
4) How to enrich the visit to Houpu with information?

Also, the questions for the student interviewees were as follows.

1) What are the problems they face in visiting the historic site in Houpu?
2) Which information do they need and what styles of the information do they prefer?
3) What is their expectation of the information platform in mobile devices?

Results of Interview Survey

A. Results from student interview

The youths' visiting style in Houpu

This study aims to suggest an attractive way of how the youth visit historic sites in Houpu. The interview results show that a popular visiting style is "target site setup" followed by development of the itinerary around the target site, e.g. good food or the recommended shops from websites. The journey plan in Houpu is connecting all targets. The other style is choosing the target site randomly after visiting the historic sites one by one and shops around them. Therefore, such site choice indicates the importance of accessibility of instant information on each historic site, which promotes the visiting experience.

Time-span of the visit Houpu for the youths

In general, the time for a tour in Houpu is determined by the information from the website, the interest of visitors, and the time to stay in Houpu. According to the interview analysis, three styles were identified.

(A) 30 minutes: visiting one or two famous historic sites for about 30 minutes, eating food and going shopping for extra time.
(B) One to two hours: most visits spend one to two hours and the visitors join a 2-hour night tour guide promoted by Kinmen government or schedule a day-time self-guide tour according to the above arrangement.
(C) Half-day: roaming the famous sites in Houpu randomly with eating food and going shopping.

The pain points of visiting Houpu for the youths

(A) The attractions include the following.
   a. Fail to find notes about the attraction in advance: For the youth who respect the rules or local customs, it is a problem if the on-site notes of an attraction are unclear or fail to read it. The young visitors would not visit the historic site.
   b. Not enough public toilets.
   c. Unclear information for attractions in maintenance.
   d. Unclear information for the irregular opening time of the shop or attraction sites and there is no notice in advance. It is convenient for visitors if the open or close time is provided in the digital environment.

(B) The part of an introduction for the attraction and tour guide
   a. Lack of integration from various websites: currently there is more than one official website introducing the historic sites and giving abundant information. However, Lacking integration of rich information makes it for visitors difficult to find complete information from a website.
   b. Audio guide costs much, giving less willingness to rent.
   c. Too much text in the introduction website causes less attraction and willingness to read throughout.

B. Results from Experts

The experts from various fields suggested ways of attracting the young to Houpu and promoting the historic sites.

(A) A cultural tour that highlights the local features around the historic sites. Attracting the youths' attention with featured shops and leading them into the historic sites.
(B) Enriching the tour by importing the quasi-historic sites that are not officially informed but have historic value and worth to visit as hidden in alleys. For example, swallow-tail roofs, horseback roofs, Tswun-Del pharmacy, Mofan Street, apotropaic, western-style buildings, and temples. These attractions are not introduced in the tour guiding brochure but are found easily in Houpu. The youths' interest to visit Houpu is enhanced if these attractions or their stories are highlighted.
(C) Making resonated feeling with storytelling. One of the features in Houpu is the historic development of the old street district and the stories of the historic sites. As the young do not visit Houpu just for amusement, an attractive way is to tell the stories. The contents of the stories consist of the background, cultural meaning, allusion, and figures in the history of the historic sites.
(D) Beautiful photos with featured and meaningful design. As the youth are usually attracted by unique images for taking pictures, the promotion to the historic sites is implemented with underlined descriptions of the featured elements or structures of the historic sites. This improves the youths' understanding and gives them an impression of the historic sites.
(E) Combining the attractions with exploratory games. Recognizing the welcomed APP "Looking for Wind Lion God in Sha-Mei", the historic sites might be promoted with games with storytelling, e.g. treasure hunting in Houpu in which the young explore with fun and purposiveness, and develop their tour mode.

Discussions

The main attractions of Houpu include of the historic sites, good food, cultural creativity district, and local arts activities.

The young people put the priority on the historic site and then, the surrounding shops, attractions, and good foods. They tend to visit many sites one by one. The platform on the mobile device provides the information in Table 3.

TABLE 3
Needed information from mobile device

Item	Information
Route	1. Route information of the target attractions 2. Route between the attractions 3. Estimating journey time between the attractions 4. The current location
Attraction	1. Information of the attraction 2. Level of population 3. Introduction and photos 4. Precautions 5. Opening and close time
Surrounding	1. Information of the surrounding shops, food, and toilets 2. Recommended sites around 3. Netizen's evaluation to the sites or the shops around
Tour Guide	1. Using multimedia, guide information given with both simple and complex levels of presentation. 2. Providing flexible manner of reading

To reduce pain points during the visit, the information should be interesting, novel, and favored by young visitors. Therefore, AR needs to be applied and allow the young to access the information with mobile phones. Also, the interactive feature of AR system enriches the acquisition of multimedia information.

By considering the results of the interview survey, the functions of AR in mobile devices for the tour in the historic site are summarized as follows.

(A) To present the tour routes
(B) To present the information on the good food and attractions around
(C) To introduce the attractions via panoramic photo
(D) To allowing interactive tour guides of attractions, including the visiting route, introduction of the historic objects and its details, and public amenities.
(E) To enable selfies to be taken with AR to composite digital effectiveness.

Moreover, a journey map from service design was employed to present the historic sites in Houpu (Fig. 2). Four pain points included the route finding, uninteresting website, not enough information, and not enough details.

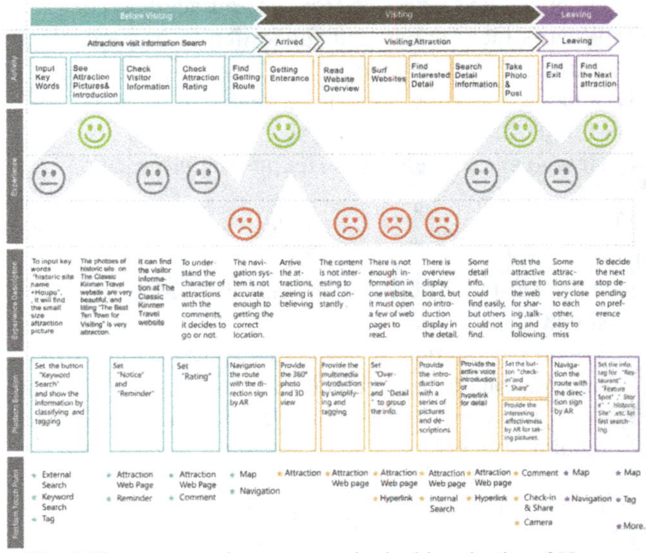

Fig. 2 The customer journey map in the historic site of Houpu

The purpose of this study is to explore the youths' pain points and expectations from information platform when they visit the historic sites and in Houpu, in terms of service design principle. The results from interview to the students and experts indicates a number of pain points and potentials to enrich the tour. These findings were then transferred into the functions needed for AR system in mobile device, which would therefore feature with the instant information provision, information accessibility with flexibility, and rich and abundant information. Further study could be suggested by focusing on the exploration of the young's acceptance and problems of using such a system as visiting in the historic sites in Houpu.

References

[1] Chen, A. L, S.Y. (2007). The pattern recognition of the digital visual tag and its application on tourism guide design. International Symposium on Culture Creativity and Design Innovation. (http://www.dirtyorange.net/v02/data/manual/manual_designer.pdf)

[2] Hong, J. C., Hwang, M. Y., Hsu, H. F., Wong, W. T., Chen, M. Y. (2011). Applying the technology acceptance model in a study of the factors affecting usage of the Taiwan digital archives system. *Computers & Education, 57*(3), 2086–2094.

[3] Henderson, R.U. (2015). The principles of UX choreography - The intersection of Disney and UX and why learning how to draw Mickey Mouse will change how you approach design. (https://medium.com/free-code-camp/the-principles-of-ux-choreography-69c91c2cbc2a#.tp46y0v82?utm_campaign=Submission&utm_medium=Community&utm_source=GrowthHackers.com)

[4] Margolin, V., & Margolin, S. (2002). A "social model" of design: Issues of practice and research. *Design Issues, 18*(4), 24-30.

[5] Norman, D. (2010). Living with complexity. Cambridge, MA: The MIT Press.

https://doi.org/10.1142/9789811238727_0094

Visual Design and Transmission of "The Book of Songs"

Chen Wei*, Liu Chang

Century College, Beijing University of Posts and Telecommunications, Beijing 102101, China
*Corresponding Author Email: Email: 11806754@qq.com, Tel: +8613811294983

Abstract

The life paintings of the ancestors in "The Book of Songs" are expressed in a visual art exhibition. The characters, symbols, and elements carried by it promote the new experience of traditional culture under the impetus of new technology. Through the analysis and study of the cultural elements of "The Book of Songs", the creative process of new media narrative, interactive animation, and mobile audiovisual is proposed by using the method of aesthetic experience and innovation integration, and the artistic innovation of interpreting the connotation of poetry and painting in the era of mobile internet is realized. In the end, under the premise of visual design and cultural satisfaction, the art of "The Book of Songs" achieves excellent cultural communication through multiple channels.

Keywords: visual design, cultural elements, innovation integration, interactive animation.

Cultural Creative Overview of "The Book of Songs"

As the source of the pre-Qin culture in China, the "Book of Songs" has a pivotal position in the pre-Qin historical books with its unique artistic charm and profound cultural accumulation. Some people have commented on their literary status, "I do not know 'The Book of Songs', it is not enough to describe the rhythm of my country's literature." It is enough to see the literary status and artistic value of the Book of Songs. It started with realism and was involved in the life of the lower class. It also expressed the emotions of the upper aristocracy. The collection of each poem came from folk singing and historical materials, showing the farming life, the political style of the times, the love marriage, the sacrifice of ancestors, the war service, etc.

The Book of Songs is summarized from the perspective of literature as "Feng, Ya, Song, Narrative, Analogy, Association". Among them, natural names refer to mountains, rivers, lakes, sun, and moon, stars, birds and beasts, grass, and woodworms. The artificial names refer to car clothing, musical instruments, architecture, flags, sacrifices, official systems, weapons, etc. The visualization of famous objects can be traced back to the "Mao Shi Gu Xun Chuan", which was the earliest concern of the famous works of the Book of Songs in the early Western Han Dynasty, and the landmark work "Mao Shi Cao Mu Niao Shou Chong Yu Shu" which is the special research done by Lu Hao in the period of the Three Kingdoms, a narrative description of the poetry culture of the pre-Qin period.

From the Original Poetry to the Spread of Visual Art

From the original interpretation to the creative description

The Book of Songs originated from the Western Zhou Dynasty to the Pre-Qin period. The author absorbed and refined according to subject matter, classification, theme, and values when studying the Book of Songs. 30 poems were selected from the chapters, Feng, Ya, and Song for the new expression of audio-visual works. The original text of each poem was translated into modern Chinese. According to the historical background, the main dialectic was formed, and the creative explanation scheme of each poem was compiled to interpret the main elements of poetry.

By studying the picture elements of poetry, the composition of the picture is determined, and the artistic laws of the false and the real, the hidden, the simple, the dense, the near and the far in the Chinese painting are appropriately applied to form the implicit and graceful artistic conception of the ancient painting.

From poetry creation to mirroring

The paintings before the pre-Qin period did not form the established artistic style. Most of them were mainly recorded in bamboo slips, caves or stone carvings. The poems in The Book of Songs used artistic expressions of "Narrative, Analogy and Association" to have natural poems. In the painting relationships, "Narrative" could be straightforward, "Analogy" could be compared to depicting, and "Association" could symbolize the meaning. It is precisely this kind of straightforward and symbolic meaning reminiscent of the mountains and rivers, clouds in ancient paintings Ethereal, poetry, songs, homesickness, and other strong images as shown in Fig. 1.

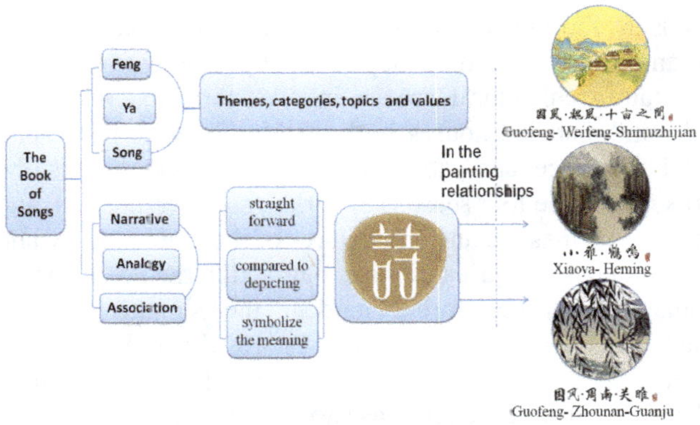

Fig. 1 Analysis of the relationship between poetry and painting.

The work is determined by interactive animation as the creative form. According to the creative description of poetry, the design and drawing of the split-screen are particularly important. The use of visual and auditory elements of audiovisual language combined with the tactile behavior of new media (mobile media) and creating a new artistic language. Take the mirror image of "Xiaoya- He Ming" and "Guo Feng, Wei Feng, He Guang" as an example. The creative idea of the former is the object of the distant mountain, Yunhe, which presents a bleak and comfortable, leisurely content and landscape painting for the audience. The latter's creative ideas are intended to express the feelings of "homesickness and no return". The audience has a scene of pride and ambition - the mountains and rivers, the rivers and rivers, the shadows of the hometown are looming, the men are looking at the mountains and rivers.

Interpretation and creation of typical shapes

For any of the "Book of Songs" animations, the vivid shape, smooth technique, and natural simplicity are all important aesthetic features. Take "Guofeng, Zhounan, Fouyi" as an example to describe the farming characters. Through the joyful collection of the pre-Qin women in the pastoral, expressing the desire for leisure and pleasure, the woman's character design is integrated with the green pastoral, the character image is simple and freehand, and the clothing is simple and unified, and the dress style is based on the "Upper garment and lower garment, a loose garment with a large girdle" of the Shang and Zhou Dynasties, the deep-seated costumes of the Spring and Autumn Period, and the "Hufu rituals" of the Warring States period. The use of the faint character shape and the scene behind it can be summed up as an abstract sketch of the ancient style.

The depiction of the architectural scene has a special meaning in the Book of Songs. The Zhou Dynasty was dominated by farming. The living conditions of the people were relatively primitive and simple. The living environment was mostly between the idyllic soil. When the tribe stabilized the land, the royal family was only the people can be led to build a house and settle down. At that time, the building of the house pays attention to the space performance, the residence of the aristocrats and the civilians are not the same, and the ancient features of the ancients belonging to the elegant. Taking "Guo Feng-Hurricane-July" as an example, the poem records the farming activities of the farmers in the land for one year and gathers a farming map of the Western Zhou Dynasty. The main architectural scenes involve farmland, mulberry fields, and thatched houses in the fields. Farmer's house and yard, burnt place, and yard. Looking at historical records, the works restore the four seasons of spring, summer, autumn, and winter, as well as the ancient features of the common city and royal layout. The house buildings outlined in the poem can be summarized as the spring garden, the summer solstice mulberry garden, the autumn harvest royal family, and the winter ridge courtyard. The four seasons all present a simple and simple spirit of the times as shown in Fig. 2.

Fig. 2 Seasonal changing scene of "July"

The Artistic Innovation and Audio-Visual Fusion of The Book of Songs

Graphic and color analysis of famous objects

These famous characters frequently appearing in poetry have obvious graphic and color characteristics are the best objects for the study of the elements of the Book of Songs. According to the statistics of the literature, there are 143 species of plants, 85 species of grasses, 58 species of woods, 109 species of animals, 35 species of birds, 26 species of mammals, 33 species of insects, and 15 kinds of fish in the Book of Songs. Besides, natural names, mountains and rivers, lake baths and other items cannot be quantified.

At this point, from the "Mao Shi Cao Mu Niao Shou Chong Yu Shu" written by Lu Hao, Wang Zongshi's "Thematic Interpretation of the Book of Songs" and Wang Yinglin's "Poetry Geography" and other research contents of the special significance of the week. Current academic figures on the famous works of the Book of Songs.

In the study, the Japanese scholar Hiroyuki published the "Thinking of Evil" and "Illustrations of objects from the Book of Songs", which is a series of books that comprehensively display the names, characteristics, and uses of animals and plants more than 2,500 years ago. It has considerable research and reference value.

In the elegant and classical visual style, the simple and natural name creation, and the return to the original color elements, the chroma of the "The Book of Songs" interactive animation and strive to achieve a beautiful and elegant style. From the analysis, the authors have made the three major color systems of the art of digitalization of the Book of Songs. The creation of each work requires both chromatographic guidelines and each the unique style of the first poem as shown in Fig. 3.

Fig. 3

Artistic innovation of interactive animation

Although interactive animation is no longer a new term, the content of The Book of Songs is presented in the art form of interactive animation, which has not been covered in the media or academic circles so far. The author selects some poetry chapters through scientific standards, matches the main creative elements in the text with visual factors such as graphics and images, interprets and analyzes the elements such as audio-visual language in film and television scripts, and digitizes them with software such as PS and Sai. The drawing design is animated with 2D animation software such as Flash, and the Unity3D engine displays the interactive plot, search, reading, reading, and saving of each poem.

Cross-media audiovisual design

On the basis of the above interactive animation works, the author mainly uses the new media communication platform to digitally reproduce the content of the Book of Songs, and combines the mobile terminal application technology to carry out multi-platform digital display, which can spread the beauty of the art of poetry and the spirit of the culture of the Book of Songs through multiple channels.

The "The Book of Songs" interactive animation builds a diversified digital display platform that integrates text, pictures, music, audio, interactive technology, etc. through a digital communication project, and hopes to establish new cognition for users with multi-sensory design methods such as touch, hearing, and vision. The use of limited specific images to express infinitely rich content, for users to experience space art, plastic arts, music art, interactive art and other multi-construction methods of new media. At the same time, the work is a high fusion of time art and language art. She is the product of the mobile internet era and is a cross-media audiovisual product.

The Aesthetic Art and Innovative Generation of the Book of Songs

The aesthetic thoughts and features of "The Book of Songs"

As a literary and cultural classic, the Book of Songs contains contemporary "harmony" thoughts, that is the sum of ethnic groups, the sum of the upper and lower, the sum of the family and the harmony between man and nature. She is a history of exploring national civilization and the realist books of the history of thought art. Compared with traditional art, the aesthetic experience of new media art has the characteristics of diversification, interactivity, virtuality, etc. These characteristics are beyond the reach of traditional art aesthetics. In Professor Li Shan's "Dialogue of the Book of Songs", it is mentioned that "Three hundred articles of 'Poetry' are an important part of the ritual and music civilization of the Zhou Dynasty, and it is the spiritual flower of the ritual activities of the Zhou Dynasty."

As everyone knows, regardless of the classification of the Feng, Ya, Song, or the artistic techniques of Narrative, Analogy, Association, for Chinese classical poetry, there is no doubt that the aesthetic characteristics have reached a very high level: that is, the language is simple, the image is vivid, the emotion is sincere, loyalty and harmony.

The aesthetic significance and technological innovation of The Book of Songs

The digital communication platform of "The Book of Songs" not only integrates a variety of media but also establishes new artistic styles through media interaction, realizing the blending of technology and art. The technological innovation here relies on the new media era. Both the content and the expression techniques have formed an innovative aesthetic experience model, allowing users to have the right to experience and speak on the digital platform of "The Book of Songs". Moreover, users can use a variety of electronic devices to interact with the new media art symbols of "The Book of Songs", and deeply appreciate the beauty of the art of "The Book of Songs".

Conclusion

It is said that in view of historical events, it is used for classics and innovation today. We study the culture of the Book of Songs in the context of the new media, and research and sort out the texts of the Book of Songs according to the composite standards of "themes, regional culture, application frequency, and aesthetic value", and form relatively complete data information. Learning history and inheriting culture are not simply adding traditional culture and science and technology, but studying media technology, tasting aesthetics and integrating artistic context in the new era, so that the art of poetry can be visualized with visual design. The wings allow culture and art to spread excellent traditional culture with a new perspective on the premise of mutual integration and mutual growth.

References

[1] Gu Taihong. General explanation of the Book of Songs [M].Beijing: Xiyuan Press, 2016.

[2] Cheng Junying. Translation and annotation of the Book of Songs [M].Shanghai: Shanghai ancient Press, 2017.

[3] Lishan, Hua Yixin, Dialogue on the Book of Songs[M]. Beijing: Zhonghua Book Company, 2013.

[4] Ke ting, Pictures of objects from the Book of Songs [M]. Hangzhou: Zhejiang people's Press, 2017.

[5] (Japan) Hiroyuki, Illustrations of objects from the Book of Songs[M]. Beijing: China pictorial Press, 2017.

[6] Zhang Daqian, Zhou Mengye. Selection of the Book of Songs: Zhang Daqian illustration collector's edition[M]. Beijing: Beijing united publishing company, 2017.

[7] Yang Xiaoyan, Li Xueqin, Peng Xiaohong. Analysis and Derivation of the Visual Features of "Book of Songs" Cultural Elements[J]. Packaging Engineering, 2018, 39 (4): 76-80.

[8] Lv Hualiang, Wang Zhouming. The value and significance of the research on famous things in the book of songs[J]. Gansu social sciences, 2010, (6): 62-65.

https://doi.org/10.1142/9789811238727_0095

Why Do Homeless People in Taiwan Not Use Social Services Provided by the Government?

Hua-Chang Lee, Chuan-Ching Hwang*

Department of Social Work, Chaoyang University of Technology, Taichung, Taiwan
*Corresponding Author Email: chuanching.hwang@gmail.com

Abstract

Many homeless do not use the services provided by the government. This article discusses the reasons for this phenomenon based on a survey conducted in 2016. After receiving training, students interviewed 150 homeless in Taichung City with a structured questionnaire. The questions asked the homeless if they had used 14 different services provided by the local government. Many homeless expressed their desire for other services that were not provided by the government. Together with the reasons for not using the services, we suggest a better design of the government services for the Taiwanese homeless, such as improved accessibility, awareness of services, and housing which have been implemented in many countries since the 1990s.

Keywords: homeless people, Taiwan, social services, services redesign

Introduction

In Taiwan, people are officially considered to be homeless if they are sleeping on the streets or living in homeless shelters. Theoretically, they need support such as shelters, medical care, good sanitary conditions, economic aid, food, and social welfare serves, and so on. However, many homeless do not use the services provided by the government. This article discusses why they do not use social welfare services. This study is based on a survey conducted during 2016–2017 on the living situations of the homeless in the city of Taichung, Taiwan [2]. Before the main reasons why many homeless are reluctant to the services are discussed, the causes of homelessness, their demographic backgrounds, and the role of government are investigated. After analyzing the reasons for using (and not using) the services, this article tries to find which services are necessary to meet the needs of the homeless.

Method

This research was conducted in 2016 with the support of the Taichung City Government. Before a structured questionnaire was constructed, experts from relevant areas were invited to discuss the living situation of the homeless in Taichung and strategies to solve their problems. Several important institutions that provide services for the homeless were visited, too. Based on the experts' views and literature reviews, homeless people in other cities were asked to answer a draft of the questionnaire. After finalizing the structured questionnaire, 20 students in the department of social work at Chaoyang University received training courses for interviewing 150 homeless in Taichung City. Due to time and accessibility limits, this study focused mainly on homeless people who were most easily accessible by outreach workers. The unregistered or those who have caused trouble for social workers were excluded.

Image of Homelessness and Role of Local Government

As of December 2019, there were officially 3,040 people who were registered as homeless. Among them, 2,194 had slept rough, including 249 in the city of Taichung, and 846 were living in shelters [1]. Most of the homeless living in the cities have been found near train or MRT stations, markets, and parking lots. In these places, it has been relatively easy to obtain assistance from passers-by or surplus food donated by food vendors or shops. Frequently, they were unwashed, disheveled, smelled unpleasant, were occupying public spaces, begging, and lying on the ground. Many passers-by would frown when they saw them. Most people think them to be dirty, stinky, and lazy and believe their misfortune is caused by their own laziness and pessimistic attitude towards life. No matter how far this is from the facts, such an impression makes the government reluctant to invest in resources to assist them.

There are two roles the government can play to assist the homeless: regulator and assistant. From the perspective of regulator, the government prevents the homeless from harassing and interfering with citizens and maintains a perspective of harmony, progress, order, and prosperity in the city. Therefore, the main goal is to reduce the presence of homeless people, and their impact on the public, and their appearance in public. Strategies for regulating them include food services to reduce begging and bathing, laundry services to improve the messy appearance of the homeless, and cost subsidization of public transportation to move them to other places. On the other hand, if the government decides to help them, more services such as resettlement, medical care, welfare applications, rental subsidies, vocational training, and job referrals need to be provided to help the homeless to cope with their difficulties and eliminate homelessness.

Finding: Living Situations of Homeless and Causes of Homelessness

From the interviews with 150 homeless, it was found that their ages were in the 40s (23%), 50s (33%), and 60s (25%).

84% of them were male. They were mostly unmarried (43%) or divorced (33%). 96% of them had received no more than a high school education or less. 65% slept rough, while 23% lived in shelters. Those who slept rough spent usually longer than a year homeless. 20% of the total respondents had been homeless for one to three years and 57% for more than three years. In total, 77% of the respondents were homeless for more than one year. The long period of homelessness shows that most of the homeless have not received proper assistance to meet their needs, meaning the problem persists.

Regarding mobility, public transportation was important for many of them. 48.3% of the respondents said that the bus was their most common method of transportation, followed by walking (42.3%) and bicycle (22.10%). 14.8% have used motorcycles. Although a considerable number of homeless were sleeping near the railway station, only 4.7% have used the train. It is reasonable for the homeless to live near the railway station since the square near the railway station is a major bus route hub. Furthermore, there are relatively many public spaces available nearby for them to sleep and lots of social service providers visit that area.

The reasons for homelessness are listed in descending order: disrupted family life 21.3%, unemployment 19.3%, physical disabilities 12.7%, insufficient income for housing 10.7%, without support of others 9.3%, physically unable to work 8%, ineligible for social welfare 7.3%, business failure 6.7%, divorce 6.7%, self-exile 4%, demolition or repossession of their accommodation 4%, inability to repay debt 3.3%, mental illness 2%, flight from domestic violence 1.3%, flight from gambling debt 1.3%, and one subject expressed unwillingness to work. According to their testimonies, 25.3% talked about family factors, unwillingness to stay at home, wanting to be self-reliant, cramped living spaces, difficulty in finding a job, the loss of savings and property, personal failure, inability to purchase a house, being treated as a troublemaker, unwillingness to list the reasons for homelessness, the enjoyment of the freedom to choose where to sleep, and personal decision to be homeless. This demonstrates that the causes of homelessness are diverse.

Social Relationship of Homeless

People who the homeless primarily contact are other homeless, friends, parents, siblings, and social workers. When they need help, most of the homeless do not seek help from the official institutions. 27.9% had asked parents, spouses, ex-spouses, siblings, other relatives, cohabitants for help. 29.3% thought that there was no one to ask for help. Only 31.3% asked social workers in social bureaus, homeless organizations, and other social welfare organizations for help. It is worth noting that the public service agencies, such as the district chief, the district officer, and the police, are not the people for the majority of the homeless to ask for help. The findings indicated that workers in the civil and police departments are not in the life circle of the homeless. However, social workers who provide outreach services have some contact with the homeless and therefore do meet some limited needs of the homeless community.

TABLE 1
Why The Homeless Are Not Using Services

Service items	% of not using, n=150	Counts of not using,	A*	B*	C*	D*	E*
1.outreach services	39%	58	43%		16%	5%	
2. catering services at fixed locations	48%	72	47%	11%	13%	6%	
3. bathing at fixed-point location	61%	91	47%	11%	11%	5%	
4. mobile bathing vehicles	75%	112	51%	17%	13%	3%	
5. laundry services	82%	123	47%	20%	8%	2%	
6. homeless shelters	64%	96	18%		55%	2%	6%
7. matching job opportunities	63%	95	42%	5%	9%		18%
8. vocational training	89%	133	40%	2%	14%		13%
9. assistance in applying for low-income aid,	73%	109	33%		16%		29%
10. free medical consultation	55%	83	42%	19%	13%		
11. subsidy for medical treatment in a city-run hospital	75%	112	41%	17%	8%	3%	
12. transportation subsidy for returning home	83%	124	23%	16%	29%		17%
13. assistance in applying for social welfare from other counties and cities	80%	120	41%		17%		28%
14. rental subsidy	91%	137	52%	3%	15%		11%

* The percentages listed in columns A, B, C, D, E are calculated by dividing the number of people giving the following reasons for not using the services, by the number in the column "counts of not using": (A) not aware of the services, (B) Confident of being able to solve the issues by themselves (C) not interested in the services, (D) services are not convenient to reach (E) ineligibility for the services.

Social Services for Homeless

In the City of Taichung, the ministry of social welfare has been cooperating with service providers for 14 different services for the homeless: outreach services, catering services at fixed locations, bathing at a fixed location, free medical consultation, homeless shelters, matching job opportunities, mobile bathing vehicles, subsidies for medical treatment in a city-run hospital, assistance in applying for low-income aid, laundry services, vocational training, rental subsidies, transportation subsidy for returning home, assistance to apply for social welfare from other counties and cities.

In the questionnaire, the homeless in the city of Taichung were asked whether and how often they had used the services above. The objective of this article is to investigate the reasons why the homeless refused to use the services. Table 1 shows the services they used. Except for outreach (39% had used) and catering services (48%), the provided services have never been used by more than 50% of the homeless. Some of the services have never even been used by more than 80% of the respondents. These services included laundry, vocational training, transportation subsidy for returning home, social welfare from other counties/cities, and rental cost subsidy.

The most frequently used service was the outreach service. This is a service provided by social workers from the social affairs bureau. As social workers pay regular visits to the homeless if they have a call, the outreach service can be seen as the main service provided directly by the government. The second most frequently used service was catering provided by three non-profit organizations.

Why didn't Homeless People Use Social Services?

The reasons why the respondents did not use the services were researched. To maintain statistical consistency and avoid excessive answers, the questionnaire listed five reasons: (A) not aware of the services, (B) confident of being able to solve the issues by themselves (C) not interested in the services, (D) services are not convenient to reach, and (E) ineligibility for the services.

As shown in Table 1, the main reason for not using the homeless services was reason A: the respondents did not know of the services at all. 8% to 52% of the respondents had no information on the 14 services. The service of homeless shelters was mostly known. Only 18% did not know about the shelters. Despite the high awareness of this service, 64% answered they had never used it and 55% were not interested in the service at all. Reason C "being not interested in the services" was the second important reason for not using the services except for the shelter service.

Reason B "confident of being able to solve the issues by themselves" was listed by a few homeless. Bathing (17%), laundry (20%), medical services (19%), and transportation subsidy for returning home (16%) were the main reasons. This shows some homeless believed they were able to solve these problems on their own. By contrast, reason D "services are not convenient to reach", was not important for not using the services with fewer than 10%. Reason E "ineligible for the services" was listed for some services, particularly that of low-income aid. Certain services require the homeless to meet preconditions set by the government. It is worth noting that 29% of the respondents believed that they did not qualify for low-income assistance.

Conclusions

The main reason for not using the services was a lack of awareness. Although the promotion of the 14 services to the homeless is needed, it is not easy to advertise the services to the homeless. Instead, a single and accessible service center integrating all the services is recommended. This helps social workers link services and resources together regardless of the homeless' awareness of the available services. Social workers may design a customized plan to help the homeless solve their issues. 77% of the respondents were homeless for longer than one year and sleeping outside. Theoretically, the majority of them needed to stay in shelters. According to the result, homeless shelters were known most among the 14 services. However, around two-thirds of the respondents claimed they had never stayed in any shelter in the city. Furthermore, 55% who had never used this service were not interested in the service at all. The main reason was they could have limited freedom due to many restrictions. For preferred living conditions, the majority of the respondents expressed a desire to be allowed to stay in places in a friendly way without interference. What the homeless truly need is a place where they stay free and safely. The housing first approach, which emphasizes providing housing before social services has been established in many countries since the 1990s [3], is worth considering in Taiwan.

References

[1] Ministry of Health and Welfare, the Handling Situation of the Homeless. Retrieved Dec 2, 2020, from https://dep.mohw.gov.tw/DOS/cp-1721-9439-113.html.

[2] H. C. Lee and C. C. Hwang, Survey on the Living Situation and Needs of Homeless people in Taichung, Report commissioned by the Social Affairs Bureau of the Taichung City Government. June 2017, unpublished.

[3] S. Tsemberis, Housing First. The Pathways Model to end Homelessness for People with Mental Health and Substance Use Disorders. Minnesota: Hazelden Publishing, 2015.

CPSIA information can be obtained
at www.ICGtesting.com
Printed in the USA
LVHW062347111021
700173LV00002B/11

9 789811 23871C